Published by the Religious Studies Center, Brigham Young University, Provo, Utah, in cooperation with Deseret Book Company, Salt Lake City
http://rsc.byu.edu

© 2011 by Brigham Young University
All rights reserved

DESERET BOOK is a registered trademark of Deseret Book Company.
Visit us at DeseretBook.com

Printed in the United States of America by Sheridan Books

Any uses of this material beyond those allowed by the exemptions in U.S. copyright law, such as section 107, "Fair Use," and section 108, "Library Copying," require the written permission of the publisher, Religious Studies Center, 167 HGB, Brigham Young University, Provo, Utah 84602. The views expressed herein are the responsibility of the authors and do not necessarily represent the position of Brigham Young University or the Religious Studies Center.

ISBN 978-0-8425-2785-9
Retail U.S. $29.99

Cover painting by Robert T. Barrett
Cover design by Carmen Cole

Library of Congress Cataloging-in-Publication Data

Brigham Young University Church History Symposium (2010) A firm foundation : church organization and administration / edited by David J. Whittaker and Arnold K. Garr.
   p. cm.
   Includes bibliographical references and index.
   ISBN 978-0-8425-2785-9 (hard cover : alk. paper) 1. Church of Jesus Christ of Latter-day Saints—History—Congresses. 2. Mormon Church—History—Congresses. I. Whittaker, David J. editor. II. Garr, Arnold K. editor. III. Title.

BX8611.B725 2010   289.3'3209—dc22

BRIGHAM YOUNG UNIVERSITY
Church History Symposium

A Firm Foundation: Church Organization and Administration

Edited by
David J. Whittaker and Arnold K. Garr

RELIGIOUS STUDIES CENTER
BRIGHAM YOUNG UNIVERSITY

DESERET BOOK

Contents

FOREWORD vii
    Elder Marlin K. Jensen

INTRODUCTION xi
    David J. Whittaker and Arnold K. Garr

The Revelatory Foundation: Revelations and Organization

1. JOSEPH SMITH AND POWER 1
    Richard Lyman Bushman

2. THE BOOK OF MORMON AS THE KEYSTONE OF CHURCH ADMINISTRATION 15
    John W. Welch

3. "THE CIRCUMFERENCE OF THE APOSTLESHIP" 59
    Richard E. Bennett

4. THE ARTICLES AND COVENANTS: A HANDBOOK FOR NEW BRANCHES 83
    Craig James Ostler

5. SEEKING AFTER THE ANCIENT ORDER: CONFERENCES AND COUNCILS IN EARLY CHURCH GOVERNANCE, 1830–34 97
    Joseph F. Darowski

Contents

6. SHARING AUTHORITY: 115
   DEVELOPING THE FIRST PRESIDENCY IN OHIO
   Mark L. Staker

7. EARLY QUORUMS OF THE SEVENTIES 139
   Susan Easton Black

8. SIX DAYS IN AUGUST: BRIGHAM YOUNG 161
   AND THE SUCCESSION CRISIS OF 1844
   Ronald W. Walker

GATHERING, ORGANIZING, AND STRENGTHENING THE SAINTS

9. MEN IN MOTION: 197
   ADMINISTRATING AND ORGANIZING THE GATHERING
   Fred E. Woods

10. A HISTORY OF MORMON CATECHISMS 223
    Kenneth L. Alford

11. PRIMARY ASSOCIATION PIONEERS: AN EARLY HISTORY 245
    RoseAnn Benson

12. YOUNG WOMEN OF ZION: AN ORGANIZATIONAL HISTORY 277
    Janet C. Peterson

BUILDING ON THE FIRM FOUNDATION

13. CHURCH ADMINISTRATIVE CHANGE 295
    IN THE PROGRESSIVE PERIOD, 1898–1930
    Thomas G. Alexander

Contents

14. CORRELATION: THE EARLY YEARS   319
    Michael A. Goodman

15. FROM RADIO TO THE INTERNET: 339
    CHURCH USE OF ELECTRONIC MEDIA
    IN THE TWENTIETH CENTURY
    Sherry Pack Baker and Elizabeth Mott

16. RELIEF SOCIETY EDUCATIONAL AND   361
    SOCIAL WELFARE WORK, 1900–29
    Dave Hall

17. JOSEPH F. MERRILL AND THE TRANSFORMATION   377
    OF CHURCH EDUCATION
    Casey P. Griffiths

18. THE CHURCH'S BEAUTIFICATION MOVEMENT, 1937–47   403
    William G. Hartley and Theodore D. Moore

19. ARDETH GREENE KAPP'S INFLUENCE ON THE YOUNG WOMEN   443
    ORGANIZATION
    Jessica Christensen and Mary Jane Woodger

20. TYING IT TO THE PRIESTHOOD: HAROLD B. LEE'S   463
    RESTRUCTURING OF THE YOUNG MEN ORGANIZATION
    Scott C. Esplin

21. N. ELDON TANNER AND CHURCH ADMINISTRATION   485
    John P. Livingstone

22. HOW TO MAKE (AND UNMAKE) A MORMON HYMNBOOK   503
    Michael Hicks

Contents

23. Events and Changes during the Administration of Spencer W. Kimball 521
    Edward L. Kimball

24. Global Lessons from a Local Stake 533
    Jessie L. Embry and A. LeGrand Richards

Administering Missions

25. Succession in German Mission Leadership during World War II 553
    Roger P. Minert

26. The Seventies' Role in Worldwide Church Administration 573
    Richard O. Cowan

27. Missions and Missionary Administration and Organization 595
    R. Lanier Britsch

A Guide to Further Study

28. Mormon Administrative and Organizational History: A Source Essay 611
    David J. Whittaker

Index 696

Elder Marlin K. Jensen

Foreword

READING the collection of symposium papers that make up the chapters of this book about the organizational and administrative history of The Church of Jesus Christ of Latter-day Saints was an exhilarating exercise for me. Part of the reason for this, I believe, is the "of the people" nature of the restored Church, a religious organization built largely upon a lay ministry. The Lord declares in the Book of Mormon, "I am able to do mine own work" (2 Nephi 27:21). How grateful we should be, however, that He chooses not to. Out of love and a desire that all of God's children have opportunity to achieve their divine potential, Christ has organized His Church so "that every man might speak in the name of God the Lord" (D&C 1:20). This unique organizational feature—allowing for individual participation in Church affairs at many levels and at all ages—effectively makes His Church our Church, and His work our work. It also makes His Church's organizational and administrative history our history. Ownership works wonders in many contexts.

It appears that the business of creating organizational and administrative structure in the Lord's work began at least as early as the time of Moses (see Exodus 18:15–26; Deuteronomy 1:9–16). Later, in

New Testament times, the Apostle Paul described a higher level of Church organization when he wrote to the Corinthians: "God hath set some in the church, first apostles, secondarily prophets, thirdly teachers, after that miracles, then gifts of healings, helps, governments, diversities of tongues" (1 Corinthians 12:28). This organization, established by God to deliver saving ordinances and covenants and to promote order, service, learning, and the personal development of Church members, was not viewed as temporary or transitory in nature. As Paul explained to the Ephesians, God's designated polity was "for the perfecting of the saints, for the work of the ministry, for the edifying of the body of Christ: till we all come in the unity of faith, and of the knowledge of the Son of God, unto a perfect man, unto the measure of the stature of the fulness of Christ" (Ephesians 4:12–13).

Although Joseph Smith was acquainted with the biblical record of Christ's Church, he and subsequent prophets in this dispensation required contemporary revelation to know how to proceed with the organization of the restored Church. In 1884, President John Taylor described the early prophets' revelatory experience: "We have embraced the Gospel of the Son of God, and God has taught us how to organize His Church. Had He not taught us we should not have known anything about its organization. Joseph Smith knew nothing about it; Brigham Young knew nothing about it; I could not have known anything about it, nor any of the Twelve, nor any man living on earth, until God introduced it and taught us in all these things."[1]

Happily, the revelation confirming the formal commencement of the restored Church on April 6, 1830, and designating Joseph Smith as the first Church officer also included what might be termed an administrative order that "there shall be a record kept among you" (D&C 21:1). For the past 180 years, a goodly portion of that record has dealt with the rise and progress of the restored Church, including the maturation of its organizational and administrative dimensions. These abundant historical sources confirm that the development of the Church's organizational and administrative structure was not an event but a process that continues to the present day. The Lord deals in matters of Church government, as He does in all other

Foreword

categories of truth and knowledge, by giving us "line upon line, precept upon precept" (D&C 98:12). Moreover, He provides refinements and innovations in Church organization and administration according to the needs and circumstances of the times.

Some of these inspired developments in the restored Church are chronicled by the skilled historians who have contributed the chapters in this book. For instance, we read of how the authority of the First Presidency and the Quorum of the Twelve Apostles was defined and how the Lord guided the Church through the succession crisis after Joseph Smith's death. We learn details about the initial founding of the Primary and Young Women organizations and are informed of later inspired changes that were made in both the Young Men and Young Women organizations. We are acquainted with adjustments in the way in which missions have been administered, the transformation of the Church Educational System in the first third of the twentieth century, the evolving role of the Seventy, the significance of the correlation program, and much more. We also come to know more intimately some of the key men and women, such as N. Eldon Tanner and Ardeth Greene Kapp, who have exerted lasting influence on Church organization and programs.

President Harold B. Lee, who had unique gifts of administration, provided insight into the evolving nature of Church organization:

> When asked for reasons for our growth, we have said, "We believe in the same organization that existed in the primitive church, founded on apostles and prophets, with Jesus Christ as the chief cornerstone." Then we have added one more dimension. While the principles of the gospel are divine and do not change, the methods in dealing with the problems change to meet the circumstances, and so our methods have had to be flexible. We have adopted a welfare program. We have adopted a family home evening program. We have intensified the work of our priesthood in home teaching in a more direct way to help the fathers.

A Firm Foundation

> We have . . . said to [members], "We want to find out what you need. It is still the same gospel, but we are endeavoring to reach those for whom we have had no adequate programs. Man wasn't made for the Church, to paraphrase what the Master said, but the Church was made for man."
>
> And so we have become flexible in adapting our methods in order to take care of the needs of our people, wherever they are. But we have built on a foundation laid down by the prophets, and we have not deviated from the principles and teachings of the gospel of Jesus Christ.[2]

As President Lee observed, the Church has been built on a foundation laid down by the prophets. There is great security in this firm foundation, but there is also, as President Lee's words and the chapters in this book confirm, a "living" dimension to the Church's organization and administration. God's hand is always outstretched, His Spirit is ever ready, apostles and prophets continue to speak, and the destiny of His Church and people in these changing and often calamitous times is therefore secure. With all the Saints of this dispensation, we can gratefully pray, "Wherefore, may the kingdom of God go forth, that the kingdom of heaven may come" (D&C 65:6).

Elder Marlin K. Jensen
Church Historian and Recorder
The Church of Jesus Christ of Latter-day Saints

NOTES

1. John Taylor, in *Journal of Discourses* (London: Latter-day Saints' Book Depot, 1884), 25:265.
2. Harold B. Lee, *Ye Are the Light of the World: Selected Sermons and Writings of President Harold B. Lee* (Salt Lake City: Deseret Book, 1974), 348–49.

David J. Whittaker and Arnold K. Garr

Introduction

THE subject chosen for the 2010 Brigham Young University Church History Symposium was the organizational and administrative history of The Church of Jesus Christ of Latter-day Saints. The response to the call for papers to the symposium was very gratifying, and we knew from the beginning that the possible topics were many because most topics in Mormon history are related to administrative history. As a divinely mandated delivery system for the saving ordinances of the gospel of Jesus Christ, the basic priesthood structure was established under the inspired direction of Joseph Smith in its earliest years. Established in Fayette, New York, on April 6, 1830, with about fifty people attending the organizational meeting, the Church has grown to over fourteen million members in countries throughout the world. The Church's success can in part be attributed to the firm foundation established by Joseph Smith.

The symposium itself was organized into sessions that traced the major developments in the organizational history of the Church. For this volume, we have arranged the papers into roughly chronological sections that deal with various themes. The first section deals with the Church's revelatory foundation, beginning with Richard Lyman Bushman's opening talk, which set the stage for the conference. Bushman's remarks show the great organizational genius of Joseph Smith that managed to combine both revelatory and bureaucratic elements into the structure of the Church from its earliest years. The other articles in this section expand on this theme, examining elements of the Church's early foundation, including the emergence of the presiding quorums and priesthood structures that remain central to the Church today.

The second section gives attention to the programs and organizations that were established in order to gather, organize, and strengthen Church members.

The third section addresses important adjustments to administration as the Church encountered the end of its isolation in the Great Basin following the Gold Rush, and later as members moved out the more rural and agricultural settings at the end of the nineteenth century. It also brings the story up to the present time with articles treating such topics as Church correlation, welfare, and education.

A fourth section examines the organization and adminitration of the Church's missions. A final section offers a bibliographic essay as a guide to further study.

Many topics are not treated in this volume, and a number of those presented during the symposium will be found elsewhere. For example, Jill Mulvay Derr's presentation on the early history of the Relief Society will be published in her forthcoming biography of Eliza R. Snow, and David J. Whittaker's abbreviated presentation on the key role of Joseph B. Keeler at the beginning of the twentieth century had already been published in full as "Joseph B. Keeler, Print Culture, and the Modernization of Mormonism, 1885–1918," in *Religion and the Culture of Print in Modern America*, ed. Charles L. Cohen and Paul S. Boyer (Madison: University of Wisconsin Press, 2008), 105–27.

Because the rich and complex history of the administration of the Church cannot be treated in just one volume, a bibliographical essay appears at the end of the volume that will direct readers to the growing literature on the topics of the symposium.

Introduction

We are grateful to Elder Marlin K. Jensen, Church Historian and Recorder, for providing a foreword to this volume. He has consistently provided encouragement and support for the serious study of Church history over the years he has served in his calling. We are also grateful for the consistent support of Kent P. Jackson, then the associate dean of Religious Education at BYU, who saw the potential for this topic when it was proposed and has consistently encouraged us as we organized the symposium and worked on the volume. Thanks also to the Religious Studies Center staff for their work on the editing and production of this volume: Robert L. Millet, R. Devan Jensen, Brent R. Nordgren, Joany O. Pinegar, Jessica S. Arnold, Jacob F. Frandsen, Jonathon R. Owen, Rosalind E. Ricks, and Jeffrey M. Wade.

"No power or influence can or ought to be maintained by virtue of the priesthood, only by persuasion, by long-suffering, by gentleness and meekness, and by love unfeigned" (Doctrine and Covenants 121:41). (Alvin Gittins, © 1959 Intellectual Reserve, Inc. All rights reserved.)

Richard Lyman Bushman

1

Joseph Smith and Power

MANY people who have led a Latter-day Saint life see Church government, as I do, as a marvel, perhaps a miracle. How can congregations function so well without professional leadership? How can we release bishops every five years and invariably find another person in the congregation to take on the assignment? Why do people work so hard in their Church jobs? Why do we trust our leaders as we do—with our money, our time, and our most confidential problems? We move from ward to ward all over the Church, and the system functions in much the same way. How can we account for the success of this lay-led church that seems to run against all expectations? What is the source and nature of its power?

The Church has been compared to a variety of organizations. When I was growing up, the Church was sometimes compared to the

---

Richard Lyman Bushman, Gouverneur Morris Professor of History Emeritus at Columbia University, was Howard W. Hunter Visiting Professor in Mormon Studies at Claremont Graduate University from 2008 to 2011.

German army. In the early thirties, before the Germans became our enemy, their army was considered the epitome of efficiency, and the Church seemed similarly effective. But that was not a convincing comparison. The Mormon Church may have been efficient, but it was voluntary, not professional, and not disciplined through extensive training. If not an army, is the Church like a monarchy, as some say, with a king to whom the people owe allegiance? The comparison does not seem quite right because the Church is run by a president, a democratic office. Or alternatively, since Mormonism grew up under American democracy, does its lay priesthood constitute a basically anti-elitist, democratic form of government as historians of American religion have argued?[1] We immediately think of objections. But if not any of these, what is the Church form of government?

CHARISMA

The German sociologist Max Weber categorized the various forms of government according to their sources of legitimacy. Why is it, Weber asked, that people submit to a government? What gives it legitimacy such that people feel they ought to obey? Of his various answers, the category that applies best to early Mormonism is charismatic authority. Weber defined *charisma* as "a certain quality of an individual personality, by virtue of which he is set apart from ordinary men and treated as endowed with supernatural, superhuman, or at least specifically exceptional powers or qualities."[2] Charismatic leaders, in most cases, rule by virtue of their divine power. The description seems to fit Joseph Smith with his unusual revelatory powers.[3] It casts light on why converts considered his leadership legitimate. They followed him because of his divine gift.

Weber considered charismatic authority the least stable of the three major types of leadership that he investigated in his classic 1922 treatise *Theory of Social and Economic Organization*. In addition to the charismatic, Weber noted the traditional (monarchs) and the rational or bureaucratic (modern business corporations). People submit to a monarch because his authority descends through the legitimate lineage—he is the bearer of the royal family's right to rule. In a bureaucratic government, people obey because the ruler occupies an office that he acquired through a rational process—in a democracy, through election or appointment.

In comparison to traditional and bureaucratic government, charismatic authority is fragile. It falters if the divine gifts or exceptional powers of the leader are brought into question during his lifetime, and after he dies a struggle may ensue among his successors who are less gifted charismatically. Moreover, charismatic government often lacks structure. Charismatic leaders collect followers; they rarely form organizations. Their successors have to devise another foundation for their authority to replace the gifts of the departed leader which they may lack. If the movement is to persist, the followers must routinize the charisma, that is, turn supernatural powers into customary roles for leaders and followers. In other words, they must create a bureaucratic or rational government; otherwise, the movement will disintegrate. Under bureaucratic government, authority comes with the office. Charismatic government must evolve into bureaucratic government or the movement will disintegrate. Charisma must be routinized.[4]

Is any of this applicable to Mormonism? Weber's analysis has naturally been applied to Joseph Smith, who was by all accounts a charismatic leader of the first order. If this label suits the Prophet, what about the evolution of authority after Joseph? Was it routinized? It is commonly said that Brigham Young's role was to routinize authority in the Church. Joseph Smith led by his prophetic gifts, we sometimes say, and Brigham Young led by his administrative genius. Young took in hand the pulsing, energetic, but somewhat chaotic young Church under its charismatic prophet and made it into a smoothly run corporate body with well-defined offices and a fixed hierarchy of power—the epitome of bureaucratic government.

ORGANIZATION

This account of administrative development, however, overlooks an important fact: Joseph Smith's preoccupation with organization. From the beginning, he did not just institute a movement; he organized a church with officers and structure. The revelation given at the organization of the Church, Doctrine and Covenants section 20, said more about offices than about doctrines (D&C 20:17–37; compare to vv. 38–84). Joseph considered the development of Church organization one of his major achievements. He thought of himself as an organization man. "This shall be your business and mission in all your lives," one revelation said, "to preside in council" (D&C 90:16). Besides his titles as seer, translator, and prophet, he was called to be an Apostle and elder of the Church (D&C 21:1). The major features of Church administration—save for wards—were in place by the time Joseph died. Brigham Young did not have to invent the office of Apostle that enabled him to assume leadership of the Church in 1844. Joseph Smith's revelations foreshadowed Apostles before the Church was organized, and he brought the Council of the Twelve into existence nine years before his death. Church organization was his mission. He was restoring, he believed, the "order of heaven in ancient councils."[5]

The most startling feature of the organization Joseph formed was its merger of the charismatic and the bureaucratic. In contradistinction to Weber's categories, the Church combined two forms of legitimacy. Joseph did not reserve prophetic gifts to himself as a person; he assigned them to an office. At the organization of the Church, he did not simply manifest the gifts of prophecy; he was appointed to that calling. He was called to be "a seer, a translator, a prophet" in the records of the Church (D&C 21:1). That was how he was to be designated in the minutes—and what is more bureaucratic than minutes? When Joseph claimed special authority for himself in the September 1830 conflict over charismatic, or revelatory, gifts, the main argument against Hiram Page's revelations was that "these things have not been appointed unto him" (D&C 28:12). Page did not occupy the prophetic office. A display of a divine gift was not enough. "All things must be done in order," a revelation said (v. 13). Joseph exercised the gifts because he had been appointed to that office: "I have given him the keys of the mysteries, and the revelations which are sealed" (v. 7). Were Joseph to fall or to die, God said, "I shall *appoint* unto them another in his stead" (v. 7; emphasis added). The gifts were not personal to Joseph, invested in him as a chosen agent of the divine. The gifts resided in the office by appointment. The minutes of the September 26, 1830, meeting quietly recorded this revolutionary transformation: "Brother Joseph Smith jr. was appointed by the voice of the Conference to receive and write Revelations & Commandments for this Church."[6] Those are startling words: the Church elected Joseph Smith to be their prophet. In the course of the very first challenge to his prophetic gifts, Joseph effectively bureaucratized charisma.

Although this event centralized revelation in the Church, Joseph also democratized the gifts. He seemed to claim a near monopoly in the Hiram Page revelation, but Joseph's impulse was to distribute charisma widely. Scarcely a year later, a revelation proclaimed that every priesthood holder was to speak by the gift of the Holy Ghost and that "whatsoever they shall speak when moved upon by the Holy Ghost shall be scripture" (D&C 68:4). The founding minutes of the first high council said it was the privilege of each council's presiding authority to seek revelation. When problems of interpretation arose, the president was "to inquire and obtain the mind of the Lord by revelation" (D&C 102:23). Revelation went with the office. Joseph admonished the Twelve Apostles to keep careful minutes since their "decision[s] will forever remain upon record, and appear an item of covenant or doctrine."[7] Eventually charisma, the gift of revelation, was invested in virtually every officer in the Church. In modern practice, thirteen-year-old deacon's quorum presidents are enjoined to seek revelation for their callings. Up and down the Church organization today, charisma and bureaucracy blend. Mormons have altered Weber's definition of *charisma* as pertaining to "exceptional powers" and have instead striven to make them common. Every Church officer at every level is to seek the gift of revelation.

These developments in Church structure laid the groundwork for Brigham Young's succession. In the crisis of 1844, Brigham Young did not have to claim prophetic gifts to undergird his claims to Church leadership. He based them on the keys of the apostleship, that is, on his office in the organization. Brigham could not have won the loyalty of the people if Joseph Smith had not created the office Young occupied. One of my favorite illustrations in *Joseph Smith: Rough Stone Rolling* is of a needlework piece stitched in the years immediately after the Prophet's death. In my mind it depicts Joseph Smith's legacy as understood by ordinary Mormons. It features two items. In the center is the "Temple of Nauvoo," and around the border are the names of the Twelve Apostles with "President Brigham Young" at the top center.[8] That is what the seamstress calculated to be Joseph Smith's legacy: the temple and the Apostles. Without the widespread loyalty to the Twelve as holders of a divinely appointed office, Brigham Young would not have succeeded. Joseph Smith is the one who restored that office.

Brigham modestly denied that he had Joseph's gifts of prophecy. In an 1852 discourse, he asked the congregation "if they ever heard him profess to be a Prophet, Seer, and Revelator as Joseph Smith was? He professed to be an Apostle of Jesus Christ, called and sent of God to save Israel."[9] In other words, he governed the Church by virtue of his place at the head of the Twelve, an office, not by personal prophetic gifts. Over and over he insisted he was not Joseph Smith's successor as prophet, but the Latter-day Saints refused to acquiesce in Young's reluctance. They insisted he was a prophet. Elder Heber C. Kimball praised Brigham Young as "a living oracle—the mouthpiece of the Almighty, to communicate line upon line, and precept upon precept . . . [who has] the word of truth constantly on hand."[10] Elder Kimball bore testimony that God would speak through Brigham Young, "and it will be like the trump of Jehovah."[11] Regardless of Brigham Young's diffidence, Elder Kimball insisted that President Young had to exercise prophetic gifts because he occupied a prophetic office.

Church members today expect the same of bishops in every ward in the Church. Modern Latter-day Saints live under the conviction that every officer, including themselves in their own offices, can partake of charisma. Charisma was not replaced by bureaucracy on the death of the first prophet; charisma was invested in the bureaucracy from the beginning. Latter-day Saints live within an anomalous and seemingly contradictory structure, a charismatic bureaucracy.

POWER

This peculiar construction recasts the problem of power that has so vexed Church leaders since the beginning. From the viewpoint of modern democracy, charismatic leadership grants altogether too much power to its central figure. Within a few years of the Church's organization, Joseph Smith was accused of authoritarian control. In 1834 he complained that the cry of his critics was "Tyrant,! Pope!! King!!!"[12] And from the point of view of American democracy, the charges were justified. Charismatic leadership almost inevitably involves unchecked power. Because authority originates in the leader's gifts, who can restrain him? The very nature of charismatic governance rules out any criticism of the leader's powers. Neither his followers nor his lieutenants can challenge the charismatic leader's will without undermining the movement. To imply that his gifts have failed and the leader has erred destroys the foundation on which the entire enterprise rests. Everyone must yield to the leader's will because his power supports everything else.

The absence of restraints on hierarchical authority troubles democratic critics of Mormonism. Church members do not seem to understand how threatening the unchecked power of the general authorities is. Why don't Mormons demand a detailed accounting of finances? Why don't they petition, lobby, and campaign for changes in out-of-date Church policies? It is inexplicable to many outside observers that Mormons comfortably reside in two opposing realms, the Church and democracy.

Underlying these accusations is the single most striking difference in church and democratic political cultures: their contrasting attitudes toward power. Democratic society's and Church society's views of power are almost polar opposites. The same person speaking as a member of one society will express contradictory views when speaking as a member of the other society. Power in democratic discourse is an aggressive force, relentlessly expanding, always seeking domination. Perhaps the single most demanding challenge in democratic theory is how to regulate power. Not trusting any kind of authority, democratic government seeks to contain it. The Bill of Rights and constitutional checks and balances are the bulwarks of democracy because they constrain power. Perhaps democracy's greatest virtue in the constellation of political forms is its preventive function. Abused power can prevail only until the next election.

In the Church, by contrast, power is trusted, even beloved. Latter-day Saints want to maximize the prophets' power, not limit it. They obey the prophets as they obey God, reverently, humbly, gratefully. Latter-day Saints feel blessed to have guidance and direction from God through the Church President. What could be better for themselves and their children than to conform their lives to the revelations? Church members are scarcely conscious of the dangers of Church power. Occasional abuses are thought of as anomalies to be quickly corrected, not as indications of power's invariable corruptions. No one talks of erecting systematic checks on power to prevent its certain abuse. Power is thought of as redemptive, not oppressive. The word *rights* rarely appears in Church discourse.

Church members are no less aware of the dangers of governmental power than other Americans. Many have libertarian tendencies. The preponderance of Latter-day Saint politicians fall on the conservative side of the spectrum. They expound on the threat of big government along with all their compatriots on the right. Their Mormonism does not numb them to the dangers of concentrated authority in the state. Yet these same individuals exhort their fellow Latter-day Saints to follow the prophet without concern for his immense power. They do not criticize Church leaders for refusing to open the financial records to inspection or call for open debate on Church policies or ask for a greater voice in Church governance. They happily embrace policies handed down from above and accept onerous Church assignments without questioning the programs they are asked to administer. They bestow a degree of confidence on Church government they would never show to the United States. How can Latter-day Saints reconcile these opposing attitudes?

If queried, Church members protest that there are checks on Church power. They refer to the sustaining vote when each officer is periodically presented to the general membership for approval. At the annual general conference in Salt Lake City, the First Presidency and the Quorum of the Twelve Apostles are named individually, and the audience is asked to raise their hands in approval. At every level, virtually every officer's name is presented for similar approval. A revelation to Joseph Smith specified that "no person is to be ordained to any office in this church, where there is a regularly organized branch of the same, without the vote of that church" (D&C 20:65). Is that not democratic?

But this is a ritual without teeth. The congregation is not given a choice in these votes. The authorities select all names in advance and offer only one choice. There is no debate, no campaigning, no examination of qualifications, not even advance knowledge of the proposed officers. Usually the vote is unanimous. This is definitely not an election. It indicates community support for the authorities who called the person to office as much as for the nominees themselves. In effect, the sustaining vote says, we are behind all of you who manage our congregation. We trust you and support each other in our callings. If sustaining turned into an election, it would be a sign of community decay.

I would argue that the preeminent check on Church power is charisma itself. Paradoxically, the very factor that seems to underlie authoritarianism in the Church is also the chief restraint on power. Church leaders at every level from top to bottom are believed to act on behalf of God. In the minds of the people, that is the source of their legitimacy. They are not elected to office, nor do they inherit their positions; they receive a call from the heavens. Their authority, therefore, is essentially godly.

The foundation principle of Church government is that godly power must be exercised in a godly manner. This conception gives the words of scripture a potency they would not otherwise command. Joseph Smith's meditation on power in Liberty Jail in 1839 has surprising practical impact. After months of contemplating his situation—the loss of many leaders, the unyielding hostility of the surrounding population, and the failure to establish the City of Zion, not to mention the likelihood of his own execution for treason—Smith wrote a long letter to the Saints gathered in Illinois. He grew angry when he considered the abuse of his people and the betrayals of his associates, but he was also hopeful and philosophic. Near the end he reflected on what he had learned about power in the preceding months.

> We have learned by sad experience that it is the nature and disposition of almost all men, as soon as they get a little authority, as they suppose, they will immediately begin to exercise unrighteous dominion.
>
> Hence many are called, but few are chosen.
>
> No power or influence can or ought to be maintained by virtue of the priesthood, only by persuasion, by long-suffering, by gentleness and meekness, and by love unfeigned;
>
> By kindness, and pure knowledge, which shall greatly enlarge the soul without hypocrisy, and without guile—
>
> Reproving betimes with sharpness, when moved upon by the Holy Ghost; and then showing forth afterwards an increase of love toward him whom thou hast reproved, lest he esteem these to be his enemy;
>
> That he may know that thy faithfulness is stronger than the cords of death. (D&C 121:39–44)

This passage frustrates the modern reader in search of a theory of government. The statement opens so knowingly with a theory of human nature we can recognize. Power corrupts virtually everyone—and quickly. "They will immediately begin to exercise unrighteous dominion." Here we have the premise of James Madison in *The Federalist* no. 10. Interest will prevail in government. What then is Joseph Smith's answer to match Madison's proposals for a large republic and many layers of elections?

To our dismay, Smith lapses into sentimental comments about the priesthood ruling by gentleness and meekness and love unfeigned. What good is that? These are precisely the human virtues, rare in the first place, that are totally unreliable in rulers. Mere words, the democratic critics will scoff. How can such sentiments regulate what the Mormon scriptures themselves admit is the very nature of humans: when they get a little authority, they will immediately "exercise unrighteous dominion"?

What the critics fail to recognize is the constraining effect of the moral terms of power. All power operates within a moral framework, that is, a sense of what values legitimize a particular authority. The king must be a protector of his people or they will turn against him, as George III learned in 1776. The democratic politician must use his office for the good of the people or he will be forced to resign, as disappointed officeholders caught in graft learn when they are forced out of office. The CEO must serve the interests of shareholders or soon be displaced, as business executives who fail to improve their company's stock price know all too well. The moral terms of power set up limitations that invisibly fix the channels of action open to officeholders in any organization.

In the Church, the bishop must act as an emissary of God. Those are the moral terms of power. The people expect it of him, as anyone thrust into this office knows. They may not set these terms vocally, but the stake president does when the call is issued. Actually, little has to be said because the person called immediately knows what is expected. "I am not worthy" is often the response when a call is issued. The moral demands of the office are higher than most men feel they can meet. They operate in the bishop's own mind without a word being uttered. He also knows they work in the minds of his congregation. They expect him to receive revelation on their behalf, to visit them when ill, to counsel them during marital trials, to inspire their young, and to watch over their moral development. The implicit moral demands are immense, and everyone, most of all the bishop, knows this. If he falls down, he will have failed in his office as surely as a CEO whose stock drops. Those expectations act as a far more powerful check on authority than any constitutional limitations. One need only compare the record of abuses of power in the Church to the same record in any branch of civic government to recognize the effectiveness of the moral terms of power.

The secret ingredient in the recipe is the expectation that leaders and people both feel. Leaders are called of God. They receive the gifts that attend their offices from heaven. The recruitment of new bishops and Relief Society presidents by the thousands every year attests to the deep understanding of these principles. Newly ordained bishops immediately assume the manner of a bishop. The ward members speak of the mantle of the office falling upon them. No one can explain exactly how the change comes about, but in actuality the transformation comes out of group wisdom. Latter-day Saints know in their bones that only leadership based on righteousness and spirituality will work, and the new officeholder knows it too. A bishop must assume the virtues of a bishop to function as one. The godliness of the office requires it.

Charisma, the gift of divine power saturating the organization, thus creates the ethos in which Church government operates. Joseph Smith had no idea of the sociology of the Church he organized. He knew only that he had a commission from God to form an organization led by revelation and priesthood. He had great confidence in his own gifts, and, remarkably, he wanted to share them with the Church. His urge was to grant the power to speak and act for God, even to see God as he had, to all. Although he lacked the Weberian language to describe what he had done, he knew he had imposed an obligation of godly behavior on those who assumed office. The result was a bold experiment in organizational form that has passed the test of time surprisingly well.

NOTES

1. Nathan O. Hatch, *The Democratization of American Christianity* (New Haven: Yale University Press, 1989).
2. Max Weber, *The Theory of Social and Economic Organization*, ed. Talcott Parsons, trans. A. M. Henderson and Talcott Parsons (New York: The Free Press, 1947), 358.
3. Weber classified Joseph Smith as a charismatic, adding that he "cannot be classified in this way with absolute certainty since there is a possibility that he was a very sophisticated type of deliberate swindler." Weber, *Social and Economic Organization*, 359.

4. Weber, *Social and Economic Organization*, 324–72.
5. Kirtland High Council Minute Book, February 17, 1834, Church History Library, The Church of Jesus Christ of Latter-day Saints, Salt Lake City. Weber said of the organization that forms around charismatic leaders: "There is no such things as 'appointment' or 'dismissal,' no career, no promotion. There is only a 'call' at the instance of the leader on the basis of the charismatic qualification of those he summons. There is no hierarchy. . . . There is no such thing as a definite sphere of authority and of competence." *Social and Economic Organization*, 360. Joseph Smith's organization was a hybrid.
6. Donald Q. Cannon and Lyndon W. Cook, eds., *The Far West Record: Minutes of the Church of Jesus Christ of Latter-day Saints, 1830–1844* (Salt Lake City: Deseret Book, 1983), 3.
7. Kirtland High Council Minute Book, February 27, 1835.
8. Richard Lyman Bushman, *Joseph Smith: Rough Stone Rolling* (New York: Knopf, 2005), gallery following p. 230.
9. Brigham Young and others, in *Journal of Discourses* (London: Latter-day Saints' Book Depot, 1854–86), 6:319. My information comes from Josh E. Probert, "'A Good Hand to Keep the Dogs and Wolves out of the Flock': Nineteenth-Century Mormon Thought on Brigham Young as Prophet," Archive of Restoration Summer Seminar paper, 2006, in author's possession.
10. Heber C. Kimball, in *Journal of Discourses*, 8:86.
11. Heber C. Kimball, in *Journal of Discourses*, 8:275.
12. Joseph Smith to Lyman Wight and others, August 16, 1834, in *Personal Writings of Joseph Smith*, ed. Dean C. Jessee, rev. ed. (Salt Lake City: Deseret Book, 2002), 348.

In Nauvoo, Joseph Smith "told the brethren that . . . a man would get nearer to God by abiding by [the] precepts [of the Book of Mormon], than by any other book." (© 1995 Intellectual Reserve, Inc. All rights reserved.)

John W. Welch

2

The Book of Mormon as the Keystone of Church Administration

The Book of Mormon serves its readers and users in many ways. On its pages are found rare and precious explanations of the gospel and doctrine of Jesus Christ, the plan of happiness and of salvation, and the Nephite prophetic worldview situating the entire world in relation to the covenants made by God with the house of Israel with promises to all of his children on this earth. Through invitations and exemplars, it provides sage tutorials in cultivating spirituality through the testimony of Jesus Christ enlivened by the power of the Holy Ghost.

Less often recognized but equally present on its pages are the foundational administrative principles of the restored gospel of Jesus Christ. Administrative principles are scattered among the revelations and experiences of Nephite religious leaders and their people, and with little

---

John W. Welch is the Robert K. Thomas Professor of Law at the J. Reuben Clark Law School and also editor in chief of BYU Studies.

difficulty an alert, interested reader can assemble from the Book of Mormon beneficial principles, practices, and procedures of Church governance.

This paper seeks to identify which of those principles were used by the earliest believers in the Book of Mormon, who often followed the Book of Mormon precisely and sometimes even explicitly. It makes sense that they would do this. By compiling textual, practical, and historical details, this paper draws attention to the foundational role that the Book of Mormon played in authoritatively establishing important principles of Latter-day Saint religious and ecclesiastical administration.

At the time it was translated in the second quarter of 1829, the Book of Mormon was the main revelation authoritatively binding on the entire congregation of the fledgling Church of Christ, as it was called from 1830 to 1834. Without delay, Joseph Smith and Oliver Cowdery and their compatriots began baptizing, worshipping together, and establishing what would become the written and unwritten order of the growing Church. Not only its doctrines and instructions for personal living but also its many administrative guidelines came to them with a seal of divine approval and investiture. Only at their peril could believers as well as nonbelievers ignore these church policies, principles, and practices.

Although most modern Latter-day Saints do not regularly recognize their deep indebtedness to the Book of Mormon for many of their institutional assets, the administrative character and personality of The Church of Jesus Christ of Latter-day Saints has indeed grown directly from the genetic material found in the Book of Mormon, which can easily be seen as the nucleus in the germination of the Restoration. Indeed, a few years after the organization of the Church, the Prophet Joseph Smith identified the Book of Mormon with the mustard seed prophetically referred to by Jesus in one of his parables in Matthew 13. The Prophet explained that this tiny seed had come forth out of the earth and would become "the greatest among herbs" (Matthew 13:32), a great tree giving shelter and nesting space to the birds of the air.[1] Said another way, Joseph Smith saw the organizational framework on which the peoples of the world would be brought together and given place as growing out of the Book of Mormon.

Most people, however, have paid little notice to the essential role of the Book of Mormon in the administrative history of the Church, perhaps for several reasons. Few people have paid enough attention to the administrative history of the Church in any regard, let alone the contributions made by the Book of Mormon to that history. Familiarity with well-established Church practices tends to obscure in modern minds the distinctiveness that many passages in the Book of Mormon would have had to its initial readers in the 1830s. Others have not thought of the Book of Mormon on par with "historical" documents, such as letters or contemporaneous journal entries. But because the writers of the Book of Mormon often assured their readers that they had seen the modern day and were writing this book to benefit modern people (as in 2 Nephi 28 or Mormon 8:26–34), the Book of Mormon would have sounded in the ears of its audiences from the outset as having been written directly to them, and therefore understanding their practical response to this book holds an important place in our efforts to reconstruct the perceptions, attitudes, motives, and practices of early Latter-day Saints.

Some people have searched for, and for the most part not found, much evidence that early Church meetings and practices were being modeled on directions taken from the Book of Mormon. But newly published documents, databases, and search engines yield more evidence than has been previously set forth. Based on the following, I believe that people should no longer ignore this elephant in the room, namely the Book of Mormon, as a persistent and even dominant source of Church administrative genius.

VERBATIM USE OF THE BOOK OF MORMON IN THE 1829 "ARTICLES OF THE CHURCH OF CHRIST"

The first evidence that the Book of Mormon was understood and used as a Church administrative guide came as early as the end of June 1829, shortly after the translation of the Book of Mormon had been completed. As initial steps were then being taken to receive divine instructions relative to "building up the church of Christ, according to the fulness of the gospel,"[2] Oliver Cowdery undertook to draft three pages entitled the "Articles of the Church of Christ,"[3] most likely late in June 1829.[4] The manuscript of this rarely seen text, preserved in the Church History Archives, identifies itself as a "true copy," apparently written a little later from an original that is no longer extant. Its full text[5] reads as follows, with bolding[6] and citation references added to show the sources Cowdery quoted:

> A commandment from God unto Oliver how he should build up his church and the manner thereof—
>
> Saying Oliver listen to the voice of Christ your Lord and your God and your Redeemer and write the words which I shall command you concerning **my Church my Gospel my Rock [D&C 18:4; cf. 3 Nephi 11:39–40 (my rock); 27:8–10 (my church, my gospel)]** and my Salvation. Behold the world is ripening in iniquity and it must needs be that the children of men are stirred up unto repentance both the Gentiles and also the House of Israel for behold I **command all men every where to repent [3 Nephi 11:32]** and I speak unto you even as unto Paul mine apostle for ye are called even with that same calling with which he was called Now therefore **whoso**ever **repenteth** and humbleth himself before me **and desireth to be baptized in my name shall ye baptize them [3 Nephi 11:23]** And after this manner did he command me that I should baptize them **Behold ye shall go down and stand in the water and in my name shall ye baptize them And now behold these are the words which ye shall say calling them by name saying Having authority given me of Jesus Christ I baptize you in the name of the Father and of the Son and of the Holy Ghost Amen And then shall ye immerse them in the water and come forth again out of the water and after this manner shall ye baptize in my name For behold verily I say unto you**

that the Father and the Son and the Holy Ghost are one and I am in the Father and the Father in me and the Father and I are one [3 Nephi 11:23–27].

And ye are also **called** to **ordain Priests and Teachers [Moroni 3:1] according to the gifts and callings of God unto men [Moroni 3:4]** and after this manner shall ye ordain them **Ye shall pray unto the Father in** my **name** and then shall ye **lay your hands upon them and say In the name of Jesus Christ I ordain you to be a Priest or if he be a Teacher I ordain you to be a Teacher to preach repentance and remission of sins through Jesus Christ by the endurance of faith on his name to the end Amen [Moroni 3:2–3]** And this shall be the duty of the Priest He shall kneel down and the members of the Church shall kneel also which Church shall be called The Church of Christ and he shall pray to the Father in my name for the church and if it so be that it be **built upon my Rock** I will **bless** it **[3 Nephi 18:12]** And after that ye have prayed to the Father in my name ye shall preach the truth in soberness casting out none from among you but rather **invite them to come [2 Nephi 26:33]** And the Church shall **oft partake of bread and wine [Moroni 6:6]** and after this manner shall ye partake of it **The Elder or Priest** shall **minister it** and after this manner shall he do he shall **kneel with the Church and pray to the Father in the name of Christ** and then shall ye **say O God the Eternal Father we ask thee in the name of thy Son Jesus // Christ to bless and sanctify this bread to the souls of all those who partake of it that they may et <eat> in remembrance of the body of thy Son and witness unto thee O God the Eternal Father that they are willing to take upon them the name of thy Son and always remember him and keep his commandments which he hath given them that they may always have his spirit to be with them Amen [Moroni 4:1–3]** And then shall ye **take the cup and say O God the Eternal Father we ask thee in the** name of thy Son Jesus Christ to bless and sanctify this wine to the souls of all those who drink of it that they may do [it] in remembrance of the blood of thy Son which was shed for them that they may witness unto thee O God the Eternal Father that they do always remember him that they may have his spirit to be with them Amen [Moroni 5:1–2] And now behold I give unto you a commandment that ye shall not suffer any one knowingly to partake of my flesh and blood unworthily when ye shall minister it for whoso eateth and drinketh my flesh and blood unworthily eateth and drinketh damnation to his soul Therefore if ye know that a man is unworthy to eat and drink of my flesh and blood ye shall forbid him nevertheless ye shall not cast him out from among you but ye shall minister unto him and shall pray for him unto the Father in my name and if it so be that he repenteth and is baptized in my name then shall ye receive him and shall minister unto him of my flesh and blood but if he repenteth not he shall not be numbered among my people that he may not destroy my people For behold I know my sheep and they are numbered nevertheless ye shall not cast him out of your Synagogues or your places of worship for unto such shall ye continue to minister for ye know not but what they will return and repent and come unto me with full purpose of heart and I shall heal <heal> them and ye shall be the means of bringing Salvation unto them Therefore keep these sayings which I have commanded [3 Nephi 18:28–33] you that ye come not under condemnation for wo unto him whom the Father condemneth—

And the church **shall meet together oft [3 Nephi 18:22]** for **prayer and sup[p]lication [Alma 31:10]** casting out none from your places of worship but rather **invite them to come [2 Nephi 26:33]** And each member shall speak and tell the church of their progress in the way to Eternal life

And there shall be no **pride** nor **envying** nor **strifes** nor **malice** nor **idoletry** nor witchcrafts nor **whoredoms** nor fornications nor covetiousness nor **lying** nor **deceits** nor no **manner of** iniquity **[very close to the lists in Alma 1:32 and 16:18]** and if any one is guilty of any or the least of these and doth not repent and show fruits mee<a>ts [meets] **for repentance [Alma 12:15]** they **shall not be numbered among my people that they may not destroy my people [3 Nephi 18:31]**

And now I speak unto the Church **Repent all ye ends of the Earth and come unto me and be baptized in my name which is Jesus Christ and endure to the end** and ye **shall be saved** Behold Jesus Christ is the name which is given of the Father and there is none other name given whereby men can be saved Wherefore all men must take upon them the name which is given of the Father for in that name shall they be called at the last at <day> Wherefore if they know not the name by which they are called they cannot have place in the Kingdom of my Father [D&C 18:22–25; cf. 3 Nephi 27:20; Mosiah 3:17; 5:12] Behold ye must walk uprightly before me and sin not [D&C 18:31] and if ye do walk uprightly before me and sin not my grace is sufficient for you [D&C 18:31] that ye shall be lifted up at the last day [3 Nephi 27:22] Behold I am Jesus Christ the Son of the liveing God I am the same which came unto my own and my own received me not [3 Nephi 9:15, 16] I am the light which shineth in darkness and the darkness comprehendeth it not these words are not of men nor of man but of me [D&C 18:34] Now remember the words of him who is the first and the last the light and the life of the world [3 Nephi 9:18] And I Jesus Christ your Lord and your God and your Redeemer by the power of my Spirit hath spoken it Amen

And now if I have not authority to write these things judge ye behold **ye shall know that I have authority when** you and I shall be brought to **stand before [Ether 5:6]** the judgment seat of Christ Now may the [*manuscript torn*] [grace] of God the Father and our Lord Jesus Christ be and abide with you all // \\ and [*manuscript torn*] [finally] save you Eternally in his Kingdom through the **Infinite atonement [2 Nephi 9:7; Alma 34:12]** which is in Jesus Christ Amen—

Behold I am Oliver I am an Apostle of Jesus Christ by the will of God the Father and the Lord Jesus Christ Behold I have written \\ the things which he hath commanded me for behold his word was unto me as a burning fire shut up in my bones and I was weary with forbearing and I could forbear no longer Amen—

Written in the year of our Lord and Saviour 1829—

A true Copy of the articles of the Church of Christ &c.

While a number of questions remain about this important document—such as the immediate circumstances that inspired Oliver Cowdery (who here identifies himself as an Apostle of Jesus Christ) to receive this revelation, or the reasons why it was not ever publically used by Oliver or Joseph Smith—for present purposes, several things can be said with confidence about this text.

First, it can certainly be described as the earliest step in preparing an administrative handbook for the Church. It is clear that, as soon as Joseph Smith and Oliver finished the translation of the books of 3 Nephi and Moroni, Oliver was on fire with the spirit of urgency to build up the Church of Christ.

Second, the great inspiration of this text, received as a revelation by Oliver, perhaps with encouragement if not direction from Joseph, was to gather out of the mass of about 608 original Book of Mormon manuscript pages[7] the basic instructions and guidelines upon which the Church should be organized and administered. That selection process alone would have been a daunting task unless aided by the guidance of the Holy Ghost to help him remember where in that sheaf of papers these administrative provisions were to be found.

Third, at a glance one can see that about two-thirds of the words in this document (bolded above) are verbatim quotes from eight chapters in the Book of Mormon, namely the words of Jesus in 3 Nephi chapters 9, 11, 18, 27, and significant quotes from Moroni chapters 3–6, along with isolated phrases from 2 Nephi 26, Alma 1, 12, 16, 31, 34, and Ether 5, and also from seven verses in Doctrine and Covenants 18 (vv. 4, 22–25, 31, and 34).[8]

Fourth, this heavy use of the Book of Mormon makes perfect sense, especially because Joseph, Oliver, and David Whitmer had sought guidance on how to build up the Church of Christ "according to the fulness of the gospel,"[9] and the Book of Mormon was generally understood to contain or to be directly associated with "the fulness of the gospel" (see D&C 14:10; 20:9; 27:5).

Fifth, the abundance of administrative topics found in this document deal with the following:

- Paragraph 1 states the need for universal repentance, baptism or rebaptism, followed by the manner of performing the ordinance of baptism and the exact words of the baptismal prayer. Before 1835,[10] the words used in the baptismal prayer were those found in 1829 in the translation of the Book of Mormon.
- Paragraph 2 gives the manner for the ordination of priests and teachers, including the very words used by the Nephite elders in performing those ordinations. Then the manner of administering the sacrament and instructions regarding not allowing people to partake of the sacrament unworthily are taken (with only one word reversal in verse 28) from six full verses in 3 Nephi 18.
- Paragraph 3 contains the definition and instructions concerning what constitutes unworthiness. A natural outgrowth of the administrative requirement to forbid people from partaking of the sacrament unworthily is the need for a definition of worthiness. This suggests that the list found in paragraph 3 may be the first effort made in the restored Church to assemble the equivalent of a list of questions to be asked of oneself or by a priesthood interviewer in

determining a person's worthiness to be baptized or to partake of the sacrament.
- Paragraph 4 extends another universal call to repentance and explains what it means to take upon oneself and bear the name of Jesus Christ, walking uprightly, and receiving the grace and testimony of Jesus, including his own declaration of his identity, which he spoke out of the darkness over the land in 3 Nephi 9.
- Paragraph 5 then ends with a seal of authority that these words will stand at the judgment seat of God, words taken from Ether 5. Oliver Cowdery had learned the necessity of speaking by divinely invested authority, and thus he certifies that he speaks as "an apostle of Jesus Christ."

The long blocks of verbatim quotes from the Book of Mormon in this 1829 text make this document the primary exhibit in demonstrating that the Book of Mormon was literally followed, and was to continue to be followed, as the initial administrative handbook of the Church.

THE CONTINUED DIRECT USE OF THE BOOK OF MORMON IN DOCTRINE AND COVENANTS 20

Revealed on April 10, 1830,[11] another document (originally known as the "Articles and Covenants of the Church") eventually became numbered as Doctrine and Covenants 20. It can easily be described as the first official handbook of the Church, focused especially on the establishment and operation of newly founded branches of the Church.[12] Although one should not see the 1829 Articles of the Church of Christ either as a source for or an early draft of section 20,[13] one clear similarity between the 1829 document and section 20 is that they both make use of numerous words and specific directives found in the Book of Mormon.

For example, the sacrament prayers are found in Doctrine and Covenants 20:77, 79, but these words were once again drawn from the Book of Mormon. In the first known printing of Doctrine and Covenants 20 in the

1831 *Painesville Telegraph*, it simply states in lieu of these verses: "And the manner of baptism and the manner of administering the Sacrament are to be done as is written in the Book of Mormon."[14] Similarly, other early iterations of Doctrine and Covenants 20, rather than spelling out the words of the sacrament prayers, mechanically refer the reader to "Book of Mormon, Page 175" (in other words, page 175 in the 1830 edition of the Book of Mormon), or they place the material from Moroni 4–5 and 3 Nephi 11 in quotation marks.[15]

Other administrative instructions in section 20 draw on the Book of Mormon. For example, those blessing the sacrament are told to kneel (20:76; compare Moroni 4:2), and the procedures for baptism are given (20:72–74; see 3 Nephi 11:23–26). The leaders of the Church are told to keep a list of the names of all members, numbering those who have been baptized (20:82; see Mosiah 6:1; 3 Nephi 30:2; Moroni 6:4) and to blot out the names of those expelled from the Church (20:83; as in Mosiah 5:11; 3 Nephi 18:31; Moroni 6:7). Members overtaken in fault are to be "dealt with as the scriptures direct" (20:80), which would seem to be an explicit reference to the unique words of the Lord on this very subject in 3 Nephi 18:28–32. Other elements in this section that relate to the Book of Mormon include the declarations that those who receive the Book of Mormon in faith will "receive a crown of eternal life" (D&C 20:14–16; compare obtaining "eternal life" in 2 Nephi 31:18; Jacob 6:11) and that all need to be baptized and endure to the end (20:25; compare 2 Nephi 33:4; 3 Nephi 27:16).

These details qualify section 20 to stand as strong supporting evidence that the Book of Mormon was consciously seen and used, in the first instance, as the basic source for priesthood and administrative instructions for the fledgling Church.

PEOPLE READ AND KNEW THE BOOK OF MORMON

It is often hard to divest ourselves of our modern perceptions of the Church when we try to imagine how it operated in the very early 1830s.

At that time, the Church had no Primary association, no Relief Society, no meetinghouses, no temples, no tithing, no Word of Wisdom, no websites, no Doctrine and Covenants, and not much to read. But they did have the Book of Mormon. Indeed, until 1835 not much else had been printed in the Latter-day Saint library. So it stands all the more to reason that the nascent Church would have made great use of the Book of Mormon for many purposes: for doctrine, for prophecy, for inspiration, for testimony, for reproof, for exhortation, and also for administrative guidance. Even if not cited nearly as often in ordinary Latter-day Saint religious discourse as was the Bible, it is evident that the Book of Mormon was seen as a record of ancient inhabitants of the Western Hemisphere, as a sign of the Restoration of the gospel and of Israel, and as a source for several religious teachings. Countering any perception that the Book of Mormon was rarely used or sidelined as a mere artifact, considerable evidence shows that the early Saints indeed made actual use of the Book of Mormon for many reasons, including administrative purposes.

Journals of William E. McLellin. Important evidence in this regard can be found in the six journals of William McLellin (1831–36), his 1831 diary being the earliest of all Mormon diaries. From these early records, first published in 1994, we can now see that the Book of Mormon was read, quoted, and drawn upon almost incessantly, at least by McLellin and most of his companions. "By far the most frequent topic in his sermons was the Book of Mormon, evidences in its behalf, prophecies about its coming forth, testimonies of its divinity, and validations of its worth in opening the glories of the latter days (his theme in over thirty-three sermons)."[16] The next most commonly treated subject in his discourses was the Articles and Covenants of the Church, which he discussed on eighteen documented occasions. Perhaps for textual and other reasons, this book and the Church were naturally and inextricably linked in his preaching.[17] Indeed, McLellin's conversion was based on his acknowledgment of "the truth and Validity of the book of Mormon" and in the same breath that he had "found the people of the Lord—The Living Church of Christ."[18]

The Book of Mormon as the Keystone of Church Administration

In 1831, McLellin's two main themes were the Book of Mormon and the coming of Christ in judgment of the world and to establish Zion among his Saints.[19] More than this is unreported, but it is not difficult to imagine McLellin using 1 Nephi 14, 2 Nephi 27–30, 3 Nephi 20–22, and 4 Nephi to proclaim and inaugurate the program of establishing Zion as the first administrative objective of the restored gospel of Jesus Christ. On Sunday, October 2, 1831, McLellin and his companion, Hyrum Smith, preached "about 2½ hours" about the Book of Mormon and "warned them of their danger"; but in spite of their warnings, "they went on in their old way to administer the sacrament."[20] Evidently he had tried to convince them that the correct way to administer the sacrament was the manner found in the Book of Mormon.

In 1832, in addition to mentioning the "evidences and testimonies concerning the coming forth of the Book of Mormon, McLellin now stressed the utility and importance of the book, . . . covenants, obedience, ordinances (particularly the laying on of hands),"[21] along with other practical elements of the plan of salvation, gathering to Zion, and the organization of the Church. All of these topics are to be found in the Book of Mormon, some primarily so, laying the foundation for preaching about other revelations, such as the recently revealed (on February 16, 1832) Doctrine and Covenants 76 on the kingdoms of glory in the heavens, which McLellin also now emphasized.

In 1833, McLellin worked with Parley P. Pratt as his companion. "Pratt's themes were much broader than McLellin's messages of fundamental simplicity and austere spirituality," but both elders taught the plainness of the gospel of Christ as found in the Book of Mormon.[22] On March 22, 1833, for example Parley P. Pratt read the account of "Alma and Amulek's teaching and sufferings" in Ammonihah, found in Alma 9–16. McLellin reported that "Br Parley was melted into tears and his words were powerful even to the cutting of those to the heart who were present and I was filled to[o] so that I walked through the room praising and blessing the name of the Lord and testifying to his word even the book of Mormon until Sister Russel spoke out and 'said that she believed it.'"[23] On March 31, McLellin records that Pratt "arose and read a number of pages concerning the personal ministry of Christ . . . on this continent, and in all he read, expounded and reasoned about 2 hours and I then spoke about one hour, and read and expounded the covenants—& articles."[24] Significantly, those particular teachings of the Savior in the Book of Mormon would have included the ordinances and administrative directives presented in the 1830 Articles and Covenants. But when Pratt "then asked if any wished to obey," or in other words follow the baptismal procedures set forth in 3 Nephi 11, no one stepped forth.

In 1834, McLellin's preaching and proselytizing emphasized virtues (such as charity, humility, endurance, forgiveness, and unity) as well as the laws of Zion. In connection with the nature of the kingdom of Christ, he spoke "about the authority given by God to the Church of the Latter-day Saints, specifically about the two priesthoods."[25] In this regard one easily imagines that (in a missionary context) he quoted 3 Nephi 11:25, "Having authority given me of Jesus Christ," and 3 Nephi 18:37, when Christ "gave them power to give the Holy Ghost," as primary texts laying the groundwork for his testimony of the restoration of the priesthoods and the revelation on priesthood in Doctrine and Covenants 84. The Church meeting described by McLellin on September 7, 1834, comports readily with the directions given for the administration of Church meetings in Moroni 6.[26] On October 12, 1834, McLellin declined to "break bread because there was such a general division in the Church,"[27] apparently following the directive in 3 Nephi 18:28–29 that the priesthood should not administer the sacrament to the unworthy. So important was the Book of Mormon to McLellin that, on November 14, 1834, he complained that his companion, John Boynton, delivered "a fine discourse but he never mentioned the book of mormon once."[28]

In 1835, McLellin traveled and served in New England together with the newly organized Quorum of the Twelve Apostles. He gladly notes when other Apostles, who shared the pulpit with him, spoke about the Book of

The Book of Mormon as the Keystone of Church Administration

Mormon, notably about the Savior's teachings in 3 Nephi, the two priesthoods, and authority to act in the name of Jesus Christ.[29] For example, on May 11, 1835, he wrote: "Elder B. Young. after reading a portion of the Saviour's teaching in the book of Mormon he spoke about 1½ hours contrasting the religions of the day with the truth."[30] Although McLellin does not report which teachings of the Savior were set in contrast with the teachings and practices of the day, the result of Brigham Young's teachings in this instance was clear: "We went immediately to the watter and Elder O. Hyde immersed 7 persons. . . . At evening we had another confirmation mee. and those baptized were confirmed by the laying on of hands and a number were blessed in order that they might be healed of infirmaties."[31] The sequential connection between faith, baptism, purification by the Holy Ghost, gifts of the Spirit, and healings is established nowhere more clearly than in 3 Nephi 17:8; 18:32; 19:13–15; and 26:14–15.

Other uses of the Book of Mormon. William McLellin's use of the Book of Mormon was not aberrational. Ample use of the Book of Mormon in Church meetings, proselyting, and in other early Latter-day Saint administrative contexts can also be documented.

In his journals, Wilford Woodruff reports that he preached about the authenticity of the Book of Mormon six times in the 1830s. On June 9, 1835, David W. Patten preached from John 10, likely regarding the "other sheep" identified in 3 Nephi 15:16–16:3 as the people at Bountiful visited by the resurrected Lord.[32] On March 23, 1837, Woodruff wrote that he was called upon in a meeting by Father Smith to read a chapter from the Book of Mormon; Woodruff then read the third chapter from the book of Jacob in the 1830 edition (today's Jacob 5), regarding the extended allegory of the tame and wild olive trees. Then in a meeting in the Kirtland Temple in April 1837, prophecies were pronounced on the heads of many of the Saints; his journal prolaims, "Rejoice O earth & Shout O heavens for the natural fruit of the tame olive tree is again manifest in the earth." On April 9, 1837, John Smith read from the twelfth chapter of 2 Nephi (today's 2 Nephi 28–30) and preached from that text. Again, on February 18, 1838, and

May 20, 1838, Wilford Woodruff preached on Zenos' allegory.[33] Although all of these occurrences do not involve administrative situations, the generously documented usage of the Book of Mormon for all of these purposes strengthens the case that the Book of Mormon was regularly on the minds and in the hearts of the Saints.[34]

This pattern of using the Book of Mormon in the preaching and practices of the early Church continued as the Apostles traveled to England to gather Zion in the British Isles. On October 18, 1840, Wilford Woodruff met for a sacrament meeting with the members; he "read in the Book of Mormon gave instructions & broke bread unto them."[35] Quite likely his instructions came from 3 Nephi 18 and from the opening chapters in the book of Moroni. On December 11, 1839, Parley P. Pratt lectured on the origins of the American Indians. On February 6, 1840, Woodruff preached to four or five hundred people on the Book of Mormon; and on October 7, 1840, he held a public debate with a minister about the Book of Mormon, all as recorded in Woodruff's journal.[36]

To the very end of the Joseph Smith era, the Book of Mormon was read, followed, and even clung to by the leaders and members of the early Church. On the way to Carthage Jail, Hyrum Smith knew right where to go to find Ether 12:37–38, which he read aloud as his final source of solace and strength before he was murdered: "Thou hast been faithful; wherefore . . . thou shalt be made strong. . . . Farewell . . . until we shall meet before the judgment-seat of Christ, where all men shall know that my garments are not spotted with your blood."[37]

Joseph Smith's use of the Book of Mormon. Moreover, in making such use of the Book of Mormon, the early Saints were following the example set by their prophet-leader. In many ways, Joseph Smith continued to be involved with and to make use of the Book of Mormon long after it was translated and published. He did not somehow leave the Book of Mormon behind as other dimensions of his ministry unfolded. On many occasions he extolled the great benefits to the world that would come through the Book of Mormon.[38] In November 1835, he expressly cited the Book of Mormon and the prophet Ether regarding the unbelief of the Gentiles and the establishment of a New Jerusalem.[39] He personally made corrections and modifications for the 1837 and 1840 editions of the book. On March 20, 1839, in Liberty Jail, Joseph testified, "The Book of Mormon is true,"[40] and on July 2, 1839, he preached on revelations in the Book of Mormon and told the Saints: "Do not betray the revelations of God, whether in Bible, Book of Mormon, or Doctrine & Covenants, or any of the word of God."[41] On June 15, 1842, he enjoined the Saints: "Seek to know God in your closets, call upon him in the fields; follow the directions of the Book of Mormon, and pray over, and for, your families, your cattle, your flocks, your herds, your corn, and all things that you possess,"[42] directly paraphrasing the words of Amulek in Alma 34:18–26.

Scouring the pages of the *Teachings of the Prophet Joseph Smith*, one finds numerous ideas and phrases that most likely originated with distinctive passages in the Book of Mormon, from 1831 to 1843.[43] For example,

- October 25, 1831: Joseph admonished the Saints to do their duty patiently and in perfect love: "Until we have perfect love we are liable to fall."[44] // This comports with Moroni 8:26, "which Comforter filleth with hope and perfect love, which love endureth by diligence unto prayer, until the end shall come."[45]
- February 16, 1832: God rewards everyone "according to the deeds done in the body"[46] // God judges "according to the deeds which have been done in the mortal body" (Alma 5:15).
- August 1832: "Ask your heavenly Father, in the name of his Son Jesus Christ to manifest the truth unto you, and if you do it with an eye single to his glory nothing doubting, he will answer you by the power of His Holy Spirit"[47] // "Ask God, the Eternal Father, in the name of Christ, if these things are not true; and if ye shall ask with a sincere heart, with real intent, having faith in Christ, he will manifest the truth of it unto you, by the power of the Holy Ghost" (Moroni 10:4); "doubting nothing" (Mormon 9:21).

- August 1832: "The Son of God came into the world to redeem it from the fall"[48] // "the Messiah cometh in the fulness of time, that he may redeem the children of men from the fall" (2 Nephi 2:26).
- January 4, 1833: Gentiles "grafted in from whence the chosen family were broken off"[49] // "grafted in the branches of the wild olive-tree" (Jacob 5:10).
- November 19, 1833: "What manner of person ought I to be?"[50] // "what manner of men ought ye to be?" (3 Nephi 27:27).
- December 1833: "puffed up, and fall under condemnation, and into the snare of the devil"[51] // "puffed up" (2 Nephi 28:15); "brought under condemnation" (Moroni 9:6); "the snares and the wiles of the devil" (Helaman 3:29).
- January 22, 1834: "committed against light and knowledge"[52] // "against the light and knowledge of God" (Alma 39:6).
- January 22, 1834: "remorse of conscience"[53] // "remorse of conscience" (Alma 29:5).
- January 22, 1834: "garments are spotless"[54] // "garments are spotless" (Alma 7:25).
- January 22, 1834: "obey the gospel with full purpose of heart"[55] // "come with full purpose of heart" (Jacob 6:5; 3 Nephi 10:6; 18:32).
- May 14, 1840: "my soul delighteth in plainness"[56] // "my soul delighteth in plainness" (2 Nephi 25:4).
- January 5, 1841: "he allways [sic] is striving to get others as miserable as himself"[57] // "he seeketh that all men might be miserable like unto himself" (2 Nephi 2:27).
- May 26, 1842: "Said Jesus: 'ye shall do the work, which ye see me do'"[58]// "for that which ye have seen me do even that shall ye do" (3 Nephi 27:21).
- June 9, 1842: "God does not look on sin with allowance"[59] // "the Lord cannot look upon sin with the least degree of allowance" (Alma 45:16).

- September 1, 1842: "There was no other name given under heaven, nor no other ordinance admitted, whereby man could be saved"[60] // "there is none other way nor name given under heaven whereby men can be saved" (2 Nephi 31:21).
- July 9, 1843: "children have no sins . . . all made alive in Christ"[61] // "all little children are alive in Christ" (Moroni 8:22).

Based on all the foregoing citations, which can collectively be clustered as the voice of a community of witnesses, I conclude that the Book of Mormon was better known and a more important source of instruction and administrative directives in the early formative days of the Church than is often realized. In the early 1830s, it was not only *the* Book of Mormon, it was indeed the *only* Mormon book; and throughout Joseph Smith's life it remained *the quintessential* Mormon book.

IMPLICIT OR PRESUMPTIVE EARLY ADMINISTRATIVE USES OF THE BOOK OF MORMON AS A HANDBOOK OF INSTRUCTIONS

Finally, the following data display numerous places where early readers of the Book of Mormon would have found on its pages clear administrative directives. There is ample reason to believe that these basic instructions and patterns of fundamental religious practices were not taken lightly, as strings in a simple narrative yarn. The Book of Mormon, written with the conditions and needs of the last days in mind, readily worked as a general handbook of Church instructions.

For example, by reading 3 Nephi 27:21, readers hear the voice of the Savior saying: "Ye know the things that ye *must do* in my *church*; . . . for that which ye have seen me do even that shall ye do. Therefore, if ye do these things blessed are ye, for ye shall be lifted up at the last day" (3 Nephi 27:21–22; emphasis added).[62] Here Jesus uses strong language. The exemplary actions and verbal instructions of the Lord *must* be followed. Thus, in general, the directives of the Book of Mormon were not optional but mandatory. In 3 Nephi, the people had seen Jesus do many things: they had seen him lead them in prayer, bless their children, ordain their leaders, show them how to baptize, heal the sick, organize and name the Church, and other such things. His instructions, examples, and procedures were to be followed.[63] How could early Church leaders and members embrace the Book of Mormon as the revealed word of God without taking all of its teachings seriously?

By 1832, however, the Saints were forgetting to follow the Book of Mormon in certain ways. Significantly, a revelation mainly "on priesthood" placed the Church under condemnation until they remembered the Book of Mormon "not only to say, *but to do* according to that which I have written" (D&C 84:57; emphasis added). This mandate would seem to reinstate and reinforce a clear direction that the Church was to use and follow the Book of Mormon as an administrative guide, for just as Jesus had said at the end of his first day among the righteous survivors at Bountiful, serious condemnation would come upon the Church if the directives given on that occasion should be ignored. Jesus said, "Keep these sayings which I have commanded you [this day] that ye come not under condemnation" (3 Nephi 18:33).

To suggest the extent to which the early Saints did, in fact, administer the affairs of the Church according to the things written in the Book of Mormon, the following materials set forth several dozen passages in the Book of Mormon that clearly provide distinctive procedural guidance. The large quantity of these passages tends to increase the likelihood that the Book of Mormon was a conscious source for this set of administrative practices. Moreover, on several occasions, historical sources are cited to show that these practices were in place early in Church history. The early presence of these practices tends to enhance the plausibility of the claim that the Book of Mormon was the primary source for these practices, for in those early days there were few other sources that could have been drawn upon. And in addition, these passages have been clustered in groups that correspond with the chapters in today's *Church Handbook of Instructions*. The strong congruence between the main administrative components of the handbook and the unmistakable directives of the Book of Mormon tends to confirm the observation that administrative order of the Church distills and instantiates the explicit and implicit administrative models woven into the essential fabric of the restored Church and gospel of Jesus Christ.

Name, leaders, and congregations of the Church. The Book of Mormon makes it clear that the name of the Church is integral to the identity of the Church of Christ. To be the Church of Jesus Christ, it must bear his name (see 3 Nephi 27:8–9). The doctrines taught must be the doctrine of Christ (see 3 Nephi 11:31–40) and the gospel of Christ (see 3 Nephi 27:13–21). His disciples must have authority to act in the name of Christ and "whatsoever [they] shall do, [they] shall do it in [his] name" (3 Nephi 27:7). Consistent with these requisites, the Church was referred to as "the Church of Christ" as early as in the 1830 Articles and Covenants (D&C 20:1); and with references to this all important nomenclature, Oliver Cowdery was authorized, in a revelation given on April 6, 1830, to become "an elder unto this church of Christ, bearing my name" (D&C 21:11).

Turning the pages of the Book of Mormon, any reader is hard-pressed to miss the will of the Lord regarding such things as following a single prophet-leader, and not a council of elders or a sea of bishops or a congregational priesthood of all believers. Sole prophet-leaders such as Nephi, Alma the Younger, Nephi the son of Helaman, and Nephi the son of Nephi (in 2 Nephi 5, Alma 1, Helaman 7, and 3 Nephi 7:25) set strong precedents that have always encouraged the Latter-day Saints to look primarily to the Lord's true prophet for guidance in all ecclesiastical matters.

Other distinctive organizational features flow from the cohesive patterns of Church structure found amidst the lines of the Book of Mormon. An indelible endorsement for the all-important body of twelve disciple-apostles (3 Nephi 12:1; 19:12) is found in the first beatitude given by Jesus to the people at Bountiful: "Blessed are ye if ye shall give heed unto the words of these twelve" (3 Nephi 12:1). Three leaders among those twelve were given exceptional powers (3 Nephi 28:2–12), and three witnesses were given extraordinary privileges (2 Nephi 27:12; Ether 5:4), as had been Peter, James, and John, all of which collectively establish the precedent that grew into the distinctive and pervasive Latter-day Saint use of three-member presidencies sitting at the head of each quorum and organization. The concept of "presiding" itself finds its religious imprimatur in Book of Mormon passages reporting the administrations of Alma, who "ordained priests and elders . . . to *preside* and watch over the church" (Alma 6:1; emphasis added).

One of the main functions of Church leaders was to create uniformity and order among the faithful. Alma the Elder "did regulate *all* the affairs of the church" (Mosiah 26:37; emphasis added), and his son and grandsons followed his example each time they made "regulations" in establishing the covenant community (Alma 6:7) or dispelled dissensions and promoted peace by making "a regulation . . . throughout the church" (Alma 45:21; see also 62:44) and by "*uniting* as many to the church as would believe in their preaching" (3 Nephi 28:18; emphasis added). To the founding members of the restored Church, passages such as these would not have been glossed over lightly. If any of them wondered whether the Church of Christ should be, on the one hand, an association of loosely connected individuals or, on the other hand, a tightly knit cohort of like-minded members, the pattern of regularized organization found in the Book of Mormon would have given them clear guidance.

Other organizational elements that quickly became constitutional in the Church are modeled in the Book of Mormon. Fundamental was the process—to say nothing of the very possibility—of legitimately introducing organizational and doctrinal changes by authoritative revelation (see Mosiah 3:3; Alma 40:11; 3 Nephi 15:1), confirmed by the voice of the people (see Mosiah 7:9; 29:25–29; Alma 2:3; 27:22). Leaders were called of God by prophecy (see 1 Nephi 2:22), so much so that Church offices and assignments were known as "callings" (Jacob 2:3; Moroni 7:2; 8:1). The body of the Church was divided into smaller congregations: at one point, there were seven local units (see Mosiah 25:19–23); on another occasion, they divided into groups of about 250 people each (see 3 Nephi 19:4–5); at a difficult time, they partitioned into flocks of 50 people per priest (see Mosiah 18:18). The pastoral duties of these Church leaders who watched over their members, teaching and fostering unity in love, are spelled out on several occasions (for example, Mosiah 18:19–23; Moroni 6:4). The creating of new congregational units is modeled in Mosiah 25:19, with the authorized formation of Alma's seven churches in the land of Zarahemla, and in Alma 27:22, with the settling of the people of Ammon in the land of Jershon.

Ordinations. Next in organizational sequence comes the administration of the ordinations of the gospel. The Book of Mormon makes it clear that priests, teachers, and elders are to be consecrated by a formal ordination (see 2 Nephi 5:26; Alma 6:1), that these priesthood ordinations must be performed by the laying on of hands (Alma 6:1; Moroni 3:2), and that priesthood authority was necessary to administer the ordinances of the gospel. "Authority" in this sense is mentioned a dozen times in the Book of Mormon (including Mosiah 18:13, 17, 18, 26; Alma 5:3; Helaman 5:18; 11:18; 3 Nephi 7:17; 11:25; 12:1; Moroni 8:28), and "priesthood" occurs in Alma 4:20 and again seven times in Alma 13. This early mandate for proper priesthood ordination in order for one to act with power and authority in behalf of God is set forth much more clearly in the Book of Mormon than in the New Testament. Indeed, Moroni 2:1–2 revealed the very words used by Jesus in 3 Nephi 18:37–38 as he gave the disciples the power to bestow the gift of the Holy Ghost.

In all these cases, many choices were open to the fledgling Church: whether to ordain, how to ordain, and which offices to install; whether to baptize, how to baptize, and when to baptize. The question here is not so much whether similar practices were followed in various sectors by Methodists or Catholics or others.[64] Many options were available and could have been embraced by the early Latter-day Saints. But in many cases, such as with the ordination and authorization of priesthood officers by the laying on of hands, the choice was already made for the Church by the scriptural instructions and requirements found in the Book of Mormon.

Indeed, the procedures and actual words used in ordaining priests and teachers are given expressly in Moroni 3:1–4. One priesthood authority is required in order to baptize (conferred in 3 Nephi 11:19–22; see also Mosiah

18:13–14), and a higher priesthood authority or power is necessary in order to bestow the gift of the Holy Ghost. Indeed, the last thing that Jesus did at the end of his first day in Bountiful was to take his twelve disciples aside and touch them, one by one (see 3 Nephi 18:36). A cloud overcame the multitude so they could not see Jesus as he spoke the sacred words (revealed in Moroni 2:2) that he used at the time when he conferred upon these disciples the power to bestow the gift of the Holy Ghost (see 3 Nephi 18:37–38). This powerful combination of instructive texts told the readers of the Book of Mormon that two priesthoods were necessary: one to baptize, another to give the Holy Ghost. Thus it would be logical to conclude that, just as Joseph and Oliver had been inspired by 3 Nephi 11 on May 15, 1829, to go to the woods in Harmony, Pennsylvania, to seek the authority to baptize,[65] they would have equally known from 3 Nephi 18 that they also needed the higher priesthood power. From the Book of Mormon, they had also already learned that the priesthood after the holy order of the Son of God was associated with Melchizedek, the greatest bearer of the high priesthood in ancient times (see Alma 13:1–15).

Ordinances. In answer to the question of what prerequisites should be required of those wishing to join the Church through the door of the new and everlasting covenant, faith was the first principle of admission as taught to the poor Zoramites by Alma and his companions in Alma 32. Working examples of the roles of study, prayer, and change of heart in the conversion process are also adeptly illustrated by the work of Ammon and his brethren in the land of Nephi in Alma 17–26. Repentance is to follow faith (see Mosiah 4:10; 11:20–25; 26:22–37; Alma 5; 9; 12; 42; Helaman 7; 13; 3 Nephi 30:2), and confession follows repentance as a concluding step before baptism (see Helaman 5:17; 16:1; Moroni 6:7).

The essence of the required baptismal commitment is an offering of a broken heart and a contrite spirit (see 3 Nephi 9:20; 12:19; Moroni 6:2), through which one may obtain forgiveness. Forgiveness must then be retained by giving to the poor and leading a life of righteousness (see Mosiah 4:26; Alma 5).

Unlike most other Christian communities, which long in the past had set aside the covenantal nature of baptism (mainly as a consequence of baptizing infants), baptism is clearly connected in the Book of Mormon with adult covenant making and the subsequent remembering and keeping of God's commandments, which are his stipulations of the covenant (see Mosiah 5:1–10; Mosiah 18:13; 3 Nephi 18). The further fact that, in this process, baptized members of the Church take upon themselves the name of Christ is repeatedly emphasized in the covenant-making texts of the Book of Mormon (see Mosiah 5:10–12; 25:23; 3 Nephi 27:25; Moroni 6:3). The point that repentance and baptism was "the gate by which ye should enter" was unequivocally established by the Book of Mormon (for example, 2 Nephi 31:17).

The words of the baptismal prayer were embedded in the Nephite record (see 3 Nephi 11:25). The rule that baptism had to be accomplished by immersion was indisputably established by the words and actions of Alma, Alma the Younger, and Jesus himself (Mosiah 18:14–17; 3 Nephi 11:26). Baptizing in the name of Jesus Christ was established in these texts as the regular order of the Church (see 3 Nephi 18:11; 27:16; 30:2; 4 Nephi 1:1).

The performance of baptisms in accordance with this very pattern, in large measure unique to the Book of Mormon, began as early as May 25, 1829, within ten days of the translation of the passages in 3 Nephi that set forth the elements of this crucially essential ordinance.[66] In April 1830, these elements were all succinctly pulled together in the Articles and Covenants: "Behold whosoever humbleth himself before God and desireth to be baptized [3 Nephi 11:23], and comes forth with a broken heart and a contrite spirit [3 Nephi 12:19], and witnesseth unto the church, that they have truly repented of all their sins and are willing to take upon them the name of Christ [3 Nephi 11:23], having a determination to serve him unto the end [Moroni 6:3], and truly manifest by their works that they have received the Spirit of Christ unto the remission of their sins, then shall they be received unto baptism into the church of Christ."[67]

Immediately arising out of the practice of baptizing only those who are willing to enter into the baptismal covenant is the question of how old a person needs to be in order to be eligible for baptism. By supplying the doctrines that only those who are "capable of committing sin" are accountable (Moroni 8:10), that children cannot repent (see Moroni 8:19, 22), and that infant baptism is abhorrent (see Moroni 8:20–21), the Book of Mormon established the principled reasons behind the concept of the age of accountability, which was spoken of as soon as the Book of Mormon was translated in 1829 (see D&C 18:42) and the Church was organized in 1830 (see D&C 20:71). In 1831, that threshold was set as the age of eight (see D&C 68:25, 27).

Giving the gift of the Holy Ghost followed baptism, as directed by the Book of Mormon (see Moroni 6:4). At the meeting at which the Church was organized in April 1830, the newly set apart elders "laid [their] hands on each individual member of the Church present that they might receive the gift of the Holy Ghost, and be confirmed members of the Church of Christ."[68]

The extensive practice of keeping "a list of the names of the several members" of the Church, which began at least as early as Doctrine and Covenants 20:82, would not have sounded unfamiliar to anyone who had read the Book of Mormon, with its frequent practice of numbering and recording the names of the people of the Church (see Mosiah 6:1; 26:35; Alma 6:3; Moroni 6:4).

The frequent administration of the sacrament among Latter-day Saints tracks the words in Moroni 6:6, "they did meet together oft to partake of bread and wine, in remembrance of the Lord Jesus." In administering the sacrament, the priesthood brings the bread, just as the disciples were told by Jesus to bring the bread and wine (see 3 Nephi 18:1). Latter-day Saint people sit to receive the sacrament (as in 3 Nephi 18:2). The ordained priesthood holder breaks the bread before, not after, it is blessed (3 Nephi 18:5). In offering the prayer, the priests kneel down in the presence of the Church (Moroni 4:2), not out of their view. The words of the two sacrament prayers are found in the Book of Mormon (3 Nephi 18:7, 10–11; Moroni 4–5);[69] two prayers are offered, not just one. The disciples then give the emblems to "all those who shall believe and be baptized" (3 Nephi 18:5). The disciples were "commanded that they should give unto the multitude" (3 Nephi 18:4), and thus holding sacrament meeting is not optional among the Saints. This pattern is followed as the order of the Church, just as Jesus commanded: "And this *shall ye always observe to do, even as I have done*" (3 Nephi 18:6; emphasis added).

The practice of blessing children began as early as 1830 (see D&C 20:70). Today, the father typically blesses his children, but in Kirtland, Reynolds Cahoon brought his son to the Prophet Joseph Smith and asked him to bless the baby. Joseph did so and named him Mahonri Moriancumer.[70]

Healing the sick, another priesthood ordinance, finds ample precedent in the Book of Mormon (see Alma 15:5–11; 3 Nephi 7:22; 17:7–9; 4 Nephi 1:5; Mormon 9:24).

Patriarchal blessings, perhaps prompted in part by the blessings given by Jacob (see Genesis 49) and Lehi (see 2 Nephi 1–4) to their sons, were given to people at a meeting on December 29, 1835. "A large company assembled, when Father Smith made some appropriate remarks. A hymn was sung and father opened the meeting by prayer. About fifteen persons then received patriarchal blessings under his hands."[71]

Righteous living. Our vision for personal and religious righteousness shines forth from the pages of the Book of Mormon. Included here are directives regarding the gifts of the Spirit and a mandate to deny not the gifts (see Moroni 10), fasting (see Mosiah 27:22; Helaman 3:35; 3 Nephi 13:16–18; Moroni 6:5), praying in private (see Enos 1:4; Alma 33–34; 3 Nephi 13:5–6, 19), praying in the name of Jesus Christ (see 3 Nephi 18:19, 23, 30), praying in whatsoever place one might be (see Alma 34:38), and living in thanksgiving daily (see Mosiah 18:23; Alma 34:38).

Regarding family life, the only place in scripture where family prayer is expressly mentioned is in the Book of Mormon (3 Nephi 18:21, "pray in your families unto the Father"; see also Alma 34:21). Parental duties to teach and care for children are clearly taught (see 1 Nephi 1:1; Mosiah 4:14–15;

Alma 37:35). Prohibited are adultery, prostitution, and all sorts of abominations and lasciviousness (see Jacob 2:23; Mosiah 2:13). Polygamy is allowed only if the Lord of Hosts specifically commands his people to do this (see Jacob 2:27, 30; 3:5).

Winebibbing and drunkenness are disapproved (see 2 Nephi 15:11, 22; Mosiah 11:15). The abuse of women and children is condemned (see Alma 14; 50:30).

Welfare. The origins of the vast welfare program of the Church are also to be found in the Book of Mormon. The need to give to the poor is stated emphatically and repeatedly (see Jacob 2:19; Mosiah 4; 18:27; Alma 1:27; 34:27–29; 35:9). Having property in common and living the principles of consecration characterized the community that saw four generations of peace and righteousness after the Savior's visits (see 3 Nephi 26:19; 4 Nephi 1:3). The payment of tithes and offerings was called for by the resurrected Lord (see 3 Nephi 24:8–10). The building of Zion, the New Jerusalem, on the American continent was foreseen (see 3 Nephi 21:22–25), even should it require moving to new lands, fleeing into the wilderness, and making great sacrifices of personal wealth and well-being (as in the repeated cases of Lehi leaving Jerusalem, King Mosiah leaving the land of Nephi, Alma's people suffering in bondage, and the people of Lachoneus gathering to the city of Zarahemla).

Church meetings. It is also not hard to construct or find in the Book of Mormon the origins of the Mormon patterns of worship. As in the modern *Church Handbook of Instructions*, the Book of Mormon spells out the purposes of Church meetings and manner of conduct for congregational worship (see Moroni 6). Included are instructions about praying together (see Alma 6:6; 3 Nephi 19; 4 Nephi 1:12; Moroni 6:5), fasting together (see Alma 6:6; 4 Nephi 1:12; Moroni 6:5), singing (see Alma 5:9, 26; Ether 6:9; Moroni 6:9), preaching and exhorting as led by the Holy Ghost (see Moroni 6:9), meeting "one day in every week" (Mosiah 18:25), keeping the Sabbath day holy (see Mosiah 18:23), keeping the commandments of the Lord (see 4 Nephi 1:12), holding conferences of large bodies of all the Saints (see Mosiah 2–5; see also Alma 5, 7; 3 Nephi 11:1), and administering covenant renewals (see Mosiah 5; Alma 5; 3 Nephi 18). Affairs of the Church or its people were conducted with the concurrence of the voice of the people, by common consent (see Mosiah 29:25–29; Alma 2:3; 4:16; 27:21–22; Helaman 1:5–8).

In April 1830, the revelation in Doctrine and Covenants 20 told the elders "to conduct the meetings as they are led by the Holy Ghost, according to the commandments and revelations of God [meaning, at least, the Book of Mormon]. . . . And see that the church meet together often, and also see that all the members do their duty. . . . It is expedient that the church meet together often to partake of bread and wine in the remembrance of the Lord Jesus."[72] On January 23, 1833, Joseph Smith recorded the following description of a typical early Mormon meeting: "Having continued all day in fasting, and prayer, and ordinances, we closed by partaking of the Lord's supper. I blessed the bread and wine in the name of the Lord, when we all ate and drank, and were filled; then we sang a hymn, and the meeting adjourned."[73] All of this follows Moroni 6.

Latter-day Saint worship services were, from the beginning, open to all, just as the Book of Mormon had invited all to hear the word of God and "none were deprived" (Alma 6:5), for "all are alike unto God" (2 Nephi 26:33). Doctrine and Covenants 46:3–5 would soon add: "Ye are commanded never to cast any one out from your public meetings, which are held before the world. Ye are also commanded not to cast any one who belongeth to the church out of your sacrament meetings; nevertheless, if any have trespassed, let him not partake until he makes reconciliation. And again I say unto you, ye shall not cast any out of your sacrament meetings who are earnestly seeking the kingdom—I speak this concerning those who are not of the church." Children were also to be included in the congregation (see Mosiah 2:5; 3 Nephi 17:25; Moroni 8), which was not always the case among the various denominations.

Volunteerism. Very significant in Latter-day Saint Church administration is the principle of volunteerism, and the strong rejection of the idea of a paid ministry is a frequent refrain in the Book of Mormon. All members are expected to labor freely for the building up of the kingdom (2 Nephi 26:31, "the laborer in Zion shall labor for Zion"). Indeed, "if they labor for money they shall perish" (2 Nephi 26:31). Priests "should labor with their own hands for their support" (Mosiah 18:24), and any form of "priestcrafts," that is, seeking honor, riches and gain, was strictly condemned (Alma 1:16; Mormon 8:33, 37). For their labor, priests were "to receive the grace of God, that they might wax strong in the Spirit, having the knowledge of God, that they might teach with power and authority from God" (Mosiah 18:26). The problem with priestcrafts was that they promoted the love of "the vain things of the world" and promoted "false doctrines" (Alma 1:16). Thus the Lord "commandeth that there shall be no priestcrafts" (2 Nephi 26:29). Richard L. Bushman correctly sees this position as having been "foreshadowed" by the Book of Mormon and as "perhaps the most radical departure" from conventional religious practices.[74] Indeed, reflecting these Book of Mormon precepts, an article published in the *Latter-day Saints' Messenger and Advocate* in 1836 expressly linked the Latter-day Saint view of priestcraft with the Book of Mormon: "It is evident that the great goddess of this generation is in danger of being exposed, in consequence of the forthcoming of the book of Mormon: which book speaks against priestcraft."[75] On December 7, 1837, the Far West high council "heard the report of their Committee on raising a revenue to pay the officers of the Church for their services, and after much discussion and adjournment from time to time, dismissed the subject as being anti-scriptural."[76]

Temples and temple worship. Latent in the Book of Mormon were also the seeds of the Latter-day Saint doctrines of temple worship. Temples are prominently mentioned on several occasions; building temples and holding sacred convocations there was a high priority among the Nephites (see 2 Nephi 5:16; Jacob 2:11; Mosiah 2:1; 3 Nephi 11:1).[77] Requirements are listed in the Book of Mormon, constituting quasi-interview lists for worthiness to stand before the Lord or enter into his covenants (see 2 Nephi 26:32; Alma 1:32; 16:18; Helaman 4:12; compare Psalm 24:3–4). On sacred occasions, white and pure garments are worn (see 1 Nephi 12:11; Jacob 1:19;

Alma 5:27; 3 Nephi 19:30). A new dispensation was greeted with a shout of "Hosanna! Blessed be the name of the Most High God!" (3 Nephi 11:17). In temple contexts, adherence to certain principles is taught and required concerning obedience (see 1 Nephi 22:30–31; Jacob 4:5; Mosiah 5:5, 8; 3 Nephi 12:19–20), sacrifice (see 3 Nephi 9:19–20), chastity (see Jacob 2:28, Mosiah 2:13; Alma 30:10; 3 Nephi 12:27–28), and consecrating wealth to the kingdom of God (see Jacob 2:18–19; 3 Nephi 13:20, 24, 33). Blessings are pronounced of peace and prosperity (see 2 Nephi 1:9, 20; Alma 36:1, 30) and upon parents and children (see 3 Nephi 17:17, 21). Sins forgiven or sealing powers given (see Enos 1:5; Mosiah 26:20; Helaman 10:7). Above all, the Nephite temple was associated with overcoming death ("death and hell must deliver up their dead," 2 Nephi 9:11–12), being lifted up at the last day (see 1 Nephi 13:37; Alma 36:3; 3 Nephi 27:22), standing before God the Eternal Judge of both the quick and the dead (see Mosiah 2:27; 16:10; Alma 5:15; Mormon 6:21; 7:6; 9:2; Moroni 8:21; 10:34), and keeping sacred things unwritten and confidential (see 3 Nephi 28:16). Thus the yearning for the temple and several of its essential components is embedded in the Book of Mormon.

Missionary work. From the outset, another integral part of the Church's implicit handbook was missionary work. The Book of Mormon not only sent people forth to proclaim the gospel to all people, it also modeled and instructed how this was to be done. Guidance was there to be found concerning missionary preparation (see Alma 17:2–4), the focus of missionary work of "labor[ing] without ceasing . . . [to] bring souls unto repentance" (Alma 36:24). Patterns of missionary work are found in many accounts (for example, Mosiah 11; 18; Alma 4–15; 31–34; Helaman 5; 3 Nephi 27:1), concerning the value of companions to serve as two corroborating witnesses (Alma and Amulek), traveling out as a group and then dividing up into different fields of labor (the four sons of Mosiah), sometimes proselytizing alone (Alma in the city of Ammonihah), taking the gospel to the Lamanites (see 1 Nephi 13; Alma 17–26; 3 Nephi 20), opening the door to the Jews and remnant of Jacob (see 3 Nephi 21), and proclaiming God's plan for the entire house of Israel and all nations of the earth (see 2 Nephi 29:11; Jacob 5; 3 Nephi 21–22). These missionary practices continue among the Saints today as parts of the written and unwritten order of the Church, just as they were inaugurated by Samuel Smith as early as 1830 and by the missionaries to the Lamanites west of Missouri in 1831.

Excommunication and discipline. An important chapter in the *Church Handbook of Instructions* deals with disciplinary procedures.[78] Some churches are strict and others are lax about joining or leaving membership. For Latter-day Saints, the basic principles of jurisdiction in judging the members (Mosiah 26:29, "him shall ye judge") and guidelines for Church disciplinary and excommunication procedures are set forth in the rules granted to Alma the Elder by King Mosiah (see Mosiah 26:12), in the instructions given by Jesus to his disciples (see 3 Nephi 18:28–32), and in the process followed in Nephite church practice (see Moroni 6:7). For example, witnesses are required in order to excommunicate (see 3 Nephi 18:28–32; Moroni 6:7), and Church leaders are commanded to reactivate those cast out, to encourage them to repent (see Mosiah 26:29–30; 3 Nephi 18:28–32).

These Church disciplinary ideals and procedures have been with the Church from its inception, just as these directives were presented on the first day of Jesus' visit to the people in Bountiful and quoted in the 1829 Articles of the Church of Christ. In 1830 the Articles and Covenants prescribed: "Any member of the church of Christ transgressing, or being overtaken in a fault, shall be dealt with as the scriptures direct" (D&C 20:80). One wonders, which "scriptures" does this passage have in mind? Matthew 18:15–20 is possible, but much more likely is 3 Nephi 18:20–32. The distinction between church jurisdiction and governmental authority, found in Mosiah in Mosiah 26:11–12 and elsewhere in the Book of Mormon, was present in 1831 in Doctrine and Covenants 42:79–87, and in 1835 in Doctrine and Covenants 134:10.

Several actual cases of excommunications could be rehearsed. For example, in 1833, "James Blanchard and Alonzo Rider were cut off from the Church by a council of Elders, in Kirtland, for repeated transgressions, and promising to reform, and never fulfiling. Nelson Acre was also cut off, on account of his absenting himself from the meetings, and saying that he wanted no more of the Church, and that he desired to be cut off. None of these being present, the council notified them of their expulsion by letters."[79] In a case on February 3, 1834, one can find evidence that Joseph Smith was following the Book of Mormon's teaching in encouraging the transgressor to return to the fold. In a letter mentioning this proceeding, the Prophet stated:

> After some investigation of the case of Bro. Wood, in council, [it] was decided that he should be cut off from the Church. [acc]ordingly the Council lifted their hands against him and [he] was excluded from the church on this 3d. day of Feb. 1834. [For] indulging an idle, partial, overbearing and lustful spirit, and [not] magnifying his holy calling whereunto he had been [det]ained. These things were plainly manifest to the satisfaction of the council, and the spirit constrained us to separate him from the church. Should bro. Joseph Wood, after learning [of the] decission [*sic*] of this council, truly repent of all his sins and bring forth fruit meet [compare Alma 12:15; 13:13; 3 Nephi 18:32] to the satisfaction of that branch of the church where he had committed the offences, he can be rebaptized and come into the church again if he desire so to do.[80]

Teaching and education. From the outset, Latter-day Saints have spent enormous time teaching one another. Administrative guidance in this regard is also present in the Book of Mormon. Teachers and teaching are often mentioned and exemplified (for example, Jacob 1:19; Mosiah 18:25). One is to "trust no one to be your teacher, nor your minister, except he be a man of God, walking in his ways" (Mosiah 23:14). Church leaders are admonished to remember and nourish members by the good word of God (see Moroni 6:4, 6). Teachers in the Church are to teach nothing except what the prophets have spoken (see Mosiah 18:19), are to teach with power and authority from God (Mosiah 18:26), and are especially to teach the youth (see 1 Nephi 1:1; Enos 1:1; Mosiah 1:2; Alma 57:21).

Record keeping. As early as section 21, the Church was commanded to keep historical records. This practice is saliently emphasized from the beginning to the end of the Book of Mormon. The Savior made the keeping of accurate records a priority (see 3 Nephi 23:7–13). The making of annual reports was formulaic during the reign of the judges (for example, Helaman 6:6, 13). Passages concerning the keeping and guarding of scriptures (see 1 Nephi 6, 9; Mosiah 1; Alma 37:1–18) and the fact that people will be judged out of the books which shall be written (see 3 Nephi 27:25) set the administrative patterns and policies that have reinforced the importance of clerks, secretaries, historians, and documentary collections in the Church from the day of its organization.

Church practices and policies. Finally, the *Church Handbook of Instructions* today also gives guidance to leaders regarding many other miscellaneous policies and practices. Although many of these deal with modern-day legal and moral concerns, they are also congruent with teachings in the Book of Mormon. Regarding civic duties of Church members, Mosiah 29 warns that great evil will follow if the voice of the people chooses iniquity and if public leaders seek personal power and gain. The duty to defend our religion, freedom, peace, wives, and children, which undergirds the Church's posture with respect to the military, is famously articulated in Alma 46:12, 20–21, together with the duty of those at home to support those in combat (see Alma 27:24).

Rather simple rules regarding the conduct of funerals seem consistent with the terse reports of the death and burial of Lehi, Benjamin, and others (see 2 Nephi 4:12; Mosiah 6:5; 29:45–46; Alma 62:52, 63:3). Disfavored cremation in general compares with the irregularity of death by fire (see Mosiah 17:20; Alma 14:8; 25:11).

Simple attire of Church leaders is preferred over the scarlet and ostentatious "fine apparel" decried in the Book of Mormon (see 1 Nephi 13:7–8; Alma 1:6, 27; 31:28; Mormon 8:37). Church buildings are to be decorated plainly and not "ornamented" with "fine work" or "precious things" (Mosiah 11:7–10), "adorning" churches more than caring for the "needy, the sick and the afflicted" (Mormon 8:37).

CONCLUSION

Thus, in four interlocking ways, it becomes fitting to see the Book of Mormon as the keystone or fountainhead of the administrative and operational principles of The Church of Jesus Christ of Latter-day Saints. First, generatively: in 1829 Oliver Cowdery drew extensively on the Book of Mormon, as soon as it was translated, as a primary source of administrative steps toward the building up of the Church. Second, constitutively: section 20 of the Doctrine and Covenants enshrined the Book of Mormon, as soon as it was available from the printer in 1830, at the heart of the Articles and Covenants of the Church. Third, historically: in the 1830s and 1840s, leaders of the Church read, knew, used, and followed the Book of Mormon, as its vocabulary shaped the administrative idiom of the Church. And fourth, programmatically: the full array of practical themes and organizational instructions found in the Book of Mormon stand congruent with the full complement of essential Church practices and programs as they have been elaborated and implemented down to the present day.

The administrative principles embedded in the Book of Mormon serve today, as they have served from the beginning, as a handbook of Church administrative instructions. Of course, the Book of Mormon is not organized as a step-by-step handbook—just as its doctrines are not set forth as a systematic theology—but when its pieces are assembled, the totality has proven to be amazingly detailed, inspired, enduring, and effective.

In its administrative functions, one may see yet another layer of divine complexity. Surely, as Joseph dictated the Book of Mormon, he was not thinking to himself, "Not only must I be sure that the story lines and the doctrinal implications of this book all hold together, but I need to leave thirteen million people with a set of administrative guidelines that will actually work, all around the world, as an effective and dynamic ecclesiastical order." These administrative stipulations fell from his lips as did the rest of the Book of Mormon, day after day, by the gift and power of God.

Here one also sees evidence that the Book of Mormon indeed contains the fullness of the gospel. The list of administrative elements spelled out above closely resembles the complete table of contents in the *Church Handbook of Instructions*. One might even say that in the Book of Mormon was to be found the administrative DNA of the Church. Many of these administrative essentials have been with the Church from its beginnings in 1829 and 1830, and at least initially in many cases it was in the Book of Mormon that the early Saints in fact found them. Latter-day Saints overlook the Book of Mormon at their peril, both to their historical jeopardy and to their spiritual condemnation, while remembering the Book of Mormon brings our administrative and eternal well-being, with its incomparable promises of celestial benefit: "Keep these sayings which I have commanded you that ye come not under condemnation" (3 Nephi 18:33). "If ye do these things blessed are ye, for ye shall be lifted up at the last day" (3 Nephi 27:22).

In a priesthood leadership meeting, training the Twelve Apostles, on Sunday, November 28, 1841, in Nauvoo, Joseph Smith "told the brethren that . . . a man would get nearer to God by abiding by [the] precepts [of the Book of Mormon], than by any other book."[81] It may be especially significant that this counsel was given to priesthood leaders, those in charge of administering the affairs of the Church. To "abide" means to "continue permanently," to "adhere to," to "maintain, defend or stand to."[82] With this instruction, the Prophet spoke not only of following the moral and ethical teachings of the Book of Mormon, but surely also its organizational and leadership principles, as well as its holy order of priesthood ministration and administration. As Joseph concluded, the Book of Mormon is indeed "the keystone of our religion,"[83] including the keystone of its administrative order. Its ordinances and administrative principles are not just convenient or optional things to do in a would-be church of Christ. They provide the essential and integral organizational principles and framework upon which the Church of Christ is truly established.

The Book of Mormon as the Keystone of Church Administration

NOTES

1. *Teachings of the Prophet Joseph Smith*, comp. Joseph Fielding Smith (Salt Lake City: Deseret News, 1938), 98.

2. Thus read the heading to chapter 15 of the 1833 *Book of Commandments*, 34, which revelation is now numbered as section 18 of the Doctrine and Covenants.

3. This document was first published by Scott H. Faulring, "An Examination of the 1829 'Articles of the Church of Christ' in Relation to Section 20 of the Doctrine and Covenants," *BYU Studies* 43, no. 4 (2004): 57–91, with black and white images on pages 58–60 and full transcription on pages 76–79. Two pages, in the handwriting of John Whitmer, found in Revelation Book 1 and recently published in color in Robin Scott Jensen, Robert J. Woodford, and Steven C. Harper, eds., *The Revelations and Translations*, vol. 1 of the Manuscript Revelation Books series of *The Joseph Smith Papers* (Salt Lake City: The Church Historian's Press, 2009), 23–24.

4. Faulring, "An Examination," dated this text sometime "during the second half of 1829" (64), the same period of time when Cowdery was preparing the Printer's Manuscript of the Book of Mormon from its original dictation manuscript. But *The Joseph Smith Papers*, 691, dates this to "circa June 1829," based on evidence now available from an original table of contents for Revelation Book 1, not printed in that volume, that tells us that the following items were found on these pages. On pages 17–21, there were four revelations given in June, namely sections 14, 18, 15, 16 (the actual pages 15–22 in Revelation Book 1 are missing); on pages 21–25 was found this revelation of the Articles of the Church of Christ (pages 23–24 are extant); then on page 25, dated June 1829, came Doctrine and Covenants 17 (pages 25–26 are missing), and on pages 25–28, dated March 1830, came Doctrine and Covenants 19. Because these Articles of the Church of Christ were recorded in Revelation Book 1 between sections 16 and 17, both revealed in June, and before section 19, received in March 1830, it would seem most likely that the Articles were written in June 1829, immediately after the completion of the translation of the Book of Mormon.

5. The relevant pages in the *Joseph Smith Papers*, Revelation Book 1, contain the text between // and // in the transcription given below, with the words after \\ scribbled out.
6. Bolded text indicates direct quotations from the Book of Mormon or from Doctrine and Covenants 18. Oliver was told in Doctrine and Covenants 18:3 to "rely upon the things which are written," which he definitely did. For details on how these quotations track the language of the Printer's Manuscript of the Book of Mormon, see Faulring, "An Examination," 89–91nn75–96.
7. Royal Skousen, ed., *The Original Manuscript of the Book of Mormon: Typographical Facsimile of the Extant Text* (Provo, UT: FARMS, 2001), 35–36.
8. Doctrine and Covenants 18 was revealed in June 1829 in Fayette, New York, after the underlying passages from Mosiah and 3 Nephi had been translated.
9. See the heading to chapter 15 of the 1833 *Book of Commandments*, 34, which revelation is numbered as section 18 in the Doctrine and Covenants.
10. "Having authority given me of Jesus Christ" was the wording used before the 1835 first edition of the Doctrine and Covenants. See the 1830 edition of the Book of Mormon and the text of Doctrine and Covenants 20 in Revelation Book 1, 57. In 1835 the words were modified to the now familiar "Having been commissioned of Jesus Christ" in Doctrine and Covenants 20:73.
11. This revelation was previously thought to have been given on April 6, 1830, but it is dated as April 10 in Revelation Book 1, 52, where it is entitled "Church Articles & Covenants."
12. On the use of section 20 in organizing and operating basic units of the Church, see Craig James Ostler, "The Articles and Covenants: A Handbook for New Branches," in this book.
13. Faulring, "An Examination," 67, says that doing so is "both inaccurate and misleading." See his analysis of the writing of section 20 in contrast to the 1829 Articles, 67–73.
14. Richard Lloyd Anderson, "The Organization Revelations (D&C 20, 21, and 22)," in *Studies in Scripture: The Doctrine and Covenants*, ed. Robert L. Millet and Kent P. Jackson (Sandy, UT: Randall, 1984), 121n26.

15. See Robert J. Woodford, "The Historical Development of the Doctrine and Covenants" (PhD dissertation, Brigham Young University, 1974), 1:343–44.
16. *The Journals of William E. McLellin, 1831–1836*, ed. Jan Shipps and John W. Welch (Provo, UT: BYU Studies; Urbana: University of Illinois Press, 1994), 19.
17. For example, on December 11, 1831, he preached for "about 2½ hours on the Covenants, the evidences of the book of Mormon," and the premillennial gatherings. *Journals of William E. McLellin*, 65; see also 184, linking "the book of Mormon and the rise of the Church," and 218, 223.
18. *Journals of William E. McLellin*, 33.
19. *Journals of William E. McLellin*, 19.
20. *Journals of William E. McLellin*, 44.
21. *Journals of William E. McLellin*, 20.
22. *Journals of William E. McLellin*, 21.
23. *Journals of William E. McLellin*, 107.
24. *Journals of William E. McLellin*, 110.
25. *Journals of William E. McLellin*, 21–22, see 145; also 177, where he spoke "on the nature of the Priesthoods and of the coming forth of 'the book.'"
26. *Journals of William E. McLellin*, 137.
27. *Journals of William E. McLellin*, 141.
28. *Journals of William E. McLellin*, 148.
29. *Journals of William E. McLellin*, 22.
30. *Journals of William E. McLellin*, 176.
31. *Journals of William E. McLellin*, 176.
32. *Journals of William E. McLellin*, 183, 205n45.
33. *Wilford Woodruff's Journal: 1833–1898 Typescript*, ed. Scott G. Kenney (Midvale, UT: Signature, 1983), 1:126, 136, 227, 252,
34. Grant Underwood, *The Millenarian World of Early Mormonism* (Urbana and Chicago: University of Illinois, 1993), 76–92, discusses and tabulates two dozen chapters, verses, and themes commonly cited in early Mormon literature. He found that "the prophetic portions" of the book, which included 3 Nephi, 2 Nephi, and Ether, "received significantly greater attention than the historical books [of] Mosiah, Alma and Helaman," and that "its earliest uses were primarily eschatological and

reflected as well as reinforced a millenarian worldview," 95–96. While to a large extent these assertions remain sound, they may need to be modified or supplemented in light of the evidences now available regarding the early administrative uses of the Book of Mormon. Eschatological themes may have been more common in proclaiming the news of the Restoration to the non-LDS, while administrative matters were more naturally at home inside the Church.

35. *Wilford Woodruff's Journal*, 1:532.
36. *Wilford Woodruff's Journal*, 1:372, 414, 526.
37. Described and cited in Jeffrey R. Holland, "Safety for the Soul," *Ensign*, November 2009, 88–89.
38. *Teachings of the Prophet Joseph Smith*, 8, 9–10.
39. *Teachings of the Prophet Joseph Smith*, 85–86.
40. Dean C. Jessee and John W. Welch, "Revelations in Context: Joseph Smith's Letter from Liberty Jail, March 20, 1839," *BYU Studies* 39, no. 3 (2000): 130, 145.
41. *The Words of Joseph Smith: The Contemporary Accounts of the Nauvoo Discourses of the Prophet Joseph*, ed. Andrew F. Ehat and Lyndon W. Cook (Provo, UT: Religious Studies Center, Brigham Young University, 1980), 8; *Teachings of the Prophet Joseph Smith*, 156; see also *Wilford Woodruff's Journal*, 1:334, on that date.
42. Joseph Smith, "Gift of the Holy Ghost," *Times and Seasons*, June 15, 1842, 825; *Teachings of the Prophet Joseph Smith*, 247.
43. I thank Bryan K. Basso for his research assistance in finding these and other such passages. Some of these phrases may have been in use in the ordinary vernacular of the 1830s, but even if that were the case their collective usage in the Book of Mormon cannot be ignored.
44. Donald Q. Cannon and Lyndon W. Cook, eds., *Far West Record* (Salt Lake City: Deseret Book, 1983), 23; *Teachings of the Prophet Joseph Smith*, 9.
45. The words "perfect love" are also found in 1 John 4:18, but in that case "perfect love" comes by knowing and believing the love that God has toward us, whereas Joseph Smith and Mormon emphasized the bestowal of this gift of God coming through living lives of righteousness. I thank Bryan Basso for his assistance in gathering the following data.

46. *History of the Church of Jesus Christ of Latter-day Saints*, ed. B. H. Roberts, 2nd ed. rev. (Salt Lake City: Deseret Book, 1971), 1:245; *Teachings of the Prophet Joseph Smith*, 11.
47. Joseph Smith, "To the Honorable Men of the World," *Evening and Morning Star*, August 1832, 22; *Teachings of the Prophet Joseph Smith*, 11.
48. Smith, "To the Honorable Men of the World," 22; *Teachings of the Prophet Joseph Smith*, 12.
49. *Personal Writings of Joseph Smith*, comp. Dean C. Jessee, rev. ed. (Salt Lake City: Deseret Book; Provo, UT: Brigham Young University Press, 2002), 296; *Teachings of the Prophet Joseph Smith*, 15.
50. *Personal Writings of Joseph Smith*, 327; *Teachings of the Prophet Joseph Smith*, 29.
51. Joseph Smith, "The Elders in Kirtland, to Their Brethren Abroad," *Evening and Morning Star*, December 1833, 120; *Teachings of the Prophet Joseph Smith*, 43.
52. Joseph Smith, "The Elders of the Church in Kirtland, to Their Brethren Abroad," *Evening and Morning Star*, February 1834, 135; *Teachings of the Prophet Joseph Smith*, 50.
53. Joseph Smith, "The Elders of the Church in Kirtland, to Their Brethren Abroad," *Evening and Morning Star*, February 1834, 135; *Teachings of the Prophet Joseph Smith*, 50.
54. Joseph Smith, "The Elders of the Church in Kirtland, to Their Brethren Abroad," *Evening and Morning Star*, March 1834, 143; *Teachings of the Prophet Joseph Smith*, 61.
55. Joseph Smith, "The Elders of the Church in Kirtland, to Tehir [sic] Brethren Abroad," *Evening and Morning Star*, April 1834, 152; *Teachings of the Prophet Joseph Smith*, 67.
56. *History of the Church*, 4:129; *Teachings of the Prophet Joseph Smith*, 164.
57. *Words of Joseph Smith*, 61.
58. *Words of Joseph Smith*, 121; *Teachings of the Prophet Joseph Smith*, 239.
59. *Words of Joseph Smith*, 123; *Teachings of the Prophet Joseph Smith*, 240–41.
60. Joseph Smith, "Baptism," *Times and Seasons*, September 1, 1842, 905; *Teachings of the Prophet Joseph Smith*, 265.
61. *Words of Joseph Smith*, 230; *Teachings of the Prophet Joseph Smith*, 314.

62. The words "must do in my church" are not quoted in the 1829 Articles, but the immediately following promise that if ye do so ye "shall be lifted up at the last day" is.
63. See, generally, John W. Welch, "Book of Mormon Religious Teachings and Practices," in *Encyclopedia of Mormonism*, ed. Daniel H. Ludlow (New York: Macmillan, 1992), 1:201–5.
64. Richard Lyman Bushman, *Joseph Smith: Rough Stone Rolling* (New York: Vintage, 2005), points out that "Joseph appointed elders, priests, and teachers, offices found in the Book of Mormon and familiar from the churches around him" (111, see also 253). While some aspects of the initial organization of the Church may not have surprised a Methodist very much (254), I do not conclude that the Church borrowed mostly from surrounding denominations and less from the precedents in the Book of Mormon. Nor would it seem that the "first appearance" of the word *priesthood* cautiously came only in 1831 somehow due to the "generally negative" meaning of priesthood among radical anti-Catholic Protestants (157). Regarding the subject of the Melchizedek Priesthood, Bushman at least concurs that Joseph Smith "was more influenced by the *Book of Mormon* and the Bible than by the learned writings of his contemporaries" (159). Indeed, here one may add another early, potent mention of priesthood, in the Book of Moses, translated in 1830, in which Adam prophesied that "this same Priesthood, which was in the beginning, shall be in the end of the world also" (Moses 6:7).
65. "After writing the account given of the Savior's ministry to the remnant of the seed of Jacob, upon this continent," it was realized acutely that "none had authority from God to administer the ordinances of the Gospel." Joseph Smith—History 1:71n.
66. *History of the Church*, 1:44, records this as the day of Samuel Smith's baptism.
67. Book of Commandments 24:30; see Doctrine and Covenants 20:37.
68. Dean C. Jessee, ed., *The Papers of Joseph Smith* (Salt Lake City: Deseret Book, 1989), 1:303.
69. See John W. Welch, "From Presence to Practice: Jesus, the Sacrament Prayers, the Priesthood, and Church Discipline in 3 Nephi 18 and Moroni 2–6," *Journal of Book of Mormon Studies* 5, no. 1 (1996): 120–29.
70. "The Jaredites," *Juvenile Instructor*, May 1, 1892, 282n.

71. *History of the Church*, 2:347. He received only a travel allowance of ten dollars per week plus expenses when he went out to give blessings, on the biblical and Doctrine and Covenants grounds that "the laborer is worthy of his hire." *History of the Church*, 2:273.
72. *History of the Church*, 1:67–69; D&C 20:45, 55, 75.
73. *History of the Church*, 1:324.
74. Bushman, *Rough Stone Rolling*, 111.
75. "Beware of Delusion!," *Messenger and Advocate*, January 1836, 251.
76. *History of the Church*, 2:527–28.
77. See John W. Welch, "The Temple in the Book of Mormon: The Temples at the Cities of Nephi, Zarahemla, and Bountiful," in *Temples of the Ancient World: Ritual and Symbolism*, ed. Donald W. Parry (Salt Lake City: Deseret Book; Provo, UT: FARMS, 1994), 297–387.
78. Bruce C. Hafen, "Disciplinary Procedures," in *Encyclopedia of Mormonism*, 1:386.
79. *History of the Church*, 1:469–70.
80. Joseph Smith Jr. and Orson Hyde to Brother Fosdick, February 3, 1834, typescript, 1–2, L. Tom Perry Special Collections Library, Harold B. Lee Library, Brigham Young University, Provo, Utah.
81. *Teachings of the Prophet Joseph Smith*, 194.
82. Noah Webster, *An American Dictionary of the English Language* (New York: S. Converse, 1828), "abide."
83. *Teachings of the Prophet Joseph Smith*, 194.

The Melchizedek Priesthood was restored to Joseph Smith and Oliver Cowdery by Peter, James, and John. (Walter Rane, Restoration of the Melchizedek Priesthood. © Intellectual Reserve, Inc. All rights reserved.)

Richard E. Bennett

3

"THE CIRCUMFERENCE OF THE APOSTLESHIP"

In Robert Bolt's classic drama *A Man for All Seasons*, the ever-principled and incomparable Thomas More, England's stout defender of the Holy Catholic faith, responded with unflinching conviction when pressed by the Duke of Norfolk about the reasonability and historicity of the Roman Catholic claim to priesthood legitimacy. "The Apostolic Succession of the Pope is—Why, it's a theory yes; you can't see it; can't touch it; it's a theory. But what matters to me is not whether it's true or not but that I believe it to be true, or rather not that I *believe* it, but that *I* believe it."¹

My intention is to discuss the restoration of the Melchizedek Priesthood. Of course, only Latter-day Saints believe in this modern-day miracle, and one must realize that expecting others to believe in such a thing would first require a conversion to the restored gospel as

---

Richard E. Bennett is associate dean of Religious Education and professor of Church history and doctrine at Brigham Young University.

we see and understand it. For those unacquainted with the miraculous, or for those unprepared to accept angelic visitations, this discussion is in the field of mere speculation and pure fantasy. Likewise, our friends in other Christian faiths, most notably those of the noble Roman Catholic persuasion, will consider such talk uncomfortable and certainly antithetical to a central tenet of their faith: the apostolic succession from St. Peter. It takes time, preparation, and faith to believe that Christ called Peter, James, and John as his Apostles, let alone to accept the uniquely Mormon doctrine that they were instrumental in restoring lost priesthood authority and the attendant keys in these latter days.

The specific details of the restoration of the Melchizedek Priesthood are admittedly difficult to ferret out. In Joseph Smith's 1832 history, he mentioned "the reception of the Holy Priesthood by the ministering of angels" but offered no other specifics. In his official history of 1838, he stated that John the Baptist "acted under the direction of Peter, James and John who held the keys of the Priesthood of Melchizedek, which Priesthood he said would in due time be conferred on us." In this same account, he offered a clue to his silence on the matter: "In the meantime we were forced to keep secret the circumstances of having received the Priesthood and our having been baptized, owing to a spirit of persecution which had already manifested itself in the neighborhood."[2] Considering the intense persecution that followed his telling of the First Vision story, such reluctance may be understandable.

Harder to comprehend is the fact that Lucy Mack Smith did not write much about the event in her writings, nor did David Whitmer or William E. McLellin. As Michael Quinn has argued, Whitmer said that he never heard "of such a thing as an angel ordaining them until I got into Ohio about the year 1834—or later" and purportedly concluded that "I do not believe that John the Baptist ever ordained Joseph and Oliver as stated and believed by some."[3] William E. McLellin, who, like David Whitmer, later left the Church, said, "In 1831 I heard Joseph tell his experiences about angel visits many times, and about finding the plates, and their contents coming to light. . . . But I never heard one word of John the baptist, or of Peter, James, and John's visit and ordination till I was told some year afterward in Ohio."[4] Quinn has even argued that Brigham Young, as President of the Church, later stated that Joseph Smith "received the Melchizedek Priesthood" after the Church was organized.[5]

It has also been argued, by Hiram Page and others, that Joseph Smith was merely "a prophet" rather than "the prophet" and that at first "nearly everyone regarded Smith as a prophet among prophets, not as *the* prophet."[6] Certainly, David Whitmer later seemed to arrive at such a conclusion, perhaps to justify leaving the Church. Furthermore, he and others argued that the term "apostle" as used in the very early days of the Church was not an administrative office but a term suggesting a charismatic calling for those who had received special manifestations of the Spirit—David Whitmer, John Whitmer, Ziba Peterson, and others—and that they felt comfortable claiming the title "apostle" (lowercase "a") independent of any ordination or priesthood setting apart.[7]

Unless additional information is discovered, we simply do not know precisely when or where the Melchizedek Priesthood was restored. Until that time, reputable scholars will probably continue to defend alternative positions with some intent in arguing that such a manifestation never occurred, that it was later contrived to justify the legitimacy of priesthood claim by later leaders of The Church of Jesus Christ of Latter-day Saints.

The purpose of this paper is to reexamine what we do know about this remarkable event in Church history. Whatever the contrary positions may be, the early missionaries of the Church taught the Apostasy and its tragic loss of authority as a terrible reality. They also spoke clearly about the restoration of priesthood authority. Furthermore, the second witness of the Restoration, Oliver Cowdery, as well as many members of the original Quorum of the Twelve asserted that (a) the vision of Peter, James, and John was a reality; (b) the gift of the Holy Ghost could not have been conferred without the Melchizedek Priesthood; (c) such authority had to have been restored before the Church was organized at Fayette, New York, on April 6, 1830;

and finally and perhaps most importantly, (d) the visit of Peter, James, and John included the restoration of priesthood keys, that Joseph Smith and Oliver Cowdery were ordained to the office of Apostle (capital "A") before the Quorum of the Twelve had been organized—and that by right of this ordination, Joseph Smith laid claim to the right of President of the Church, thereby establishing the pattern of apostolic succession.

"THE BLINDNESS THAT HAD HAPPENED"

One cannot discuss the restoration of priesthood authority without first reviewing what early missionaries taught about the Apostasy and the original Christian Church. With the Church still in its infancy, many of its newest converts sought to spread the word while gathering to Zion. Jonathan Crosby, for instance, prayed that "the Lord would rend the heavens and come down, and remove the darkness which covers the earth, and gross darkness the minds of the people."[8] Among the doctrines these earliest converts preached, the Apostasy was prominent, if not paramount.[9] Teachings about the Apostasy included the loss of truth, resultant false religion, the absence of authority, and the scattering of Israel.

The early missionaries spoke of the Apostasy in very strident tones. They taught that it was a reality, long prophesied and now fulfilled, that the Christian world had lost its way and that the results of the Apostasy were spiritually and morally devastating. Samuel Smith, Joseph's younger brother wrote: "I have written . . . to prove that the Gentiles have broken the everlasting covenant and that darkness has covered the earth since the days of the Apostles and to show the calamity that is coming upon them and to prove that while in this situation, the Lord was to lift up a standard to the people which should . . . come forth to throw light into the minds of the people and to deliver them from the darkness that happened unto them and to show the way of deliverance from the judgments that are coming upon the Gentiles."[10] He then reported how Elder Orson Hyde spoke of "the blindness that had happened in consequence of the falling away from the faith that was delivered to the Saints."[11] And Sylvester Smith, writing in May 1833 from his missionary assignment in southern New York, added the following:

> I am sensible that the word will not grow and flourish upon the barren rocks of pride and unbelief, which is almost the only characteristic of the old churches.
>
> When I view the situation of the sectarians of the day, my heart cries, wo, wo, wo, to the scribes and pharisees, hypocrites, who build and garnish the sepulchers of the apostles! but alas! Their building upon the old covenant, will not save them if they reject the new! Their crying out against the murderers of Christ and his apostles, will not save them, while they stone those whom the Lord sends to warn them of the desolation which await the wicked![12]

In 1834, William McLellin quoted from Jude 1:3 when he addressed a congregation "about an hour and ¼ on the situation or confusion of the world and on the faith once delivered to the saints."[13] In another account, Orson Hyde referenced the same scripture to "show them the blindness that had happened in consequence of the falling away from the faith that was once delivered to the Saints."[14] Said W. W. Phelps in 1834: "The world . . . was to wander far from God, and righteousness was so far to depart from the earth and the true principles of the religion of heaven to be so neglected, as to leave the world in a state of apostasy. . . . Isaiah says in [60:2], 'For behold, the darkness shall cover the earth, and gross darkness the people.' . . . Any man who will read this . . . will see . . . it was at this time, that darkness was to cover the earth and gross darkness the minds of the people."[15]

Elder Orson Pratt, who had proselyted actively since late 1830, summarized his teachings of the Apostasy and of "the falling away of the Church" of Christ,[16] and the fact that "there could not but one church be correct."[17] In the following jubilant letter of 1835, he wrote to Oliver Cowdery: "Who could have supposed five years ago that truth would have spread so rapid . . . it moves in majesty and power, and continues its steady course, pulling down the strong holds of Babylon, and leaving her mighty towers, exposing the creeds, systems and inventions of men, exhibiting the extreme ignorance, follies and errors of all sects, which causes their priests to rage and their mighty ones to tremble."[18]

Elder Parley P. Pratt admitted: "At the commencement of 1830, I felt drawn out in an extraordinary manner to search the prophets, and to pray for an understanding of the same. . . . I began to understand the things which were coming on the earth—the restoration of Israel, the coming of the Messiah, and the glory that should follow. I was so astonished at the darkness of myself and mankind on these subjects that I could exclaim with the prophet: surely, '*darkness covers the earth, and gross darkness the minds of the people.*'"[19]

The early missionaries believed that the Apostasy had thoroughly corrupted virtually all of mankind. And because of it, "surely, gross darkness covers the earth, and wickedness greatly prevails among the people, and the truth makes them angry, for they are joined to their idols."[20] The Apostasy was something far more than a loss of truth or even priesthood; it was the ushering in of a time of sin and corruption, a terrible state of affairs which these early missionaries viewed as confirmation of that calamity. Such talk of the Apostasy begged the need for a restoration of priesthood authority and priesthood keys that were necessary to change mankind for the better.

"THE FIRST LIGHT OF THE MORNING"

Of all aspects of the Prophet Joseph Smith's early visions, the ones shared most by early missionaries were the visitations of the angel Moroni, the coming forth of the Book of Mormon, and the restoration of priesthood authority.

A careful review of early missionary journals indicates that priesthood restoration was not as much preached as other topics were, at least not explicitly. For instance, several spoke of the "authority" of the revelations Joseph Smith had received and less about their own authority. And little seemed to be said about the specific visits of John the Baptist and Peter, James, and John. Nevertheless, priesthood and its restoration were important points of discussion. For instance, William E. McLellin wrote in May 1833, "Today I preached in the schoolhouse to a tolerably large congregation, on the Priesthood, on the operation of the Holy spirit and on the nature of communion."[21] Later he spoke on "the confusion on the earth" and "on the plainness of the Gospel and on the Authority which God has given to his church."[22] And in one setting he preached "on the dealings of God with men, on the plainness of the Gospel and on the two Priesthoods."[23]

Elder Orson Pratt wrote in July 1833, during one of his earliest missions, "I preached upon the Priesthood and more revelations and miracles, the 29th of Isaiah and the two sticks."[24] In March 1834, he and Elder Orson Hyde read from the Articles and Covenants of the Church (now found in section 20 of the Doctrine of the Covenants) with its emphasis on priesthood ordinations, quorums, and responsibilities and went on to give them "a proclamation of the first principles of the Gospel."[25] He went on to "prove from the scriptures that miracles, gifts of healings, prophecies, revelations, and all the spiritual gifts which were in the Church in the days of the Savior and Apostles were necessary for the Church of Christ now, and that there never was nor ever will be a true church on the earth in a state of mortality without them."[26] Implicit in their many discussions on the first principles and performances of baptism was the doctrine of the restored priesthood.

And in the specific charge to Parley P. Pratt on the eve of his mission to the Eastern States in 1835, "President" Oliver Cowdery said, "Brethren, you have your duty presented in this revelation. You have been ordained to the holy priesthood; you have received it from those who have their power and authority from an angel; you are to preach the gospel to every nation."[27] And when preaching to John Taylor and others in Toronto, Upper Canada, Pratt reasoned as follows: "How often the Lord may have restored his priesthood and ordinances, the true Church and its gifts to the earth, among the humble, is not known. But this much we know, . . . nothing short of a new dispensation—a new revelation to commission apostles as at the first could give any religious body a claim, or a shadow of claim, to be the Church of Jesus Christ, or entitle them to the spiritual gifts." [28]

A Firm Foundation

And by 1851 we read the following: "The first light of the morning, in this age, and the time referred to by the Savior, was the angel who had the everlasting Gospel, which was to be preached to all people, preaching and ministering . . . to others, even as he had received of the angel; and the light continued to shine and spread, as others believed on the testimony of Joseph, for they repented of their sins, and were baptized by him; and he, having received the Holy Priesthood from the angels, conferred the same Priesthood on the believers."[29]

THE WITNESS OF OLIVER COWDERY

More specific to the restoration of the "two priesthoods," Oliver Cowdery wrote the following just two years before his return to the Church:

> I have cherished a hope, and that one of my fondest, that I might leave such a character, as those who might believe in my testimony, after that I should be called hence, might do so, not only for the sake of the truth, but might not *blush* for the private character of the man who bore that testimony. I have been sensitive on this subject, I admit; but I ought to be so—you would be, under the circumstances, had you stood in the presence of John, with our departed Brother Joseph, to receive the Lesser Priesthood—and in the presence of Peter, to receive the Greater, and looked down through time, and witnessed the effects these two must produce,—you would feel what you have never felt, were wicked men conspiring to lessen the effects of your testimony on man, after you should have gone to your long sought rest.[30]

Ten years after leaving the Church, Cowdery arrived in Kanesville, Iowa, in 1848 and sought permission to enter in the door of baptism and be restored to membership. Elder George A. Smith, in a letter to Elder Orson Pratt in October 1848, described Oliver's comments this way:

Oliver Cowdery, who had just arrived from Wisconsin with family, addressed the meeting. He bore testimony in the most positive terms of the truth of the Book of Mormon—the restoration of the priesthood to the earth and the mission of Joseph Smith as the Prophet of the last days; and told the people if they wanted to follow the right path to keep the main channel of the stream—where the body of the church goes, there is the authority; and all these lo here's and lo there's, have no authority; but this people have the true and holy Priesthood; for the angel said unto Joseph Smith, Jr., in his hearing, that "this priesthood shall remain on the earth until the end!" His testimony produced quite a stir among the gentlemen present, who did not belong to the church, and it was gratefully received by all the Saints.[31]

Cowdery gave even more precise details of the restoration of two priesthoods in a follow-up letter to Samuel W. Richards in 1849. "While darkness covered the earth and gross darkness the people," he wrote:

> long after the authority to administer in holy things had been taken away, the Lord opened the heavens and sent forth his word for the salvation of Israel. In fulfillment of the sacred Scripture the everlasting Gospel was proclaimed by the mighty angel (Moroni), who, clothed with the authority of his mission, gave glory to God in the highest. This Gospel is the "stone taken from the mountain without hands." John the Baptist, holding the keys of the Aaronic Priesthood; Peter, James and John, holding the keys of the Melchizedek Priesthood, have also ministered for those who shall be heirs of salvation, and with these ministrations ordained men to the same Priesthoods. These Priesthoods with their authority, are now, and must continue to be, in the body of the Church of Jesus Christ of Latter-day Saints. Blessed is the elder who has received the same and thrice blessed and holy is he who shall endure to the

end. Accept assurances . . . of him who, in connection with Joseph the Seer, was blessed with the above ministrations.[32]

Oliver Cowdery died soon after these testimonials as a member of the Church he helped establish. It was a deliberate act on his part to come back and to bear testimony to what he had seen and heard—the restoration of both the Aaronic and Melchizedek Priesthoods. His personal integrity would allow him to do no less.

THE GIFT OF THE HOLY GHOST

After Joseph Smith and Oliver Cowdery had baptized one another under the direction of John the Baptist, each began to prophesy, although neither had yet received the gift of the Holy Ghost. "Accordingly we went and were baptized, I baptized him first, and afterwards he baptized me. . . . The messenger . . . said . . . he acted under the direction of Peter, James and John, who held the keys of the Priesthood of Melchizedek, which Priesthood, he said, would in due time be conferred on us." Immediately after their baptism, the Holy Ghost fell upon them, and Oliver prophesied of "many things which should shortly come to pass," and Joseph prophesied "concerning the rise of this Church, and many other things connected with the Church, and this generation of the children of men." They then "began to have the scriptures laid open" to their understanding, "and the true meaning and intention of their more mysterious passages revealed in a manner which we never could attain to previously" (Joseph Smith—History 1:71–74). Even though they had used the Urim and Thummim as a remarkable instrument of translation and revelation, it was now the Holy Ghost that began to instruct them in marvelous ways.

But they had not yet received the gift of the Holy Ghost. "He [John the Baptist] said this Aaronic Priesthood had not the power of laying on hands for the gift of the Holy Ghost, but that this should be conferred on us hereafter" (Joseph Smith—History 1:70), a clear indication that a further priesthood endowment was forthcoming. As simple as it may appear, they looked forward to the restoration of the Melchizedek Priesthood as the essential prerequisite to receiving the gift of the Holy Ghost, without which no officer in the Church could be called or established, or lasting testimony secured.

According to revelation given the day the Church was organized, Joseph Smith had been "inspired of the Holy Ghost to lay the foundation thereof, and to build it up unto the most holy faith" (D&C 21:2). And again, as per the Articles and Constitution of the Church (D&C 20), no officer in the new Church—whether elder, priest, teacher, or deacon—could have been ordained unless "by the power of the Holy Ghost, which *is in the one* who ordains him" (D&C 20:60; emphasis added). Put another way, there could have been no ordinations and no Church without first the bestowal of the gift of the Holy Ghost upon the first and second elders. As President George Q. Cannon much later remarked, "[Joseph] was unable to seal the gift of the Holy Ghost or to ordain an elder, until after Peter, James and John had endowed him with the priesthood after the holy order of Melchizedek."[33]

Unlike their baptism under the direction of John the Baptist, Joseph and Oliver recorded very little about the formal bestowal of the Holy Ghost upon them. If, however, Peter, James, and John acted in accordance with the previous pattern, they would have first conferred the Melchizedek Priesthood upon both men and then directed them to ordain one another and bestow upon each other the gift of the Holy Ghost by the power and authority of their newly received priesthood.[34]

THE VOICE OF PETER, JAMES, AND JOHN

If this matter of the Holy Ghost attains, it stands to reason that the Melchizedek Priesthood was restored some time before the organization of the Church. The exact date and place of the restoration of this higher priesthood authority, in what B. H. Roberts has called the "fourth vision" of the Restoration, have yet to be discovered; however, there are clues. As Professor Larry C. Porter has skillfully argued, it was likely restored near

Harmony, Pennsylvania, for Oliver Cowdery wrote of hearing "the voice of Peter, James, and John in the wilderness between Harmony, Susquehanna county, and Colesville, Broome county, on the Susquehanna river, declaring themselves as possessing the keys of the kingdom, and of the dispensation of the fulness of times" (D&C 128:20). Just where the spot was between Harmony and Colesville, New York, a distance of twenty-seven miles, is impossible to say.[35]

In a now-famous 1882 letter to President Joseph F. Smith, Addison Everett, a bishop in Winter Quarters and later in Salt Lake City, recalled hearing the Prophet in Nauvoo relate the circumstances surrounding the restoration of the priesthood. "Said as they ware tran[s]lating the Book of Mormon at His Father In Laws in Susqauhanah County Penny. T[h]ey ware thretned By a Mob and in the same time Falther Kn[i]ghts came Down from Cole[s]vill[e] County New York and Desired them to go home with him and preach to them in his Neighbourhood And on Account of the Mob Spirit prevailing they concluded to goe." Everett recalled that even in Colesville persecution continued, forcing the pair to return to Harmony. His letter continues:

> And they wandered in a dense Forest all night and often times in Mud and water up to thare Knees. And Brother Oliver got quite exausted in the After Part of the Night and Brother Joseph had to put his arm arround him and allmost carry him. And Just as the day Broke in the East Brother Oliver gave out Entirely and he[,] Br Joseph[,] leaned him against an Oake tree Just out side a field fenc[e] Br Oliver Crying out how long O Lord O how Long Br Joseph hav[e] we got to suffer these things[?] Just this moment Peter James & John came to us and Ordained [us to] the Holy Aposleship and gave [unto] us the Keys of the Disp[e]nsation of the fullness of times. And we had some 16 or 17 miles to goe to reach our place of residence and Brother Oliver could travel as well as I could . . . Now as to time and Place. I heard the Name of the Banks of the Susquehanah river spoken [of] But whare it was

pla[c]ed I cannot till. No doubt the Oake tree and the field fence was ajacent to the river. As to time I cannot Be Very Explsit. But as the Mob spirit had not abated when they returned they had to remove to Father Whitmores [Whitmers] [Fayette, Seneca Co] to finish the Translation.[36]

How much credence can be given to a reminiscence written almost forty years after the fact is debatable. Nonetheless, it is true that the Knights assisted in the translation of the Book of Mormon by supplying paper and provisions, that persecution attended the translation, that by June 1, 1829, Joseph and Oliver had removed north to Harmony, and that the two were never together again in the wilderness of the Susquehanna.

And further to the matter of timing, revelations from as early as June 1829 speak of Joseph and Oliver having already received the apostleship. "And I speak unto you, even as unto Paul mine apostle, for you are called even with that same calling with which he was called" (D&C 18:9). In the Articles and Covenants of the Church—section 20 of the Doctrine and Covenants—reference is made to Joseph and Oliver as having already been "called of God, and ordained an Apostle of Jesus Christ" *before* the Church was organized on April 6, 1830 (D&C 20:2).[37]

THE KEYS OF THE APOSTLESHIP

A careful reading of scriptural text and of the statements of the earliest Church Apostles reveals that Joseph and Oliver received from Peter, James, and John something even more than priesthood authority: they also received the "keys" pertaining to and governing that priesthood. While some may err in thinking that this is unnecessary nuance and an overly subtle differentiation, it is of great importance to distinguish the two, for the keys meant everything to Church government, the matter of apostolic succession, and even the timing or chronology of the coming of Peter, James, and John.

If priesthood is Christ's authority delegated unto man to perform ordinances, miracles, and other works in his stead, then keys represent the governing authority, the power over the priesthood, the permitting or consenting power to direct, confirm, revoke, and be accountable for all matters of ecclesiastical administration and ordination. The keys may also represent sealing powers that "whatsoever ye shall bind on earth shall be bound in heaven" (Matthew 18:18).

Just as Joseph Smith and Oliver Cowdery had obtained not only the Aaronic Priesthood from John the Baptist but also the "keys" pertaining thereto, they received from the Apostles Peter, James, and John the keys of the apostleship which they themselves possessed. Possessing the keys to the Melchizedek Priesthood, Joseph Smith and Oliver Cowdery were prepared to enter into the operation, ordinances, and government of that priesthood. They could baptize not only for the remission of sins but also into Church membership, being able to *confer* the gift of the Holy Ghost to baptized believers and to *confirm* them members of the Church. So too they could set apart and ordain other officers in the Church.

Section 27, given in August 1830, states:

> And also with Peter, and James, and John, whom I have sent unto you, by whom I have ordained you and confirmed you to be apostles, and especial witnesses of my name, and bear the *keys* of your ministry and of the *same things* which I revealed unto them;
>
> Unto whom I have committed the keys of my kingdom, and a dispensation of the gospel for the last times; and for the fulness of times, in the which I will gather together in one all things, both which are in heaven, and which are on earth. (D&C 27:12–13; emphasis added)

The "same things" which God had revealed unto his ancient Apostles, the same powers, commissions, and endowments given unto them were now to be entrusted with these modern Apostles. Joseph and Oliver were to be more than mere disciples or followers, but Apostles, leaders, and directors over the work of the Lord in this, the final time, or dispensation, before Christ's Second Coming.

"The Circumference of the Apostleship"

This argument was presented by many of the early Apostles of this Church. The Articles and Covenants, originally published in the Book of Commandments,[38] speaks of Joseph Smith and Oliver Cowdery having been "called of God and ordained an apostle of Jesus Christ, an elder of this church" (D&C 20:2). Their ordination to the apostleship preceded their being called, set apart, and sustained by the membership at the inauguration of the Church on April 6 in Fayette, New York. In fact, they could not have become the first or second presiding elders over the Church or could not have organized and established the Church without first having been Apostles. At least this is how many of the original Quorum of the Twelve came to understand the process. The argument that the original Apostles, Joseph Smith and Oliver Cowdery, were mere disciples, not much different than any other early leaders in an egalitarian forum of charismatic coequals does not square with statements made by the original Twelve. Elder Parley P. Pratt, a member of the original Quorum of the Twelve and a member of the Church since 1830, responded this way: "Who ordained our first founders to the Apostleship, to hold the keys of the kingdom of God, in these the times of restoration? Peter, James, and John, from the eternal world."[39] Added Elder Heber C. Kimball, another original Quorum member: "Joseph Smith was a Prophet of God, a Seer, a Revelator, an Apostle of Jesus, and was ordained directly under the hands of Peter, James, and John."[40]

Brigham Young, while President of the Church, elaborated further on the perfect sequence of events so far discussed and on the order and importance of the priesthood and its keys:

> When the Lord called upon His servant Joseph, after leading him along for years until he got the plates, from a portion of which the Book of Mormon was translated, "by and bye," said he, "you are going to organize my church and establish my kingdom. I am going to have a church on the earth. All these churches you have inquired about are wrong; they have truth amongst them, but not the Priesthood. They lack a guide to direct the affairs of the Kingdom of God on the earth—that is the keys of the priesthood of the Son

of God." This tells the story. We possess the Priesthood. The Lord sent John to ordain Joseph to the Aaronic Priesthood, and when he commenced to baptize people he sent a greater power—Peter, James, and John, who ordained him to the apostleship, which is the highest office pertaining to the Kingdom of God that any man can possess on the face of the earth, for it holds the keys of the Kingdom of Heaven, and has power to dispense the blessings of the kingdom.[41]

In light of the fact that the Quorum of the Twelve was not formed until 1835, it is significant that men in large part chosen by Joseph Smith with the aid of the Three Witnesses received and were "ordained," in President Young's words, to the "office" of apostleship. In other words, President Young and most of his colleagues believed that there were Apostles before there was a Quorum of the Twelve Apostles, indeed *before* there was, or could have been, an organized Church. The argument that the government of the Church was a later self-imposition of authority to justify the claims of second-generation Church leaders and that Peter, James, and John gave them no special governing authority or commission disregards the statements of a great many original Church leaders.

Said Elder Orson Pratt, another original member of the Twelve: "This Church never could have arisen had the Lord stopped with the mere translation of the Book of Mormon and the restoration of the lesser priesthood. It is true that with the latter we could baptize, but it does not impart the power to confer the Holy Ghost; and that this Church might have the power to administer in every ordinance of the Gospel, the apostleship was again restored, which holds all the keys, authorities and powers to administer, not only in the outward ordinances, but also to confer the spirit of the living God."[42]

One of the finest and most comprehensive statements on the nature of this apostleship and of the sequence of events culminating in the final organization of the Church was given by yet another member of the original

"The Circumference of the Apostleship"

Quorum, President Brigham Young, who made this statement in 1853 while laying the cornerstone of the Salt Lake Temple:

> I speak thus to show you the order of the Priesthood. We will now commence with the Apostleship—where Joseph commenced. Joseph was ordained an Apostle, that you can read and understand. After he was ordained to this office, then he had the right to organize, build up the kingdom of God, for he had committed unto him the *keys* of the *Priesthood*, which is after the order of Melchizedek, the *High priesthood*, which is after the order of the Son of God. And this, remember, *by being ordained an Apostle.*
>
> Could he have built up the kingdom of God without first being an Apostle? No, he never could. The keys of the Eternal Priesthood, which is after the order of the Son of God, is comprehended by being an Apostle. All the Priesthood, all the keys, all the gifts, all the endowments, and everything preparatory to entering back into the presence of the Father and the Son, is in, composed of, circumscribed by, or I might say incorporated within the circumference of the Apostleship.
>
> Now, who do we set, in the first place, to lay the Chief, the South East Corner Stone: the corner from whence light emanates to illuminate the whole fabric that is to be lighted? We begin with the First Presidency, with the Apostleship, for Joseph commenced, always, with the keys of the Apostleship; and he, by the voice of the people, presiding over the whole community of Latter Day Saints, officiated in the Apostleship, as the First President.
>
> . . . I know that Joseph received his Apostleship from Peter, James and John, before a revelation on the subject was printed, and he never had a right to organize the Church before he was an Apostle.[43]

Consequently, Joseph Smith was the "first," "chief," or senior Apostle *before* he was established, confirmed, and set apart as President of the

Church. "Joseph Smith was the first Apostle of this Church, and was commanded of Jesus Christ to call and ordain other Apostles," President Young later affirmed, and

> these other Apostles are Apostles of Jesus Christ, and of Joseph Smith the chief Apostle of this last dispensation. . . . Joseph told us that Jesus was the Christ, the Mediator between God and man, and the Saviour of the world. He told us that there was no other name in the heavens nor under the heavens, neither could there be, by which mankind could be saved in the presence of the Father, but by and through the name and ministry of Jesus Christ, and the atonement he made on Mount Calvary. Joseph also told us that the Saviour requires strict obedience to all the commandments, ordinances and laws pertaining to his kingdom, and that if we would do this we should be made partakers of all the blessings promised in his Gospel.[44]

While preparing for the reorganization of the First Presidency some three and a half years after the death of Joseph Smith, Brigham Young taught his fellow Apostles at Winter Quarters in December 1847 that the pattern of succession in the presidency was laid down at the very beginning. Joseph Smith could not have become president without first being an Apostle and in his case, the first Apostle or chief elder with the keys. President Young, with "seven thunders rolling within him," said that as senior Apostle, now to become President in December 1847, he was doing nothing more than what his predecessor, Joseph Smith, had done seventeen years before, for the Twelve collectively had "received my kingdom" (D&C 136:41) and could govern and appoint.

During the intensive deliberations at Winter Quarters, President Young argued that it was past time for them to reorganize the First Presidency with him, as senior Apostle, as the next President and successor to Joseph Smith. Never one to campaign for the office, President Young nevertheless felt that government by a First Presidency was preferable to that of the

Twelve for many scriptural and logistical reasons, efficiency being one of them. Because they collectively held the keys, they had the right to reorganize. "Oliver Cowdery ordained Joseph an apostle," Brigham Young argued, and "Oliver [was] ordained an apostle by Joseph. They received their ordinations by Peter, James and John before there was a Church. . . . Peter, James and John constituted a First Presidency, Joseph said so many times."[45] His convincing argument was that an election or an appointment of any other potential candidate could not preempt what was rightfully now his by ordination. "You can't make me President: I am President; you can't give me power because I [already] have it."[46]

Thus Brigham Young believed that the pattern of apostolic succession was established in the very ordination of Joseph Smith by Peter, James, and John: the senior Apostle becomes President of the Church upon his ordination as such with the unanimous approval of the remaining Twelve. And while others of the Twelve held to somewhat differing methods of succession, none contested that Joseph Smith had been first ordained an Apostle under the hands of Peter, James, and John before he became President of the Church.

SUMMARY

To summarize, the early missionaries of this Church taught repeatedly the reality and awful dimensions of the Apostasy and, because of it, the need for and reality of a restoration of priesthood authority—"two priesthoods." The return of the angel Moroni with his message of the Book of Mormon was likewise primary in their early messages, and while some have argued that very little was said about a higher priesthood being restored, a great many of the original members of the Quorum of the Twelve believed differently—that the return of Peter, James, and John and their restoration of priesthood and priesthood keys were prerequisite to the bestowal of the Holy Ghost, to the organization of the Church, to the ordination of all later priesthood officers, and to a proper understanding of the pattern of succession in the presidency. Furthermore, Joseph Smith could not have attained the Presidency of the Church without first being the senior Apostle of this dispensation. Such discussion has necessitated a reexamination of the timing of the restoration of the Melchizedek Priesthood, one which these early Apostles contended must have occurred at least sometime before the Church was organized in April 1830.

In the end, I suppose if one could find bushels of letters and statements about the return of Peter, James, and John and priesthood authority, it would not be convincing to those who are intent on asserting otherwise. Essentially, these are matters of faith made as historically reasonable as possible. Thus we return to paraphrase Thomas More: "The restoration of priesthood authority in our day?—Why, it's a historical question yes; you can't see it; can't touch it; it's a history. But what matters to me is not only whether it can or cannot be substantiated but that I believe it to be true, or rather not that I *believe* it, but that *I* believe it."

NOTES

1. Robert Bolt, *A Man for All Seasons* (Toronto: Bellhaven House, 1960), 53.
2. Joseph Smith, comp., *History of the Church of Jesus Christ of Latter-day Saints*, ed. B. H. Roberts, 2nd ed. rev. (Salt Lake City: Deseret Book, 1971), 1:40, 43–44.
3. David Whitmer, interviewed by Zenos H. Gurley, January 14, 1885, in D. Michael Quinn, *The Mormon Hierarchy: Origins of Power* (Salt Lake City: Signature Books, 1994), 19.
4. William E. McLellin statement, in Quinn, *Mormon Hierarchy*, 19.
5. *Journal of Discourses* (London: Latter-day Saints' Book Depot, 1865), 10:303, in Quinn, *Mormon Hierarchy*, 26.
6. Quinn, *Mormon Hierarchy*, 8.
7. See Quinn, *Mormon Hierarchy*, 10–12.
8. Letter from Jonathan Crosby Jr., in *Evening and Morning Star*, August 1834, 181.
9. According to their diaries, twelve of sixteen missionaries who served in the period from 1830 to 1834 taught various elements of the Apostasy. The sixteen missionaries were Calvin Beebe, Jonathan Crosby Jr., Peter Dustin, William Draper, William Huntington, Joseph G. Hovey, Orson Hyde, Joel Hills Johnson, Wandle Mace,

William E. McLellin, John Murdock, W. W. Phelps, Parley P. Pratt, Samuel H. Smith, Sylvester Smith, and Brigham Young.

10. Journal of Samuel H. Smith, L. Tom Perry Special Collections, Harold B. Lee Library, Brigham Young University, Provo, UT, 22–23.
11. Journal of Samuel H. Smith, August 27, 1832, 17.
12. Sylvester Smith, "Letter from a Missionary Werving in Chenango Point, New York," *Evening and Morning Star*, July 1833, 109.
13. *The Journals of William E. McLellin, 1831–1836*, ed. Jan Shipps and John W. Welch (Provo, UT: BYU Studies, 1994), August 31, 1834, 136.
14. Journal of Samuel H. Smith, August 27, 1832, 17.
15. *Evening and Morning Star*, June 1834, 162 and July 1834, 169. Again from Phelps: "In consequence of the religious world having lost the power of getting revelations for themselves they have fallen into their present state of confusion, each partly manufacturing duties for themselves. For instance, the Presbyterian, the Episcopalian, the Methodist, and the Catholic god with the god of some other sects, requires them, (or at least they think he does,) to sprinkle their children, while the Baptist . . . god is greatly offended with it."
16. *The Orson Pratt Journals*, comp. Elden J. Watson (Salt Lake City: Elden Jay Watson, 1975), March 13, 1835, 52; and June 2, 1835, 65.
17. *Orson Pratt Journals*, August 23, 1835, 70.
18. Orson Pratt to Oliver Cowdery, February 16, 1835, in *Orson Pratt Journals*, 47.
19. *Autobiography of Parley P. Pratt*, ed. Parley P. Pratt Jr. (Salt Lake City: Deseret Book, 1980), 33; emphasis in original.
20. Letter from "Calvin and Peter," *Evening and Morning Star*, February 1833, 69. These missionaries are understood to be Calvin Beebe and Peter Dustin from a letter dated December 11, 1832, 63.
21. *Journals of William E. McLellin*, May 19, 1833, 122.
22. *Journals of William E. McLellin*, October 19, 1834, 142.
23. *Journals of William E. McLellin*, October 28, 1834, 145.
24. *Orson Pratt Journals*, July 7, 1833, 20.
25. *Orson Pratt Journals*, March 27, 1834, 37.
26. *Orson Pratt Journals*, March 1, 1835, 49.

27. *Autobiography of Parley P. Pratt*, 122.
28. *Autobiography of Parley P. Pratt*, 149.
29. "Sixth General Epistle of the Church . . . to the Saints Scattered Abroad," September 22, 1851, in Church Historian's Office, History of the Church, 1839–about 1882; see also Journal History of the Church of Jesus Christ of Latter-day Saints, September 22, 1851, 71, Church History Library, The Church of Jesus Christ of Latter-day Saints, Salt Lake City.
30. Oliver Cowdery to Phineas Young, March 23, 1846, in Scott H. Faulring, "The Return of Oliver Cowdery," in *Oliver Cowdery: Scribe, Elder, Witness*, ed. John W. Welch and Larry E. Morris (Provo, UT: Neal A. Maxwell Institute for Religious Scholarship, Brigham Young University, 2006), 331.
31. George A. Smith to Orson Pratt, about November 1848, 78, correspondence in Church Historian's Office.
32. Oliver Cowdery to Samuel W. Richards, January 13, 1849, in *Improvement Era*, October 1914; see Journal History, January 13, 1849, 2.
33. George Q. Cannon, *Life of Joseph, the Prophet* (Salt Lake City: Deseret Book, 1972), 75. According to the private journal of Oliver B. Huntington, President Wilford Woodruff once grappled with the question of the timing of the restoration of the higher priesthood. "Some people suppose that [1831] was the time that Joseph and Oliver [were] ordained to the Apostleship by Peter, James and John, thereby inferring that the Church was organized before [the] Melchizedek Priesthood was given; which is all wrong simply because some people want to criticize and find something wrong. The Melchizedek Priesthood was given before the Church was organized, in 1829 or March 1830." Diary of Oliver B. Huntington, March 3, 1883, 210–11, L. Tom Perry Special Collections, Harold B. Lee Library.
34. J. Reuben Clark Jr., *On the Way to Immortality and Eternal Life* (Salt Lake City: Deseret Book, 1961), 144.
35. For a fuller discussion of this topic, see Richard E. Bennett, *School of the Prophet: Joseph Smith Learns the First Principles, 1820–1830* (Salt Lake City: Deseret Book, 2010), 83–108.
36. Addison Everett to Oliver B. Huntington, February 17, 1881, in Oliver Boardman Huntington, journal 14, January 31, 1881, L. Tom Perry Special Collections,

Harold B. Lee Library. See also O. B. Huntington, diary 15, February 18, 1883, 44–47, where the letter is again recorded with few additional particulars. See also Addison Everett to Joseph F. Smith, January 16, 1882, Joseph F. Smith Collection, Church History Library. I am indebted to Larry C. Porter for the above information. For a full discussion of the Everett letters and the restoration of the Aaronic and Melchizedek Priesthoods, see Larry C. Porter, "The Restoration of the Aaronic and Melchizedek Priesthoods," *Ensign*, December 1996, 30–47.

37. In the original Book of Commandments, section 20 shows the word "Apostle" capitalized. Robin Scott Jensen, Robert J. Woodford, and Steven C. Harper, eds., *Revelations and Translations*, vol. 1 of the Manuscript Revelation Series of *The Joseph Smith Papers*, ed. Dean C. Jessee, Ronald K. Esplin, and Richard Lyman Bushman (Salt Lake City: The Church Historian's Press, 2009), 77.

38. See *Revelations and Translations*, 76–77.

39. Parley P. Pratt, in *Journal of Discourses*, 2:44.

40. Heber C. Kimball, in *Journal of Discourses*, 6:256.

41. Brigham Young, in *Journal of Discourses*, 12:70.

42. Orson Pratt, in *Journal of Discourses*, 12:361.

43. Journal History, April 6, 1853, 6–8.

44. Brigham Young, in *Journal of Discourses*, 9:364–65.

45. Minutes of a Meeting of the Twelve and Seventy, November 30, 1847, Brigham Young Papers, Church History Library.

46. Minutes of a Meeting of the Twelve, December 5, 1847, Brigham Young Papers, Church History Library; see also Richard E. Bennett, *Mormons at the Missouri— Winter Quarters, 1846–1852* (Norman: University of Oklahoma Press, 2004), 210, 308.

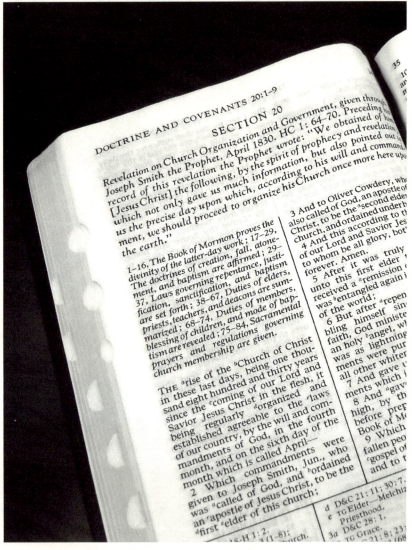

The Articles and Covenants of the Church of Christ (D&C 20) are the basic foundation for the government of The Church of Jesus Christ of Latter-day Saints.

Craig James Ostler

4

THE ARTICLES AND COVENANTS: A HANDBOOK FOR NEW BRANCHES

THE Articles and Covenants of the Church of Christ (D&C 20) are the basic foundation for the government of The Church of Jesus Christ of Latter-day Saints. The importance given to the revelation is reflected in early publications of the Church. This revelation guided early Church members in organizing and directing branches of the newly restored Church in the 1830s and continues in that function within the basic unit program today. A brief review of its early history gives insight into its importance and use. The value of the revelation today is demonstrated in the answers it provides to many basic questions regarding Church government, ordinances, record keeping, and expectations for Church members.

Craig James Ostler is a professor of Church history and doctrine at Brigham Young University.

A Firm Foundation

WRITING AND REVEALING THE ARTICLES AND COVENANTS

Students of the Doctrine and Covenants easily discover that section 20 does not read like most of the revelations of the Restoration. That is, the Lord does not speak in first person, but rather, this revelation was written under the inspiration of the Lord from the perspective of two individuals, the Prophet Joseph Smith and Oliver Cowdery. Declarations and instructions in the Articles and Covenants include such phrases as "the Lord has spoken it; and we, the elders of the church have heard, and bear witness" (D&C 20:16) and, multiple times, "we know that . . ." (D&C 20:17, 29, 30, 31, 35). As an inspired foundational document for branches of the Church, the Articles and Covenants might be likened to an early document in American history: the Constitution of the United States. The Lord did not dictate the words of that document. Nevertheless, he declared that he "established the Constitution of this land, by the hands of wise men whom I raised up unto this very purpose" (D&C 101:80). Similar to the Constitution of the United States, the Articles and Covenants of the Church required several written drafts from Oliver Cowdery and the Prophet Joseph Smith as the Spirit of the Lord worked within them to produce the final copy. On the other hand, distinct from the Constitution, there is sufficient evidence that much of the Articles and Covenants came by direct revelation to the Prophet Joseph Smith.[1]

In June 1829, the Lord gave Oliver Cowdery instructions to write a document that would serve as the Articles and Covenants of the Church.[2] Oliver sought further information from the Lord as to what should be included in that document. In response the Lord taught Oliver: "Behold, I have manifested unto you, by my Spirit in many instances, that the things which you have written [as scribe for the Book of Mormon translation] are true; wherefore you know that they are true. And if you know that they are true, behold, I give unto you a commandment, that you rely upon the things which are written; for in them are all things written concerning the foundation of my church, my gospel, and my rock" (D&C 18:2–4). Thus the manuscript of the soon-to-be-published Book of Mormon served

The Articles and Covenants: A Handbook for New Branches

as a primary source for the Articles and Covenants of the Church. In addition, through the Holy Ghost, the voice of the Lord guided Oliver Cowdery and later the Prophet Joseph Smith in writing this revelation.

It had long been assumed that the Articles and Covenants were written for and possibly read at the initial organizational meeting of the Church on April 6, 1830, held in the Peter Whitmer Sr. home in Fayette, New York. However, the manuscript of the printer's copy for the Book of Commandments and Revelations dates the Articles and Covenants to April 10, 1830.[3] In addition, it appears that the first reading of the document was three months later at the first Church conference. Further, the document contains information that meets the needs of newly organized branches of the Church rather than the general organization overseeing the various branches. Thus it may be better to reference this revelation as the handbook for branches of the Church, which is supported by the manner in which it was used in the early days of the Restoration and in which it continues to be used today.

PRIORITY GIVEN TO THE ARTICLES AND COVENANTS IN THE EARLY DAYS OF THE RESTORATION

The table of contents in the manuscript for the Book of Commandments places the Articles and Covenants between current sections 38 and 39 of the Doctrine and Covenants, which date to early January 1831, the same time that a third conference of the Church was held. In the printer's manuscript of the Book of Commandments, there is no number assigned to the revelation, unlike most other commandments. However, the title "Church Articles and Covenants" is the heading given to the revelation. The Book of Commandments (1831) placed the current section 20 following section 22. However, in the first edition of the Doctrine and Covenants (1835), the revelation is placed prominently as section 2, the first section following the preface (D&C 1). Further underscoring the prominence of this section is that it was the first canonized revelation of the Restoration and the first revelation to be printed. The record for the June 9, 1830, conference states, "Minutes of the first Conference held in the Township of Fayette, Seneca County, State of New York. by the Elders of this Church, June 9th 1830. according to the Church Articles and Covenants. . . . Ezekiel 14th read by Joseph Smith jr. and prayer by the same Articles and Covenants read by Joseph Smith jr. and received by unanimous voice of the whole congregation."[4]

This pattern was repeated at the second conference of the Church held September 26, 1830, which was also held at the Peter Whitmer Sr. home. Minutes from the conference indicate, "Articles and Covenants read by br. Oliver Cowdery and remarks by Brother Joseph Smith jr."[5]

The earliest known printed copy of section 20 "appeared in the non-Latter-day Saint press just a year after church organization, antedating known Latter-day Saint printings and manuscripts by about a year: *Painesville* [Ohio] *Telegraph*, 19 April 1831, p. 4."[6] The first known printings by Latter-day Saints are those in the *Evening and Morning Star* in 1832 and again in 1833. In the initial issue of the Church newspaper, the lead article under the heading of "Revelations" was "The Articles and Covenants of the Church of Christ."[7] It seems fair to surmise from the priority given to them as the first article, on the first page, of the first issue of the paper, that the most urgent revelation to put into the hands of Church members at that time was the Articles and Covenants of the Church. A second printing of the Articles and Covenants carried the following explanation: "We have again inserted the articles and covenants according to our promise in a previous number, for the benefit of our brethren abroad who have not the first number of the first volume. As there were, some errors which had got into them by transcribing, we have since obtained the original copy and made the necessary corrections."[8]

EARLY MEMBERS' RELIANCE UPON THE ARTICLES AND COVENANTS

Although there is not an abundance of evidence from historical documents and records regarding the availability of the Articles and Covenants, those few references in Church publications point to the likelihood that the Articles and Covenants were accessible to new members and were used in

The Articles and Covenants: A Handbook for New Branches

organizing and regulating branches. Missionaries sent to spread the message of the Restoration often baptized a few individuals in a given locality and moved on to other locations. Without uniform instructions, the Church organization in any given area could have soon become very independent and distinctive from other branches of the Church. It is evident that early members of the Church recognized the need to follow the instructions and explanations provided in the Articles and Covenants as published in the Church newspaper, and subsequently, when it was published as a section of the Doctrine and Covenants. This appears to be especially true of small branches that were organized according to the directive in the revelation. For example, the editors of the *Evening and Morning Star* shared the following letter from Robert Cullertson, an early Church member, along with a prefacing explanation:

> New churches are continually rising as the light spreads, and it is our peculiar privilege to hear, frequently, from different individuals, calling themselves our brethren, of whose names we have before never heard, and whose faces we have never seen, and learning of saints where we had not heard that the gospel had been preached. The following letter was received a few days since, and though the writer is a stranger, he will pardon us for taking the liberty of copying it into the Star.
>
> "May 2, 1834. Dear Brother—I take this opportunity of writing to let you know what the Lord is doing for the children of men in these last days. Last winter, one year ago, brother Simeon Carter came through our section of country, preaching the everlasting gospel of our blessed Savior. . . .
>
> "The church I spake of is on Sugar Creek, Shelby county, Indiana.—One brother and myself, with our families, moved into Kentucky, seven miles from Cincinnati, last month, and are trying to serve the Lord according to the Articles and Covenants of the church of Christ. We have established a church of eight members,

who agree to serve the Lord with full purpose of heart. Last Lord's day but one, I baptized two, and there is a prospect of more. . . ."[9]

In a later article appearing in the *Evening and Morning Star* titled "The Church of Christ," the Saints were cautioned, "A private member has no authority to preach, neither administer ordinances; nor has a teacher or deacon, authority to baptize, or confer blessings; nor has a priest power to confirm the members, for all things must be done according to the articles and covenants, which are from the Lord."[10] Further reference was made in that same article regarding the duty of members as given in the Articles and Covenants. Members were to "manifest before the church, and also before the elders, by a godly walk and conversation, . . . walking in holiness before the Lord" (D&C 20:69). The editors explained, "When a saint walks in holiness before the Lord, he will love his neighbor as himself, he will pray for his enemies; he will visit the sick, and comfort them; he will feed the hungry, and clothe the naked as long as he has means to do with; and when they are exhausted he will pray for more; and while pitying the poor and strengthening the weak, the angels will rejoice over his acts of goodness."[11] Such explanations of required authority of proper priesthood offices and exhortations to members are evidence of efforts to educate members regarding principles recorded in the Articles and Covenants.

Following the publication of the Doctrine and Covenants in 1835 and the placement of the Articles and Covenants as the first revelation after the preface, members continued to be instructed concerning the specifics of record keeping addressed in the revelation. At a general conference held on Damond's Creek, Calloway County, Kentucky, September 2, 1836, Thomas B. Marsh, President of the Twelve, presided and addressed the conference, "showing the necessity of there being kept by the Tennessee conference, a church record of all names belonging to the several branches of said conference, and also a record of all the proceedings of all courts and conferences held within the bounds of said conference. And that a clerk should be chosen, or appointed, by this conference, to keep the records, and be a standing clerk while the church should remain in this region. And also, that the priests and teachers

The Articles and Covenants: A Handbook for New Branches

bring from their several branches, the names of such as had been added since the last conference &c. agreeable to the articles and covenants."[12]

At a general conference held in Philadelphia, April 6, 1841, President Hyrum Smith indicated the continued importance of then Doctrine and Covenants section 2 as new branches were organized and possibly needing regulation or reminders of the government of the Church. Under the direction of Hyrum Smith, the minutes note, "The president then addressed the conference and congregation of the duty of the elders, and on the different orders on the priesthood; the Articles and Covenants were read, and again the president addressed the congregation on the same."[13]

A REVELATION OF ANSWERS TO QUESTIONS ON CHURCH GOVERNMENT AND PROCEDURES

A brief consideration of questions that might be asked by missionaries or new members in organizing a branch of the Church and the answers found in the Articles and Covenants emphasizes the value this revelation had and continues to have. The following list of questions with answers from Doctrine and Covenants section 20 may be helpful in better revealing the significance of this revelation.

Question: When should Church members meet? Why?

Answer: "It is expedient that the church meet together often to partake of bread and wine in the remembrance of the Lord Jesus" (D&C 20:75).

Question: What will they do in their meetings, and who will preside at the meetings?

Answer: "The elders are to conduct the meetings as they are led by the Holy Ghost, according to the commandments and revelations of God. [The priest's] duty is to take the lead of meetings when there is no elder present; but when there is an elder present, he is only to preach, teach, expound, exhort, and baptize" (D&C 20:45, 49–50).

Question: Who has authority to administer the sacrament?

Answer: "An apostle is an elder, and it is his calling to baptize; and to administer bread and wine—the emblems of the flesh and blood of Christ.

[Also,] the priest's duty is to . . . administer the sacrament" (D&C 20:38, 40, 46).

Question: What is the proper way to bless the sacramental emblems, and what words will you use in the sacramental prayers?

Answer: "It is expedient that the church meet together often to partake of bread and wine in the remembrance of the Lord Jesus; and the elder or priest shall administer it; and after this manner shall he administer it—he shall kneel with the church and call upon the Father in solemn prayer, saying: O God, the Eternal Father, we ask thee in the name of thy Son, Jesus Christ, to bless and sanctify this bread to the souls of all those who partake of it, that they may eat in remembrance of the body of thy Son, and witness unto thee, O God, the Eternal Father, that they are willing to take upon them the name of thy Son, and always remember him and keep his commandments which he has given them; that they may always have his Spirit to be with them. Amen" (D&C 20:75–77). The words for the blessing of the wine or water also follow in the revelation.

Question: How will you determine if investigators, who request baptism, qualify for baptism?

Answer: "*And again, by way of commandment to the church concerning the manner of baptism*—All those who humble themselves before God, and desire to be baptized, and come forth with broken hearts and contrite spirits, and witness before the church that they have truly repented of all their sins, and are willing to take upon them the name of Jesus Christ, having a determination to serve him to the end, and truly manifest by their works that they have received of the Spirit of Christ unto the remission of their sins, shall be received by baptism into his church" (D&C 20:37; emphasis in original).

Question: Who has authority to baptize?

Answer: "An apostle is an elder, and it is his calling to baptize. . . . [Also,] the priest's duty is to . . . baptize (D&C 20:38, 46, 50).

Question: How will you administer baptism?

Answer: "Baptism is to be administered in the following manner unto all those who repent—the person who is called of God and has authority from Jesus Christ to baptize, shall go down into the water with the person who has presented himself or herself for baptism, and shall say, calling him or her by name: Having been commissioned of Jesus Christ, I baptize you in the name of the Father, and of the Son, and of the Holy Ghost. Amen. Then shall he immerse him or her in the water, and come forth again out of the water" (D&C 20:72–74).

Question: Who can confirm baptized individuals as members of the Church and confer the gift of the Holy Ghost by the laying on of hands?

Answer: "An apostle is an elder, and it is his calling to . . . confirm those who are baptized into the church, by the laying on of hands for the baptism of fire and the Holy Ghost, according to the scriptures" (D&C 20:38, 41).

Questions: Do you confirm individuals as members of the Church immediately after baptism or do you wait?

Answer: "*The duty of the members after they are received by baptism.*— The elders or priests are to have a sufficient time to expound all things concerning the church of Christ to their understanding, previous to their partaking of the sacrament and being confirmed by the laying on of the hands of the elders, so that all things may be done in order" (D&C 20:68; emphasis in original).[14]

Question: Who can ordain new elders, priests, teachers, and deacons?

Answer: "An apostle is an elder, and it is his calling . . . to ordain other elders, priests, teachers, and deacons; . . . [a priest] may also ordain other priests, teachers, and deacons" (D&C 20:38–39, 48).

Question: What contacts will Church members have with each other outside of Church meetings, and who will make that contact?

Answer: "The priest's duty is to . . . visit the house of each member, and exhort them to pray vocally and in secret and attend to all family duties" (D&C 20:46–47).

Question: How should you handle problems that might arise such as backbiting and hurt feelings?

Answer: "The teacher's duty is to watch over the church always, and be with and strengthen them; and see that there is no iniquity in the church, neither hardness with each other, neither lying, backbiting, nor evil speaking" (D&C 20:53–54).

Question: When do you hold conferences combined with other branches of the Church?

Answer: "The several elders composing this church of Christ are to meet in conference once in three months, or from time to time as said conferences shall direct or appoint; and said conferences are to do whatever church business is necessary to be done at the time (D&C 20:61–62).

Question: What say do members of the Church have concerning those that are ordained to offices in the Church?

Answer: "No person is to be ordained to any office in this church, where there is a regularly organized branch of the same, without the vote of that church" (D&C 20:65).

Question: Suppose that a new baby has been born to one of the member families. What should be done regarding baptism of the infant, if anything?

Answer: "Every member of the church of Christ having children is to bring them unto the elders before the church, who are to lay their hands upon them in the name of Jesus Christ, and bless them in his name. No one can be received into the church of Christ unless he has arrived unto the years of accountability before God, and is capable of repentance" (D&C 20:70–71).

Question: How do you keep track of who the members of the Church are?

Answer: "It shall be the duty of the several churches, composing the church of Christ, to send one or more of their teachers to attend the several conferences held by the elders of the church, with a list of the names of the several members uniting themselves with the church since the last conference; or send by the hand of some priest; so that a regular list of all the names of the whole church may be kept in a book by one of the elders, whomsoever the other elders shall appoint from time to time" (D&C 20:81–82).

Questions: What should happen, if one of the members of the branch chooses to leave the Church or is expelled for misconduct and then they move and claim to be good members of the Church? For that matter, what if a faithful member moves to another branch? How do the members of the new branch know that these are faithful members of the Church?

Answer: "If any have been expelled from the church, so that their names may be blotted out of the general church record of names. All members removing from the church where they reside, if going to a church where they are not known, may take a letter certifying that they are regular members and in good standing, which certificate may be signed by any elder or priest if the member receiving the letter is personally acquainted with the elder or priest, or it may be signed by the teachers or deacons of the church" (D&C 20:83–84).

BASIC UNIT PROGRAM

Where the Church is in its beginnings within any given area, the Articles and Covenants are the basis for Church organization. A branch with few members does not need volumes of instructional handbooks and teaching manuals for various age groups. The basic unit program handbooks and publications of the Church today depend and cite liberally from the Articles and Covenants.[15] John P. Livingstone describes the program: "The simplified program now used in many small Church units worldwide was pioneered in the 1970s in response to the needs that had long concerned Church leaders. Beginning among the native North Americans, this approach now serves the Church in many parts of the world."[16] Similar to the instructions in Doctrine and Covenants section 20, the *Branch Guidebook* instructs members: "Branches where the branch president is the only one who holds the Melchizedek Priesthood or who is a priest in the Aaronic Priesthood hold sacrament meeting and a Sunday gospel instruction meeting for members."[17] Under the heading "Priesthood Ordinances and Blessings," the *Family Guidebook* quotes previously cited sections from the Articles and Covenants. For example, Doctrine and Covenants 20:70 is excerpted regarding the "Naming and Blessing of Children"; verse 73 is cited under directions regarding "Baptism"; verse 41 is cited regarding "Confirmation";

and verses 77 and 79 are cited concerning the "Sacrament."[18] Care is given to see that branches are organized and directed according the instructions revealed in the Articles and Covenants of the Church. The organizations of branches throughout the world hearken to the original inspired instructions given at the beginning of the Restoration. As a firm foundation, the instructions in the Articles and Covenants can be built upon and added to as the branch grows to the point of becoming a ward in one of the stakes of Zion.

CONCLUSION

It is a marvel that the foundational revelation of Church government given in 1830, at a time when there were very few members, is still the basis for the Church government today. The guidelines and instructions in the Articles and Covenants have been added to in governing the Church as the Lord revealed offices in the priesthood such as bishop, high councilor, high priest, patriarch, and seventy (see D&C 20:66; 107). However, the revelation itself stands intact without needing to change the basic government of Church branches. From the time that branches of the Church were first organized to the present, leaders of the Church have assured that the government and basic practices and principles of the Church follow the instructions in the Articles and Covenants.

NOTES

1. See Scott H. Faulring, "An Examination of the 1829 'Articles of the Church of Christ' in Relation to Section 20 of the Doctrine and Covenants," *BYU Studies* 43, no. 4 (2004): 57–91.
2. Lyndon W. Cook, *The Revelations of the Prophet Joseph Smith* (Deseret Book: Salt Lake City, 1985), 125, section 20, note 3. See an early draft of section 20, dated 1829 (Joseph Smith Collection, Church History Library), which states that Oliver Cowdery was commanded to write section 20.
3. Robin Scott Jensen, Robert J. Woodford, and Steven C. Harper, eds., *Manuscript Revelation Books*, vol. 1 of the Revelation and Translation series of *The Joseph Smith*

Papers, ed. Dean C. Jessee, Ronald K. Esplin, and Richard Lyman Bushman (Salt Lake City: Church Historian's Press, 2009), 74–75.

4. Donald Q. Cannon and Lyndon W. Cook, eds., *Far West Record* (Deseret Book: Salt Lake City, 1983), 1.
5. Cannon and Cook, *Far West Record*, 3.
6. Richard Lloyd Anderson, "The Organizational Revelations," in *Studies in Scripture, Vol. One: The Doctrine and Covenants*, ed. Robert L. Millet and Kent P. Jackson (Salt Lake City: Deseret Book, 1989), 119n3.
7. "Revelations," *Evening and Morning Star*, June 1832, 1.
8. "The Book of Mormon," *Evening and Morning Star*, June 1833, 98.
9. "Progress of the Church of the Latter Day Saints," *Evening and Morning Star*, May 1834, 156.
10. "The Church of Christ," *Evening and Morning Star*, March 1833, 74.
11. "The Church of Christ," 74–75.
12. "Extract from the proceedings of a general conference . . ." *Messenger and Advocate*, January 1837, 441.
13. Minutes, *Times and Seasons*, May 15, 1841, 413.
14. Note that at a later time, when missionaries journeyed to Missouri, they were instructed to "preach by the way in every congregation, baptizing by water, and the laying on of the hands by the water's side" (D&C 52:10).
15. The publications include *Family Guidebook* (1999), *Branch Guidebook* (1993), *Priesthood Leader's Guidebook* (1992), and *Teaching Guidebook* (1994), all published in Salt Lake City by The Church of Jesus Christ of Latter-day Saints.
16. John P. Livingstone, "Establishing the Church Simply," *BYU Studies* 39, no. 4 (2000): 133.
17. *Branch Guidebook*, 15.
18. *Family Guidebook*, 19–22.

Conferences and councils have always been a part of the Church, but not always in the same form that we may think of them now. (© 2000 by Intellectual Reserve, Inc. All rights reserved.)

Joseph F. Darowski

5

SEEKING AFTER THE ANCIENT ORDER: CONFERENCES AND COUNCILS IN EARLY CHURCH GOVERNANCE, 1830–34

As I reviewed the record of council minutes for 1833 in Minute Book 1 (Kirtland Council Minute Book) for future inclusion in the Joseph Smith Papers series, it became apparent that conferences and councils were routinely used to resolve administrative matters and problems facing the early Church, especially before 1834, when the first Church high council was established at Kirtland. As I immersed myself in the question of exactly what role Church conferences and councils played in the Church, I discovered three things. First, an appraisal of the minutes of the quarterly meetings held during the first years of the Church's existence as an institution reveals not a narrow hierarchical leadership but a shared, even symbiotic, collaboration. This relationship remained the essence of the genius of Church organization and structure throughout the lifetime of Joseph Smith. Second, it was interesting

---

Joseph F. Darowski is a research historian in the Church History Department and is a volume editor with the Joseph Smith Papers Project.

to discover that Joseph Smith was not always as prominent a participant as might be expected. I had previously labored under the assumption that Joseph Smith primarily governed the early Church through the power of his charismatic personality and priesthood authority, sanctioned by revelatory endorsement from on high. My notion was that Joseph Smith stood at the head of everything and therefore ultimately decided everything. Govern he did, but not quite as exclusively as I had supposed. Finally, over time, even as the complexity and scope of Church governance expanded, the conference/council model was retained. An important watershed was reached with the ratification of a constitution for the "High Council of the Church of Christ" on February 19, 1834, which formalized this arrangement. Another occurred in 1835 with the calling of the Quorum of Twelve Apostles and the First Quorum of Seventy. In many respects, the basic structure of the Church was in place by March 1836 when the Church's extant organizational structure was sustained by the membership at the dedication of the Kirtland "House of the Lord."

During the Kirtland era and beyond, two factors became driving forces behind the development of Church government. First, Joseph Smith experienced considerable internal resistance to his control, both temporal and ecclesiastical, regarding the affairs of the Church. Contemporary correspondence and personal accounts attest to the difficulties he encountered in his dealings with fellow Church leaders such as Edward Partridge, William W. Phelps, Sidney Rigdon, and others. In apparent response, a series of revelations reiterated his appointment to be even as Moses and to hold the keys of the mysteries of the kingdom. Simultaneously, the nature, duties, and offices of the priesthood were elaborated, particularly in revelations given in September 1832 and spring 1835 (D&C sections 84 and 107). These and other developments had to be accommodated as institutional organization and administration were gradually rationalized.

This article focuses on the dynamic convergence of issues surrounding early Church conceptions of priesthood, authority, and governance that generated a flow of revelations and refinements which, over time, yielded a hierarchal, yet consensual, institution in which all official members were able to appreciably participate; I trace specific steps critical to the unfolding of these developments in an effort to illuminate the historical, ecclesiastical, and social dimensions of that process. I also provide historical evidence of Joseph Smith's and the Saints' commitment to a collaborative, council-based response to ecclesiastical and institutional demands.

CONFERENCES AND COUNCILS

Two words—*conference* and *council*—need clarification. Initially, Church business was conducted by elders at meetings called conferences. By 1833, the terms *conference* and *council* sometimes seem almost synonymous, at least in regard to gatherings of high priests in Kirtland. At that point, the nature of the meetings and the business attended to appear outwardly similar regardless of the designation; a distinction between them is not clearly apparent. Pre-1834 meetings convey a sense of "a conference" as a setting in which the elders, high priests, or both groups conferred with each other and conducted "Church business" as directed in the April 1830 Articles and Covenants. Several meetings were designated as "general conferences" or "special conferences" as well. After the high council was formed in February 1834, the term *council* was generally applied to its meetings.

Webster's 1828 dictionary offers definitions that seem to fit hand in glove. For *conference* it proposes as a primary meaning "the act of conversing on a serious subject; a discoursing between two or more, for the purpose of instruction, consultation, or deliberation." For *council* we are given "an assembly of men summoned or convened for consultation, deliberation and advice." In this regard and given the limited numbers in attendance at many of the early Church gatherings, *council* really seems the more applicable term, but at the same time it also has a somewhat more formal connotation—a bishop's council, a president's council, and so forth.

Of course, other denominations held "conferences" and "councils," and a more thorough investigation of those usages may shed appreciable light on the subject. Given the early Church's penchant for borrowing Protestant terms and then repurposing them, it seems likely that the term *conference* carried a contemporaneous cultural meaning, regardless of the challenge we may encounter in trying to parse fine distinctions today. It is also possible that the gradual shift toward the term *council* for a certain class of meetings represented a passage from a less formal to a more structured institution with the introduction of bishops and presidents in addition to the first and second elders. In this sense, the term *council* came more prominently into play as the Church grew and offices and officers multiplied. However, forcing a distinction between the use of *conference* and *council* for the period through February 1834 is essentially unnecessary. Under either usage, Church business was conducted, the mind and will of the Lord sought, and instruction given. After that period it may be advantageous to qualify the terms to an extent, as *conference* seems to take on a more familiar connotation, as does *council*.

Commencing with the founding or organization of the Church of Christ as an institution in April 1830, guidelines, designated as the Articles and Covenants of the Church of Christ, were drafted and soon thereafter adopted. An early version states, "The elders are to conduct the meetings as they are led by the Holy Ghost. . . . The several elders composing this church of Christ are to meet at each of its meetings to do church business, whatsoever is necessary, &c."[1] Another iteration specifies, "The several elders composing this Church of Christ are to meet in conference once in three Month[s] or from time to time as they Shall direct or appoint—to do Church business whatsoever is necessary."[2]

THE FIRST CHURCH CONFERENCES

The first actual conference of the Church met on June 9, 1830, at Fayette, Seneca County, New York. The fairly succinct minutes of this meeting, which were later copied into Minute Book 2 (Far West Record), begin, "Minutes of the first Conference held in the Township of Fayette, Seneca County, State of New York, by the elders of this Church, June 9th 1830. According to the Church Articles and Covenants." The pattern or format of the meeting was rigorously consistent with the instructions in the Articles and Covenants, which were formally adopted at the conference. Joseph Smith played a leading role, as did Oliver Cowdery, both of whom stood at the head of the Church as first and second elders. But the only duty acknowledged was Cowdery's, who was to "keep the Church record and Conference minutes until the next conference."[3] An adjustment to this order occurred at the September 26, 1830, conference. Two months prior to this meeting, a revelation received in July 1830 mandated that "all things shall be done by common consent in the Church."[4]

A subsequent revelation received on behalf of Oliver Cowdery responded to issues raised by Cowdery's questioning of Joseph Smith's wording of a passage in the Articles and Covenants and Hiram Page's purported receipt of revelations for the Church. It explicitly asserted that "no one shall be appointed to receive commandments and revelations in this church excepting my servant Joseph Smith, Jun., for he receiveth them even as Moses." It further stipulated that Cowdery "not leave this place until after the Conference" and that "my servent Joseph shall be appointed to rule the Conference by the voice of it."[5] The conference record reads, "Minutes of the second Conference held by the Elders of this Church according to adjournment. . . . Br. Joseph Smith jr. appointed leader of the Conference by vote. Brother Joseph Smith jr. was appointed by the voice of the Conference to receive and write Revelations & Commandments for this Church."[6] By these resolutions the conference both acknowledged and ratified the import of the revelations which preceded it.

Though the September conference had further defined and refined Church governance, it did not modify the essential practice of conducting important Church business at such gatherings. At the same time, Joseph Smith's role in these sessions was more clearly established. He would provide the Church with revealed knowledge and counsel while standing at its head and holding the keys of the mysteries of the revelations. Yet it remained for the conference of elders as a body to "do Church business, whatsoever is necessary, &c."

The following year, in October 1831, Joseph Smith raised concerns regarding the elders' understanding of the purpose and potential of Church conferences. At a preliminary meeting on October 11, he echoed instructions from the Articles and Covenants and promised to instruct the elders regarding the "ancient manner of conducting meetings as they were led by the Holy Ghost."[7] The subsequent "general Conference" held at the Town of Orange, Cuyahoga County, Ohio, on October 25 began with exhortations by Sidney Rigdon and Joseph Smith concerning the need for unity, faith, and reliance on God. Rigdon observed, "When God works all may know it, for he always answers the prayers of the Savior for he makes his children one, for he by his Holy Spirit binds their hearts from earth to heaven. . . . God always bears testimony by his presence in counsel to his Elders when they assemble in perfect faith and humble themselves before the Lord and their will being swallowed up in the will of God." Joseph Smith added, "It is the privilege of every Elder to Speak of the things of God &c, And could we all come together with one heart and one mind in perfect faith the vail might as well be rent to day as next week or any other time."[8]

The tenor of Sidney Rigdon's and Joseph Smith's remarks, especially when considered in light of the October 11, 1831, conference, apparently bore immediate fruit, elevating the elders' understanding of their authority and access to the "mind and will of God." On November 1, 1831, at a conference held in Hiram, Ohio, "Oliver Cowdery made a request desiring the mind of the Lord through this conference of Elders to know how many copies of the Book of commandments it was the will of the Lord should be published in the first edition."[9] That same day a revelation to Joseph Smith for Elder Orson Hyde and others commenced: "The mind & will of the Lord as made known by the voice of the Spirit to a confrence held November first, 1831, concerning certain Elders, who requested of the Lord to know his will." In that revelation the instruction received at the October 25, 1831, conference was reiterated on a personal level. Elder Hyde was specifically taught, "Lo this is my ensample unto all those who are ordained unto this priesthood whose mission is appointed unto them to go forth & this is the ensample unto them that they shall speak as they are moved upon by the Holy Ghost & whatsoever they shall speak when moved upon by the Holy Ghost shall be Scripture shall be the will of the Lord shall be the mind of the Lord shall be the word of the Lord shall be the voice of the Lord & the power of God unto Salvation."[10]

At a "Special Conference" held on November 8, 1831, Sidney Rigdon raised the issue of "errors or mistakes which are in commandments and revelations." Significantly, the minutes of the meeting record how his issue was addressed by noting, "Resolved by this conference that Br Joseph Smith Jr correct these errors or mistakes which he may discover." Further, it was "Resolved by this conference that br Oliver Cowdery shall [copy, correct, and select] all the writings which go forth to the world."[11] In this instance, the conference, through the passing of resolutions, gave explicit direction to the Church's first and second elders, and they willingly complied. This example illuminates the role Joseph Smith intended conferences and councils to play in the affairs of the early Church and the degree to which he and Oliver Cowdery sustained the principle of Church governance through such means.

Language such as "the mind and will of the Lord" and "resolved by this conference" was repeated over the ensuing months in the record of subsequent meetings as copied into Minute Book 2. It reflected a refinement in the early Saints' understanding of the symbiotic relationship between revelation and administration, between the authority of Joseph Smith and the authority of the elders of the Church meeting in conference. Joseph Smith stood like Moses at the head of the priesthood and the Church—prophet, seer, and revelator. The elders, when they met in conference per the Articles and Covenants, stood charged to "do church business, whatsoever is necessary &c" as guided by the Spirit. Melded together in a mutually supportive bond and collaboration, Joseph Smith and the elders in conference constituted the governing council of the Church. Moreover, conferences and councils were not to just conduct "Church business" in some conventional administrative sense, they were to come together to learn the mind and will of the Lord and implement it. Joseph Smith was to provide revelations, commandments, and inspired direction to the Church, while conferences and councils were to direct its ecclesiastical and temporal activities as guided by the Holy Ghost.

THE PRESIDENT OF THE HIGH PRIESTHOOD

At the very time these refinements in the operation of Church conferences became the practice, additional elements and dimensions were added to the Church's organizational structure. Though the authority and office referred to as the "high priesthood" was introduced at a conference held in Geauga County, Ohio, in June 1831, it was not until a revelation received on November 11, 1831, that it took on specific connotations in regard to Church governance. That revelation begins, "To the Church of Christ in the Land of Zion in addition to the Church Laws respecting Church business." The various offices in the Church were reviewed and the need for presiding officers identified. Much of the revelation addressed the high priesthood, establishing its preeminence in the Church. The phrasing could not be plainer: "Then cometh the high Priesthood, which is the greatest of all." A new office was mandated to preside over this order of the priesthood and over the Church as a whole: "Wherefore it must needs be that one be appointed of the high Priest hood to preside over the Priesthood; & he shall be called President of the high Priest hood of the Church; or in other words the Presiding high Priest over the high priesthood of the Church; from the same cometh the administring of ordinances & blessings upon the church." The president's ultimate authority, however, did not derive just from presiding over the high priests, per se; rather, it also flowed from a broader administrative and judicial responsibility. After reiterating that the office of bishop was not equal to that of president of the high priesthood, the revelation specifies that "the most important business of the church, & the most difficult cases of the church, . . . shall be handed over, & carried up unto the court of the church before the president of the high Priesthood; & the president of the Court of the high Priesthood shall have power to call other high priests, even twelve to assist as counselors; & thus the president of the high priesthood & his councellors, shall have power to decide upon testimony, according to the laws of the church; . . . for this is the highest court of the church of God & final desision upon controvers[i]es, there is not any persons belonging to the church who is exempt from this court of the church." Finally, Joseph Smith's standing and authority is restated once more by way of an allusion to Moses: "And again the duty of the President of the office of the high Priesthood is to preside over the whole [Church] and to be like unto Moses. Behold here is wisdom yea to be a seer a revelator a translator and a prophet having all the gifts of God."[12]

Joseph Smith was sustained and ordained to the office of president of the high priesthood of the Church in a conference at Amherst, Ohio, on January 25, 1832. On March 8, 1832, he selected Jesse Gause and Sidney Rigdon "to be my councellers of the ministry of the presidency of the high Priesthood."[13] The authority to call such counselors was reaffirmed in a revelation regarding the role of the bishops: "unto the office of the presidency of the high Priesthood I have given authority to preside with the assistance of his councellers over all the Concerns of the church."[14]

The Missouri high priests acknowledged Joseph Smith as president of the high priesthood on April 26, 1832, during a series of council meetings held there that formally established the Literary and United Firms.[15] In the minutes for these meetings the terms *council* and *conference* were referenced, and Joseph Smith was identified at one point as "President of Conference & also of the High priesthood." A number of resolutions and orders were issued in the name of the "council." Though the practice of "conferences/councils" directing the business of the Church was apparently adhered to, those who held the office of high priest expressly took the lead.

On July 3, 1832, the leadership in Missouri (Zion) endorsed the November 11, 1831, revelation, resolving "that the mode and manner of regulating the Church of Christ Take effect from this time, according to a Revelation received in Hiram Portage County Ohio Nov 11, 1831."[16] In subsequent meetings, leaders reorganized the Church in Missouri into branches and called presiding officers over the elders and high priests.

THE ORGANIZATION OF COUNCILS

Eventually, at a conference of high priests in Zion, a presiding council was organized. On March 26, 1833, it was determined that "seven High Priests, who were sent from Kirtland to build up Zion, viz.—Oliver Cowdery, W. W. Phelps, John Whitmer, Algernon Sidney Gilbert, Bishop Partridge, and his two counselors—should stand at the head of affairs relating to the Church, in that section of the Lord's vineyard."[17] Later that year, on September 11, according to further minutes of a council of high priests on that date, Edward Partridge was "acknowledged to be at the head of the Church of Zion at present."[18] Partridge was the first bishop called in the Church and was apparently recognized as the ranking or presiding officer in Zion, in contrast to Joseph Smith, who had been previously sustained president of the high priesthood of the Church.

During the same period, Minute Book 1 records a succession of conferences and councils of high priests at Kirtland, Ohio, beginning December 5, 1832, and continuing until the organization of the high council of the Church of Christ, as it was initially styled, in February 1834. The Kirtland high priest conferences and councils were witness to several seminal events in early Church history. Among these were the receipt of the "Olive Leaf" revelation in late December 1832 and early January 1833 (D&C section 88); the inauguration of the School of the Prophets on January 22–23, 1833; the ordination of Sidney Rigdon and Frederick G. Williams to the presidency of the high priesthood, "to be equal in holding the Keys of the Kingdom with Brother Joseph Smith Jr," on March 18, 1833; the purchasing of the French Farm, where the Kirtland "House of the Lord" was to be constructed; Doctor Philastus Hurlbut's disciplinary councils; revelations concerning the "House of the Lord" and its design; information concerning the plat of Zion and Kirtland; and the establishment of F. G. Williams & Co.[19]

It is in the light of the unfolding of principles and practices of Church government received and implemented over a four-year period that these assemblies are best understood. These meetings were, in effect, president's councils, presided over by the president of the high priesthood of the Church. They reflect a culmination of the early Saints' efforts to respond to the directives initially received and ratified in the Articles and Covenants in 1830 and subsequently amplified in October and November 1831. They further demonstrate that the institutional Church was governed through conferences/councils founded on the principles of divine guidance and common consent. Though Joseph Smith stood at the head of the Church, he envisioned, endorsed, and participated in a conference/council system of Church government.

Even though much had been accomplished in 1833 through these president's council meetings, Joseph Smith was still concerned about their form and structure, and about the conduct he observed when priesthood leaders met. All was not yet according to the ancient order. At a council meeting held in his home on February 12, 1834, Joseph Smith hearkened back to the instruction given in October 1831, observing, "I shall now endeavor to set forth before this council, the dignity of the office which has been conferred upon me by the ministering of the Angel of God, by his own will and by the voice of this Church. I have never set before any council in all the order in which a Council ought to be conducted, which, perhaps, has deprived the Council of some, or many blessings." He then proceeded to explain the ancient order for the conducting of councils. He related that "in ancient days, councils were conducted with such strict propriety, that no one was allowed to whisper, be weary, leave the room, or get uneasy in the least, until the voice of the Lord, by revelation, or by the voice of the council by the Spirit was obtained; which has not been observed in this Church to the present."[20] In this respect, his discourse to the gathered high priests and elders further amplified and elaborated his October 25, 1831, instructions.

THE ORGANIZATION OF THE FIRST HIGH COUNCIL

Five days later, a conference of high priests assembled, again at Joseph Smith's house. On this occasion the minutes state that "they proceeded to organize the President's Church Council, consisting of twelve High Priests, and this according to the law of God."[21] Thus what would subsequently be known as the first "High Council of the Church of Christ" was organized. It consisted of "twelve high priests, and one, or three presidents, as the case may require, . . . appointed by revelation, for the purpose of settling important difficulties which might arise in the Church." With the organizing of a formal high council, a new phase in Church governance commenced. As part of his instruction, Joseph Smith explained that "he would show the order of councils in ancient days as shown to him by vision." He also observed that this would be a model for the high priests "abroad" to follow, though they should be careful to send a copy of their actions to the seat of Church government, that is, to the council presided over by the president of the high priesthood of the Church. Such councils abroad were also authorized to appoint a president to preside over their meetings. The process for conducting deliberations was explained to the twelve counselors selected to serve on the president's Church council. Then, as the minutes relate, "It was then voted by all present that they desired to come under the present order of things which they all considered to be the will of God." And it was also voted "by all present that Bro. Joseph should make all necessary corrections by the Spirit of inspiration hereafter."[22] The meeting then adjourned until February 19.

By the time the corrected minutes were presented for consideration and ratification, Joseph Smith had significantly revised them. As noted on February 19, "he had labored the day before with all the strength and wisdom that he had given him in making the corrections necessary in the last council minutes."[23] The "president's church council" was restyled the "High Council of the Church of Christ." The purpose of the council was to settle "important difficulties which might arise in the Church, which could not be settled by the Church, or the Bishop's council to the satisfaction of the parties," language that mirrored the November 11, 1831, revelation regarding the office of president of the high priesthood of the Church. Another provision provided for the selection of the president of the high council of the Church. It explicitly affirmed that Joseph Smith was to serve in that office. As expressed in the revised minutes, "The president of the Church, who is also the President of the Council, is appointed by the voice of the Saviour and acknowledged in his administration by the voice of the Church, and it is according to the dignity of his office that he should preside over the High Council of the Church." It was again specified that high priests abroad who organized a council after this model were to report their proceedings to "the High Council at the seat of government of the Church," which at that time was wherever Joseph Smith resided. If any party was dissatisfied with the results of such a council they could appeal to the high council "at the seat of the general Church government" of the Church for a rehearing. In addition, "the President or Presidents at the seat of general Church government shall have power to determine whether any such case . . . is justly entitled to a rehearing." After some further minor revisions, the minutes were presented to the council by Joseph Smith. According to the record of the meeting, "The questions were asked whether the present Council acknowledged the same, and receive them for a form or constitution of the High Council of the Church of Christ hereafter. The Document was received by the unanimous voice of the Council." These provisions made it clear that the high council at the seat of Church government was a presiding high council for the Church, or to use earlier terminology, the president of the high priesthood of the Church's court or council.[24] To reiterate, during the Kirtland period, the high council of the Church at Kirtland was also the high council of the Church itself when functioning as the president's Church court or council. By implication, the stake high council wherever Joseph Smith resided, became, by default, the president's council.

This became the practice during much of Joseph Smith's lifetime. The intention, of course, was for Joseph Smith to reside in Zion and thus make the high council there the presiding high council for the Church. This aim was later reflected in language incorporated into section III of the 1835 Doctrine and Covenants (currently section 107), which adopted much of the November 11, 1831, revelation regarding the president of the high priesthood of the Church. Once organized, the high council of the Church of Christ met frequently to conduct disciplinary councils and other Church business as directed. On February 24, 1834, Joseph Smith assembled the council at his home to receive the report of Elders Lyman Wight and Parley Pratt, who had just arrived from Zion. It was at this gathering that the initial plans for Zion's Camp emerged. According to the minutes for this occasion, "Bro. Joseph . . . arose and said that he was going to Zion to assist in redeeming it. He then called for the voice of the council to his going, which was given without dissenting vote."[25]

After the arrival of Zion's Camp in Missouri in June 1834, the Missouri high priests met together. The minutes from Minute Book 2 note that on July 3, 1834, "The High Priests of Zion assembled for the purpose of organizing a general Council of High Priests, agreeable to the revelation for the purpose of settling important business that might come before them which could not be settled by the Bishop and his council. Proceeded to make choice of President."[26] These actions reflect both the constitution of the high council as ratified on February 19 in Kirtland, and the November 11, 1831, revelation.

There remains some question whether Joseph Smith was present in the meeting on that date. The minutes do not list him specifically. Only the three presidents appointed—David Whitmer, William W. Phelps, and John Whitmer, along with twelve high priests as counselors and Frederick G. Williams as clerk—are identified. He may have been present, and some later recollections place him there, though they may simply reflect a conflation of events from July 3 to 7.[27] In any event, the actions taken were fully consistent with the provisions of the constitution of the high council regarding high priests abroad—that is, outside the boundaries of the seat of Church government or an organized stake. At that moment, Kirtland was technically the seat of Church government and the only organized stake, per se. So in that sense, it is something of a moot point whether Joseph Smith was physically present or not.

However, matters were quite different on July 7, 1834. At that assembly of high priests, Joseph Smith ordained the three presidents and twelve counselors appointed on July 3. Interestingly, after that high council was organized and business conducted, another action was taken by those present. As the minutes relate, "High Priests, Elders, Priests, Teachers, Deacons & members covenanted with uplifted hands to heaven that they would uphold Brother David Whitmer as President, head and leader in Zion (in the absence of br. Joseph Smith jr.) & John Whitmer & W. W. Phelps as assistant Presidents and Counselors."[28] Thus it seems that David and John Whitmer with W. W. Phelps were first sustained and ordained as presidents of the high council at Zion and then as presidents of the Church in Zion. In a sense, this structure paralleled locally that of the Church in general, with Joseph Smith, Sidney Rigdon, and Frederick G. Williams as presidents of the high priesthood of the Church and also as presidents of the high council of the Church.

At the close of this period of Church growth and institutional development, Joseph Smith offered two observations that summed up the early Church's accomplishments in regard to governance by conference and council. On February 19, following the ratification of the constitution of the high council of the Church of Christ, he noted with satisfaction that "the Council was organized according to the ancient order, and also according to the mind of the Lord."[29] Subsequently, on July 7, 1834, when Joseph Smith ordained the presidency and counselors of the high council in Zion, he informed them that "if he should now be taken away . . . he had accomplished the great work which the Lord had laid before him, . . . and that he now had done his duty in organizing the High Council, through which Council the will of the Lord might be known."[30]

NOTES

1. Attributed to Martin Harris, *Painesville Telegraph* (Painesville, OH), April 19, 1831.
2. Book of Commandments and Revelations, 56, Church History Library, The Church of Jesus Christ of Latter-day Saints, Salt Lake City; facsimile copy in Robin Scott Jensen, Robert C. Woodford, and Steven C. Harper, eds., *Manuscript Revelation Books*, vol. 1 of the Revelations and Translations series of *The Joseph Smith Papers*, ed. Dean C. Jessee, Ronald K. Esplin, and Richard Lyman Bushman (Salt Lake City: Church Historian's Press, 2009), 83; currently D&C 20:61–62; see also *The Evening and the Morning Star*, June 1832, 1–2.
3. Minute Book 2 (Far West Record), June 9, 1831, 1, Church History Library.
4. Book of Commandments and Revelations, 34; see also Jensen and others, *Revelations and Translations*, 39; currently D&C 26:2.
5. Book of Commandments and Revelations, 40–41; see also Jensen and others, *Revelations and Translations*, 51, 53; currently D&C 28:2, 10.
6. Minute Book 2, September 26, 1830, 2.
7. Minute Book 2, October 11, 1831, 8–9.
8. Minute Book 2, October 25, 1831, 10–14.
9. Minute Book 2, November 1, 1831, 15–16.
10. Book of Commandments and Revelations, 113; see also Jensen and others, *Revelations and Translations*, 199; currently D&C 68:2–3.
11. Minute Book 2, November 8, 1831, 16–17.
12. Book of Commandments and Revelations, 122–23; see also Jensen and others, *Revelations and Translations*, 217, 219; currently D&C 107:59, 64–67, 78–81.
13. Kirtland Revelation Book, 10–11, Church History Library, Salt Lake City; facsimile copy in Jensen and others, *Revelations and Translations*, 433, 435. In 1833, Jesse Gause was replaced by Frederick G. Williams after Gause was excommunicated on December 3, 1832.
14. Revelation, March 10, 1832, "Duties of Bishops &c to Joseph and Sidney March 1832," Newel K. Whitney Collection, L. Tom Perry Special Collections, Brigham Young University, Provo, UT.
15. Minute Book 2, April 26–30, 1832, 24–26.

Seeking After the Ancient Order

16. Minute Book 2, July 3, 1832, 28.
17. Joseph Smith History, Vol. A-1, p. 282.
18. Minute Book 2, September 11, 1833, 36–37.
19. See specific dates in Minute Book 1 (Kirtland Council Minute Book), Church History Library, Salt Lake City.
20. Minute Book 1, February 12, 1834, 27–29.
21. Minute Book 1, February 17, 1834, 29–31.
22. Minute Book 1, revised minutes, February 17, 1834, 32–35.
23. Minute Book 1, February 19, 1834, 36–39.
24. Minute Book 1, revised minutes, February 17, 1834, 32–35.
25. Minute Book 1, February 24, 1834, 41–42.
26. Minute Book 2, July 3, 1834, 43.
27. Richard Lloyd Anderson finds convincing George A. Smith's later recollection of Joseph Smith being in attendance on July 3, 1834. He also credits accounts by Wilford Woodruff, Levi Jackman, and Newel Knight that suggest Joseph Smith was present on that occasion as well. However, the copy of the minutes of the meeting available in Minute Book 2 do not acknowledge Joseph Smith's presence, leaving open the possibility that later recollections may be in error or conflated.
28. Minute Book 2, July 7, 1834, 43–45.
29. Minute Book 1, February 19, 1834, 37.
30. Minute Book 2, July 7, 1834, 43–45.

On December 27, 1847, Brigham Young was sustained as President of the Church in the Kanesville Tabernacle, where he reorganized the First Presidency with Heber C. Kimball and Willard Richards as counselors. (Brigham Young daguerreotype by Marsena Cannon, ca. 1851–52, enhanced by artist Charles DeForest Fredricks, ca. 1857, NPGSI.)

Mark L. Staker

6

Sharing Authority: Developing the First Presidency in Ohio

On Tuesday, November 30, 1847, Joseph Young organized a meeting of Quorum of the Seventy leaders at 11 a.m. in the log Council House just east of Brigham Young's cabin in Winter Quarters, Iowa. He invited the six Apostles in the settlement at that time, including Brigham Young, to join the meeting and give counsel. Thomas Bullock served as the clerk for the Apostles and kept the minutes, rapidly capturing the discussion as it unfolded. Robert L. Campbell was there as clerk for the Quorum of Seventy and took a second set of detailed notes.

Brigham Young's mind was clearly on other matters than business among the Seventy, and the conversation often drifted to the subject of a First Presidency. He frequently led out in asking questions and sharing his thoughts, but others also freely expressed their views. They discussed who could appoint a First Presidency and how its members

---

Mark L. Staker is a senior researcher in the Church History Department, The Church of Jesus Christ of Latter-day Saints.

should be selected and organized. Brigham Young recognized that Joseph Smith had shaped how that office should function. Throughout their meeting the men looked to the revelations Joseph had received and his own example in governing the Church for a model to follow. Brigham Young recognized that they had all the authority they needed to continue Joseph's pattern of governance and establish a First Presidency. Joseph Young acknowledged that his brother Brigham "has suggested a new thought to me that the church have the authority and can make a Presidency."[1] Brigham Young reasoned that "Joseph [Smith] was ordained an Apostle, but the church elected him as a President, Prophet, Seer, & Revelator, but he never was ordained to that office, why the one that ordained him would have to take his own hat off & put it on him [Joseph] & then go to hell[.] Oliver Cowdery ordained Joseph an Apostle. Oliver [was] ordained an Apostle by Joseph. they received their ordinations by Peter James & John before there was a church[.] take them that are ordained & elect them and they [are] selected & upheld by the church & therefore elected[.]"[2]

Brigham Young's insistence that Peter, James, and John ordained Joseph and Oliver Apostles before there was a Church emphasized the fact that the Church did not give its President authority or permission to govern but that his authority originated from an independent source. Even with independent authority, however, they were still "selected & upheld." The Church was also to play an important role in approving its leaders.

During the discussion, Orson Pratt took this concept further by arguing that "the 1st President has not the right of choosing his 2 Councillors . . . the three are chosen by the body."[3] Brigham Young insisted the President could choose his own counselors, "only he must be backed up by the church[.] the President has the right to make his selection or nomination & if the church won't back him up he may continue nominating till he has every male member in the church & if they won't back up his nomination he may preside alone—and the Church has no right to nominate for him."[4] Ezra T. Benson added later in the discussion, "I consider the Prest. can select just whom he pleases, even a lay man." Brigham Young stated:

Sharing Authority: Developing the First Presidency in Ohio

"Go back a little further to the time of the 3 Wit[nesses]: when O. Cowdery had nearly as much power as Joseph—he went & bapd [baptized] a man & then [Joseph] sd. [said] I want you to be my 1st Cor.[Counselor]—that was (Fredrick Gee) [Williams]."[5]

The discussion by these Latter-day Apostles continued for some time and included a number of references to the early Apostles of Jesus Christ—Peter, James, and John. Heber C. Kimball asked rhetorically, "If Peter Jas & Jon had the right to come were they not a Prescy[?]" to which Brigham Young responded, "Joseph said so many a time."[6] The three early Apostles not only provided the authority to direct the Church but had served as a model for its administration. Peter, James, and John had become a symbol for Church governance.

Although Brigham Young and his fellow Apostles still had much to learn about Church administration and may have been imperfectly familiar with events that occurred before they became members, Joseph's teachings and example were clear enough that they could move forward less than a month after their discussion at Winter Quarters and reestablish the office of First Presidency on December 27, 1847. On that day, Brigham Young was sustained as President of the Church in the Kanesville Tabernacle, where he reorganized the First Presidency and called as his counselors two men who were also in that November 30 meeting, Heber C. Kimball and Willard Richards.

Brigham Young and his associates had personal experience and an oral tradition to help shed light on the published revelations they used to support their action. When Joseph Smith initially established the office of First Presidency, he had much less information to build on. It clearly took some time and continuing revelation before Joseph fully realized the model he would follow, and the governance system rapidly changed during the first three years of the Church's existence to meet the needs of a fast-growing membership. As this system took shape, Joseph Smith shared increasing levels of authority to govern with an expanding group of individuals that eventually took shape as three Presidents modeled on the leadership of Peter, James, and John.

BEGINNINGS

The development of a First Presidency in Kirtland, Ohio, began with the restoration of priesthood authority to Joseph Smith and Oliver Cowdery on May 15, 1829. Joseph later related how, after John the Baptist conferred priesthood authority and he and Oliver baptized each other, "I laid my hands upon his [Oliver Cowdery's] head and ordained him to the Aaronic Priesthood, and afterwards he laid his hands on me and ordained me to the same Priesthood—for so we were commanded" (Joseph Smith—History 1:71). Oliver recalled that when they "received the office of the lesser priesthood," the angel had made a promise that he would be "ordained to the Presidency."[7] The messenger, John the Baptist, noted that "he acted under the direction of Peter, James, and John, who held the keys of the priesthood of Melchisedeck," which would be conferred on them "in due time."[8]

At that point, both men shared equal priesthood authority and looked toward receiving additional authority from heavenly messengers. Although the Church was later formally organized on April 6, 1830, Oliver Cowdery believed that when he and Joseph Smith received the priesthood and baptized each other, this initiated the restoration of the Church of Jesus Christ on earth and that Oliver was "the first received into this church, in this day" upon his baptism.[9] After their baptisms, both men received revelation and prophesied the rise and progress of the Church.

Both men continued to receive exactly the same keys of authority as previously promised. Joseph Smith noted that in addition to the "lesser priesthood," both men received the Melchizedek Priesthood according to a prophecy that it "should come upon the Seer of the last days and the Scribe that should sit with him, and that should be ordained with him, by . . . those who had been held in reserve for a long season."[10] Oliver Cowdery wrote that both he and Joseph "received the high and holy priesthood" from these Apostles.[11] Every time Joseph Smith received priesthood keys, Oliver did

Sharing Authority: Developing the First Presidency in Ohio

also—including in Ohio in 1836 when Moses, Elias, and Elijah conferred "the keys of this dispensation" (D&C 110:16).[12]

Even though Oliver understood he was the first person baptized into the Church of Jesus Christ when he went down into the Susquehanna River, he recognized the existence of the Church did not mean it was fully organized. Based on scriptural precedent, most Christian congregations require a confirmation by "the imposition of hands" to become a full member of the respective church.[13] Oliver Cowdery observed, "I was also present with Joseph when the Melchisedeck priesthood was confered by the holy angles of god," he recalled, " . . . which we then confirmed on each other by the will and commandment of god."[14] This confirmation was considered necessary to make them fully members of the congregation. Finally, when the Church was officially organized on April 6, 1830, members were rebaptized and confirmed, and specific individuals were acknowledged to have authority to lead the congregation.

It was this gradual development of an official Church organization through stages that Brigham Young likely referenced when he summarized, "This was a slow business, but at last he [Joseph] organized the Church, for the Lord had revealed to him the Aaronic priesthood upon which the Church was first organized; after that he received the Melchisedek priesthood, when the Church was more fully organized, and a few more believed, and then a few more and a few more."[15] The process of organization continued to expand as the Church grew.

JOSEPH THE SEER AS FIRST ELDER

From the very beginning, however, while Joseph and Oliver always shared priesthood keys, it appears Joseph still held a unique position as revelator. John Whitmer used the title "Joseph the Seer" in the introduction to his copies of the earliest revelations and in the earliest pages of his history of the Church.[16] Joseph used this same language when identifying himself along with Oliver as "the seer of the last days and the Scribe that should sit with him."[17] This title seems to focus on Joseph Smith's charismatic role as a revelator of God's will and translator of God's word rather than as an administrator in the new Church, but it also confirms Joseph's special status.

Even during this early period, however, there were clear attempts by Joseph to share his role. He sought inspiration and received revelation that invited Oliver Cowdery to assist in translating (see D&C 8, 9). Although the translation attempt failed, Joseph received a number of revelations jointly with Oliver Cowdery and sometimes others that placed them in similar roles.

This joint sharing of authority between Joseph and Oliver was reflected in their calls by revelation and subsequent ordinations to the office of first and second elder at the organization of the Church on April 6, 1830 (see D&C 20:2–3).[18] In revelation given on that day, Joseph's title of seer was affirmed and expanded when he was told, "Thou shalt be called a seer, a translator, a prophet, an apostle of Jesus Christ" (D&C 21:1). Oliver was to ordain Joseph first elder, and in turn he was to be an elder "and the first preacher of this church" (D&C 21:12).

Joseph Smith's position as first elder and Oliver Cowdery's position as second elder separated them from other men in the Church who were also given priesthood authority. The nature of the authority given to others during the early period is not clear, but Heber C. Kimball came to understand that at least some others were ordained as Apostles of Jesus Christ. "Peter comes along with James and John and ordains Joseph to be an Apostle, and then Joseph ordains Oliver, and David Whitmer, and Martin Harris; and then they were ordered to select twelve more and ordain them."[19] Heber C. Kimball was not a member of the Church when it was headquartered in New York and may have imperfectly understood the events of that early period.[20] He placed Oliver as receiving his ordination from Joseph rather than directly from heavenly messengers, as Oliver recalled; but their apostolic ordinations may have been similar to the two men ordaining each other after John the Baptist gave them the Aaronic Priesthood, as Joseph Smith described. Heber C. Kimball placed the Three Witnesses in a special category similar in office to Peter, James, and John but not with the same authority to govern. Other early members may also have held the title of Apostle, but this seems to have been a reference to the source of their authority rather than the office they held.[21] The Three Witnesses would later select twelve men in Kirtland and ordain them as Apostles.[22]

Available sources leave many unanswered questions about the nature of early Church administration, but it is clear that Joseph and Oliver held the two most prominent offices as first and second elder. The wording of the revelation directing their ordination (see D&C 21), however, suggests that Joseph and Oliver's relative positions in the Church were already subtly different from each other when the Church was organized and by September 26, 1830, these differences had become more pronounced. By September, Oliver had received five revelations jointly with Joseph in addition to their initial shared visitation by John the Baptist.[23] After Oliver Cowdery's criticism of one of Joseph Smith's revelations that summer, followed by Oliver's acceptance of revelations received by Hiram Page as valid,[24] Joseph received a revelation in September directed specifically at Oliver that affirmed, "No one shall be appointed to Receive commandments & Revelations in this Church excepting my Servent Joseph for he Receiveth them even as Moses."[25] In antiquity, Moses had Aaron to serve as his voice, and thus the revelation did not specifically restrict Oliver's involvement in receiving revelations jointly as long as they came through Joseph. Oliver could even receive revelations alone if they were not written "by way of commandment" (D&C 28:8). However, the practice of Joseph and Oliver receiving joint revelations immediately stopped. Oliver never shared in receiving a published revelation again, even though he shared all priesthood keys conferred on Joseph, including those keys conferred almost six years later during a joint visitation by Moses, Elias, and Elijah (see D&C 110).

Following Joseph's receipt of the revelation specifically appointing him to receive commandments and revelations, the Church conference met and "Br. Joseph Smith jr. [was] appointed leader of the Conference by vote" and "appointed by the voice of the Conference to receive and write Revelations & Commandments for this Church."[26] The participants in the conference affirmed what Joseph had received in revelation. Although Oliver Cowdery's name was listed second among the names of the elders who attended the conference, he was not appointed to preside in the same manner.

The term "vote" fits comfortably with Brigham Young's later use of the word "elected" to describe their manner of affirming leaders, but the selection of Joseph Smith as the authority was not a democratic process where other candidates were considered. Less than three months before Joseph's appointment, revelation directed that "all things shall be done by common consent" (D&C 26:2). The phrase "common consent" was used as a legal phrase in the Middle Ages in England to express a joint approval of the lord of a manor and his tenants to legally binding bylaws that would govern them.[27] The word "vote" in 1828 still reflected this unifying agreement when it was used to mean "united voice in public prayer."[28] It was this united expression of support and dedication done through raising a hand that seems to have been the "voice of the Conference" formally appointing Joseph to receive and write revelations rather than a divisive expression of will through selecting one of several candidates. Even the term "election," as later used by Brigham Young, was defined in 1828 to include more than just a process for selecting from a range of choices. It acknowledged that an election could be the expression of approval for a king, president, or other leader to govern—sometimes through the raising of hands. It could also be the acknowledgment of approval of an individual by God, who "elected" that person for salvation.[29]

Less than four months after the conference, Joseph Smith began sharing in revelations with Sidney Rigdon in a practice that continued from December 1830 until February 1831, when Joseph received another revelation noting that there was "none other appointed . . . to receive commandments and revelations" than him (D&C 43:3). These joint revelations stopped for the rest of the year.

Sharing Authority: Developing the First Presidency in Ohio

BISHOP OF THE CHURCH

The revelations addressing Joseph's role as revelator did not clarify how the Church should be governed. Revelations specifically addressing Church governance began when Joseph Smith first arrived in Kirtland and received a revelation directing the elders of the Church to assemble together to receive the law "that ye may know how to govern my church" (D&C 41:3). Significantly, the resulting revelation provided a specific list of commandments to govern behavior but also directed that Edward Partridge was to "be appointed by the voice of the church, and ordained a bishop unto the church . . . to see to all things as it shall be appointed unto him in my laws" (D&C 41:9–10).

Partridge was a convert drawn from the Reformed Baptist movement (or Disciples of Christ), as were many other newly baptized members in Kirtland. Their former religious denomination viewed bishops as overseers of distinct congregations. Some Kirtland members, including Joseph Smith, were exposed to denominations such as Methodism, which typically viewed bishops as overseers of multiple congregations. The revelation seemed to have this more broadly applied understanding by calling Partridge as the bishop of the Church rather than of a congregation. Partridge approached his calling in this way by immediately visiting multiple congregations, where he read and implemented the law of the Church.[30] Congregations or branches of the Church had overseers responsible for the temporal and spiritual needs of their community, but although *overseer* is the English equivalent of the Greek-derived term *bishop*, these individuals did not seem to share the same authority to govern that Partridge held.[31]

Edward Partridge's calling as bishop was the first one directing an individual to leave his business and "spend all his time in the labors of the church" (D&C 41:9). The same revelation reaffirmed Joseph Smith's calling as a translator in which he would still spend all of his time on behalf of the Church, but Partridge's calling as bishop gave him the only administrative position in the nascent Church of Christ. In fact, it was not until ten months later, on November 11, 1831, when Joseph first received a revelation establishing the office of President of the high priesthood, that he learned in revelation that "the office of a Bishop is not equal unto it,"[32] clarifying that the bishop of the Church was not the highest office in the Church. This suggests that, between Partridge's ordination at the June 1831 conference and the establishment of a new office at the November 1831 conference, he held the highest specific Churchwide office available. At Kirtland's June conference, Lyman Wight ordained Edward Partridge and a number of others, including Joseph Smith, to the high priesthood. After these ordinations, Bishop Partridge blessed all those who were ordained, including Joseph Smith.[33] Then John Corrill and Isaac Morley, who had also been ordained to the high priesthood, were ordained by Lyman Wight as assistants to Bishop Partridge. Meanwhile, Oliver Cowdery, who was not at the conference, remained an elder in Missouri.

This arrangement created a potential for conflict where one leader, Joseph Smith, had never repudiated his title of first elder and was the only person authorized to receive revelation for the entire Church, while the other leader, Edward Partridge, had specific authority over the Church. Potential confusion became a reality during the next five months when Edward Partridge "insulted the Lord's prophet in particular & assumed authority over him in open violation of the Laws of God."[34]

Oliver Cowdery's position as second elder was also apparently never repudiated, and in every instance where he took minutes during the next year, he consistently recorded Joseph Smith's name first and his second in the list of what otherwise appears to be a random order of participants.[35] When Joseph did not attend a priesthood conference several times, clerks listed Oliver Cowdery's name first in the record.[36] A few months after Partridge's insult and assumption of authority over Joseph, Oliver Cowdery, who had been ordained a high priest on August 28, 1831,[37] took lead in a conference held in Missouri. Oliver sent his minutes of the conference to Kirtland and received a stinging rebuke that his minutes were not "binding on [t]his church neither . . . of God nor yet according [to] the mind of the holy Spirit." The conference, rather than Cowdery directly, was soundly criticized for insulting Bishop Partridge by appointing him as moderator when Partridge had already been given that responsibility "by commandment." The correcting letter noted, "When God appoints authorities in his church let no conference take it upon them to reappoint these authorities." The written protest then took direct umbrage with Oliver Cowdery for "discarding the order established" by overstepping his bounds and infringing on the rights of the bishop and his counselors through transacting business that was rightfully theirs.[38] It was clear Cowdery did not have authority over Partridge.

The final two charges leveled condemned the conference for appointing Cowdery clerk rather than allowing Bishop Partridge that prerogative and for giving the bishop's counselor John Corrill additional responsibilities that were not the conference's prerogative to give. Although the evidence is sparse enough that it is difficult to draw specific conclusions about the relationship between Oliver Cowdery and Edward Partridge in Missouri, it is abundantly clear that there were unresolved issues about leadership and authority over the whole Church that continued until March 1832.

JOSEPH SMITH AS THE PRESIDENCY OF THE CHURCH

The resolution of this confusion began seven months after Partridge was called as bishop during the November 1831 conference held at the Johnson home in Hiram, Ohio. Joseph Smith received revelations at the Hiram conference that both shared authority much more widely and clarified priesthood governance. Although Joseph's earlier revelations emphasized that he was the only one authorized to receive revelation and commandments for the Church, in November he received a revelation directed to "all those who were ordained unto this priesthood whose mission is appointed unto them to go forth . . . [that] whatsoever they shall speak when moved upon by the Holy Ghost shall be Scripture."[39] This document dispensed authorization to receive revelation to all priesthood holders fulfilling their appointed mission within the context in which they served. Rather than consolidating revelatory authority within an ever-tightening circle, this played the opposite role in placing responsibility for creating scripture on those who were acting in their specific spheres of authority. One month later, Sidney Rigdon began receiving joint revelations again with Joseph Smith, apparently in his role as a scribe.

The same November 1 revelation also addressed priesthood governance. It initially instructed that bishops were to be appointed "by a confrenc of high priests" and that these bishops could only be tried for infractions to the law of the Church "before a conference of high priests."[40] The revelation in this original form suggested a specific body of high priests was responsible for appointing bishops and sitting in judgment on them. Two days later, on November 3, the high priests attending the conference signed a document which affirmed that the revelations had come through Joseph Smith, "who was appointed by the vos [voice] of the Church for this purpose."[41]

A week later, on November 11, Joseph Smith received a revelation that provided order to the growing number of priesthood office holders. Although the term "quorum" would not become part of the discourse for another two and a half years, this revelation directed "there must needs be presiding Elders to preside over them who are of the office of an Elder." It went on to outline the same pattern for other priesthood holders: presiding priests would preside "over them who are of the office of a Priest," presiding teachers would preside "over them who are of the office of a Teacher, in like manner. And also the deacons." None of these individuals was initially identified as a president. That term was reserved for a specific office: "Then cometh the high Priest hood, which is the greatest of all wherefore it must needs be that one be appointed of the high Priest hood to preside over the Priest hood & he shall be called President of the high Priest hood of the Church or in other words the Presiding high Priest over the high Priesthood of the Church."[42] As if to emphasize the significance of the office of President, the revelation continued, "And again the duty of the president of the office of the High Priesthood, is to preside over the whole church, & to be

Sharing Authority: Developing the First Presidency in Ohio

like unto Moses . . . to be a Seer, a revelator, a translator, & a prophet, having all the gifts of God, which he bestoweth upon the head of the church."[43]

The revelation made it clear that the President of the high priesthood would fill a different role from that expected of presiding officers of other priesthood groups. Not only would he be over the bishop (whom previous revelation had already directed was to be an ordained high priest and thus naturally under the jurisdiction of the high priesthood), but he was to "preside over the whole church" (D&C 107:91) and thus was over the other priesthood offices and general membership as well.

Although the revelation directed that Joseph Smith was to be the President of the high priesthood, the conference of high priests meeting at the Johnson home in Hiram, Ohio, did not act on it. A general conference held in Orange, Ohio, the month before, in October of 1831, had already determined that the next general conference of the Church would be held in Amherst, Ohio, fifty-five miles west of Kirtland, on January 25, 1832.

Joseph Smith waited to act until that conference. Two days before the scheduled Amherst conference an unscheduled general conference was held in Kaw Township, Missouri. It was at the Missouri conference where Partridge was appointed moderator and Cowdery served as clerk, eliciting sharp criticism from leaders in Kirtland as previously discussed. Although Oliver Cowdery wrote a cursory account of the Missouri conference in the minute book and then produced detailed minutes of the meeting which were sent to Kirtland, both sets of which survive, no minutes of the more important Amherst conference survive. It is through a brief reference made in passing in a letter and in later minutes that we know what occurred. At the Amherst "conference of High Priests, Elders and members," Joseph was ordained President of the high priesthood, with authority to preside over the whole Church.[44]

The November revelation had not mentioned assistants, counselors, or other positions of authority associated with the office, and there is no evidence that the concept of counselors was presented at the Amherst conference. Even when the term "presidency" was used six weeks later, it referred to a single individual. The term "presidency" was seen as equivalent to "the office of president."⁴⁵

Members in Missouri apparently received no advance notification that the ordination of Joseph Smith as President would take place in Amherst because the letter responding to the minutes of the Missouri conference that occurred at the same time specifically pointed out the charges leveled at Oliver and his companions in Missouri were brought "against that conference to the president of the high Priesthood our beloved brother joseph who has been ordained unto this office by the conference held in Amherst Lorain County Ohio on the 25 of January 1832."⁴⁶

Six weeks after Joseph Smith's ordination, he noted during a meeting held in Hiram on March 8, 1832, "[I] Chose this day and ordained brother Jesse Gause and Broth[er] Sidney to be my councellors of the ministry of the presidency of the high Priesthood."⁴⁷ Jesse was a recent convert and unfamiliar to the general membership. This may be why his last name was specifically mentioned in the notation. Jesse Gause and Sidney Rigdon were not called to be *in* a Presidency but they were to be "of the ministry of the presidency"; in other words, they were to help with the management of the Presidency, an office that Joseph Smith held. This relationship is clear in a revelation Joseph Smith received on or about the same day that noted that Joseph was the sole holder of the office of the Presidency of the high priesthood. The revelation reads in part, "And unto the office of the Presidency of the high priesthood I have given authority to preside with the assistance of *his* councilors over all the concerns of the Church. . . . For *unto you* [Joseph] I have given the keys of the Kingdom."⁴⁸ Although Oliver Cowdery clearly also held priesthood keys, Joseph held the office of Presidency alone.

A week after he selected his counselors, Joseph Smith received a revelation urging Jesse Gause to "hearken to the calling wherewith you are called even to be a high Priest in my Church & counsellor *unto* my Servant Joseph *unto whom* I have given the keys of the Kingdom which belongs always to the presidency of the high Priest Hood."⁴⁹ Gause and Rigdon were clerks or scribes to Joseph Smith, who held the keys of the Presidency. This shift in

Sharing Authority: Developing the First Presidency in Ohio

organization also seems to have changed Joseph Smith's relationship with his scribes because his last joint revelation received with Sidney Rigdon was on February 16 (see D&C 76), twenty-one days before Rigdon became a counselor to the Presidency.

The nature of the revelation addressed to Jesse Gause suggests some reluctance on his part to accept the calling he was given. Gause was a new convert to the Church and newly ordained as a high priest when the call was extended. He was unfamiliar to the Church in Missouri, as expressed in the minutes of the Literary Firm, which listed the names of Joseph Smith Jr. as President, followed by Sidney Rigdon with no special identification, and then a list of the rest of the participants, ending with "Jesse Gauss, one of the President's councillors," as if to identify him to the reader.[50] Later on the same day, Oliver Cowdery noted the participants in the minutes and gave the title of each, beginning with Joseph Smith as "President of Conference & also of the Highpriesthood," followed by his own name as "Clerk of Conference, and printer to the Church" and then the two bishops, Edward Partridge and Newel K. Whitney, each of which had stewardship over multiple branches. In the middle of the list he added Sidney Rigdon as "Counsillor of President," and the last name on the list was "Jesse Gauss Counsillor to the President."[51]

On or around the same day that Joseph selected Sidney Rigdon and Jesse Gause to serve as counselors to the Presidency, these two men signed a written protest, joined by several others, complaining about irregularities in Church administration in Missouri as previously discussed.[52] Sometime between March 8 and March 20, Joseph determined to go to Missouri.[53]

Although travel to Missouri was primarily to address issues connected to the publication of the revelations, which Oliver Cowdery, W. W. Phelps, and John Whitmer were overseeing, it also addressed Church governance issues. As soon as Joseph arrived he met on April 26 with "a general council of the Church" that included nine high priests and four elders.[54] The high priests at the meeting acknowledged that Joseph was "President of the High Priesthood, according to commandment and ordination in Ohio, at the

Conference held in Amherst."⁵⁵ Sidney Rigdon and Jesse Gause attended this meeting and had their names listed immediately after Joseph's. However, there was no reference to their positions, and they were not presented for the same affirmation of common consent that Joseph was. Because only the high priests acknowledged Joseph's role as President, even though the general membership attended the Amherst conference, it may be that only high priests sustained him there as well; a lack of minutes of the conference makes it impossible to determine.

After acknowledging Joseph's ordination, Bishop Partridge offered "the right hand of fellowship . . . in the name of the Church."⁵⁶ Bishop Partridge and Sidney Rigdon then patched up their differences during a break in the meeting. Jesse Gause, who was at the April 26 Missouri conference, then left on a mission on August 1 and went to the nearby Shaker community. Ten days later, one of his acquaintances in the Shaker community wrote that Jesse Gause "is yet a Mormon—and is second to the Prophet or Seer—Joseph Smith."⁵⁷ This suggests that although he did not hold the office of Presidency with Joseph Smith, the position of counselor gave Jesse prominence. On August 20, Jesse Gause parted from Zebedee Coltrin and soon left the Church. He likely had some kind of contact with Church leaders after this and is probably the Brother Jesse mentioned in Joseph Smith's journal that was excommunicated on December 3, apparently in absentia.⁵⁸

A FIRST PRESIDENCY

Frederick G. Williams had been a scribe for Joseph Smith as early as February 1832. On January 5, 1833, he was formally called to replace Jesse Gause. The revelation reads, "I say unto you thou art called to be a councillor & scribe unto my servant Joseph."⁵⁹ Two weeks later, on January 22, Frederick was listed with the high priests, who attended a special conference, including "Joseph Smith Jun President, Sidney Rigdon chief scribe and High Councilor, Frederick G. Williams assistant scribe and counselor."⁶⁰ This reference to Joseph as president and his two counselors as scribes, with Rigdon clearly filling a more significant position, suggested that the

Sharing Authority: Developing the First Presidency in Ohio

counselors played a supporting role with an emphasis on their scribal functions but were not considered Presidents in the same way.

A little over a month later, on March 8, 1833, exactly one year after Rigdon and Gause were called as counselors, Joseph received a revelation that transformed his relationship with Rigdon and Williams. The Lord revealed, "I say unto thy brethren, Sidney and Frederick . . . they are accounted as equal with thee in holding the Keys of this last kingdom . . . that through your administration, they may receive the word, and through their administration, the word may go forth unto the ends of the earth."[61]

The counselors were still to serve as scribes and Joseph was still to receive the word, but no longer were they counselors *to* Joseph—they were now counselors *with* him. They also held keys and used the title President. Ten days later, on March 18, 1833, "Bro Sidney arose and desired that he and Bro Frederick should be ordained to the office that they had been called to Viz of President of the High Priesthood and to be equal in holding the Keys of the Kingdom with Brother Joseph Smith Jr according to a revelation given on the 8th day of March 1833 in Kirtland."[62] Williams then copied the relevant portion of the revelation into the minute book and noted, "Acordingly, Bro Joseph proceded . . . and ordained them by the laying on of the hands to be equal with him in holding the keys of the Kingdom and also the Presidency of the High Priesthood."[63]

Frederick G. Williams had signed every minute entry up to that point with his name followed by "Clerk" or "Clerk of Conference." At the end of the minutes on the day he was ordained, and for the next nine months, Frederick G. Williams added after his name "Clerk P[ro] T[em]," identifying himself as a temporary clerk as an indication that his status had now changed. Even though he continued to keep the minutes of meetings for the rest of the year, he was no longer a clerk. Now Frederick G. Williams was a President. During the remainder of the year, Sidney and Frederick used the title "President" after their names in a variety of contexts.[64]

When Joseph Smith organized the Kirtland high council on February 17, 1834, he clarified how the presidents were both selected and approved. He noted, "The president of the Church, who is also the president of the Council, is appointed by the voice of the Saviour and acknowledged in his administration by the voice of the Church, . . . and it is his privilege to be assisted by two other presidents, appointed after the same manner."[65] Joseph then added that if the two other presidents were absent, he could preside "without an assistant, and in case that he himself is absent, the other presidents have power to preside in his stead, both or either of them."[66] Although the term "First Presidency" does not appear in a document until Oliver Cowdery used it as he prepared the November 1, 1831, revelation (now D&C section 68) for publication in 1835,[67] by February 17, 1834, the office of First Presidency was firmly established as Brigham Young and his associates would come to recognize it.

Later that same year, on Friday, December 5, 1834, Oliver Cowdery was "ordained an assistant President of the High and Holy Priesthood."[68] Hyrum Smith replaced him in this office in 1841 and received "the keys whereby he may ask and receive, and be crowned with the same blessing, and glory, and honor, and priesthood, and gifts of the priesthood, that once were put upon him that was my servant Oliver Cowdery" (D&C 124:95).[69] In July 1835 the *Messenger and Advocate* identified Peter, James, and John as "forming the first presidency of the church of Christ,"[70] and by the following month the same newspaper identified "O. Cowdery and S. Rigdon, [as] Presidents of the first presidency."[71] When Brigham Young restored the office of First Presidency after Hyrum's death, he never filled the office of Assistant President. Instead he built on the pattern initially set with Joseph Smith, Sidney Rigdon, and Frederick G. Williams in Kirtland.

NOTES

I am grateful to Jenny Lund, Gary Boatright, Robin Scott Jensen, Richard Jensen, Harold Hoyal, and LaJean Carruth, who all showed small kindnesses while I prepared this article.

1. First Council of Seventy Minutes, November 30, 1847, 4, Church History Library, The Church of Jesus Christ of Latter-day Saints, Salt Lake City.

Sharing Authority: Developing the First Presidency in Ohio

2. First Council of Seventy Minutes, November 30, 1847, 8–9. Thomas Bullock's minutes at this point read: "Joseph was ordd. [ordained] an Apostle—but the ch[urch] elected him as a Prest. [President], Prophet Seer & Revr. [Revelator]—but he never was ordd. to that office[.] Josh. [Joseph] was ordd. an Apostle by O. Cowdery—they recd. [received] their ords. [ordinations] by Peter James & John bef[ore] there was a ch.[urch] They r taken & selected & upheld by the ch[urch] & therefore elected." Historian's Office, General Church Minutes, November 30, 1847, 2, Church History Library.
3. First Council of Seventy Minutes, 4.
4. First Council of Seventy Minutes, 4–5.
5. Historian's Office, General Church Minutes, 3. Robert Campbell recorded Brigham Young's comment as follows: "Go a little farther back to the time of De Witt—Oliver Cowdery came within a hair breadth of as much influence as Joseph but he went took a man & baptized him & then said I want you to be my first Councillor that is (Frederick Gee) [Williams]." First Council of Seventy Minutes, 5. While Brigham Young could have been referencing January 26, 1838, when Oliver Cowdery was removed from his position as President in Far West, Missouri, the context of the discussion suggests that Bullock's minutes were correct and he was referencing the Three Witnesses. See Donald Q. Cannon and Lyndon W. Cook, eds., *Far West Record: Minutes of The Church of Jesus Christ of Latter-day Saints, 1830–1844* (Salt Lake City: Deseret Book, 1983), 135–36.
6. First Council of Seventy Minutes, 9.
7. *The Papers of Joseph Smith*, ed. Dean C. Jessee (Salt Lake City: Deseret Book, 1989), 1:21.
8. *Papers of Joseph Smith*, 1:291.
9. Oliver Cowdery to W. W. Phelps, September 7, 1834, Norton, OH, in *Messenger and Advocate*, October 1834, 14.
10. Brian Q. Cannon, "Seventy Contemporaneous Priesthood Restoration Documents," in *Opening the Heavens: Accounts of Divine Manifestations, 1820–1844*, ed. John W. Welch (Provo, UT: Brigham Young University Press), 236.
11. Cannon, "Priesthood Restoration Documents," 243.

12. Note that Joseph Smith observed in the revelation that Moses "committed unto *us* [Joseph and Oliver] the keys of the gathering of Israel" and that Elijah "stood before *us*. . . . Therefore, the keys of this dispensation are committed into your hands." D&C 110:11, 13, 16; emphasis added.
13. Noah Webster, *An American Dictionary of the English Language* (New York: S. Converse, 1828), "confirm." This was based on biblical precedent found in Acts 8:14–17 and Acts 19:2–6. Protestants generally consider that this confirmation includes reception of the influence of the Holy Ghost. Catholics and Eastern Orthodox Christians also confirm members of their congregations by the laying on of hands but the gifts of the Holy Ghost are received at baptism.
14. Cannon, "Priesthood Restoration Documents," 244. Joseph Smith also noted when they received the Aaronic Priesthood that they had yet to receive "the authority of the laying on of hands for the gift of the Holy Ghost." *Papers of Joseph Smith*, 1:299.
15. Brigham Young, in *Journal of Discourses* (London: Latter-day Saints' Book Depot, 1854–86), 10:303.
16. Robin Scott Jensen, Robert J. Woodford, and Steven C. Harper, eds., *Manuscript Revelation Books*, vol. 1 of the Revelations and Translations series of *The Joseph Smith Papers*, ed. Dean C. Jessee, Ronald K. Esplin, and Richard Lyman Bushman (Salt Lake City: The Church Historian's Press, 2009), 9. He also referred to Joseph as "the Seer" in other contexts as well. See Bruce N. Westergren, *From Historian to Dissident: The Book of John Whitmer* (Salt Lake City: Signature Books, 1995), 4.
17. Cannon, "Priesthood Restoration Documents," 236.
18. Joseph noted that he and Oliver received revelation jointly when "the word of the Lord, came unto us in the Chamber, commanding us; that I should ordain Oliver Cowdery to be an Elder in the Church of Jesus Christ, And that he also should ordain me to the same office . . . and have them decide by vote whether they were willing to accept us as spiritual teachers, or not." *Papers of Joseph Smith*, 1:299. Joseph also noted that the command indicated that they were to ordain other individuals as elders as well, but the revelation was clearly only directed to the two men, and they were the only two presented for a sustaining vote.
19. Heber C. Kimball, in *Journal of Discourses*, 6:29.

Sharing Authority: Developing the First Presidency in Ohio

20. Heber C. Kimball's account identifies Peter as the individual who came and gave Joseph and Oliver authority to baptize each other and ordain one another as priests. However, later in the same account he identifies Peter as coming with James and John to ordain Joseph as an Apostle. Heber C. Kimball may have not understood the details of those early events well and believed that Peter appeared both times, but it is also possible that he misspoke or that Leo Hawkins made a mistake while recording the sermon and that Elder Kimball understood that John the Baptist had made the first visit. In *Journal of Discourses*, 6:28–38.

21. Greg Prince discusses the practice of calling various early priesthood holders "apostles." While he suggests the possibility that twelve individuals were specifically identified as Apostles in the early months of the Church's existence and thus filled a specific office, with the exception of the Three Witnesses, the individuals referred to seem to have used the terms as elders or holders of the Melchizedek Priesthood. *Power from on High: The Development of Mormon Priesthood* (Salt Lake City: Signature Books, 1995), 11–14. Thus John Whitmer's license identified him as "an Apostle of Jesus Christ, an Elder of this Church of Christ" while the Articles and Covenants of the Church noted that "an apostle is an elder." Prince, *Power from on High*, 13. Further complicating an understanding of priesthood office, the term may have had a more general use such as that applied by a New York newspaper editor who indiscriminately referred to all of Joseph Smith's followers as "'Gold Bible' apostles." Abner Cole, "The Age of Miracles Has Again Arrived," *Reflector* (Palmyra, NY), June 30, 1830, 53.

22. Most members of the Quorum of Twelve Apostles were called on February 14, 1835. Parley P. Pratt, who was not at that initial meeting, was ordained an Apostle on February 21, 1835, and his brother Orson was ordained sometime afterward. See *Autobiography of Parley Parker Pratt*, ed. Parley P. Pratt Jr. (Salt Lake City: Deseret Book, 1979), 118–19.

23. The joint revelations are published as D&C 6, 7, 18, 24, and 26, while the visitation of John the Baptist is recorded in D&C 13.

24. Richard Lyman Bushman, *Joseph Smith: Rough Stone Rolling* (New York: Knopf, 2005), 120–21.

25. Jensen, Woodford, and Harper, *Manuscript Revelation Books*, 51; compare D&C 28:2.
26. Cannon and Cook, *Far West Record*, 3.
27. Warren O. Ault, "Village By-Laws by Common Consent," *Speculum: A Journal of Mediaeval Studies* 29, no. 2 (April 1954): 378–94, especially 381–83.
28. *Dictionary of the English Language*, "vote."
29. *Dictionary of the English Language*, "election"; see also "elected." Webster acknowledges that the act of choosing is the central element of election, but his examples focus on the expression of assent rather than the element of choice.
30. Westergren, *From Historian to Dissident*, 37.
31. Benjamin Shattuck, "Letter to the Editors," *Telegraph* (Painesville, OH), April 26, 1831, 3. Shattuck identifies Edson Fuller as an overseer in the Chardon branch but also says that he is "one of the prophets or apostles, as they are called." The identification of Fuller as a prophet or apostle seems to be a general descriptive term applied to others as well (perhaps as Melchizedek Priesthood holders) but the use of the word overseer is a specific function to which he was appointed by "a majority of the society in Chardon."
32. Jensen, Woodford, and Harper, *Manuscript Revelation Books*, 217.
33. Cannon and Cook, *Far West Record*, 7.
34. Cannon and Cook, *Far West Record*, 41. A reply to these charges was produced November 14, 1831, in Hiram, Ohio, but since Partridge was in Missouri the charges were clearly made before Joseph Smith received his November 11 revelation addressing the office of President of the High Priesthood and its relationship to that of Bishop.
35. See examples in the *Far West Record* during 1831 under September 1, September 12, October 11, October 21, October 25, November 1, November 8, November 9, and November 11–13. Cannon and Cook, *Far West Record*, 11–12, 16, 18–19, 26, 28, 30–31.
36. See, for example, Cannon and Cook, *Far West Record*, 15.
37. Cannon and Cook, *Far West Record*, 10.

Sharing Authority: Developing the First Presidency in Ohio

38. "Charge Preferred Against [the] High Council Held in Zion Jany 1832," holograph, Joseph Smith Papers, Church History Library; transcription provided by Robin Scott Jensen.
39. Jensen, Woodford, and Harper, *Manuscript Revelation Books*, 199.
40. Jensen, Woodford, and Harper, *Manuscript Revelation Books*, 201.
41. Jensen, Woodford, and Harper, *Manuscript Revelation Books*, 215. Later, additional high priests signed this declaration.
42. Jensen, Woodford, and Harper, *Manuscript Revelation Books*, 217.
43. Jensen, Woodford, and Harper, *Manuscript Revelation Books*, 219.
44. *History of the Church of Jesus Christ of Latter-day Saints*, ed. B. H. Roberts, 2nd ed. rev. (Salt Lake City: Deseret Book, 1971), 1:267.
45. *Dictionary of the English Language*, "presidency." The phrase "his Presidency" was specifically used to describe Frederick G. Williams's office as one of the Presidents of the Church. *History of the Church of Jesus Christ of Latter-day Saints*, ed. B. H. Roberts, 2nd ed. rev. (Salt Lake City: Deseret Book, 1961), 444.
46. "Charge Preferred Against [the] High Council Held in Zion Jany 1832."
47. Kirtland revelation book, 10, quoted in Robert J. Woodford, "Jesse Gause, Counselor to the Prophet," *BYU Studies* 15, no. 3 (Spring 1975): 363.
48. Revelation given to Joseph Smith March 1832, Newel K. Whitney Papers, L. Tom Perry Special Collections, Harold B. Lee Library, Brigham Young University; emphasis added.
49. Jensen, Woodford, and Harper, *Manuscript Revelation Books*, 255.
50. Cannon and Cook, *Far West Record*, 46.
51. Cannon and Cook, *Far West Record*, 47.
52. "Charge Preferred Against [the] High Council Held in Zion Jany 1832."
53. Joseph Smith asked for inspiration on March 20, 1832, based on a previous decision to travel to Missouri. Jensen, Woodford, and Harper, *Manuscript Revelation Books*, 273.
54. *History of the Church*, 1:267.
55. Cannon and Cook, *Far West Record*, 44.
56. Cannon and Cook, *Far West Record*, 44; see also *History of the Church*, 1:267.

57. Matthew Houston to Seth Y. Wells, from North Union, OH, August 10, 1832, Shaker Manuscripts, Western Reserve Historical Society, quoted in D. Michael Quinn, "Jesse Gause: Joseph Smith's Little-Known Counselor," *BYU Studies* 23, no. 4 (Fall 1983): 490.
58. *Personal Writings of Joseph Smith*, ed. Dean C. Jessee, rev. ed. (Provo, UT: Brigham Young University Press, 2002), 22.
59. Revelation, Kirtland, OH, January 5, 1833. Frederick G. Williams Papers, Church History Library.
60. Kirtland High Council minutes, December 1832–November 1837, in *Selected Collections from the Archives of The Church of Jesus Christ of Latter-day Saints* (Provo, UT: Brigham Young University Press, 2002), DVD, January 22, 1833, 6.
61. Jensen, Woodford, and Harper, *Manuscript Revelation Books*, 313–15.
62. Kirtland High Council minutes, March 18, 1833, 16–17.
63. Kirtland High Council minutes, March 18, 1833, 11.
64. Joseph Smith and Frederick G. Williams to John Smith, July 1, 1833, in *History of the Church*, 1:370; see also 1:443–44.
65. Kirtland High Council minutes, February 17, 1834, 27.
66. Kirtland High Council minutes, February 17, 1834, 27.
67. At that time, he crossed out the phrase "a confrenc of high priests" from the manuscript. He generally wrote in "the presidency" or "the presidency of high priests" but in one case he wrote "the first presidency of the chich [church]" recording for the first time a new title for the principal governing body. Jensen, Woodford, and Harper, *Manuscript Revelation Books*, 201.
68. *Personal Writings of Joseph Smith*, 49.
69. See *Personal Writings of Joseph Smith*, 49n93.
70. "Dear Brother in the Lord, Letter No. 9," *Messenger and Advocate*, July 1835, 145.
71. General Assembly, *Messenger and Advocate*, August 1835, 181.

Susan Easton Black

7

Early Quorums of the Seventies

"Brethren, I have seen those men who died of the cholera in our camp," said Joseph Smith to Brigham Young and his brother Joseph. "And the Lord knows, if I get a mansion as bright as theirs, I ask no more."[1] The Prophet then wept and for a time was unable to continue. After gaining composure, he told Brigham that he would be one of twelve men appointed to spread the good news of Jesus Christ to the nations of the world. Turning to thirty-seven-year-old Joseph Young, the Prophet said, "Brother Joseph, the Lord has made you President of the Seventies."[2]

Brigham's elder brother was startled by the prophetic announcement. He knew something of Moses and the seventy elders of Israel and of Jesus appointing other seventy, but it had never occurred to him that men would be called to be seventies in the dispensation of the fulness

---

Susan Easton Black is a professor of Church history and doctrine at Brigham Young University.

of times.³ Yet Joseph Young and 3,129 other men were ordained seventies during the early years of the Church. In this paper, read of the early beginnings, the vision, and purpose of the first quorums of the seventies. Learn of the rapid expansion in both the number of men called and quorums organized under the direction of Brigham Young. Discover why the seventies were willing to sacrifice their time and talents to build the first priesthood hall in the Church.

BEGINNINGS OF THE FIRST QUORUM OF THE SEVENTIES

Latter-day Saint historians claim that the First Quorum of the Seventy was composed of veterans who marched with Zion's Camp.⁴ The *History of the Church* lists the names of forty-one Zion's Camp members in the original quorum. Joseph Young, Senior President of the Quorum, adds twenty-nine additional men not named on the earlier list.⁵ By combining and reviewing these lists, it is more accurate to say that sixty-seven members of the First Quorum marched with Zion's Camp. Jesse Huntsman, William D. Pratt, and Jezehi B. Smith were exceptions.⁶ Newly called seventies were not selected from the youngest (Bradford Elliott or George Fordham, both age ten years) or the oldest in the camp (Noah Johnson, age seventy-one years). The average age of the first seventies was 25.6 years. The average age in Zion's Camp was 29.6 years. The oldest man ordained a seventy was Elias Hutchings, age fifty-one. The youngest was Daniel Stephens, age sixteen. From their number, seven men were selected Presidents of the seventies, with Joseph Young appointed Senior President.⁷ Young was responsible for overseeing the purpose and function of the Quorum, an assignment he held until his death in 1881. If for any reason Young failed to carry out his responsibilities, the next senior by ordination would take the leadership role, and so on.⁸ (As occasions arose, those appointed to temporary leadership positions were referred to as alternates.)

When the First Quorum and their Presidency were in place, Joseph Smith spoke of the central role these men now held in the kingdom of God.

"If the first Seventy are all employed, and there is a call for more laborers," Joseph said, "it will be the duty of the seven presidents of the first Seventy to call and ordain other Seventy and send them forth to labor in the vineyard, until, if needs be, they set apart seven times seventy, and even until there are one hundred and forty-four thousand thus set apart for the ministry." Joseph then instructed the Presidency of their right to "choose, ordain, and set . . . apart from among the most experienced of the Elders of the Church" other seventies or especial witnesses of Christ.[9] And on March 28, 1835, in a "revelation on Priesthood, given through Joseph Smith the Prophet, at Kirtland, Ohio," the Lord revealed that the First Quorum was "equal in authority to that of the Twelve special witnesses or Apostles" (D&C 107:26).[10]

The responsibility that Joseph rolled onto the shoulders of the newly called seventies was surprising, if not startling, to men relatively young in age and in understanding of the gospel. Comprehending Joseph's vision of equality with the Twelve and the "seven times seventy" was foreign to men who knew little of the Restoration and even less of the world that awaited their message. They were economically poor, lacking in formal education, and devoid of experience with cultures and nations. Most contended that their Christian upbringing had little prepared them for a leadership role in the Restoration. It seemed only yesterday that men of the cloth led their congregations. Now they were expected to be leaders of the newfound religious faith. Did the Lord not see their weakness in oratory skills and understanding of the nuances of the Bible? How could they rise beyond their natural ability to be messengers of God and share the good news with a world steeped in unbelief?

Although many of their questions went unanswered, the newly ordained seventies left Kirtland to share the gospel of Jesus Christ. Without purse or scrip, and often not knowing where to go or whom to speak with, the seventies began their missionary travels. Many were turned out of doors, abused and frustrated. Others found listeners and a few grateful converts. To those who accepted the gospel and entered baptismal waters, Kirtland beckoned. Converts packed their belongings and headed to the central gathering place of the Church. As for the seventies, they came and went as traveling missionaries that first season and the next. Their determination to share the gospel was great, even though their ability to bring others to the water's edge was not remarkably successful.

As the seventies returned to Kirtland, they knew intuitively that an accounting was expected of their missionary travels. Most reported or spoke with a member of the Presidency of the seventies. The Presidency, in turn, reported to the Twelve, and on a more informal basis to Joseph Smith. On December 28, 1835, President Sylvester Smith[11] told Joseph Smith that the seventies were "worthy young men, strong, active, energetic, determined in the name of the Lord to go forward and persevere to the end." He assured the Prophet that they had been traveling missionaries "in various States and generally with good success; many have been convinced, and 175 baptized into the Kingdom of Jesus."[12] Joseph wrote of this conversation, "My heart was made glad while listening to the relation of those that had been laboring in the vineyard of the Lord, with such marvelous success. And I pray God to bless them with an increase of faith and power, and keep them all, with the endurance of faith in the name of Jesus Christ to the end."[13] With an endowment of power, Joseph knew the seventies could magnify their ability to preach to a fallen world and reap a bountiful harvest. Joseph also knew that there was only one place on earth that this singular gift could be bestowed—the Kirtland Temple.

Could the seventies wait until the temple was finished? It appears not. In January 1836, two months shy of the temple dedication, Joseph invited the Twelve Apostles and the Presidents of the seventies to meet him in the unfinished temple. In that holy house, Joseph gave these leaders an endowment, or anointing of power, to enhance their ability to carry out their priesthood assignments. After each had received his anointing, Joseph instructed them to call upon God with uplifted hands to seal the promised blessings. It was then that three of the seventies witnessed holy manifestations. Sylvester Smith saw "a pillar of fire rest down and abide upon the heads of the quorum as they stood in the midst of the Twelve," Roger Orton saw "a mighty angel riding upon a horse of fire, with a flaming sword in his hand, followed by five others, encircle the house, and protect the Saints, even the Lord's anointed from the power of Satan and a host of evil spirits, which were striving to disturb the Saints," and Zebedee Coltrin saw the "Savior extended before him as upon a cross, and, a little after, crowned with glory upon his head, above the brightness of the sun."[14] These manifestations, a precursor to Pentecostal events that followed two months later at the temple dedication, were spiritual outpourings from God. When the manifestations ceased, the Presidents of the seventies were instructed to anoint quorum members with the same power they had received so that they too could fulfill their important role in carrying the gospel of Jesus Christ to the world. By so doing, Joseph Smith again rolled responsibility from himself to the Presidency, giving them the administration of blessings in addition to the responsibilities of calling, ordaining, and overseeing the function of the quorum.

EXPANSION OF THE SEVENTIES QUORUMS BEGINS IN KIRTLAND

Ten days later, on Sunday, February 7, 1836, Joseph Smith met with the Presidency of the seventies once again. This time, the meeting place was a loft in the printing office located near the Kirtland Temple. The purpose of the meeting was to organize the Second Quorum from among faithful elders of the Church.[15] As Joseph spoke with the Presidents, he recalled an earlier day when each had marched with Zion's Camp:

> Let me tell you, God did not want you to fight. He could not organize His kingdom with twelve men to open the Gospel door to the nations of the earth, and with seventy men under their direction to follow in their tracks, unless He took them from a body of men who had offered their lives, and who had made as great a sacrifice as did Abraham. Now the Lord has got His Twelve and His Seventy, and there will be other quorums of Seventies

called, who will make the sacrifice, and those who have not made their sacrifices and their offerings now, will make them hereafter.[16]

Although some historians claim that the Second Quorum was composed of Zion's Camp veterans, such is not entirely true. Only eleven of the men called to the Second Quorum marched with Zion's Camp—the most famous being Wilford Woodruff, Truman O. Angell, King Follett, and Erastus Snow. Thus Joseph's statement, "Those who have not made their sacrifices and their offerings now, will make them hereafter," had direct bearing on most called to the Second Quorum and subsequent quorums thereafter. The average age of the new quorum members was thirty-five years. Despite seniority in age over those serving in the First Quorum, the Second Quorum was told to look to the First Quorum as leaders. When vacancies occurred in the First Quorum, those in the Second Quorum were invited to take their place.[17] Caroline Crosby, wife of Jonathan Crosby, wrote of her husband's call to the Second Quorum: "I well recollect the sensations with which my mind was actuated when I learned the fact that my husband had been called and ordained . . . and would undoubtedly be required to travel and preach the gospel to the nations of the earth. I realized in some degree the immense responsibility of the office, and besought the Lord for grace and wisdom to be given him that he might be able to magnify his high and holy calling."[18]

On December 20, 1836, the Third Quorum of the Seventy was organized, about ten months after the Second Quorum.[19] Thereafter, Wilford Woodruff noted that "the seventies will meet every Tuesday evening through the winter [of 1837] in the Kirtland Temple. He also noted on one occasion "about one hundred seventies were present."[20] In their weekly meetings, instruction was given to improve effectiveness in missionary labors until mid-March 1837, when the Kirtland Safety Society Anti-Banking Company collapsed. The financial collapse of the society triggered an outcry against Joseph Smith and Mormonism that was slow to mend. Twenty-seven members of the First Quorum joined dissidents and abandoned their faith. About a third in the two other quorums followed suit. Benjamin Johnson, a witness to the disintegration of the quorums, lamented, "Like Judas, [they were] ready to sell or destroy the Prophet Joseph and his followers. And it almost seemed to me that the brightest stars in our firmament had fallen."[21]

Adding to the problems in the quorums, a controversy over priesthood authority arose. The controversy centered on which priesthood body—high priests quorums or seventies quorums—had higher preeminence or authority in the Church. Carved initials on temple pulpits suggested the seventies held the higher authority, for immediately above the initials representing Presidency of the high priests quorum (PHPQ) were the letters PSZ, which referred to the Presidents of the seventy.[22] This same issue arose again and again through the succeeding years. In spring 1837, Joseph Smith resolved the difficulty by reorganizing the Presidency of the seventies. Presidents previously ordained to the office of high priest were placed in the high priests quorum. Five of seven Presidents were released, and five ordained to take their place.[23]

On March 6, 1838, with a new Presidency in place, the seventies again met in the Kirtland Temple. Their purpose in meeting was to discuss the benefits and perils associated with moving as a group to Missouri. Without reaching a decision in this meeting, they planned a follow-up meeting on March 10. At this meeting, "the Spirit of the Lord came down in mighty power, and some of the elders began to prophesy" that if they traveled together and kept the commandments of the Lord, the expedition would succeed. James Foster, a new President of the seventies, spoke of seeing a company of about five hundred starting from Kirtland and traveling and camping together, concluding that it was the will of God that the seventies should travel as a body to Missouri.[24] With the affirmation of Hyrum Smith, specific plans for the journey ahead were made. However, most seventies abandoned the plans. They moved from Kirtland in separate family groupings, seemingly unmindful of their earlier decision to journey in a large contingency.

When the camp finally moved forward, only 30 percent of the men claimed membership in one of the three seventies quorums.[25] The fact that so few seventies joined the camp is evidence that unity and brotherhood were waning. It may further evidence that the collapse of the Kirtland Safety

Society and the controversy over authority had taken their toll. What was once a determined, anointed, and cohesive brotherhood was no more. Yet Joseph Young, Senior President of the quorums, had little time to lament problems within his ranks. It was time to move the remaining members of his quorums, their families, and the poor to Missouri. Under his leadership, the camp consisting of 515 pioneers left Kirtland in July 1838. John Pulsipher wrote, "On the first day of July 1838 we started for Missouri in the largest company of Saints that ever traveled together in this generation, and all the people in the country, town, and cities through which we passed were surprised. It certainly was wonderful at that time to see a company of men, women and children a mile long, all traveling together in order, and pitching their tents by the way."[26]

The initial plan was to settle the traveling party in Adam-ondi-Ahman, Missouri. En route to Diahman, the camp tarried at Haun's Mill. Unfortunately, many in the camp suffered from atrocities committed during a terrible slaughter that occurred in October 1838 at Haun's Mill. Following the tragedy, a decentralized settling plan was put in place for those in the Kirtland Camp. Some ran to Far West, the main Latter-day Saint settlement. Others scattered. For many, the once cherished brotherhood was lost in the extremities. Regular quorum meetings became a remembrance of the past. Few seventies were called on missions, and even fewer accepted the call. However, amid the strident persecution and scattering of 1838, uncalled and unassigned seventies served self-appointed missions. Neither the sword nor the musket could destroy the spirit of missionary work.

Not long after the seventies found refuge in Quincy, Illinois, Joseph Young once again held meetings and called and ordained seventies. Was he doing so under the direction of the Twelve? Records do not substantiate that fact. Perhaps Joseph Young, like Joseph Smith before him, had reached the conclusion, "What power shall stay the heavens? As well might man stretch forth his puny arm to stop the Missouri river in its decreed course, or to turn it up stream, as to hinder the Almighty from pouring down knowledge from heaven upon the heads of the Latter-day Saints" (D&C 121:33). With renewed courage, even the strength of dedication, Joseph Young filled vacancies in the first three quorums and created other quorums.

Such vigor did not last long. Limitations to the function and calling of the seventies were forthcoming. In May 1839, after fourteen seventies had joined the Twelve on their mission to England, it was resolved that "those of the Seventies who have not yet preached, shall not for the future be sent on foreign missions."[27] To many, such a resolution countered the purpose of the seventies to take the gospel to all the world. Nevertheless, Joseph Young and his quorums complied. Yet Young and his Presidency kept ordaining more men until they increased their number to 490 in hopes that one day the resolution would be lifted. Instead of being lifted, further restraints to the activities of Young and his Presidency followed. On July 19, 1839, Joseph Smith asked Young "not to ordain any into the quorum of the Seventies."[28] Why? The answer is not readily known. In retrospect, it appears that the Prophet was rethinking the work of the seventies.

When the Latter-day Saints moved from Quincy to the swampland of Commerce, Illinois, seventies were asked to dig drainage ditches and reclaim the swampland—a far cry from their initial purpose. The assignment appears more individual based than quorum based. Individually, the seventies erected cabins, homes, stores, and public buildings. The only collective building built was the Seventies Hall—the first priesthood hall in the Church. Pennsylvania native Edward Hunter[29] gave land "for use and benefit of the Quorums of Seventies as President."[30] Architect William Weeks drew plans for the building, and quorum secretary, John D. Lee, supervised construction. Of his assignment, Lee penned:

> [In] Fall [1843] I was appointed on a committee, with Brigham Young as counselor, to build a hall for the Seventies, the upper story to be used for the Priesthood and the Council of Fifty. Previous to my being appointed on the committee two committees had been appointed, but had accomplished nothing, and we commenced without a dollar. My plan was to build it by shares, of the value of five dollars each. Hyrum Smith, the Patriarch, told

me that he would give the Patriarchal Blessing to any that labored on the foundation of the building. The Seventies numbered about four hundred and ninety men. I was to create the material. That is, I would watch, and when I could get a contract to take out lumber from the river, as rafts would land at the city, I would take common laboring men, and the portion of the lumber that we got for our pay we would pile up for the building. In this way we got all the lumber needed. The brick we made ourselves, and boated the wood to burn them and our lime from the island.[31]

Donations for the Seventies Hall came in the form of cash or subscriptions. Subscriptions were a type of stock in the sum of five dollars. For example, Hosea Stout purchased stock certificate no. 207 dated December 22, 1844. The certificate reads, "This is to certify that Hosea Stout is entitled to one share $5.00 of the capital stock of the SEVENTIES HALL. Transferable by endorsement Jos. Young, Pres, John D. Lee, Secretary."[32] With others also purchasing certificates and still others donating goods such as lumber and bricks, progress on the hall moved forward until March 1844, when a tornado blew down the unfinished west wall. Supervisor Lee wrote of this event:

> In the month of March, 1844, we had the building up on the west side nearly two stories high. One day when the wall was built up nine feet high and forty-five feet long, and was of course green, a tornado came that night and blew the wall down, breaking columns and joists below, doing a damage of several thousand dollars. I was inclined to be down in the lip, but Brigham Young laughed at me, and said it was the best omen in the world; it showed that the Devil was mad, and knew that the Seventy would receive the blessing of God in that house; and as they were special witnesses to the nations of the earth, they would make his kingdom quake and tremble; that when Noah was building the ark he was mobbed three times, but he persevered, and finally they said, "Let the d———d old fool, alone, and see what he

will accomplish." "Just so with you; double your diligence and put her up again. If you do not you will lose many a blessing."[33]

Lee and a team of seventies "threw the wall down flat, and commenced a new one, another brick thicker than the former."[34] By May 1844, the Seventies Hall, measuring twenty-eight feet wide by forty feet long, was enclosed. Two inscriptions on the front of the building "high up in italics was the word (Priesthood) another over the lower doors in Roman characters was Seventies Hall No 1," indicating this was the first hall, but others would follow.[35] Double doors at the entrance led to a vestibule. A second set of doors gave access to the lecture-preaching room. The second floor was reached by two quarter-turn stairways in the vestibule. There was such promise in the building that none foresaw a reason to stop construction. But within the month, Joseph Smith and his brother Hyrum lay dead in Carthage. News of their deaths brought a deafening halt to the construction of the hall. The moratorium had nothing to do with supplies, materials, or time. Laying aside hammers and saws was a choice. The hall, and indeed the very city of Nauvoo, mourned the death of their Prophet and Patriarch.

THE SEVENTIES MEMBERSHIP AND QUORUMS EXPAND

It was not until Brigham Young returned to Nauvoo that the seventies and their friends picked up tools and returned to construction sites. The silence that had brooded over the city for weeks was broken by the sound of hammers, evidencing that Mormonism had not ended in Carthage. At this time, Joseph's words "Brethren, shall we not go on in so great a cause? Go forward and not backward" took on new meaning (D&C 128:22). An October 8, 1844, announcement gave added strength to that meaning. Heber C. Kimball urged, "elders who are under the age of thirty-five, and also all the priests, teachers deacons, and members, who are recommended to be ordained, to withdraw and receive an ordination into the seventies."[36] Within hours, Joseph Young and his Presidency had ordained approximately four hundred men to the office of seventy. They filled eleven quorums and created a twelfth with forty members. Pleased by their actions, Brigham Young said to the newly ordained seventies:

> You must now magnify your calling. Elders who go to borrowing horses or money, and running away with it, will be cut off from the church without any ceremony. They will not have as much lenity as heretofore. The seventies will have to be subject to their presidents and council. We do not want any man to go to preaching until he is sent. . . . *You are all apostles to the nations to carry the gospel*; and when we send you to build up the kingdom, we will give you the keys, and power and authority. If the people will let us alone we will convert the world, and if they persecute us we will do it the quicker. . . . Inasmuch as you will go forth and do right you will have more of the spirit than you have heretofore.[37]

Joseph Young's reaction to the announcement is viewed as the beginning of the great expansion or what historian William G. Hartley calls the "mushrooming of the seventies." As to the reason for expanding, Hartley contends that "the Twelve had in mind a massive missionary labor in the near future."[38] It is presumed that the barrier placed on foreign missions was soon to be lifted and a large missionary initiative launched in fulfillment of the January 19, 1841, revelation, which called for "traveling elders to bear record of my name in all the world, wherever the traveling high council, mine apostles, shall send them to prepare a way before my face" (D&C 124:139).

To provide seasoned leaders for the newly called quorums, Brigham Young ordained sixty-three members of the First Quorum of the Seventies, not serving in the Presidency, as Presidents over the Second to the Tenth Quorums.[39] In the Eleventh Quorum, Presidents were elected from within its ranks. Whether appointed or elected, all quorum Presidents met regularly with or reported to Joseph Young and his Presidency, now referred to as the Council of the Seventy. This was more than a title change. The Council of the Seventy was considered one of the three great councils of the Church—The

First Presidency, Twelve, and Seventies.[40] As for the Seventies Hall, it now progressed at a rapid pace. By Christmas 1844, "all the finished carpentry and painting was done and the heating stoves installed." With all things in place, dedicatory services were planned for December 26 to December 30, 1844. On the designated days, morning and afternoon sessions were held to accommodate the now fifteen quorums and their families. On Thursday, December 26, services commenced under the direction of Joseph Young. Seated on the stand were the Council of the Seventy and members of the Quorum of the Twelve Apostles. The Senior President of each quorum was seated on the right, a choir of singers on the left, and the brass band in front. The Second and Third Quorums sat in order of ordination. The remaining seats were filled with family members. A hymn composed by W. W. Phelps for the dedication titled "A Voice from the Prophet: Come to Me" was sung. Brigham Young then offered the dedicatory prayer. His prayer is known as "A Supplication to the Throne of Grace." In the prayer, he asked the Lord to "increase our knowledge, wisdom, and understanding, that we, thy servants, may be enabled to administer salvation to thy people, even as thou hast committed a dispensation of the same unto us." He pled, "May we feel the prelude of that power and authority with which thy servants shall be clothed, when they shall go forth and open the door of salvation to the nations and kingdoms of the earth; even thy servants, the seventies, upon whom the burden of thy kingdom does rest." He asked the Lord to "sanctify [the hall] and make it holy, . . . that it may be filled with thy Spirit that it may be called the gate of heaven." He prayed that the Lord would "pour out thy Spirit upon the Presidency of the Seventies; wilt thou endow them with knowledge and understanding that they may be enabled to instruct thy servants over whom they are called to preside." Of his prayer, historian B. H. Roberts wrote, "It is doubtful if Brigham Young ever did anything better in oral expression than this beautiful and timely prayer."[41]

On the second day of dedication, John Taylor told the seventies that "no other people can possibly do this work, for unto us the keys of this last dispensation with the power of the priesthood is given." He explained that the world does not know God's laws or ways: "They don't know enough in reality to save a mosquito." He admonished the seventies, "Never shrink from your calling, nor succumb to the learned because of the advantage they have over you by reason of literary attainments for God is with you. . . . You are the heralds of salvation."[42] It was not until the fourth day of dedication that Joseph Young gave a second dedicatory prayer. In his prayer, he explained the reason why the seventies had built the hall: "The quorums of the seventies, who have built this hall, not particularly by thy commandment, but in honor of thy name." He asked the Lord to "let them become mighty men in pulling down the strongholds of satan, and bursting the prison doors of darkness, and spread the light of the everlasting gospel to earth's remotest bounds."[43] As the dedicatory ceremonies ended, John D. Lee, secretary of the quorums, wrote, "Truly this was a time and season of rejoicing with the saints. Peace and harmony, brotherly love, kindness and charity prevails throughout. The remembrance of this glorious jubilee will never be erased from the minds of those who were participants. Each family was provided with fruits, nuts and every desert that heart could wish. Well might it be said that the saints enjoyed a feast of fat things."[44] The *Times and Seasons* reported, "The excellent melody of the Choir and Band, mingling with the devout aspirations of a congregation of *all saints*, gave the commencement of [the] services an air of interest, felicity and glory, at once feeling, touching, pathetic, grand, sublime!"[45]

Adding to the sublimity of that occasion was the call for additional seventies. The following excerpts reveal how quickly that call was embraced:

- The *Nauvoo Neighbor* on October 29, 1845, reported, "The Seventeenth Quorum of Seventies, are requested to meet at the Masonic Hall, on Saturday the 8th of November, at 2 o'clock, P.M. All the members of the quorum are requested to attend, as there will be business of importance. D. M. Repsher, Sen. Prest."[46]
- When the April conference of 1845 began, there were twenty-four quorums. By the end of conference, there were twenty-five full quorums.[47]

- On Sunday June 1, 1845, "the Presidents of the Seventies met and preached to each other, and ordained four presidents for the twenty-seventh quorum."[48]
- On Sunday June 29, 1845, "This day the twenty-eighth quorum of the seventies has been organized, and is nearly full."[49]
- On October 8, 1845, twenty-two members were ordained to the Thirty-first Quorum.[50]
- In December 1845, the Thirty-second Quorum was organized.[51]

By early January 1846, there were thirty-four quorums, and by late January, thirty-five. The total number of men serving in one or more of the thirty-five quorums was 3,129. They varied in age from teenagers to men in their early fifties. They hailed from the East, South, and Midwest, from states as far away as Maine and as close as Iowa. Over a fourth of the seventies claimed nativity in overseas countries such as England, Scotland, Ireland, France, and Germany. In spite of their diversity, these men shared a common cause and brotherhood in the seventies quorums.

Knowing that mission calls were forthcoming, the seventies sought opportunities to increase their knowledge of countries and peoples and to improve their speaking and writing skills. They invited James M. Monroe, one of their number, to teach English grammar[52] and George D. Watt, another seventy, to teach classes in shorthand.[53] They devoted a portion of their hall to a circulating library with Amasa Lyman as librarian and John D. Lee as registrar. Lee received 675 donated books, including works on science, philosophy, religion, and history. This later effort was praised in the *Nauvoo Neighbor* on January 1, 1845: "Among the improvements going forward in this city, none merit higher praise, than the Seventies' Library. . . . It looks like old times, when they had "Kirjath Sapher," the city of books."[54] The seventies also founded a museum in the hall. Addison Pratt, a former whaler, donated "the tooth of a whale, coral, bones of an Albatross' wing, and skin of a foot, jaw-bone of a porpoise" as the first exhibit in the museum.[55] But the hall, with all its learning possibilities, could not provide the seventies with power to open the doors of nations to the gospel of Jesus Christ. For that endowment, there was no substitute for a temple.

Knowing the importance of this power, seventies worked round the clock to expedite construction on the house of the Lord. But try as they might, labor was slow. Could they wait for the temple to be finished before receiving an endowment, a gift from God that would endow them with power to fulfill their missionary role? Brigham Young, hearkening to an earlier day in Kirtland, did not believe a further wait necessary. On Friday, December 12, 1845, the Council of the Seventy and the Presidencies of quorums and their wives, numbering in all twenty-eight men and twenty-seven women, gathered on the third floor of the unfinished temple to receive their endowment.[56] After receiving this endowment, "the Twelve delegated to them [the Presidents of the Seventy] the government of the Temple, while the ordinances were being administered to their quorum."

What has heretofore been interpreted as men and women receiving the endowment must now be reinterpreted as the endowment being received by quorums and family members of quorum members. The *Nauvoo Neighbor* reported, "We have now twenty seventies already organized, waiting for their endowment, and by the time they get it there will be as many more waiting to receive theirs, and thus there will be an eternal increase in the kingdom of God."[57] There were 1,858 seventies who received their endowments in the Nauvoo Temple. Counting their wives and extended relatives who joined them, out of the 5,595 receiving endowments in Nauvoo, the vast majority were seventies and their loved ones. Recording their endowments was the quorum secretary, John D. Lee.

CONCLUSION

After receiving their endowments, the seventies left Nauvoo. Of their number, 294 marched with the Mormon Battalion in the Mexican War. Eighty-seven joined the vanguard company of 1847. Most became leaders in small settlements throughout the Intermountain West. Two-thirds served as traveling missionaries. But with the passage of time, their accomplishments have been attributed to individuals, not to quorums of brethren with assignments to fulfill. As such, much of the great work of the early seventies quorums has been obscured.

The same was once true of the Seventies Hall. In 1846, real estate entrepreneur James E. Furness of Quincy purchased the hall.[58] Under his ownership, the hall was known as the First Presbyterian Church of Nauvoo. On July 5, 1847, Furniss sold the hall to William Quarter, a Roman Catholic bishop in Chicago.[59] The hall then became a Catholic facility. By 1866, the top floor of the hall was removed and the first floor divided into two rooms to make way for the Nauvoo First Ward School. In October 1915, the *Nauvoo Independent* reported, "The First Ward School properties were put up for sale Saturday. Nobody bid on the school house and lot, but the site of the old school house was sold to L. K. Parker for $50.50." Parker razed the hall for materials and used the land for agricultural purposes.[60] And thus it remained until 1962. In that year, J. LeRoy Kimball of Salt Lake City acquired the agricultural site. He had bigger plans for the site than farming. An excavation crew was brought in to discover if foundation stones of the once-proud Seventies Hall remained. When stones were found just below the plowline, plans were made to rebuild the hall. Today, a reconstructed hall is open for interpretive and historical tours in Nauvoo.[61]

But what of those who built the hall or served in the thirty-five quorums? Efforts have been made to identify each seventy in a reference format so that visitors to the Seventies Hall can find their ancestors.[62] Should more be done? A reference entry is a notation of remembrance, but only a notation. Underneath the note lies a story of brethren committed to their faith and quorums. It is a story of Joseph Young and thousands of young men who sacrificed to share the gospel of Jesus Christ and build Nauvoo. It is a legacy of quorum activity that was unparalleled in its time. It is hoped that the saga of the largest priesthood organization in Nauvoo will one day be told in great detail.

NOTES

1. Historian William G. Hartley refers to the vision as "an unrecorded revelation 'showing the order of the Seventy.'" "Nauvoo Stake, Priesthood Quorums, and the Church's First Wards," *BYU Studies* 32, no. 1 (1991): 71; Joseph Smith, *History of the Church of Jesus Christ of Latter-day Saints*, ed. B. H. Roberts, 2nd ed. rev. (Salt Lake City: Deseret Book, 1976), 2:181.
2. Smith, *History of the Church*, 2:181; see also Levi Edgar Young, "Joseph Young," *Utah Genealogical and Historical Magazine* 5 (July 1914): 105–7.
3. See Milton V. Backman Jr., *The Heavens Resound: A History of the Latter-day Saints in Ohio, 1830–1838* (Salt Lake City: Deseret Book, 1983), 252; Joseph Young Sr., *History of the Organization of the Seventies* (Salt Lake City: Deseret News, 1878), 1–2; Smith, *History of the Church*, 2:181; Andrew Jenson, "Church General Authorities: First Council of Seventy," 1925, Church History Library, The Church of Jesus Christ of Latter-day Saints, Salt Lake City. Exodus 24:2, 9, 22 and Numbers 11:16–30 reveal little of the definition or function of the seventy. It is conceivable that the Sanhedrin (consisting of seventy members and a high priest) at the time of Jesus had some relationship to the ancient council of seventy, but a historical connection is not affirmed. The Gospel of Luke reveals that "the Lord appointed other seventy also, and sent them two and two before his face into every city and place" (Luke 10:1). For modern scriptural references to the office of Seventy, see Doctrine and Covenants 107:23, 25, 34, 38, 90, 94, 95–98; 27:12; 103:33–34.
4. See Karl Ricks Anderson, *Joseph Smith's Kirtland: Eyewitness Accounts* (Salt Lake City: Deseret Book, 1989), 143.
5. Smith, *History of the Church*, 2:203–4.
6. There were 228 participants in Zion's Camp, of which 205 were men. Half the camp participants were below age thirty-one. See James L. Bradley, *Zion's Camp 1834: Prelude to the Civil War* (Logan, UT: Publishers Press, 1990): xxi.
7. According to an 1835 revelation, the Seventy were to be led by seven Presidents (see D&C 107:93).
8. Smith, *History of the Church*, 2:202.
9. Smith, *History of the Church*, 2:221–22.

10. The Community of Christ (RLDS) claims that Doctrine and Covenants 107:96 limits the number of seventies quorums to seven quorums. See "History, Calling, and Function of the Seventy," *Saints' Herald*, November 7, 1955, 10–11.
11. Sylvester Smith left the Church and took with him early records of the seventies quorums. Hazen Aldrich was appointed to take his place as a president and a clerk. Like Sylvester Smith, Hazen Aldrich left the Church. However, in 1837, when Elias Smith was appointed clerk of the seventies, Aldrich allowed Elias to copy records from December 20, 1836, to April 6, 1837. See Jenson, "Church General Authorities: First Council of Seventy," 6.
12. Sylvester Smith, "Report on Meeting of the Seventy December 27, 1835," *Messenger and Advocate*, January 1836, 253–54.
13. Smith, *History of the Church*, 2:346.
14. Andrew Jenson, "A History of the Third Quorum of Seventy," 3–4, Church History Library.
15. B. H. Roberts, ed., *The Seventy's Course in Theology: First Year* (Salt Lake City: Deseret News, 1907), 5.
16. Young, *History of the Organization of the Seventies*, 14; Smith, *History of the Church*, 2:182n.
17. Antoine R. Ivins, "The Seventy," *Improvement Era*, April 1935, 214.
18. "Caroline Barnes Crosby (1807–1884)," in Kenneth W. Godfrey, Audrey M. Godfrey, and Jill Mulvay Derr, *Women's Voices: An Untold History of the Latter-day Saints* (Salt Lake City: Deseret Book, 1982), 48.
19. Twenty-seven men were ordained to the Third Quorum. It is assumed that other men were ordained later to fill up the Quorum. Antoine R. Ivins points out that on "May 6, 1839, forty-five men were ordained seventies without designation to any particular quorum." He suggests that they became members of the Third Quorum of Seventies. See Ivins, "The Seventy," *Improvement Era*, April 1935, 214; Dean C. Jessee, "The Kirtland Diary of Wilford Woodruff," *BYU Studies* 12, no. 4 (Summer 1972): 375.
20. Jessee, "Kirtland Diary of Wilford Woodruff," 376.

21. Benjamin F. Johnson, "Autobiography of Benjamin F. Johnson," typescript, L. Tom Perry Special Collections, Harold B. Lee Library, Brigham Young University, Provo, UT.
22. See Roger D. Launius, *The Kirtland Temple: A Historical Narrative* (Independence, MO: Herald Publishing, 1986), 48.
23. The five high priests released as Presidents of the First Quorum of the Seventies were Hazen Aldrich, Leonard Rich, Zebedee Coltrin, Lyman Sherman, and Sylvester Smith. This left Joseph Young and Levi Hancock in the Presidency. Hazen Aldrich, Leonard Rich, and Sylvester Smith were disfellowshiped. The following five elders were called to fill the vacancies in the Presidency of the seventies: James Foster, Josiah Butterfield, John Gaylord, Daniel S. Miles, and Salmon Gee. See Minutes of the Seventies, Book A (1835–1838), 18, in Young, *History of the Organization of the Seventies*, 4–5.
24. Smith, *History of the Church*, 3:87–89.
25. See Smith, *History of the Church*, 3:91–93.
26. "A Short Sketch of the Biography of John Pulsipher," Seventies Quorums Genealogical Records, Part I, Second Quorum Biographies, 220–21 (microfilm), in James M. Baumgarten, "The Role and Function of the Seventies in L.D.S. Church History" (master's thesis, Brigham Young University, 1960), 27. See also Gordon Orville Hill, "A History of Kirtland Camp: Its Initial Purpose and Notable Accomplishments" (master's thesis, Brigham Young University, 1975), 22; Smith, *History of the Church*, 3:98–100.
27. Smith, *History of the Church*, 3:347.
28. Smith, *History of the Church*, 4:162.
29. Edward Hunter (1793–1883) was the bishop of the Nauvoo Fifth Ward from 1844 to 1846. He became the third Presiding Bishop of the Church. See "Autobiography of Edward Hunter," in Kate B. Carter, *Our Pioneer Heritage* (Salt Lake City: Daughters of Utah Pioneers, 1963), 5:319–26.
30. On February 6, 1844, Edward and Ann Hunter, grantors, sold to Joseph Young ("for use and benefit of the Quorum of Seventies as President"), Lot 3, Block 127 in Nauvoo for one dollar. In the description that followed, the Hunters stipulated that they did "convey and confirm unto the said Joseph Young, President of the Quorum of

Seventies, or his successor in office, for the use and benefit of said Quorum of Seventies, his assigns forever." Nauvoo Municipal Court, Book B, February 19, 1844, 73 (entry 300) and Nauvoo Recorder's Office, Deed Book B, 73, in Susan Easton Black, Harvey B. Black, and Brandon Plewe, *Property Transactions in Nauvoo, Hancock County, Illinois and Surrounding Communities, 1839–1859* (Wilmington, DE: World Vital Records, 2006), 3:1958. Although there is evidence that Edward Hunter and his wife sold the property to Joseph Young, on June 1, 1846, Edward and Ann Hunter, grantors, sold to James E. Furness, grantee, for $1,400 Lot 3, Block 127, Nauvoo Plat, Town of Nauvoo, and all of Block 130 in the same plat and town. See Hancock County Deeds, Book P, June 2, 1846, 419–20 (entry 8459), in Black, Black, and Plewe, *Nauvoo Property Transactions*, 3:1961.

31. John D. Lee, *The Life and Confessions of John D. Lee* (Philadelphia: Barclay & Co., 1877), 145–46.
32. Stout Papers, no. 8, 71, Utah Historical Society, Salt Lake City.
33. Lee, *Life and Confessions of John D. Lee*, 145–46.
34. Lee, *Life and Confessions of John D. Lee*, 145–46.
35. Journal of Peter M. Wentz, 6–7, Nauvoo Restoration Files, Land and Record Office, Nauvoo, IL.
36. *Times and Seasons*, November 1, 1844, 695–96.
37. B. H. Roberts, ed., *History of the Church of Jesus Christ of Latter-day Saints, Period 2: Apostolic Interreganum*, 2nd ed. rev. (Salt Lake City: Deseret Book, 1932), 7:307–8. See "Dedication," *Nauvoo Neighbor*, December 25, 1844, 2.
38. Hartley, "Nauvoo Stake," 72.
39. See Roberts, *History of the Church*, 7:279.
40. Roberts, *History of the Church*, 7:260n.
41. See Roberts, *History of the Church*, 7:332–33; "Dedication of the Seventies Hall," *Times and Seasons*, February 1, 1845, 794–99.
42. Roberts, *History of the Church*, 7:340–41.
43. Roberts, *History of the Church*, 7:343.
44. Roberts, *History of the Church*, 7:345.
45. "Dedication of the Seventies Hall," 794.
46. "Notice," *Nauvoo Neighbor*, October 29, 1845, 3.

47. "The Conference," *Nauvoo Neighbor*, April 16, 1845, 2.
48. Roberts, *History of the Church*, 7:424.
49. Roberts, *History of the Church*, 7:432.
50. Roberts, *History of the Church*, 7:481.
51. Roberts, *History of the Church*, 7:549.
52. Roberts, *History of the Church*, 7:365.
53. In 1837, Isaac Pitman published *Stenographic Sound-hand*. Shorthand at that time was called "phonography." George D. Watt was proficient in the use of Pitman shorthand. See Ida Watt Stringham and Dora Dutson Flack, *England's First "Mormon" Convert: The Biography of George Darling Watt* (Salt Lake City: David J. Ellison, 1958).
54. "Seventies' Library," *Nauvoo Neighbor*, January 1, 1845, 3.
55. Smith, *History of the Church*, 5:406; Louisa Barnes Pratt, "*Journal and Autobiography of Louisa Barnes Pratt, 1801–1880*"; "The History of Louisa Barnes Pratt: Being the Autobiography of a Mormon Missionary, Widow, and Pioneer," in Addison Pratt Family Collection, 1831–1924, Church History Library.
56. Roberts, *History of the Church*, 7:544.
57. "Elder Kimball's Remarks at the Music Hall during the Concert on the Evening of the 5th ult.," *Nauvoo Neighbor*, April 7, 1845, 3.
58. See Black, Black, and Plewe, *Nauvoo Property Transactions,* 3:1961.
59. See Hancock County Deeds, Book T, August 16, 1847, 2 (entry 10722), in Black, Black, and Plewe, *Property Transactions in Nauvoo*, 2:1439.
60. See *Nauvoo Independent*, October 1915 (reprint October 18, 1965), in Ida Blum Collection, L. Tom Perry Special Collections, Harold B. Lee Library, Brigham Young University, Provo, UT.
61. "In the Warranty Deed of Purchase, Hugh R. Whitlock and his wife, Kathryn B. Whitlock of Nauvoo, acting as grantors, . . . paid, convey, and warrant to J. LeRoy Kimball of Salt Lake City all four lots of Block 127 on May 12, 1962." Hugh R. Whitlock to J. LeRoy Kimball, Warranty Deed, May 12, 1962, Hancock County Records, Book of Deeds.
62. See Harvey B. Black, *Seventy Quorum Membership, 1835–1846: An Annotated Index of Over 3,500 Seventies Organized in the First Thirty-Five Quorums of the Seventy in Kirtland, Ohio, and Nauvoo, Illinois* (Provo, UT: Infobases, 1996).

Ronald W. Walker

8

SIX DAYS IN AUGUST: BRIGHAM YOUNG AND THE SUCCESSION CRISIS OF 1844

Every Latter-day Saint knows the importance of the six days in August 1844 when Brigham Young and the Twelve Apostles were sustained at Nauvoo as Joseph Smith's successors. Yet no narrative has a daily summary of what went on using the rich documents compiled at the time or the growing body of historical literature on the topic. Such a day-by-day approach yields new understanding. We learn, for example, the uncertainty of the times. *Crisis* is a strong word, but it comes close to describing events surrounding the succession. During these days, the Church might have taken several paths or, with the passing months, fractured beyond remedy. As we look at the different positions leading men and women took on what the Church should be, we also learn more about early Mormonism and its leaders. Joseph Smith's recent revelations about plural or eternal marriage, the temporal kingdom of

---

Ronald W. Walker is a professional historian living in Salt Lake City.

God, the endowment, and the apostolic keys were important issues in the succession. And no leader was more important than Brigham Young, whose religious experience and leadership were crucial. In particular, Young's earlier religious experience at Peterborough, New Hampshire, had a major role in the events that unfolded.

SIDNEY RIGDON

On Saturday, August 3, 1844, Sidney Rigdon arrived in Nauvoo, the Church headquarters, located on the big bend of the Mississippi just above the Des Moines rapids. "Few, if any, locations along this mighty river can compare with Nauvoo," said one man who had made the circuit from St. Paul to New Orleans.[1] The city sat on a promontory that rose to the east. It was known for its religion but also for its work and workers. However, grief, uncertainty, and hard economic times had wrung from the Latter-day Saints much of their bustle.[2] Six weeks earlier, a black-faced mob had killed Joseph and Hyrum Smith, the brothers who served as Prophet and Patriarch. What lay ahead for the Saints, and who would be the new shepherd? Was there a future for them and their religion?

Some looked to fifty-three-year-old Rigdon to lead the Saints. He had credentials. He had been with the Church almost from the beginning. For the past eleven years, he had served as Joseph Smith's First Counselor in the First Presidency, the Church's highest quorum. He had helped to shape events and played a role in them, even joining in some of Smith's visions.[3] Few could match his words once he stood behind a speaker's stand. His words flowed with natural eloquence, seldom as friends might talk, but with storm and stir. He was a preacher's preacher, full of history and learned scripture references. One of his fortes was the last days.[4]

Rigdon had been gone from the city for a month and a half. In the middle of June, nine days before his death, Joseph and other well-wishers had walked Sidney to the Nauvoo quay, not far from where Rigdon kept a public house for river travelers.[5] Rigdon had a new duty: Joseph wanted him to raise up a branch of Saints at Pittsburgh. About forty converts were already there, and perhaps Rigdon could make it an important center. With Rigdon was his son-in-law, Ebenezer Robinson, who had been asked to begin a new Latter-day Saint newspaper. "He is a good man," Robinson remembered Smith saying of his counselor as they walked down to the river, "and I love him better than I ever loved him in all my life, for my heart is entwined around him with chords that can never be broken."[6]

There was another reason for Rigdon's Pittsburgh mission. Joseph Smith was a candidate for the United States presidency and had chosen Rigdon as a running mate. Law and reason said that the two men should come from different states and even different parts of the country. Smith's motives for his improbable electioneering are unclear to this very day. Did he wish to awaken the country to Mormonism and to its past grievances? Neighbors had mistreated the Saints from the beginning. Or was the campaign a part of Smith's millennial expectation—some kind of step or sign of the last days? Whatever the reason, the political campaign was neither a stunt nor a "symbolic gesture," one historian concluded. Smith was serious. During the April 1844 general conference, 244 volunteered to be campaigners, and by April 15 the number had risen to 337.[7] By summer the best of the Latter-day Saint talent was barnstorming through the United States to support Smith's candidacy.[8]

Rigdon arrived in Pittsburgh on June 28, the day after the murder of the Smith brothers, and spoke to the local people several times before rumors of the assassination began to catch up with him. George J. Adams, the official Nauvoo courier, was asked to carry the news but failed to complete his mission.[9] But within a week, Elder Jedediah M. Grant sent Rigdon an "Extra" edition of the *Nauvoo Neighbor* announcing the murders, and followed up with a personal visit. At last, Rigdon's reluctance to believe reports of Smith's death gave way to "stern reality."[10] Rigdon was soon doing what he knew best: he was preaching on "Mr. Broadhurst's green, and directed the whole tide and strength of his eloquence to extol and eulogize Joseph Smith, and also the city and people of Nauvoo."[11]

At first Rigdon said that he wanted to work on postassassination events with members of the Quorum of Twelve of Apostles. Two of the Apostles had been in the same room at Carthage, Illinois, when the Smith brothers had been killed, and they remained in Nauvoo. Elder John Taylor, editor of the *Times and Seasons*, received in a "savage manner" four balls, while Elder Willard Richards, Smith's secretary, had miraculously escaped with only a forehead wound from a bullet graze (see D&C 135). The rest of the Apostles were out preaching and electioneering. Parley P. Pratt and George A. Smith were in the Midwest, while seven were in the eastern states: Orson Hyde, Heber C. Kimball, Orson Pratt, William Smith, Lyman Wight, and Wilford Woodruff, as well as Brigham Young, the Apostles' president and leader. Elder John E. Page was in Pittsburgh with Rigdon.

Rigdon asked Jedediah Grant, who was going east, to invite the Apostles to come to Pittsburgh as they returned to Nauvoo. He wanted to hold a council.[12] Young and the Apostles in the Boston area declined. They wanted to return to Nauvoo "immediately," they explained in a letter, and believed the route through the Great Lakes was quicker and safer. The Smith murders had not cooled the fierce anti-Mormonism in the Midwest. Moreover, it was the desire of the Twelve, the Apostles' letter continued, that Rigdon and Page should meet them at Nauvoo, and "after we had rested and mourned for our martyred brethren, we would sit down together and hold a council on the very ground where sleeps the ashes of our deceased friends."[13] The careful words of both Rigdon and Young had a subtext: each of the men wanted to control the succession, and the issues of the location of the meeting and who would organize it were important.

Once Rigdon got Young's letter, Rigdon hurried to Nauvoo.[14] William Marks, president of the Nauvoo Stake, may have sent him a letter encouraging him to come quickly.[15] Rigdon would also claim that religious visions and revelations had summoned him, including, as one historian later wrote, the "voice of Joseph Smith."[16]

When Rigdon arrived in Nauvoo, there were four Apostles in town. Elders Richards and Taylor had been joined by Parley P. Pratt and George A.

Six Days in August: Brigham Young and the Succession Crisis of 1844

Smith, the men closest to headquarters when the killings took place. Pratt immediately sought out Rigdon, who was crowded by the handshaking of well-meaning friends. "You are busy today," Pratt told Rigdon. "We will not interrupt you today, but tomorrow morning the few of the Twelve who are here will want to meet with you, and sit down in council together."[17] The two men agreed to meet the following morning at 8:00 a.m.—Sunday—at the home of John Taylor, who was still convalescing and bedridden.

The appointment came and went—without Rigdon. The Apostles sent Pratt to find out why. Pratt found Rigdon talking to a Nauvoo outsider not very far from Taylor's home. As near as Pratt could tell, the conversation was rather aimless, but Rigdon refused to be pulled away. Rigdon and Pratt had known each other from their pre-Mormon days in Ohio's Western Reserve when the two men were ministers in the Primitive Christian movement of Barton W. Stone and Thomas and Alexander Campbell (which became one wing of today's Church of Christ). Pratt had introduced Rigdon to Mormonism. "Well, well! Brother Pratt," Rigdon finally said, "I must go with you now without delay." But as the two men started toward Taylor's home, there was another excuse. A large crowd was gathering to worship at 10:00 a.m., and Rigdon claimed he had to preach. A meeting between Rigdon and the Apostles would have to wait. The Apostles were left to "do their own counselling," Pratt said sourly. He felt that Rigdon had avoided their meeting, and he felt misused.[18]

Some said that as many as six thousand Saints were at the meeting grounds east of the rising temple that Sunday. Many knew that Rigdon had arrived in town and wanted to hear what he had to say. He chose as his text a verse from the ancient prophet Isaiah, "my ways [are] higher than your ways" (Isaiah 55:9). He wanted to prepare the Saints for something new. He told them of an extraordinary vision he had received in the upper room of his Pittsburgh lodging. He announced that he "was the identical man that the ancient Prophets had sung about, wrote and rejoiced over; and that he was sent to do the identical work that had been the theme of all the Prophets in every preceeding generation."[19] Again, he turned to Isaiah's poetry:

"The Lord shall hiss for the fly that is in the uttermost part of the rivers of Egypt, and for the bee that is in the land of Assyria," he quoted (Isaiah 7:18). He gave these words apocalyptic meaning. The day would come when he would see "one hundred tons of metal per second thrown at the enemies of God, and that the blood would be to the horses bridles." At that time, Rigdon "expected to walk into the palace of Queen Victoria and lead her out by the nose."[20]

The report of Rigdon's sermon was preserved by his rivals and no doubt did not reflect his humor or the full meaning of his words. But one claim was clear. He wanted to be Joseph's successor, or as he phrased it, the Church's "guardian." He had seen Joseph in the heavens, he said, and he, Rigdon, held the "keys of this dispensation." He would stand as a "god" to the people, like Moses, and he would preserve the Church as Joseph "had begun it."[21] These last words seemed to indicate Rigdon's willingness to go back to the first teachings of Smith, whose ministry had been progressive and unfolding.

The argument was part of his claim for succession. According to Rigdon, the death of Joseph Smith had not dissolved the First Presidency. As the last surviving member of this group, Rigdon should be the new leader. After all, one of Joseph Smith's revelations described Rigdon (and another counselor) as "equal" with Smith in "holding the keys of this last kingdom. . . . And this shall be your business and mission in all your lives, to preside in council and set in order all the affairs of this church and kingdom" (D&C 90:6, 16). Still another revelation had made Rigdon the Prophet's "spokesman" (D&C 100:9–11), and in 1841, Rigdon had been ordained to the office of "Prophet, Seer and Revelator"—the series of titles reserved for the Church's most important leaders.[22]

That afternoon, after his dramatic speech, Rigdon and his allies made another move. As Elder Charles C. Rich preached in the worship meeting, he was interrupted by President Marks with a surprising announcement. Marks declared that on Thursday morning, August 8, President Rigdon would hold a "special meeting" of the Saints to consider his claims. Rigdon.

wanted the succession question settled in four days. Such a meeting had been on the lips of the Nauvoo Saints since the death of the Smith brothers, only the assumption had been that the Twelve Apostles would conduct the meeting, not Rigdon.[23]

After Rigdon's forenoon address, the Apostles continued to hope for a meeting with Rigdon, but Marks's announcement showed that events were moving rapidly and might spin out of control. Rigdon and Marks had consulted neither with the Apostles nor with the local high council of elders, who normally might help decide on a special meeting—nor with Rich, who served as Marks's counselor. Pratt, who apparently was in the afternoon congregation, tried to challenge Marks. Weren't Brigham Young and the other Apostles expected to return to Nauvoo soon, he asked, perhaps within several days or even hours? Shouldn't a special meeting wait for their arrival? Marks replied that Rigdon actually wanted the special meeting to take place on Tuesday. Marks had granted two extra days and was unwilling to go further. Rigdon had family matters in Pittsburgh that required his immediate attention, Marks explained.[24]

By evening, William Clayton, one of Joseph Smith's personal secretaries and a close friend, was upset. Both Bishop Newel K. Whitney and Charles C. Rich had come to his home with news and questions. "It seems a plot [has been] laid for the saints to take advantage of their situation," Clayton wrote in his diary.[25]

The best that the Apostles could do was to meet with Rigdon the following day. They arrived in force—Parley P. Pratt, Willard Richards, and George A. Smith, and, if one source is to be believed, the ailing John Taylor. With them was Bishop Whitney and Elder Amasa Lyman, whom Smith had chosen to be his counselor, though the Saints never had the chance to sustain him formally. Everyone agreed to meet that evening at Elder Taylor's home.[26]

On Monday evening, whether because of his excitable personality or perhaps by strategy, Rigdon paced furiously before the Church leaders. The local political situation was out of control, he warned. The coming election might bring into office anti-Mormons who might further hurt the Saints.

"You lack a great leader," he said. "You want a head, and unless you unite upon that head you're blown to the four winds, the anti-Mormons will carry the election—a guardian must be appointed."[27]

The Apostles and their friends were not convinced. They continued to ask Rigdon to put off any meeting of the Saints until the Apostles arrived from the eastern missions.[28] But the only thing that they could wring from Rigdon was the promise that the coming meeting on Thursday would be a "prayer meeting" for discussion, an "interchange of thought and feeling . . . [to] warm up each other's hearts." It would not be a business meeting to make binding decisions.[29]

On Tuesday, August 6, at 2:30 p.m., Rigdon once again sermonized. The audience and the occasion is unclear, but he seemed to continue to be agreeable. He spoke of mobs coming upon Nauvoo and remembered old Missouri difficulties. These events no longer were a context for his claims to leadership, however. He insisted that he wanted no office "in the kingdom of god," even if it were offered. Instead, he would rather be a "constable upon earth" than a priestly king.[30] Things seemed to be settling down.

That evening, Brigham Young and four other Apostles—Elders Kimball, Orson Pratt, Wight, and Woodruff—came down the river on the steamboat *St. Croix*. The name of the vessel was apt: Rigdon and Young with their respective parties were on a mission that would determine the future of the Church. Two days before landing, Elder Kimball, Young's closest friend, had a dream of a natural-looking Joseph Smith. Smith was preaching to a large congregation, Kimball reported, and when morning came and Kimball woke, he told his friends that he believed he understood what the dream meant. Joseph had "laid the foundation for a great work and it was now for us to build upon it."[31] The dream was meant to remind the Apostles of their own leadership claims.

The Apostles had done just as they told Rigdon they would do, only their trip to Navuoo took longer than they at first had hoped. While still in the East, Elder Young wanted as many of the Apostles as possible at Nauvoo when the succession would be decided, and he had waited a week in Boston for a straggling Elder Wight. The Apostles joined together in upstate New York and went by railroad to Buffalo, where they secured passage on Lake Erie to Cleveland and then to Detroit. They continued on the lake route to Chicago. The company of fellow passengers was not congenial. Elder Woodruff complained of the passengers' "prejudice" and "nonsens[e] and folly." He noted that they "wish to speak evil of us while we walk uprightly."[32] The 160-mile leg across Illinois was a grueling forty-eight hours as their coach stopped only for food, fresh teams, and to pry themselves and other wagons from the mud. At one point, a heavily loaded wagon belonging to Norwegian immigrants was bogged in the mire, and the Norwegians were whipping and bawling at their oxen. According to one account, Young looked over the situation, stepped from the coach, and coaxed the animals in a language unknown to either the Norwegians or the Americans. Then a light touch of the whip got the calmed animals to lift the wagon, and the Norwegians went ahead with their journey—to "the surprise and amusement of the passengers" in the coach.[33]

The last 120 miles downriver from Galena to Nauvoo were pleasant because of the Apostles' excitement to return home. The men had been gone for more than three months and longed for the last bend of the river that would reveal their city and their families. "We were hailed with Joy by all the Citizens we met," remembered Elder Woodruff, when they stepped from the wharf near Nauvoo's landmark, "the upper stonehouse." Despite their happiness, Woodruff felt something else. "When we landed in the City," he reported in his diary, "there was a deep gloom [that] seemed to rest over the City of Nauvoo which we never experi[en]ced before."[34] The place was a deposit of not only grief and sorrow but also fear of the future.

BRIGHAM YOUNG

Brigham Young had no idea events would turn so badly when he left Nauvoo on May 21. From Nauvoo, he took a side trip to Kirtland, Ohio, where Mormonism had first really begun to mold him. Kirtland was also the place where he began his friendship with Joseph Smith, which became the lodestone for the rest of Young's life. Young visited the old sites in Kirtland and preached in the temple, trying to breathe new life into the old disciples who had let the Church go on without them. He found them "dead and cold to the things of God." Continuing his trip, Young visited his brother, John Young, and also his sister, Nancy Kent, who lived in Chester, Ohio. He then headed for Boston, the center of his operations for the next several months.[35] Joseph Smith had given him the duty of drawing up the fields of labor for all the missionaries involved in the political campaign. He had chosen Boston for himself.[36]

Young was now forty-three years old, and the spring in his step for long preaching tours was not what it had once been. Just outside of Kirtland while waiting for an eastbound boat, he had confessed as much in a letter to his wife Mary Ann, who was back home in Nauvoo. "I feele lonsom," he began his letter. "O that I had you with me this somer I think I should be happy. Well I am now [happy] because I am in my cauling and duing my duty, but [the] older I grow the more I desire to stay at my own home insted of traveling."

Once at Albany, New York, he continued his writing. He had not gotten much sleep on his way east and was "perty well tired out," he said. "Last night I felt for somtime as though I had got to get a new const[it]jution or [I would] not last long. How I due want to see you and [the children]. Kiss them for me and kiss Luny [Luna] twice or mor. Tel hir it is for me. Give my love to all the famely. I nead not menshion names. . . . Don't you want for eney thing. You can borrow monney to get what you want. . . . After taking a grate share of my love to your self then deal it out to others as you plese."[37]

Once in Boston, his routine included the familiar duties of traveling and preaching. "We have Baptized a good many since we left," he wrote in still another letter.[38] Whenever possible, he went to Salem to visit his daughter Vilate, who was being schooled there. And there were the demands of the political campaign. The famed Boston Melodeon Concert Hall on Washington Street held one Latter-day Saint rally, which was supposed to elect delegates to the upcoming Baltimore Convention. The meeting began promisingly. The seats were crowded and the business going forward when Abigail Folsom, a feminist and abolitionist, staged a protest. Rowdies in the galley continued the uproar. Soon the meeting was broken up and had to be adjourned until the next day to the green at Bunker Hill.[39]

These were the perils of Latter-day Saints on the campaign circuit. Several days later, Young had the chance to look back on events. Elder Erastus Snow was at the speaker's stand delivering one of his long sermons, and Young, sitting in an alcove, had a chance to write to Willard Richards in Nauvoo. He wanted Richards to stop in on his family and speak words of comfort to them. He reported favorably on William Smith and Lyman Wight, with whom he had never before had the opportunity to serve. Wight "is a great, good, noble-hearted man," he wrote. "I love my brethren more and more."

Many of his words to Richards were about the campaign trail, and he wrote with irony, "I should suppose that there is an election about to take place or the Prophet had offered himself for some office in the United States, for of all the howlings of Devils and Devil[s] whelps." The rumors were thick. "Sometimes the Mormons are all killed; sometimes they are half killed, and sometimes the blood is knee deep in Nauvoo. Sometimes old Joe, as they call him is taken by the mob and carried to Missouri, sometimes he is gone to Washington, sometimes he has runaway, given up to the authorities, etc. etc. One might suppose him to be a sectarian God, without body, parts or passions—his center everywhere and his circumference no where." If Young thought Smith's election prospects were dim, he did not acknowledge it. "We shall do all we can [with the campaign]," he told Richards, "and leave the event with God."[40]

There was a terrible irony working. Young's letter to Richards was written on July 8, a week and a half *after* the assassinations. Several days before their deaths and with events closing in on them, Joseph and Hyrum Smith had written a plaintive letter asking Young and other Church leaders to return to Nauvoo and help in this moment of great crisis.[41] But the mail was not getting through—in either direction.

In the next day or two, Young heard other rumors about the deaths of the Smiths, which he again dismissed.[42] Traveling with Orson Pratt, Young went on Church business to out-of-the-way Peterborough, New Hampshire, a few miles north of the Massachusetts border. His sermon there suggested that he might be coming to grips that some of these awful rumors. "The death of one or a dozen could not destroy the priesthood," he told the local Saints, "nor hinder the work of the Lord from spreading throughout all nations."[43]

The ambiguity ended on July 16. Young and Pratt were leaning back in their chairs at Brother Bement's house in Peterborough when a letter arrived from Nauvoo telling of the killings. Later in the day, Elder Woodruff's letter with the same news arrived. "I felt then as I never felt bef[ore]," Young later said. There were no tears but an awful, paralyzing headache. "My head felt as tho my head [would] crack." His thoughts went everywhere. Had Joseph and Hyrum taken the keys or the authority of the Church with them?

At last, his despair lifted "like a clap," he said. The answer came to him like revelation: "The keys of the kingdom [are] here." He brought his hand to his knee to make the point.[44] He later confessed that the idea of assuming Joseph's office had never occurred to him.[45] It had been an interesting psychological study, resisting reality until he could resist it no longer—followed by an emotional and religious outburst of feeling.

There was another meaning to Young's revelation. It showed that the Church's procedures for succession were by no means clear, even to the leading Apostle. Young, of course, had been present during those almost daily private council meetings with Smith earlier in the year. During these councils, Smith had laid out the endowment or temple rituals step-by-step, the capstone of his revelation. He concluded with what should have been a portentous warning: "Brethren, the Lord bids me hasten the work in which we are engaged. . . . Some important scene is near to take place. It may be that my enemies will kill me, and in case they should, and the keys and power which rest on me not be imparted to you, they will be lost from the Earth." Joseph and Hyrum Smith then anointed the Apostles and other men who were present in the room, after which Joseph paced before them and dramatically pushed back upon his shoulders the collar of the coat he was wearing. "I roll the burden and responsibility of leading this church off from my shoulders on to yours," he said. "Now, round up your shoulders and stand under it like men; for the Lord is going to let me rest a while."[46]

This event, now known in Church history as the "last charge," was memorialized by several of the men who were present, but perhaps most significantly by an unpublished and unsigned statement that currently resides in the Church History Library. "Joseph Smith did declare that he had conferred upon the Twelve every key and every power that he ever held himself before God," the statement said. "This our testimony we expect to meet in a coming day when all parties will know that we have told the truth and have not lied, so help us God."[47] For Young, the last charge was a final act in a series of events. "Joseph more than one score of times told . . . [the apostles] both in private and in public, that he rolled the Kingdom on to their shoulders," Young would later say.[48] Joseph's conferral of authority included priesthood keys of authority but also a fullness of the endowment ritual, "everything necessary for the salvation of man."[49]

Young and a majority of the other Apostles had been present during these occasions and heard Joseph's words. But their hopes and wishes, like those of Jesus' disciples before Calvary, did not permit them to accept the last charge at face value. Only the actual killings, months later, made Joseph Smith's warning clear.[50]

But Young's religious experience at Peterborough was more certain, especially as the days wore on and he continued to feel religiously prompted. He was convinced that he, as President of the Twelve, had authority to lead the Church, or to at least name Joseph's successor. He also believed that at some point a new First Presidency of three men would be required, though he was willing to let that issue rest for the moment.[51] And he hoped that a general assembly of the Saints would give its approval to the succession. One of Joseph's revelations declared such a gathering to be the highest authority in the Church—the collective inspiration of leaders and members (D&C 107:32).[52]

The day after hearing of the Smith brothers' deaths, Young hurried from Peterborough to Boston. That night he shared a room with Elder Woodruff at Sister Voice's home. Young slept in the bed while Woodruff, who was grieving the Prophet's death, slept in a large chair and did his best to shield his convulsive tears.[53] Young's grief, in contrast, was clear-eyed and determined. On July 18, he held a council with the Apostles who could be quickly gathered together in the East. The result was a letter that the Church's eastern newspaper, the *Prophet*, soon published. The Apostles told Church leaders to head quickly to Nauvoo for the general council.[54] That evening Young briefly preached. He tried to cheer the local Saints: "When God sends a man to do a work all the devils in hell cannot kill him untill he gets through his work. So with Joseph[.] He prepared all things[,] gave the keys to men on the earth[,] and said[,] I may be soon taken from you."[55] He was already using the last charge as a text.

DECIDING THE SUCCESSION

On Wednesday, August 7—the fifth day of the succession crisis—the Apostles spent much of the day huddled in conference at John Taylor's house. They held two meetings early in the day. It was the first time that a legal quorum of seven or more Apostles gathered since Carthage—and they actually had not met since months before that because of their missions. Richards had been the Saints' "principal counselor" during the previous five anxious weeks, answering "calls and inquiries" by the hundreds.[56] Before the others returned, he had been the only healthy Apostle in Nauvoo. He knew the Church's business as well as anyone in the city and had a reputation for good judgment and good works.

People may have deferred to Richards for another reason. Less than two weeks after the killings, Richards, in the course of his usual correspondence, signed one preacher's license as "Clerk and *acting President*." Other preaching licenses reportedly had a still more interesting signature. An entry in the historical record of these licenses explained, "From the murder of President Joseph Smith to this Date [September 2, 1844] licenses were signed

Six Days in August: Brigham Young and the Succession Crisis of 1844

'*Twelve Apostles, President.*'" This last piece of evidence was confirmed by the Church's official chronological history.[57] Since these materials were written weeks and even years after the succession controversy and may represent a later view of events, they require some skepticism. On the other hand, they may also suggest that Richards, early on, was asserting the leadership claims of a united Quorum of the Twelve and some people were accepting them.

It is unfortunate that someone who attended the meetings held on Wednesday did not leave a record of the issues discussed. These two meetings had to be among the most important during the succession crisis. For one thing, the newly arrived Apostles had to be brought up to date. There had been difficulties in Nauvoo from the first week of the murders. "The greatest danger that now threatens us is dissensions and strifes amongst the Church," William Clayton had written on July 6. Clayton reported that the Saints were discussing four or five possible successors to Smith in his twin offices as Church President and trustee-in-trust.[58] Clayton regrettably did not identify these men, though they may have included Rigdon and Young as well as William Marks and Samuel Smith, another of the Smith brothers.

The office of trustee-in-trust, which managed the Church's property, posed a serious problem. Someone had to receive property and pay the bills for the temple, which meant an immediate appointment. More explosive was the conduct of Emma Smith, the Prophet's widow, who was determined that the family's property should not be swallowed by the Church's claims—Joseph had mixed personal and official accounts and many of his debts were unresolved. Emma opposed the stopgap idea of having Clayton serve until the Apostles returned, and during July repeatedly inserted herself into the trustee-in-trust issue.[59] Her feelings were deep. She accused such opponents as Richards of not treating her "right" and warned if they should "trample upon her," she would "look to herself"—lawyers were obviously on her mind. By the middle of July, she threatened that she "would do the church all the injury" she could if a new trustee-in-trust were appointed without her approval. Her choice, apparently, was Marks, whose views on Church policy and doctrine more closely agreed with her own. Clayton, in the middle of controversy, despaired. Bills were coming due, and Lucy Mack Smith, the Prophet's mother, was also restive.[60] Clayton felt that a public disturbance over Smith's estate and the trustee would bring clamoring creditors and a costly settlement. With proper management, however, there was enough "to pay the debts and plenty left for other uses."[61]

There were other topics that the Twelve must have discussed in their Wednesday meetings. Some were crucial to the future of Mormonism. Did the Smith family have a special claim to the Church's leadership? For several months Joseph and Hyrum Smith had been acting closely together, and Hyrum, as the Church's Assistant President and Patriarch, had the authority to carry on had he survived Carthage.[62] The Old Testament and the Book of Mormon were full of examples of prophetic primogeniture—passing a prophet's mantle of leadership to a son or perhaps to a family member. For the moment, this question of family succession was not pressing. Joseph Smith's brother, Samuel Smith, had died on July 30, and Joseph Smith's sons were young. Another brother, William Smith, was erratic, and no one saw him as a serious candidate.

There were underground issues, too. Historian Ronald K. Esplin has argued that Nauvoo in early 1844 had been a city of secrets. During the several years before his death, Joseph Smith had introduced a breathtaking array of new doctrines and practices: "The plurality of gods, new temple ordinances, new theocratic practices, and even plural marriage." This "Nauvoo 'package'" was known unevenly among the Saints, according to Esplin. The result were insider Saints who possessed a "private *gnosis*," while the majority of Church members were either unaware or not fully informed.[63]

In addition to new doctrines, Smith had also created three new organizations. The first was the Female Relief Society. This organization was publicly known and open to the women living in Nauvoo, though most of its members were drawn from the city's leading women. The two other organizations were semisecret. The Council of Fifty sought to redress past wrongs, increase the Church's political influence, and expand Mormonism's borders into the American West. The Council of Fifty also was a contingency plan for the last days when earthly governments would fall at Christ's Second Coming and a new religious and political order would be necessary. While some historians have suggested that this new council was not much more than a symbol, the weight of inconclusive evidence suggests that Joseph Smith was serious about his political outreach. His 1844 political campaign and the later Mormon settlement in the Great Basin were not speculative patterns or decorations.[64]

The second semisecret group was Joseph Smith's prayer circle. Known in furtive references in diaries and minutes as the "Holy Order," the "Quorum of the Anointed," the "First Quorum," or still more often as the "Quorum" or "Council," this group was making Church decisions in July along with Richards.[65] He was a member of the group and influenced many of its decisions, but not without some tension and hurt feelings along the way.[66]

Like the Council of Fifty, the Quorum of the Anointed began in 1842 and two years later was meeting weekly and sometimes daily.[67] Members were the first initiates of the empowering "ancient order of things," or the endowment, that later was introduced in the Nauvoo Temple. By the summer of 1844, membership was limited to about sixty-five specially devoted men and women. These anointed members met in special priesthood robes, discussed the matters of the kingdom, and offered special prayers. Their July devotions were fervent. According to Brigham Young, a few of the select group met twice "every day . . . to offer up the signs and pray to our heavenly father to deliver his people." It had been the "cord which bound the people together."[68] Some of their soulful petitions were pleas to return the Apostles back to the city.[69]

Many of Smith's new teachings went against the grain of commonplace or sectarian Christian tradition—and the views of conservative Saints. But within this circle, the Prophet felt at ease.[70] "Brother Joseph feels as well as I Ever see him," wrote Heber C. Kimball to Parley P. Pratt in 1842. "One reason is he has got a Small company, that he feels safe in thare ha[n]ds. And that is not all, he can open his bosom to[o] and feel him Self safe."[71] The groups who knew of Smith's advanced teaching were the Twelve Apostles, the Council of Fifty, and the Anointed Quorum, as well some of the officers of the Relief Society. Sometimes their meetings merged into a single assembly—an informal fusion of the three or four groups—and as a result there were disorderly lines of authority. The March 1844 meeting in which Smith gave his last charge almost certainly was such an example. On that occasion, there had been an assembly of about sixty men—probably a meeting of the Council of Fifty and the Twelve Apostles with others.[72] Altogether, there were probably no more than one hundred such select disciples in Nauvoo, and perhaps only one member in twenty knew about them.[73] But these few members held in their bosom knowledge of the explosive ideas of plural marriage and the temporal kingdom.[74]

Understandably, Smith's last agenda had little space on the public stage. But privately it gave context to the events surrounding the succession. The succession of 1844 was not simply about appointing a man or group of men to lead the Church. Rather, it was about what kind of Church would survive. When Marks was being pushed for the position of trustee-in-trust, Bishop Whitney objected. He remembered Marks's past association with William Law and Emma Smith, both of whom had a recent history of opposing Joseph Smith and the Twelve. "If Marks is appointed Trustee our spiritual blessings will be destroyed inasmuch as he is not favorable to the most important matters," Whitney told Clayton, referring to the temple ordinances. Moreover, Whitney believed the office of trustee was inseparably tied to the Presidency. One office entailed the other, and that combination put Joseph Smith's last teachings in jeopardy. Whitney favored the appointment of Samuel Smith before Samuel died.[75]

As the events leading to Joseph Smith's death closed in on Joseph in June, he seemed to retreat from some of his advanced teachings. According to D. Michael Quinn, immediately before he went to Carthage, Smith turned his back on polygamy, the endowment, and the Council of Fifty.[76] Whether the retreat was meant to be temporary or permanent, or whether the steps were expedient or heartfelt, the most likely conclusion was that Smith was stabilizing Nauvoo while privately holding firmly to his teachings. His closest disciples accepted this view. But the possibility of a turnabout gave comfort to Emma Smith and Marks during the succession crisis. A rumor circulated through Nauvoo on August 7 claiming that Rigdon had cemented his alliance with Marks by offering him the office of Patriarch, while Rigdon would become the Church's President.[77] Emma Smith could be expected to lend her quiet support. Still more likely, these people never worked out an agenda of offices or goals. They were united vaguely by their lack of belief in Joseph Smith's last teachings and probably never organized themselves into a formal group or opposition.

The Apostles concluded their meetings on August 7 with a decision: a general assembly would be convened within the week on Tuesday, August 13, at 10:00 a.m. They intended to put forward their claims and follow it with a formal, ratifying vote.[78] For the Apostles, there was no turning back. Most had accepted plural marriage at great emotional and psychological cost. Their days of fervent councils with the founding Prophet were at odds with a pre-Nauvoo program and a pre-Nauvoo Church. The idea of Joseph Smith conducting a fallen ministry was out of the question.

The Apostles made two other decisions. They wanted a semipublic airing of Rigdon's claims and scheduled a meeting at Nauvoo's still uncompleted Seventies Hall later in the day. Rigdon would have the opportunity of speaking before the Church's local and general leaders. The Apostles also agreed to meet the following morning, August 8, for another private meeting.

Minutes and reports of the 4:00 p.m. meeting at the Seventies Hall are incomplete, but it is possible to reconstruct what took place. Rigdon once more put forward his claims and gave more detail about the vision he revealed earlier about putting the Church in order. It was not an "open vision," he explained, but a stirring that had come to his mind—a continuation of what Joseph Smith and he had experienced in their vision revealing the three degrees of heaven.[79] His future calling, Rigdon said, was to build up the Church for Joseph, because all future blessings must come through Joseph. He was again asserting his position as Joseph Smith's councilor and spokesman. Elder Wilford Woodruff probably spoke for his fellow Apostles with a curt dismissal. "A long story," Woodruff said, and a "second class vision."[80]

William Clayton, who attended the meeting, said that Brigham Young concluded with a few blunt sentences that had his characteristic sting. He did not care who led the Church, he told the Church leaders; even old Ann Lee would do if that was the mind of God. (Ann Lee had helped found the Believers in Christ's Second Appearing, or Shakers, a century before.) But on the question of who would manage the succession, there was no compromise. Young alone held "the keys and the means of knowing the mind of God," he said.[81] On these grounds, Young did not accept Rigdon's claims.

Young's claim was extraordinary. During the last years of Joseph Smith's life, Smith had increasingly turned to Young. He was the first to receive his full endowment, and Smith later allowed him to perform the endowment ceremonies in his absence. Young was given many other prominent duties as he became one of Smith's closest colaborers.[82] But the last charge had not singled Young out—Smith had spoken expansively about most members of the Twelve and some members of the Council of Fifty having the full blessings of the endowment or patriarchal power. Still more important, Smith recognized the Apostles' special priesthood authority, and one of his revelations described the Twelve (along with other quorums) as forming a group "equal in authority and power" to the First Presidency (D&C 187:24). But this revelation described the Apostles' collective power and said nothing about their president being a special revelator. Nor did Young use this revelation as a source for his authority. The one thing that seemed to give Young assurance in the early days of August was his Peterborough experience, though he did not say a word about it.

By Thursday, August 8, events were finally coming to a climax. The Apostles had scheduled their private meeting for 9:00 a.m. Rigdon's prayer meeting was to take place an hour later, though there was a great deal of confusion about it. Some Saints recalled that Rigdon had pledged that the gathering would be an informal worship session like most midweek meetings at the time. Still others claimed that Rigdon had shifted back and forth about the meeting and at last called it off.[83] One thing appears certain: the Apostles did not think Rigdon's meeting would be important enough for them to attend.

What happened was happenstance—one of those imponderables that intrude into human affairs that men and women often call chance, fortune, luck—or providence. The Apostles gathered at Richards's office, but Young did not show up. Several years later when his colleagues reminded him of his error, Young was disbelieving. "Does any of you know of my making an appointment & not being there?" he bristled. "I don't own to that & if such an item goes into the history [of the Church] I'd tear it out if written in [a] book of Gold." But a recollection came after this outburst. "By talking about it, I begin to recollect it."[84] Young, in fact, had missed a meeting. The exhaustion of the past month had caught up with him.

By midmorning, Young saw people streaming into the grove where the Saints held their public meetings and must have known it was Rigdon's prayer meeting. Young decided to go although the meeting had already started. Apparently no Church minutes survive, and probably none were taken. What does exist are several dozen reminiscences describing events that took place. Helen Mar Whitney, Heber C. Kimball's daughter, remembered a large multitude, half of whom were standing.[85] People were concerned about the succession. A stiff wind was blowing, which tossed Rigdon's words back upon him. In order to go on speaking, he stepped out into the congregation and stood on a wagon bed either opposite to the speaker's stand or to one side. Before he was through, he spoke for an hour and a half.[86]

One narrative of the event emphasized its drama, and it may be true. As Rigdon was concluding and about to call for a vote, Young stepped to the speaker's stand, and his sudden appearance must have been electrifying.[87] The people had not seen him for almost four months, and many were unaware he had returned. At first he was not in the angle of their vision, and they turned at the sound of his voice. "I did not ask . . . if I might speak," Young remembered. "I just spoke as I did."[88]

"I will manage this voting for Elder Rigdon," Young said. "He does not preside here. This child [Young himself] will manage this flock for a season."[89] Young complained of "a hurrying Spirit" and spoke of "the true Organization of the Church," which required a formal voting by the people in a special seating arrangement. Anxious to forestall a morning vote, he on the spot announced such a meeting for 2:00 p.m. the same day. After hearing Rigdon, he was unwilling to wait for the coming week.[90]

"Who of the Apostles defended this Kingdom when Sidney was going to lead this people to hell?" he would later ask rhetorically. "I magnified my calling and scarce a man stood by me to brunt the battle."[91] In fact, his confused fellow Apostles remained at Richards's office until they came looking for him just as he was ending his brief remarks.[92] Woodruff gave his reading of the situation: "In consequence of some excitement among the People and a disposition by some spirits to try to divide the Church, it was thought best to attend to the business of the Church in the afternoon."[93]

What would have happened had Young not taken charge at the grove that morning? Would the people have voted to sustain Rigdon? Today it is easy to dismiss Rigdon because the flow of history makes past events seem inevitable. However, historical records and recent scholarship suggest that many Saints were uncertain about who should be their new leader and the question of succession was fluid.[94] James Blakesley, a Church member who lived a few miles up the river at Rock Island, Illinois, wrote of the confusion: "The church is left without an earthly head, unless the promise of the Lord shall be fulfilled, which saith, that if he removed Joseph, he would appoint another in his stead. But as this has not yet been done, what is the church to do? Now sir, if I have been correctly informed, some of the members of the church at Nauvoo, want Stephen Markham for their head, and others Sidney Rigdon, and others President Marks, and others Little Joseph [Joseph Smith's son], and others B. Young, and some others P. P. Pratt, and if they can all have their choice, we shall soon have a multiplicity of church[e]s of Latter Day Saints."[95] Still another view was that of Ezra T. Benson, who at the time of Smith's death was in New Jersey campaigning. "The question arose by Bro[ther] Pack [his companion] who will now lead the Church," Benson later wrote. "I told [him] I did not know but I knew who would lead me and that would be the twelve apostles."[96] Benson would later become a member of that body.

Rigdon's claims were not easily put aside. He still held many Church titles and was easily among the most accomplished of the Saints. His pulpit voice remained strong. Rigdon spoke "with all the eloquence possible for a man to have," recalled George Romney, who was in the congregation. His remarks left "quite an impression," said Maria Wealthy Wilcox. Latter-day Saint stalwart Benjamin F. Johnson's account had the overtone of apology. "I sat in the assembly near President Rigdon, closely attentive to his appeal," Johnson said. "And was, perhaps, to a degree, forgetful of what I knew to be the rights and duties of the apostleship."[97]

Events were moving rapidly. At the Apostles' meeting, Elder Kimball, probably acting on a decision made the previous day, instructed Clayton to pay Emma Smith $1000 to quiet the simmering trustee-in-trust matter. Together with Richards and Kimball, he delivered the money and assured her of the "good feelings of the Twelve towards her. She seemed humble and more kind."[98]

The afternoon general assembly meeting started forty-five minutes late. No doubt much hurrying was needed to get everyone in place. Rigdon and Young and at least seven members of the Twelve were on the stand, and apparently also Marks and his high council. The high priests were seated nearby to the right. Seventies had the front seats, and the Aaronic Priesthood the rear seats. Elders were to the right of the seventies, and the sisters were on the left. Around this formal assembly were other Saints, many standing.[99] The wind continued to blow. The congregation included perhaps six thousand or more. The meeting was what Latter-day Saints later called a solemn assembly, the Church's highest authority on matters of teaching and doctrine.

Young looked at the people and tried to take their pulse.[100] While grieving and a bit uncertain, they also appeared hopeful. They were sheep without their shepherd, he said to himself. When Young spoke to the people, he tried to catch this spirit. He began by likening the congregation to the days of King Benjamin, the Book of Mormon prophet who blessed his people before his death (see Mosiah 2–4). "We have all done the best we could," he said encouragingly. Without Joseph Smith, the Saints would now have to walk "by faith and not by sight." He did not like doing Church business so soon after the murders. If he could have had his way, he would have postponed the assembly for more mourning. "I feel to want to weep for 30 days—& then rise up & tell the people what the Lord wants with them." But Rigdon had forced his hand.

No shorthand reporter was present during the assembly, and surviving records preserve only sporadic phrases and sentences. But it is clear that Young wanted everyone to understand the order of the Church and the authority of the Apostles. "The Twelve [were] appointed by the finger of the Almighty," he insisted. They were "an independent body" that held "the keys of the Kingdom to all the whole world so help me God." Together, they were the Church's new "first presidency." The congregation might choose Rigdon or another man, but such an action "would sever all." "You can't put any one at the head of the 12 again." And Young wanted the people to remember his own service. Had he ever faltered? Along the way, Young's remarks, or perhaps those of some of the speakers who followed him, flatly challenged Rigdon's standing. He had lost his position as "prophet, seer, and revelator" due to "unfaithfulness."[101]

Young's speech had humor, anecdotes, and some bite directed at his opponents. But it also taught, blessed, and uplifted. Young remembered his feeling. As he began to speak, he felt "compass[s]ion" and a "swol[l]en" heart for the Saints. "The power of the Holy G[h]ost even the spirit of the Prophets" seemed to rest upon him. It had been a difficult speech to deliver: It was "a long and laboras [laborious] talk of a bout two [h]ours in the open air with the wind blowing."[102]

Usually Young's sermons flowed from one idea to the next to the next. This address, however, lacked order. "For the life of me," said one of Young's critics, Bishop George Miller. "I could not see any point in the course of his remarks other than a wish to overturn Sidney Rigdon's pretensions." Everything seemed "anarchy and boisterous confusion."[103] The independent-minded Miller had earlier shown a willingness to go against the Apostles, and nothing he now heard turned him from his course.[104] The criticism of Latter-day Saint historian Elder B. H. Roberts was more thoughtful. Roberts wondered why Young had not given a more scriptural defense. Neither Young nor others who spoke on Thursday afternoon, Roberts believed, offered a discussion of the "relationship of the respective presiding councils."[105] Roberts wanted a defense based upon Joseph Smith's revelation on Church government, now published as section 107 in the Doctrine and Covenants.

There was a good reason why Young spoke as he did. When section 107 was given in 1835, few regarded it as a blueprint for the Apostles' succession—or for that matter, that the revelation established the Twelve as the Church's second most important quorum.[106] These ideas came during the early years at Nauvoo when Joseph Smith for the first time made the Apostles his right-hand men.[107] It was during these years that Smith had given them the full endowment and the commission to lead out in his absence. These last teachings were private and wrapped around sensitive issues such as plural marriage, theocracy, and the endowment ordinances, which, if known, might have turned some men and women in the congregation against Young and the Apostles. In short, there were many things that Young did not say because they were neither appropriate nor timely.

Elder Amasa Lyman spoke later in the meeting. He wanted the people to know that he had no special claims because he had served as Joseph Smith's recent (but unsustained) counselor. Lyman's remarks were aimed at Rigdon. When it finally came time for Rigdon to defend his claims, he asked Elder W. W. Phelps to speak in his behalf—Rigdon's hour-and-a-half morning speech had worn him out. The choice of Phelps was a disaster. Phelps stunningly defended the Twelve, as did the popular Parley P. Pratt a few moments later.

After so much confusion and hand-wringing during the past six days, the matter ended rather easily. Looking back, the reasons appear clear. There really was no viable alternative to the Twelve. From the Church's early days at Kirtland, Rigdon had been brilliant but unsteady, which biographer Richard S. Van Wagoner suggested was the result of a manic-depressive illness that grew more serious with age.[108] In Kirtland, he had once declared that God's keys no longer rested with Joseph Smith or perhaps even in the Church. Smith swiftly removed him from his office as counselor, but Rigdon, after repenting "like Peter of old and after a little suffering by the buffiting of Satan," was restored.[109] Rigdon's experiences in Missouri in the late 1830s brought episodic bouts of malaria and still more depression. Rigdon's illness was so severe by the time he settled at Nauvoo there were times that he did not function. At the Church's October 1843 conference, Joseph Smith suggested that Rigdon might step down, and Smith appears to have questioned his loyalty. But the conference (and eventually Smith himself) hoped that Rigdon might do better, and Rigdon continued to be sustained as First Counselor.[110]

While those who saw Rigdon up close during the first week of August knew that his moods and behavior seesawed, neither insiders nor outsiders understood the nature and extent of his illness. In contrast, there was the strong figure of Brigham Young. His experience at Peterborough increased his already high self-confidence. He felt driven. The events of succession were a time when the "power of the priesthood sat upon me," he later said. It was a time when he could "sling mountains."[111]

The people felt it too. The sensation began when Young spoke at Rigdon's prayer meeting and continued in the afternoon and even through several months after. William Burton, a missionary returning to Nauvoo in the spring of 1845, was surprised. The places of Joseph and Hyrum Smith had been taken "by others much better than I once was supposed," he wrote in his diary. "The spirit of Joseph appeared to rest upon Brigham."[112] For many Saints, Young and the Twelve held and personified Joseph Smith's last doctrines. Said one Saint, "The twelve have been ordained[,] sealed and anointed[,] in fine have received all the Power necessary to preside." It was a matter of ordination—and more.

The idea that Young had been transformed (or transfigured) by the spirit of Joseph Smith became one of the great traditions of Latter-day Saint history. The story has been told many times and with many variations. A recent compilation has more than one hundred testimonies, fifty-seven of them firsthand, and many written by men of women of ability and reputation. For some, the confirmation had been a "feeling" or "spiritual witness" that they had felt during one of those long meetings of August 8 or in the days that came later. This version often used the word *mantle* to describe what they had seen—the symbolic cloak of the Old Testament prophet Elijah falling upon his successor Elisha. "It was evident to the Saints that the mantle of Joseph had fallen upon [Young]," said Wilford Woodruff less than a year later, and "the road that he pointed out could be seen so plainly."[113]

Within a decade, the Saints were building upon these memories and describing the event with many details. When Young first rose to speak, it was said, he had cleared his voice just like Joseph Smith used to do. Others said that Young's gestures and voice were Smith's, or perhaps it was the manner of Young's reasoning or the expression on his face that seemed so remarkable. Still others claimed to have seen the "tall, straight and portly form of the Prophet Joseph Smith." Young's body had grown larger before their spiritual eyes.[114] "If you had had your eyes shut, you would have thought it was the Prophet," said one man.[115] These memories were remarkable for their detail and their number, and they are hard to put aside.

Some skeptical historians have a different view. "When 8 August 1844 is stripped of emotional overlay, there is not a shred of irrefutable contemporary evidence to support the occurrence of a mystical event either in the morning or afternoon gatherings of that day," writes Van Wagoner. "A more likely scenario was that it was the force of Young's commanding presence, his well-timed arrival at the morning meeting, and perhaps a bit of theatrical mimicry."[116]

Young himself never made any special claims about his transfiguration beyond saying that on August 8 he had felt the Holy Ghost and the spirit of the prophets.[117] He recognized as well as any modern social scientist the power of memory to transform events and give memories details and meaning. He sat through several recitals of the event in later years without giving them his approval. It was enough for him, and many of his closest associates too, that the solemn assembly had worked God's will. Whatever else happened on that afternoon—the mysteries of spiritual feeling and experiences can only be narrated but not verified by the historian—the people had been drawn together and for the moment had assurance. "The church was of one h[e]art and one mind," Young said of the events, which, after all, was miracle enough.[118] Many years later, President Woodruff wrote that this highly celebrated day in August 1844 and Brigham Young's role in the succession became the "pivot" on which the rest of Latter-day Saint history turned—and he was right.[119]

NOTES

1. O. F. Berry, "The Mormon Settlement in Illinois," in *Papers in Illinois History and Transactions: Illinois State Historical Society* (Springville, IL: Illinois State Journal, 1906), 91.
2. Statement of George Edmunds, a longtime settler, in Berry, "Mormon Settlement in Illinois," 97. For want and hard economic times, see William Huntington, "Reminiscences and Journal, April 1841–August 1846," July 8 and 11, 1844, 16, Church History Library, The Church of Jesus Christ of Latter-day Saints, Salt Lake City.
3. Richard S. Van Wagoner, *Sidney Rigdon: A Portrait of Religious Excess* (Salt Lake City: Signature Books, 1994), ix.
4. "Veritas to James G. Bennett," *New York Herald*, February 19, 1842.
5. J. Wickliffe Rigdon, "Life of Sidney Rigdon," 178–79, Church History Library. *Speech of Elder Orson Hyde, Delivered Before the High Priest's Quorum, in Nauvoo, April 27th, 1845* (City of Joseph, IL: John Taylor, 1845), 27.

6. *Latter Day Saints' Messenger and Advocate* (Pittsburgh), December 6, 1844, 4, in Richard S. Van Wagoner, "The Making of a Mormon Myth: The 1844 Transfiguration of Brigham Young," *Dialogue* 28, no. 4 (Winter 1995): 4.
7. *Manuscript History of Brigham Young, 1801–1844*, comp. Elden Jay Watson (Salt Lake City: by the compiler, 1969), 165; D. Michael Quinn, *The Mormon Hierarchy: Origins of Power* (Salt Lake City: Signature Books, 1994), 119, 145; Glen M. Leonard, *Nauvoo: A Place of Peace, A People of Promise* (Salt Lake City: Deseret Book; Provo, UT: Brigham Young University Press, 2002), 339; Joseph Smith, *History of the Church of Jesus Christ of Latter-day Saints* (Salt Lake City: Deseret Book, 1957), 6:325, 335–40.
8. Quinn, *The Mormon Hierarchy*, 119, 145; see also Leonard, *Nauvoo*, 339.
9. Willard Richards, statement, in Church Historian's Office, History of the Church, July 2, 1844, 7:249, Church History Library, also found in *Selected Collections from the Archives of The Church of Jesus Christ of Latter-day Saints*, http://ldsarch.lib.byu.edu/CD%20Volume%201/Disc1/v1/seg13.htm; Willard Richards, certificate, about July 2, 1844, Willard Richards Papers, Church History Library, also found in *Selected Collections from the Archives*, http://ldsarch.lib.byu.edu/CD%20Volume%201/Disc31/MS 1490/b3f1-14/seg5.htm.
10. Jedediah M. Grant, *A Collection of Facts, Relative to the Course Taken by Elder Sidney Rigdon . . .* (Philadelphia: Brown, Bicking & Guilbert, 1844), 16.
11. *Speech of Elder Orson Hyde*, 11.
12. Grant, *Collection of Facts*, 17.
13. Church Historian's Office, General Church Minutes, September 8, 1844, Church History Library, also found in *Selected Collections from the Archives*, http://ldsarch.lib.byu.edu/CD%20Volume%201/Disc18/CR%20100%20318/b1f1-38/seg13.htm.
14. Church Historian's Office, General Church Minutes, September 8, 1844.
15. David B. Clark, "Sidney Rigdon's Rights of Succession," *Restoration*, April 6, 1987, 9.
16. Van Wagoner, "Making of a Mormon Myth," 5; see also Andrew F. Ehat, "Joseph Smith's Introduction of Temple Ordinances and the 1844 Mormon Succession Question" (master's thesis, Brigham Young University, 1982), 197.

17. Church Historian's Office, General Church Minutes, September 8, 1844.
18. Church Historian's Office, General Church Minutes, September 8, 1844; *Speech of Elder Orson Hyde*, 11–12.
19. Church Historian's Office, History of the Church, August 4, 1844, 7: addenda, p. 10; also found in *Selected Collections from the Archives*, http://ldsarch.lib.byu.edu/CD%20Volume%201/Disc1/v7/seg17.htm.
20. Church Historian's Office, History of the Church, August 4, 1844, 7: addenda, p. 10.
21. William Clayton, *An Intimate Chronicle: The Journals of William Clayton*, ed. George D. Smith (Salt Lake City: Signature Books in association with Smith Research Associates, 1991), 140; Huntington, "Reminiscences and Journal," July 14 to August 4, 1844, 17–18.
22. Notice, *Times and Seasons*, June 1, 1841, 431.
23. Huntington, "Reminiscences and Journal," July 8 and 11, 1844, and July 14 to August 1, 1844, 16–18.
24. Church Historian's Office, General Church Minutes, September 8, 1844; *Speech of Elder Orson Hyde*, 12–13.
25. Clayton, *Intimate Chronicle*, 140.
26. Church Historian's Office, History of the Church, August 5, 1844, 7:294, also found in *Selected Collections from the Archives*, http://ldsarch.lib.byu.edu/CD%20Volume%201/Disc1/v7/seg16.htm.
27. Church Historian's Office, History of the Church, August 5, 1844, 7: addenda, p. 10.
28. Clayton, *Intimate Chronicle*, 140.
29. Church Historian's Office, History of the Church, August 5, 1844, 7:294.
30. Church Historian's Office, General Church Minutes, April 6, 1844, also found in *Selected Collections from the Archives*, http://ldsarch.lib.byu.edu/CD%20Volume%201/Disc18/CR%20100%20318/b1f1-38/seg10.htm.
31. Wilford Woodruff, journal, August 6, 1844, Wilford Woodruff Journal and Papers, 1831–1898, Church History Library.
32. Woodruff, journal, July 30, 1844.

33. Church Historian's Office, General Church Minutes, August 3, 1844, 7:293, also found in *Selected Collections from the Archives*, http://ldsarch.lib.byu.edu/CD%20Volume%201/Disc1/v7/seg15.htm.
34. Woodruff, journal, August 6, 1844.
35. *Manuscript History of Brigham Young*, May 21, 1844, to June 30, 1844, 167–69.
36. *Manuscript History of Brigham Young*, May 10 and 15, 1844, 165.
37. Brigham Young to Mary Ann Young, June 12, 1844, original in possession of Dr. Wade Stephens, Bradenton, Florida, in Dean C. Jessee, "Brigham Young's Family: Part I, 1824–1845," *BYU Studies* 18, no. 3 (Spring 1978): 326.
38. Brigham Young to Willard Richards, July 8, 1844, Willard Richards Papers, Church History Library, also found in *Selected Collections from the Archives*, http://ldsarch.lib.byu.edu/CD%20Volume%201/Disc31/MS%201490/b3f15-23/seg29.htm.
39. Woodruff, journal, July 1, 1844.
40. Brigham Young to Willard Richards, July 8, 1844; spelling and punctuation standardized.
41. Joseph Smith, *History of the Church of Jesus Christ of Latter-day Saints*, ed. B. H. Roberts, 2nd ed. rev. (Salt Lake City: Deseret Book, 1957), 6:486–87, 519.
42. *Manuscript History of Brigham Young*, July 9, 1844, 170.
43. Church Historian's Office, History of the Church, August 14, 1844, 7:266–67; Brigham Young, journal, July 14, 1844, Brigham Young Office Files, 1832–1878, Church History Library; Journal History of The Church of Jesus Christ of Latter-day Saints, July 9 and 14, 1844, Church History Library.
44. Church Historian's Office, General Church Minutes, February 12, 1849, also found in *Selected Collections from the Archives*, http://ldsarch.lib.byu.edu/CD%20Volume%201/Disc18/CR%20100%20318/b2f1-20/seg12.htm; *Manuscript History of Brigham Young*, July 16, 1844, 170–71; Church Historian's Office, History of the Church, July 16, 1844, 272–73, also found in *Selected Collections of the Archives*, http://ldsarch.lib.byu.edu/CD%20Volume%201/Disc1/v7/seg14.htm, also Church Historian's Office, journal, June 22, 1863, 27:81–82, Church History Library, also found in *Selected Collections from the Archives*, http://ldsarch.lib.byu.edu/CD%20Volume%201/Disc17/b3v26-27/seg55.htm.

45. Brigham Young, "Remarks Before a Family Gathering," December 25, 1857, Brigham Young Papers, Church History Library.
46. Declaration of the Twelve, about 1844, in "The Work of God Rolls Forward," http://josephsmith.net/josephsmith/v/index.jsp?vgnextoid=e8b5fe1347df1010Vgn VCM1000001f5e340aRCRD&vgnextfmt=tab3; spelling standardized.
47. Declaration of the Twelve, about 1844; see also Church Historian's Office, General Church Minutes, September 8, 1844.
48. Brigham Young, discourse, October 7, 1866, in Brigham Young, *The Complete Discourses of Brigham Young, Volume 4: 1862–1867*, ed. Richard S. Van Wagoner (Salt Lake City: Smith-Pettit Foundation, 2009), 4:2379.
49. Samuel W. Richards to Franklin D. Richards, August 23, 1844, quoting Elder Orson Hyde, Church History Library.
50. Orson Hyde, in *Journal of Discourses* (London: Latter-day Saints' Book Depot, 1854–86), 13:180; Wilford Woodruff, in *Journal of Discourses*, 13:164. Andrew F. Ehat summarizes, "The full meaning of this meeting [when the last charge was given] at first escaped all those who attended it and only after the Martyrdom was it appreciated" ("Joseph Smith's Introduction of Temple Ordinances," 96).
51. Church Historian's Office, General Church Minutes, December 5, 1847; see also Brigham Young to Orson Spencer, January 23, 1848, Brigham Young Papers. Describing the establishment of the First Presidency consisting of Young, Kimball, and Richards, Young wrote, "Nothing more has been done to day than what I knew would be done when Joseph died."
52. B. H. Roberts, *Comprehensive History of the Church*, 6 vols. (Salt Lake City: Deseret News, 1930), 2:416; see also Doctrine and Covenants 20:65.
53. Woodruff, journal, July 17, 1844.
54. Journal History, July 18, 1844, quoting the *Prophet*.
55. Woodruff, journal, July 18, 1844.
56. Church Historian's Office, History of the Church, August 6, 1844, 7: addenda, p. 10. Examples of this correspondence may be found in the Willard Richards Papers, also found in *Selected Collections from the Archives*, http://ldsarch.lib.byu.edu/CD%20Volume%201/Disc31/MS 1490/contents.htm.

57. General Church Recorder, Far West and Nauvoo Elders' Certificates, Church History Library; emphasis added. Smith, *History of the Church*, 7:212–13.
58. Clayton, *Intimate Chronicle*, 137.
59. Clayton, *Intimate Chronicle*, 137–39.
60. Clayton, *Intimate Chronicle*, 139; Ehat, "Joseph Smith's Introduction of Temple Ordinances," 13.
61. James B. Allen, "One Man's Nauvoo: William Clayton's Experience in Mormon Illinois," *Journal of Mormon History* 6 (1979): 57–58n57.
62. Leonard, *Nauvoo*, 428.
63. Ronald K. Esplin, "Joseph, Brigham and the Twelve: A Succession of Continuity," *BYU Studies* 21, no. 3 (Summer 1981): 304–6.
64. The topic of the Council of Fifty has elicited much scholarly attention. The authoritative secondary sources are Klaus J. Hansen, *Quest for Empire: The Political Kingdom of God and the Council of Fifty in Mormon History* (East Lansing, MI: Michigan State University Press, 1967); D. Michael Quinn, "The Council of Fifty and its Members, 1844 to 1845," *BYU Studies* 20, no. 2 (Winter 1980): 163–97; and Quinn, *Mormon Hierarchy*, especially 120–34, 137–41, and 196–97.
65. Allen, "One Man's Nauvoo," 47; Devery S. Anderson and Gary James Bergera, eds., *Joseph Smith's Quorum of the Anointed, 1842–1845: A Documentary History* (Salt Lake City: Signature Books, 2005), 80–82.
66. Clayton, *Intimate Chronicle*, 137–39.
67. Quinn, "Meetings and Initiations of the Anointed Quorum (Holy Order), 1842–45," appendix 4, in *Mormon Hierarchy*, 491–519; Anderson and Bergera, eds., *Joseph Smith's Quorum of the Anointed*, 80–82.
68. Allen, "One Man's Nauvoo," 47, 48n29.
69. Church Historian's Office, General Church Minutes, October 8, 1848, also found in *Selected Collections from the Archives*, http://ldsarch.lib.byu.edu/CD%20Volume%201/Disc18/CR%20100%20318/b2f1-20/seg10.htm.
70. This is the argument of Esplin, in "Joseph, Brigham and the Twelve," 303.
71. Heber C. Kimball to Parley P. Pratt, June 17, 1842, Parley P. Pratt Papers, Church History Library.

72. Hyde, in *Journal of Discourses*, 13:180; Ehat, "Joseph Smith's Introduction of Temple Ordinances," 93.
73. In *Mormon Hierarchy*, 170, Quinn suggested that 5 percent of the Saints knew about these practices.
74. Todd Compton, foreword, in Anderson and Bergera, *Joseph Smith's Quorum of the the Anointed*, ix–xii.
75. Clayton, *Intimate Chronicle*, 138.
76. Quinn, *Mormon Hierarchy*, 145–48.
77. Clayton, *Intimate Chronicle*, 141.
78. Woodruff, journal, August 7, 1844.
79. Clayton, *Intimate Chronicle*, 141. The vision that Rigdon mentions is recorded in Doctrine and Covenants 76.
80. Woodruff, journal, August 7, 1844.
81. Clayton, *Intimate Chronicle*, 141.
82. Ehat, "Joseph Smith's Introduction of Temple Ordinances," 112–13, 118, 121, 147.
83. Church Historian's Office, General Church Minutes, December 5, 1847.
84. Church Historian's Office, General Church Minutes, December 5, 1847.
85. Helen Mar Whitney, "Scenes in Nauvoo after the Martyrdom of the Prophet and Patriarch," *Woman's Exponent*, February 1, 1883, 130. Van Wagoner notes that the multitude was of more than five thousand Saints ("Making of a Mormon Myth," 9).
86. Van Wagoner, "Making of a Mormon Myth," 9.
87. *Speech of Elder Orson Hyde*, 13–14. See also Van Wagoner, "Making of a Mormon Myth," 9.
88. Church Historian's Office, General Church Minutes, December 5, 1847.
89. Jacob Hamblin statement as cited in Lynne Watkins Jorgensen and *BYU Studies* staff, "The Mantle of the Prophet Joseph Passes to Brother Brigham: A Collective Spiritual Witness," *BYU Studies* 36, no. 4 (1996–97): 162.
90. Joseph Fielding, in Andrew F. Ehat, "'They Might Have Known That He Was Not a Fallen Prophet': The Nauvoo Journal of Joseph Fielding," *BYU Studies* 19, no. 2 (Winter 1979): 155.
91. Church Historian's Office, General Church Minutes, October 8, 1848.

92. Church Historian's Office, General Church Minutes, December 5, 1847.
93. Woodruff, journal, August 8, 1844.
94. Quinn, *Mormon Hierarchy*, 143–85.
95. James Blakesley to Jacob Scott, August 16, 1844, in Heman C. Smith, "Succession in the Presidency," *Journal of History* 2, no. 1 (January 1909): 3–4. Blakesley wrote before learning of the meetings on August 8.
96. Ezra Taft Benson, "A Brief History of Ezra Taft Benson Written by Himself," in Church Historian's Office, Histories of the Twelve, 1856–1858, Church History Library.
97. These memories are respectively those of George Romney and Maria Wealthy Wilcox, as well as Johnson. They are printed in Jorgensen and *BYU Studies* staff, "Mantle of the Prophet," 174, 178, and 167.
98. Clayton, *Intimate Chronicle*, 142.
99. Church Historian's Office, General Church Minutes, August 8, 1844, also found in *Selected Collections from the Archives*, http://ldsarch.lib.byu.edu/CD%20Volume%201/Disc18/CR%20100%20318/b1f1-38/seg12.htm. There are four copies of proceedings, and each has unique details.
100. In addition to the four summaries of the August 8 afternoon meeting in the Church History Library, Wilford Woodruff left an account in his diary. My narrative is a reconstruction based upon these five sources.
101. Huntington, "Reminiscences and Journal," August 8, 1844, 18.
102. Brigham Young, journal, August 8, 1844, Church History Library. While parts of the diary were written by secretaries, these sentences, significantly, were written in Young's own hand. See Dean C. Jessee, "The Writings of Brigham Young," *Western Historical Quarterly* 4, no. 3 (July 1873): 284.
103. H. W. Mills, "De Tal Palo Tal Astilla," *Historical Society of Southern California: Annual Publications* 10, no. 3 (1917): 135.
104. William Huntington, "Reminiscences and Journal," July 8 and 14, and August 4, 1844, 17–18.
105. B. H. Roberts, *History of the Church of Jesus Christ of Latter-day Saints, Period 2: Apostolic Interregnum*, 2nd ed. rev. (Salt Lake City: Deseret Book, 1932), 7:234n.
106. Quinn, *Mormon Hierarchy*, 156–60.

107. Esplin, "Joseph, Brigham and the Twelve," 308–12.
108. Van Wagoner, *Sidney Rigdon*, viii.
109. Joseph Smith to W. W. Phelps, July 31, 1832, *Personal Writings of Joseph Smith*, ed. Dean C. Jessee, rev. ed. (Salt Lake City and Provo, UT: Deseret Book and Brigham Young University Press, 2002), 273.
110. Van Wagoner, *Sidney Rigdon*, 323–24.
111. Church Historian's Office, General Church Minutes, December 25, 1857.
112. Cited in Jorgensen and *BYU Studies* staff, "Mantle of the Prophet," 135.
113. Wilford Woodruff, "To the Officers and Members," *Millennial Star*, February 1845, 138.
114. Jorgensen and *BYU Studies* staff, "Mantle of the Prophet," 167. For more accounts of the mantle of Joseph, see Jorgensen's full article.
115. Rachel Ridgeway Ivins, cited in Jorgensen and *BYU Studies* staff, "Mantle of the Prophet Joseph," 167.
116. Van Wagoner, "Making of a Mormon Myth," 21; see also Reid L. Harper, "The Mantle of Joseph: Creation of a Mormon Miracle," *Journal of Mormon History* 22, no. 1 (Fall 1996): 35–71.
117. Brigham Young, journal, August 8, 1844, Church History Library.
118. Sermon, December 25, 1847, Church minutes.
119. Wilford Woodruff, in *Journal of Discourses*, 15:81.

Fred E. Woods

9

Men in Motion: Administering and Organizing the Gathering

Shortly after the restored Church of Jesus Christ was officially established, the Prophet Joseph Smith received a revelation that focused on the doctrine of gathering Israel in modern times: "And ye are called to bring to pass the gathering of mine elect; for mine elect hear my voice and harden not their hearts; wherefore the decree hath gone forth from the Father that they shall be gathered in unto one place upon the face of this land, to prepare their hearts and be prepared in all things against the day when tribulation and desolation are sent forth upon the wicked" (D&C 29:7–8).

A decade later, in 1840, thousands of European converts began to flow to America to join the body of Saints gathering in Nauvoo. Less than a year after the first vessel of Latter-day Saint British converts embarked for America,[1] the Quorum of the Twelve made a key

---

Fred E. Woods is a professor of Church history and doctrine at Brigham Young University.

decision that significantly aided the emigration process when they selected a man to serve in Liverpool as the first Latter-day Saint emigration agent. On April 5, 1841, Wilford Woodruff recorded that the Twelve "resolved that Elder Amos Fielding be appointed to superintend fitting out the Saints from Liverpool to America under the instructions of Elder [Parley] P. Pratt."[2] This same month, the Church periodical *Latter-day Saints' Millennial Star* published an "Epistle of the Twelve," which discussed the appointment and the advantages of having such a representative:

> We have found that there are so many "pick-pockets," and so many that will take every possible advantage of strangers, in Liverpool, that we have appointed Elder Amos Fielding, as agent of the church, to superintend the fitting out of Saints from Liverpool to America. Whatever information the Saints may want about the preparations for a voyage, they are advised to call on Elder Fielding, at Liverpool, as their first movement, when they arrive there as emigrants. There are some brethren who have felt themselves competent to do their own business in these matters, and rather despising the counsel of their friends, have been robbed and cheated out of nearly all they had. A word of caution to the wise is sufficient. It is also a great saving to go in companies, instead of going individually. First, a company can charter a vessel, so as to make the passage much cheaper than otherwise. Secondly, provisions can be purchased at wholesale for a company much cheaper than otherwise. Thirdly, this will avoid bad company on the passage. Fourthly, when a company arrives in New Orleans they can charter a steam-boat so as to reduce the passage near one-half. The measure will save some hundreds of pounds on each ship load. Fifthly, a man of experience can go as leader of each company, who will know how to avoid rogues and knaves.[3]

Regarding these agents, historian Craig S. Smith wrote, "The monumental efforts of the Church agents in implementing and achieving a

Men in Motion: Administering and Organizing the Gathering

successful Mormon emigration are generally not considered in most studies. Stories of the Mormon emigration typically focus on the faith, sacrifices, and hardships of the emigrants themselves." Smith further explains, "What is usually not examined is the tremendous amount of behind-the-scenes organizing, planning, and preparing required for a successful emigration."[4]

The focus of this paper, therefore, is to examine the pivotal role these agents played in concert with Church leaders. Under the inspired leadership of Joseph Smith and especially his able administrative successor Brigham Young, tens of thousands of foreign converts were successfully directed to Nauvoo (1840–46) and to the Great Basin (1847–77).[5] In addition, members of the Twelve and other local Church leaders were assigned duties pertaining to the gathering, and these leaders worked hand in hand with the appointed agents and, in some instances, as the agents themselves.

Among the many resources aiding Mormon migration was the *Millennial Star*, which served as an important tool in arranging for the transport of converts across the Atlantic during the latter half of the nineteenth century.[6] The first editor of the *Millennial Star*, Elder Parley P. Pratt, indicated in a prospectus issued May 27, 1840, that the purpose of the periodical was to spread the truth, gather Israel, and be as a star of light for the faithful to prepare for the Second Coming of Jesus Christ. This publication was established in Manchester in April 1840, two months before the first emigration of foreign converts from Liverpool. Just two years later, in April 1842, the *Star* began to be published from Liverpool, which had become headquarters for the British Mission.[7]

Within its pages, the *Star* created the feeling that the Second Coming was nigh at hand. The first article of the opening issue discussed the Millennium and reviewed the teachings of ancient prophets regarding the restoration and gathering of Israel in the last days.[8] This periodical not only stimulated a desire to gather; it also served as an essential instrument for Church leaders and agents in providing a continual stream of information and direction to the passing migrants. Even the departure times of the chartered vessels were published in various editions of the *Star*.

Very detailed guidance was regularly provided on each aspect of the emigrants' journey to Zion. For example, in August 1841, the *Star* published an article titled "Information to Emigrants." After furnishing several pages of general information regarding immigration to North America, the following practical counsel guided the emigrants on what they should take on their voyage: "Those intending to emigrate will do well to take no furniture with them except the necessary articles of beds, bedding, wearing apparel, pots, cooking utensils, &c., which will come in useful both on the ship and on the steam-boat, and after they arrive. . . . Every thing which is not designed for use on the passage should be carefully packed in strong boxes or trunks."

Advice was also given on the best routes and travel costs, including specific guidelines for the purchase of tickets and the avoidance of extra lodging expenses:

> New Orleans is by far the cheapest route for emigrants to Illinois; and much more money may be saved by emigrating in large companies. . . . When all things are prepared, they can go immediately on board, and begin to arrange the berths, beds, provisions, &c., and avoid the expense of living a while in the town of Liverpool.
>
> Perhaps the passage money and provisions for each passenger from Liverpool to New Orleans will be not far from four pounds. Children under fourteen years of age, half-price; under one year nothing. . . .
>
> When the ship arrives in New Orleans the company will need to send their foreman, or leader, or committee, to charter a steam boat for Nauvoo or St. Louis, which will probably be from 15s. [shillings] to 25s. per head, and provisions to be purchased for about two weeks; so the whole passage money from Liverpool to Nauvoo will probable [sic] be from £5 to £7.[9]

Men in Motion: Administering and Organizing the Gathering

The *Millennial Star* also encouraged emigration with reports from those who had reached America. An article titled "Emigration" notes, "The news from the emigrants who sailed from this country last season, is so very encouraging that it will give a new impulse to the spirit of emigration."[10] Written instructions especially encouraged emigration to Nauvoo so that the Saints might build the temple and partake of its blessings.[11] British converts were also encouraged by the excellent organization and dependability of Church leaders, both at Liverpool and Nauvoo, and later at Salt Lake City, as well as at the frontier outfitting posts along the way.

Such excellence was not achieved without a price. Whether the agents dealt with transportation by land or by sea, there were always challenges to contend with. For example, one Mormon agent in Liverpool had this to say concerning his assignment: "There is much to do when a vessel is preparing to sail for some days; from ten to twenty emigrants coming to the office; one wants this and one wants that, and the third wants to know where he shall sleep all night, with a dozen or more women and children in the office to run over; one wants tin ware, another is short of cash and their children are hungry."[12]

Following the Nauvoo exodus of 1846, the Saints began to stream into the Salt Lake Valley instead of Nauvoo. As the Saints gathered to Utah, each emigration agent continued to provide valiant service, and the *Millennial Star* continued to offer instruction to emigrants:

> We beg to inform the Saints intending to emigrate, that we are now prepared to receive their applications for berths. Every application should be accompanied by the names, age, occupation, country where born, and £1 deposit for each one named, except for children under one year old. . . .
>
> Passengers must furnish their own beds and bedding, their cooking utensils, provision boxes, &c.
>
> Every person applying for a berth or berths should be careful to give their address very distinct, in order to insure the delivery of our answer to them by letter carriers.[13]

Such exemplary administration soon caught the eye of those who were not of the faith. A London newspaper correspondent reported that Mormon emigration agent Samuel W. Richards had been interviewed by the House of Commons concerning the agents' success in bringing Mormon converts across the Atlantic: "I heard a rather remarkable examination before a committee of the House of Commons. The witness was no other than the supreme authority in England of the Mormonites, and the subject upon which he was giving information was the mode in which the emigration to Utah, Great Salt Lake, is conducted. . . . There is one thing which . . . they [the Mormons] can do, viz., teach Christian shipowners how to send poor people decently, cheaply, and healthfully across the Atlantic."[14]

This promising system launched by the Prophet Joseph Smith was later buttressed by what may be referred to as an emigration revelation received by Brigham Young at Winter Quarters on January 14, 1847. Following the Nauvoo exodus, with thousands of Saints strung out across Iowa Territory, Young received "The Word and Will of the Lord concerning the Camp of Israel in their journeyings to the West" (D&C 136:1). Among other things, the Lord revealed that the Mormon companies were under covenant "to keep all the commandments" and to be organized with captains "under the direction of the Twelve Apostles" (D&C 136:2–3).

As Mormon Trail historian Richard E. Bennett has noted, this inspired document clearly emphasized the important doctrinal point that the gathering was to take place under apostolic supervision.[15] Further, those selected as captains (or others assigned to assist with migration matters) clearly understood their vital roles under the direction of the Twelve, and emigrants knew they were under covenant to obey. This emigration revelation provided not only a much-needed administrative map to guide the Mormon pioneers across the plains to the Salt Lake Valley but also a divine pattern of principles and promises for all segments of the journey, whether by sail, rail, or trail.

Apostles and prophets designated trail captains and later appointed emigration agents to ensure efficiency and safety. The general Church

Men in Motion: Administering and Organizing the Gathering

membership now benefited from a revelation that provided a model of migration from ports to outfitting posts or by tracks or trail. All along the journey—from the time converts left their native lands until their arrival in Zion—the Lord's inspired system was to be followed. This system was wisely administered under Brigham Young, the American Moses, for three decades. President Young's skill and concern regarding migration issues are manifest in hundreds of letters. Correspondence demonstrates that he kept a watchful eye on all aspects of the emigration business during his years as Church President. This carefulness is evident from a letter which President Young sent to his nephew Joseph W. Young, who had been assigned to be the emigration agent at the town of Wyoming, Nebraska, in 1864: "I trust you will always frankly and fully express to me your views upon any and every subject of importance in your official operations, for that gives me a chance to sanction or correct, as my judgement may direct."[16]

Although the system was inspired, sometimes challenges arose—for example, mail delivery was slow and took weeks or even months. William Gibson, who oversaw emigration as a local Church leader in St. Louis, reported the following in 1852:

> Fall I received a letter from S [Samuel] W Richards in Liverpool saying that there would be a large Emigration next spring & he would need from 300 to 500 waggons & he desired me [to] look around & find out where they could be got best & cheapest; the waggons before this, [they] had mostly come from Cincinnati[,] so I wrote there to find out their prices now & having got that I went around to all the wagon makers in St. Louis & round about it I found that the Cheapest, best & most reliable waggons were made by Mr. [Louis] Espenschied of St. Louis; they cost about ten dollars less each waggon than those from Cincinatti &, to judge from those we had received from there were much superior waggons; accordingly I wrote back to Br Richards but some how he delayed sending me on the final order for them, which in the end was the cause of the loss of several thousand dollars to the Emigration Fund.[17]

Even though those involved with the emigration operation were certainly dedicated, they were not perfect. A few instances arose in which those who administered the program may have used poor judgment, though this was certainly more the exception than the rule. Such seems to be the exception with the Willie and Martin handcart company tragedies, for which President Young publicly reproved two of his agents for allowing the Saints to cross the plains so late in the season.[18]

Another challenge in the effort to get Saints to Utah was cost. Thousands of Latter-day Saints who desired to come to Zion simply did not have the means to do so. To address this problem, the Church initiated the Perpetual Emigrating Fund (PEF) in 1849, a revolving loan system that transported nearly one-third of the nineteenth-century European emigrants to Utah.[19] This same year, the Church also launched the *Frontier Guardian* from Kanesville, Iowa, with Elder Orson Hyde as editor. Like the *Millennial Star* and other Church periodicals of the mid-nineteenth century, the *Frontier Guardian* provided advice for the migrant Saints and others heading west. At the conclusion of its first volume, the *Guardian* explained the purpose of the PEF in two separate articles written by the First Presidency (Brigham Young, Heber C. Kimball, and Willard Richards). The first, titled "Second General Epistle," specified that the PEF was created for the purpose of gathering the poor, "agreeably to our covenants in the [Nauvoo] Temple that we would never 'cease our exertions, by all the means and influence within our reach, till all the saints . . . should be located at some gathering place of the saints.'"[20] The second, a letter from the Presidency to Orson Hyde, noted, "The Funds are to be appropriated in the form of a loan, rather than a gift; and this will make the honest in heart rejoice, . . . while the lazy idlers, if any such there be, will find fault, and want every luxury furnished them for their journey, and in the end pay nothing."[21]

There is evidence that Church leaders and agents were often pressed financially in administering the migration program on both sides of the Atlantic. Such conditions required both practical experience as well as inspiration and sometimes unconventional methods. Such appears to be the case

Men in Motion: Administering and Organizing the Gathering

with Lucius Scovil, who served as an emigration agent in New Orleans. As the 1849 winter dragged on, Scovil grew a bit despondent as he considered his own financial circumstances as well as the poverty of the local Saints, some of whom were emigrants who needed funding to reach Zion. This undesirable condition was augmented by the fact that cholera had once again attacked the inhabitants of New Orleans.

Scovil recalled that on March 2, 1849, he meditated on the difficult conditions. While he pondered, he was impressed to go to Caliboose Square.[22] Further, he should walk to a nearby bookstore and buy a lottery ticket from a Frenchman employed there. Although he conceded "the thought was foreign to my natural feelings as anything could be," he explained:

> Yet I walked forward and 15 minutes later I found myself at the book store. when I entered the store I felt that I had been very familiar with the Frenchman at some previous time. I therefore inquired if he had lottery tickets for sale. He asked me who told me that he had lottery tickets for sale, as there was no lottery tickets for sale in Louisiana, it being contrary to law, "but," said he, "I have lottery tickets for sale and the drawing is tomorrow." He then spread out the tickets before me on the counter and I soon discovered a half ticket of the number I wanted, No. 9998. I asked him the price, and he said $2.50. I took the ticket and paid for it.

Ten days later, Scovil, on learning that he had won one hundred times his money, expressed gratitude to God that he had opened up the way for Scovil to perform his appointed task in New Orleans and advance the immigrants to St. Louis.[23]

Because of the high volume of British Saints passing through St. Louis, it was deemed necessary to establish temporary lodging for these Saints. Minutes from a meeting held in the spring of 1849 indicate that many of the brethren "urged the propriety of procuring some place, as a rendezvous for the saints emigrating from Europe so that the Poor might have some place to put up at until they would be enabled to get Houses. [It] was recommended that the Mound House if Possible be procured for the purpose."[24] The following month, Nathaniel H. Felt, the local Church leader who oversaw emigration, suggested that another building be rented, and eventually the Concert Hall in St. Louis was leased for the price of twenty-five dollars per year.[25]

St. Louis Mormon emigration agents like Felt were diligent in attending to the emigrants' various needs, which ranged from employment and housing to arranging vessels for steamboat travel, as well as preaching the importance of the gathering. At the close of 1849, Felt spoke on this theme, urging the Saints to move to Salt Lake City as soon as possible. He further desired that the local branch leaders "let this idea go forth, that all gather up, if it be only to the Bluffs [Council Bluffs, Iowa]." Just two months later, Felt advised the Saints who had temporarily congregated in St. Louis to "go to the Valley go to the Bluff. . . . Go; Go; as far as you can."[26]

The many who were unable to go because of economic hardship remained in St. Louis for several months or even years.[27] Thus, in April 1854, President Young and other Church leaders designated St. Louis as a location where the "Saints might gather with approbation who were unable to go directly through to Utah."[28] Apostle Erastus Snow was chosen to journey to St. Louis, organize a stake, preside over the region, and oversee general emigration matters in Iowa and Missouri.

Before his arrival, Elder Snow already had plans to establish and edit a Latter-day Saint periodical, which he called the *St. Louis Luminary*.[29] As with the *Millennial Star* and the *Frontier Guardian*, Elder Snow intended that the paper be used as an emigration guide of sorts for the many scattered Saints, offering news from the Valley, support, and instruction.[30] Just one month after the organization of the St. Louis Stake, he published a cry for assistance in the December 2, 1854, issue of the *Luminary*, explaining, "Soon we will have a great many of our foreign emigration here, and some of them perhaps destitute. I wish . . . every man in Israel . . . consider themselves a vigilance committee, to keep their eyes and ears open, and learn of every opening and avenue by which they can throw their employment in the hands of those who stand in need."[31]

Moreover, Elder Snow gave instructions to the European converts and Eastern States Mormon emigrants who planned to stop just briefly in St. Louis before continuing forward to the Salt Lake Valley. In an article titled "Emigrants for Utah," he counseled:

> My assent will not be given for any Saint to leave the Missouri River, unless so organized in a company of at least fifty effectual *well armed* men, and that too under the command of a man appointed by me; one who will carry out my instruction. . . .
>
> Choice wagons made to order and delivered at the point of outfit, with bows, projections, &c., will be about $78, without projections, $75. Oxen, with yokes and chains, from $70 to $85 per yoke; cows from $16 to $25 each.
>
> My experience, derived by six journeys over the plains enables me to know what kind of teams and outfits are wanted for the plains.[32]

Yet the number of Mormons coming up the Mississippi, passing through St. Louis, and heading west on the Missouri River would soon be curtailed when the port of arrival for incoming foreign converts changed from New Orleans to the East Coast as a result of a letter written in 1854 by President Young to Elder Franklin D. Richards, who then presided over emigration from Liverpool. Because of the threat of diseases such as cholera, President Young directed Elder Richards as follows: "You are aware of the sickness liable to assail our unacclimated brethren on the Mississippi river, hence I wish you to ship no more to New Orleans, but ship to Philadelphia, Boston, and New York, giving preference in the order named."[33]

In 1855, the Saints began using eastern ports and soon found that New York was the best choice, thanks to the Castle Garden Immigration Depot, which opened that same year. The European converts also benefitted from the Latter-day Saint emigration agents stationed in New York, who arranged temporary employment or lodging for emigrants.[34] The first New York agent appointed by President Young was Elder John Taylor, who oversaw emigration matters and presided over the Eastern States Mission. Elder Richards was stationed in Liverpool, with stewardship over Latter-day Saints embarking for America as well as over all issues pertaining to the Saints in Europe. Each man was heavily involved in gathering the Saints to Zion and was in contact with the other as well as with President Young.

In a letter, Elder Taylor reminded Elder Richards of the emigration instructions that President Young and his counselors had previously sent which had been published in two Latter-day Saint periodicals: the *Mormon*, published in New York and edited by Elder Taylor, and the *St. Louis Luminary*.[35]

> Whenever you ship a company, whether it be small or large, be careful to forward to Elder John Taylor, at New York City, a correct list of the names of the persons in each company with their occupation and approximate amount of property or means, & forward it in season for Elder John Taylor to receive it before the company arrive in port, that he may be so advised as to be able to meet them, or appoint some proper person to do so & counsel them immediately on landing as to the best course for each and all in every company to pursue; viz, whether to tarry for a season, to work in the place, or immediate neighbourhood of their landing or to proceed.[36]

Such a superior emigrant location system was evident by both land and sea,[37] as is readily apparent in the manner in which Elder Taylor used the *Mormon* to assist these European converts upon their arrival on the Eastern Seaboard. In its first issue, dated February 17, 1855, Elder Taylor articulated that a primary purpose of the new periodical was "to impart the latest information relative to the best course to be pursued by Emigrants on their arrival in Boston, New York and Philadelphia."[38]

Men in Motion: Administering and Organizing the Gathering

Besides serving as a directory for routing emigrants west, the *Mormon* included dates of port arrivals as well as employment opportunities for those who needed to raise money to continue their journey to the Salt Lake Valley. Two weeks after the establishment of the *Mormon*, local missionaries received the following instruction from Elder Taylor via this newspaper: "As there will shortly be many of our brethren here from Europe who will be in want of employment, in various trades and occupations, you are requested to send to this office, directions whereby we may know where to send those that are in need of employment, on their arrival in this country."[39]

Though the *Mormon* was short lived,[40] the system of using a Latter-day Saint periodical to find much-needed jobs for the incoming European immigrants proved most effective. For example, the *Mormon* reported an abundance of mining jobs in a local area.[41] In a letter to Church headquarters, Elder Taylor soon reported, "We have been doing what we could lately in assisting the emigrating operations, and not withstanding the bad times, with the united efforts of the brethren, we have succeeded in obtaining work for all, with very few exceptions, and they are provided for by the others." Further, "I am in hopes we shall be as successfull with the remainder; You will see by the published lists, in the 'Mormon' the names of those coming."[42] Less than two months later, Elder Taylor informed President Young that "although 30,000 persons have been out of work in New York and the same proportion in Phila[delphia], yet our brethren I believe have all got employment."[43]

For the incoming who could not find employment, Elder Taylor devised a plan to assist them in their stranded condition on the East Coast. In a letter to President Young dated February 20, 1856, Elder Taylor remarked, "We have had pretty hard times here with many poor saints here; but shall see it through. I am raising a loan fund something after the order of the P.E.F. to be kept for the purpose of assisting those that are poor untill they get employment, & then to be returned."[44]

Elder Taylor continued to provide direction and aid to improve conditions for the migrant Saints.[45] In his multifaceted assignment and in all his plans and demands for sail, rail, and trail travel, Elder Taylor was also assisted in New York by his son George and other elders. One elder of particular note was Nathaniel H. Felt, who, as previously noted, assisted with emigration in St. Louis. Felt, an experienced, wealthy tailor from Salem, Massachusetts, eased the heavy responsibilities pouring into Elder Taylor's New York office.[46] Elder Taylor informed President Young, "Br. Felt & my son George are with me, as I found their assistance absolutely necessary. They are all well & doing well."[47]

Elder Taylor regularly corresponded with President Young, whose counsel he valued and implemented.[48] For example, an extract from a letter written to President Young in April 1855 gives a glimpse at Elder Taylor's concerted efforts to assist in the emigration process. Having just informed the President that the ship *Siddons* had not yet arrived in Philadelphia, Elder Taylor offered the following plan for the remaining 1855 season of emigrant rail travel: "Concerning emigration I have made all the enquiries I can & am decidedly of the opinion that the best rout[e] at present will be by Burlington Iowa to which place a railroad goes direct."[49]

Other New York Mormon agents succeeded Elder Taylor, and they likewise made suggestions to improve the process of gathering Saints to the Salt Lake Valley. For example, Mormon emigration from the East Coast was redirected through Quincy, Illinois, thanks to a letter written to President Young by George Q. Cannon, then serving as an agent in New York on the eve of the 1859 migration season. After Cannon had made a trip from the East to St. Louis, he discovered that it was a more economical and better route to channel the gathering Saints through Quincy to Florence, Nebraska, rather than to send them to Iowa City on the Chicago and Rock Island Railroad, which had been the established route since this railroad reached Iowa City in the spring of 1856.[50]

In addition, William C. Staines, another New York agent, acted faithfully in this position from 1867 until his death in 1881. Notwithstanding, Staines faced the same challenges as did other agents who offered advice as they observed thousands of incoming emigrants. For example, in a letter to

Men in Motion: Administering and Organizing the Gathering

Albert Carrington in England, Staines advised, "If any Saints emigrate to New York without means to go to Utah, they should be competent to take care of themselves, and not rely upon us, as I have not means to further them with. Their luggage should not be mixed up on the ship with that of those who are going through to Utah."[51]

During his tenure of service, Brother Staines "made regular annual trips between Salt Lake City and New York, his duties requiring his presence in the East during the spring, summer, and fall, after which he would return to spend the winter with his family and friends in Utah."[52] In the spring of 1871, before his annual departure to the East, he was given a special blessing under the hands of Lorenzo Snow, Franklin D. Richards, and Wilford Woodruff, who acted as voice. Brother Staines was commended and received the following promises:

> You shall be greatly blessed in the emigration, in laboring for the benefit of your brethren and sisters. The angels will be round about you; you shall be preserved while attending to this mission, and the Lord will open your way in many respects. Whenever you come to a position where all may seem dark, you shall see your way open up before you. Whenever danger shall lie in your path, whether upon rail-roads or else-where, the Spirit of God shall reveal unto you that danger and you shall escape the same. Whenever it shall be right to make contacts for the emigration it shall be clearly made known to your mind. Your labors will be accepted of the Lord God of Israel, and you shall be preserved by His power.[53]

In the spring of 1881, James H. Hart was set apart by now-President John Taylor as emigration agent at New York City to replace Staines. Hart kept President Taylor informed of his labors through his seven-year tenure, as evidenced by sixty-two letters he wrote to the president. During the years Hart served as an agent, he commuted back and forth from Bloomington, Idaho, between emigration seasons. This was apparently necessary as he served as first counselor to William Budge in the Bear Lake Stake presidency and spent two years as a prosecuting attorney.[54] Hart had previous experience working with emigration matters in St. Louis, where he had served as president of the St. Louis Stake from 1855 to 1857.[55] His earlier experience as a lawyer—coupled with his work as a farmer, eight years as a postmaster, and three terms in the Idaho Territorial Legislature—provided a wealth of experience for his assignment on the East Coast.[56]

Upon arrival at New York City, and continually thereafter, Brother Hart was interviewed by newspaper reporters. One of his grandsons, Edward L. Hart, noted, "He was, in that metropolis, the visible Mormon—the genuine specimen that could be seen and interviewed."[57] Besides his challenge of facing the media and thousands of passing emigrants, James Hart also had to deal with continual correspondence from Church members, a task that must have kept him very busy and at times tried his patience. Such correspondence included the following letter sent by James H. Johnson on July 3, 1883: "Dear Brother I have sent you $37 dollars for you to purchase my ticket from Chicago to Salt Lake City Utah. I would like to leave St. Catherine's on the 6 or 7 that is next Friday or Saturday. I will Saturday the 7 of July. Please and rite back how to go on, yours very truly."[58]

Three months later an engaging request from a Brother Scofield inquired, "Will you be kind enough to hand the enclosed seven dollars to Sister Sarah Woodenden or any of her family who are emigrants (on the next company) from Brighouse Yorkshire and you will confer a great favor. P.S. They are my relatives."[59]

In addition to such correspondence, Brother Hart also effectively handled important decisions that affected emigration on a much broader scale. One of the most notable changes was his suggestion that the Saints no longer use the New York trains to travel west. In light of the city emigration procedures, costs, and the passage of the Interstate Railway Act of 1887, Hart suggested that the Church transport Latter-day Saint emigrants from New York to Norfolk, Virginia, by ship and then proceed through the port of Norfolk west on Norfolk's railroads. This suggestion was implemented, and over five thousand converts traveled west through Norfolk to Utah between 1887 and 1890.[60]

As the nineteenth century came to a close, the Mormon gathering, which once flowed at a rapid rate, slowed to a trickle. Antipolygamy laws had an impact, and in 1887 the Edmunds-Tucker Act, in effect, halted the Perpetual Emigrating Fund. Yet by this time, tens of thousands of European converts had been successfully transported to Zion through the wise guidance of Church leaders and a number of dedicated Mormon agents who provided timely advice. These men in motion had propelled the Church forward into the twentieth century and left a great legacy of inspired, consecrated priesthood service.

APPENDIX: NINETEENTH-CENTURY PRESIDENTS OF THE BRITISH MISSION[61]

President	From	To
Heber C. Kimball	July 1837	April 1838
Joseph Fielding	April 1838	July 1840
Brigham Young	July 1840	April 1841
Parley P. Pratt	April 1841	October 1842
Thomas Ward	October 1842	November 1843
Reuben Hedlock	November 1843	February 1845
Wilford Woodruff	February 1845	October 1846
Orson Hyde	October 1846	January 1847
Franklin D. Richards	January 1847	February 1847
Orson Spencer	February 1847	August 1848
Orson Pratt	August 1848	January 1851
Franklin D. Richards	January 1851	May 1852
Samuel W. Richards	May 1852	June 1854
Franklin D. Richards	June 1854	August 1856
Orson Pratt	August 1856	October 1857
Samuel W. Richards	October 1857	March 1858
Asa Calkin	March 1858	May 1860

President	From	To
Nathaniel V. Jones	May 1860	August 1860
Amasa M. Lyman and Charles C. Rich	August 1860	May 1862
George Q. Cannon	May 1862	August 1864
Daniel H. Wells	August 1864	August 1865
Brigham Young Jr.	August 1865	June 1867
Franklin D. Richards	June 1867	September 1868
Albert Carrington	September 1868	June 1870
Horace S. Eldredge	June 1870	June 1871
Albert Carrington	June 1871	October 1873
Lester J. Herrick	October 1873	March 1874
Joseph F. Smith	March 1874	September 1875
Albert Carrington	September 1875	June 1877
Joseph F. Smith	June 1877	July 1878
William Budge	July 1878	November 1880
Albert Carrington	November 1880	November 1882
John Henry Smith	November 1882	January 1885
Daniel H. Wells	January 1885	August 1887
George Teasdale	August 1887	October 1890
Brigham Young Jr.	October 1890	June 1893
Alfred Solomon	pro tem	
Anthon H. Lund	June 1893	July 1896
Rulon S. Wells	July 1896	December 1898
Platt D. Lyman	November 1898	May 1901

NOTES

1. The British Saints launched their first maritime emigration to Nauvoo, Illinois (via New York), with the voyage of the *Britannia* on June 6, 1840, with English convert John Moon leading a group of forty Saints from the port of Liverpool. Joseph Smith, *History of the Church of Jesus Christ of Latter-day Saints*, ed. B. H.

Roberts, 2nd ed. rev. (Salt Lake City: Deseret Book, 1966), 134. This maiden voyage ended in New York. The migrants then traveled by rail and steamboat to Nauvoo. This trip was the first of thirty-four chartered voyages to Nauvoo. In addition, at least thirteen non-chartered Latter-day Saint voyages consisted of small groups of families or individuals. For a list of each voyage and the story of their maritime journey, see Fred E. Woods, *Gathering to Nauvoo* (American Fork, UT: Covenant Communications, 2002).

2. *Wilford Woodruff's Journal, 1833–1898 Typescript*, ed. Scott G. Kenney (Midvale, UT: Signature Books, 1983–85), 2:79. Parley P. Pratt was then serving as the president of the British Mission. With the exception of the first British Mission president (Heber C. Kimball, 1837–38), each of the presidents had the ultimate responsibility to oversee the emigration of European converts bound for America, which commenced in 1840. Church agents worked under the direction of and in concert with each president, as in the case of Amos Fielding and President Pratt. For example, in the *Autobiography of Parley P. Pratt*, ed. Parley P. Pratt Jr., 3rd ed. (Salt Lake City: Deseret Book, 1938), 315, Pratt notes, "In the month of September, 1841, Brother Amos Fielding and myself chartered a large new ship called the 'Tyrean' . . . for New Orleans." See also appendix for a list of each of the British Mission presidents during the nineteenth century.

3. "Epistle of the Twelve," *Millennial Star*, April 1841, 311.

4. Craig S. Smith, "Wyoming, Nebraska Territory: Joseph W. Young and the Mormon Emigration of 1864," *BYU Studies* 39, no. 1 (2000): 31.

5. See Richard L. Jensen, "Brigham Young and the Gathering to Zion," in *Lion of the Lord: Essays on the Life and Service of Brigham Young*, ed. Susan Easton Black and Larry C. Porter (Salt Lake City: Deseret Book, 1995), 209–26, for an excellent treatment of Young's emigration administrative efforts.

6. This information has been culled from the *Millennial Star* and other primary sources, all available on the *Mormon Immigration Index* CD-ROM, comp. Fred E. Woods (Salt Lake City: The Church of Jesus Christ of Latter-day Saints, 2000). With the exception of a few voyages out of Southampton in 1894, the Mormons continued to use Liverpool as their main port of embarkation throughout the nineteenth century. Additional research reveals that the Church continued to keep

a record of voyages from Liverpool to America until 1925. During this first quarter of the twentieth century, Liverpool continued to be the main point of embarkation for European converts voyaging to America. These voyage and passenger records are contained in the "'British Mission Registers" (Church History Library, Salt Lake City), which the author has been compiling and analyzing since 2000.

7. The April 1842 issue of *Millennial Star* indicates the change of publication location from Manchester to Liverpool. This move certainly made it much easier for Church leaders and agents to supervise emigration affairs, which were often tied in with news from the *Star*.

8. Alan K. Parrish, "Beginnings of the *Millennial Star*: Journal of the Mission to Great Britain," in *Regional Studies in Latter-day Saint Church History: British Isles*, ed. Donald Q. Cannon (Provo, UT: Department of Church History and Doctrine, Brigham Young University, 1990), 135–39. Parrish also notes that the *Millennial Star* was "published as a monthly, biweekly, or weekly publication for 130 years, . . . the longest continuous publication in the history of the Church, terminating in 1970" (133). It is also of interest that the name of the periodical certainly fits the scriptural theme contained in Doctrine and Covenants 29:8, which states that one purpose of gathering the faithful to one place is "to prepare their hearts and be prepared in all things against the day when tribulation and desolation are sent forth upon the wicked."

9. "Information to Emigrants," *Millennial Star*, August 1841, 60–61. For instructions to emigrants in the years 1840–54, see Frederick H. Piercy, *Route from Liverpool to Great Salt Lake Valley*, ed. by James Linforth (London: Latter-day Saints' Book Depot, 1855), 19–22.

10. "Emigration," *Millennial Star*, February 1841, 263.

11. *History of the Church*, 4:186; 5:296; D&C 124:25–7.

12. British Mission History, January 16, 1844, in Philip A. M. Taylor, "Mormons and Gentiles on the Atlantic," *Utah Historical Quarterly* 24, no. 3 (July 1956): 204.

13. "Notice to Intending Emigrants," *Millennial Star*, November 20, 1852, 618.

14. London correspondent of *Cambridge Independent Press* (May 24, 1854) concerning Mormon emigration agent Samuel W. Richards, in "Missionary Experience,"

Contributor, February 1890, 158–59. Pages 155–59 of this article also contain a firsthand account of this unusual evidence by Richards himself.

15. Richard E. Bennett, *Mormons at the Missouri, 1846–1852* (Norman: University of Oklahoma Press, 1987), 157.

16. Brigham Young to Joseph W. Young, May 10, 1864, Correspondence of Brigham Young, Church History Library, The Church of Jesus Christ of Latter-day Saints, Salt Lake City.

17. Journals of William Gibson, Fall 1852, 108; Spring 1853, 112, Church History Library. Louis Espenschied was a German immigrant who, at age twenty-two, opened up his St. Louis wagon factory in 1843. His grandson Lloyd Espenschied, in "Louis Espenschied and Family," *Bulletin of the Missouri Historical Society* 18, no. 2 (January 1962): 91–92, noted, "Strangely enough, it appears to have been a religious sect that gave Louis his first considerable business in 'prairie schooners.' When the Mormons sallied forth westward from Nauvoo, Illinois, in 1846, bound across the vast plains toward the Great Salt Lake, they were desperately in need of wagons. They themselves built most of them, it seems, but they were obliged to call upon others." Further, Lloyd noted that the eldest grandchild of Espenschied wrote, "Grandfather had made wagons for the Mormons when they left Illinois, and had made a special box on the back to hold fruit trees ready to plant." In addition, the author, drawing upon correspondence he received dated June 9, 1943, from Church assistant historian A. W. Lund, maintained that by 1855, Louis was still working with Mormon emigration. Lund uncovered a letter written by John Wardle and Elder Erastus Snow to Espenschied that noted, "Paid $2,000.00 to Louis Espenschied and Co., for Wagons." Finally, later letters between President Brigham Young and Louis Espenschied revealed that President Young and Espenschied were in correspondence with each other as late as 1859. See outgoing letter from Young to Espenschied dated June 1, 1857, and incoming letter from Espenschied to Young, dated August 29, 1859. See also July 14, 1859, letter by Jeter Clinton to President Young, wherein Clinton discusses with President Young a $258.00 debt owed to Espenschied. Brigham Young Correspondence, Church History Library.

18. David Roberts, *Devil's Gate: Brigham Young and the Great Mormon Tragedy* (New York: Simon & Schuster, 2008) has recently tried to pin the blame of the Willie and Martin handcart disasters on President Young. Not only does Roberts jump to conclusions regarding Young's knowledge of the incident, he fails to examine carefully decades of correspondence between the Mormon prophet and his agents, which reveals that President Young continually provided meticulous instructions on emigration matters. While Roberts is quick to point out that President Young contributed to the greatest tragedy of American emigration by land, he fails to note the maritime migration safety record during President Young's administration. It is certainly impressive that none of the hundreds of vessels carrying Mormon passengers across the Atlantic ever sank, and only one such vessel sank in the Pacific. This safety record is quite remarkable, as evidenced by the fact that between the years 1847 and 1853 alone, at least fifty-nine other immigrant vessels sank crossing the Atlantic. Conway B. Sonne, *Saints on the Seas: A Maritime History of Mormon Migration 1830–1890* (Salt Lake City: University of Utah Press, 1983), 139.

19. Fred E. Woods, "Perpetual Emigrating Fund," in *Encyclopedia of Latter-day Saint History*, ed. Arnold K. Garr, Donald Q. Cannon, and Richard O. Cowan (Salt Lake City: Deseret Book, 2000), 910. See also Richard L. Jensen and William G. Hartley, "Immigration and Emigration," in *Encyclopedia of Mormonism*, ed. Daniel H. Ludlow (New York: Macmillan, 1992), 2:674.

20. "Second General Epistle" from the First Presidency, *Frontier Guardian*, December 26, 1849, 1.

21. "Letter to Orson Hyde" from the First Presidency, October 16, 1849, in *Frontier Guardian*, December 26, 1849, 2.

22. The caliboose, or "jailhouse," was located in the French Quarter of New Orleans.

23. Journal History of The Church of Jesus Christ of Latter-day Saints, March 12, 1849, Church History Library, 2–3.

24. Record of the Saint Louis Branch, 1847–50, Church History Library, May 3, 1849.

25. Record of the Saint Louis Branch, 1847–50, June 2, 1849.

26. Record of the Saint Louis Branch, 1847–50, February 16, 1850.

Men in Motion: Administering and Organizing the Gathering

27. For a complete history of the Saints in St. Louis, see Fred E. Woods and Thomas L. Farmer, *When the Saints Came Marching In: A History of the Latter-day Saints in St. Louis* (Orem, UT: Millennial Press, 2009).
28. Piercy, *Route from Liverpool to Great Salt Lake Valley*, 57.
29. Andrew Karl Larson, *Erastus Snow: The Life of a Missionary and Pioneer for the Early Mormon Church* (Salt Lake City: University of Utah Press, 1971), 257–58.
30. St. Louis Records, 1852–56, Church History Library, October 3, 1854, 186.
31. "To the Saints in St. Louis," *St. Louis Luminary*, December 2, 1854, 6.
32. "Emigrants for Utah," *St. Louis Luminary*, February 17, 1855, 50.
33. Brigham Young to Franklin D. Richards, "Foreign Correspondence," *Millennial Star*, October 28, 1854, 684.
34. For more information on the role of Latter-day Saint emigration agents at New York, see Fred E. Woods, "The Knights at Castle Garden: Latter-day Saint Immigration Agents at New York," in *Regional Studies in Latter-day Saint Church History: New York and Pennsylvania*, ed. Alexander L. Baugh and Andrew H. Hedges (Provo, UT: Religious Studies Center, Brigham Young University, 2002), 103–24.
35. Although emigration was certainly a key issue in these periodicals and others established during this period, this topic was not the primary reason they were launched. Richard D. McClellan, "Polemical Periodicals," in *Encyclopedia of Latter-day Saint History*, 907, noted, "Soon after the Church formally announced the practice of plural marriage [1852], Brigham Young appointed several men to go to various cities to establish periodicals to respond to anti-polygamy polemic. . . . *The Seer* was edited by Orson Pratt and published from 1853 to 1854 in both Washington D.C., and Liverpool, England. It was followed by the *St. Louis Luminary* (November 1854–December 1855), established by Erastus Snow; the *Mormon*, founded by John Taylor in New York City in February 1855; and the *Western Standard* of San Francisco, edited by George Q. Cannon, beginning in February 1856." For more information on the role of the *Luminary* in St. Louis concerning emigration and Church matters in general, see Woods and Farmer, *When the Saints Came Marching In*, 45–55.
36. John Taylor to Franklin D. Richards, March 4, 1856, Correspondence of Brigham Young, Church History Library.

37. For an excellent overview of the operations behind Mormon migration during this period, see Piercy, *Route from Liverpool to Great Salt Lake Valley*.
38. "To the Emigration and Our Readers Generally," *Mormon*, February 17, 1855, 3.
39. "To the Saints Scattered Abroad," *Mormon*, March 3, 1855, 3.
40. Andrew Jenson, "Taylor, John," in *Latter-day Saint Biographical Encyclopedia* (Salt Lake City: Andrew Jenson Publishing Company, 1887), 1:18, points out that the *Mormon* was discontinued as a result of Elder Taylor and other elders being called home to the Salt Lake Valley because of the threat of the Utah War.
41. "Mormonism Revised," *Mormon*, March 24, 1855, 3.
42. John Taylor to Brigham Young, May 18, 1855, Correspondence of Brigham Young, Church History Library.
43. John Taylor to Brigham Young, July 15, 1855, Correspondence of Brigham Young, Church History Library. Two months later, Elder Taylor again wrote President Young, stating, "Since I last wrote you, part of another ship load of Emigrants have arrived, numbering 162. All poor, they have most of them obtained employment. Monetary and mercantile affairs are looking up a little, and prospects are brightening for laboring people." See John Taylor to Brigham Young, September 16, 1855, Brigham Young Correspondence, Church History Library.
44. John Taylor to Brigham Young, February 20, 1856, Correspondence of Brigham Young, Church History Library.
45. For more information on the role of Elder Taylor in supervising emigration, see Fred E. Woods, "A Gifted Gentleman in Perpetual Motion: John Taylor as an Emigration Agent," in *Champion of Liberty: John Taylor*, ed. Mary Jane Woodger (Provo, UT: Religious Studies Center, Brigham Young University, 2009), 171–91.
46. For a biographical treatise of Nathaniel H. Felt, see Fred E. Woods, "Nathaniel H. Felt: An Essex County Man," in *Regional Studies in Latter-day Saint Church History: The New England States*, ed. Donald Q. Cannon, Arnold K. Garr, and Bruce A. Van Orden (Provo, UT: Religious Studies Center, Brigham Young University, 2004), 219–36.
47. John Taylor to Brigham Young, April 11, 1855, Correspondence of Brigham Young, Church History Library.

Men in Motion: Administering and Organizing the Gathering

48. In the Correspondence of Brigham Young collection located in the Church History Library, there are twenty-one known letters which John Taylor wrote to Brigham Young during the period of April 1855–57. There are also seventeen, possibly eighteen, known letters from President Young to Elder Taylor during these same years. These outgoing letters from President Young are full of information regarding emigration. In fact, one lengthy letter dated October 30, 1856, is entirely devoted to this theme and carefully treats the challenges of a triangular correspondence between Franklin D. Richards in Liverpool, Elder Taylor in New York, and President Young in Salt Lake City. Perhaps more letters would have come to Elder Taylor from the Salt Lake Valley, but getting the mail across the nation in a timely fashion was a continual problem in the mid-nineteenth century. For example, in a letter to Elder Taylor dated July 28, 1856, President Young wrote, "In regard to the emigration, whatever we could say . . . would be long past before it reached you." In any case, the Brigham Young Correspondence provides a wealth of information not only on the dialogue between Elder Taylor and President Young but also the dialogue with other Mormon emigration agents assigned at such ports and posts as Liverpool; New Orleans; New York; Kanesville; Florence; Wyoming; Nebraska; Mormon Grove; Kansas Territory; St. Louis; and Iowa City in their correspondence sent to Salt Lake City during the years that President Young presided over the Church (1847–77). The author is currently involved in writing a book about these dedicated "men in motion."

49. John Taylor to Brigham Young, April 11, 1855, Correspondence of Brigham Young, Church History Library.

50. See George Q. Cannon to Brigham Young, April 23, 1859, 1–2, Correspondence of Brigham Young, Church History Library; and Fred E. Woods, "Two Sides of a River: Mormon Transmigration through Quincy, Illinois, and Hannibal, Missouri," *Mormon Historical Studies* 2 (Spring 2001): 120–21.

51. William C. Staines to A. [Albert] Carrington, *Millennial Star*, August 14, 1869, 536. Mormon emigration historians Richard L. Jensen and William G. Hartley note, "There were three categories of immigrants: the independent, who paid their own way to Utah; 'states' or 'ordinary' immigrants, who paid only enough to reach a port of entry or other intermediate stopping place in the United States, hoping

to earn enough there to finish the journey; and PEF immigrants, assisted by the Perpetual Emigrating Fund." "Immigration and Emigration," in *Encyclopedia of Mormonism*, 2:674.

52. Jenson, "Staines, William Carter," in *Latter-day Saint Biographical Encyclopedia*, 2:517.
53. "Blessing," Papers of William Carter Staines, Church History Library, item 1, 1–2.
54. Edward L. Hart, *Mormon in Motion: The Life and Journals of James H. Hart, 1825–1906, in England, France and America* (Salt Lake City: Windsor Books, 1978), 191–92, 194. Jenson, "James Henry Hart," in *Latter-day Saint Biographical Encyclopedia*, 2:28, notes that James Hart was a prosecuting attorney from 1883 to 1884.
55. Stanley B. Kimball, "The Saints and St. Louis, 1831–1857: An Oasis of Tolerance and Security," *BYU Studies* 13, no. 4 (Summer 1973): 514–15. For an account of James Hart's years at St. Louis, see Hart, *Mormon in Motion*, 124–51.
56. Hart, *Mormon in Motion*, 182, 188–89.
57. Hart, *Mormon in Motion*, 202. The same page states, "For the most part he was treated fairly by the New York press." See pages 201–6 for examples of his image as presented by the reporters.
58. James H. Johnson to Mr. James Hart, July 3, 1883, collected material concerning James H. Hart, n.d., Church History Library.
59. Jno. Scofield to Elder J. H. Hart, October 24, 1883, New York Emigration Office Records, Church History Library.
60. For details of Latter-day Saint immigration through Norfolk, see Fred E. Woods, "Norfolk and the Mormon Folk: Latter-day Saint Immigration through Old Dominion (1887–1890)," *Mormon Historical Studies* 1, no. 1 (Spring 2000): 73–91.
61. "World Missions and Their Presidents," unpublished manuscript, Church History Library. The *Deseret News 1997–98 Church Almanac* (Salt Lake City: Deseret News, 1996), 411, notes that on June 28, 1854 (commencing with Franklin D. Richards), the British Mission took additional administrative responsibilities, overseeing not only the British Isles but also Europe.

Kenneth L. Alford

10

A History of Mormon Catechisms

When I first heard the term *catechism* as a young grade-school student, I had no idea what it meant. I later learned that the word comes from two ancient Greek words, *kata*, which means "down," and *echein*, which means "to sound." Literally, *catechism* means "to sound down (into the ears)"; in other words, a catechism is "instruction by word of mouth."[1] Catechisms can take two different forms—either a series of questions and answers or simply a series of questions.[2] Catechisms are most frequently associated with religion, but they have also been used for centuries in a variety of scientific, political, military, and other fields.

The *Encyclopedia of Mormonism* observes that "conspicuously absent from LDS language . . . are many terms of other Christian cultures, such as 'abbot,' 'archbishop,' 'beatification,' 'cardinal,' '*catechism*,'

Kenneth L. Alford is an associate professor of Church history and doctrine at Brigham Young University.

'creed,' 'diocese.'"³ However, the word *catechism* was actually used frequently by Latter-day Saints during the nineteenth and early twentieth centuries.

Imagine that President Thomas S. Monson were called to Washington DC and asked to testify before a Senate committee regarding whether the Church uses catechisms. Strange as this may seem today, that situation actually occurred in the first decade of the twentieth century. President Joseph F. Smith traveled to Washington DC and testified in hearings before the United States Senate Committee on Privileges and Elections to determine if Reed Smoot, one of the Twelve Apostles and the senator-elect from Utah, should be seated in the Senate. One of the questions he was asked by Senator Lee S. Overman, a first-term senator from North Carolina, was, "Do you have catechisms for the children?" President Smith answered, "Yes, sir." The hearing transcript reveals that the next several questions from Senator Overman addressed the Church's use and understanding of catechisms.⁴

A CHRISTIAN CATECHISTIC TRADITION

A rich Christian catechistic tradition stretches back hundreds, if not thousands, of years. Thomas Aquinas and other theologians developed and encouraged the use of catechisms. Catechisms also played an important role during the establishment of the American colonies.

> Puritan and Pilgrim alike in the early days in New England had family religious instruction through catechism, questions and answers. . . . One of the earliest catechisms among the Puritans and Pilgrims was that by John Cotton, . . . issued in London in 1646. Cotton Mather call[ed] it, "The Catechism of New England," and fifty years after its issue [said], 'The children of New-England are to this day most usually fed with this excellent catechism.' It contained sixty questions and answers which became familiar as household words in New England, and it was made a part of the famous *New England Primer* in the next century, thus continuing its popularity for more than a hundred years.⁵

Religious catechisms were especially popular in the nineteenth century among a variety of American Christian denominations, including Roman Catholics, Lutherans, Episcopalians, and Methodists.[6] There were also numerous nondenominational Christian catechisms published. Catechism societies—groups whose members met for the purpose of reciting religious catechisms—were organized across the United States. For example, the preface to *A Short Biblical Catechism*, published in Boston in 1816, briefly outlines how the catechism societies functioned. "At each meeting the members severally may answer the questions succeeding those which they answered at the previous meeting."[7]

Catechisms also figured prominently in much of popular nineteenth-century literature. Books such as *Jane Eyre* (Charlotte Brontë), *Walden* (Henry David Thoreau), *Treasure Island* (Robert Louis Stevenson), *Uncle Tom's Cabin* (Harriet Beecher Stowe), *Les Misérables* (Victor Hugo), *The Scarlet Letter* (Nathaniel Hawthorne), and *Hard Times* (Charles Dickens) all included references to catechisms.[8]

A LATTER-DAY SAINT CATECHISTIC TRADITION

It should not be surprising that early converts to The Church of Jesus Christ of Latter-day Saints often brought with them a catechistic background. Commenting on his Anglican and Methodist childhood, President John Taylor said, "I learned and said my prayers; was taught the catechism; knew the litany and a great many of the church prayers by rote; repeated week after week."[9] President Wilford Woodruff explained that when he was a child, "I dared no more go out to play on a Sunday than I dared put my hand in the fire. It would have been considered an unpardonable sin. We could not attend a ball and dance; we did not dare attend a theatre, and from Saturday night, at sundown, to Monday morning, we must not laugh or smile, but we must study our catechism."[10]

Truths taught to children through catechisms often made a lasting impression upon their lives. As Elder George A. Smith noted in 1855, "It may be said of me that I never knew anything else but 'Mormonism,' yet I have found that some of the traditions of my early education (as I was piously educated at the Sunday school in the doctrine and principles of Presbyterianism)—some of these principles which I received in my youth have clung to me so closely that I have had to stop at times and reflect whether I had learned that from the proper source, or whether it was part of my old catechism."[11]

Thus catechisms were a familiar religious educational device to many early Latter-day Saint converts. It was a natural extension, therefore, for Latter-day Saints to create and use catechisms to teach the doctrines of the Restoration. The *Lectures on Faith* (until 1921 the doctrine portion of the Doctrine and Covenants) contain what may be the earliest examples of Latter-day Saint catechisms.[12] The first five lectures each end with a formal catechism that reiterates the key concepts, doctrines, and scriptural facts from the preceding lecture in a question-and-answer format. Many questions are doctrinal in nature. For example:

Q. Is faith anything else beside the principle of action?
A. It is.
Q. What is it?
A. It is the principle of power, also.
Q. How do you prove it?
A. First, It is the principle of power in the Deity, as well as in man. Heb. 11:3. Through faith we understand that the worlds were framed by the word of God.[13]

Some questions and answers are factual, including many that most gospel students today would probably consider to be gospel trivia.

Q. How many noted righteous men lived from Adam to Noah?
A. Nine; which includes Abel, who was slain by his brother.
Q. What are their names?
A. Abel, Seth, Enos, Cainan, Mahalaleel, Jared, Enoch, Methusalah, and Lamech.

Q. How old was Adam when Seth was born?
A. One hundred and thirty years. Gen. 5:3
Q. How many years did Adam live after Seth was born?
A. Eight hundred. Gen. 5:4.[14]

The two final lectures in the *Lectures on Faith* did not contain a catechism. A note to readers at the end of lecture six states, "This lecture is so plain and the facts set forth so self-evident that it is deemed unnecessary to form a catechism upon it: the student is, therefore, instructed to commit the whole to memory."[15]

In 1835, Oliver Cowdery explained why catechisms were added to the *Lectures on Faith*. He suggested that "in giving the following lectures we have thought best to insert the catechism, that the reader may fully understand the manner in which this science was taught. It was found, that by annexing a catechism to the lectures as they were presented, the class made greater progress than otherwise; and in consequence of the additional scripture proofs, it was preserved in compiling."[16]

The treatise "Of Governments and Laws in General," authored by Oliver Cowdery and canonized as Doctrine and Covenants section 134, is written as a form of implicit catechism, with the individual questions missing and each of the answers beginning with either "We believe" or "We do not believe." With the questions made explicit, it might look something like this:

1. Q. *Why were governments instituted?*
   A. We believe that governments were instituted of God for the benefit of man; and that he holds men accountable for their acts in relation to them, both in making laws and administering them, for the good and safety of society.
2. Q. *Do governments have the right to establish laws?*
   A. We believe that rulers, states, and governments have a right, and are bound to enact laws for the protection of all citizens in the free exercise of their religious belief.[17]

The Articles of Faith, written by Joseph Smith in 1842, follow this same implicit catechistic format.

THE REFORMATION

From 1856 to 1857, the Church, especially within the Utah Territory, enacted a religious "reformation" to help members return to fundamental doctrines and practices. Church members were often called to repentance by specially called missionaries who used a formalized set of questions that they regularly referred to as a catechism. There were several versions of reformation catechisms. Members were asked questions regarding their spiritual life, such as, "Do you pray in your family night and morning and attend to secret prayer? Do you pay your tithing promptly? Do you teach your family the gospel of salvation? Do you and your family attend Ward meetings? Have you lied about or maliciously misrepresented any person or thing? Have you borne false witness against your neighbor? Have you taken the name of the Deity in vain?"

They were also asked questions of a more legal nature: "Have you committed murder, by shedding innocent blood, or consenting thereto? Have you betrayed your brethren or sisters in anything? Have you committed adultery, by having any connection with a woman that was not your wife or a man that was not your husband? Have you coveted anything not your own? Have you taken and made use of property not your own, without the consent of the owner? Have you been intoxicated with strong drink?"

Some questions reflected living conditions in the mid-nineteenth century: "Do you wash your body and have your family do so as often as health and cleanliness require and circumstances will permit? Have you cut hay where you had no right to, or turned your animals into another person's grain or field, without his knowledge and consent? Have you taken water to irrigate with, when it belonged to another person at the time you used it? Have you taken another's horse or mule from the range and rode it without the owner's consent? Have you branded an animal that you did not know to be your own?"[18]

Historian Paul Peterson noted, "The administration of the catechism was a particularly sensitive problem. It would appear that initially, at least in some instances, it was administered publicly, and the confession that followed was likewise public. Most often, however, teachers and home missionaries went to individual homes and catechized families as units. This naturally led to embarrassing moments."[19]

Commenting on the reformation catechism in a letter to Elder Orson Pratt, President Brigham Young stated, "Those missionaries go from house to house, and examine every individual therein separately; and, as a consequence, we have had this people examining themselves minutely; much honest confession and restitution have been made. The catechism has been as a mirror to the Saints, reflecting themselves in truth."[20]

LATTER-DAY SAINT CATECHISM PUBLICATIONS

Beginning in 1845, the *Millennial Star*, an influential Church publication in Great Britain, published a series of catechisms—"The Mormon Creed" by Orson Pratt (1845), "Questions and Answers" by Thomas Smith (1848), "The Child's Ladder" by David Moffat (1849), and "Catechism for Children" by John Jaques (1853–54).[21] Jaques, who was baptized at age eighteen in England in 1845, published fourteen catechism chapters serially in the *Millennial Star*. In 1854, Jaques combined those chapters into a book, *Catechism for Children, Exhibiting the Prominent Doctrines of the Church of Jesus Christ of Latter-day Saints*, which became the most famous Latter-day Saint catechism book.[22]

Jaques's book was printed and reprinted for thirty-five years, including editions in Samoan, Danish, German, Swedish, Hawaiian, Dutch,[23] and the Deseret alphabet.[24] "*Catechism for Children* is the first broadly distributed LDS children's book. Its importance, however, goes beyond this bibliographical footnote: for by claiming to list the doctrines of Mormonism, it . . . helped to standardize Mormon theology."[25] By 1888, Jaques's *Catechism for Children* was in its tenth printing and had sold over thirty-five thousand

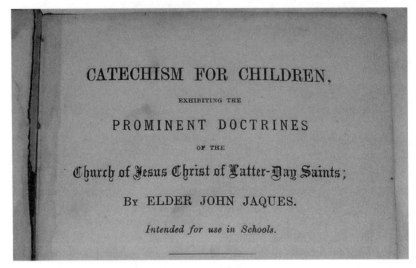

Written by John Jaques, Catechism for Children *was the most popular and influential of all Latter-day Saint catechism books. (Courtesy of Kenneth L. Alford.)*

copies—almost one copy for every five members of the Church (equivalent to selling almost three million copies today). Sales were helped, no doubt, by comments such as Elder George A. Smith's during the April 1872 general conference: "The catechism for children, exhibiting the prominent doctrines of the Church of Jesus Christ of Latter-day Saints, should be in every family, school and Bible class."[26]

The eighteen chapters in Jaques's *Catechism for Children* covered a wide variety of gospel doctrines and topics—the basic principles and ordinances of the gospel, the Council in Heaven, the Fall, the Atonement, the Ten Commandments, the Word of Wisdom, the organization of the Church, the priesthood, and other subjects. Here is a sample from chapter 5 ("Person, Character and Attributes of God"):

1. Q. What kind of a being is God?
   A. He is in the form of a man.
2. Q. How do you learn this?

    A. The Scriptures declare that man was made in the image of God. Gen. i. 26, 27.
Repeat the passage.

    And God said, Let us make man in our own image, after our likeness. * * * So God created man in his own image, in the image of God created he him: male and female created he them.

3. Q. Have you any further proof of God's being in the form of man?

    A. Yes. Jesus Christ was in the form of man, and was at the same time in the image of God's person. Heb. i. 3.[27]

The influence of Jaques's *Catechism for Children* was widespread and long lasting. On August 18, 1901, Elder B. H. Roberts delivered a lecture to the Mutual Improvement Association conference. His discourse was published in the *Deseret News* and the *Improvement Era*, and a copy "fell into the hands of the Reverend C. Van Der Donckt, of Pocatello, Idaho, a priest of the Roman Catholic Church,"[28] who wrote a reply that was also published in the *Improvement Era*. Elder Roberts answered his reply, and the entire exchange was published in 1903 in Elder Roberts's book *The Mormon Doctrine of Deity: The Roberts–Van Der Donckt Discussion*. The influence of Jaques's book is shown by the fact that some of their debate centered on questions and answers from his book.[29] Roberts also quoted Jaques's *Catechism* in his *Seventy's Course in Theology* and *Defense and the Faith of the Saints*.[30] Furthermore, the first serious scriptural commentary on the Doctrine and Covenants, written from 1913 to 1916 by Hyrum M. Smith and Janne M. Sjodahl, quoted John Jaques's definition of the term *dispensation* in helping to expound on Doctrine and Covenants 27:13.[31]

PROLIFERATION OF CATECHISMS

The 1880s saw the height of Latter-day Saint catechism popularity. On Christmas Day in 1881, Eliza R. Snow wrote to Robert Welch, a Primary secretary who had earlier written to her, saying, "I am now devoting what

Examples of popular nineteenth-century Latter-day Saint catechism books. (Courtesy of Kenneth L. Alford.)

time I can to a series of three books for the Primary Associations, especially for recitations. These books are very much needed, and I feel anxious to get them out as soon as possible."[32] She had recently completed and published *Bible Questions and Answers for Children*, a book of questions and answers about both the Old and New Testaments. Her book begins with this catechism:

1. Q. Who made this world?
   A. The Gods.
2. Q. How long did it take to make the world all things in it?
   A. Six days.
3. Q. At that time, how many years long was a day?
   A. One thousand.

A History of Mormon Catechisms

4. Q. What was the world called?
   A. The earth.
5. Q. What was the great deep?
   A. Water.
6. Q. What was on the face of the water?
   A. Darkness.[33]

Eliza R. Snow's book of Bible catechisms is especially interesting because it included an explanatory note informing readers how her book of catechisms was to be used with students. She said, "This book is designed to assist those who have charge of the children. The president, or one whom she shall appoint, is expected to read a question, and another appointee read the answer, and all the children present repeat the answer in concert.

Eliza R. Snow spent the final years of her life authoring catechisms for Latter-day Saint youth.

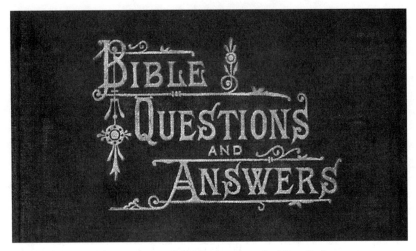

Cover of a Latter-day Saint catechism book written by Eliza R. Snow.

As soon as the children can answer the questions the prompting may be dispensed with. One chapter, or part of a chapter, may be taken for a lesson, and be repeated week after week until it is well committed."[34]

In the 1880s, the Deseret Sunday School Union published several catechism books. The first of these—*Questions and Answers on the Life and Mission of the Prophet Joseph Smith*—was published in 1882.[35] It contained thirteen chapters that began with Joseph Smith's birth and boyhood and ended with the Martyrdom. In 1886, Abraham H. Cannon, the son of Apostle George Q. Cannon and one of the seven Presidents of the Seventy, authored *Questions and Answers on the Book of Mormon*, which was "designed and prepared especially for the use of the Sunday Schools in Zion."[36] In the preface, the publishers stated, "The importance of a careful study of writings so fraught with historical and religious truths as the volume translated by the Prophet Joseph Smith, cannot be overestimated. And our most earnest desire will be gratified if these questions and answers can but induce the young people of Zion to search with greater diligence for the valuable truths contained in the revelations of ancient and modern times, all of which are given the Latter-day Saints for their instruction."[37] The catechism questions and answers begin with the background and history of the Book of Mormon:

1. Q. What is the Book of Mormon?
   A. The sacred history of ancient America.
2. Q. By whom was it written?
   A. A succession of ancient prophets who inhabited the continent.
3. Q. On what was it written?
   A. On plates which had the appearance of gold.[38]

The first two chapters discuss the coming forth of the Book of Mormon, the Three Witnesses, the Eight Witnesses, and even the Jaredites. The questions in chapter 3 start with 1 Nephi 1:

1. Q. Whose writings are found in the first part of the Book of Mormon?
   A. Those of Nephi.
2. Q. Who was his father?
   A. Lehi, who was a descendant of Manasseh, the son of Joseph, who was sold into Egypt.
3. Q. How many brothers did he have older than himself, and what were their names?
   A. Three, Laman, Lemuel and Sam.[39]

The remaining chapters walk the reader through the remainder of the Book of Mormon, concluding with Moroni's promise, his farewell, and Joseph Smith's testimony:

18. Q. How does Moroni say people can learn of the truth of the Book of Mormon?
    A. By asking God, with a sincere heart, in the name of Christ.
19. Q. What is Moroni's last exhortation to all people?
    A. To come unto Christ, and lay hold upon every good gift.
20. Q. What is the testimony of the Prophet Joseph concerning the Book of Mormon?

A. "I told the brethren that the Book of Mormon was the most correct of any book on earth, and the keystone of our religion, and a man would get nearer to God by abiding by its precepts, than by any other book."[40]

During the 1880s, the *Juvenile Instructor* published numerous catechisms[41] as well as a series of six "Motto Catechism Cards"—small cardboard cards with catechisms of various gospel topics printed on them.[42] Card number one was about wisdom, number two about the knowledge of God, and so forth. Other catechism cards were published during the 1880s and 1890s by various Church organizations and private individuals.

Speaking during general conference in October 1899, Elder Francis M. Lyman stated, "With pleasure we refer to the value that the Juvenile Instructor . . . has been in aiding the great Sunday school work. . . . The publication in its columns of the catechisms on the Bible, Book of Mormon, Church History, etc. . . . have rendered it a necessity in our Sunday schools whose influence can scarcely be over-estimated."[43]

In 1898, the Deseret Sunday School Union published *The Latter-day Saints' Sunday School Treatise.* A section devoted to catechisms informed Sunday School teachers and officers that catechization was "the art of asking questions in accordance with the laws of the most rapid proportionate development and culture of the pupil." Readers were informed that catechism questions should be "adapted to the capacity of the pupil. Questions should lead the pupil from the known to the unknown. From the concrete to the abstract. From the simple to the complex." Catechisms could help teachers with "the correcting of errors. The drawing out of new ideas. The inculcation of the principles of the Gospel. The training in obedience to the will of God."[44] The discussion of catechisms also included these fourteen "Rules of Catechization" to assist teachers in creating and using their own gospel-centered catechisms:

1. See that every question and every answer is a complete sentence.
2. Aim to have every question bear directly on the subject in hand.
3. Be clear, concise and logical.
4. Aim to never use more than three questions explanatory of the same point.
5. Repeat no pupil's answer habitually.
6. Have no habitual expletives, as, for instance, "Just so," "Right," etc.
7. Avoid direct questions, that is, such as can be answered by "Yes" or "No."
8. Ask more reflective than mere memorative questions.
9. Be natural, avoiding all affectation.
10. Avoid peculiarities in speech, gestures or voice.
11. Do not place yourself at the mercy of your class by non-preparation or by unguarded questions.
12. Prefer pupil's own language to mere quotations, but encourage exact quotations of scriptural passages.
13. Put the same question in several forms occasionally.
14. Be pointed in your questions, so that they will admit of but one perfect answer.[45]

Sunday School teachers were informed that "pupils should feel as anxious to answer as the teacher to ask, and they should feel as free in asking questions."[46]

THE INFLUENCE OF CATECHISMS

Nineteenth-century Latter day Saint catechisms had a large influence on members of the Church, including future Church presidents. For example, Joseph Fielding Smith said, "I remember that one thing I did from the time I learned to read and write was to study the gospel. I read and

As a child, Joseph Fielding Smith memorized much of John Jaques's Catechism for Children.

committed to memory the children's catechism and primary books on the gospel."[47] Future Church President Heber J. Grant "took advantage of the ward's new school. In fact, the ambitious and assertive boy was often at front stage. Excelling at memorization, he quickly mastered the Articles of Faith; the first five pages of John Jaques's *Catechism*; and Joseph Smith's health revelation, the Word of Wisdom, a frequent Sunday School recitation. . . . On one occasion, Heber pitted his declamatory skills against Ort [Orson F.] Whitney [and lost] . . . But 'Heber had another card up his sleeve,' Orson Whitney recalled many years later. 'He answered more questions from the

Catechism than any other student in school, and won a prize equal to mine, which was the *Autobiography of Parley P. Pratt.*"[48]

In an October 1874 session of general conference, Elder George A. Smith promised the young men of the Church "that if they will attend the Bible classes and study the catechism in use in our schools, and make themselves familiar with it, they will become so thoroughly informed in the principles of the Gospel and the evidences of it, that when called upon to go abroad to defend the doctrines of Zion they will be well prepared to do so."[49]

Almost thirty years later, during the October 1903 general conference, Elder Reed Smoot approvingly noted, "Not later than last Wednesday, September 30, Chancellor McCracken of New York University, in his address to the student body, made the following statement: 'I wish we could require from every freshman a Sunday school diploma that would certify that he knew by heart the ten commandments, the sermon on the mount, a church catechism of some kind, a score of scripture psalms and best classic hymns.'"[50]

The experience of Eli Peirce illustrates the effect that catechisms had on many members of the Church. On October 5, 1875, Peirce was working at the railroad office instead of attending general conference. He later explained:

> One of my fellow employees was at the conference; I was not, because I did not care to be. He heard my name called [to serve as a full-time missionary], abruptly left the meeting and ran over to the telegraph office to call and tell me the startling news. This was the first intimation I had received that such a thing was contemplated. At the very moment this intelligence was being flashed over the wires, I was sitting lazily thrown back in an office rocking chair, my feet on the desk, reading a novel and simultaneously sucking an old Dutch pipe, of massive proportions, just to vary the monotony of cigar smoking.
>
> As soon as I had been informed of what had taken place, I threw the novel in the waste basket, the pipe in a corner and started up town to buy a catechism. Have never read a novel nor smoked a pipe from that hour. Sent in my resignation the same day, to

take effect at once, in order that I might have time for study and preparation.

Remarkable as it may seem, and has since appeared to me, a thought of disregarding the call, or of refusing to comply with the requirement, never once entered my mind.[51]

To Eli Peirce, purchasing and studying Latter-day Saint catechisms seemed to be closely linked with mission preparation and righteous living.

THE DECLINE OF LATTER-DAY SAINT CATECHISMS

Catechisms quickly faded from popular Latter-day Saint culture in the first decades of the twentieth century. Influential leaders such as Elder James E. Talmage spoke out against rote memorization, the favored method for teaching catechisms. He believed that religion "is more than knowledge, though that knowledge be classified and codified, and annotated to perfection. Religion is the application of the laws of God in our lives, the living up to all we have learned as to our duty, and it entails the obligation to so live until right life is a part of our natures and calls not for rule and rote at every turn."[52]

CATECHISMS TODAY

Catechisms can still be found today in many forms and in many places. For example, hymn 11 in the current hymnbook, "What Was Witnessed in the Heavens?," is a catechism.[53] The Primary children's song "He Sent His Son," by Mabel Jones Gabbott, is also in the form of a catechism:

> *How could the Father tell the world of love and tenderness?*
> He sent his Son, a newborn babe, with peace and holiness.
> *How could the Father show the world the pathway we should go?*
> He sent his Son to walk with men on earth, that we may know.
> *How could the Father tell the world of sacrifice, of death?*

He sent his Son to die for us and rise with living breath.
What does the Father ask of us? What do the scriptures say?
Have faith, have hope, live like his Son, help others on their way.
What does he ask?
Live like his Son.[54]

Primary children continue to memorize the Articles of Faith. The current missionary manual, *Preach My Gospel*, has several catechistic elements, as does the pamphlet *For the Strength of Youth*. In a manner reminiscent of the worthiness questions asked during the 1856–57 reformation, every two years, members of the Church who wish to receive or renew a temple recommend are asked to answer—not just once, but twice—a series of questions that Saints in the nineteenth century would have recognized as a catechism. Catechisms may have faded from the collective consciousness of Latter-day Saints, but they can still easily be found.

NOTES

1. *Oxford English Dictionary*, "catechism" and "catechesis."
2. *The American Heritage College Dictionary*, 4th ed., "catechism."
3. Robert W. Blair, "Vocabulary, Latter-day Saint," in *Encyclopedia of Mormonism*, ed. Daniel H. Ludlow (New York: Macmillan, 1992), 4:1537; emphasis added.
4. *Testimony of Important Witnesses as Given in the Proceedings before the Committee on Privileges and Elections of the United States Senate in the Matter of the Protest Against the Right of Hon. Reed Smoot, a Senator from the State of Utah, to Hold His Seat* (Salt Lake City: Salt Lake Tribune, 1905), 207.
5. Edwin Wilbur Rice, *The Sunday-School Movement 1780–1917 and the American Sunday-School Union, 1817–1917* (Philadelphia: American Sunday-School Union, 1917), 73.
6. In the nineteenth century, catechisms were even produced for those who could not read. See Barbara H. Jaye and William P. Mitchell, eds., *Picturing Faith: A Facsimile Edition of the Pictographic Quechua Catechism in the Huntington Free Library* (Bronx, New York: Huntington Free Library, 1999); and *A Catechism to Be Taught*

Orally to Those Who Cannot Read; Designed Especially for the Instruction of the Slaves (Raleigh: Office of "The Church Intelligencer," 1862).

7. Hervey Wilbur, *A Short Biblical Catechism, Containing Questions, Historical, Doctrinal, Practical and Experimental* (Boston: Samuel T. Armstrong, 1816), v.

8. See Charlotte Brontë, *Jane Eyre* (New York: Dodd, Mead and Company, 1924), 58. "The Sunday evening was spent in repeating, by heart, the Church Catechism, and the fifth, sixth, and seventh chapters of St. Matthew; and in listening to a long sermon, read by Miss Miller, whose irrepressible yawns attested her weariness." See also Henry David Thoreau in *Walden and Other Writings of Henry David Thoreau*, ed. Brooks Atkinson (New York: The Modern Library, 1992), 8. Thoreau introduced one of his arguments with an appeal to catechisms: "When we consider what, to use the words of the catechism, is the chief end of man, and what are the true necessaries and means of life, it appears as if men had deliberately chosen the common mode of living because they preferred it to any other."

9. Dean C. Jessee, "The John Taylor Nauvoo Journal," *BYU Studies* 23, no. 3 (Summer 1983): 2.

10. *The Discourses of Wilford Woodruff*, ed. G. Homer Durham (Salt Lake City: Bookcraft, 1969), 181.

11. George A. Smith, in *Journal of Discourses* (London: Latter-day Saints' Book Depot, 1854–1886), 2:361.

12. Doctrine and Covenants section 77, received by Joseph Smith Jr. in March 1832 at Hiram, Ohio, is in the form of questions and answers about the book of Revelation, but there do not appear to be any indications that it was used as a catechism for educational purposes.

13. *Doctrine and Covenants of the Church of the Latter Day Saints: Carefully Selected from the Revelations of God* (Kirtland, OH: F. G. Williams, 1835), 10.

14. Doctrine and Covenants (1835), 28.

15. Joseph Smith, comp., *Lectures on Faith* (Salt Lake City: Deseret Book, 1985), 71.

16. Oliver Cowdery, *Messenger and Advocate*, May 1835, 122.

17. See Doctrine and Covenants 134:1–2.

18. Paul H. Peterson, "The Mormon Reformation" (PhD diss., Brigham Young University, 1981), 75–76.

19. Paul Peterson, "The Mormon Reformation of 1856–1857: The Rhetoric and the Reality," *Journal of Mormon History* 15 (1989): 72.
20. Brigham Young to Orson Pratt, January 31, 1857, in *Brigham Young: The Man and His Work*, comp. Preston Nibley, 4th ed. (Salt Lake City: Deseret News, 1936), 269.
21. Davis Bitton, "Mormon Catechisms," *Task Papers in LDS History*, no. 15 (Salt Lake City: Historical Department, The Church of Jesus Christ of Latter-day Saints, 1976), 4–7.
22. John Jaques, *Catechism for Children, Exhibiting the Prominent Doctrines of the Church of Jesus Christ of Latter-day Saints* (London: F. D. Richards, 1854).
23. Bitton, "Mormon Catechisms," 8.
24. Deseret Alphabet Manuscripts, ca. 1869, Church History Library, The Church of Jesus Christ of Latter-day Saints, Salt Lake City.
25. Peter Crawley and Chad J. Flake, *A Mormon Fifty: An Exhibition in the Harold B. Lee Library in Conjunction with the Annual Conference of the Mormon History Association* (Provo, UT: Friends of the Brigham Young University Library, 1984), 32.
26. George A. Smith, in *Journal of Discourses*, 14:376.
27. Jaques, *Catechism for Children*, 15.
28. B. H. Roberts, *The Mormon Doctrine of Deity: The Roberts-Van Der Donckt Discussion* (Salt Lake City: Deseret News, 1903), vi.
29. See Roberts, *Mormon Doctrine of Deity*, 87–89.
30. See B. H. Roberts, *The Seventy's Course in Theology, Second Year: Outline History of the Dispensations of the Gospel* (Salt Lake City: Deseret News, 1907), 11: and *Defense of the Faith and the Saints* (Salt Lake City: Deseret News, 1912), 2:266.
31. Hyrum M. Smith and Janne M. Sjodahl, *The Doctrine and Covenants: Containing Revelations Given to Joseph Smith, Jr., the Prophet*, rev. ed. (Salt Lake City: Deseret Book, 1973), 136.
32. Eliza R. Snow to Robert Welch, December 25, 1881, Church History Library, The Church of Jesus Christ of Latter day Saints, Salt Lake City.
33. Eliza R. Snow, *Bible Questions and Answers for Children*, 2nd ed. (Salt Lake City: Juvenile Instructor Office, 1883), 10.
34. Snow, *Bible Questions and Answers*, explanatory note.

35. Deseret Sunday School Union, *Questions and Answers on the Life and Mission of the Prophet Joseph Smith* (Salt Lake City: Juvenile Instructor Office, 1882).
36. A. H. Cannon, *Questions and Answers on the Book of Mormon* (Salt Lake City: Juvenile Instructor Office, 1886).
37. Cannon, *Questions and Answers*, preface.
38. Cannon, *Questions and Answers*, 9.
39. Cannon, *Questions and Answers*, 15–16.
40. Cannon, *Questions and Answers*, 62.
41. See "Questions and Answers on the Bible" and "Questions and Answers on the Book of Mormon," *Juvenile Instructor*, May 15, 1875, 116.
42. "Motto Catechism Cards," *Juvenile Instructor*, Church History Library.
43. Francis M. Lyman, in Conference Report, October 1899, 79–80.
44. The Deseret Sunday School Union, *The Latter-day Saints' Sunday School Treatise*, 2nd ed. (Salt Lake City: George Q. Cannon & Sons, 1898), 110.
45. The Deseret Sunday School Union, *Latter-day Saints' Sunday School Treatise*, 111.
46. The Deseret Sunday School Union, *The Latter-day Saints' Sunday School Treatise*, 110.
47. Joseph Fielding Smith, *Answers to Gospel Questions* (Salt Lake City: Deseret Book, 1963), 4:vi.
48. Ronald W. Walker, "Young Heber's Years of Passage," *BYU Studies* 43, no. 1 (2004): 43.
49. George A. Smith, in *Journal of Discourses*, 17:257.
50. Reed Smoot, in Conference Report, October 1903, 61.
51. Eliza R. Snow Smith, *Biography and Family Record of Lorenzo Snow* (Salt Lake City: Deseret News, 1884), 408, 415. Eli left for his mission on November 1, 1875. He served in the Pennsylvania area for ten months, baptized fifty-six people, and organized three branches.
52. James E. Talmage, in Conference Report, April 1905, 78.
53. John S. Davis, "What Was Witnessed in the Heavens?," *Hymns* (Salt Lake City: The Church of Jesus Christ of Latter-day Saints, 1985), no. 11.
54. Mabel Jones Gabbott, "He Sent His Son," *Children's Songbook* (Salt Lake City: The Church of Jesus Christ of Latter-day Saints, 2000), 34–35; emphasis added.

RoseAnn Benson

11

Primary Association Pioneers: An Early History

Many names could be mentioned in conjunction with the organization of the Primary Association; however, three women—Aurelia Spencer Rogers (1834–1922), Eliza R. Snow[1] (1804–87), and Louie B. Felt[2] (1850–1928)—played key roles in its early establishment. They recognized the problems at hand and dedicated their lives to assure the success of this program. Aurelia addressed the need for an organization. Eliza expanded the organization to branches and wards throughout the Utah Territory and provided a variety of materials to be used in weekly meetings for teaching, reciting, and singing. Louie faced her own challenges in finding a place in the shadow of Eliza. She honed her service in Salt Lake City's Eleventh Ward and overcame any feelings of shyness to emerge as one who encouraged others and was beloved by her counselors, board members, and the children. All three

---

RoseAnn Benson is an adjunct professor in ancient scripture and Church history and doctrine at Brigham Young University.

of them showed a willingness to step forward, initiate, and contribute. They broke new ground and left a lasting legacy.

Aurelia was forty-four years old when she became president of the first Primary in Farmington, Utah, and held that position for nine years. Later she became president of the Davis Stake Primaries, a member of the general Primary board, and finally an honorary member of the general Primary board.[3]

Eliza was seventy-four years old when she began traveling throughout the territory of Utah organizing Primaries in conjunction with her general Relief Society responsibilities. She remained active in her calling as general Relief Society president and in organizing the Young Ladies and Primary Associations until her death at age eighty-three.

Louie was twenty-eight years old when Eliza selected her to be the president of the second Primary Association in the Eleventh Ward, and she was thirty years old when Eliza chose her to preside over all the Primary Associations in the Utah Territory.[4] Louie served as general Primary president for forty-five years, even during poor health, until age seventy-five.

BEGINNINGS: AURELIA SPENCER ROGERS

As a young mother, Aurelia met President Heber C. Kimball while she was visiting Salt Lake City. She records that he spoke with her and "seemed to read me like a book, and to understand my inmost thoughts." He spoke a little of her future. Aurelia remembered, "I did not begin to know what was before me; but [he] told me to continue as faithful as I had been, and all would be well, for there was a great work for me to do."[5] Many years later, she concluded, "With all the difficulties encountered, I have indeed had joy in my Primary labors; and feel that it was this work that President Heber C. Kimball saw when conversing with me."[6]

In a brief sketch of the creation of the Primary Association, Aurelia described some of the children in her Farmington community as being "allowed to be out late at night," some even deserving the designation "hoodlum." In addition, some children were guilty of "carelessness in the extreme, not only in regard to religion, but also morality." She identified the causes for parents' negligence in training their children as exhaustion of people who had been driven out of Illinois and suffered persecution of every kind and the fact that they could barely provide sustenance for their children. Nevertheless, she refused to accept any excuse for a lack of spiritual upbringing in what she considered "the most sacred duty of parentage."[7]

Similarly concerned, Farmington bishop John W. Hess called a meeting of the mothers in the ward and gave them instructions on training and guiding children. He laid this responsibility on the mothers, but in Aurelia's mind, without a united effort of all ward members, it appeared not all would embrace his counsel. Aurelia reported that she initially considered speaking to the leaders of the Young Men's Mutual Improvement Association; however, she did not. Nevertheless, her concern for the youth and especially for young boys did not end. In fact she described her distress about the young boys as "a fire [that] seemed to burn within me." She continued to ponder the idea of "an organization for little boys wherein they could be taught everything good, and how to behave."[8]

Shortly thereafter, in March 1877, a Farmington Relief Society conference was held. Sisters Eliza R. Snow and Emmeline B. Wells attended from Salt Lake City.[9] Providentially, these two women and others stopped at Aurelia's home after the meeting while they awaited the train back to Salt Lake.[10] The conversation turned to the topic of young people and especially "the rough, careless ways [of] many of the young men and boys."[11] According to Eliza, Aurelia was desirous to do something more to effect the "cultivation and improvement of the children morally and spiritually than was being done through the influence of day and Sunday-Schools."[12] Now Aurelia had the ear of the most powerful woman in the Church, Eliza R. Snow, the de facto general president of the Relief Society, under whose purview fell the concerns of all women in the Church. Aurelia asked Eliza, "What will our girls do for good husbands, if this state of things continues?" As Eliza contemplated this question, Aurelia pressed on: "Could there not be an organization for little boys, and have them trained to make better men?" In Aurelia's words, Eliza "was silent a few moments, [and] then said there might be such a thing and that she would speak to the First Presidency about it."[13] Before this could be done, however, President Brigham Young died on August 29, 1877.

According to Aurelia's notes, Eliza continued to believe that the idea of an organization for young boys was a good one and in time presented it to the senior Apostle and soon-to-be Church President, John Taylor, and to others of the Quorum of Twelve.[14] After they approved the proposal, Eliza wrote a letter to Bishop Hess of the Farmington Ward explaining the matter to him. Soon afterward, Bishop Hess met with Aurelia and, after they had talked a while on the subject, he asked her if she "would be willing to preside over an organization of the children."[15] Up until this point, Aurelia's focus had been on an organization for the young boys; girls had not been mentioned. Aurelia realized almost immediately, however, that the organization would not be complete without the young girls too. Among other reasons, singing was necessary, and "it needed the voices of little girls as well as boys to make it sound as well as it should."[16]

Aurelia wrote to Eliza to ask "her opinion in regard to the little girls taking part." In a letter dated August 4, 1878, Eliza responded with these encouraging words: "The spirit and contents of your letter pleased me much. I feel assured that the inspiration of heaven is directing you, and that a great and very important movement is being inaugurated for the future of Zion. . . . The importance of the movement and its great necessity is fully acknowledged by all with whom I have conversed on the subject. . . . We think that at present, it will be wisdom to not admit any under six years of age, except in some special instances. You are right—we must have the girls as well as the boys—they must be trained together. . . . The angels and all holy beings, especially the leaders of Israel on the other side [of] the veil will be deeply interested." At a visit to Farmington shortly thereafter, "Sister Snow suggested that the organization be called 'Primary.'"[17]

With no directions from a presiding organization and without personal academic training, Aurelia learned what to do from the Spirit and from her experience as a mother. She described pondering "over what was to be done for the best good of the children. I seemed to be carried away in the spirit . . . which lasted three days and nights. . . . This was a testimony to me that what was being done was from God."[18] More than a year after Aurelia's initial inspiration and questions regarding children, the first Primary Association was organized.

On Sunday, August 11, 1878, at a public meeting, Bishop Hess set apart Aurelia and two counselors to preside over the Primary Association in Farmington. The minutes of the organizational meeting called for the "Primary Mutual Improvement Association to include children of both sexes from six to fourteen years of age." At the meeting, Bishop Hess charged the parents to "feel the importance of this movement." In his mind, "if anything in this life should engage the attention of parents it should be the care of their children." He reminded those present that "elders by hundreds and thousands travel the world over to convert people and thousands of dollars are spent to emigrate them. . . . We have here with the L.D. Saints a host of spirits that we are the parents of, and when we awake to their interest we will wonder what we have been thinking of in neglecting those little ones and letting their untrained minds take their own course."[19]

The new president spoke next. Aurelia testified, "I believe the Lord is preparing the way and blessed is the name of the Lord. . . . Over one year ago Bishop Hess called the sisters together, feeling that the young people were being led astray, and threw the responsibility upon the sisters to look after their daughters. I felt then if he had called the Brethren together also, to advise together with them it would have been better." Aurelia's greatest concern was for the boys and young men, the future "Elders in Israel and who are running in the streets, their mothers hardly able to control them. . . . While they are running loose, the adversary will feel that he can instill into their tender minds such influences that in their youth will make them subject to him. But I feel that in this he will be baffled, but he will not cease his efforts." Nevertheless, she was certain that "when children are taught in the right way, they will notice the course of their parents more and more.

When asked if I would lead out in this movement I felt that I could not refuse. . . . My intentions are to speak and act with the Spirit of the Lord." She concluded with the desire that all "pray to the Lord to bless those in authority with wisdom to direct aright" the new Primary organization.[20]

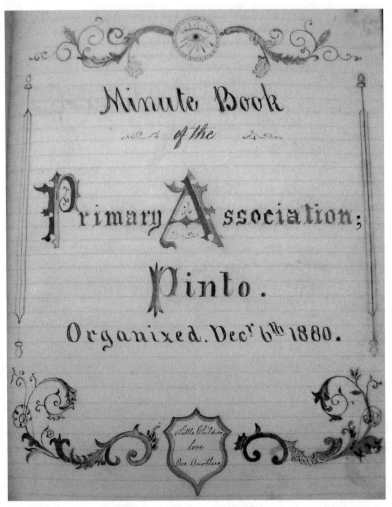

The decorations on the first page of this Primary Association minute book illustrate how important this organization was to its participants. (L. Tom Perry Special Collections, Harold B. Lee Library, Brigham Young University.)

Although Aurelia's initial pondering had brought peace, she wrote, "After the organization I was nearly overcome by the opposite power, and was sunken, as it were, into the very depths of misery; I felt my unworthiness so keenly that I could scarcely attend to my duties; and went to my meetings weeping by the way, being humbled to the very earth. . . . I had been made to feel my entire dependence on God the Eternal Father."[21]

Nine days later, on August 25, the children were called together for the first time and the purpose of the meeting explained to them. Thereafter, beginning September 7, meetings were held on Saturday at 2:00 p.m. at the meetinghouse. She described her early thoughts in this new responsibility: "It would be impossible for one who had never experienced anything of the kind, to imagine our feelings as we stood before an audience of children who had come there to receive instructions from us. We were very weak indeed, but felt to lean upon the Lord in all humility."[22] The leaders felt that Primary meetings were a school for them as well as for the children. They depended on the Lord to assist them and enlighten their minds by the Holy Spirit, "that they might be in very deed the teachers of life and salvation unto the children committed to their care."[23]

Not all supported Primary. From a number of editorials and letters in the *Woman's Exponent* and Eliza R. Snow's several personal exhortations, it appears that support for the Primary Association was not unanimous even after more than a year of organizing associations throughout the territory.[24] Thomas G. Alexander writes, "Reports from the 1880s indicate that attendance averaged about half the number of children enrolled."[25]

In advocating support for the Primary organization, an editorial in the *Woman's Exponent* counseled:

> It is evident that to correct the evils that exist in the world today a great reformation is needed, of a kind unlike any other, and many wise people believe it must commence with the children. . . . Everything for the better education of little children in all that is most excellent should be done, and because of the indelible impressions made upon the infant mind in its earliest years, the

greatest care should be taken in the development of their moral and spiritual faculties. Many people do not believe that children possess any positive spiritual faculties that can possibly be cultivated so young as under eight, nine, or ten years. . . . There has been too much neglect of these spiritual qualities in the young, yet they are of vital importance in the perfecting and harmonizing of the human soul. . . . But a new movement has been made to put into active exercise the spiritual elements of the children's character. For this purpose the organizations called Primary Associations have been formed, and already much has been accomplished in this direction. But there is not sufficient interest awakened upon the subject; many parents are indifferent in regard to the matter. Some good people think this getting the children together to teach them of the things of God, and help develop in them at a very early period the latent germ of spirituality, is superfluous. . . . To all, or any, who feel any doubt on this subject, we would suggest that they take the trouble to visit one of these same Primary Associations, and listen to the teachings given, note the spirit and manner in which they are imparted; hear the sweet voices of the children singing, and see the eyes sparkle with innocent pleasure and the little faces brighten as they answer their questions; and better still, hear them speak in their childish manner of faith and other principles.[26]

Six months later, another editorial warned parents, "A deep sleep seems to have fallen upon some, and they are indifferent to the evil influences that are fast gaining ground, and perchance creeping stealthily into their own households." The editorial reminded parents that "to aid mothers in the spiritual education of the children, the Primary Associations have been organized among the Saints. They will have an influence to lead them into the channel of a proper education. As a people we cannot be too particular in training the children. . . . The children of Zion have God's work to do and their discipline and education should be administered accordingly."[27]

Primary Association Pioneers: An Early History

Later that same year, Eliza, in speaking to the Sanpete County Relief Society, asked the women two questions: "Mothers, do you realize the importance of the early training of your children? What can be of so much consequence to parents than that their children shall be so cultivated as to grow up to be men and women of God?" She promised the sisters, "The Primary organizations are designed to assist the mothers in their most responsible duties in this direction, and mothers should not think their work at home more important, than sending their children to the Primary meetings."[28] The next month, in Kanosh, Eliza declared that Primary "was one of the most important organizations. The youth of Zion were thirsting for knowledge." She expressed her great concern that "our children have been neglected in the past and many have grown up infidels. Their minds have been charged with knowledge and their mental capacities have been crowded to the exclusion of spiritual life."[29]

President Taylor lent his support and the weight of his office to the fledgling Primary Association by attending an 1880 Weber Stake sisters conference with Elder Franklin D. Richards of the Quorum of the Twelve Apostles, Eliza R. Snow, and Zina D. Young. "Pres. Taylor was specially invited by the children of the Primary Association"[30] and at their request offered the opening prayer. The program included singing by the children, questions posed by Eliza and answered by the children, and a recitation of the Lord's Prayer in concert. President Taylor directed his remarks mostly to the children: "When the Lord Jesus was upon the earth, the children crowded around him, and when they were told to retreat by His disciples, Jesus said, 'Suffer little children to come unto me, for of such is the kingdom of Heaven.'" By this example, President Taylor taught that Jesus loved little children and that "He loved them still, and when they were good He would hear their prayers, and answer them, though in person He was not with them on the earth." At this point in the meeting, he asked Elder Richards to read from 3 Nephi, telling the story about Jesus commanding the people to bring their children that he might bless them. President Taylor pointed out the signs—fire and angels descending out of heaven—as evidence of the depth of Jesus' love for little children. He concluded his remarks by urging the children to heed the truths restored by Joseph Smith and taught to them by their parents: "Upon the children would soon rest the responsibility of carrying on the work of their parents; therefore they should be good and kind, and avoid being harsh and of a fighting nature, in order to prepare themselves for the work before them."[31]

The prophet's response to the Primary children was an especially important signal to Church members, as some still resisted the idea of this new organization. He taught about the Savior's love of little children and demonstrated his own love for them by coming at their invitation. The attendance of two members from the presiding quorums of the Church was an unspoken indication of their support for the Primary Association. Nevertheless, not all Church members responded to their example.

In a retrospective look at her first seven years as Primary president, Aurelia lamented how little success she had with getting the boys to attend the weekly meetings. She felt that all her "anxiety and labor to get the boys to attend" had largely failed. Her keen disappointment reflected her thoughts on why the Primary had been instituted in the first place: "for the good of the little boys especially." She thought greater parental support, especially encouragement from fathers, was necessary to get the boys to attend. She chose, however, to put her worries "in the hands of the Lord, and when He saw fit to wake the people up things might be different."[32]

EXPANSION: ELIZA R. SNOW

Eliza organized the second Primary in the Salt Lake Eleventh Ward on September 14, 1878, only weeks after the organization of the Farmington Primary. She selected Louise B. Felt to be the president, training her for her call two years later as the general president of the Primary. The organization of local Primary Associations began in earnest thereafter, with Eliza traveling throughout the territory of Utah. As the head of the Relief Society, all the women in the Church were her responsibility, and she therefore took the lead in organizing the Young Ladies' Mutual Improvement Associations and the Primary Associations, considering them auxiliaries under the responsibility of the Relief Society.[33]

It appears that Eliza often selected the Primary presidents. In fact, she "spoke on the subject of organization," although she prefaced her remarks by informing the priesthood brethren present that they might "correct us if need be." She declared that "there were some societies which women had a right to organize, such as the Y. L. and Primary Associations."[34] Bathsheba Smith, later Relief Society general president, "was present at the [organizing] meeting [of the Relief Society] when the Prophet Joseph Smith told the sisters to adopt parliamentary rules."[35] Evidently these same procedures were followed in organizing the early Primary Associations. Ward and stake minute books and reports in the *Woman's Exponent* show that Primary Associations were "organized by" Eliza R. Snow Smith, Emmeline B. Wells, or Zina Huntington Young; that Eliza "called for a show of hands of the children who wished to be organized into a Primary Association"; that women were "nominated" to be Primary presidents; and that these women chose to "resign" after a period of time.[36]

Emmeline B. Wells noted in a biographical sketch of Eliza that as the first secretary of the Relief Society, she was "brought prominently forward as one of the founders of the institution, and [this] helped to prepare her as an organizer." Her organizational skills were legendary and were called "strong features of her character." Eliza's executive ability was a great strength to the Relief Society, "and she has had much to do in this capacity. When one calls to mind the fact that there are three hundred branches of the Relief Society, almost as many Young Ladies' Associations, and hundreds of Primary Associations for the children, now in working order, and that she has done a large proportion of the organizing, one cannot but acknowledge that she must have possessed extraordinary power and ability in this direction."[37] Eliza was recognized as the leader of the women's organizations and stood preeminent among women in organizing.[38] Both men and women of the Church recognized that Eliza was a talented and respected organizer, yet she had a clear understanding of the boundaries between her responsibilities and those of priesthood holders in organizing Relief Societies, Young Ladies' Mutual Improvement Associations, and Primary Associations.

Eliza's zeal for the new Primary organization is illustrated by the string of meetings she attended during September and October 1878 in Provo, Spanish Fork, and Pleasant Grove, Utah.[39] Similarly, 1879 and 1880 saw Primaries organized in Nephi, Levan, Morgan, Croyden, and Beaver.[40] In order to maximize her efforts, several Primaries in relatively close proximity would be organized within a few days. In a report to the *Woman's Exponent*, Eliza wrote that in February 1881, she and Zina D. Young traveled from St. George to Kanab, Long Valley, Orderville, Johnson, Glendale, and back to St. George to organize ward and stake Primary Associations.[41] The organization of a Primary was accompanied by instructions to the children, such as these noted in the Parowan minutes: "Sister Eliza than gave some good instructions to the rising generation upon the principles of the gospel and the benefits to be derived by keeping the Word of Wisdom which would enable them to become strong and mighty pillars in Zion."[42] Part of this five-month trip to southern Utah included traveling "one thousand [miles] by team over jolting rocks and through bedded sand"[43] and camping out for three nights.[44] Although both women had made the trek west in 1847 and 1848 respectively and were no strangers to camping, Eliza was seventy-seven years old, Zina was sixty, and it was winter. Nevertheless, Eliza R. Snow traveled the length of the Utah Territory during the snowy winter months.

As soon as Primary Associations were organized they became part of the Relief Society quarterly meetings. These meetings already included the Young Ladies' Mutual Improvement Association. The meetings were held over two days, with the Primary meeting often held on Saturday afternoon. Sometimes visitors from Salt Lake came to address the women, teenagers, and children. Later, when the general presidencies were organized, Primary likely had its own separate conference. The minutes of these meetings with women and Primary children record sacred experiences.

Utah Stake Primary Association Conference, Provo, Utah, 1881. In 1881, the first countywide Primary conference held in Provo, Utah, created great interest. Such a conference for children was new, and the house was crowded. Margaret T. Smoot, stake Relief Society president, presided, with Zina D. H. Young as the Salt Lake visitor.

The meeting was described as moving; tears ran down the faces of many of the mothers. Sister Smoot spoke of having "received an answer to a question I have asked many times and received no answer. In the Bible, I have read these words: 'Out of the mouths of babes and sucklings shall his name be praised.'" She testified, "My heart is full to overflowing. I thank my Heavenly Father that I have lived to see the day when the little children of Zion are praising his name." She then blessed the sisters of the Primary placed in "charge of the children that they might be filled with the Spirit of the Lord to lead and guide them in this ways." Sister Young then spoke and said, "The gift of tongues is resting upon some of the sisters here, also the gift of interpretation." Sister Dwyke, the wife of the bishop, arose and spoke in tongues, and Sister Young gave the interpretation: "It was a blessing and prophecy concerning the children of the primaries, . . . that the children given in their charge were the hope of Israel and the heirs to the kingdom of God." The secretary closed her minutes with this heartfelt comment: "It was a time to be long remembered."[45]

Primary Conference of Cache Stake, Logan Tabernacle, September 2, 1882. During this conference, Eliza R. Snow and Zina D. H. Young were the Salt Lake visitors. Following the reports given by leaders, Eliza spoke to the children. Sister Snow's love for the children, as if they were her own, was evident in her delight at their ability to answer gospel questions and at learning that some were paying tithing. She admonished "the children to pray for the sick, for the Lord heard their prayers as soon as any other persons." Sister Young also spoke briefly to the children encouraging them to come home early at night in order to avoid bad company and to be missionaries by inviting their playmates to attend Primary. She promised that "all who do right will enter Heaven [but] others would be shut out. Never fear to do right and God will bless you."

Primary president Jane E. Hyde Molen expressed her hope that the children would not be too tired or cold to sit and listen to the instructions from the sisters. She requested all present "to pray for Sister Snow to speak in tongues that they might know the gift of tongues was still with the Church." Sister Snow desired to have the gift of tongues manifest, but first she would make certain the children would not make light of this gift of the Spirit and would ask them to pray for her. In this meeting,

> Sister Snow arose and told of the meetings little children had when the Prophet Joseph was alive. Little children then spoke in tongues and she said the time would come again when children would have the gift of tongues. . . . She then spoke to them in tongues after which Sister Young gave the interpretation. . . . Brothers and Sisters be good, if you could see the angels that are here you would be astonished. God loves you [and] he will bless you if you are faithful. Live humble before the Lord. Oh Father bless these little ones that they may have peace. She then spoke to the mothers and said Oh Father bless the mothers of these little ones. Thou knowest my agony and the tears I have shed on my pillow by night. Mothers extend thy faith that the Spirit of God may rest upon you and them. The meeting was closed with singing and prayer.[46]

Primary Conference of Cache Stake, July 27, 1885. During this conference, Sister Eliza R. Snow remarked how she loved the sweet singing of Primary children and requested they sing her favorite hymn, "In Our Lovely Deseret." Jane E. Molen asked the children if they realized who had just spoken to them. "First think little children, we have the privilege of having the prophet's wife to teach us." At the afternoon session, Eliza gave the opening prayer, which was "repeated in concert by the children." Eliza's example of having the children repeat in unison her prayer taught them to unite their faith and focus their hearts on the Savior and was sometimes practiced in weekly meetings, especially when the children prayed for those who were ill.[47] In her address to the children, she declared that "Primary meetings are to improve the children and prepare them to go on missions." Their mission now was "to bring a boy or girl with them to meeting; those who are not in the habit of attending." She urged each one to have mighty faith and to pray night and morning. In particular she desired the boys to learn to sing and praised those who were "trying to do right," remarking that she would rather have them administer to her than one of their fathers. Eliza spoke to the Primary presidents and encouraged them to continue with meetings even if but one child attended.

During her many visits, Eliza listened to the singing and recitations of the children. She often expressed her pleasure in seeing so many bright faces and hearing the various exercises and her joy in meeting with the children and hearing them sing.[48] Then she would speak and instruct the children on behavior. For example, on one occasion she advised, "When we come to meeting we should sit very still and look at the speaker and not turn our head around to see who comes in."[49] She would relate stories such as the story of Samuel the prophet, drawing a comparison between Samuel and the little children.[50] She would ask questions like "Who was the first prophet in this dispensation?"[51] She would tell the children and their leaders what other Primary Associations were doing. Often she blessed the children and promised them, "If we are good and pray and be obedient to our parents we will raise up to be good men and women."[52]

A clear structure slowly developed as Primaries were incorporated into the existing Relief Society organization and ideas from other Primaries were shared. Nevertheless, regular lessons, division into classes, and a standard weekly program were not implemented for many years.

Primary materials. The following passage is from a typewritten copy of the history of the Provo Utah Fourth Ward Primary from October 12, 1878, to 1900. It was written in April 1957 by Beatrice Young Moore, granddaughter of President Brigham Young and a member of that ward's Primary in the 1890s. She provides insight into a typical weekly Primary meeting:

> In all these years there were no regular lesson outlines as we have now. A program was arranged a week in advance, either by officers or a number of children as a program committee. Bible stories were told by the sisters, poems by the children. Sometimes verses from

the Sermon on the Mount, some of the Articles of Faith or Ten Commandments were recited in unison or sometimes by one or two children. Also dialogues were quite popular with two, three or four children participating. I joined Primary in the Fourth Ward in 1890. We met in the old chapel on Second North between University Avenue and First East on the north side of the street. . . . We met in the vestry in back. . . . On Sept. 26, 1896 the children were asked to each bring a nickel as a donation to Elias Gee to help him on his mission. . . . On January 30, 1896 a letter was sent to Sister Smoot [Relief Society President] from the matron of the Deseret Hospital thanking them for a box of fruit which was sent by Primary children. In minutes from 1895 on, I wasn't on the program very often but I guess the officers called on volunteers to pray, and of course *I always* offered to do it. Was glad when I was old enough to go to M.I.A. at 14, but I learned much in Primary.[53]

Early on, the "untrodden and obscure way" of running the weekly meeting meant that each Primary presidency had to "catch the Spirit of their calling" and then determine their own program.[54] As one large group, the children sang, were taught, and learned to bear testimony. The Primary presidency and their assistants taught the children on a wide variety of topics, from lessons on honesty, punctuality, and good manners to obedience, faith in God, and prayer.[55] According to the minutes, mainstays of the weekly meeting included a great deal of singing, stories from the Bible or the Restoration, recitations by the children, and occasional outings to a park. Other activities included such things as sewing rags to help make carpet, planting beans and corn, and hosting a yearly concert.[56] Although many good activities were taking place, the Primary associations needed greater organization on many levels. Eliza recognized this need for Primary materials and stepped in to fill it. During a very short period of time, between the years 1880 and 1882, she published two music books, a Bible question-and-answer book, and two Primary speaker books.

Eliza R. Snow, recognizing the need for music within the Primary organization, put together two books of music for the Primary Association. One of them was the Children's Primary Tune Book *pictured above.*

Children's music books. On June 17, 1880, Eliza addressed the Relief Societies of Weber County during a quarterly conference held in the Ogden Tabernacle. Among other things she declared that "something greatly needed was a hymn book for the young, and she was occupied in getting up one for this purpose. The books would be sold at 12½ cents per copy, as she did all her own work free in the interest of the kingdom. Thus the books could be sold at cost." She thought "we should have prophets and prophetesses among the young."[57] On November 27, 1880, Emmeline B. Wells, speaking at the ninth quarterly meeting of Relief Society in the Provo meetinghouse, promoted "the Primary Hymn Books and Tune Book for the children. [She] thought they were well adapted for the use of the little folks and would be a great blessing to them."[58] Within one year, Eliza published two books of music for the Primary Association.

In 1880, *Hymns and Songs: Selected from Various Authors for the Primary Associations of the Children of Zion* was published. It was bound in a 3 × 5-inch blue cloth jacket with a gold-embossed title, *Children's Primary Hymn Book.* The book consisted of 124 pages, sixty-five hymns (beginning with "We Thank Thee, O God, for a Prophet" and forty-four songs (beginning with "Joseph Smith's First Prayer").[59] Neither category included music. Eliza's contributions to this book of music include "Annie's Sympathy," "Angel Whisperings," "A Precious Jewel," "Children, Obey Your Parents," "Gold and Tinsel," "I'll Serve the Lord," " In Our Lovely Deseret," " Little Betty," "Looking at the Stars," "My Father Dear," "My Own Home," "Our Heavenly Father, We," "O My Father, Thou That Dwellest," "Sing the Sweet and Touching Story," "To a Star," "To Santa Claus," "The Tool and the Gem," "The World's Jubilee," and "Youthful Sonnet."[60]

Eliza's other book, the *Tune Book for the Primary Associations of the Children of Zion*, was bound in a 7 × 8¼-inch green cloth jacket with a gold-embossed title, *Children's Primary Tune Book*. The book consisted of forty pages and ninety-one hymns of one verse each and included music. Some hymns are still popular today; however, most are found only in the adult hymnal. These include "All Things Bright and Beautiful," "Dearest Children, God Is Near You," "Do What Is Right," "Hope of Israel," "How Firm a Foundation," "Joseph Smith's First Prayer," "Love at Home," "My Mother Dear," "Praise to the Man," "Sweet Hour of Prayer," "The Spirit of God Like a Fire is Burning," "Today [While the Sun Shines]," and "We Thank Thee, O God, for a Prophet."[61] Eliza's "O My Father," "Our Heavenly Father," and "I'll Serve the Lord While I Am Young" became Primary favorites.[62] Eliza's favorite song, however, was "In Our Lovely Deseret," which she would often request the children to sing. Given her history with the development of the Primary Association and its early music books, it is surprising that not one of Eliza's lyrics is found in the current *Children's Songbook*.

Children's catechism. Eliza published *Bible Questions and Answers for Children* in 1881 as a catechism, or a book of basic principles and beliefs in the form of questions and answers. The book was 119 pages long, bound in black cloth, and divided into forty-four chapters. The book included questions from the Old and New Testaments; however, there were only seven questions on Isaiah, Joel, and Malachi and nearly ninety questions on the last days of Christ's ministry on earth. The following are seven questions and answers from the last chapter:

> Q.—What did Isaiah, an ancient prophet, say should speak out of the dust?
> A.—Truth.
> Q.—What did he say should look down from heaven?
> A.—Righteousness.
> Q.—What did the Prophet Joel say the Lord will do in the last days?
> A.—Pour out His Spirit upon all flesh.
> Q.—Who did he say shall prophesy?
> A.—The sons and the daughters.
> Q.—What did the prophet Malachi say of the last days?
> A.—That the day should come that shall burn as an oven.
> Q.—Who shall be burnt up?
> A.—The proud and all that do wickedly.
> Q.—Where will the righteous be?
> A.—In the holy city—the New Jerusalem.[63]

In an explanatory note for how the book was to be used, Eliza wrote:

> This book is not designed to be placed in the hands of children for them to study, but to assist those who have charge of the children. The president, or one whom she shall appoint, is expected to read a question, and another appointee read the answer, and all the children present repeat the answer in concert. As soon as the children can answer the questions the prompting may be dispensed with. One chapter, or part of a chapter, may be taken for a lesson, and be repeated week after week until it is well committed. In getting up this book, historical order has not been the aim; but to impress the minds of the children with important facts contained in the Old and New Testaments. E. R. Snow Smith.[64]

Recitations. Eliza compiled two books of poetry, dialogues, and speeches to be used by children as recitations during Primary meetings.[65] The *Primary Speaker Book No. 1* was "adapted to the capacities of members from the age of four to ten years." The 178 pages included the following seven contributions from Eliza: "Elegy," "Honesty the Best Policy," "I Want to Be Good," "To Santa Claus," "The Honest Boy," "The Repentant," "Well, If We Make It So." The *Primary Speaker Book No. 2* was also a compilation of poetry, dialogues, and prose. It was to be used for those from age ten to fifteen. In this 196-page volume, Eliza contributed many more pieces of literature to this volume, including "A Precious Jewel," "Annie's Sympathy," "Assassination of Generals Joseph and Hyrum Smith," "A New Year's Speech," "Beauty Everywhere," and "Camp of Israel."

Eliza wrote an introduction to the two *Speaker* books titled "A Few Hints to Presiding Officers." In it she laid out the purpose of recitations, the behavior to be expected from the children, the importance of memorization, the need for proper expression, and the connection to learning to read, stating, "The object of recitation is not only to cultivate the heart and intellect, but also to improve the manners." She encouraged dignity and eschewed "careless, rude, and swaggering motions." In her opinion, "short recitations, with their meaning explained so as to be fully understood, and recited with proper tone and gesture, are very much more cultivating than lengthy ones committed to memory and recited in a monotonous manner. . . . Instead of encouraging children to exhibit *how much* they can commit to memory, they should be taught *how*, and be inspired with an ambition to manifest *how well* they can recite what they have memorized. This will greatly assist them in acquiring the art of reading, which is very desirable. E.R.S.S."[66]

GREATER ORGANIZATION: LOUIE B. FELT

Aurelia Rogers records that at an April 1880 meeting, Eliza thought "it best to have some one appointed to preside over all the Primary Associations in the Territory. She suggested that the person should reside in Salt Lake City, as that was the center; and asked me whom I would propose to fill the office." Upon a few moments' reflection, "the name of Sister Louie B. Felt came to [Aurelia's] mind." Eliza confirmed that that was also her feeling. The first time Louie and Aurelia met, they had "an unusually warm feeling of sympathetic friendship." When others suggested that it was Aurelia's rightful place to preside, she declared that she "never had a moment's jealousy over anyone holding office; for no person will ever take my honors from me; I shall have all that I deserve."[67] Louie recorded Eliza's words in calling her to this position: "Sister Felt, we have chosen you for this place." Louie's surprise was evident in her response: "I am not worthy and I am so ignorant. I could not fill that position. I'm sure I could not." Eliza reassured her with this comment: "If you thought you could we would not want you." Louie was finally comforted when the sisters gathered around her and Eliza gave her a "grand blessing."[68]

During the time Louie worked in the Salt Lake City Eleventh Ward Primary and Young Ladies' Mutual Improvement Association, Eliza R. Snow, Zina D. Young, Mary I. Horn, and other stake members took note of her "great ability and charm as a leader and speaker in the Stake MIA, and as the ward primary president."[69] Lillie Tuckett Freeze, who was to become Louie's general Primary secretary, wrote, "Louie had a most wonderful influence over the little children of the Eleventh Ward. They were fascinated by her gracious manner. Every child was willing and anxious to do whatever she suggested."[70] Louisa White, Louie's Eleventh Ward Primary counselor, also wrote that "President Felt was beloved by officers and children alike. She was continually studying up something that would be of benefit or interest to the children. Many times I have been summoned to her home to discuss some plan pertaining to their welfare or entertainment."[71]

Louie was originally from Connecticut and was sent with her husband to settle the Muddy River (in Nevada), so she was a relative newcomer to Salt Lake City.[72] Nevertheless, her two years of training as ward Primary president combined with natural talent caused Eliza to decide that Louie would make an excellent general Primary president.[73]

Several important responsibilities became official callings on June 18 and 19, 1880, at a conference of the Sisters Associations of the Salt Lake Stake. On the morning of June 19, "the middle seats of the Tabernacle were filled with the children of the Primary Associations of the city." As part of the business, "'Sister Eliza,' then nominated Mrs. Louie Felt as General Superintendent to preside over all the Primary Associations of all the Stakes of Zion, which was unanimously carried."[74] President John Taylor lauded the ladies of the Relief Society, especially the Primary presidents, for teaching the children correct principles. At the afternoon session, President Taylor spoke and closed his remarks by blessing the children and the sisters "with Sister Snow at their head. Mrs. M. I. Horne moved, and Mrs. S. M. Kimball seconded the motion that President Taylor publicly appoint 'Sister Eliza' as president of all the Relief Societies.... P. Taylor then nominated her and she was sustained as president."[75] Eliza, who had long been recognized as the leading lady in the Church and was referred to as the "president of the entire Female Relief Societies,"[76] had never previously had been sustained as general president.

Louie learned how to lead from Eliza, Aurelia, Emmeline, Zina, and other prominent sisters.[77] From the reports recorded in the *Woman's Exponent*, it does not appear that she traveled to organize any of the early Primary Associations, apparently lacking authority to do so.[78] In fact, for a time, she seems to have concentrated on her responsibilities as the Eleventh Ward Primary president, as a counselor to Mary Ann Freeze on the Salt Lake Board for the Young Ladies' Mutual Improvement Association, and as ward treasurer.[79] Further, early in her presidency, in response to the 1882 Edmunds-Tucker Act, Lillie Tuckett Freeze recorded that "the raid began and we all scattered for nearly four years.... Nothing much could be done; only as the stakes and wards kept the work going." During this time approximately fifteen hundred men were imprisoned, and Louie's husband, Joseph (who had two wives), went "underground." Louie traveled east twice to avoid testifying against her husband.[80]

Nevertheless, "from 1880 to 1890 Louie visited a number of stakes. Some of them a number of times in company with the leading sisters for all went together in those days and helped each other."[81] In October 1880, Louie, in company with Mary Ann Freeze and Clara Conrad, took the train from Salt Lake to Provo to visit, "by invitation, the Primary Mutual Improvement Associations of Spanish Fork." She remarked on the quiet and attentive order of the children in the meeting, on their ability to answer gospel questions, and particularly on the singing of the small children.[82] The minutes of the meeting report, "Mrs. Louie Felt addressed the meeting, praising and encouraging the little ones; engaging their attention by her pleasing and lovable manner."[83] It appears that she traveled only when invited and without her counselors, perhaps because there were no general Church operating funds to pay for travel. Louie's husband was willing to pay her expenses.[84]

Louie's friend and secretary, Lillie Tuckett Freeze, confirmed the sentiments of the Spanish Fork Primary: "Louie, because of her charming magnetic personality, her sweet winning ways, her peculiar adaptability in handling and appealing to children made her the idol of the day—she was sought after by women and children, feted, praised, honored, and adored—no woman in the church has been more beloved, no woman has received such manifestations of loving admiration from co-workers—especially her own board—no woman filled her positions better—no one is entitled to more honor. With Louie, as with all persons in active public life—there is always much unwritten history."[85]

CONCLUSION

Aurelia Rogers was honored throughout her lifetime by her own Farmington Primary children, her Primary coworkers, and the general Primary presidency.[86] A tribute to her attested: "[She] heeded the inspirations of her heart and there came into existence the Primary Association, an organization we love so much. Had she not trusted in God, how much she never could have known or realized. . . . Who can measure the joy and satisfaction of Sister Rogers' heart today when she understands that by one of her important obediences to the inspirations of her Maker, she can again serve His purposes. . . . She is so great, and yet so humble; so worthy, and yet so modest, we are happy to honor her. And for all us Primarians, God bless our own Aurelia S. Rogers. May she live her days in continued service and joy."[87]

For fifty years, Eliza R. Snow was honored among Latter-day Saints as "The Elect Lady."[88] As part of a birthday tribute to Eliza on her seventy-seventh year, Susa Young Gates praised Eliza, declaring, "Her monument will be upreared in woman's heart, and children will look back to her as she who, by the grace of God first gave them their dear Primaries. We love thee—E. R. Snow! The magic name—I hear it whispered by the wind, and children's voices catch the sound and sing it high and free. The hearts of thousands stir and murmur out a prayer. Old hands are held to Heaven to call down years upon her life, and little babies coo the song of love they cannot speak. All join our anthem as we pray—God bless thee, E. R. Snow."[89]

In honor of Louie B. Felt, Ruth May Fox wrote:

"Suffer the children to come unto me."
    Through the years of my life I have striv'n
To teach them the words Thou gavest, dear Lord,
    "For of such is the kingdom of heav'n."

She added, "Although she has no children of her own, thousands, yes, tens of thousands, love to look upon her beautiful face and call her 'Mother' because she has loved them and she has reared them in the work of the Lord."[90] For her Primary officers and children, Louie had "lived, worked, wept, and prayed for nearly half a century. She has grown old and young again doing for others."[91]

Aurelia, Eliza, and Louie were strong and capable women, yet there is no evidence of jealousy or vying for power or position. Each woman played her own unique and integral role in the organization of the Primary Association. Each had spiritual impressions, gifts, and talents that helped develop and further the organization. Eliza freely credited Aurelia with the initial idea of a children's organization. Aurelia leaned on Eliza for guidance in making sure she did not overstep her bounds. Eliza asked Aurelia's opinion before selecting the first general Primary president, and Aurelia was delighted that

Louie was chosen. Louie willingly sought advice and counsel from Eliza, Aurelia, and others on how to fulfill her responsibilities as the General president and felt a keen loss of "good support and council" when Eliza passed away.[92] Each woman wore out her mortal life in service to the Primary children and to others. They organized, encouraged, exhorted, and sought for gifts of the Spirit to bless the lives of the future leaders of the Church, and their legacy lives on today. The president of the Huntsville Relief Society wrote to the *Woman's Exponent*, summarizing what many felt: "We are very thankful to have a Primary Association; we can already see the benefit of that spiritual education which all need to make good fathers and mothers. Truly it was the Spirit of God that inspired the Primary organization."[93]

NOTES

For a more complete history of the Primary Association, see Carol Cornwell Madsen and Susan Staker Oman, *Sisters and Little Saints: One Hundred Years of Primary* (Salt Lake City: Deseret Book, 1979); and Conrad A. Harward, "A History of the Growth and Development of the Primary Association of the LDS Church from 1878 to 1928" (master's thesis, Brigham Young University, 1976).

1. Eliza Roxcy Snow often was referred to as "Aunt Eliza" or "Sister Eliza" or "Miss Eliza R. Snow" until May 1880. At this time she took Joseph Smith's name and was called Eliza R. Snow Smith. See Jill Mulvay Derr, *Mrs. Smith Goes to Washington: Eliza R. Snow Smith's Visit to Southern Utah* (St. George, UT: Dixie State College, 2004), 4.
2. Although everyone called her Louie, her full name is Sarah Louise Bouton Felt.
3. See "Lesson Department: Aurelia Rogers," *Children's Friend*, September 1919, 287.
4. See Emmeline B. Wells, "Salt Lake Stake Relief Society Conference," *Woman's Exponent*, July 1, 1880, 21–22.
5. Aurelia Spencer Rogers, *Life Sketches of Orson Spencer and Others, and History of Primary Work* (Salt Lake City: George Q. Cannon and Sons, 1898), 165.
6. Rogers, *Life Sketches*, 233.
7. Rogers, *Life Sketches*, 205–6.

8. Rogers, *Life Sketches*, 207.
9. See Rogers, *Life Sketches*, 207.
10. See *The Personal Writings of Eliza Roxcy Snow*, ed. Maureen Ursenbach Beecher (Salt Lake City: University of Utah, 1995), 36–37.
11. Rogers, *Life Sketches*, 208.
12. *Personal Writings of Eliza Roxcy Snow*, 36–37.
13. Rogers, *Life Sketches*, 208.
14. See Rogers, *Life Sketches*, 208–9. Eliza remembers asking "Mrs. R. if she was willing to take the responsibility and labor on herself of presiding over the children of that settlement, provided the Bishop of the Ward sanctioned the movement." Before this could be done, however, the train arrived and Bishop Hess could not be consulted. Eliza omits presenting the idea to members of the Quorum of Twelve. Instead, she states, "Directly after arriving home, I wrote the Bishop, and by return Mail received from him a very satisfactory response, in which he, (Bishop Hess) not only gave his permission but hearty approval accompanied with his blessing. I then informed Mrs. Rogers that she might consider herself authorized to proceed, and organize in Farmington, which she did." *Personal Writings of Eliza Roxcy Snow*, 37. Another account records that it was at dinner following a July 1878 Relief Society conference in Farmington that Aurelia "talked to us about an Association for little boys. We all spoke to Bishop Hess and he approved & on the way home on the train we decided to go to [President John] Taylor and take the matter before him." Emmeline B. Wells, *Diaries*, July 10, 1878. See also Jill Mulvay Derr, Janath Russell Cannon, and Maureen Ursenbach Beecher, *Women of Covenant: The Story of Relief Society* (Salt Lake City: Deseret Book, 1992), 118.
15. Rogers, *Life Sketches*, 209.
16. Rogers, *Life Sketches*, 209.
17. Rogers, *Life Sketches*, 209, 210–12.
18. Rogers, *Life Sketches*, 212.
19. Farmington Ward, Davis Stake, Primary Association minutes and records, August 11, 1878, Church History Library, The Church of Jesus Christ of Latter-day Saints, Salt Lake City; emphasis in original.

20. Farmington Ward, Primary Association minutes and records, August 11, 1878; emphasis in original.
21. Rogers, *Life Sketches*, 214.
22. Rogers, *Life Sketches*, 215.
23. Provo Fourth Ward, Utah Stake, Primary Association minutes and records, September 1878, Church History Library.
24. See Homespun, "Talk," *Woman's Exponent*, December 15, 1880, 106; and M.J.C., "Education and Occupation," *Woman's Exponent*, December 15, 1880, 106.
25. Jill Mulvay Derr, "Sisters and Little Saints: One Hundred Years of Mormon Primaries," in *The Mormon People: Their Character and Traditions*, ed. Thomas G. Alexander (Provo, UT: Brigham Young University, 1980), 80.
26. "The Children," *Woman's Exponent*, November 15, 1879, 92.
27. "Education of the Young," *Woman's Exponent*, May 1, 1880, 180.
28. Eliza also warned, "The 'civilization' of the world, which is a spirit of corruption creeping in among us, and it will require all the protection that can be imparted by filling their minds with good, so there will be no place for evil—not only should the children understand the principles of the Gospel, but they must have its spirit in their hearts." "R.S., Y.L.M.I.A., Primary Associations," *Woman's Exponent*, October 1, 1880, 110.
29. "R.S., Y.L.M.I.A., Primary Associations," *Woman's Exponent*, December 1, 1880, 102.
30. "Home Affairs," *Woman's Exponent*, April 1, 1880, 164.
31. "Primary Associations' Quarterly Conference at Ogden," *Woman's Exponent*, May 1, 1880, 8:23.
32. Rogers, *Life Sketches*, 230.
33. See "Lesson Department: Eliza R. Snow," *Children's Friend*, April 1919, 72.
34. Eliza, however, maintained that the women "had no right [to organize a] Relief Society; but they could assist the priesthood in doing so. If we were living up to our duties we were helpmeets to the priesthood." Papers of Lillie Tuckett Freeze, 1886–1928, Church History Library. Later Eliza "explained that she had been given a mission to *assist* the priesthood in organizing the Relief Societies; hence, some had conceived the idea that she organized." "R.S., Y.L.M.I.A. and Primary

Reports," *Woman's Exponent*, November 15, 1880, 94; emphasis in original. For further comment on the unique role Eliza played at this time, see Derr, *Mrs. Smith Goes to Washington*, 11.

35. Papers of Lillie Tuckett Freeze, 1886–1928.
36. For an interesting example of resigning, see Derr, *Sisters and Little Saints*, 80.
37. Emmeline B. Wells, "Pen Sketch of an Illustrious Woman," *Woman's Exponent*, October 15, 1880, 73.
38. Wells, "Pen Sketch of an Illustrious Woman," 73.
39. See Provo Fourth Ward, Primary Association minutes and records, September 1878; and Spanish Fork Ward, Utah Stake, Primary Association minutes and records, October 17, 1878, Church History Library; and Pleasant Grove Branch, Utah Stake, Primary Association minutes and records, October 19, 1878, Church History Library.
40. See Morgan Utah Stake Primary Association minutes and records, manuscript, October 28, 1879, Church History Library; see also Harriet Welch, "Relief Society Reports," *Woman's Exponent*, June 1, 1880, 6.
41. Although Eliza's report only includes six settlements, the trip included thirty-two settlements "organizing at least thirty-five [Primaries] during their trip south, and perhaps as many as thirty-eight." Derr, *Mrs. Smith Goes to Washington*, 14.
42. Parowan Utah Stake Primary Association minutes and records, March 27, 1881, Church History Library, Salt Lake City.
43. *Personal Writings of Eliza Roxcy Snow*, 37.
44. Eliza R. Snow Smith, "Trip to Kanab," *Woman's Exponent*, March 15, 1881, 157; see also "R.S., Y.L.M.I.A.," *Woman's Exponent*, June 1, 1881, 1. Although Southern Utah often enjoys a relatively mild winter, at an elevation of 3,200 feet, Hurricane, Utah, can also have snow. Susa Gates Young recorded that they were not prepared for cold weather. See Susa Gates Young to Lucy Bigelow Young, December 6, 1880, Susa Young Gates Collection, Utah Historical Society, Salt Lake City, in Derr, *Mrs. Smith Goes to Washington*, 15.
45. Provo Fourth Ward Minutes, 1881.
46. Logan Utah Cache Stake Primary Association minutes and records, September 2, 1882, Church History Library.

47. See also Pleasant Grove Ward Minutes, Church History Library; Nephi Ward Minutes, Church History Library; Pinto Ward Records, 1880–1889, L. Tom Perry Special Collections, Harold B. Lee Library, Brigham Young University; and Scipio Ward, Millard Stake, Primary Association minutes and records, November 9, 1889, Church History Library.
48. See Provo Fourth Ward, Primary Association minutes and records, November 4, 1881.
49. Spanish Fork Ward, Primary Association minutes and records, November 1881, Church History Library.
50. See Provo Fourth Ward, Primary Association minutes and records, November 4, 1881.
51. Spanish Fork, Utah Stake, Primary Association minutes and records, November 1881, Church History Library.
52. Spanish Fork, Primary Association minutes and records, November 1881.
53. Provo Fourth Ward, Primary Association minutes and records; emphasis in original.
54. Louisa Morris White, "Recalling the Past," manuscript, Church History Library.
55. See Rogers, *Life Sketches*, 215–16.
56. See Rogers, *Life Sketches*, 220–21.
57. "Relief Society Reports," *Woman's Exponent*, July 1, 1880, 22.
58. "R.S., Y.L.M.I.A.," *Woman's Exponent*, January 15, 1881, 127.
59. Eliza R. Snow, *The Children's Primary Hymn Book* (Salt Lake City: Deseret News, 1880).
60. Eliza wrote some of these songs when the Sunday School's *Juvenile Instructor* began publication in 1866.
61. Eliza R. Snow Smith, *Tune Book for the Primary Associations of the Children of Zion* (Salt Lake City: Juvenile Instructor Office, 1880).
62. "Lesson Department: Eliza R. Snow," *Children's Friend*, April 1919, 73.
63. Eliza R. Snow Smith, in *Bible Questions and Answers for Children* (Salt Lake City: Juvenile Instructor Office, 1881), 119.

64. Eliza R. Snow Smith, "Explanatory Note," in *Bible Questions and Answers for Children*, 120. At this time in Church history there was little emphasis on the "facts" of the Book of Mormon although the story of the Restoration was often taught.
65. Eliza wrote some of the poems when the Sunday School's *Juvenile Instructor* began publication in 1866.
66. Eliza R. Snow, *Recitations for the Primary Associations in Poetry, Dialogues and Prose* (Salt Lake City: Deseret News, 1882), 1; emphasis in original. (The title page of book one has a publication date of 1891, an apparent typographical error.)
67. Rogers, *Life Sketches*, 222–23.
68. L. B. Felt's History, Church History Library, Salt Lake City. Part of the grand blessing was given by the gift of tongues.
69. Papers of Lillie Tuckett Freeze, 1886–1928; see also Susan Staker Oman, "Nurturing LDS Primaries: Felt and May Anderson, 1880–1940," *Utah Historical Quarterly* 49, no. 3 (1981): 265.
70. Papers of Lillie Tuckett Freeze, 1886–1928; see also "Lesson Department: Louie B. Felt," *Children's Friend*, December 1919, 413.
71. White, "Recalling the Past."
72. See "Lesson Department: Louie B. Felt," 409.
73. See Papers of Lillie Tuckett Freeze, 1886–1928.
74. "Salt Lake Stake Relief Society Conference," *Woman's Exponent*, July 1, 1880, 21. Lillie Tuckett Freeze recorded that "Joseph F. Smith blessed Louie." Papers of Lillie Tuckett Freeze, 1886–1928.
75. "Salt Lake Stake Relief Society Conference," 21.
76. "Woman's Exponent," *Woman's Exponent*, June 15, 1872, 16; see also Jill Mulvey Derr, "Strength in Our Union," in *Sisters in Spirit: Mormon Women in Historical and Cultural Perspective*, ed. Maureen Ursenbach Beecher and Lavina Fielding Anderson (Urbana: University of Illinois Press, 1987), 172.
77. See Papers of Lillie Tuckett Freeze, 1886–1928.
78. See Derr, *Sisters and Little Saints*, 30.
79. See "R.S., Y.L.M.I.A.," 7; see also Papers of Lillie Tuckett Freeze, 1886–1928, and White, "Recalling the Past."
80. Papers of Lillie Tuckett Freeze, 1886–1928.

81. Papers of Lillie Tuckett Freeze, 1886–1928.
82. L. B., "A Pleasant Visit to Spanish Fork," *Woman's Exponent*, November 15, 1880, 91.
83. Hannah Cornaby, "Meeting at Spanish Fork," *Woman's Exponent*, November 15, 1880, 95.
84. See Papers of Lillie Tuckett Freeze, 1886–1928; see also *Children's Friend*, December 1919, 414; Janet Peterson and LaRene Gaunt, *The Children's Friends: Primary Presidents and Their Lives of Service* (Salt Lake City: Deseret Book, 1996), 13.
85. Papers of Lillie Tuckett Freeze, 1886–1928; emphasis in original.
86. Aurelia records one such "crowning evidence of love" in Rogers, *Life Sketches*, 322–24.
87. Adelaide U. Hardy, "Librarians' Department," *Children's Friend*, September 1919, 358–59.
88. "Lesson Department: Eliza R. Snow," 73.
89. Susa Young Gates, "Address to Eliza R. Snow Smith," *Woman's Exponent*, February 15, 1881, 141.
90. "Lesson Department: Louie B. Felt," 404.
91. "Lesson Department: Louie B. Felt," 415.
92. Papers of Lillie Tuckett Freeze, 1886–1928; see also Oman, "Nurturing LDS Primaries," 266.
93. "R.S., Y.L.M.I.A.," 127.

Though it has been known by different names, the Young Women Organization has always sought to help young women improve themselves, develop their talents, serve others, and strengthen their testimonies of Jesus Christ. (© Intellectual Reserve, Inc. All rights reserved.)

Janet Peterson

12

Young Women of Zion: An Organizational History

The Young Women program of The Church of Jesus Christ of Latter-day Saints has grown from the desires of young women to improve themselves, develop their talents, serve others, and strengthen their testimonies of Jesus Christ. The various names of the organization are listed below:

- The Young Gentlemen and Ladies' Relief Society of Nauvoo, 1843
- The Young Ladies' Department of the Cooperative Retrenchment Association (Young Ladies' Retrenchment Association), 1869
- Young Ladies' National Mutual Improvement Association, 1877

Janet Peterson is a member of the Church Correlation Committee, Materials Evaluation Division.

- Young Ladies' Mutual Improvement Association (YLMIA), 1904
- Young Women's Mutual Improvement Association (YWMIA), 1934
- Aaronic Priesthood MIA, Young Women, 1972
- Young Women, 1974

Though the name has changed several times over the years, the purposes have not. Marba C. Josephson, editor of the *Improvement Era* and general board member, described the goals as "aiding the LDS girl to gain a testimony of the gospel through wholesome lesson work and spiritualized recreation."[1] Church leaders have long recognized the vital role that this auxiliary fills in helping adolescent girls to develop testimonies of the Savior and to become faithful, covenant-keeping women.

The programs and procedures have changed to meet the needs of an ever-growing Church population and to help young women face the challenges of their particular eras. Guided by inspiration from the Lord, each of the thirteen general presidents has built upon the foundations laid by her predecessors. The organizational history of Young Women can be divided into three major periods: (1) Getting Started, 1843–80; (2) Setting the Pattern, 1880–1961; (3) Maturing with the Worldwide Church, 1961–Present.

GETTING STARTED, 1843–80

The first Church organization for the youth, the Young Gentlemen and Ladies' Relief Society of Nauvoo, arose from a gathering of young men and women in January 1843 at Elder Heber C. Kimball's home. The group lamented "the loose style of their morals—the frivolous manner in which they spent their time—and their too frequent attendance at balls, parties, etc."[2] Elder Kimball suggested a more formal meeting be held so that he could instruct them about their duties to their parents, their worthiness, and their avoidance of "evil company."[3]

The name was soon shortened to the Young People's meetings. Officers were elected, and resolutions adopted to be charitable and to help the poor. Membership required a person to be under thirty years of age and of "good moral character." Meetings were held the last Tuesday of each month until the Saints were driven from Nauvoo.

More than twenty-five years later and in another setting, the young ladies and gentlemen were again organized, but this time separately. On November 28, 1869, President Brigham Young rang a prayer bell to gather the women in his family into a parlor of the Lion House. He told them:

> All Israel are looking to my family and watching the example set by my wives and children. . . . I desire to organize my own family first into a society for the promotion of habits of order, thrift, industry, and charity; and . . . to retrench from their extravagance in dress, in eating, and even in speech.
>
> I have long had it in my mind to organize the young ladies of Zion into an association. . . . There is need for the young daughters of Israel to get a living testimony of the truth. . . . Retrench in everything that is bad and worthless, and improve in everything that is good and beautiful. Not to make yourselves unhappy, but to live so that you may be truly happy in this life and the life to come.[4]

President Young thus organized the Young Ladies' Department of the Cooperative Retrenchment Association, whose aim was to help young women "set an example before the world."[5] He charged Eliza R. Snow, then Relief Society president and his plural wife, to organize and direct associations along the Wasatch Front. The Nineteenth Ward formed the first ward association in 1870, followed by scores of other ward groups for the Juniors, or younger women. The Seniors, or older sisters, remained as one organization.[6] The Salt Lake Stake organized the first stake board in 1878.

Every group endeavored to follow Brigham's admonitions. However, members quickly abbreviated the name to the Retrenchment Ladies, Young Ladies, YL, or Juniors and Seniors.[7] Each ward association was an independent entity as there was no general presidency nor approved guidelines.

To commemorate Brigham Young's birthday in June 1880, President John Taylor called a sisters' conference and announced separate general presidencies for the Relief Society, Primary, and young women, with Elmina Shepard Taylor leading the Young Ladies' National Mutual Improvement Association.

SETTING THE PATTERN, 1880-1961

During this eighty-year period, the young women societies developed an organizational structure with a centralized presidency, uniform lessons, age-group divisions, a magazine, achievement awards, music and dance festivals, and a camping program. The patterns set during this formative period shaped programs and procedures even to this day. Each general president added to the program.

Elmina Shepard Taylor, 1880–1904. Presiding over an organization with no precedents to follow and no previous experience to rely on posed a significant challenge to Elmina S. Taylor. Susa Young Gates noted, "There was no General Board, no aids, no guides, no magazine nor other publications for their work; no quarterly or yearly conferences nor conventions, either stake or general; no headquarters, not even any regular meetings of the general officers."[8]

Sister Taylor strived to bring uniformity and unity to the young women organization, for each ward had its own program. The presidency and central board met periodically and developed lessons in theology, literature, domestic science, parliamentary procedure, and good manners. The general leaders traveled by team and wagon, making hundreds of visits to give instructions and to gather ideas from the field. The first printed lessons appeared in the *Guide* in pamphlet form, then in the *Young Woman's Journal*, begun in 1889. This journal also included spiritually oriented materials as well as recipes, sewing patterns, and short stories. Tuesday night was designated as Mutual night, and the weekly program included the following:

1. Singing (Association choir), prayer, roll call
2. Miscellaneous business
3. Bible lecture

4. Historical narrative or biographical sketch
5. Musical exercise
6. Book of Mormon, alternating with Church History
7. Answering questions
8. Declamation, alternating with select reading
9. Report of current events or an essay
10. Scientific lecture
11. Distribution of queries and reading programme
12. Closing exercise, singing, benediction[9]

By the turn of the century, twenty thousand young women were enrolled in Mutual programs in the Intermountain West as well as Canada, Mexico, England, New Zealand, and Hawaii.[10]

Martha Horne Tingey, 1905–29. Both Sister Taylor and her counselor Martha H. Tingey, who succeeded her, served twenty-four years as president. Thus Sister Tingey served for nearly fifty years. Early in Sister Tingey's administration, board meetings moved from quarterly to weekly, and in 1909 the general auxiliary offices were housed in the just-completed Bishop's Building at 40 North Main Street. The central board was renamed the general board in 1912.

Sister Tingey's presidency instituted leadership week in 1914. Those involved in YLMIA referred to the weekly meetings as "Young Ladies." Girls fourteen years and older were enrolled until they entered Relief Society. They were placed in either the Juniors or Seniors.

Because the Mutual year only ran from September to June, leaders sought a new endeavor for the summer months. Patterned after the Camp Fire program and considered a sister organization to the Boy Scouts, the Beehive program, announced in 1915, involved girls ages fourteen to eighteen. Requirements for advancement included knowing "the proper use of hot and cold baths," mending and caring for clothing, doing "one good turn" daily, and memorizing Doctrine and Covenants 89.[11] The Beehive experience, so well received, was incorporated into the general program.

During Sister Tingey's tenure, cultural avenues of music, drama, dance, speech, and road shows expanded. Beginning in 1924, lessons appeared in manuals. Operational funds came from subscriptions to the *Young Woman's Journal* and the annual dime fund (later twenty-five and then thirty-five cents).

To encourage more physical activity among young people, the First Presidency assigned the recreational program to the youth leadership. After the Liberty Stake initiated a summer camp in 1912, the general board suggested that each stake develop a summer program, including hiking and camping, although such was not universally adopted.

Ruth May Fox, 1929–37. At age seventy-five, Ruth May Fox was surprised when called to lead the young women. President Heber J. Grant said that age was a quality of mind and blessed her to have "the same vigor of body and of mind in the future" that she experienced in the past.[12]

As many older Primary girls wanted to attend Mutual, parents could choose whether their daughters attended one or the other or both. At this time, the twelve- to thirteen-year-old group was called Nymphs. Later, the entrance age was determined by a girl's twelfth birthday. Over time, the older girls were divided into Seniors and Advanced Seniors. Then a Junior class was added. From the story of Ruth in the Bible, the Seniors were renamed the Gleaners.

Sister Fox announced a Churchwide summer camping program at June Conference in 1929. Another announcement followed: the *Young Woman's Journal* would be merged with the *Improvement Era*, the YMMIA magazine.

Sister Fox penned the words for a new anthem for the Church's centennial in 1930. Thousands of young people gathered in the Tabernacle to sing "Carry On" as they waved banners of gold and green, the official colors of the MIA. In 1931, the renovated Lion House became a social center for girls, offering classes in writing, speech, charm, and religion. To parallel the name of the young men's organization, the YLMIA was renamed the Young Women's Mutual Improvement Association in 1934.

Young Women of Zion: An Organizational History

The first dance festival, held during the 1936 June Conference, became a popular and long-lasting annual event. Until that year, youth repeated slogans such as "We stand for the non-use and non-sale of tobacco" and "We stand for the preservation of our heritage through obedience to law."[13] Scripture themes then replaced slogans.

Lucy Grant Cannon, 1937–48. Lucy Grant Cannon, a daughter of President Grant, served for eleven years, a challenging era to administer as the Depression drew to a close and World War II began. YWMIA enrollment had grown to seventy-six thousand, concentrated in the United States but with increasing numbers in international areas. Lucy's presidency gave each class its own manual, code, and symbol—a beehive for the Beehives, a rose for the Junior Class, and a sheaf of wheat for the Gleaners. The Gleaner class included young women up to age twenty-two, and earning a Golden Gleaner award was their crowning achievement. Those twenty-three and older belonged to a special interest group, nicknamed "Spingro."

Never a static organization, the young women's auxiliary at times adopted programs for the general Church that had originated in various stakes. Youth conferences were one endeavor, and firesides, another, when Gleaners and M-Men in California wanted more opportunities for socializing.[14]

The war deeply affected the program and the participants. With paper shortages hindering the publication of manuals, the MIA communicated to local leaders through the *Improvement Era*. Gas rationing significantly reduced travel to stakes, and June Conference was suspended. With the war introducing more worldly influences to young people, leaders sought to strengthen them through lessons and firesides, with an increased emphasis on moral standards, the Word of Wisdom, and temple marriage. Because many young women living in smaller towns had migrated to larger cities to work, the YWMIA developed a "Big Sister" program, so that local leaders could watch over and assist these girls. The Beehive House continued to house young women who had come to Salt Lake for work or school and was nicknamed the "Behave House."

Still, in the midst of war, the MIA provided vital spiritual direction and a social life for the youth of the Church. Wallace Stegner, a non-Mormon observer, wrote in 1942:

> The social life of Mormondom is centered in the Ward House as surely as the religious life is, and every Mormon child from the age of twelve upward is a member of . . . the M.I.A., or Mutual. . . .
>
> Designed as a faith-promoting scheme among the young people, the M.I.A. is in practice a highly-developed youth movement. . . .
>
> All the way from hikes, outings, picnics, swimming parties, and hayrides to movies, dances, community singing, amateur theatricals, and athletic contests, the M.I.A. is the orbit within which the young Saint's life moves.[15]

When the great war ended in 1945, the restored peace allowed the MIA to return to its former programs, including June Conference. Three thousand dancers celebrated the war's end during the 1946 conference. The next year the centennial of the pioneers' arrival in the Salt Lake Valley was honored throughout the Church. Many of the one hundred thousand young women participated in parades, square dances, and pioneer treks in their various locales.

Bertha Stone Reeder, 1948–61. When Bertha S. Reeder was called in 1948, young women were enrolled simultaneously in YWMIA and the Girls' Program, the latter functioning as a separate auxiliary. Begun in the Granite Stake, the Girls' Program had been adopted for the entire Church in 1946. Sister Reeder asked the First Presidency to merge the two programs. Girls who attended 75 percent of their meetings and fulfilled other requirements, including keeping the Word of Wisdom, paying tithing, and giving service, received an Individual Award. According to general board member Ruth Hardy Funk, this incentive program resulted in "a great increase in the attendance of young women, . . . not only in Mutual but in all of the meetings. . . . It also had a parallel effect on the whole Church."[16]

Sister Reeder's presidency realigned the age-groups: Beehives for ages twelve and thirteen; Mia Maids, ages fourteen and fifteen; Junior Gleaners, sixteen and seventeen; and Gleaners, eighteen to twenty-nine. The recreation department, renamed the sports committee, emphasized physical activity. Sister Reeder, an avid outdoorswoman herself, organized a general camp committee, suggested that all stakes purchase campsites, and visited many camps each summer.

"Be Honest with Yourself" posters, a forerunner to the current *For the Strength of Youth*, were displayed in meetinghouses, and wallet-sized cards were given to the youth.

June Conference continued to be the highlight of the MIA year, bringing thousands of youth and their leaders to Salt Lake City. Ruth Funk reported that 80 percent of stakes sent representatives to June Conference. She commented, "Of course we must remember that except for maybe ten stakes, all the stakes were in the United States."[17]

In 1959, the Special Interests group was divided into the Young Marrieds and the Mutual Study, for single adults. The Junior Gleaners were renamed the Laurels.

MATURING WITH THE WORLDWIDE CHURCH, 1961–PRESENT

Advent of correlation. During the 1950s, President David O. McKay had appointed Elder Harold B. Lee to chair the General Priesthood Committee and to study all Church programs and organizations. Starting in 1961, all curriculum planning and writing would be directed by the priesthood. As President Spencer W. Kimball would later explain, "The Church does not have several organizational lines running from headquarters leaders to their local counterparts. There is only one fundamental organizational channel, and that is the priesthood channel."[18]

Among the many facets of the correlation process, committees evaluated lesson and magazine materials.[19] Ardeth G. Kapp, then serving on the Youth Correlation Committee, felt that young women "needed to be taught 'matters of eternal consequence' at an earlier age, [and that] they needed Sunday instruction."[20] Previous lessons had been broader in scope, often with an emphasis on such self-improvement aims as good grooming and manners, or loyalty. Sister Kapp commented, "There were no *poor* lessons by way of principle or conduct . . . but many lessons were taught at the sacrifice of things [young women] couldn't get anywhere else except in the Church."[21]

Whereas the MIA generally had been considered the activity arm of the Church for girls, with Sunday School lessons bearing the main responsibility for spiritual instruction, by 1977 scripturally oriented manuals were introduced, with activities reinforcing lessons on gospel principles.[22] Auxiliaries ceased to be financially self-sustaining, thus allowing leaders to focus more on the spiritual and leadership development of the young women.

Church growth and counterculture influences. By 1961, membership had risen to three hundred thousand, with more and more young women living beyond the Intermountain area and outside the United States. A number of factors influenced Church growth worldwide: the postwar baby boomers were of age to serve missions; President McKay emphasized every member a missionary; many Church members moved away from Utah for schooling and employment; the Church became less obscure due to media attention and the prominence of members in a variety of endeavors.

As the Church became a greater force for good in the world, evil influences also increased. The so-called Sexual Revolution was accelerated by the introduction of the birth-control pill in 1960, drugs, more daring themes in TV shows and movies, and the strident questioning of women's roles and the family as an institution. This atmosphere was a significantly challenging moral climate for young women. To counter these moral assaults, the young women leaders focused even more on girls developing spiritually, gaining strong testimonies, strengthening the family, and preparing to make sacred temple covenants.

Florence Smith Jacobsen, 1961–72. Florence S. Jacobsen began her service expressing the hope "that we can be so dedicated that not one single girl in this great Church will be forgotten."[23] Her presidency and seventy-five-member board oversaw a myriad of activities with dance and music festivals, leadership training, youth conferences, and producing new manuals. She did all this while still having charge over the Young Marrieds and Special Interest groups.

Sister Jacobsen presided over the YWMIA's centennial in 1969 with a program in the Lion House, where Brigham Young had organized his daughters. Under her careful supervision, the Lion House had been restored with authentic details and furnishings.

Since 1960, a section titled "The Era of Youth" was included in the *Improvement Era*. However, the auxiliaries no longer published their own magazines when the Church launched a new set of magazines in 1971, with the *New Era* designated just for youth.

Recent general presidents have served for about five years while the early presidents served a quarter of a century and their immediate successors around a dozen years. General boards dropped from a high of seventy-five members to about thirty and then to ten.

Ruth Hardy Funk, 1972–78. A few months after Ruth Hardy Funk was called, the First Presidency announced the organization of the Melchizedek Priesthood MIA, responsible for single adults over eighteen, and the Aaronic Priesthood MIA, for youth ages twelve to eighteen. As Presiding Bishop Victor L. Brown, who would supervise the MIA, explained, "The MIA under this reorganization becomes part of the priesthood and is no longer an auxiliary."[24]

Over the next few years the organizational structure continued to be refined and adjustments made in establishing the roles of the Young Women leadership, on both the general and local levels. Sister Kapp recalled, "I think that it was [an] interim period focusing primarily on the difference between local leaders looking to the general level for direction and local leaders . . . look[ing] to their own local priesthood leaders for direction. And that's quite a dramatic change after a history of looking to Salt Lake for direction."[25]

In 1974, President Kimball divided the Aaronic Priesthood MIA into two organizations: the Aaronic Priesthood and the Young Women. All in all, three major organizational changes to the Young Women program took place during this period.[26]

Sister Funk introduced peer leadership, with youth leading out supported by adult advisers. President Lee suggested that shadow leadership would take at least five years to implement; thus, the years of Sister Funk's administration were a time of sorting out processes and establishing procedures.[27] Yet groundwork was laid for youth taking greater leadership roles in class presidencies and youth councils.

Replacing the Individual Award program, the Young Womanhood Recognition encouraged girls to achieve goals in the areas of spiritual awareness, homemaking arts, service and compassion, recreation and the world of nature, cultural arts and education, and personal and social refinement. The first version of *For the Strength of Youth* listed standards for young people.

In 1975, President Kimball announced that June Conference would be replaced by regional conferences to "take the program to the people."[28] More responsibility was then placed on local leaders; for example, the general board no longer wrote scripts and programs for local use. Despite the trepidation of some local leaders about creating their own productions, the result was beneficial, with one leader saying their program was "better than June conference."

Elaine Anderson Cannon, 1978–84. With the 1978 revelation on the priesthood, missionary work exploded in some African nations and such countries as Brazil. The scope of the Young Women program thus became more international and meeting the needs of developing areas an even higher priority.

Elaine A. Cannon organized the first general women's meeting (for ages twelve and up) held at the Tabernacle in September 1978 and broadcast to fourteen-thousand gatherings around the world. Elaine, Ruth Funk, and Barbara B. Smith spoke, followed by President Kimball. He said, "This is an unique and significant gathering. Nothing like it has ever been held before in the Church—and as far as I know, in the world."[29]

The consolidated meeting schedule, instituted in 1980, significantly changed the complexion of the Young Women program. The three-hour block thus provided Sunday instruction for girls at the same time the Aaronic priesthood met in their quorums.

Ardeth Greene Kapp, 1984–92. Ardeth G. Kapp's administration further refined the Personal Progress program and introduced the Young Women values, theme, and motto ("Stand for Truth and Righteousness") during a satellite broadcast in 1985. Sister Kapp said, "I see the crest of a great wave forming . . . that will move across the earth, reaching every continent and every shore, I call upon you to stand with me to prepare to take your place in a great forward movement among the young women of the Church—a movement of renewed commitment—a movement in which you are destined to shape history and participate in the fulfillment of prophecy."[30]

To foster a worldwide sisterhood among the young women, the first Worldwide Celebration was held in 1987, with celebrations continuing every three years until the year 2000. Reviewing her time in Young Women, Sister Kapp stated, "One thing I hope our administration will be remembered for was changing the mindset from saying 'What shall we do?' to the question 'What do we want to have happen?', so that we're not focusing on activities but looking at outcomes."[31]

Janette Callister Hales (Beckham), 1992–97. Janette C. Hales directed the publication of a new camp manual, with a focus on the Young Women values, service, and spirituality. The introduction states: "[Young women] can find joy in an outdoor setting that will strengthen their love for each other and the gospel and their commitment to stand together as 'witnesses of God at all times and in all things, and in all places.'" [32]

From 1994 on, general Young Women meetings, separate from the Relief Society meetings, have been held a week prior to April general conference. At the first of these meetings, Sister Hales encouraged each girl to become "a righteous, problem-solving woman of faith."[33] She also encouraged adults to learn the names of the youth in their wards, to call them by name and support them.³⁴ The 125th anniversary of the Young Women organization was observed in 1994, though not through a Churchwide celebration.

Margaret Dyreng Nadauld, 1997–2002. Margaret D. Nadauld reiterated the purpose of the girls' organization: "It is the mission of Young Women . . . to help young women grow spiritually and to assist their families in preparing them to come unto Christ."³⁵ Throughout her tenure, Sister Nadauld counseled young women to recognize and live up to their roles as daughters of God, that "women of God can never be like women of the world."³⁶

As the twenty-first century opened, refinements to the Young Women program developed with the revised *For the Strength of Youth* and the words *strengthen home and family* added to the Young Women theme. With many revisions to simplify the program and make it more fitting to the worldwide Church, Personal Progress was published in a smaller format.

Reminiscent of June Conference, youth again participated in dance and music festivals. According to Margaret, "It is strengthening to youth to establish a wider circle of friends than many have in their small wards or branches. This can be accomplished while they are *doing* and *learning* new skills."³⁷

Susan Winder Tanner, 2002–8. Whereas in the early days young adults were still a part of MIA, beginning in 1972 young women moved to Relief Society when they turned eighteen or completed high school. How to effectively help young adult women make this transition during a critical period of their lives was a prime concern of Susan W. Tanner, who worked closely with Relief Society president Bonnie D. Parkin. Together they presented workshops to suggest ways to help make this transition successful.

From the time camping was incorporated into the program in 1929, it has been a vital and fun part of Young Women. With camping property scarce to purchase and expensive to rent, many local units were unable to find suitable camps. The Church thus developed various large camping properties for use by multiple stakes.

Young Women of Zion: An Organizational History

Today's challenges. Today's young women are bombarded with immoral behaviors and icons through the media, the Internet, and text messages. Commenting on the current moral climate, Angela Kays-Burden in the *Christian Science Monitor* wrote:

> The purveyors of our pop culture often portray marriage itself as an arcane institution that our progressive society should move beyond.
>
> In recent years, television shows and Hollywood movies have promoted our acceptance of—and even our appetite for—infidelity. Major networks are complicit in helping to erode the significance of lifelong commitments and loving relationships between husbands and wives.[38]

President Boyd K. Packer commented, "Nothing in the history of the Church or in the history of the world . . . compares[s] with our present circumstances. Nothing . . . exceeds in wickedness and depravity that which surrounds us now."[39] Though confronted by moral assaults, the youth, according to an earlier statement of President Gordon B. Hinckley, "are . . . the finest [and strongest] generation of young people ever in the history of the Church."[40] Elaine S. Dalton told the young women, "There has never been a better time to live on the earth than this."[41]

Elaine Schwartz Dalton, 2008–. As the new general president, Sister Dalton stated, "We [unfurl] our banner calling for a return to virtue. We believe that if there is anything that keeps people away from the Savior and . . . the temple it is not being worthy or pure and morally clean."[42] On the 139th anniversary of Young Women, the First Presidency approved Virtue as a new value and represented by the color gold. Elaine remarked, "The date is not a coincidence. . . . The Lord had His hand in this decision. It has been divinely inspired."[43] The revised *Personal Progress* book, including the value of Virtue, came out in January. As part of the Brand New Year program and utilizing the positive aspects of the Internet, the Church launched a website for youth (youth.lds.org).

CONCLUSION

"The Church moves on and programs change," President Thomas S. Monson said, "but the basic responsibility of helping youth to choose the right . . . is as cardinal a rule today as it has ever been."[44] Over its 140-year history, the young women's auxiliary has grown from one small group in Utah to an organization of a half million worldwide. It has developed through inspiration from the Lord and under the leadership of thirteen faithful, dedicated women. From its inception, this auxiliary has striven to help young women mature in the gospel, gain testimonies of the Savior, prepare for the temple and for their later roles as wives, mothers, and Church leaders. As Susa Young Gates stated, "Mortality has no scales with which to weigh, no rule by which to measure, the value of the Mutual Improvement work to the young women of Zion!"[45]

NOTES

1. Marba C. Josephson, *History of the YWMIA* (Salt Lake City: Young Women's Mutual Improvement Association, 1955), 42.
2. Joseph Smith, "A Short Sketch of the Rise of the Young Gentlemen's and Ladies' Relief Society of Nauvoo," *Times and Seasons*, April 1, 1843, 154, in "An Interesting Outgrowth of the Relief Society in Nauvoo," *Relief Society Magazine* 4, no. 3 (March 1917): 123.
3. Smith "Short Sketch," quoted in "Interesting Outgrowth," 124.
4. Susa Young Gates, *History of the Young Ladies' Mutual Improvement Association* (Salt Lake City: Deseret News, 1911), 8–10.
5. Josephson, *History of the YWMIA*, 2.
6. Gates, *History of the Young Ladies' Mutual Improvement Association*, 36.
7. *A Century of Sisterhood: Chronological Collage, 1869–1969* (Salt Lake City: Young Women's Mutual Improvement Association, 1969), 15.
8. Gates, *History of the Young Ladies' Mutual Improvement Association*, 93–94.
9. *Century of Sisterhood*, 29–30.
10. *Century of Sisterhood*, 36.

11. Josephson, *History of the YWMIA*, 55.
12. Ruth May Fox, *My Story* (privately published, December 1973), 59.
13. *Century of Sisterhood*, 48, 58.
14. Josephson, *History of the YWMIA*, 82–83.
15. Wallace Stegner, *Mormon Country* (Lincoln, NE: University of Nebraska Press, 1970), 16–18.
16. Ruth H. Funk, interview by Gordon Irving, February 6, 1979, 33, James Moyle Oral History Program, Church History Library, The Church of Jesus Christ of Latter-day Saints, Salt Lake City.
17. Funk, interview, 11.
18. Spencer W. Kimball, "Living the Gospel in the Home," *Ensign*, May 1978, 101.
19. Daniel H. Ludlow, "Correlation," in *Encyclopedia of Latter-day Saint History*, ed. Arnold K. Garr, Donald Q. Cannon, and Richard O. Cowan (Salt Lake City: Deseret Book, 2000), 250.
20. Janet Peterson and LaRene Gaunt, *Keepers of the Flame: Presidents of the Young Women* (Salt Lake City: Deseret Book, 1993), 150.
21. Ardeth G. Kapp, oral history, July 1983, 55, James Moyle Oral History Program, Church History Library, Salt Lake City.
22. Kapp, oral history, 71.
23. Florence S. Jacobsen, "Women, This Is Our Time," *Ensign*, March 1972, 39.
24. Victor L. Brown, "The Aaronic Priesthood MIA," *Ensign*, July 1973, 80.
25. Kapp, oral history, 129.
26. Peterson and Gaunt, *Keepers of the Flame*, 114–15.
27. Kapp, oral history, 90.
28. In Kapp, oral history, 104.
29. Spencer W. Kimball, "Privileges and Responsibilities of Sisters," *Ensign*, November 1978, 101.
30. Ardeth G. Kapp, "Stand Up, Lead Out," *New Era*, November 1985, 23.
31. Personal interview with Ardeth G. Kapp, August 6, 1990.
32. *Young Women Camp Manual* (Salt Lake City: The Church of Jesus Christ of Latter-day Saints, 2002), 1.
33. Janette C. Hales Beckham, "Growing Up Spiritually," *Ensign*, May 1994, 96.

34. Janette C. Hales, "You Are Not Alone," *Ensign*, May 1992, 79.
35. Margaret D. Nadauld, "Come unto Christ," *Ensign*, May 1998, 65.
36. Margaret D. Nadauld, "The Joy of Womanhood," *Ensign*, November 2000, 16.
37. Margaret D. Nadauld, e-mail message to author, January 8, 2010.
38. Angela Kays-Burden, "Media Portrayal of Adultery Challenges Traditional Values," *Deseret News*, December 13, 2009, G-3.
39. Boyd K. Packer, "The One Pure Defense," address to Church Educational System religious educators, February 6, 2004, 4.
40. Gordon B. Hinckley, in Elaine S. Dalton, "It Shows in Your Face," *Ensign*, May 2006, 109.
41. Dalton, "It Shows in Your Face," 109.
42. "Standing for Virtue," *New Era*, November 2008, 18.
43. "Standing for Virtue," 18.
44. Sarah Jane Weaver, "Building on a Firm Foundation," *Church News*, November 28, 2009, 3.
45. Gates, *History of the Young Ladies' Mutual Improvement Association*, 299.

Thomas G. Alexander

13

CHURCH ADMINISTRATIVE CHANGE IN THE PROGRESSIVE PERIOD, 1898–1930

B ETWEEN 1898 and 1930, The Church of Jesus Christ of Latter-day Saints undertook a number of significant administrative changes that helped it to function more effectively. Perhaps the most significant began during the administration of President Lorenzo Snow. Financial distress of oppressive magnitude compounded the problems that the Church faced during the 1890s. Through provisions of the Edmunds-Tucker Act of 1887, the federal government had confiscated most of the Church's secular properties. Later, in an effort to save members from the effects of the depression that followed the international financial collapse of 1893, the Church incurred debts that could not easily be repaid to found various business enterprises. Moreover, in part because members knew that the federal government was confiscating Church properties, tithing receipts declined from an average of more than

---

Thomas G. Alexander is the Lemuel Hardison Redd Professor of Western American History emeritus, Brigham Young University.

$500,000 a year in the 1880s to approximately $350,000 in the year 1890. The depression caused tithing revenues to decline even more, and as early as 1893, Church leadership had begun borrowing funds from stakes to try to finance various activities. This borrowing proved only a stopgap measure, and by mid-1898 the Church stood $2.3 million in debt, principally to investment bankers outside of Utah.[1]

By late 1898, the excessive debt had become intolerable, and President Lorenzo Snow moved in several ways to promote the Church's financial solvency. First, to refinance the debt, the Church issued $1.5 million in 6 percent bonds. Church leaders estimated revenues from tithes at just under $1 million per year at the time, and they estimated the value of Church property at $4 million to $6 million. They knew that the Church's income had been increasing at a rate of about 10 percent per year. They planned to retire the bonds by pledging $80,000 from tithing revenues—including $30,000 for interest—annually.[2] Second, President Snow revived a policy inaugurated by President Woodruff in the late 1880s. He decided to sell the Church's interest in some businesses. Unlike Woodruff, however, he did not engage in deficit financing to invest in other enterprises. In December 1899, Church officers found that the Sterling mining property in Nevada had proved unproductive, and instead of pouring more money into the venture, they let their claims lapse at a loss of more than $300,000. They also authorized Elder Heber J. Grant to wind up affairs of the Utah Loan and Trust Company of Ogden, also at a considerable loss.[3]

The efforts to promote increased financial stability had their spiritual side as well. In May 1899, Lorenzo Snow and a large party of General Authorities traveled to St. George, which was experiencing a prolonged drought. In a sermon that has become legendary in Mormon history, President Snow promised the Saints that if they would pay a full tithing the Lord would "open the windows of heaven" and bless them. On the way home he witnessed to his associates that the Lord had given him a revelation. He admonished them, under covenant, to obey the law of tithing. On June 12 and again on July 2, 1899, in special meetings, President Snow and other

Church Administrative Change in the Progressive Period, 1898–1930

General Authorities emphasized the need for Church members to pay a tenth. Brigham Young Jr., one of the Twelve, recorded in his journal that "the spirit of the Lord testified that all this was His mind."[4]

In line with this reemphasis, the Twelve sought out bishops and stake presidents who had failed to contribute their own tithing and "labor[ed] with them kindly . . . [to] help them to recover lost ground." By 1900, Anthon H. Lund of the Twelve commented on the increase in tithing. Previously he had said that he once thought there was a great deal of formality in preaching the word. After seeing the increase in revenues that preaching brought, he believed that preaching carried a great deal of power as well. Tithing revenues had increased from $800,000 to $1.3 million in just one year.[5]

Until 1899 the Church had instituted virtually no budgetary control. Church leaders seem to have made expenditures on an ad hoc basis. In December 1898, when Lorenzo Snow gave Brigham Young Jr. papers on the Church's debt, Young had to admit, "It is a mystery to me where these millions have gone to say nothing of the 6 or 700,000 dollars income we have every year which for years has vanished like the rest."[6] President Snow himself acknowledged he had worked in the dark. On January 5, 1899, Elder John Henry Smith suggested that the Church appoint an auditing committee to oversee expenditures. The First Presidency and the Twelve agreed. The First Presidency called Elders Franklin D. Richards, Francis M. Lyman, John Henry Smith, Rudger Clawson, and Heber J. Grant, of the Twelve, for the task. By December 1901, although the committee had been operating for nearly three years, the First Presidency still found accounts of the Church somewhat in disarray, and the committee persuaded them to open a new set of books. The Church had not closed the books for many years, and they erroneously showed the Church to be $43,000 in debt! The new books showed that the Church actually held more in property and income than it owed, and Lorenzo Snow found he had rightly estimated that the Church could begin to pay off obligations held by private creditors.[7]

By 1908, the Church had not only retired its debt but had sufficient cash flow to complete a reform first contemplated in 1888. In January 1908, the Presiding Bishopric and First Presidency agreed that they would no longer use tithing scrip (essentially Church-issued paper money). This meant that Church transactions were to be made entirely on a cash-only basis. The Church also began to discourage members from paying tithing in kind—that is, in commodities such as wheat, eggs, and livestock. Part of the reason for the change appears to have been the substantial loss in the value of commodities as they remained in storage. The system seems also to have made easier the valuation of funds transferred between units.[8]

Though the First Presidency and Twelve considered the Church's temporal affairs, principal responsibility for many of these matters fell upon the Presiding Bishopric. By December 1907, reports indicated that seventy-seven-year-old Presiding Bishop William B. Preston had become so ill and weak that he could no longer function. He died in August 1908. First counselor Robert T. Burton had carried most of the burden of the office, but after his death in November 1907, the whole load fell upon second counselor Orrin P. Miller.[9] The First Presidency and Twelve gave the matter prayerful consideration, and in December 1907 President Smith called Charles W. Nibley to his office. "Charlie," he addressed his old friend, "The Church of Jesus Christ of Latter-day Saints needs a Presiding Bishop and you have been chosen for the place." Nibley accepted the call and chose Orrin P. Miller as his first counselor and David A. Smith, a son of Joseph F. Smith, as his second counselor.[10]

Nibley, a successful businessman, inaugurated many reforms that modernized and rationalized Church administration, including the shift from scrip to cash and improvements in record keeping. All of these things had become second nature to Nibley in his secular business career. Previously, though wards kept membership records, the Church expected members to carry their own records, called recommends at the time, from ward to ward as they moved. In many cases records went unexamined and carried inaccuracies. In 1901, following a recommendation by the Church auditing committee, the Church had inaugurated a ward "Record Day" during the annual ward conference. Members were to come in at that time and examine their records. In addition, a circular letter of February 1902 encouraged wards, stakes, and auxiliaries to keep their records in order. The Church encouraged ward officers to contact members before they moved to see that "they procure their recommends" to take with them.[11]

Bishop Nibley addressed problems of inaccuracies and misplaced records by instituting centralized records management. He assigned responsibility for record keeping to the wards rather than the members. The Church expected the wards to maintain membership records, and when a member moved from one ward to another, bishops were to send the records to the Presiding Bishop's Office, which served as a clearinghouse. In addition, instead of waiting for members to come in to examine their records, the bishops were required to make a house-to-house canvass of their wards at least once per year to correct individual records.[12]

Before 1901, local trustees had held the titles to ward property. They registered the title in their names with county authorities. Beginning in 1901, however, Utah law allowed a bishop to establish a corporation sole. The title to his ward's property vested in him and transferred to his successor upon his death or release.[13] Stake presidents made similar arrangements for stake property.

For members today who recognize the central role of priesthood quorums in the lives of Church members, it may be difficult to understand the relative insignificance of quorums in the late 1890s. Between Brigham Young's 1877 priesthood reorganization and the priesthood reorganization of the first decade of the twentieth century, the general Church, the ward, and, to a lesser extent, the auxiliary organizations, carried out virtually all functions that directly affected the lives of Church members. Many members received gospel instruction at Primary, Sunday School, religion classes, Relief Society, Mutual Improvement Association, and sacrament meeting. The bishop organized and supervised ward teaching, and the bishopric and Relief Society coordinated virtually all welfare and Church-service functions. In short, members—including priesthood holders—functioned as ward and auxiliary members rather than as quorum members. Indeed, many were not enrolled in a quorum, and many quorums met infrequently in poorly attended Monday evening meetings.

Auxiliaries played a less important role as well. Unlike the situation today where all members belong to auxiliary organizations according to their gender and age, in the early twentieth century, membership in auxiliaries was voluntary. Many members belonged to none. Many women did not belong to the Relief Society. Attendance at ward sacrament services was very low by present standards, generally under 15 percent. As late as 1900, most members seemed to perceive their primary community to be the general Church, and because of that Saints could be seen as active members whose lives were quite different from those we tend to view as active today.[14]

Perhaps to strengthen the Church in the time of transition and in the increasingly pluralistic society in which the Church members lived, the First Presidency and Twelve recognized the need for increased priesthood activity. The change originated with the quorums of the seventies. In 1900, Lorenzo Snow taught that seventies owed primary allegiance to their quorums rather than to the wards and auxiliaries. In 1901, the First Presidency and Twelve urged elders, high priests, and other quorums to hold regular meetings and to enroll in their quorums all priesthood holders living within the ward or stake's jurisdiction. If a priesthood holder refused enrollment, the quorum leader was to report him to the high council for possible ecclesiastical court action.[15]

To a large extent, the organization of the seventies quorums made their leadership in vitalizing their quorums easier than other priesthood quorums. In part, this was possible because although the role of members of the First Council of the Seventy as General Authorities was not well defined, they had a clear function as leaders of seventies' work in the Church. Unlike other quorums, the First Council provided central direction for the seventies and could develop and disseminate programs and lead out in priesthood reorganization.

In October 1902, the First Council proposed measures to promote systematic instruction and activation. The seven presidents called J. Golden

Kimball, Brigham H. Roberts, Rulon S. Wells, and Joseph W. McMurrin from among their number to plan a course of action. By October 15, Roberts reported that he and Kimball had completed a rough draft of a proposed series of lessons. This draft eventually led to the publication of a course of study entitled *The Seventies Course in Theology*, apparently a first for any of the priesthood quorums in the Church.[16]

Throughout 1903, as the seventies tried to bring about increased activity, they encountered opposition from stake presidents and bishops who had traditionally directed local Church activities. Because the quorums had functioned ineffectively as missionaries, the local authorities had called seventies to serve as Sunday School or MIA teachers and as members of bishoprics. One seventy suggested, in fact, that instead of holding regular quorum meetings, the members might just as well attend and study the MIA lessons. The First Council ruled, however, that seventies should conduct their own meetings and follow the outlined course of study instead of merging with auxiliary organizations.[17]

After leading out in the development of a course of study, the seventies turned to the reform of their meeting schedule. Like most other quorums, the seventies held their infrequent meetings on Monday evenings. However, since seventies were called as missionaries and other assignments infringed upon this primary responsibility, they could make the case for holding meetings on Sunday as a means of invigorating the quorums. In January 1907, the First Council asked the First Presidency and Twelve to approve a change in seventies quorums' meeting times from Monday evening to the more convenient Sunday morning between nine and twelve. This was such a radical proposal that three hours of discussion preceded approval. The First Presidency then sent a circular letter to local ecclesiastical officers emphasizing that seventies might determine the time of their meeting on Sunday morning and that if any seventies taught Sunday School, which also met on Sunday mornings, bishops should release them. Seventies held the first meetings under this new schedule on November 3, 1907, with B. H. Roberts's *Seventies Course* as the lesson manual.[18]

The seven presidents recognized that the new procedure and new lessons might create some problems, and in an effort to assist in resolving difficulties, the *Improvement Era* added a new section, "The Seventy's Council Table," edited by Roberts. But the anticipated difficulties still surfaced. In June 1908 members of the seventies quorum of the Union Stake objected to bishops attending their meetings. The stake presidency felt, however, that bishops had a right to attend any meeting held in the ward. In addition, seventies interpreted this emphasis on quorum meetings as releasing them from the responsibility of attending weekly sacrament meetings. Some also thought themselves relieved from allegiance to a stake since the seventies quorums were general Church rather than stake organizations.[19]

Because other priesthood quorums met on Monday evening, a number of stake presidents felt that Sunday seventies' meetings caused too much confusion and that the First Presidency ought to switch the meeting back to Monday. After consideration, the First Presidency and the Twelve agreed, and a delegation met with members of the First Council to secure their approval. Because the percentage of attendance at quorum meetings had increased after the change, the seventies refused to go back to Monday even though most Apostles thought they ought to.[20]

Where the seventies led, other quorums followed. After Brigham Young's 1877 reorganization, twelve-year-olds were supposed to be ordained deacons. Regular movement to teacher at age fourteen and priest at age sixteen was not the rule, however, and by the turn of the century irregularities still existed in deacon ordinations. Some bishops delayed ordinations, and some followed such lax procedures that in at least one case a boy was ordained at age three. Between 1903 and 1906, the First Presidency and Twelve began strongly emphasizing the need to reorganize and regularize Aaronic Priesthood activity. Like other quorums, the Aaronic Priesthood met only irregularly on Monday evenings, and some authorities suggested that inactivity in the Aaronic Priesthood was partly responsible for the "evils in Elders Quorums."[21]

After urging the revitalization of the Aaronic Priesthood quorums for three years, the Twelve, through President Francis M. Lyman, laid out the approved procedure at the October general conference in 1906, that the Church followed for some time. Ordination to deacon at age twelve was to be the rule for all worthy young men. They were to serve as deacons for three years when they were eligible for ordination as teachers, who were to serve for three years. This was followed by three years as priests. Advancement to the Melchizedek Priesthood could follow at age twenty-one, but only those who were worthy were to be advanced.[22]

Following the success of the seventies in revitalizing their quorums, in November 1907 a circular letter outlined the procedure which the Melchizedek Priesthood should follow under what came to be called the new priesthood movement. Stake presidents were to recommend prospective priesthood holders to the high council for approval. In the case of seventies, because some quorums covered more than one stake, the stake presidents were to consult with each other and make certain that they called only men suitable for missionary work. When seventies could no longer serve as missionaries, the stake president was to recommend them for ordination as high priests in recognition of their faithfulness. Bishops were to recommend men for ordination to elder to the stake president after securing the sustaining votes of ward members. Final approval for any Melchizedek Priesthood office required an affirmative vote at a stake priesthood meeting.[23]

The Twelve followed the seventies' lead by formulating regular lessons and other procedures for the other Melchizedek and Aaronic Priesthood quorums. During the fall and winter of 1908, the Apostles spent time reviewing lessons designed for use by the Aaronic Priesthood in 1909. At the same time the General Authorities placed quorums under closer control of bishops and stake presidents. High priests and seventies quorums were henceforth to be contained within the boundaries of one stake, though the seventies could have more than one quorum per stake. More than one elders quorum might exist in a stake, but each quorum must have at least a majority of the number required for a full quorum, which was ninety-six.

Quorums of deacons, teachers, and priests were to be organized within one ward and presided over by the bishops, though the teachers and deacons were to have their own president.[24]

Each quorum except the seventies, who met on Sunday, was to meet every Monday evening for "instruction in the formal study of the doctrines, principles and history of the gospel." In some cases neither the instructors nor the quorum members were taking time to prepare for a discussion of the lessons, and the General Authorities attempted to deal with these pedagogical and other problems through the "Priesthood Quorums Table" in the *Improvement Era*.[25]

Since the general Church organization had not resolved the question, a number of stakes tried rearranging the time of priesthood meeting, Sunday School, sacrament meeting, and MIA. The St. Johns Stake, for instance, held priesthood meeting on Sunday evening on three Sundays of the month in connection with YMMIA. On the fourth Sunday, the wards held a joint YM-YLMIA meeting. In 1913 the Ensign Stake adopted a plan of holding MIA and priesthood meeting on alternate Tuesday nights, but this produced disappointing results. In the Liberty, Ogden, and Fremont stakes, the other quorums joined the seventies on Sunday mornings. Those stakes found this arrangement to be "satisfactory," producing better-than-average attendance. After these reports, the Twelve reconsidered its reluctance to hold priesthood meeting on Sundays and agreed with the possibility of having the Aaronic Priesthood classes as part of Sunday School.[26] The shift of priesthood meeting from Monday night to Sunday morning not only helped priesthood attendance but also boosted Sunday School activity. In fact, in light of the results, the MIA considered shifting its meeting to Sunday as well.[27]

Perhaps the most noticeable change which took place with the new priesthood movement was increased activity. The General Priesthood Committee of the Church reported in October 1913 that priests especially paid greater attention to priesthood work. Most quorums held regular meetings, where five years before not more than 5 percent of the wards had. Attendance at weekly priesthood meeting increased from 16 percent in 1913 to 18 percent in 1915. Sacrament meeting attendance, which stood at 14.5 percent in 1913, increased to 17 percent in 1915. Ward teaching visits increased from 42 percent to 63 percent over the same period.[28]

For members today, this may seem like an extremely poor showing, but the early twentieth century was a time of transition and change which one must judge on its own terms, not by the standards we would apply today. The statistics meant that, for the average Latter-day Saint, attendance at priesthood or sacrament meeting was not an important part of Church commitment. In the nineteenth century, Church leaders expected members to give their lives to the Church in the development of new communities and in the creation of new Church enterprises. This tied them to the general Church community. Church attendance and priesthood activities were secondary since members' entire beings were wrapped up in the Church. The changing statistics and the development of new programs and procedures by the general and local authorities reveal an increasing reorientation in the Church. At the present time, commitment is measured by willingness to devote time to the Church for such things as accepting mission calls; attending meetings; and participating in teaching, temple attendance, compassionate service, and welfare work. In effect, the Saints of the early twentieth century were laying the groundwork for the Church as we know it today.

Moreover, the changes that were taking place had the effect of strengthening both the general Church and the local organizations. The reemphasis on tithe paying and the reorganization of record keeping efforts increased the importance of the presiding and local bishops, moving primary responsibility over the definition of Church activity from the member as part of the community to the bishop as presiding authority of the ward. The priesthood reorganization, while vitalizing the quorums, also tied them more closely to the ward and stake organization, subordinating them even more to bishops and stake presidents.

The changes also had the effect of narrowing the scope of Church organization by defining the Church as part of the larger society rather than as a separate community. This is most apparent in the changes which took place in Church courts. After the first two decades of the twentieth century, Church members were expected to take secular disputes to civil and criminal rather than Church courts. Concern for the time local Church leaders could spend in their business interests led in part to the reduction of the size of stakes and the willingness to release longtime officers for reasons other than unfaithfulness or incapacity.

On November 19, 1918, the Church lost its sixth President. Seriously ill since mid-summer, Joseph F. Smith had been unable to fill all his responsibilities, and day-to-day supervision of Church affairs had fallen on first counselor Anthon H. Lund.[29]

One might assume that the question of succession in the First Presidency had been settled in the minds of all by 1918, but that was not the case. In early July 1918, during President Smith's incapacity, Presiding Patriarch Hyrum G. Smith discussed his belief that by virtue of his patriarchal office he ought to become the presiding authority of the Church upon the death of Joseph F. Smith. On July 3, 1918, Joseph Fielding Smith, David O. McKay, and Heber J. Grant of the Twelve called on Presidents Lund and Charles W. Penrose. The three Apostles said that the Twelve differed with the presiding patriarch on the question of succession but that they did not want a controversy. To help settle the matter, they presented a letter that Wilford Woodruff had written on March 28, 1887.[30]

The letter was extremely important because it had come into Grant's possession under similar circumstances. At the death of John Taylor, a controversy had surfaced over the reorganization of the First Presidency. Several Apostles discussed the matter with Wilford Woodruff, then President of the Quorum of the Twelve, and he wrote the letter to them, stating that in the absence of direct revelation from the Lord to the contrary, he believed that the president of the Quorum of the Twelve should become President of the Church. Presidents Lund and Penrose expressed pleasure at the letter but decided not to discuss the matter with Joseph F. Smith in view of his poor health.

Church Administrative Change in the Progressive Period, 1898–1930

This letter seems to have resolved any doubt that others in the Twelve or the Presidency might have had at the time, and on November 21, 1918, the day before President Smith's funeral, the counselors in the First Presidency and the Twelve met together. No one occupied the presidency's chairs in the council room in the Temple, but the Apostles took their places according to seniority in the Twelve. The meeting was both a memorial for Joseph F. Smith and an expression of love and confidence in Heber J. Grant, whom all seemed to recognize as the next President.[31] Following the meeting, Elder Grant met with Presidents Penrose and Lund to plan the Church's reorganization. He asked the two to continue to serve as his counselors and asked that Elder Lund, the senior Apostle, serve as President of the Twelve. On November 23, the Twelve reorganized the First Presidency and their own quorum.[32]

Confirmation of President Grant's call followed. Because of the international flu pandemic, no general conference was held in October 1918 or in April 1919, but the Apostles called a general conference for June 1, 1919, to sustain the new presidency. In the meantime, in late May 1919 several people reported spiritual confirmations. President Lund reported that at a temple meeting on May 25, 1919, events took place similar to those reported at the meeting "held in Nauvoo when President Brigham Young was transfigured to look like Joseph Smith and the people took it as a sign that he was the true successor to the martyred prophet." Several people at the meeting said that at recent meetings Heber J. Grant had looked like Joseph F. Smith. Theodore Robinson said that at the fast meeting the preceding Sunday at the Granite Stake conference he was astonished that although Heber J. Grant was speaking, he looked exactly like Joseph F. Smith. Several others, including Brigham F. Grant and Edward H. Anderson, said the same thing.[33]

The deaths of several long-established leaders, changes in the First Presidency, and calls to new positions led to changes in the Church hierarchy. President Lund, who had suffered for some time from a hemorrhaging duodenal ulcer, died of that disease on March 2, 1921. President Grant was in California at the time, and on March 5, on the way home to attend the funeral, he discussed possible counselors with Presiding Bishop Charles W. Nibley. Nibley said that everyone expected he would select his cousin Anthony W. Ivins. Grant remarked that if this were done "the Presidency would be strictly Democratic." Bishop Nibley indicated that this would make no difference because Elder Ivins was the wisest man among the Apostles. After President Lund's funeral on March 6, Grant spoke with President Penrose, who told him that Ivins was the only one he had thought of. President Grant said that his mind had rested on Ivins and that unless the Lord indicated someone else, he would undoubtedly select Ivins. On March 8, after a discussion with President Penrose, he decided to wait for the "impression of the Spirit" until April conference. On March 10, 1921, at a meeting of the first Presidency and the Twelve, he proposed that Charles W. Penrose become his first counselor and Anthony W. Ivins his second. Rudger Clawson became President of the Twelve, George F. Richards was called as Salt Lake Temple president, and the First Presidency and Twelve chose John A. Widtsoe to fill the vacancy in the Twelve.[34]

President Penrose died on May 16, 1925, and that evening President Grant did not get to sleep until well after midnight as he prayed earnestly for guidance in the selection of a successor. By May 28 he felt impressed to call Anthony W. Ivins to fill President Penrose's place and to select Presiding Bishop Charles W. Nibley as second counselor. He discussed possible replacements for Nibley with Reed Smoot on that day, and on June 4 proposed the call of Sylvester Q. Cannon, then city engineer of Salt Lake City.[35]

Between 1918 and 1930, leaders continued making changes to Church administration. Church leaders recognized that they needed first to implement the separation of the Church's estate from that of the President of the Church and of ecclesiastical and secular properties. This mixing of Church properties and finances with the President's personal estate had caused some concern at the death of Lorenzo Snow as it had with the death of every previous president. Nevertheless, by 1930 the Church still had not separated policy making from administrative functions. In fact, administrative modernization was not completed until the 1970s, when the President of the Church withdrew from active involvement in Church-owned businesses and the Twelve ceased to administer Church departments.³⁶ In large part, the financial difficulties of the Church made administrative reform impossible. The First Presidency was constantly forced into taking an active part in routine matters such as negotiating loans and allocating funds for building construction. Still, in view of the difficulties the Church faced during this period, the accomplishments were significant.

Immediately after assuming the Presidency of the Church, Heber J. Grant began several measures of reorganization which were to have far-reaching effects on Church administration. On November 27, 1918, he announced that the First Presidency would relinquish the presidency of various auxiliary organizations. He intended, he said later, "to give all the auxiliary boards a full organization independent of the President of the Church, though, of course each [would be] under the direction of the General Authorities." David O. McKay became the president of the Deseret Sunday School Union with Stephen L Richards and George Pyper as assistants. Anthony W. Ivins became general superintendent of the YMMIA with Brigham H. Roberts and Richard R. Lyman as assistants. President Joseph F. Smith had been general superintendent of both organizations. At the death of Anthon H. Lund, Joseph Fielding Smith became Church historian instead of vesting that job in the First Presidency. Some positions, however, the President of the Church retained. Heber J. Grant became president of the General Church Board of Education and retained the presidency of Church-related businesses such as the Utah National Bank, ZCMI, and U and I Sugar.³⁷

Previous difficulties, together with the increasing complexity of Church financial commitments, brought about the establishment of two legal entities to administer Church property. The First Presidency, the Presiding Bishopric, and Church legal advisers completed arrangements on February 7, 1922, for the creation of Zion Securities Corporation, which was to administer all taxable and nonecclesiastical property. Directors were Heber J. Grant, Anthony W. Ivins, Stephen L Richards, Charles W. Nibley, and

Arthur Winter. As a companion measure, on November 26, 1923, the Corporation of the President, a corporation sole, was organized to hold ecclesiastical property of the Church.[38]

The first three decades of the twentieth century were extremely important in the development of Church policy on buildings, monuments, and historic sites.[39] Largely on the initiative of President Joseph F. Smith, the Church expanded its support of charitable and recreational facilities like hospitals and gymnasia, and it constructed buildings in downtown Salt Lake City to house administrative offices. Church leaders moved rather aggressively to acquire sites at which important occurrences in the early history of the Church had taken place, particularly in Vermont, western New York, and Illinois, and to erect monuments to people and events of the past.[40]

Perhaps most important were the creative innovations of the period. The Church leadership moved from an ad hoc system in which varying contributions, usually ranging about 30 percent under Joseph F. Smith, were appropriated from general Church revenues for the construction of local meetinghouses and stake houses to a system under Heber J. Grant in which the Church contributed a standard amount—ordinarily 50 percent—of the cost of a building. The Church added to the four temples constructed in Utah by constructing new temples outside Utah at Laie, Hawaii; Cardston, Alberta, Canada; and Mesa, Arizona. The leadership acted vigorously to make certain that they used the best possible designs and decorations, invited competitive bidding among Mormon architectural firms—generally consisting of men with training in the best traditions of Europe and the United States—and hiring the best available Mormon artistic talent to paint and produce the murals, paintings, and other decorative features of the temples.[41] In particular, two developments epitomize the administrative modernization of the Church and its response to the pluralization of the society around the Mormons—the construction of Deseret Gymnasium and the reorganization of the Church architect's office.

Church Administrative Change in the Progressive Period, 1898–1930

As the Mutual Improvement Association expanded its physical education program, a number of general board members favored the construction of a gymnasium in Salt Lake City for young men. Some men had begun to frequent the YMCA gym, and many neglected Sunday services and drew away from the Church. To counteract this tendency, the General Authorities encouraged ward officers throughout the Church to see that ward buildings provided light gymnastic facilities to keep young men near their homes and "away from town influences." By late February 1908, the First Presidency and Twelve approved the construction of Deseret Gymnasium in collaboration with Latter-day Saints University, a high school with some collegiate work in Salt Lake City. Completed in 1910, the facility received general Church funds for about a third of the cost and obtained the remainder in contributions from Church members in the Salt Lake area.[42]

The Church also experimented with a system of standard plans for meetinghouses. In November 1919, the Church announced the appointment of Willard Young as superintendent of the Church Building Department. Perhaps in response to problems found in some buildings like the Blackfoot Tabernacle, which exhibited atrocious acoustics, Young began to standardize plans for buildings using colonial and neoclassical models. In April 1924, however, Joseph Nielson, who had served as architect for the science building at Brigham Young University and had designed the Beaver meetinghouse in 1918, called on President Grant to complain. He said that having an architectural department was not fair to local architects and that often the little work an architect could get locally made the difference between his success and failure. Several months later, after considering the situation, President Grant changed the policy and on August 27, 1924, notified architects that the officers of the various wards and stakes could hire local architects to design their buildings should they choose to do so.[43]

In the twenties, principally because of depressed economic conditions, the First Presidency approved new buildings only reluctantly. During the financial crisis of 1920–21 and the Great Depression beginning in 1929, President Grant faced problems in meeting all the demands upon Church resources. In November 1921, the First Presidency wrote that the "finances of the Church here at home have not been at such a low ebb for ten or twelve years." Conditions improved by August 1922, but by mid-1930 the Church had again fallen into severe financial difficulty. On June 9, President Grant had to tell the presidency of the Panguitch Stake that he could not appropriate money for a seminary building because he had not yet been able to fulfill promises for assistance made in 1929. He agreed, however, to try to help the stake get a loan to finance the construction. In late December 1930, the Church leadership announced a new policy of stopping the erection of "costly L.D.S. meeting houses." By April 1931, the Church Auditing Committee reported that expenditures for Church buildings and other needs amounted to "much more" than its income. The First Presidency then resolved to curtail new construction even more.[44]

Though most money seems to have gone toward capital improvements, full-time general authorities received a living allowance. Officers with outside business interests seem to have done well. Those like James E. Talmage and John A. Widtsoe, who had worked as educators and had few sources of outside income, had to rely upon the Church allowance to subsist and found themselves in constant financial difficulty. In July 1916, Talmage recorded preparations for a party at Joseph F. Smith's home. "In preparation for this visit the brethren of the twelve were divided into two classes—the Haves and Haven'ts or the withs and withouts—one class comprising those who own autos and the other consisting of those who have no such means of conveyance. Members of the second class were assigned with their families to the care of their betters. Wife and I were conveyed to and from the Smith home by Brother and Sister Anthony W. Ivins in their splendid Packard Car."[45]

Widtsoe reported that his allowance as an Apostle was one-third his salary for the previous two decades while serving as a professor and president at two educational institutions. He had been forced to sell his car and discharge his servants. Some increases were made in the allowance in 1925, but it remained modest.[46]

Church Administrative Change in the Progressive Period, 1898–1930

An important development during the 1920s was the increasing expansion of the Church outside the Utah core area. In July 1922, the First Presidency called George W. McCune of Ogden to move to Los Angeles to become president of the newly created stake. By 1929, the Church had organized two stakes in the Los Angeles area, and the tremendous growth that had taken place in Los Angeles impressed Heber J. Grant.[47]

In general, however, the Church leadership was not particularly happy with the out-migration of Mormons from Utah. Though exceptions existed, particularly in the case of other Mountain West states, the General Authorities expressed a general feeling of discomfort with the idea of dispersion.[48] In point of fact, the General Authorities had little dispersion to worry about by 1930. Most Church members still lived in the intermountain region, and a day's train ride from Salt Lake City followed by a short buggy or auto ride would take the General Authorities to most Mormons. General Authority visits to the Church's 1,000 wards had become less frequent, but one or more visited virtually every quarterly conference of the 104 stakes, most of which were in Utah, Arizona, and Idaho. Certainly the Church had grown in size and complexity since 1900, but it was still a relatively homogeneous intermountain organization of 672,000, more easily administered, in spite of its problems, than the diverse organization of today, with more members outside then inside the United States.

The evidence presented here would seem to indicate that while the modernization of the Church's relationship to politics and the business community had been largely accomplished by 1930, its organizational forms still remained in transition. The Church evidently accomplished its greatest success in ecclesiastical rather than managerial fields. The General Authorities had revitalized the priesthood quorums and set them on track to assume a greater portion of the burden for instruction and governance on the local level. The Church achieved signal achievements in the organization of Zion's Securities Corporation and the Corporation of the President, but trivial decisions, to which subordinates might more efficiently have attended, still burdened the First Presidency. The Church leadership had made some efforts to solve this problem, at least in connection with the funding for building construction, but the financial stringencies of the period made the proposed solutions impossible to completely implement.

NOTES

1. For a general discussion of the Church's debt in the 1880s and 1890s, see Leonard J. Arrington, *Great Basin Kingdom: An Economic History of the Latter-day Saints, 1830–1900* (Cambridge: Harvard University Press, 1958), 400–403; see also Ronald W. Walker, "Crisis in Zion: Heber J. Grant and the Panic of 1893," *Arizona and the West* 21 (Autumn 1979): 257–78.
2. Heber J. Grant, diary (hereafter cited as Grant, diary), January 4 and August 8, 1898, Church History Library, The Church of Jesus Christ of Latter-day Saints, Salt Lake City (hereafter CHL); Brigham Young Jr., journal (hereafter cited as Young, journal), July 12, 1898, CHL.
3. Young, journal, July 14, 1900; Anthon H. Lund, journal (hereafter cited as Lund, journal), September 6, 1900, CHL; Arrington, *Great Basin Kingdom*, 403–9.
4. Young, journal, July 2, 1899; Marriner W. Merrill, journal (hereafter cited as Merrill, journal), July 2, 1899, LDS Archives; John Henry Smith, journal (hereafter cited as J. H. Smith, journal), July 2, 1899, Smith Family Papers, Western Americana Collection, University of Utah Library.
5. Young, journal, April 12, May 6, 1900; Lund, journal, June 26, 1900.
6. Young, journal, December 21, October 13, 1898.
7. Grant, diary, January 5, 1899; Lund, journal, December 5, 1901; Joseph F. Smith to Nancy L. Richards, July 19, 1901, Joseph F. Smith Letterbooks, CHL; J. H. Smith, journal, December 12, 1901.
8. Lund, journal, January 13, 1908, October 12, 1913, and passim; Presiding Bishop, Annual Reports, 1903, 1908, 1909, CHL (hereafter PBO Report); Journal History of The Church of Jesus Christ of Latter-day Saints, photocopy, CHL, May 1910.
9. Grant, diary, December 4, 11, 1907; Lund, journal, December 4, 11, 1907; Joseph F. Smith to Charles W. Penrose, December 12, 1907, Joseph F. Smith Letterbooks.
10. Charles W. Nibley, "Reminiscences of Charles W. Nibley" MS, CHL, 81, 83.

11. Anthony W. Ivins, journal, April 8, 1901, Ivins Family Papers, Utah State Historical Society, Salt Lake City (hereafter USHS); James R. Clark, comp., *Messages of the First Presidency* (Salt Lake City: Bookcraft, 1965–75), 4:34, 46.
12. First Presidency, circular letter, January 1, 1910, Clark, *Messages*, 4:213–14.
13. Circular letter, September 12, 1901, cited in Clark, *Messages*, 3:341; Lund, journal, January 22, 1904.
14. PBO Report, 1903, 1908, 1909. For a discussion of the change in this basic orientation, see Jan Shipps, "In the Presence of the Past: Continuity and Change in Twentieth Century Mormonism" in *After 150 Years: The Latter-day Saints in Sesquicentennial Perspective*, ed. Thomas G. Alexander and Jessie L. Embry (Midvale, UT: Charles Redd Center for Western Studies, 1985), 3–35.
15. First Council of the Seventy Minutes (hereafter FCS Minutes) March 14, October 10, and passim, 1900; December 4, 1901, CHL; Lund, journal, December 1, 1901.
16. FCS Minutes, October 1, 15, 1902. For a discussion of the later manifestations of this movement, see William G. Hartley, "The Priesthood Reform Movement, 1908–1922," *BYU Studies* 13, no. 2 (Winter 1973): 137–56. From the currently available evidence on the work of the seventies, it is clear that Hartley dates the origins of this movement too late.
17. FCS Minutes, September 30, 1903.
18. George F. Richards, journal, January 30, May 31, 1907, CHL; First Presidency, circular letter, June 12, 1907, in Clark, *Messages*, 4:157–59.
19. *Improvement Era*, December 1907, 147–50, and September 1908, 893–94; Grant, diary, June 10, 1908.
20. Grant, diary, December 17, 1908; Richards, journal, December 2, 22, 23, 1908.
21. William G. Hartley, "The Priesthood Reorganization of 1877: Brigham Young's Last Achievement," *BYU Studies* 20, no. 1 (Fall 1979): 3–36; Lund, journal, August 9, 1906, October 6, 1903; Richards, journal, July 15, 1906; see also D. Michael Quinn, "The Evolution of the Presiding Quorums of the LDS Church," *Journal of Mormon History* 1 (1974): 21–37.
22. Ivins, journal, October 8, 1906.
23. First Presidency to First Council of the Seventy, October 26, 1907, and idem, circular letter, November 6, 1907, in Clark, *Messages*, 4:159–62.

24. Richards, journal, December 26, 1908; Grant, diary, November 30, 1908; J. H. Smith, journal, December 3, 1908; Journal History, November 29, 1908.
25. *Improvement Era*, March 1909, 397, April 1909, 498, and July 1909, 749; Grant, diary, March 20, 1909.
26. Richards, journal, May 27, 1911, March 5, 1913; Lund, journal, June 10, 1913.
27. Lund, journal, August 13, 1913.
28. *Improvement Era*, November 1913, 61, and September 1915, 1024.
29. Lund, journal, November 17, 8, 19, 22, 1918.
30. The following is based on Grant, diary, July 3, 1918.
31. Lund, journal, November 21, 1918.
32. Lund, journal, November 23, 1918.
33. Lund, journal, May 25, June 1, 1919; Journal History, June 1, 1919.
34. Grant, diary, March 5, 6, 8, 10, 17, 1921; Richards, journal, March 10, 14, 1921.
35. Grant, diary, May 16, 1925; Reed Smoot, diary, L. Tom Perry Special Collections, Harold B. Lee Library, Brigham Young University, June 4, 1925 (hereafter Smoot, diary).
36. Talmage, journal, January 7, 1918; Lund, journal, November 27, 1918, January 13, 1919.
37. Lund, journal, November 27, December 29, 1918.
38. Grant, diary, January 28, 1919, April 25, September 20, 21, 1921, January 31, February 7, 1922; Smoot, diary, April 10, 1919; Journal History, February 8, 1922, November 26, 1923.
39. On the importance of Church sites, see Kathleen Flake, *The Politics of American Religious Identity: The Seating of Senator Reed Smoot, Mormon Apostle* (Chapel Hill: University of North Carolina Press, 2004), 109–37.
40. On the acquisition of sites, see B. H. Roberts, *Comprehensive History of the Church of Jesus Christ of Latter-day Saints, Century 1* (Salt Lake City: Church of Jesus Christ of Latter-day Saints, 1930), 6:319, 426–30, 525–26; James B. Allen and Glen M. Leonard, *The Story of the Latter-day Saints*, 2nd ed. (Salt Lake City: Deseret Book, 1992), 453, 511.
41. On architectural development, see Allen D. Roberts, "Religious Architecture of the LDS Church: Influences and Changes Since 1847," *Utah Historical Quarterly*

43 (Summer 1975): 321–27; Peter L. Goss, "The Architectural History of Utah," *Utah Historical Quarterly* 43 (Summer 1975): 223–39; and Paul L. Anderson, "The Early Twentieth Century Temples," *Dialogue* 14 (Spring 1981): 9–19. The statistical information on the amounts appropriated by the Church comes from Lund, journal, and Grant, diary.

42. Grant, diary, February 26, March 15, 25, 31, June 9, 1908; Lund, journal, April 25, 1912; First Presidency to Nephi L. Morris, October 31, 1910, cited in Clark, *Messages*, 4:218–19; Journal History, February 27, 1908.

43. On the development of standard plans, see Martha Sonntag Bradley, "'The Church and Colonel Saunders': Mormon Standard Plan Architecture" (master's thesis, Brigham Young University, 1981), 31–50; see also Allen and Leonard, *Story of the Latter-day Saints*, 509–10; Grant, diary, April 18, August 27, 1924.

44. First Presidency to Serge Ballif, November 19, 1921; and Heber J. Grant to Reed Smoot, August 26, 1922; Grant, diary, June 9, 1930, April 3, 1931; Journal History, December 29, 1930.

45. Talmage, journal, July 13, 1916.

46. Grant, diary, December 19, 1919, January 20, 1921, June 1, 9, 1921; Smoot, diary, September 21, 1918, December 25, 1919; D. Michael Quinn, "The Mormon Hierarchy, 1832–1932: An American Elite" (PhD diss., Yale University, 1976), 127–30; Talmage, journal, July 13, 1916; Widtsoe, *In a Sunlit Land*, 161; Richards, journal, January 30, 1925.

47. Grant, diary, July 13, August 14, 1922, February 24, 1929.

48. Heber J. Grant to Nephi L. Morris, May 8, 1922; Journal History, February 3, April 25, 1923, May 26, 1930; Grant, diary, April 14, 1923, July 20, November 27, July 20, 1929.

The formation of correlation provides a powerful witness to how God guides and directs his work through inspired servants, such as Presidents David O. McKay and Harold B. Lee using their agency to act to the best of their abilities.

Michael A. Goodman

14

CORRELATION: THE EARLY YEARS

Elder Bruce C. Hafen has stated, "Few superlatives could overstate the historical importance of correlation, both as a doctrinal concept and as an organizational movement."[1] Yet, despite the importance of correlation, little has been published regarding its history. Though included as a topic in biographies about David O. McKay, Harold B. Lee, and Neal A. Maxwell, each account focused more on the individuals' involvement in correlation than the history of correlation itself. Therefore, each account had large gaps in the history. This article will present the history of correlation from the turn of the twentieth century until 1960. Though access to some primary sources is limited, the information and documentation illuminates not only the basic early history of correlation but also the processes and inspiration that led to its creation.

Michael A. Goodman is an associate professor of Church history and doctrine at Brigham Young University.

The formation of correlation provides a powerful witness to how God guides and directs his work through inspired servants using their agency to act to the best of their abilities. Elder Maxwell explained that "revelation works in a natural way. There is an unmet need [such as Church growth]. As we ponder over it, the mind and experience can put forward an adequate alternative [for the season, and] the confirmation is the inspiration."[2] Man's best efforts, combined with direct inspiration, and at times intervention from above, allows God to direct his work on earth. It is important to remember that God works through his chosen servants living in a specific time and place who use their agency to bring to pass things the Lord reveals to them. It has been stated that Church correlation did not spring forth, Minerva-like, in the mid-1960s. It came line upon line, precept upon precept, born of necessity and after a long process filled with inspiration and hard work.

PROPHETIC VISION

Many people played a crucial role in the early history of correlation. Almost all of them were members of the First Presidency and Quorum of the Twelve Apostles. Few had a more profound impact than David O. McKay and Harold B. Lee. For the first fifty-plus years of correlation's history, President McKay either led out in the actual effort or directed others as one of the presiding authorities. Harold B. Lee, often considered the father of correlation in the modern era, was profoundly influential as well. In fact, in his biography, his son-in-law states that "some historians may well argue that President Harold B. Lee's most significant lifetime work for the Church, though not generally understood by the membership, was the reorganization of the kingdom under the direction of President David O. McKay."[3]

To view correlation as those who were responsible for it did is to see God's hand throughout. These men, in their public discourses and their private writing, acknowledged the historical realities they were working through and the agency and personalities of those involved. As will be seen from the frequent correlation initiatives that came to a stop almost as fast as they started, the history of correlation is full of what might be called failed attempts. However, some of the leading Brethren saw it instead as laying the groundwork needed for future successes which would come when the time was ripe and the need was much greater. They did not see correlation as simply an administrative or organizational matter. They saw it as the kingdom of God rolling forward. They believed it was much larger than simply an effort to correlate curriculum and adjust organizational charts. President N. Eldon Tanner emphatically stated as much when he said, "Priesthood Correlation is the closest blueprint yet in mortality to the plan presented in the Grand Council of Heaven before the world was created and is the most effective utilization thus far of special keys given to the Prophet Joseph Smith in the Kirtland Temple."[4]

NEW BEGINNINGS

When God restored his Church in the latter days through the Prophet Joseph Smith, he did so line upon line, precept upon precept. Most Church organization we are familiar with today developed in answer to specific time-and-place needs with guidance and inspiration from above. There were no First Presidency, Quorum of Twelve, Quorums of Seventy, stake presidencies, or bishops when the Church was organized in 1830. Each of these offices developed as the need arose and as God directed. Not only were the offices not in existence when the Church was organized, their form, structure, and duties have also evolved through the years. As early as 1835, the basic governing structure recognized today was revealed to the Prophet Joseph. The Lord dictated that the First Presidency was the presiding organization of the Church, followed by the Quorum of Twelve Apostles, followed by the Seventy. However, the role and function of each of these presiding quorums has evolved in accordance with the needs of the Church. For example, the First Quorum of Seventy as we know it today was not organized until 1975 and 1976 under the inspiration of President Spencer W. Kimball. Even after its organization, the number, structure, and function of the Quorums of Seventy have changed to meet the needs of a growing Church.

As the Church continued to expand, it became clear that the presiding quorums would need help if they were to accomplish the work God had given them. As a result, the Relief Society was organized in March 1842 by the Prophet Joseph. The Sunday School was organized December 9, 1849, by Richard Ballantyne. The Young Women's Mutual Improvement Association was organized on November 28, 1869, as the Young Ladies' Retrenchment Society by Brigham Young. The Young Men's Mutual Improvement Association was formed on June 10, 1875, also by Brigham Young. Finally, the Primary was organized on August 25, 1878, by John Taylor.

Each auxiliary was created to help the presiding authorities accomplish the work of the ministry. As each auxiliary grew in size, it also grew in complexity. Though each auxiliary was intended to meet the needs of distinct groups, it soon became evident that much of what they did overlapped and at times complicated the work as a whole. By the turn of the twentieth century, these auxiliaries had grown so large and complex that they presented two distinct but connected challenges. First, through their diligent efforts, the auxiliaries were supplanting the priesthood quorums in their divinely commissioned responsibilities to minister to the Saints. Second, as each auxiliary grew, so did the amount of training material and curriculum each produced. The expense in time and money of constantly developing new training and curriculum materials, along with the challenge of avoiding overlapping, ineffective, or misdirected material, constantly challenged the Brethren. These two challenges gave rise to one other unintended consequence. With so many organizations often working in so many directions and requiring great amounts of time from individual members, the family unit began to suffer.

PRIESTHOOD AND CURRICULUM

The presiding Brethren felt it necessary to reemphasize the divinely appointed and central role of the priesthood with the auxiliary organizations functioning in a supporting role. President Lee stated that a main purpose of correlation was to place "the Priesthood as the Lord intended, as the center core of the Kingdom of God, and the auxiliaries as related thereto; including a greater emphasis on the Fathers in the home as Priesthood bearers in strengthening the family unit."[5]

Early on, the need to correlate a rapidly expanding curriculum may have been its most visible role. By the early 1900s, many Church organizations, including Young Men, Young Women, Sunday School, and the Seventies, were already publishing their own instructional material, often annually. Other than the Sunday School, which began publishing curriculum in the beginning, the other auxiliaries did not begin the work of curriculum or instructional development right away. For example, though the Relief Society was organized in 1842, they did not begin publishing a unified curriculum until 1913.[6] However, as each organization produced more and more instructional material, the lack of correlation led to inevitable duplication, disparity, and expense. These curricular challenges, coupled with the ever-increasing overlap of each auxiliary's efforts with the priesthood, led to a realization by the presiding Brethren of the need of greater correlation of efforts. Though some early attempts at correlation focused more strongly on one or the other challenge, most sought to address both priesthood and curricular issues.

GENERAL PRIESTHOOD COMMITTEE ON OUTLINES

By the beginning of the twentieth century, President Joseph F. Smith began to correlate the efforts of the auxiliaries and to restore the priesthood quorums to the more prominent role they were created to fill. At the April 1906 general conference, President Smith prophesied:

> We expect to see the day, if we live long enough (and if some of us do not live long enough to see it, there are others who will), when every council of the Priesthood in the Church of Jesus Christ of Latter-day Saints will understand its duty, will assume its own responsibility, will magnify its calling, and fill its place in the Church, to the

uttermost, according to the intelligence and ability possessed by it. When that day shall come, there will not be so much necessity for work that is now being done by the auxiliary organizations, because it will be done by the regular quorums of the Priesthood. The Lord designed and comprehended it from the beginning, and He has made provision in the Church whereby every need may be met and satisfied through the regular organizations of the Priesthood.[7]

In the beginning, the effort was not to minimize the work of the auxiliaries as much as it was to get the priesthood actively engaged in correlating their efforts. Within two years, President Smith took the first step by creating the General Priesthood Committee on Outlines on April 8, 1908, and appointing recently called Apostle David O. McKay as chair.[8] The major assignment of this committee was to write the curriculum for the deacons, teachers, priests, elders, and high priests. By this time, most of the auxiliaries were beginning to work on their own curriculum, but there was no curricular committee to take care of the priesthood quorums.

The committee was also tasked with helping the priesthood "understand its duty, . . . assume its own responsibility, . . . magnify its calling, and fill its place in the Church, to the uttermost," as Joseph F. Smith stated above. In a report, the committee declared that the major problem in getting the priesthood quorums to function was a loose organizational structure and quorums that were not functioning properly.[9] As part of their efforts to correct these problems, the committee did write curriculum for each of the quorums. In May of 1912, they also published an article in the *Improvement Era* detailing the need for greater diligence and organization of Aaronic Priesthood quorums, especially teachers and priests quorums.[10] After four years of effort, they felt that their work in spurring the priesthood forward was successful. In a report given to the general priesthood conference in 1913, the committee reported great satisfaction at the results of their efforts from 1908 through 1913. They list several impressive accomplishments during this time period. According to their report, in 1908 only thirty bishops were actively presiding over the priests quorum in their ward. By 1913, about 500 of the 715 Church bishops were now doing so. Over 258 new priests quorums had been organized. In a single year over 1,000 new priests were ordained, making a total of 7,578 priests. The report also mentioned an overall increase in ordained priesthood members who attended quorum meetings. Finally, it spoke of an increase of quorum officers doing their work and thus lightening the loads of the bishops.[11] Clearly they felt that their work had produced good results.

Less information is available regarding the success of the committee in correlating the curriculum of the different auxiliaries. A note in the minutes indicated that the committee was later enlarged to include members of the general boards of Sunday School, the Young Men's Mutual Improvement Association, and the Church School System in an attempt to enhance the correlation between these organizations.[12] However, no records have yet been found documenting either the efforts or the results of this correlation effort.

THE CORRELATION COMMITTEE

In 1912, President Smith organized the Correlation Committee and once again assigned David O. McKay as the chair.[13] Steven L Richards, who would become one of the major contributors to the Church's correlation efforts, was called to serve on this committee with Elder David O. McKay while he was serving as a member of the General Sunday School Board. While serving on this committee, Brother Richards was called as an Apostle on January 18, 1917.[14] This committee was tasked to do more than simply correlate curriculum. The heads of each auxiliary were also called to serve on this committee. "The purpose of the committee was to prevent the unnecessary and undesirable duplication of work [of all kinds] in the various auxiliaries of the Church . . . and for the general purpose of unifying the work and advancing the cause of each organization."[15] Records indicate that this committee met at least quarterly from 1912 to 1918.[16] They met more frequently during the first and last year of their time together, approximately every month. Though the minutes do show an effort to correlate the studies of each auxiliary, they do not definitely indicate how successful these efforts were. They worked for several years to create a teacher improvement program written by Howard R. Driggs. He wrote a book entitled *Teacher Training Course*, which was recommended for use throughout the Church.[17]

SOCIAL ADVISORY COMMITTEE OF GENERAL BOARDS

By 1916 the Social Advisory Committee was formed, consisting of three members each from the general boards of the Relief Society, YLMIA, and the Primary.[18] Within a month, the First Presidency recommended that the General Sunday School Board be added. Stephen L Richards, then serving on the General Sunday School Board, was chosen as chairman.[19] As has been noted, within a year he was also called as an Apostle. The work of this committee overlapped with some of the work of the Correlation Committee headed by Elder McKay. Though the Social Advisory Committee was originally tasked to bring about reforms of dress and social conduct, they found themselves working on some of the same issues as the Correlation Committee.[20] Elder Richards suggested that the two committees be combined and that the "amalgamated committee be instructed to consider and report on the relationship of the quorums to each other, and the auxiliaries to each other, to define their functions and fields of endeavor and outline a program or survey of their work."[21] Elder Richards then moved that Elder McKay be named chair of the combined committees. However, Elder McKay felt that Elder Richards should be made the chair of the combined committee. Ultimately, Elder Richards was appointed as chair.

THE AMALGAMATED CORRELATION– SOCIAL ADVISORY COMMITTEE

This combined committee, the Amalgamated Correlation–Social Advisory Committee, was tasked with trying to correlate the work of each of the auxiliaries and the priesthood quorums.[22] By April 1921, they submitted a comprehensive twenty-seven-page recommendation to the First Presidency.[23] They recommended the creation of correlation committees, like their own, on several different levels in the Church. These committees, to be staffed with both priesthood and auxiliary officers, would carry on the work of correlation at every level. A second recommendation was made to resolve a conflict between stake and ward conferences and the annual general auxiliary conferences. They recommended that the stake and ward conferences be adjusted to make room for the auxiliary conferences that were regularly held at the same time each year.

The amalgamated committee made an even bolder recommendation regarding the correlation of gospel instruction and curriculum development. They recommended that the Sunday School take over all "theological and doctrinal instruction for the whole membership of the Church in an authoritative, standardized course."[24] The reason given for this recommendation included the "pronounced need for a well organized, well administered course of study which will be adequate to insure to the membership of the Church a comprehensive, coherent conception of the fundamental principles of the gospel."[25] Though this course of action would have largely eliminated the need to correlate curriculum, as only one organization would be writing and delivering it, it was a radical departure from Church practice.

Though these recommendations would have moved the work of correlation and simplification forward, as will be seen by the response of the First Presidency, they would have moved in a direction contrary to what the First Presidency had outlined as the primary objective. A week before formally submitting his report, Elder Richards had read and given details on the report to the full Quorum of the Twelve and the First Presidency.[26] On April 28, Elder James E. Talmage moved that further discussion of the Correlation–Social Advisory Committee recommendations be tabled until the First Presidency had a chance to go over it first. The First Presidency of Heber J. Grant, Charles W. Penrose, and Anthony W. Ivins responded almost immediately to the committee's recommendation that stake and ward conferences be moved so as not to conflict with the auxiliaries' conferences.

In their response they stated, "We think it the wisest plan to not make the change."[27] However, they did not respond to the other recommendations for another thirteen months.

On June 7, 1922, the First Presidency advised the Quorum of Twelve Apostles that they felt it would be unwise to adopt the recommendations regarding the Sunday School taking over all curriculum development and delivery or the establishment of correlation committees on the various levels.[28] In this letter, and a letter which was given to Elder Richards on June 26, the First Presidency gave several reasons why they declined acting on the recommendations. Regarding permanently organizing correlation committees at each level of the Church, the First Presidency stated they felt it would simply be "unnecessary and undesirable." They further emphasized the importance of maintaining the organization the Lord had revealed of direct priesthood direction in all aspects of correlation:

> All these organizations were presided over and their fields of activity outlined by the Presidency of the Church, the details of their work being directed by the general and local officers who were chosen to preside over them.
>
> While the present administration has relinquished the direct presidency of the Sunday Schools and the Young Mens Mutual Improvement Associations, it still retains its right of presidency over all of the quorums and auxiliary organizations of the Church. Under the Presidency of the Church, are the General Boards, which have been chosen to direct, in detail, the various associations. These General Boards are expected, in all that they do, to act in harmony with the Stake Presidencies, and the Stake Presidencies act in harmony with the Bishoprics of the various wards. Thus all of the agencies through which the activities of the Church are controlled come under the direct supervision of the Priesthood.[29]

In letters sent out to the wards and stakes dated January 13 and March 8, 1923, the First Presidency announced that the General Correlation

Committee and the Social Advisory Committee had completed their assigned tasks and have "therefore, been released with the commendation of the Presidency for the splendid work accomplished by them." They went on to emphasize the importance of maintaining direct priesthood direction to all work done in the Church. Rather than another administrative level being placed between the stake and ward leaders and the auxiliaries, the First Presidency stated, "We wish also to have it clearly understood that all auxiliary associations operate under the direct presidency and supervision of stake and ward priesthood authorities, who carry the ultimate responsibility for the work of these organizations."[30] They recommended that stake and ward leaders hold a monthly meeting to correlate the work of the auxiliaries under their stewardship. This step seems to have been a precursor to the present stake and ward council system.[31]

The First Presidency also chose not to implement the recommendation regarding the Sunday School taking over all gospel instruction and curriculum development. In explaining why, they emphasized that the major purpose for each organization was that "the doctrines of the Gospel might be taught, . . . that faith in the Lord, in Christ His Son, and in Joseph Smith, His Prophet might be burned into the souls of the people."[32] Though there was a great need to correlate the efforts of the different organizations, the First Presidency chose not to accomplish it by assigning responsibilities to one organization.

PRIESTHOOD/SUNDAY SCHOOL COOPERATIVE

The next effort at correlation focused largely on Church curriculum and again involved Elder McKay. In 1928, while serving as both Apostle and general superintendent of the Sunday School, Elder McKay announced that the curricula of all quorums and the Sunday School would be reviewed and authorized by a common committee.[33] He announced that in doing so, the Sunday School would take up its role as a "helper" to the priesthood.[34] No records have been found which indicate the success or failure of this endeavor. However, one notable simplification in Church publications did occur around this time. In 1929, the magazines of the YMMIA and YWMIA, the *Improvement Era* and the *Young Woman's Journal*, were combined into one publication called the *Improvement Era*.[35]

Though the work of these early committees did not accomplish their intended aim of Churchwide correlation, the First Presidency felt that they did redirect Church thinking toward priesthood leaderships rather than auxiliary control.[36] Efforts to strengthen the priesthood continued through the 1930s. As early as 1932, the First Presidency reported gratifying results.[37]

COMMITTEE OF CORRELATION AND COORDINATION

Though the earlier Churchwide correlation committees had been discontinued, the need to correlate the work of the priesthood and the auxiliaries continued to grow. On September 23, 1938, Elder John A. Widtsoe wrote a memorandum for President J. Reuben Clark Jr., reiterating the need to have all policy decisions made by the Twelve, not the auxiliary heads.[38] In that same year, the First Presidency of Heber J. Grant, J. Reuben Clark, and David O. McKay was again considering ways to correlate the work of the Church. In January of the following year, the First Presidency organized the Committee of Correlation and Coordination and asked three members of the Twelve—Joseph Fielding Smith, Stephen L Richards and Albert E. Bowen—to take the lead.[39] The committee was made up of members of the Twelve, the First Council of the Seventy, the Presiding Bishopric, the Relief Society, the Department of Education, the Sunday School, the YMMIA and YWMIA, the Primary, and the Genealogy Committee. The First Presidency letter calling this committee sheds light on their purpose:

> The continuing expansion and the increasing overlapping of these fields, . . . the failure always to hew to the line in matters of doctrine and Church discipline, with the final result that the youth of the Church are left with too fragmentary information, sometimes, almost chaotic notions regarding the principles of the gospel,

and the organization and history of the Church, the necessity to provide a course of study and of activities that will bring the young people of missionary age to a substantial and rounded knowledge of the principles of the gospel—all require that the work of the auxiliary organizations and of our educational institutions should be coordinated, unified, and standardized to avoid duplication and overlapping, and to provide the training which is required by the young people.... In order to accomplish the purposes herein stated, the First Presidency desire that this Committee shall outline courses of study and activities for each of the organizations named above, and report, with recommendations, to us.[40]

Not many records have been found detailing the actual work of this committee. We know that they chose to start by asking each organization to report on their current status. They arranged to have a letter sent to each General Auxiliary leader asking that they submit a report of their general objectives, plans, procedures, and lesson courses. A copy of the letter to the president of the Relief Society is contained in the history compiled by Antone K. Romney.[41]

UNION BOARD OF THE AUXILIARIES

March 29, 1940, was a watershed moment in the correlation efforts of the Church. President Clark, under assignment by President Grant, called the leaders of the Relief Society, Sunday School, Young Men, Young Women, Primary, and Genealogy Society together and presented detailed instructions on correlation principles. A follow-up letter signed by all three members of the First Presidency, entitled "Memorandum of Suggestions," was sent thereafter.[42] In large measure, it summarized past and current correlation challenges and outlined suggestions on how best to address each of them. At this meeting President Clark announced the formation of the Union Board of the Auxiliaries and called President George Q. Morris, then general YMMIA superintendent, to be president. In his presentation,

President Clark listed four specific correlation challenges that needed to be addressed. First, there was an ever-increasing burden being placed on the membership of the Church, both financial and otherwise, to carry out the various activities of the Church. Second, the bishops of the Church were being overwhelmed not only with their scripturally mandated duties but also with the numerous activities of the auxiliaries. Third, there was beginning to be a great disparity between the "near ins" and the "far outs" of the Church created by the fact that those who lived near Church headquarters had vast and elaborate organizations competing to fill their needs and that those same organizations could not function in an equal manner for those who lived farther out. Finally, the financial burdens placed on the Church had created large debts in 1937 and 1938. The ever-expanding activities of each of the organizations constantly strained the Church's ability to live within its means.

In order to address these concerns, the First Presidency suggested that the "auxiliaries might consolidate, cooperate, eliminate, simplify, and adjust their work so as to cooperate with the Presidency."[43] They further suggested that auxiliaries should operate on a budget supplied by the First Presidency and that all surplus funds be returned to the First Presidency. The First Presidency recommended that auxiliaries cease to solicit funds except for magazines. Finally, they recommended that travel and visits by members of the auxiliary boards be reduced to a minimum and that the Union Board plan all new work so as to curtail the ever-increasing burden that their activities had been putting on the Church membership.[44]

At the creation of the Union Board of Auxiliaries, President Clark made several recommendations regarding the restructuring of Church curriculum. He reminded those in attendance that "the sole ultimate aim and purpose of the Auxiliary organizations of the Church is to plant and make grow in every member of the Church a testimony of the Christ and of the Gospel."[45] He reminded everyone that the Church auxiliaries exist to aid the family in their work and that the family was the basic unit in the Church.[46] Though this suggestion would not bear fruit immediately, it would form the basis of future efforts. The First Presidency recommended that each auxiliary consider home life as divisible into three periods: birth to fifteen, fifteen to marriage or early twenties, and from this point forward. They then suggested a division of responsibility by organization based on these three age periods.

The First Presidency felt that there was no need for completely new curriculum to be written every year for each auxiliary and recommended a different approach to curriculum development. Finally, they suggested combining all Church magazines into three magazines that could contain all of the curricular material for the Church and could be managed and printed under the direction of the Union Board of Auxiliaries. It appears that with the onset of America's involvement in World War II, most of these suggestions were not implemented. In fact, the union meetings held by the auxiliaries were discontinued for a time.[47] However, we know that President Clark continued to mentor and teach others regarding these and other correlation principles. From Harold B. Lee's biography, we learn that Elder Lee and Elder Romney were invited to President Clark's home July 10, 1941, where he continued to share this vision regarding the "simplification of the present Church programs."[48]

COMMITTEE ON PUBLICATIONS

Four years later, the First Presidency set up a committee to evaluate all Church publications. In a letter dated August 9, 1944, the First Presidency formed the Committee on Publications, made up of Elders Joseph Fielding Smith, John A. Widtsoe, Harold B. Lee, and Marion G. Romney. "The function of this Committee is to pass upon and approve all materials . . . to be used by our Church Priesthood, Educational, Auxiliary, and Missionary organizations in their work of instructing members of the Church."[49] The First Presidency also named a Reading Committee to assist the Committee on Publications. They then gave strict guidelines for evaluating all published materials. These guidelines and committees were the forerunners of the modern evaluation committees within the Correlation Department.

A Firm Foundation

HAROLD B. LEE COMMITTEE

One of the final attempts at correlation in the first half of the century began on December 15, 1947. The First Presidency assigned Elder Harold B. Lee to head a committee of Apostles to look at work in the Melchizedek Priesthood quorums and the auxiliaries and recommend changes.[50] The committee was tasked with four specific objectives. First, they were to work toward a greater emphasis and enlarging of the field of priesthood activity. Second, they were to work toward better supervision of the auxiliary boards and coordination of their work. Third, they were to preserve the good being done by the Sunday School and MIA programs but remove overlapping and redundant responsibilities. And finally they were to come up with a simplified Church meeting schedule.[51] On January 22, 1948, they made several recommendations. First was that the First Presidency and Quorum of the Twelve maintain general supervision of priesthood quorums and work; second, that full-time assistants to the Twelve as well as members of the First Council of Seventy and Presiding Bishopric be called to help in the correlation work; third, that Melchizedek and Aaronic Priesthood boards of assistants be organized; and finally, that the Church's meeting schedule be modified. The First Presidency of George Albert Smith chose to take the recommendations under consideration.[52] No record has been found indicating that the First Presidency acted on the recommendations at that time.

Though no other formal correlation committees were organized until 1960, there was some continued correlation work done. Elder Lee continued to suggest a redesign of ward teaching program to bring it under the supervision of the Quorum of the Twelve instead of the Presiding Bishopric in 1948 and again in 1949.[53] Next, when Elder Richards was called to the First Presidency in April 1951, he met with the Twelve to review unsolved business, including several correlation issues. He promised to seek for decisions on several of these issues.[54] Finally, in 1956, Elders Delbert L. Stapley and Adam S. Bennion met with the First Presidency and suggested a new general committee that would again attempt to correlate the course of study given by the quorums and auxiliaries of the Church. President McKay instructed them to submit their proposal as a formal request, which they did.

Clearly, the early years of correlation did not bring to fruition many of the stated goals and objectives the First Presidency and Quorum of Twelve had suggested. However, the stage was being set and the groundwork was being laid for the time when those same principles would be even more crucial. With the end of World War II, the Church began to expand at a dramatically faster rate internationally. The expansion further exacerbated the challenges facing the Church. As President Lee once stated, the whole problem of correlation becomes more acute as the Church grows and develops."[55] Though the realization of many of the First Presidency and Quorum of Twelve's ideas would have to wait till the 1960s and '70s to come to full fruition, the principles were taught as early as the first decade of the 1900s. When the need for correlation became even more acute, it could be built on the foundation laid during the first sixty years of the twentieth century.

NOTES

1. Bruce C. Hafen, *A Disciple's Life: The Biography of Neal A. Maxwell* (Salt Lake City: Deseret Book, 2002), 318.
2. Hafen, *Disciple's Life*, 324.
3. L. Brent Goates, *Harold B. Lee: Prophet and Seer* (Salt Lake City: Bookcraft, 1985), 363.
4. N. Eldon Tanner, Minutes of the Priesthood Genealogy Committee Training Session, December 1963, quoted in Daniel H. Ludlow, "Correlation," in *Encyclopedia of Latter-day Saint History*, ed. Arnold K. Garr, Donald Q. Cannon, and Richard O. Cowan (Salt Lake City: Deseret Book, 2000), 251.
5. Harold B. Lee, regional representatives seminar, 2–3, quoted in Hafen, *Disciple's Life*, 325.
6. Antone Kimball Romney, August 1961, "History of the Correlation of L.D.S. Church Auxiliaries, Section A," Church History Library, The Church of Jesus Christ of Latter-day Saints, Salt Lake City.
7. Joseph F. Smith, in Conference Report, April 1906, 3.

8. Dale Mouritsen, 1974, "Efforts to Correlate Mormon Agencies in the Twentieth Century: A Review," 6, Church History Library.
9. Mouritsen, "Efforts to Correlate Mormon Agencies," 6–7.
10. David O. McKay, David A. Smith, and Joseph J. Cannon, "Priesthood Quorums Table" *Improvement Era*, May 1912, 655–60.
11. David O. McKay, "Priesthood Quorums' Table: Report of the Committee on Priesthood Outlines," *Improvement Era*, May 1913, 734–39.
12. General Priesthood Committee, Minutes of Meetings, 1908–22, 1, 11, quoted in Mouritsen, "Efforts to Correlate Mormon Agencies," 6.
13. Gregory A. Prince and William Robert Wright, *David O. McKay and the Rise of Modern Mormonism* (Salt Lake City: University of Utah Press, 2005), 141.
14. Minutes, 1913–20, Correlation Committee, Church History Library.
15. Joseph F. Smith, in Marion G. Romney, Correlation Items, "The Basics of Priesthood Correlation," address at general priesthood board meeting, November 15, 1967, 2, Church History Library.
16. Minutes, 1913–20, Correlation Committee.
17. Minutes, 1913–20, Correlation Committee.
18. Minutes, 1916–120, Social Advisory Committee, Church History Library.
19. Minutes, 1916–1920, Social Advisory Committee.
20. Minutes, 1916–1920, Social Advisory Committee.
21. Minutes of a Temple Meeting, November 4, 1920, in Romney, Correlation Items, "The Basics of Priesthood Correlation," 4, Church History Library.
22. Romney, Correlation Items, "The Basics of Priesthood Correlation," 5.
23. Stephen L Richards, Report of the Amalgamated Correlation–Social Advisory Committee, April 21, 1921, in Antone Kimball Romney, "History of Correlation of L.D.S. Church Auxiliaries, D," Church History Library.
24. Richards, Report of the Amalgamated Correlation–Social Advisory Committee.
25. Richards, Report of the Amalgamated Correlation–Social Advisory Committee.
26. Romney, Correlation Items, "The Basics of Priesthood Correlation," 6.
27. First Presidency letter, April 20, 1921, in Romney, Correlation Items, "The Basics of Priesthood Correlation," 6.

28. First Presidency letter, June 26, 1922, in Antone Kimball Romney, "History of Correlation of L.D.S. Church Auxiliaries, E."
29. First Presidency letter, June 26, 1922.
30. First Presidency letter, June 26, 1922.
31. Romney, Correlation Items, "The Basics of Priesthood Correlation," 12.
32. First Presidency letter, June 7, in Romney, "History of Correlation of L.D.S. Church Auxiliaries, E."
33. Prince and Wright, *Rise of Modern Mormonism*, 142.
34. David O. McKay, *Improvement Era*, July 1928, 792–94.
35. Richard O. Cowan, *Priesthood Programs of the Twentieth Century* (n.p., 1974), 157.
36. First Presidency letter to stake presidents, January 13, 1923, in Romney, "History of Correlation of L.D.S. Church Auxiliaries, E."
37. *Deseret News, Church Section*, July 9, 1932, 1, 3.
38. John A. Widtsoe, Memorandum for J. Reuben Clark, in Romney, "History of Correlation of L.D.S. Church Auxiliaries, F."
39. First Presidency letter, January 1939, in Romney, "History of Correlation of L.D.S. Church Auxiliaries, F."
40. First Presidency letter, January 1939, in Romney, "History of Correlation of L.D.S. Church Auxiliaries, F."
41. First Presidency letter, January 1939, in Romney, "History of Correlation of L.D.S. Church Auxiliaries, F."
42. Heber J. Grant, J. Reuben Clark Jr., David O. McKay, Memorandum of Suggestions, in Romney, "History of Correlation of L.D.S. Church Auxiliaries, G."
43. Grant, Clark, and McKay, Memorandum of Suggestions.
44. Grant, Clark, and McKay, Memorandum of Suggestions.
45. Grant, Clark, and McKay, Memorandum of Suggestions.
46. Grant, Clark, and McKay, Memorandum of Suggestions.
47. Heber J. Grant, J. Reuben Clark Jr., David O. McKay, circular letter, January 15, 1944, in *Messages of the First Presidency of The Church of Jesus Christ of Latter-day Saints*, ed. James R. Clark (Salt Lake City: Bookcraft, 1975), 6:206.
48. Goates, *Harold B. Lee: Prophet and Seer*, 365.

49. Heber J. Grant, J. Reuben Clark, and David O. McKay to Joseph Fielding Smith, John A. Widtsoe, Harold B. Lee, and Marion G. Romney, August 9, 1944, in Clark, *Messages of the First Presidency*, 6:209.
50. First Presidency and Council of the Twelve, Temple Meeting Minutes, January 22, 1948, in Romney, "History of Correlation of L.D.S. Church Auxiliaries, H."
51. First Presidency and Council of the Twelve, Temple Meeting Minutes, January 22, 1948.
52. First Presidency and Council of the Twelve, Temple Meeting Minutes, January 22, 1948.
53. Goates, *Harold B. Lee: Prophet and Seer*, 365.
54. Goates, *Harold B. Lee: Prophet and Seer*, 366.
55. Harold B. Lee, quoted by Marion G. Romney in Correlation Items, "The Basics of Priesthood Correlation," 3.

Sherry Pack Baker and Elizabeth Mott

15

From Radio to the Internet: Church Use of Electronic Media in the Twentieth Century

LEADERS of The Church of Jesus Christ of Latter-day Saints have proactively adopted and made use of media—both print and electronic—as means to achieve the Church's organizational purposes. In the Latter-day Saint worldview, these media-related activities are not only practical and prudential but also religious in nature. The very existence of electronic media is considered providential with divinely appointed purposes. According to this view, God has inspired the invention of communications technologies in these latter days, and there is a God-given commission and responsibility to use them in furthering the work of the Church. Speaking of an older technology, the telegraph, President Brigham Young said, "We should bring into requisition every improvement which our age affords, to facilitate our intercourse and to render our inter-communication more easy."[1]

Sherry Pack Baker is an associate professor of communications at Brigham Young University. Elizabeth Mott is a doctoral student of American religious history at Claremont Graduate University.

A Firm Foundation

The zeal with which the Church uses media can best be understood within this combined prudential and providential framework. The belief that "we *should* bring into requisition every improvement which our age affords" suggests media use to spread the gospel is not only a wise and efficacious thing to do but also a commandment from the Lord. President David O. McKay said, for example, "The Lord has given us the means of whispering through space, of annihilating distance. We have the means in our hands of reaching the millions in the world. . . . We're in the business of broadcasting to learn how to use it to further the work of the Lord."[2] President Spencer W. Kimball said, "The Lord is anxious to put into our hands inventions of which we laymen have hardly a glimpse. . . . Our Father in Heaven has now provided us mighty towers—radio and television towers, with possibilities beyond comprehension—to help fulfill the words of the Lord that 'the sound must go forth from this place unto all the world.'"[3]

This chapter reviews the Church's history of the use of electronic media in the twentieth century. It places landmark events within the framework of the administrations of each Church President who presided over them. It identifies a philosophy and foundational principles and strategies that emerged in the first stages of the Church's use of broadcast media early in the twentieth century that have affected all subsequent Church efforts in broadcasting and electronic communications. It also looks to the future and identifies a new strategy and principle that has emerged in the twenty-first century in response to the Internet environment.

RELIGION AND MEDIA TECHNOLOGIES

Scholars have taken an interest in the matter of the adoption and use of media by organized religions. In the book *Communication and Change in American Religious History*, Leonard I. Sweet discusses the "interplay in American history between the emergence of new communication forms and religious and social change."[4] He cites scholars such as Averil Cameron, Roger Finke, and Rodney Stark, who concluded that "those religious leaders who have made the biggest advances have been those who worked out of their tradition to express their faith through innovative ways and means, idioms and technologies accessible and adapted to the times in which they lived."[5] Sweet also cites Colin Morris's book on Christian communications, which suggests that "many of the exciting new twists in the Christian story over the centuries have occurred because advocates for Christianity have exploited developments in communications technology."[6] Further, Sweet refers to historian Nathan Hatch, who has written that success in America's religious marketplace is explained by "the ability of religious groups to adopt and adapt to the democratic and populist impulses of American culture, and to use popular forms of communication to reach the widest possible audience."[7] Conversely, mainline Protestantism, which made excellent use of print technology throughout its history, did not successfully adapt to and exploit broadcast technologies.[8]

While there is no well-developed theory of media and religion, this observation of the relationship between the successful use of communications technologies and the success of organized religions is worth consideration. This relationship is consistent with the views of communications theorists like Harold Innis, Marshall McLuhan, and Walter Ong. They held, according to Sweet, that "communications structures are more than mediums of transmission" in that they affect "every nook and cranny of society, including the intellectual and social girders that underpin that society."[9] This view is summarized by Marshall McLuhan's well-known statement that "the medium is the message."[10] This means essentially that "communications media themselves, apart from their content and programming, are dynamic and even determinative forces. The medium changes and shapes history and culture; it creates and alters perceptions of reality and truth."[11]

In a related view, Neil Postman has argued that "technological change is not additive; it is ecological," adding, "What happens if we place a drop of red dye into a beaker of clear water? Do we have clear water plus a spot of red dye? Obviously not. We have a new coloration to every molecule of water. That is what I mean by ecological."[12] Postman had argued earlier: "One significant change generates total change. . . . A new technology does not add or subtract something. It changes everything. . . . After television, the United States was not America plus television; television gave a new coloration to every political campaign, to every home, to every school, to every church, to every industry."[13] Consistent with this ecological view is James B. Allen's observation that older Latter-day Saints living in the year 2000 experienced "a different Church than they had known 50 years earlier"[14]—not the same church plus new technologies but a different church.

The assumption of the centrality of communications media to the success of religions is a useful backdrop to any narrative about use of the media, and about the progress of the LDS Church in the twentieth century. The following chronology briefly outlines major events in Church use of broadcast media in the administrations of Church Presidents, beginning with Heber J. Grant. This chronology confirms historian Leonard J. Arrington's observation that "at every stage of our history, the leaders of the Latter-day Saints have sought to use every communication facility that civilization afforded."[15]

HEBER J. GRANT, 1918–45

Church broadcast history begins with Heber J. Grant, who became President of the Church in 1918 at almost the precise historical moment that commercial radio burst upon the scene. The Church began experimenting with radio in its very earliest stages and was among the first organizations to receive a broadcast license.

In 1920, the same year in which KDKA, the first commercial radio station, began broadcasting in Pittsburgh, the *Deseret News* began nightly wireless news flashes in Salt Lake City. In 1921, the Latter-day Saints University received the first US broadcast license issued to an educational institution, and in 1922 the school station broadcast the first Tabernacle organ concert.

On May 6, 1922, the station that later became KSL was dedicated, with President Grant giving the dedicatory address from a tin shack on the roof of the Deseret News Building. Thus began radio broadcasting in the Church and in the region. It was "the first full time commercial broadcasting operation between the Mississippi Valley and the Pacific Coast."[16] A year later, the first successful radio broadcast from the Tabernacle was of a speech by US President Warren G. Harding, and the first radio broadcast of portions of general conference also took place.

The Church began almost immediately to be a producer of radio programming. For example, the "Church Hour"—a series of Sunday evening programs—began in 1924. This was before the national radio networks had been established (NBC in 1926 and CBS in 1927). In 1928, the half-hour weekly program *Sunday Evening on Temple Square* began. In 1929, KSL radio affiliated with NBC, and on July 15 the Tabernacle Choir began its weekly network radio broadcasts.

By 1933, KSL-AM had become one of the first Federal Communications Commission (FCC) class 1-A clear-channel stations, transmitting at 50,000 watts—the maximum allowable power. Also by that date, KSL Radio had changed its affiliation from NBC to CBS. President Grant took advantage of other opportunities to reach national audiences as well. For example, in 1935 he spoke on *The Church of the Air*, a national Sunday-morning radio program produced by Columbia Broadcasting Company.

Also in 1935, the Church Radio, Publicity, and Mission Literature Committee was organized with Gordon B. Hinckley as its executive secretary and day-to-day director. Most members are familiar with the story of Gordon B. Hinckley's visit to the Church Office Building shortly after returning from his mission to report on the need for literature to support the missionary effort.[17] This meeting resulted in his being hired by the Church, his appointment to the Radio Committee, and his subsequent influence on Church media from 1935 until his death in 2008. The organization of this committee is also of note because it is one marker of President Grant's recognition of the importance of outreach and publicity efforts in improving the image of the Church in the early twentieth century. Under his direction, the Church made full use of radio technology. In 1936, portions of general conference were broadcast to Europe through international shortwave radio; in 1938, *The Fulness of Times* series of half-hour radio programs produced by Gordon B. Hinckley was broadcast in the United States, Canada, South Africa, Sweden, and New Zealand. This series continued until 1942.

The Tabernacle Choir participated in the first overseas broadcast to the British Isles through the US Army Special Services radio network in 1944, and in 1945 the choir performed on the nationwide radio broadcast of the memorial service for President Franklin D. Roosevelt.[18] This is one example of the many instances in which the choir sang on radio and television at the deaths or inaugurations of US presidents throughout the twentieth century.

These events during the Grant administration demonstrate some of the ways in which radio both reflected and contributed to the Church's transition from a history of ridicule and isolation in the West to a respected participant in the national and international experience.

President Grant died in May of 1945 after serving for nearly twenty-seven years. Ronald W. Walker wrote that President Grant commanded "the national media unlike any other contemporary Utahn."[19] As the Church's broadcasting pioneers, Grant and his administration created the foundation for all subsequent media activities, accomplishments, and successes throughout the twentieth century. Due in part to the longevity of his tenure as the President of the Church at the key moment of the dawn of broadcasting, Heber J. Grant and his administration were able to develop a philosophy and foundational principles and strategies, affecting all subsequent Church efforts in broadcasting and electronic communications:

- Early adoption of new media technologies by the Church
- Church ownership of media outlets
- Church production of media content
- Use of media to create a favorable image of the Church
- Use of electronic media to reach and communicate with Church members
- Use of electronic media to introduce and explain the Church to those not of our faith
- Establishment of and enduring commitment to Tabernacle Choir broadcasts

- Use of the Tabernacle Choir for Church public relations purposes in media and in mediated national and international events
- Establishment and development of the Church as a broadcast entity

GEORGE ALBERT SMITH, 1945–51

George Albert Smith became President of the Church at the end of World War II. He delivered the first Church sermon by shortwave radio to servicemen in Japan in 1946. He served his presidency during the postwar years in which television emerged and began its rapid development. President Smith presided over the first live general conference broadcast over commercial television in 1948.[20] He presided also over the Church's adoption of television when KSL-TV, the first commercial TV station in Utah, went on the air in June 1949 and presided over the first live local broadcast of general conference on KSL television in October.[21] That year *Music and the Spoken Word* was first broadcast on television.[22]

It is interesting to note that the Church had only about one million members when it began television broadcasting in 1949, having reached that milestone in 1947.[23] Membership numbers become significant if one is looking for evidence of a correlation between use of media technology and Church growth during the twentieth century.

DAVID O. McKAY, 1951–70

President David O. McKay's administration was proactive in making use of all available media, including telephone wire transmissions, videotape, commercial and shortwave radio, television and film, and even satellite. His administration took place right in the heart of the age of mass media that many consider to be synonymous with the period known as modernism. While the groundbreaking pioneers had set the stage, it was up to President McKay to see that Church broadcasting became viable.

Gregory A. Prince and William Robert Wright wrote, "When David O. McKay became president in 1951, he inherited a nascent broadcasting apparatus with largely unrealized potential. Gradually he moved to unleash that potential."[24] They added, "Clean-shaven, immaculately dressed, and movie-star handsome, McKay immediately caught the attention of member and nonmember alike, and held it."[25] Francis M. Gibbons wrote, "This new mass communications medium . . . seemed tailor-made for the appearance, personality, and dominating presence of President David O. McKay."[26]

General conference was televised outside of the Intermountain area for first time in October 1953,[27] marking the expansion of the Church's broadcasting footprint as it moved into the second half of the century. In 1954, President McKay oversaw the development of film production facilities at Brigham Young University, thus moving the Church deeply into that medium.[28]

Of significance to future events is that President McKay kept Gordon B. Hinckley on as head of the Radio Committee. Then in 1958, McKay called Hinckley to be an Assistant to the Twelve and in 1961 called him to be an Apostle.

The decade of the 1960s was important for the expansion of Church media use, as well as for the development of satellite technologies. Early in the 1960s, the Church moved even further into broadcast ownership through the development of radio and television properties at Brigham Young University. In 1960, KBYU-FM began broadcasting, and in 1962, BYU acquired the Provo station KLOR-TV and changed the call letters to KBYU-TV.[29] The establishment of Church-owned broadcasting properties at BYU was an important strategic move that has had deep implications for the Church and for BYU—and continues to have far-reaching effects due to the launch of BYU-TV International in 2007.[30]

In 1962, the Church's April general conference was broadcast on television nationwide for the first time. July 1962 marked the dawn of the satellite age. That was the date that the first worldwide satellite broadcast of a live television program took place over the recently launched Telstar 1 satellite (owned by AT&T and flown by NASA).[31] Viewership of the program was reportedly about three hundred million people.[32] "Featured on the program were excerpts from a baseball game in Chicago, a live news conference by President John F. Kennedy, and a concert by the Mormon Tabernacle Choir, singing from Mt. Rushmore."[33]

In October 1962, the live telecast of *Music and the Spoken Word* debuted, reaching over eight hundred radio and television stations worldwide.[34] Also in 1962, the Church purchased five international shortwave radio transmitters from a New York shortwave radio station, with the objective of communicating with Church members in Europe and South America.[35] But new and more effective technologies were soon to make themselves available.

In 1963, the Church reached the two million mark in membership. This was only sixteen years after it had reached the one million mark in 1947. By way of comparison, that initial million member milestone (in 1947) had taken 117 years to accomplish, beginning with the foundation of the Church in 1830. Membership growth continued to accelerate.

In 1964, Bonneville International Corporation was created with Arch Madsen as president and Gordon B. Hinckley as a vice president. Bonneville was created to consolidate Church-owned commercial broadcasting stations and operations. With this action the Church truly became a permanently committed and established media entity.[36]

In October of 1965, general conference was first heard live in Europe. KBYU-TV began broadcasting in 1965, and it later became affiliated with the Public Broadcasting System.[37]

In 1967, some radio and TV stations in Mexico started carrying general conference,[38] and 1968 marked the first general conference satellite broadcast to South America.[39]

President McKay died in January of 1970. He served as President of the Church for nineteen years. Prince and Wright wrote of President McKay, "Under his leadership, the church experienced unparalleled growth, nearly tripling in total membership and becoming a significant presence throughout the world."[40] Surely the media contributed to that presence.

JOSEPH FIELDING SMITH, 1970–72

There were no major broadcasting events to make note of during President Joseph Fielding Smith's administration, although the reconfiguration of all the Church magazines in January 1971 dramatically changed the landscape in terms of the Church's print media. This was the year in which the first issues of the *Friend*, the *New Era*, and the *Ensign* were published (replacing several previous Church publications). It also was the year in which Church membership reached three million.

HAROLD B. LEE, 1972–73

Some landmark communications events took place during President Harold B. Lee's short administration. These included the beginnings of the Bonneville production of the *Homefront* series, which eventually won several prestigious awards, including back-to-back Emmy awards in 1997 and 1998.[41] President Lee also presided over the establishment of the Church's Public Affairs Department, which included divisions for news and information and for electronic media. Gordon B. Hinckley also was deeply involved with this initiative to present the "Church's image more professionally."[42]

SPENCER W. KIMBALL, 1973–85

The Church moved aggressively with its media use and strategy during President Spencer W. Kimball's administration. During the early years of his administration, upon the recommendation of Gordon B. Hinckley,[43] all the Church-owned shortwave radio properties purchased since 1962 were sold because they were not meeting their objectives.

In the 1970s, the Church was involved in a diverse variety of media-related activities. In 1976, it produced an hour-long TV special "*The Family . . . and Other Living Things*," which aired in the US and Canada.[44] By 1977, general conference broadcasts were reaching all of the US, Latin America, Australia, the Philippines, and parts of Africa, Europe, and Asia.[45] Also by 1977, the Church owned sixteen radio and television stations, an international broadcast distribution system, a Washington news bureau, a cable TV system, and production and consulting divisions.[46] Bonneville Entertainment Inc. was organized in 1977 to produce films and television features but was later dissolved in 1982.[47] In 1978, President Kimball addressed the first Churchwide closed-circuit meeting for women in the Tabernacle on Temple Square. The meeting was broadcast via satellite to meetinghouses throughout the world, as were general priesthood meetings."[48]

By 1978, just seven years after the previous million-member landmark, Church membership reached four million.

In the 1980s, the Church entered one of the most important periods in its broadcast and electronic media history—the satellite era. President Kimball's administration made a substantial investment and commitment to satellite technology during this decade. In March 1980, the Bonneville Satellite Corporation was formed.[49] Then in April, the Church's first satellite broadcast in conjunction with general conference occurred in commemoration of the Church's sesquicentennial celebration. During this broadcast, President Kimball dedicated the reconstructed Peter Whitmer Sr. log home on the original site in Fayette, New York.[50] That event is a significant marker not only for the Church's 150th anniversary but also for its progress in its adoption of media technologies—from the single-pull press[51] that was used to print the first copies of the Book of Mormon in 1830 to the satellite delivery of general conference in 1980.

The step into satellite technology was one of the ways in which President Kimball's administration "lengthened the stride" of the Church.[52] In January 1981, the Tabernacle Choir participated in the inaugural festivities for US President Ronald Reagan, and Gordon B. Hinckley was called by President Kimball in July to serve as a third counselor in the First Presidency. That same year the Church installed a satellite station in City Creek Canyon, three and a half miles from downtown Salt Lake City, and began installing satellite receivers in stake centers throughout Utah.[53] In October the Church announced that it would create a network of five hundred satellite dishes to be placed at stake centers outside of Utah, linking Church headquarters with members throughout the United States and Canada. One newspaper reported that this was the world's largest network via satellite at that time and that the order placed for the satellites had been the largest single order for a single television network.[54]

President Hinckley was deeply involved in this satellite initiative. His biography by Sheri L. Dew reports:

> This development was particularly gratifying to him [Hinckley] as he had, with Bonneville executives, for years investigated various technologies to develop just such a network. . . . Of that experience he said, "As I learned what a satellite and a transponder were, how far above the earth they would orbit, that they worked through the conversion of sunlight to electricity through voltaic cells, and so forth, I got the picture. I could envision the tremendous impact a network of satellites would have on our people. This was the culmination of years of effort in trying to find a way to communicate with our members."[55]

In 1982, the new satellite system was used for the first time for a Church-wide youth fireside, with President Hinckley speaking.

EZRA TAFT BENSON, 1985–94

A wide variety of broadcasting and electronic media events took place during the Benson administration. In 1988, the National Interfaith Cable Coalition, of which the Church was a founding member, launched the Vision Interfaith Satellite Network (VISN) which carried several Church programs and specials.[56]

In January 1989, "eight large city television stations in the United States [began] airing *Together Forever,* a program produced by the Church. Within four months of this event, every commercial station in the United States where mission headquarters [were] located [had broadcast] the program."[57] Also in January, the Tabernacle Choir performed at the inaugural events for President George H. W. Bush, who called the choir a "National Treasure."[58]

From Radio to the Internet

In February, President Hinckley spoke at the Church's first fireside broadcast by satellite for single-adult members.[59] In December, Church membership was reported to be seven million, and by 1990 more than 2,500 Church satellite dishes in North America were able to receive general conference.[60]

The Church also was responsive to the emerging computer age. In 1991, Church records were completely digitized.[61] Also in 1991, the Church Audiovisual Department was formed. This consolidated all Church-owned audiovisual facilities and production efforts,[62] and control of the BYU Motion Picture Studio also passed to this department.[63] In 1991, Church membership reached eight million. In October 1992, "*On the Way Home*, a Church video production, premiered over the Church satellite network as part of missionary open houses held in Church meetinghouses throughout North America."[64]

HOWARD W. HUNTER, 1994–95

President Howard W. Hunter engaged in a first-ever event; he addressed the full-time missionaries via satellite.[65] Also during his tenure, a Church-produced Public Affairs radio program called *Music and Values* won a 1994 Gabriel Award.[66]

GORDON B. HINCKLEY, 1995–2008

One of the most unique characteristics of media-related events in President Hinckley's administration was his own presence in the media—in news conferences and in public appearances and interview shows. Due to the focus of this chapter, however, only a few key events in the Church's institutional use of the media during President Hinckley's tenure will be highlighted. These events will exemplify the continuing reach and expansion of broadcast media and also the beginnings of the Church's entry into the Internet age. The events mentioned here do not begin to convey the full reach of President Hinckley's contributions to Church media innovations because his administration also stretched well into the first decade of the twenty-first century.

As an example of the wide variety of issues and concerns the Church dealt with during President Hinckley's administration in its role as a media entity, in 1995 alone, the first year of his presidency, KSL-TV switched its affiliation to NBC after forty-five years with CBS, the Church began broadcasting a series of worldwide missionary firesides via satellite,[67] and the *Church News* went online at ldschurchnews.com.[68] These three events alone touch on the Church's use of media in traditional broadcasting, satellite, and Internet.

A year later, in December 1996, the Church's official website lds.org was launched.[69] This event was the official and landmark beginning of the Internet age for the Church.

In 1997, PBS aired *Ancestors*, a ten-part series on family history produced by KBYU-TV, an example of the continuing importance of Church involvement in television content.[70]

In 1999 (May 24), the genealogy website familysearch.org was launched and was immediately successful and popular.[71]

At the end of the twentieth century and the beginning of the twenty-first, broadcasting was still very important to the Church. In 1999, Bonneville International Corporation holdings included seventeen radio and television stations, and in the year 2000, BYU-Television began broadcasting nationally 24/7 on the DISH Network satellite system, allowing people across the United States and southern Canada to pick up the station. By the end of the year, BYU-TV was available in about seventeen million homes because by then it was being carried by cable companies and DirecTV.[72]

The Church's entry into the Internet age during President Hinckley's administration was a fitting culmination to his career after all he had done in every other media format throughout the history of the Church's adoption, acquisition, and use of electronic media. President Hinckley was involved for nearly the whole journey, except for the first twelve years of radio. He worked in and was a driving force in Church media matters for seventy-three years. He epitomized the zeal by which Church leaders and their administrations adopted electronic media in sharing the message of the restored gospel.

CONCLUSION

This conclusion focuses on four succinct points. First, the four Church Presidents covered in this brief history who held office for the longest tenures were positioned at precise periods in media emergence and development to make use of those new technologies for Church purposes: Heber J. Grant during the radio era, David O. McKay during the mass media era of TV and film, Spencer W. Kimball during the satellite era, and Gordon B. Hinckley during the height of all of the traditional electronic media and the dawn of the Internet era.

Second, as discussed above, theorists have attributed the success of organized religions in part to their ability to adopt and make use of emerging media. Church leadership must have anticipated the positive effects to be achieved from media adoption, ownership, use, and production, or they would not have invested so much time and treasure in their development. The Church was successful in adopting and making use of media in the twentieth century, and it also was successful in terms of growth in membership. These issues have been juxtaposed in this discussion, but are they truly related? To the authors' knowledge, the possible effects of Church media use on growth in membership during the twentieth century have not been studied systematically and analytically. In order to approach this question, a variety of studies and analyses are needed. For example, what can be documented about the effect on Church growth of the aggressive move into satellite technology in the 1980s, both within the United States and in other countries? Or of the use of television and film in the 1960s and '70s? Such analyses would need to include also comparative studies with other religions relating to their media use and membership increase (or decrease) during the twentieth century.

Third, this brief history and the time line[73] on which it is based provide only a skeleton around which full histories beg to be written. There are fascinating stories to be told about every media innovation and event highlighted in these chronologies. The content, personalities, historical circumstances, obstacles, and conflicts (technological, financial, institutional, organizational, and interpersonal) that surrounded each of these events should be documented. The subject matter of this chapter (the Church's use of electronic media in the twentieth century) deserves careful and close examination in all of its aspects, just as historians have so carefully studied all issues relating to nineteenth-century Mormon print media issues.

Finally, with regard to the past, this chapter began with the theoretical assumption that changes in communications technologies are ecological. They affect everything. The academic study of twentieth-century Mormonism has only just begun. One key element and common thread that will need to run through these studies will be a consideration of the ways in which things changed in Mormondom as new media technologies were introduced. What were those changes, and how did they make the institutional Church and the experience of being a Mormon different than they previously had been?

SPECULATION ABOUT THE FUTURE

In September 2000, Church membership reached eleven million with more than half the members being non-English speakers.[74] This demographic in itself raises important questions about how the Church will and should make the best use of all forms of media in the twenty-first century.

If indeed the past is prologue, one can anticipate that the Church will continue to embrace new media, whatever they might look like in the coming years. One evidence of the Church's continued commitment to media in the twenty-first century is that it has entered headlong into the Internet with its websites (lds.org, mormon.org, familysearch.org), its Internet radio (radio.lds.org), and its presence on YouTube (youtube.com/mormonmessages).

The twenty-first century presents the Church with an entirely different communications environment. Nevertheless, it seems likely that the strategies that were developed and that endured throughout the twentieth century will continue to guide future media activities: early adoption of new media technologies, Church ownership of media outlets, Church production of media content, use of the media to create a favorable image of the Church, use of electronic media to reach and communicate with Church members, and use of electronic media to introduce and explain the Church to those not of our faith.

But the twenty-first century also saw a new media principle and strategy that departs dramatically from the past. Much of the Church's focus in the twentieth century for both print and broadcast media initiatives was to control its own message. The new principle, introduced in the twenty-first century in response to the new media environment, is for individual members to use the Internet to help the Church achieve its purposes. Elder M. Russell Ballard made this clear in his graduation speech at BYU–Hawaii in December 2007. He said on that occasion:

> There are conversations going on about the Church constantly. Those conversations will continue whether or not we choose to participate in them. But we cannot stand on the sidelines while others, including our critics, attempt to define what the Church teaches. While some conversations have audiences in the thousands or even millions, most are much, much smaller. But all conversations have an impact on those who participate in them. Perceptions of the Church are established one conversation at a time. The challenge is that there are too many people participating in conversation about the Church for our Church personnel to converse with and respond to individually. We cannot answer every question, satisfy every inquiry, and respond to every inaccuracy that exists. . . . *May I ask that you join the conversation by participating on the Internet, particularly the New Media, to share the gospel and to explain in simple, clear terms the message of the Restoration.*[75]

The ultimate effects of this strategy, as well as of the Church's own new media initiatives and activities, are only beginning to unfold. The Internet has changed the world even more dramatically than did the radio, film, broadcast, and satellite technologies of the twentieth century. How it will change the Church and its members remains to be seen.

NOTES

1. Brigham Young, "Circular Letter of Instruction," November 9, 1865, in Leonard J. Arrington, "The Deseret Telegraph—A Church-Owned Public Utility," *Journal of Economic History* 11, no. 2 (1951): 122, 118.
2. Gregory A. Prince and Wm. Robert Wright, *David O. McKay and the Rise of Modern Mormonism* (Salt Lake City: University of Utah Press, 2005), 124, 127.
3. Spencer W. Kimball, "When the World Will Be Converted," *Ensign*, October 1974, 10.
4. Leonard I. Sweet, *Communication and Change in American Religious History* (Grand Rapids, MI: Eerdmans, 1993), 1.
5. Sweet, *Communication and Change*, 2.
6. Colin Morris, *Wrestling with an Angel: Reflections on Christian Communications* (London: Collins, 1990), 63–64, in Sweet, *Communication and Change*, 2.
7. Nathan O. Hatch, *The Democratization of American Christianity* (New Haven, CT: Yale University Press, 1989), in Sweet, *Communication and Change*, 2.
8. Sweet, *Communication and Change*, 61.
9. Sweet, *Communication and Change*, 50.
10. Marshall McLuhan, *Understanding Media: The Extensions of Man* (New York: McGraw-Hill, 1964), 7.
11. Sherry Baker, "Mormon Media History Timeline, 1827–2007," *BYU Studies* 47, no. 4 (2008): 118.
12. Neil Postman, "Five Things We Need to Know about Technological Change," Proceedings of the New Technologies and the Human Person: Communicating the Faith in the New Millennium Conference (1998), 5.
13. Neil Postman, *Technopoly: The Surrender of Culture to Technology* (New York: Vintage Books, 1993), 18.
14. James B. Allen, "Technology and the Church: A Steady Revolution," *Church Almanac, 2007* (Salt Lake City: Deseret Morning News), 120.

15. Leonard J. Arrington, "The Deseret Telegraph," *This People*, January 1989, 53.
16. Wendell J. Ashton, *Voice in the West: Biography of a Pioneer Newspaper* (New York: Duell, Sloan, & Pearce, 1950), 270–72, 407.
17. Sheri L. Dew, *Go Forward with Faith: The Biography of Gordon B. Hinckley* (Salt Lake City: Deseret Book, 1996), 85.
18. R. L. Miller, "Mormon Tabernacle Choir," http://www.media.utah.edu/UHE/m/MORMONTABCHOIR.html.
19. Walker wrote: "Commanding the national media unlike any other contemporary Utahn, Grant managed to alter long-standing negative stereotypes about Utah and her people. He frequently spoke before influential national groups, personally guided nationally prominent Americans through Utah, boosted Utah's tourism, and quietly assisted sympathetic Hollywood production such as *Union Pacific* and *Brigham Young*. Symptomatic of these public relations efforts, Grant cultivated the friendship of leading national opinion makers and visited U.S. presidents Warren G. Harding, Calvin Coolidge, Herbert Hoover, and Franklin D. Roosevelt in Washington, D.C." "Heber J. Grant," in *Utah History Encyclopedia*, http://www.media.utah.edu/UHE/g/GRANT,HEBER.html.
20. Craig K. Manscill, Robert C. Freeman, and Dennis A. Wright, eds., *Presidents of the Church* (Springville, UT: Cedar Fort, 2008), 210.
21. M. Dallas Burnett, "Conferences: General Conferences," in *Encyclopedia of Mormonism*, ed. Daniel H. Ludlow (New York: Macmillan, 1992), 1:307–8.
22. Lloyd D. Newell, "Seventy-five Years of the Mormon Tabernacle Choir's *Music and the Spoken Word*, 1929–2004: A History of the Broadcast of America's Choir," in *Mormon Historical Studies* 5, no. 1 (2004): 135.
23. "Church Growth," http://www.mormon.org/mormonorg/eng/basic-beliefs/membership-in-christ-s-church/church-growth.
24. Prince and Wright, *Rise of Modern Mormonism*, 124.
25. Prince and Wright, *Rise of Modern Mormonism*, 404.
26. Francis M. Gibbons, *David O. McKay: Apostle to the World, Prophet of God* (Salt Lake City: Deseret Book, 1986), 329.
27. Gibbons, *David O. McKay*, 329; Lynn Arave, "Historic Moments in LDS Broadcasts," *Deseret News*, April 5, 2002.

28. David Jacobs, "A History of Motion Pictures Produced by the Church of Jesus Christ of Latter-day Saints, 1912–1967" (master's thesis, Brigham Young University, 1967).
29. Norman Tarbox, "The History of Public Television in the State of Utah" (PhD diss., University of Utah, 1979), 238. The station remained dark due to construction problems with the antenna, and it took a number of years for KBYU-TV to begin broadcasting in November 1965.
30. "BYU Television International" (2007), http://history.cfac.byu.edu/index.php/BYU_Television_International.
31. "Telstar" (2010), *The Internet Encyclopedia of Science* http://www.daviddarling.info/encyclopedia/T/Telstar.html.
32. Prince and Wright, *Rise of Modern Mormonism*, 129.
33. Allen, "Technology and the Church," 136.
34. R. B. Josephson, "Russ Josephson's Salt Lake Mormon Tabernacle Choir Discography" (2005), http://www.josephsons.org/slmtc/mtchist.htm.
35. Fred C. Esplin, "The Church as Broadcaster," *Dialogue* 10, no. 3 (1977): 25–45.
36. Prince and Wright, *Rise of Modern Mormonism*, 135.
37. Tarbox, "History of Public Television"; O. S. Rich, *BYU Broadcast Education: The Beginning, an Autobiographical Sketch* (Provo, UT: Brigham Young University, 1992), 127.
38. Arave, "Historic Moments in LDS Broadcasts."
39. W. Dee Halverson, *Bonneville International Corporation Historical Record, 1922–1992* (Salt Lake City: Heritage Associates), 5.
40. Prince and Wright, *Rise of Modern Mormonism*, front cover flap.
41. Allen, "Technology and the Church," 140.
42. Dew, *Go Forward with Faith*, 318. BYU's application to acquire Provo's KLOR-TV (Channel 11) was accepted by Beehive Broadcasting Co. in March (KLOR-TV had gone bankrupt under its first owners); call letters were changed to KBYU-TV in September. The station was still dark due to construction problems with the antenna, and it took a number of years for KBYU-TV to begin broadcasting in November 1965. Tarbox, "History of Public Television," 238–44.
43. Dew, *Go Forward with Faith*, 283.

44. Richard O. Cowan, *The Church in the Twentieth Century* (Salt Lake City: Bookcraft, 1985), 290; "Church to Produce Television Special," *Ensign*, November 1976, 89; Esplin, "The Church as Broadcaster," 25–45.
45. Victor L. Ludlow, "The Internationalization of the Church," in *Out of Obscurity: The LDS Church in the Twentieth Century* (Salt Lake City: Deseret Book, 2000), 221–22.
46. Esplin, "The Church as Broadcaster," 25–45.
47. Halverson, *Bonneville International Corporation Historical Record*, 53.
48. Richard Neitzel Holzapfel and others, *On This Day in the Church: An Illustrated Almanac of the Latter-day Saints* (Salt Lake City: Eagle Gate, 2000), 180.
49. Halverson, *Bonneville International Corporation Historical Record*, 57.
50. Rodney H. Brady, "Bonneville International Corporation," in *Encyclopedia of Mormonism*, 1:132.
51. Steven L. Olsen, "Centennial Observances" (1992), http://www.lightplanet.com/mormons/daily/holidays/Centennial_EOM.htm.
52. Peter Crawley, *A Descriptive Bibliography of the Mormon Church* (Provo, UT: Religious Studies Center, Brigham Young University, 1997), 1:30–31; Larry C. Porter, "The Book of Mormon: Historical Setting for Its Translation and Publication," in *Joseph Smith: The Prophet, the Man*, ed. Susan Easton Black and Charles D. Tate Jr. (Provo, UT: Religious Studies Center, Brigham Young University, 1993): 49–64.
53. Edward L. Kimball, *Lengthen Your Stride: The Presidency of Spencer W. Kimball* (Salt Lake City: Deseret Book, 2005).
54. Allen, "Technology and the Church," 136.
55. "Mormon Church Establishing World's Largest Satellite Television Network," *Evening Independent* (St. Petersburg, Florida), January 22, 1983, http://news.google.com/newspapers?nid=950&dat=19830122&id=lucLAAAAIBAJ&sjid=IVkDAAAAIBAJ&pg=3844,1554068.
56. Dew, *Go Forward with* Faith, 388.
57. Holzapfel and others, *On This Day in the Church*, 181.
58. Holzapfel and others, *On This Day in the Church*, 18.
59. Gordon B. Hinckley, "To Young Single Adults," *Ensign*, June 1989, 72.
60. Holzapfel and others, *On This Day in the Church*, 40.

61. Arave, "Historic Moments in LDS Broadcasts."
62. Manscill, Freeman, and Wright, *Presidents of the Church*, 367.
63. *Ensign*, June 1992, 79.
64. Peter N. Johnson, "Motion Pictures, LDS Productions," in *Encyclopedia of Mormonism*, 2:964–65.
65. Holzapfel and others, *On This Day in the Church*, 207.
66. Richard Neitzel Holazpfel and William W. Slaughter, *Prophets of the Latter Days* (Salt Lake City: Deseret Book, 2003), 193.
67. Holzapfel and others, *On This Day in the Church*, 221.
68. "Thousands Watch Church Satellite Broadcast," *Ensign*, May 1996, 109.
69. Russell C. Rasmussen, "Computers and the Internet in the Church," in *Out of Obscurity: The LDS Church in the Twentieth Century* (Salt Lake City: Deseret Book, 2000), 280.
70. Rasmussen, "Computers and the Internet," 280.
71. Holzapfel and others, *On This Day in the Church*, 14.
72. Rasmussen, "Computers and the Internet," 282; Holzapfel and others, *On This Day in the Church*, 102.
73. Holzapfel and others, *On This Day in the Church*, 6; "New BYUTV Network Widens Reach of LDS, BYU Programs," *Ensign*, April 1996, 79; Kimberly Demucha, "KBYU Programming to Go National, International" (February 3, 2000), http://newsnet.byu.edu/story.cfm/7616; "BYU TV Now Carried on DIRECTV," *Ensign*, March 1997, 77–78.
74. Terryl L. Givens, *The Latter-day Saint Experience in America* (Westport, CT: Greenwood, 2004), 314.
75. M. Russell Ballard, "Using New Media to Support the Work of the Church" (2007); emphasis added, http://newsroom.lds.org/ldsnewsroom/eng/news-releases-stories/using-new-media-to-support-the-work-of-the-church.

Dave Hall

16

Relief Society Educational and Social Welfare Work, 1900–29

In the first decades of the twentieth century, the general leadership of the Relief Society built an organizational structure that facilitated what was perhaps the greatest era of accomplishment in the history of the society. Seeking to attract younger women, its presidency and general board developed an educational curriculum that drew upon up-to-date methods espoused by experts in the fields of education and social work. Manifested through weekly lessons, special training sessions, and regular conference addresses delivered by a wide range of speakers, these educational innovations proved extremely successful in drawing new generations of women into the Relief Society. The organization's leadership marshaled these growing numbers into a structured pursuit of a wide range of activities that improved public health and social services in communities throughout the Intermountain West. The Relief Society's

---

Dave Hall lectures in history at California State University–Fullerton and Cerritos Community College.

trained army of well-informed paraprofessionals brought local and even national attention and praise for both the Relief Society and the Church.

This paper examines the institutional development of these programs and the structures that were used to implement them as well as the benefits they provided to the Church and community. In doing so, it will demonstrate that these efforts emerged in consequence of a convergence of factors involving community needs, the interests of Relief Society women, and the support of priesthood leaders.

The Relief Society's entry into modern public health and social work was rooted in the changing social environment of turn-of-the-century Utah. At that time, the Church was moving away from previous efforts to establish a semi-independent commonwealth in the West toward assimilation into the national economic and social mainstream.[1] During this period, a number of activities practiced by the Relief Society—such as sericulture and grain storage—were seen as increasingly anachronistic to younger women, who responded by staying away from the organization in droves. Many instead turned to women's clubs with their interesting programs of self-education and community reform, or they simply refused to "move up" from the Mutual Improvement Association. Ultimately, declining membership rolls forced the Relief Society to adjust its agenda to meet changing circumstances.[2]

With the support and encouragement of priesthood leaders, the Relief Society began to move forward into a new era of its existence, a process that accelerated in 1914 with the creation of a new centralized curriculum and the adoption of a new official organ, the *Relief Society Magazine*. Important movers and shakers in these developments included Susa Young Gates, former editor of the *Young Woman's Journal* and new editor of the *Relief Society Magazine*; longtime Relief Society leader and counselor to Emmeline B. Wells, Clarissa Smith Williams; Jeannette Acord Hyde; former state legislator Alice Merrill Horne; and Relief Society general secretary Amy Brown Lyman. Together they created a study curriculum that included genealogy, literature, home economics, theology, and eventually social work.

Relief Society Educational and Social Welfare Work, 1900–29

Over the previous decades, the Relief Society had developed a regular series of meetings that included biannual general conferences held the week before the Church's general conferences, quarterly stake conferences, and regular stake auxiliary meetings. The new standardized curriculum fleshed out the organization's meeting schedule by facilitating regular weekly meetings in the wards. The *Relief Society Magazine*, first created to disseminate the lessons, also carried a wide variety of articles and information of interest to women. It soon came to resemble many popular women's magazines of the day, serving both to entertain and to inform, but with the difference that it was assembled by and for Mormon women.[3]

The new curriculum and the magazine proved successful as recruiting devices, and the organization's agenda increasingly appealed to younger members. Of particular importance was a focus on home economics, broadly defined, that included not only housekeeping and homemaking but also information on health and nutrition. National interest in home economics had led to federal funding for extension work on the subject, which was provided through state land-grant colleges as part of the 1914 Smith-Lever Act.[4] The president of the Utah State Agricultural College (now Utah State University) was future Apostle John A. Widtsoe, who convinced Relief Society president Emmeline B. Wells to allow Agricultural College representatives to attend Relief Society meetings, where they would lecture on health and nutrition.[5] This in turn led Relief Society women to organize informational roundups in their communities and to host clinics where young children could be examined for health problems.[6]

Yet this was just the opening through which the Relief Society would become a vital player in the development of public health and social welfare work. Beginning in 1913, the Relief Society general board agreed to assist Salt Lake officials in sponsoring several "milk depots" during the summer months on the city's poorer east side. These limited efforts, involving only a handful of Relief Society women, were designed to provide pure milk to young children during the hot summer months and health and nutritional information to their mothers.[7] But new activities were about to involve many more in social welfare work.

Surprisingly, it was the First World War that drove the Relief Society forward on a number of fronts.[8] On the one hand, infant health work, billed as a patriotic endeavor aimed at securing the nation's long-term defense by providing healthy children to serve in the military, was promoted by the US Children's Bureau in the Department of Labor as part of its national Year of the Child campaign in 1918. Its intent was to address the unusually high rate of infant and maternal mortality in the United States in comparison to other industrialized nations.[9] With the support of Church leaders and through the *Relief Society Magazine* and promotional activities carried out in Relief Society conferences, ward Relief Societies joined in organizing clinics where babies could be examined and weighed (to establish a national baseline) and where information on maternal and infant health and nutrition could be disseminated.[10]

An even bigger development came when the Relief Society sent representatives to the meeting of the National Council on Social Work in 1917, which was devoted to Red Cross activities in support of the war effort. Again, as coordinated through general Relief Society conferences and through the magazine, this had a multipronged result: On the one hand, Relief Society women throughout the nation joined in forming local branches of the Red Cross (often identical to ward organizations), where they rolled bandages and sewed bed linens for wounded soldiers. At the same time, ward and stake organizations also became the focus of local efforts to promote home production and canning of food and were where bond drives took place in behalf of the war effort.[11] The Pittsburgh conference also played an important role in the adoption of modern social work techniques in the Church. This conference occurred as a consequence of government and Red Cross efforts to provide aid for servicemen and their families using up-to-date methods.[12] Relief Society general secretary, Amy Brown Lyman, took the lead here and with other Relief Society representatives received intensive training at a six-week institute in Denver.[13] Lyman and the others returned home to supervise assistance for servicemen and their families, and at the request of President Joseph F. Smith, Lyman began to utilize these techniques in

Relief Society Educational and Social Welfare Work, 1900–29

Church charity projects. This work outlived the war; in fact, in the decade following it led to intensive training for over 2,900 special social service aides who directed charity efforts in local stakes. An even broader-based effort was promoted through lessons incorporated into the organization's curriculum, articles in the *Relief Society Magazine*, and addresses in general and local Relief Society conferences designed to educate the rank and file sisters in social work methods and aims.[14] Through this process, tens of thousands of Relief Society women were molded into a veritable army of social work paraprofessionals and interested supporters working to improve public health and social welfare in both church and community.

As this took place, a change in the Relief Society presidency placed Clarissa Smith at the head of the Relief Society. She then named Lyman as managing director over the organization.[15] With the focused attention of these Relief Society leaders and the support of the president of the Church, the organization moved aggressively forward into the 1920s—an era of even greater accomplishment. A new federal initiative played a role in this process, leading to even greater involvement by Relief Society women in matters relating to public health and social reform.

The Federal Maternity and Infancy Act of 1921, better known as the Sheppard-Towner Act, was the first national legislation aimed specifically at improving social welfare. It provided a modest amount of federal funds to the states on a matching-grant basis to facilitate educational work in health and nutrition, on a much larger scale than that provided for under Smith-Lever. These monies were also intended to encourage the creation of clinics where expectant mothers and young children could receive screenings for health problems.[16]

Working in cooperation with state officials and with the support of the Relief Society general board, local Relief Societies took up projects that attacked the gravest threats to mothers and children in even the poorest regions. In counties too poor to support a health department or even a public health nurse, Relief Society leaders sought to aid women by sponsoring itinerant health conferences organized in cooperation with the state board of health under Sheppard-Towner auspices.[17] Preventative measures were also adopted: As elsewhere, infections caused by unsanitary conditions during childbirth—a condition commonly known as puerperal fever—was still the largest single cause of maternal mortality in the nation. To facilitate a clean, safe environment for women in areas without access to hospitals or maternity homes, the general board urged local societies to stockpile sterile bedding and instruments necessary for safe childbirth. The *Relief Society Magazine* carried plans for maternity closets to be set up in Relief Society halls in which such items could be stored, along with lists of instruments to be included and instructions, secured from the state board of health, for proper sterilization techniques. Local societies provided these supplies at minimal or no cost to those in need, who then returned them for resterilization and reuse.[18]

Within a few years Relief Society women had installed such closets in nearly every community in Utah. Physicians serving rural areas discovered that these supplies met "their every need," and some even required their maternity patients to have such supplies at the ready during their delivery.[19] While most beneficial in sparsely settled districts, maternity closets also proved useful to physicians in larger towns. Of the 163 deliveries reported in Brigham City between January and November 1924, for example, 75 used Relief Society maternity bundles.[20]

Nationally, prominent backers of Sheppard-Towner had been convinced that relatively simple measures could work a revolution in infant and maternal health in America. Through local initiatives such as the maternity closets, Relief Society women working under the direction of the general board began to bring this vision to reality. Yet this marked only the beginning of the society's contributions. Elsewhere in the nation, states such as Pennsylvania and New York already possessed rudimentary systems of public health. Coupled with their larger populations, which brought a proportionately larger share of Sheppard-Towner funds, much of the maternity and infancy work in these areas could be managed by state employees alone.[21] But in Utah's case, a small population made it eligible for a maximum of only $13,000 in federal funds annually. Its small tax base also meant that state and local initiatives to provide public health services were necessarily limited.²² For this reason the volunteer work of the Relief Society proved absolutely critical to Sheppard-Towner's success. State officials involved in its administration came to rely on local Relief Society volunteers to perform a number of tasks, including the organization of conferences. These women arranged for locations, often schools, where mothers and children could be examined and counseled, and provided the necessary publicity and preparations to make sure clinics and classes ran smoothly. State workers especially valued these Relief Society volunteers because they grasped the work quickly—perhaps due to their studies of related issues in their educational curriculum. Inasmuch as they were also well acquainted with local fears and prejudices, they were able to effectively explain matters of concern to women in attendance. In fact, understaffed and stretched state public health nurses soon learned that, with a little additional training, Relief Society women could be counted on to run conferences even in the absence of paid professionals.²³

Relief Society women also helped address many of the health problems discovered at these conferences. Children during this period were routinely confronted by a variety of debilitating and life-threatening diseases. Some, like diphtheria and smallpox, could be prevented through vaccination; others, like goiter and rickets, could be cured with proper diet. Problems like poor vision were often easily rectified if diagnosed and treated in a timely manner. When attending physicians or nurses spotted such treatable maladies, Relief Society women saw that follow-up treatment was provided and even helped with financial arrangements when necessary. In addition, they kept records of examinations and gave "health talks" stressing nutrition, hygiene, and vaccination. State officials deemed their contributions extremely valuable as they allowed the state to make the most of limited resources and freed public health nurses to develop follow-up work in selected areas.²⁴

An example is found in Utah County, whose Relief Society stake president reported on her experiences at the organization's October 1926 general conference. Working under the direction of the state board of health and assisted by local physicians serving on a voluntary basis, she joined with other

Relief Society women to organize health conferences and clinics in each of five stakes in the county. Aware of their need for a trained professional, these women successfully petitioned county commissioners for funding to hire a public health nurse. However, a dispute arose between local physicians and the state board, resulting in the withdrawal of the doctors and the resignation of the nurse. Undaunted, local Relief Society leaders drew upon their growing expertise in government affairs and contacted the state's head of maternity work, who advised that a county health unit be established, staffed by a full-time doctor and nurse and funded by the state and county.

Despite conditions in which heavy expenditures and a limited tax base already strained county budgets, Relief Society leaders of the five Utah County stakes solicited the support of civic groups and clubs to achieve their goal. Under the new arrangement, seventeen health conferences were held each month. From January to September 1926, over 2,300 expectant mothers and young children received initial examinations. Over 560 had follow-up exams from county health care professionals, through which nearly four thousand health concerns of various kinds were discovered. In those cases where the problems were correctable and where families themselves were unable to meet the costs, the stake Relief Societies arranged for low-cost services or used local donations and central maternity funds to cover expenses. In this manner the organization supplied medical treatment or surgery for sixty-six cases during the first nine months of 1926.[25]

A year later, the Utah Stake Relief Society president eloquently summed up the value of the educational work made possible through the unique partnership of the Relief Society, the state, and the federal government through Sheppard-Towner: "Our health centers have been invaluable in helping us to discover people in sore need of health opportunities," she noted. "Women who suffered almost constantly and were dependent because of it, have been freed from their ailments and made happy and self-supporting." As for children, the "defects" of the ill and handicapped had been corrected and "they have been put on an equal footing with their associates."[26]

Relief Society Educational and Social Welfare Work, 1900–29

Infant and maternal mortality figures support such anecdotal accounts. By the first year following the passage of the act, infant mortality rates in Utah (among Mormon and non-Mormon women) began to decline noticeably, from 69 to 59 per 1,000 live births, where they would hover for the duration of Sheppard-Towner. As Clarissa Williams reported in conference, the decline in mortality rates for children of Mormon women throughout the Church—those most affected by the full range of Relief Society health work—were even more impressive: from 53 per 1,000 in 1921 to 39 per 1,000 in 1923. By 1929, Utah was one of nine states with the lowest infant mortality rates in the nation, with only four states reporting lower levels. During the same period, maternal mortality declined from 59 to 49 per 10,000, with only Iowa attaining a lower rate.[27] The verdict was in: Utah, understaffed and underfunded, had achieved one of the lowest combined rates of infant and maternal mortality of any state in the nation, a matter of great satisfaction to Relief Society women.

All this forged the Relief Society into a unified and self-aware force for reform in the West. Such sentiments were summed up early on when general board member Jeannette A. Hyde spoke in the organization's April 1923 general conference. Speaking of the importance of the contributions of Relief Society women to the social reforms of the period, "You may ask, 'Would not the men . . . have done the same?' I shall only answer you by asking: 'Have they done it in the past?'"

Women of the organization used their new sense of unity to pursue a variety of additional reforms; perhaps most impressive was their successful mobilization in behalf of a state training school for people with mental disabilities. Gathering 25,000 signatures to present to the state legislature, they took pride when the measure creating the school was approved by lawmakers, and doubly so when Amy Brown Lyman herself was named to the board supervising the institution.[28]

In light of these impressive accomplishments, it would seem that the Relief Society was mobilized for action and poised for yet greater accomplishment as it prepared to enter a new decade. For a number of reasons, such was not the case. Among the first was antipathy that arose among some Americans toward the sort of efforts that had captured the energies of Relief Society women during the 1920s. In particular, the Sheppard-Towner Act, despite its impressive results in lowering infant and material mortality, drew the ire of the American Medical Association as well as social conservatives across the nation (including Utah's own senator William H. King), who saw it as the first step toward socialized medicine. In consequence, funding for the measure was left to expire in 1929. And Sheppard-Towner was only one among many reform measures that lost support during the 1920s, a factor which left fewer venues open for organized women, like those in the Relief Society, to assert their influence.[29]

Another factor, indeed the most important in many ways, was the massive shock of the Great Depression. All across the nation the economic downturn overwhelmed the efforts of private and public charities who struggled valiantly but in vain to assist those in need. In the Relief Society's case, the central offices of the Relief Society were swamped with new aid applicants, while local leaders were overwhelmed and even demoralized by their inability to help even those most desperate for assistance.[30]

Of course, as time went on, beginning under the Hoover administration and then more so under Franklin Roosevelt's New Deal, the federal government moved forward in providing relief. The Church followed suit, introducing the Church Welfare Plan. As this occurred, Relief Society women, like their non-Mormon sisters across the nation, sought to adjust to these new realities in a way that still allowed them to make meaningful contributions. However, as they did so, they found themselves now as followers rather than initiators in social welfare matters. Amy Brown Lyman sought to again expand the role of Relief Society women during her presidency, which spanned the years 1940–45, but was unsuccessful. Wartime restrictions limited her options while personal tragedy undermined her authority. More importantly, Church leaders began to envision a role for Mormon women that was linked less to community reform and more focused on safeguarding home and family. Under this new reality, there was little room for the kind of activism that characterized the 1910s and 1920s.[31]

The first decades of the twentieth century thus stand as a unique period of focused activism among Relief Society women, a time when the full resources of the organization were devoted to making improvements in charity work and public health. With the support of Priesthood leaders and with a united leadership backed up by a focused curriculum urging them on toward meaningful action, Relief Society women gave countless hours of selfless service during these years and left behind an impressive legacy of accomplishment that was of great worth to their own and to future generations.

NOTES

1. For an overview of this process, see Thomas G. Alexander, *Mormonism in Transition: A History of the Latter-day Saints, 1890–1930* (Urbana: University of Illinois Press, 1986).

2. Jill Mulvay Derr, Janath Russell Cannon, and Maureen Ursenbach Beecher, *Women of Covenant: The Story of Relief Society* (Salt Lake City: Deseret Book, 1992), 154–61.

3. Derr, Cannon, and Beecher, *Women of Covenant*, 189–91; Amy Brown Lyman, *In Retrospect: Autobiography of Amy Brown Lyman* (Salt Lake City: General Board of Relief Society), 50–52.

4. US Department of Agriculture, *Report on Agricultural Experiment Stations and Cooperative Agricultural Extension Work in the United States for the Year Ended June 30, 1915* (Washington, DC: US Government Printing Office, 1916), 145–46; US Department of Agriculture, *Cooperative Extension Work in Agriculture and Home Economics, 1917: Part II of Report on Experiment Stations and Extension Work in the United States* (Washington, DC: Government Printing Office, 1919).

5. *Coerced* might be a better term, as Widtsoe stated he might have to organize rival women's organizations if Wells did not go along with the plan. Carol Cornwall Madsen, "A Mormon Woman in Victorian America" (PhD diss., University of Utah, 1985), 393; Janette A. Hyde, "Home Economics Department," and "Home

Economics Work under the Smith-Lever Act," *Relief Society Magazine*, February 1916, 85–90.

6. "Guide Lessons, Home Economics: Mother's Condition and Diet," *Relief Society Magazine*, December 1916, 728–30; "Guide Lessons, Home Economics: Correct Nursing Habits," *Relief Society Magazine*, January 1917, 56–59; and Amy Brown Lyman, "Notes from the Field: Wasatch Stake," *Relief Society Magazine*, April 1922, 214.

7. Derr, Cannon, and Beecher, *Women of Covenant*, 184; Amy Brown Lyman, "Notes from the Field: Milk Stations," *Relief Society Magazine*, August 1916, 460–62.

8. Amy Brown Lyman, "Social Service Work in the Relief Society, 1917–1928, Including a Brief History of the Relief Society Social Service Department and Brief Mention of Other Relief Society and Community Social Service Activities," 3–4, Amy Brown Lyman Papers, L. Tom Perry Special Collections, Harold B. Lee Library, Brigham Young University, Provo, UT.

9. Robyn Muncy, *Creating a Female Dominion in American Reform* (New York: Oxford University Press, 1991), 96–97; J. Stanley Lemons, *The Woman Citizen: Social Feminism in the 1920s* (Urbana: University of Illinois Press, 1973), 16.

10. Clarissa Smith Williams, "Patriotic Department," *Relief Society Magazine*, April 1918, 218; "Weigh Your Child for the Government," in Clarissa Smith Williams, "Patriotic Department," *Relief Society Magazine*, June 1918, 347–49.

11. Derr, Cannon, and Beecher, *Women of Covenant*, 207–8.

12. For the Pittsburgh conference on Home Service work, see Eugene T. Lies, "Red Cross Work Among Families of Soldiers and Sailors," *Proceedings of the National Conference of Social Work at the Forty-Fourth Annual Session held in Pittsburgh, Pennsylvania, June 6–13, 1917* (Chicago: National Conference of Social Work), 140–43.

13. "Mrs. Lyman, Delegate, Reports Proceedings Pittsburg Convention," *Deseret News*, June 19, 1917; Lyman, "Social Service Work," 3; and Amy Brown Lyman, "The Red Cross Conference in Denver," *Relief Society Magazine*, December 1917, 687–790.

14. Lyman, "Social Service Work," 1–2; Amy Brown Lyman, "General Relief Society Conference," *Relief Society Magazine*, December 1920, 712; Lyman, *In Retrospect*, 64–65.
15. "General Conference of Relief Society," *Relief Society Magazine*, June 1921, 353; Annie Wells Cannon Diary, April 14, 1921, Annie Wells Cannon Collection, L. Tom Perry Special Collection, Harold B. Lee Library, Provo, UT.
16. For Shepherd-Towner, see Theda Skocpol, *Protecting Soldiers and Mothers: The Political Origins of Social Policy in the United States* (Cambridge: Belknap Press of Harvard University Press, 1992); and Muncy, *Creating a Female Dominion*. For useful and detailed descriptions of the activities of Lyman and the Relief Society during this period, see Loretta L. Hefner, "This Decade Was Different: Relief Society's Social Services Department, 1919–1929," *Dialogue* 15 (Autumn 1982): 64–73; and Hefner, "The National Women's Relief Society and the U.S. Sheppard-Towner Act," *Utah Historical Quarterly* 50 (Summer 1982): 255–67.
17. H. Y. Richards, "The Cooperation of Lay Organizations in Maternity and Infancy Work," *Proceedings of the Third Annual Conference of State Directors in Charge of the Local Administration of the Maternity and Infancy Act*, Department of Labor, Children's Bureau Publication No. 157 (Washington, DC, 1926), 184–86.
18. "Recommendations of General Board Respecting Maternity and Health," *Relief Society Magazine*, January 1924, 27–30.
19. Richards, "Cooperation of Lay Organizations," 185.
20. Amy Brown Lyman, "Notes from the Field," *Relief Society Magazine*, May 1925, 275.
21. New York and Pennsylvania, the states with the largest possible federal appropriations under Sheppard-Towner's matching grant provisions, were eligible for a maximum of $80,041.78 and $68,810.99, respectively. These are not large sums by any means, but when coupled with already-existent public health systems and larger tax bases, were a distinct advantage nevertheless. See *The Promotion of the Welfare and Hygiene of Maternity and Infancy: The Administration of the Act of Congress of November 23, 1921, Fiscal Year Ended June 30, 1926*, Children's Bureau Publication No. 178 (Washington, DC: Government Printing Office, 1927), 2.

22. *The Promotion of the Welfare and Hygiene of Maternity and Infancy*, US Department of Labor, Children's Bureau Publication No. 156 (Washington, DC, 1925), 58.
23. "Semi-Annual Report of Maternity and Infancy Work, July 1–December 31, 1925," Utah State Board of Health, Children's Bureau files, Utah folder, National Archives, 1, 2, table 23; Richards, "Cooperation of Lay Organizations," 185.
24. H. Y. Richards, "Semi-Annual Report of Maternity and Infancy Work, July 1–December 31, 1926," Shepherd-Towner Papers, Children's Bureau Records, Utah file, National Archives.
25. Mrs. Electa S. Dixon, "Relief Society Conference: Utah Stake Report," *Relief Society Magazine*, December 1926, 628–30.
26. Dixon, "Utah Stake Report," 630.
27. *The Promotion of the Welfare and Hygiene of Maternity and Infancy: Administration of the Act of Congress of November 21, 1921, for Fiscal Year Ended June 30, 1929*, U.S. Department of Labor, Children's Bureau Publication no. 203 (Washington, DC, 1931), 132–38; "Relief Society Conference Report," *Relief Society Magazine*, June 1925, 312. Accurate infant mortality figures are not available for Utah before 1917, when the state began full cooperation in the Children's Bureau sponsored birth and death registry system. Baseline figures for 1917 were 69 per 1,000; in 1918, they were 64 per 1,000. The 1919, 1920, and 1921 figures climbed to 71, 71, and 73 respectively, which can likely be attributed to the effects of the influenza epidemic. In 1922, they returned to the pre-war level of 69. Similar figures for maternal mortality were 59 in 1917—jumping to 86 and 84 in 1918 and 1919 during the epidemic—before declining to 73 in 1921 and down to 55 in 1922. The year 1924 marked the lowest figure for maternal mortality in Utah, with a rate of 45 per 10,000 live births, while 1927 was the low point for infant mortality, with 54 deaths per thousand births.
28. Lyman, *In Retrospect*, 71; Relief Society Circular Letter, Louise Y. Robison and Julia A. F. Lund to the Utah Stakes, December 31, 1928, Relief Society Circular Letter Files, Church Historical Department, Salt Lake City; Louise Y. Robison, "Officers' Meeting, Morning Session," in Julia A. F. Lund, "Relief Society Conference," *Relief Society Magazine*, June 1929, 290–91; Amy Brown Lyman, "Training School for the Feeble-Minded," *Relief Society Magazine*, January 1930, 22–24.

29. J. Stanley Lemons, *The Woman Citizen: Social Feminism in the 1920s* (Urbana: University of Illinois Press, 1973), 11–12, 172–73; Muncy, *Creating a Female Dominion*, 139–143.
30. Annie D. Palmer, "The Social Worker in the Unemployment Emergency," *Relief Society Magazine*, January 1932, 17–19; Jill Mulvay Derr, "Changing Relief Society Charity to Make Way for Welfare," in *New Views of Mormon History: A Collection of Essays in Honor of Leonard J. Arrington*, ed. Davis Bitton and Maureen Ursenbach Beecher (Salt Lake City: University of Utah Press, 1987), 242–72.
31. For an overview of developments affecting the Relief Society during these years, see Derr, Cannon, and Beecher, *Women of Covenant*, 248–313.

Joseph F. Merrill, an individual fairly unknown to the contemporary Church, was a key figure in the development of many of the educational programs now taken for granted by Church members. (© Intellectual Reserve, Inc. All rights reserved.)

Casey Paul Griffiths

17

JOSEPH F. MERRILL AND THE TRANSFORMATION OF CHURCH EDUCATION

In the history of the Church there is no better illustration of the prophetic preparation of this people than the beginnings of the seminary and institute program. These programs were started when they were nice but not critically needed. They were granted a season to flourish and to grow into a bulwark for the Church. They now become a godsend for the salvation of modern Israel in a most challenging hour.—Boyd K. Packer[1]

Looking over the vast international reach of the Church Educational System today, with thousands of dedicated teachers serving the needs of Latter-day Saints in dozens of different countries, it is difficult to imagine that less than a century ago the educational program of the Church consisted of a few struggling schools confined to the Intermountain West.

Casey Paul Griffiths is a seminary teacher in Sandy, Utah.

Church education at the beginning of the twentieth century was largely based around the academy system, a group of loosely associated Church schools begun by local stakes and found in larger Latter-day Saint population centers. Because of the geographical limitations of this system, thousands of LDS students had no access to Church education. As Church members began to expand beyond the mountain strongholds of the Church, there was no clear plan to bring religious education to them. Like a number of other Church programs, the educational program of the Church underwent a radical transformation in the early decades of the century. Understanding the historical and prophetic threads that led to the formation of a system of education flexible enough to allow the Church to reach all of its members is a critical part of the administrative history of the Church. Thousands of Church members and leaders deserve the credit for this miraculous undertaking. Heber J. Grant, David O. McKay, and a host of other Church leaders played crucial roles in this endeavor. One individual whose life was inextricably woven into the fabric of this great work was Joseph F. Merrill. A crucial figure in the twentieth-century history of the Church, he shepherded many Latter-day Saint educational programs through the crucial transitional changes they experienced at the beginning of the century.

Joseph F. Merrill, an individual fairly unknown to the contemporary Church, was a key figure in the development of many of the educational programs now taken for granted by Church members. He was responsible for the creation of the first seminary program, played a key role in creating the institutional guidelines of the first institute of religion, and helped to keep Brigham Young University open in the midst of the worst economic crisis the nation has ever faced. He assisted in the painful but necessary task of transferring Church schools to state control. When members of the Utah State Board attempted to strike down the seminary program while it was still in its relative infancy, Merrill waged a public battle to allow the weekday religious program of the Church to survive and mature. Understanding Merrill's background, his labors, and his leadership provides a window into understanding how the current system of Church education came to be.

Joseph F. Merrill and the Transformation of Church Education

EDUCATIONAL BACKGROUND

Joseph F. Merrill was born in 1868 in Richmond, Utah, the son of Apostle Marriner W. Merrill. His early years were devoted to difficult work on the family farm, occasionally broken by stints of labor in railroad camps operated by his father in Idaho and Montana. Marriner was the father of a large family because of plural marriage, and he realized his property could not be easily divided among his large progeny. Marriner explained that "all his life he had been handicapped because of a lack of education and that years ago he had concluded that the best thing he could do for his children was to give them all the opportunities of an education rather than to leave them material things to quarrel over after he was gone."[2] He urged his sons to receive as much education as possible, even going so far as to hire a private teacher to run his own family school. As a result, the Merrill family produced a large number of highly educated individuals. Of twelve brothers younger than Joseph, ten later graduated from college, three received PhDs, four earned master's degrees, and two others obtained medical degrees—a family record almost unprecedented for the time and place.[3]

Joseph Merrill was the beneficiary of his father's love of learning. As soon as he was of age he attended the University of Utah. Falling in love with the academic environment of the university, he decided to further his education by traveling to the eastern United States to attend school. Merrill spent the better part of the 1890s performing graduate work at the University of Michigan, University of Chicago, and Johns Hopkins University. In 1899 he received a PhD, becoming the first native Utahn to do so.[4]

Running parallel to Merrill's intellectual development was his spiritual growth. Although raised in a faith-filled home, he noted his frustration as he strove to receive a divine witness of his religion. Beginning at age ten, he began praying for his own answer. For nine years he prayed without receiving any special feelings or manifestations. At the age of nineteen, shortly before he left for college, he received a spiritual witness. Commenting on the fortunate timing of the incident, he later said, "A few weeks later I left home to go to the University. Had I left without an answer, I may have forgotten to continue to pray, for college life is none too helpful to a religious faith. Many students begin to study science, as I did, and many students of science begin to feel sooner or later that there is no personal God. I always remembered the remarkable way in which the Lord answered me, so I never forgot to pray."[5]

During his schooling in the East, his faith was challenged by the isolation he felt being one of the only Latter-day Saints present. Engaged in an intense courtship with Annie Laura Hyde, he sent letters to her that reflect some of the isolation he felt and guilt over occasional lapses in his Sabbath observance. With no Latter-day Saint meetings to attend, he was frequently present at the worship services of other faiths. He later wrote, "I usually attended one non-Mormon church service, sometimes two services, every Sunday. For a considerable number of years I was out of intimate contact with my own Church so I went to all the churches in the communities where I lived . . . and attended their services at least 350 times during that period."[6]

While there is no indication that Merrill's faith in the Church ever seriously faltered during this period, Merrill did experience firsthand the tension which could sometimes exist between the realms of faith and academia. Even during his early years at the University of Utah he felt this strain. Reflecting back on this time he wrote, "We at the University felt we were between 'the devil and the deep blue sea.' The Gentiles regarded us as a Mormon institution. The Mormons (some of them) looked upon our school as an 'infidel factory.' Hence we did not enjoy the whole-hearted support of either faction."[7] Returning from his education in the East, he had made up his mind to remain true to the faith privately but to remain neutral publicly. He believed he could have a greater influence in the scholarly community if he displayed no partisanship and therefore accepted no calls to Church service for a time. Laboring under this dilemma, Merrill experienced what he would consider the second great theophany of his life.

Riding on a train across Wyoming, Merrill read in a newspaper a notice that Richard R. Lyman, an old friend from his time at the University of

Michigan, had been called to be stake superintendent of YMMIA. To himself he said, "Congratulations, Richard." That instant a sign came suddenly that radically altered the course of his life. "No sooner had these words passed through my mind than I was surprised by the words 'You are to be his first counselor.' These last words were not read from the paper or audibly spoken in my ears but they were forcibly impressed upon my consciousness as if they had been uttered in thunderous tones."[8] When he arrived in Salt Lake City, Richard Lyman was at the train station to deliver the expected call. Merrill accepted unhesitatingly. He came to regard this experience as the spiritual bookend to his higher education. Merrill would spend the rest of his life striving to build a bridge between the realms of scholarship and faith.

THE FIRST SEMINARY, 1912

Finished with his education, Merrill took up a teaching position at the University of Utah. He also enthusiastically accepted any call to serve in the local Granite Utah Stake, eventually becoming a member of the stake presidency. As the counselor given stewardship over education, Merrill was troubled by the increasing number of youth in his stake attending public high schools without the kind of religious education offered at the Church academies.[9] Possibly inspired by the religious seminaries he saw during his education at the University of Chicago, Merrill struck upon the idea of requesting the release of students from their studies for one class in order to receive instruction at a local Church-owned facility.[10] After receiving approval from the Granite Stake presidency and the Church Board of Education, Merrill launched into the process of searching for the right teacher, designing the curriculum, and building a home for the new institution. Describing his ideal candidate to the stake presidency, Merrill laid down a set of standards still largely observed today in the selection of seminary teachers:

May I say that it is the desire of the Presidency of the Stake to have a strong young man who is properly qualified to do the work in a most satisfactory manner. By young we do not necessarily mean a teacher young in years, but a man . . . who can command their respect and admiration and exercise a great influence over them. We want a man who can enjoy student sports and activities as well as one who is a good teacher. We want a man who is a thorough student, one who will not teach in a perfunctory way, but who will enliven his instruction with a strong winning personality and give evidence of thorough understanding of and scholarship in the things he teaches. It is desired that this school be thoroughly successful and a teacher is wanted who is a leader and who will be universally regarded as the inferior to no teacher in the high school.[11]

Thomas Yates, a forty-one-year-old electrical engineer, member of the high council, and graduate of Cornell University, was selected as the first seminary teacher.[12]

Working together, Merrill and Yates designed the first seminary curriculum using the scriptures as the primary texts for the course. Merrill made arrangements with the school district for the students to receive academic credit for biblical studies, and a noncredit course in Church history and Book of Mormon studies was included as well. A $2,500 loan from Zion's Bank financed the first seminary building, and construction was begun only a few weeks before school started. It was not fully finished until three weeks into the school year. The limited finances resulted in the most spartan of accommodations. The building consisted of four rooms: a cloak room, an office, a small library, and a classroom. While the building was equipped with blackboards and a stove for heating, there were no electric lights. The seminary's entire library consisted of a Bible dictionary owned by Yates. Students used their scriptures as the textbooks and made their own maps to decorate the room.[13] Despite the rough conditions, seventy students enrolled the first year. The program found even greater success in its second year when Guy C. Wilson, a professional educator who had recently moved to Salt Lake City from the Latter-day Saint colonies in Mexico, arrived and took over for Yates.

In the years following the launch of the released-time program at Granite, the concept of released-time seminary spread rapidly throughout the Church. The expense involved in operating the Church academies meant they would always be geographically limited, but seminaries could be brought quickly and inexpensively to every stake in the Church. As the number of seminaries grew rapidly, the academies declined. The Church Board of Education made a major decision in 1920 to close most of the academies. However, the Church continued to maintain Brigham Young University and a few of the larger academies, which were converted into Church-sponsored junior colleges. Ricks became a junior college in 1918. Weber, Dixie, and Snow Colleges in Utah, as well as Gila College in Arizona, became junior colleges in 1923. During the same time, the seminary program continued to grow rapidly. Between 1922 and 1932, seminary enrollment rose from 4,976 to 29,427 students.[14] Looking back on the explosive growth of the released-time system, Merrill modestly commented, "We sometimes 'build better than we know.'"[15]

CHURCH COMMISSIONER OF EDUCATION, 1928

After thirty-five years as a professional educator at the University of Utah, a new call came to Joseph Merrill in 1928. Adam S. Bennion, the Church superintendent of schools, had chosen to resign and Merrill was asked to fill his post. Based on Bennion's recommendation, the title "Superintendent of Church Schools" was dropped in favor of "Commissioner of Church Schools."[16] Merrill brought a wealth of experience to the position. As head of the School of Mines at the University of Utah, he had been involved with the state legislature. His long career in higher education brought many connections throughout the academic community as well.[17] It also helped that many of his close associates from the University of Utah, among them James E. Talmage, John A. Widtsoe, and Richard R. Lyman, were serving as members of the Quorum of the Twelve Apostles.

Merrill also brought a unique perspective to the work. His experiences during his own education had convinced him of the absolute necessity of providing religious education to every youth of the Church. Speaking in general conference, he said, "I believe that I have been called to the finest and the best educational position in America." Waxing prophetic, he continued, "The time will come, I verily believe, and before very many years, when week-day religious education will be offered to every high school boy and girl, to every college and university boy and girl in this Church."[18]

Just as vital as Merrill's deep feeling of the importance of the work was the perspective he brought as an outsider to the system. As a newcomer to the Church hierarchy, he had been removed from the battles already fought to streamline the educational programs of the Church. This allowed him to diagnose the problems facing Church education dispassionately and seek solutions. Not having been present at earlier discussions on educational policy, Merrill also pushed the board to clarify their positions on items where no clear decision of policy had been made. Merrill's service over the next five years would provide numerous opportunities to make major shifts in the educational policies of the Church.

BEGINNINGS OF THE INSTITUTE PROGRAM

As Church commissioner of education, Merrill inherited several vital projects from his predecessor, Adam S. Bennion. Among the most important was the launch of a new "collegiate seminary" program in Moscow, Idaho. Prior to Merrill's call as commissioner, Church leaders had already sent J. Wyley Sessions, a returning mission president from South Africa, to Moscow to begin working within the community to prepare the way for the new program. Sessions faced a difficult task. In his own recollection, he was given no guidance other than a directive from the First Presidency to "take care of our boys and girls that are up there and to see what the Church ought to do for our college students who are attending state universities."[19]

Joseph F. Merrill and the Transformation of Church Education

Initially meeting with opposition in the community from those who feared he would "mormonize"[20] the university, Sessions dove into his assignment with gusto, winning friends for the Church and paving the way for the program to be launched.

By the time the program was handed off to the incoming Merrill administration, Sessions had spent several years preparing the community. At the same time he was finalizing the plans to construct the first building and working to design the curriculum for the new venture. Feeling overwhelmed, Sessions wrote to Merrill, "I have been working on a plan for the organization for our Institute and the courses we should offer in our weekday classes. I confess that the building of a curriculum for such an institution has worried me a lot and it is a job that I feel unqualified for." Perhaps reflecting on his own experiences during his education in the East, Merrill wrote to Sessions, advising him to keep sight of what the program was meant to accomplish. In Merrill's mind, the objective of institute was to "enable our young people attending the colleges to make the necessary adjustments between the things they have been taught in the Church and the things they are learning in the university, to enable them to become firmly settled in their faith as members of the Church." Merrill saw the need for an institution that could help students reconcile the truths of secular learning with spiritual things. He continued, "You know that when our young people go to college and study science and philosophy in all their branches, that they are inclined to become materialistic, to forget God, and to believe that the knowledge of men is all-sufficient. . . . Can the truths of science and philosophy be reconciled with religious truths?" Reflecting on his own hard-won testimony, he concluded, "Personally, I am convinced that religion is as reasonable as science; that religious truths and scientific truths nowhere are in conflict; that there is one great unifying purpose extending throughout all creation; that we are living in a wonderful, though at the present time deeply mysterious, world; and that there is an all-wise, all-powerful Creator back of it all. Can this same faith be developed in the minds of all our collegiate and university students? Our collegiate institutes are established as means to this end."[21]

Deeply involved in the project, Merrill maintained a close eye on the construction of the building, pushing Sessions to keep costs under budget. Years later, Sessions would recall Merrill's involvement with shades of admiration and even exasperation, calling Merrill "the most economical, conservative General Authority of this dispensation."[22] Sessions even went so far as to visit the First Presidency, stating he couldn't "build a little shanty at the University of Idaho."[23] After a fair amount of wrangling, a beautiful building was completed, and the new structure opened its doors in 1928. It was soon followed by similar programs in Logan, Utah; Pocatello, Idaho; Laramie, Wyoming; and a host of other locations. Initially referred to as collegiate seminaries, Merrill approved the name "Latter-day Saint Institute of Religion" after it was suggested by Jay G. Eldridge, the non-LDS dean of faculty in Moscow.[24]

Born in the midst of opposition in Moscow, the institutes were received warmly. Some educators hailed them as the solution to the problem of Church and State in collegiate education. F. J. Kelly, the president of University of Idaho, wrote of the institute program, "All the great churches should recognize their responsibility of providing this religious training at state supported colleges and universities. These church institutions should be recognized as an intrinsic part of the educational scheme."[25]

SAVING THE CHURCH SCHOOLS

Perhaps the most controversial actions of Merrill's tenure as commissioner involved the transfer or closure of the existing Church schools. Most of the Church network of academies were closed or turned over to state control in 1920, when Adam S. Bennion became the head of the Church school system. By the time Merrill was called as commissioner, however, it was clear that Church finances could no longer support the schools, and changes needed to be made. The successful launch of the institute program also provided reason to believe that the Church could provide for the spiritual needs of its youth while allowing Latter-day Saint youth to attend state universities. When Merrill became commissioner, his instructions were clear. Remembering this period, he wrote to his brother, "When I was asked by the First Presidency if I would accept the position being vacated by Dr. Bennion, I asked for a statement of policy. They replied, 'We have concluded to spend all the money we can afford for education in the field of religious education.' My first duty would be to eliminate the junior colleges from the Church School system . . . and to promote the extension of the seminary system, just as widely as our means would permit. . . . The First Presidency told me that this was the plan they would like to see followed. But the junior colleges were to be closed."[26]

Merrill's earlier work with the Utah State legislature during his time at the University of Utah was a key asset in arranging for the majority of the Church colleges to be transferred to state control rather than be closed outright. Merrill's style was markedly different from his predecessor, Adam S. Bennion. Where Bennion was an English literature major and an eloquent speaker and writer, Merrill's background in science lent itself to communicating in blunt facts. Soon after his call as commissioner, Merrill began negotiating with the state to take over the Church junior colleges, leaving no room for error. Utah legislators were initially enthusiastic to receive an entire system of junior colleges free of charge. However, some began to waver when the darkening shadows of the Great Depression brought the viability of state finances into question. During this time, Merrill wrote to C. R. Hollingsworth, a state senator, "In the Church colleges there are now enrolled approximately fourteen hundred junior college students. I am telling you only the plain truth when I say the Church will no longer carry this burden and it will drop it much sooner than otherwise if the University and the State do not care to accept our offer."[27] Advising the proponents of other schools, Merrill organized community support for the survival of every school he felt could be saved. When a school superintendent in Ogden wrote regarding the possibility of the closure of Weber College, Merrill replied, "Does Ogden want a junior college? If so, my suggestion is that Ogden get its coat off and go to work."[28]

While the closure or transfer of most of the Church schools was certain, questions still remained: How far Church leaders were willing to carry the transformation of the Church school system? Were *all* of the Church schools, including Brigham Young University, to be eliminated in favor of the seminary and institute system? Finding no clear answer in the minutes of the Church Board of Education, Merrill asked for a clear statement of policy. This in turn led to a lively discussion among board members as to the policy. Board members had mixed feelings concerning what should happen next. President Heber J. Grant felt Church policy should be to close schools as quickly as possible. David O. McKay, a member of the Quorum of the Twelve at the time, felt strongly that the junior colleges should be retained in order to allow Church influence in teacher training throughout the state. McKay also felt that the seminary system was untested and that more time was needed to prove that they were a suitable replacement for the Church schools. The meeting ended with President Grant declaring that the policy covered *all* Church schools, including BYU. President Grant expressed remorse, saying that it "almost breaks one's heart" to close all the schools but that Church finances simply could no longer support the school system.[29]

What were Merrill's feelings in that matter? While it is clear that Merrill felt some school closures were inevitable, it is also clear that he felt a university was a vital component of the Church Educational System. The day after the board meeting where the decision was made, he wrote to a BYU official, expressing his own desires for the university: "At the Board meeting yesterday it was not definitely stated so, but it seemed to be the minds of most of those present that the BYU as a whole was included in the closing movement; and that is specially the reason why I am writing you. My own hope and fondest desire is that we may retain the BYU as a senior and graduate institution, eliminating its junior college work, and make the University outstanding, a credit to the Church, and a highly serviceable and necessary institution."[30] Writing to BYU president Franklin S. Harris,

Merrill expressed similar hopes: "As I have told you before, I think it perfectly feasible and logical to make the BYU the most outstanding institution between the Mississippi and the Pacific coast."[31]

Merrill also defended the need for a Church school in the press. Part of reasoning for keeping BYU under Church control stemmed from the need of an institution where seminary teachers could be trained. Merrill may have been attempting to tie the seminary system and BYU together, making the survival of both vital to the future of Church education. In the *Deseret News* he laid out three key reasons for the retention of BYU:

> A university is an essential unit in our seminary systems. For our seminary teachers must be specially trained for their work. The Brigham Young University is our training school....
>
> We need in the Church a group of scholars learned in history, science, and philosophy, scholars of standing and ability who can interpret for us and make plain to us the results of research and the reasoning of the human mind....
>
> I offer as a third reason why we need a university the fact that Latter-day Saints' ideals are in many respects different from and higher than those of the average non-Latter-day Saints.... Do we not need a university that shall hold up Latter-day Saint ideals so high in the educational world that all students in all schools of all grades may see beauty thereof, and perhaps be influenced by them?[32]

Considering the considerable pressure placed on Church expenditures during some of the darkest days of the Great Depression, Merrill's vision for the Church school system was remarkably farsighted.

During Merrill's tenure as commissioner, arrangements were made to transfer Weber, Snow, and Dixie Colleges to state control. Through a process of delicate negotiations, each school was successfully transferred to state control, along with Gila College in Arizona. The two most difficult schools to save were Ricks College in Idaho and LDS College in Salt Lake

City. Attempts were made to transfer control over Ricks College to the state of Idaho, but the state legislature rejected the offer several different times. Merrill persisted in trying to save Ricks College. He wrote to one school official, "The cause of the College is just. Let the support of the people be so generous that the College shall never die."[33] When Merrill left the commissioner's office in 1933, the fate of Ricks College was still unresolved. However, strong community support and Church funding, as meager as circumstances allowed, kept the school on life support until the situation improved. Today renamed BYU–Idaho, the school serves as a vital component of the Church Educational System.

The only outright school closure during Merrill's service was LDS College in Salt Lake City in 1931. More of a Church-sponsored high school than a college by this point, the school may have met its fate because alternative schools were already abundant in the Salt Lake City area. The closure of the school may have also acted as a kind of sacrificial lamb to convince the Utah State legislature of the seriousness of Merrill's intentions to close schools outright if the state would not accept them.[34] Though the school closed, a portion of it still endures today. The business department of the school was allowed to stay open and eventually grew into the LDS Business College.

The closure or transfer of Church schools was among the most difficult tasks Merrill was asked to oversee during his service. It does, however, illustrate an important principle of Church administration. While the available minutes from the period show that different opinions existed over the issue, Church leaders presented a united front once the decisions were made. Even Elder McKay, the most concerned opponent of the schools' closure, was willing to defend Merrill in his labors. When Elder McKay attended a particularly rancorous meeting dealing with the possible closure of Ricks College, Merrill was harshly criticized. One witness recorded that she thought "Br. McKay would go through the ceiling" when one official criticized Merrill.[35] Even though McKay and Merrill may not have seen eye to eye every issue surrounding the educational system, McKay supported Merrill in his actions.

Joseph F. Merrill and the Transformation of Church Education

The battles waged over the fate of the Church schools did leave some lingering questions. Educationally, the Church had placed all its eggs in one basket: the seminary and institute systems. As David O. McKay had pointed out, the seminary system was still relatively young and untested. A return to the Church schools would be difficult, if not impossible. If anything threatened the seminaries, the entire educational program of the Church could be at risk.

THE 1930–31 CHURCH EDUCATION CRISIS

Merrill's worst fears seemed to have materialized in January 1930. A report to the state school board from Isaac L. Williamson, the state inspector of high schools,[36] was issued on January 7, 1930. The report was a scathing critique of the relationship between Utah high schools and seminaries. At the time there were few indications that the attack was coming. Merrill had tried to meet with Williamson's committee before it made its report to the state board but had been refused permission.[37] Church leaders, Merrill included, found themselves blindsided by the report and quickly organized themselves to issue a response.

The report was published in full in the *Salt Lake Tribune* the next day, taking up an entire page of the paper. Williamson's concerns with the seminary program were quite lengthy, but in summary he felt that the Church educational program was a violation to constitutional law, a barrier to the academic achievement of Utah students, and an unfair financial burden to the taxpayers of the state. Williamson charged that sectarian doctrine was taught in Latter-day Saint classes where credit was offered and that inappropriate sharing of resources between seminaries and public schools was also happening in some areas. He even accused the state of giving financial support to the seminaries by providing buses to take them to their schools located near the seminaries. He charged, "The school and the seminary are so intimately linked together that in the minds of the public, pupils, and patrons, they are thought of as one institution."[38]

Recognizing the danger of the situation, Merrill fired back by publishing a lengthy response in the *Deseret News* the next day. He accused Williamson of "straining at a gnat and swallowing a camel." Rather than costing the state money, Merrill countered, the Church system *saved* the state thousands of dollars by providing teachers and facilities for a portion of the school day, without any charge to the state.[39] Other prominent educators rushed to defense of the seminary system as well. D. H. Christensen, a former superintendent of Salt Lake City schools, wrote another *Deseret News* piece stating, "A high school student who spends one-fifth of his school time in the study and discussion of things spiritual, loses nothing and he may gain much by the uplifting and wholesome influence of such effort."[40]

Meanwhile, things turned from bad to worse with the state board. Responding to the Williamson report, the Utah State Board of Education assigned a three-man subcommittee to investigate the seminary system. When the committee returned with its results in March 1930, two of the three subcommittee members recommended a complete disassociation between schools and seminaries, the end of credit for Bible studies, and refusal of permission to excuse students during the day for seminary studies. Joshua Greenwood, the only Latter-day Saint on the subcommittee, refused to sign the report. If the committee's suggestions were enacted, it would have effectively ended the released-time program in Utah, a devastating blow to the Church's educational efforts. With the Church schools gone, there were few alternatives left. Experimental early-morning classes had begun in the Salt Lake school district, where released-time was not allowed, but enrollment in the early morning programs was about 10 percent, compared to 70 percent in areas where released-time was available.[41]

With so much at stake, Merrill and other Church leaders began to plead their case to the public. At a meeting for Church educators held in conjunction with the April 1930 general conference, President Grant addressed the conflict directly, saying, "It is up to us who hold a vote to see that this liberty [seminary] is granted." Milton Welling, the Utah secretary of state, stated, "We can't be successful without such institutions and in my judgment if they are lost to the state it will be the fault of the people of the Church." The proceedings of the entire meeting were published in the *Deseret News* under the headline "Pres. Grant Calls on Saints to Defend Rights."[42]

A month later, Merrill took the fight to the state board itself. Merrill used his connections in the Utah educational system to construct a firm response to Williamson's charges.[43] Contacting officials at BYU and Utah State University, Merrill cited statistics showing that seminary graduates had higher grades, on average, than their non seminary counterparts. Further, Merrill showed that in 1928 only *one* high school dropout in the entire state of Utah had listed seminary as a cause for his academic difficulties. The next year, only three listed seminary as a factor. Citing these statistics, Merrill charged, "Can there be any justification for a school official making grave charges against an institution without having facts to substantiate his charges?"[44]

Regarding the charges of a financial burden placed by the seminaries, Merrill responded with written statements from sixteen different Utah superintendents, with none citing seminary as an additional burden. The superintendent of the Cache School District cited thousands of dollars saved by the seminary program and continued: "The seminaries were expected to give the high school pupil a foundation for moral integrity and character development. They are doing so to a surprisingly successful extent. They seem one thing that is coming up to expectations."[45] Pointing out the absurdity of some of Williamson's charges, Merrill wrote, "As to bus transportation, we admit frankly that the seminary is benefited by the transportation system of the high school. So is the corner grocery, the refreshment stand, the shop, the business house, and the town as a whole." Merrill argued, "No sane person would assert that because these places are benefited by the presence of the high school in the community they are therefore supported, in part, in any legal sense whatsoever, by the money of the taxpayers."[46]

Merrill continued by pointing out all the states where released-time was allowed without sanction. He further argued that seminaries were technically private schools, and acceptance of credit from private schools had been standard in public education for years. Recognizing that similar programs proceeded unmolested by other denominations in other states throughout the country, Merrill finally raised the ugly possibility of religious intolerance as a motivating factor behind the report. He wrote:

> The adoption of the Committee's suggestions means the death of the seminary, and the enemies of the seminary all know it. But why do they want to kill something that every high school principal and school superintendent of experience says is good, being one of the most effective agencies in character training and good citizenship that influences the student? Is religious prejudice trying to mask in legal sheep's clothing for the purpose of stabbing the seminary, this agency that has had such a wonderful influence in bringing a united support to the public schools?[47]

Merrill's defense sent a clear message to the state board that the Church was willing to fight for the seminary program and held compelling legal reasons to believe they would win if the question came to a court decision.

In the aftermath of Merrill's rebuttal, the board did not show much inclination to back down, though it now had to consider the consequences of legal action if it did move to end credit and released time. In June 1930, the board briefly considered the possibility of a "friendly lawsuit" to answer the constitutional questions raised by the Williamson report, briefly initiating a search to find a taxpayer who would bring the suit.[48] Merrill expected that the fate of seminary might ultimately have to be decided in court, and he was ready for the challenge. In July 1930, he told a gathering of BYU students that the Church would "fight to the last ditch" to save its seminaries and that the controversy might eventually end up in the Supreme Court.[49]

Fortunately, such measures were unnecessary. In September 1931, the Utah State Board voted six to three in favor of retention of credit and released time. Williamson argued passionately before the state board several times against the seminaries but appears to have been ineffective.[50] The conflict served as an uncomfortable reminder of the religious rift still existing in the state. All six of the board members who voted in favor of retention were Latter-day Saints, while the three dissenters were not.[51] Minor skirmishes continued over the seminary issue in the ensuing decades. At a 1932 meeting of Utah educators, one school principal called the seminaries an "evil more subtle, farther reaching, more dangerous, and unwise than the cigarette evil."[52] The lawsuit desired by the state board never materialized, and the seminary system continued and operated relatively free of controversy for several decades. The legal issues over released time and credit were finally resolved in 1978 when a lawsuit brought by the American Civil Liberties Union in Logan, Utah, established through trial the legal operational boundaries for the Church program.[53]

The battle over the seminary system caused significant reverberations in Church education. In truth, the Williamson report had raised some legitimate concerns over the way the system operated. Even while the controversy was raging, administrative changes were initiated to comply with the wishes of the state board. New policies ensured that seminary registration was carried out in separate buildings, seminary photographs and activities were not allowed to be shown in high school yearbooks, and seminary teachers were forbidden from seeking any privileges not already available to any citizen in their respective communities.[54] The episode also radically altered the mindset of Church educators for a brief time. The conflicts with the state board may have in part inspired Merrill to create the Department of Religion at BYU in order to prevent Church teachers from making the same errors that had led to Williamson's report.[55] Several outside scholars from the University of Chicago were brought in to instruct the Church's religious educators, and several promising young teachers were sent to the University of Chicago Divinity School to receive advanced training.[56] After Merrill's departure, the rising secularism in Church education caused some concern among Church leaders. However, during the crisis years of 1930–31, it cannot be disputed that Merrill succeeded brilliantly in securing the future of the Church's educational program. With his connections throughout the Utah educational system and his extensive experience working in higher education, there may have been no person better suited to fight the battle to save the seminary program.

A Firm Foundation

FROM EDUCATOR TO APOSTLE

The crisis of 1930–31 represented a kind of climax in Merrill's tenure as commissioner. Less than a week after the state board made its decision, Merrill was called to serve as a member of the Quorum of the Twelve Apostles. He continued to serve in his capacity as commissioner until 1933, when he was called to preside over the European Mission of the Church. In his service there, he continued his tradition of innovation, pioneering the use of media in presenting the message of the gospel. One of the missionaries he worked most closely with was the young Gordon B. Hinckley, future President of the Church.[57] After his return from Europe, Merrill continued to work as a passionate advocate of Church education until his death in 1952.

What was the institutional impact of Merrill's service? He was critical to the survival of Church education for several reasons. First, he has rightly been called as "the father of the Church Seminary."[58] The institute program, largely an application of seminary principles to the college level, was also deeply influenced by him. With his experience working as an administrator in Utah higher education, Merrill also played a vital role in the final stages of shepherding the Church Educational System from Church schools to the seminary and institute program. Without this change, it is difficult to imagine that the Church education could have the kind of worldwide impact it enjoys today. Merrill was a key player in the retention of BYU and the inception of a professional department of religion at the school. It is all the more amazing to consider that Merrill carried out all of these changes under the most trying of economic circumstances. From a high of $958,440 spent on education in 1925, expenditures declined to a record low of $459,580 in 1934, the year after Merrill left office.[59] In 1930–31 alone, Church expenditures on education were lowered by $100,000.[60] Merrill's emphasis on thrift has had an impact even into our day. Faced with his own difficult financial decisions, President Hinckley often recalled hearing Merrill's voice ringing in his ears: "I will be more careful with the Church's money than I will with my own."[61]

Joseph F. Merrill and the Transformation of Church Education

Today the effect of Church educational programs is immeasurable. At the present time, over 363,000 students worldwide are enrolled in seminary programs.[62] Early-morning seminary and the home-study programs both grew out of these early efforts and then expanded across the globe to bless the lives of scores of young Latter-day Saints. The institute program expanded along with the Church as well, allowing religious education to be brought to college-age youth almost anywhere they chose to attend school. Today over 150,000 students are taught the gospel in institute at over 500 different locations.[63] Merrill's vision has become a transformative factor not only in Church education but in the lives of countless numbers of Latter-day Saints.

Merrill believed strongly in the power of education to change people's lives. As one who had successfully navigated the treacherous shoals of intellectualism and survived with his faith intact, he felt an obligation provide as much guidance as possible to those who would follow. To this end, he labored tirelessly to create an educational system which could do just that. Expressing the value of this, he wrote:

> Many of us believe that a sound religious faith, practically applied in our daily living, gives a balance, a guide and an inspiration to the believer that makes his life meaningful, courageous, and sweet—therefore entirely worth while. But such a faith comes to most people only by effort. They are not born with it. This faith is of such a nature, however, that those who possess it always have joy in helping their fellows to acquire it. If they succeed a priceless service has been rendered, some of us believe. "If it so be that you should labor all your days . . . and bring save it be one soul unto me, how great shall be your joy with him in the kingdom of my Father!"[64]

NOTES

1. Boyd K. Packer, "Teach the Scriptures," address to Church Educational System full-time religious educators, October 14, 1977, 1–9, in Boyd K. Packer, *Mine*

Errand from the Lord: Selections from the Sermons and Writings of Boyd K. Packer (Salt Lake: Deseret Book, 2008), 358–59.

2. Richard R. Lyman, "Dr. Joseph F. Merrill of the Council of the Twelve," *Improvement Era*, November 1931, 10; see also Gordon B. Hinckley, "Church Mourns the Passing of Elder Joseph F. Merrill," *Improvement Era*, March 1952, 146; and Melvin Clarence Merrill, *Utah Pioneer and Apostle; Marriner Wood Merrill and His Family* (n.p.: privately published, 1937), 341.

3. Lyman, "Dr. Joseph F. Merrill of the Council of the Twelve," 10.

4. *Dedication of the Joseph F. Merrill Engineering Building* (Salt Lake City: Utah State Historical Society, n.d.), 1; see also Alan K. Parrish, *John A. Widtsoe* (Salt Lake City: Deseret Book, 2003), 117. Parrish notes that John A. Widtsoe was studying in Germany at the same time, completing his doctoral work only a few months after Merrill. I have been unable to verify absolutely that Merrill was the first native Utahn to earn a PhD, though in the source cited, which was produced by the University of Utah, he is cited as such.

5. Joseph F. Merrill, "Boyhood Experiences," *Improvement Era*, May 1944, 146.

6. Joseph F. Merrill, "Knowing the Gospel Truth by Personal Revelation," *Church News*, December 7, 1946.

7. Joseph F. Merrill, "The Lord Overrules," *Improvement Era*, July 1934, 413.

8. Merrill, "The Lord Overrules," 413.

9. Joseph F. Merrill, "A New Institution in Religious Education," *Improvement Era*, January 1938, 54–56.

10. Richard O. Cowan, *The Church in the Twentieth Century* (Salt Lake City: Bookcraft, 1985), 89.

11. Charles Coleman and Dwight Jones, comps., *History of Granite Seminary*, unpublished manuscript, 1933, MS 2237, Church History Library, The Church of Jesus Christ of Latter-day Saints, Salt Lake City, 5–6.

12. Thomas Jarvis Yates, *Autobiography and Biography of Thomas Jarvis Yates*, Church History Library, Salt Lake City, 78; see also Casey Paul Griffiths, "The First Seminary Teacher," *Religious Educator* 9, no. 3 (2008): 114–29.

13. Coleman and Jones, *History of Granite Seminary*, 6–7.

Joseph F. Merrill and the Transformation of Church Education

14. James B. Allen and Glen M. Leonard, *The Story of the Latter-day Saints*, 2nd ed. (Salt Lake: Deseret Book, 1992), 502.
15. Merrill, "A New Institution in Religious Education," 55.
16. William Peter Miller, *Weber College, 1888–1933* (n.p., 1975), MSS 7643, Church History Library, Salt Lake City, 31. David O. McKay was appointed the first Church commissioner of education in 1919. He was succeeded by John A. Widtsoe in 1922. In 1925 the commission was disbanded, and Adam S. Bennion, who had been serving as Church superintendent of education, became the executive officer of Church education, still serving under the direction of the Church Board of Education. In 1927, Widtsoe's departure for the European Mission, which closely coincided with Bennion's resignation, opened the way for another restructuring. The creation of a new office of commissioner was designed mainly to shorten the lines of communication between Church leaders and the chief educational officer of the Church. See Parrish, *John A. Widtsoe: A Biography*, 357–59.
17. "New Superintendent of Church Schools," *Improvement Era*, February 1928, 325–26.
18. Joseph F. Merrill, in Conference Report, April 1928, 37.
19. J. Wyley Sessions and Magdalene Sessions, June 29, 1965, interviewed by Richard O. Cowan, transcript and audio recording in author's possession (hereafter Sessions 1965 oral history); James Wyley Sessions, August 12, 1972, interviewed by Marc Sessions, MS 15866, Church History Library, Salt Lake City (hereafter Sessions 1972 oral history); see also Leonard Arrington, "The Founding of LDS Institutes of Religion," *Dialogue* 2, no. 2 (Summer 1967): 137–47, and Ward H. Magleby, "1926, Another Beginning, Moscow, Idaho," *Impact*, Winter 1968.
20. Sessions 1972 oral history, 5.
21. Magleby, 31–32. As one of the first native Utahns to obtain a PhD, Merrill was intimately familiar with the struggles he describes in his letter. He experienced them himself as a young man as he attended Johns Hopkins University. See Merrill, "The Lord Overrules," 413, 447.
22. J. Wyley Sessions, *J. Wyley Sessions Remembrance*, January 6, 1967, Laguna Hills, UA 156, box 2, folder 5, L. Tom Perry Special Collections, Harold B. Lee Library, Brigham Young University.

23. Magleby, "Another Beginning," 23.
24. Magleby, "Another Beginning," 23, 27.
25. Gary A. Anderson, "A Historical Survey of the Full-Time Institutes of Religion of the Church of Jesus Christ of Latter-day Saints, 1926–1966" (PhD diss., Brigham Young University, 1968), 65.
26. Joseph F. Merrill to Amos N. Merrill, Salt Lake City, December 13, 1951, Joseph Francis Merrill Collection, MSS 1540, box 4, folder 2, L. Tom Perry Special Collections, BYU.
27. Joseph F. Merrill to C. R. Hollingsworth, Salt Lake City, February 6, 1929, Merrill Collection, MSS 1540, box 5, folder 1, L. Tom Perry Special Collections, Harold B. Lee Library, BYU.
28. Joseph F. Merrill to W. Karl Hopkins, Salt Lake City, February 9, 1929, Merrill Collection, MSS 1540, box 5, folder 3, L. Tom Perry Special Collections, BYU.
29. William E. Berrett, CES History Resource Files, 1899–1985, CR 102 174, Church History Library, Salt Lake City. This meeting is also discussed in Ernest L. Wilkinson, ed., *Brigham Young University: The First One Hundred Years* (Provo, UT: Brigham Young University Press, 1975), 2:87.
30. Wilkinson, *Brigham Young University*, 2:87.
31. Joseph F. Merrill to Franklin S. Harris, January 8, 1930, Harris Presidential Papers, in Wilkinson, *Brigham Young University*, 2:221; emphasis added.
32. William E. Berrett and Alma P. Burton, *Readings in L.D.S. Church History from Original Manuscripts* (Salt Lake City: Deseret Book, 1958), 3:341–42.
33. David L. Crowder, *The Spirit of Ricks: A History of Ricks College* (Rexburg, ID, 1997), 113.
34. Miller, *Weber College, 1888–1993*, 40–41. While the minutes of the Church Board of Education are currently restricted to researchers, Miller's history of Weber College contains many of the minutes crucial to understanding this critical period of transformation in Church education.
35. T. Edgar Lyon to parents, February 15, 1933, Rexburg, ID, T. Edgar Lyon Collection, MSS 2341, box 13, folder 3, reel 10, L. Tom Perry Special Collections, BYU.
36. Williamson was a non-Mormon and a former superintendent of the Tintic School District. He had previously served as superintendent over the Wakita, Oklahoma,

school district after obtaining his degree from Harvard University. Shortly after the 1930–31 crisis was resolved, he left Utah to return to the Midwest. "Prof. Adams Will Go To Park City," *Eureka Reporter*, May 31, 1912; see also Frederick S. Buchanan, "Masons and Mormons: Released-Time Politics in Salt Lake City, 1930–56," *Journal of Mormon History* 19, no. 1 (1993): 77.

37. William E. Berrett, *A Miracle in Weekday Religious Education* (Salt Lake City: Salt Lake Printing Center, 1988), 43.
38. "Seminaries of LDS Church Put Under Study by School Officials," *Salt Lake Tribune*, January 9, 1930.
39. "Head of System Answers Attack upon Seminaries," *Deseret News*, January 9, 1930, 1.
40. D. H. Christensen, "Seminary Students Not Deficient in Scholarship," *Deseret News*, January 21, 1930, 3.
41. Allen and Leonard, 502–3.
42. "Church Leaders Protest Battle on Seminaries," *Deseret News*, April 7, 1930.
43. Church of Jesus Christ of Latter-day Saints, *A Reply to Inspector Williamson's Report to the State Board of Education on the Existing Relationship Between Seminaries and Public High Schools in the State of Utah and Comments Thereon by a Special Committee of the Board*, issued as a letter to the Utah State Board of Education, May 3, 1930, box 57, folder 13, Buchanan Collection, AO149.xml, Special Collections, Marriott Library, University of Utah, 4 (hereafter referred to as Merrill Report*)*. While it is likely that several figures authored this report, it was sent under Merrill's signature. For the sake of clarity, and so as to not confuse this report with the Williamson report, I will refer to the words in this report as Merrill's work, knowing other unidentified Church officials may have also had a hand in writing them.
44. Merrill Report, 8.
45. Merrill Report, 7.
46. Merrill Report, 9.
47. Merrill Report, 23–24.
48. "Status of Church Seminaries Seek Court Decision," *Deseret News*, June 28, 1930, 3.
49. "L.D.S. Church to Wage Seminary Fight to Finish," *Salt Lake Telegram*, July 3, 1930, 6.

50. Utah State School Board Minutes, June 28, 1930, courtesy of Twila Affleck, Utah State Board of Education.
51. Buchanan, "Masons and Mormons," 80.
52. "Teacher Flays Seminaries at U.E.A. Session," *Deseret News*, October 29, 1932, 1.
53. Berrett, *A Miracle*, 188.
54. Berrett, *A Miracle*, 46.
55. Minutes of the Church General Board of Education, February 5, March 5, 1930, copies in author's possession; see also Wilkinson, *Brigham Young University*, 2:286. The decision to send Guy C. Wilson, the first full-time religious instructor to BYU, occurred during the days immediately following the Williamson Report.
56. See Russel B. Swensen, "Mormons at the University of Chicago Divinity School: A Personal Reminiscence," *Dialogue* 7, no. 2 (Summer 1972): 39.
57. See Rob Taber, "The Church Enters the Media Age: Joseph F. Merrill and Gordon B. Hinckley," *Journal of Mormon History* 35, no. 4 (Fall 2009): 218–32.
58. "New Superintendent of Church Schools."
59. Wilkinson, *Brigham Young University* 2:211.
60. General Board Minutes, November 4, 1931, cited in Thomas Alexander Scott, "Eastern Arizona College: A Comprehensive History of the Early Years" (EdD diss., Brigham Young University, 1985), 638; see also Milton L. Bennion, *Mormonism and Education* (Salt Lake City: The Department of Education of the Church of Jesus Christ of Latter-day Saints, 1939), 200–1, 223, 225.
61. Sheri L. Dew, *Go Forward with Faith: The Biography of Gordon B. Hinckley* (Salt Lake City: Deseret Book, 1996), 218–19.
62. "Seminary Program," http://www.newsroom.lds.org/ldsnewsroom/eng/background-information/seminary-program.
63. http://institute.lds.org/faq/index.
64. Merrill, *The Truth-Seeker and Mormonism* (Salt Lake: Zion's Press, 1946), vii.

William G. Hartley and Theodore D. Moore

18

THE CHURCH'S BEAUTIFICATION MOVEMENT, 1937–47

WHEN LeGrand Richards became the Church's Presiding Bishop in April 1938, he found that there were "very few ward buildings with shrubs or flowers around them. They thought the boys would destroy them." In Utah and Idaho, "many buildings had never been painted and . . . a lot of old dilapidated outhouses and chicken coops and fences and barns" near ward buildings caused some tourists to ask, "Is there something in the Mormon Church against the use of paint?" In a run-down ward building in Idaho, Bishop Richards asked the bishop, "Bishop, would you dare invite the girls of your ward to come here to a party in a party dress?" "No, I don't think so," the bishop replied. "Well, you fix it up," Bishop Richards said.[1] Because of an abundance of unattractive meetinghouses, the Church promoted a decade-long beautification movement starting in 1937 that generated much

---

William G. Hartley is a professor emeritus of history at Brigham Young University. Theodore D. Moore is an assistant professor of history at Salt Lake Community College.

energy at all Church levels and produced improvements big and small. To spearhead the program, the Church created the Improvement and Beautification Committee. Initially it functioned under the Church Security or Welfare Committee, but it soon shifted to the Presiding Bishopric's Office.

For a decade, the program's two primary concerns were to have wards make their meetinghouses and grounds attractive and to motivate members to beautify their homes. The program sought to utilize unemployed and underemployed Church welfare recipients. It hoped to improve the image outsiders gained while visiting Mormon communities.[2] The program involved men, women, children, priesthood quorums, and every Church auxiliary—Sunday School, Primary, Relief Society, and the MIAs. Regularly it produced articles and before-and-after photographs in the Church section of the *Deseret News* and the *Improvement Era*, *Relief Society Magazine*, *Children's Friend*, and Presiding Bishopric's monthly *Progress of the Church*. It worked in cooperation with other community groups promoting beautification, especially with the Utah Centennial Commission. The Centennial Commission wanted Utah to look good for a World's Fair–type celebration planned for 1947 to celebrate the centennial of the pioneers' arrival in Utah.

BEAUTIFICATION EFFORTS UNDER WAY

Periodically, run-down urban and rural conditions prompted national and local groups to undertake improvement projects.[3] Agencies responsible for roads and highways, parks, forests, tourism, and urban renewal projects pushed such efforts. Nationally, women's groups, civic organizations, the Junior Chamber of Commerce, cities, counties, 4-H clubs, and others did the same. In Salt Lake City, municipal leaders made periodic attempts to better the city's physical appearance, and in 1936 those goals began anew, driven by groups such as the Salt Lake Women's Chamber of Commerce, which took on the task of purifying the city's polluted air.[4] During the 1930s, Utah's state health inspectors promoted annual spring cleanup drives for sanitation purposes. In 1936, for example, they produced successful spring cleanups in forty Utah towns and cities. Just two months before the Church launched its program in June 1937, the Utah Junior Chamber of Commerce (Jaycee) conducted an annual cleanup drive involving more than fifty communities. The Jaycee campaign also prodded homeowners to "clean-up, paint-up, and cut down weeds."[5]

CONNECTION WITH THE WELFARE PROGRAM

In April 1936, the Church organized a centrally directed welfare program called the Church Security Plan. In 1937 that program, headed by the General Security Committee, launched a campaign to beautify Latter-day Saint buildings and grounds. That committee met weekly and included the First Presidency, Elders Melvin Ballard and Albert Bowen of the Twelve, and the Presiding Bishopric—Sylvester Q. Cannon, David Asael Smith, and John Wells. Three subcommittees oversaw projects and industries, agriculture, and beautification. Highland Stake president Marvin O. Ashton chaired the beautification subcommittee.[6] The Church Security Plan was soon renamed the Church Welfare Plan.

CONNECTION TO THE PLANNED 1947 PIONEER CENTENNIAL

This Church beautification effort linked directly with plans percolating in 1937 for a grandiose 1947 Mormon pioneer centennial commemoration. A Utah Trails Centennial Commission headed by President David O. McKay, counselor in the First Presidency, worked on centennial ideas and lobbied the state government to also participate. By June 1938, Governor Henry H. Blood had named one hundred men and women to a Utah Centennial Committee that was to design a plan to present to the governor and legislature by January 1939.[7] Then in 1939 the legislature funded and authorized a fifteen-person Utah Centennial Commission to voluntarily serve until the centennial. President David O. McKay was chairman; other members included Gus P. Backman from the Salt Lake Chamber of Commerce

Marvin O. Ashton, chairman of Church Improvement and Beautification Committee (left). James M. Kirkham, secretary of Church Improvement and Beautification Committee (right). (Courtesy of Church History Library.)

and former governor Charles R. Mabey.[8] The commission's charge was to create centennial activities to properly honor the pioneer arrivals and "portray fittingly the natural resources and scenic wonders of Utah, the prehistoric culture of the west, the development of irrigation, farming, mining, forestry, transportation, culture and the arts." Expecting thousands of tourists for the centennial, planners wanted Utah cleaned up and beautified by that time.[9]

Two contemporary World's Fairs, both expected to be tourist draws, influenced the planners. In San Francisco the Golden Gate International Exposition opened on February 18, 1939, and continued through October, with a repeat the next year. Among its features was a forty-nine-mile scenic drive so visitors could visit many of the city's major attractions and historic structures. Also, in April 1939 a World's Fair opened in New York City, the largest such fair to that point. With those fairs in mind, the Utah Centennial Commission proposed a World's Fair–caliber event for Utah for 1947, but with a unique twist. It would center in Salt Lake City but have as major "expositions" several scenic wonders throughout the state, such as Arches National Monument and the Bonneville Salt Flats. To ready Utah for the flood of tourists this "World's Fair" would attract, the commission promoted beautifying campaigns.[10]

CHURCH IMPROVEMENT AND BEAUTIFICATION COMMITTEE

Gathered in the office of Presiding Bishopric counselor David A. Smith, the Church Improvement and Beautification Committee held its first meeting on May 27, 1937, with Marvin O. Ashton as chairman. Members included builder Howard J. McKean, Irving T. Nelson of a "special landscape committee," and Church auxiliary representatives Jennie B. Knight (Relief Society), Mary R. Jack (Primary), Rose W. Bennett (YWMIA), Axel A. Madsen (YMMIA), and George A. Holt (Sunday School). This group's task was to launch a vigorous program to beautify LDS meetinghouses and grounds. For buildings and maintenance, the Church already funded 60 percent of major projects, a major incentive for wards deciding to "spruce up." These auxiliary representatives discussed how their groups could promote the cause. Chairman Ashton asked all of them to discuss the project with their general boards and return with their reactions.[11]

LAUNCHING AND PROMOTING THE PROGRAM

Chairman Ashton announced the new "Church-wide Improvement Program" in the June *Improvement Era*. It was designed, he said, to (1) find work for unemployed men, (2) beautify Church property, (3) raise the standards of people in their lives, homes, and communities, (4) encourage industry, and (5) save the Church insurance liability. "The thing to be decidedly emphasized is to make use of those out of employment who are able to work," he said. "There are wards where many people are on relief who could be doing something for what they receive but who are now in downright idleness. The slogan for our whole Church should be 'Work for Everybody and Everybody Work.'" "Let us banish from our communities discouragement and idleness," he urged, "and put our Church buildings, inside and out, in the proper condition of repair and beautification."[12]

He announced two contests as enticements. The first lasted until October 1937 to clean up meetinghouse grounds and paint, repair, and renovate Church *buildings*. The other ran from October 1937 to October 1938 to beautify meetinghouse *grounds*. Cash prizes were offered to first, second, and third place winners, and criteria for judging the contest were spelled out. Within weeks, however, the committee dropped the contests and cash prizes, deciding that awards for all rather than competition was the better approach.[13]

Immediately the committee launched a publicity campaign. In June they sent letters to newspapers in Utah, Idaho, and other western states where meetinghouses were located, asking them to publish articles about beautification projects. It also sent letters to lumber, hardware, and paint stores soliciting their cooperation. Early in July, local newspapers announced the Church's beautification program. One newspaper praised the "generous offer of the First Presidency to provide material assistance from the general funds of the Church."[14] July issues of the *Relief Society Magazine* and the *Children's Friend* carried beautification articles. Throughout the year, committee members, by assignment, published beautification messages in the *Improvement Era* and the *Deseret News*.[15]

Committee member Howard McKean recommended that the committee "take a ward badly run down that needs a lot of work done, and under the committee's direction it be beautified and the pictures before and after publicized throughout the Church showing what can be done."[16] For that purpose, through regular and special visits, committee members inspected several meetinghouses along main highways into Utah that should be beautified and could be used as examples. But that raised questions about how much authority the committee had to ask wards to improve. It was determined that the committee could make suggestions and then let the

Presiding Bishopric do the prodding. Committee records do not document what the targeted wards were asked to do or how well they responded.[17]

Despite the initial push coming from the top down, it is notable that General Authorities left a great deal of autonomy to the local wards, bishops, and members regarding what and how to beautify, including chapel planning and design. The Church provided 60 percent of funding for projects, but rather than mandate what improvements a ward should make, it asked wards to submit their own plans and estimates for approval by the Presiding Bishopric.

The committee needed beautification committees at the stake and ward levels, so it formulated and distributed organizing ideas and asked that such committees be assembled.[18] Stakes and wards responded well.

With First Presidency approval, the committee created a questionnaire and sent it to all bishops. Two pages long, it asked scores of questions about a ward's building, grounds, and custodian: when was the building built; what kind of construction; how many rooms; general condition of exterior masonry and cement work; was the water piped or irrigation water; did the meetinghouse have lavatories and plumbing; what kind of heating; what was the condition of furniture, carpets, roofs, and windows; what kind of soil was in the grounds, what trees and shrubs; what kind of walks, fences, parking, and outbuildings; was there a separate amusement hall; how long had the custodian served, what was his pay, and had he outside employment? The form also asked about the ward's employment situation, and, if the ward undertook an improvement program, did they have sufficient skilled unemployed members to help. Final questions dealt with what kind of improvements the bishop anticipated, cost estimates, how the ward would spend the Church's 60 percent share, and how the Beautification Committee could help with the project.[19]

In a July 1937 Church Security meeting, Brother Ashton, based on ward questionnaires that had been returned, said that most church buildings were in good shape but some needed "blasting."[20] One example of a completed questionnaire is that of Preston Idaho Fourth Ward bishop J. H.

Larsen, who said that his building had ten rooms but needed an amusement hall. The building's side entrances needed repair, the lavatories were unfit to use, the walls needed plastering and cleaning and painting, the building had no curtains or carpets, and the roof and exterior needed paint. The bishop wanted to clean, paint, and remodel the chapel and classrooms, carpet all rooms, and install new seats on the stand in the chapel. He estimated the projects' costs at $5,500.[21]

At the end of the year, the First Presidency wanted to know the Church's estimated 1938 beautification costs based on the returned questionnaires. Of 1,085 wards and branches contacted, 1,014 returned the questionnaires and in most cases provided photos, as requested, of the front and rear of the meetinghouses. First, the committee reassured the First Presidency that "our work must of necessity be one of encouraging and stimulating, not presuming to say how much a Ward should spend." Then they reported that in total the bishops requested $353,082 for ward improvements, meaning the wards' 40 percent share would be $141,249 and the Church's 60 percent share would be $211,833. Not knowing how much the Church had at its disposal for the projects, the committee asked the First Presidency what the committee could tell wards to expect. The committee also recommended "that more men be available" to visit bishops and help them to plan and to supervise their improvement projects.[22]

1938: BEAUTIFICATION COMMITTEE EFFORTS

Early in 1938, the committee issued an eight-page brochure, *Our Churches Shall Be Beautiful*, to serve as a beautification primer for wards.[23] On the cover, a First Presidency message said that the appearance of the Saints' church and community buildings and homes should properly reflect the ideals and high standards of the faith, and stake presidents and bishops should see that this happened. The booklet explained that the Church would cover 60 percent of cash costs and that donated ward labor, materials, or cash could cover the other 40 percent. To form a ward beautification committee, wards should expand their security committees to include

The Church's Beautification Movement, 1937–47

Cleanup by Nibley Park Ward Primary boys. (Deseret News, *Church section, August 7, 1937.*)

auxiliary representatives. "Bishop, investigate!" the pamphlet urged, which meant to survey what needed to be done and then to divide up the work. "Let us resolve that the old shabby church building shall disappear. . . . Let us raise the standard of our communities by beginning with the Church." Listed were project ideas women and children could do. Pictures illustrated beautification results. A scriptural reminder, often repeated by the committee, underscored the importance of the program: "For Zion must increase in beauty, and in holiness; her borders must be enlarged. . . . Zion must arise and put on her beautiful garments" (D&C 82:14).

To tie beautification to the pioneer centennial, the committee's publicity frequently reminded that beautification "started with the arrival of Pioneers in Utah," who labored to make the desert "blossom as a rose."[24]

In April 1938, LeGrand Richards became the new Presiding Bishop. He chose beautification committee chairman Marvin O. Ashton as his first counselor and Joseph B. Wirthlin as second counselor. During 1938 the flow of beautification-related articles in Church publications continued. For example, a March *Improvement Era* article, "Clean-Up! Paint-Up! Rake-Up!," told the YMMIA adult classes how to get involved.[25] The Church Security Program's page in each Church section of the *Deseret News* regularly offered beautification advice. On September 24, for example, Mary R. Jack's article "Children's Part in Church Beautification" said that "up to June 1st of this year, 283 Primaries reported children taking part helping to clear the grounds of rock and weeds, raking and carrying off rubbish, mowing lawns, digging dandelions, sweeping walks, cleaning class rooms, dusting, washing curtains, and in innumerable ways helping to clear, to keep clean and to beautify meeting houses and grounds."[26]

Early in 1939, the committee published a report about a 1938 St. George Temple beautification project for which members used local materials. Parowan members contributed evergreen trees valued at over $1,400 and spent the equivalent of eighteen work days to find and dig up the trees in local canyons and transport them to and plant them on the temple grounds. Some Cedar City members even donated trees from their own yards.[27]

1939: DEVELOPMENTS UNDER THE PRESIDING BISHOPRIC

In mid-1939, the Presiding Bishopric took over direction of the Church Improvement and Beautification Committee, which Bishop Ashton still headed. James M. Kirkham became the committee's secretary, basically an executive secretary, and served as a prime voice, expert, and promoter for the beautification program.[28] Also in 1939, the Landscape Department of the Presiding Bishop's Office was created to assist wards, stakes, and other units.[29] Sometime before November 1939, perhaps because of mounting beautification costs, the Church changed the cost share percentage with wards to fifty-fifty.[30]

Throughout 1939, the committee placed pictures and articles in the *Improvement Era* and *Progress of the Church*, praising beautification projects recently completed. One was the small Moreland Ward in Portland Stake that finished a beautiful chapel in six months by remodeling an older building.[31] Church headquarters, to set an example, beautified the grounds between the Church Office Building and the Hotel Utah and put new varnish on the Salt Lake Temple's doors, causing many to comment on the building's improved appearance. As of September of 1939, approximately 350,000 tourists had already visited Temple Square that year.[32]

The Grandview Ward chapel, dedicated on July 10, 1938, lacked landscaping, so members undertook a beautification program. With the help of some Church funding, they installed a watering system and planted donated shrubs, trees, lawn seed, and flowers. Thirty-seven men spread sixty-seven loads of mountain soil on the grounds in half a day. In less than a year members completed the landscaping.[33]

The Milton Ward of the Morgan Stake, noted a December 9 article, "takes a well-deserved place on the rapidly growing list of successes under the Church beautification program directed by the Presiding Bishopric." In 1930 the ward tore down its 1875 building and in subsequent years completed and paid for a new building. Then they landscaped the grounds and installed an attractive fence around the property.[34]

As 1939 ended, an article in the *Deseret News* reviewed the prior decade's chapel building and beautification efforts. That period witnessed a "progressive building program," the article said, matched in recent years by a strong beautification program by which "many wards have produced outstanding results to date."[35]

Meanwhile, many state organizations supporting beautification, led by the state agricultural extension service, began to unite and coordinate their efforts for an eight-year plan (preparing for the state's centennial), among them the Centennial Commission, the Farm Bureau, garden clubs, Utah's Nurserymen's Association, state highway people, the State Board of Health, and others.[36]

A Firm Foundation

1940: MANY NON-LDS ORGANIZATIONS PUSH BEAUTIFICATION

During 1940, many secular Utah organizations pushed beautification, encouraged by the state's Centennial Commission. On January 31, 1940, the Salt Lake County Beautification Committee, which Bishop Ashton chaired, held a "Beautification Fiesta" in the Salt Lake Tabernacle to raise funds and promote civic beautification. Local high school students provided musical numbers, and local businesses donated money in return for Fiesta tickets. The Fiesta's printed program included a logo that read, "Let's talk about BEAUTIFICATION until everyone is doing it," and this promotional statement: "One of the major projects to be put over by the STATE CENTENNIAL CELEBRATION COMMITTEE this year, is to clean up, improve, and beautify our homes, public places and surroundings. . . . This Fiesta is the opening 'gun,' our start in a campaign to make every Salt Lake City and Salt Lake County citizen beautification minded."

The Utah Landscape Improvement Committee, formed in 1938, cooperated with numerous state organizations by 1940, which shows how extensive the movement was statewide. These included:

- Junior Chamber of Commerce (Jaycees)
- Farm Bureau
- Future Farmers of Utah
- US Forest Service
- Utah Federated Women's Clubs
- The Church of Jesus Christ of Latter-day Saints
- *Salt Lake Tribune*
- American Legion
- Utah elementary and secondary schools
- Catholic Church
- Brigham Young University
- State Board of Health
- Southern Civic Clubs
- Northern Civic Clubs

The Church's Beautification Movement, 1937–47

- Presbyterian Church
- Utah Nurseryman's Association
- Salt Lake Council of Women
- State Rural Service
- Utah State Agricultural College Extension Service
- Utah Highway Commission[37]

An April 1940 *Relief Society Magazine* editorial noted the "vigor with which both state and Church are conducting improvement and beautification campaigns." It said that plans for 1947 called for a gigantic statewide celebration, "but in order that our highways, our homes, and our cities be equally attractive, and reflect a refined and cultured people, the Utah Centennial Beautification Committee is enthusiastically laying the ground work for an extensive beautification program." The Church, the editorial assured, is working in close cooperation with the Centennial Committee.[38] That same month the Salt Lake City Jaycees sponsored a cleanup drive called "Reside in Pride." Their campaign, supported by the Centennial Commission, involved school children and asked home owners and business owners to clean up and paint.[39]

THE MOVEMENT IN HIGH GEAR IN 1940

Church beautification promotions brought results. By January 1940, most stakes and wards had beautification committees, and during the year wards and stakes submitted 150 landscape plans to Church headquarters.[40] All that year Church publications promoted beautification and cited examples of what members were accomplishing.

The Church committee's beautification announcements by then followed a calendar cycle. During springtime, the push was for postwinter cleanups, pruning, and planting, including lawns. Summer encouragements dealt with outdoor and indoor construction, repairing, painting, and thorough cleaning of buildings. Fall focuses were on postsummer cleanups, planting of shrubs and trees, and planning for winter indoor improvements. For example, regarding "the importance of a fall clean-up" the *Relief Society*

Magazine's October 1940 issue warned that "during the summer months there has been an accumulation of trash, waste and debris in many places. Weeds and other growths should be removed and burned. All the breeding and hibernating places of insects should be destroyed before fall and winter storms come."[41] Winter counsel dealt with keeping local committees organized, thorough inspections of buildings, pruning, drafting plans for the next year, and submitting applications to the Church for landscaping and improvement expenditures.

Church periodicals continued to feature beautification examples. January 1940's *Progress of the Church* posted photographs of men on a truck with shovels and women serving lunch outside a ward building, and an accompanying article told about members beautifying the grounds for the Shelley Idaho Stake Tabernacle. In the spring of 1939, according to the article, about two hundred members brought their teams, trucks, and tractors with which they leveled and prepared the grounds and installed a sprinkler system.[42] In another January article, custodian Robert C. Marchant of the Yalecrest Ward told how he landscaped a plot north of the chapel's east wing, measuring seventy by one hundred and ten feet, that had been a weed patch and dumping area. In the fall of 1938, the bishop decided that area should be planted with flowers, so Brother Marchant cleared, plowed, and fertilized the soil. He bought $2.10 worth of flower seeds, nursing some starts in the boiler room that winter. In the spring he planted and transplanted. By mid-June, the different colored flowers began to bloom and his carefully designed color scheme emerged.[43]

From Duchesne County in Utah's hinterlands came a remarkable story of students beautifying their newly built seminary building, for which funds had run out before it could be painted, furnished, and landscaped. The stake was unable to help, so Altamont Seminary teacher Walter Kerksiek turned to the Church Beautification Committee for assistance. Learning that his 40 percent share of costs could be in labor, he rallied the students. Students planned exterior and interior improvements. They needed lawns, flowers, bulbs, a fence, sidewalk, and shrubbery outside, and electrical fixtures, drapes, curtains, and shades inside. Tables and a desk needed painting. By summer of 1937, they received Church approval. A contractor donated time and oversaw seminary boys who poured seven hundred square feet of cement walks around the building. Because it was too late to seed a lawn, that fall they planted bulbs—tulips, hyacinths, and daffodils—and applied three coats of paint to the building and roof. In November they painted the interior. Students selected colors for the curtains and drapes and stains for the woodwork. They became so invested in the project that when it was finished, seminary attendance went up and increased respect for the building was evident.[44]

Seminary teacher Kerksiek, as bishop of the Mount Emmons Ward, also led a campaign to beautify its chapel and grounds. When he started, "people had disrespect for the buildings and grounds. Cars were parked anywhere." Rooms were dirty, and weeds grew around the chapel. Bishop Kerksiek made beautification plans and motivated ward members to get involved. "We had the deacons plant lawn under supervision and they also

Chapel project in Wayne Stake. (Deseret News, *Church section,* December 21, 1940.)

dug the holes and carried water for the shrubs we planted. The Relief Society and the young girls of the town planted the flowering plants. We had as high as thirty women and girls on their knees sorting out plants." "It just thrills me to note the change in attitude," the bishop said. "They are proud of the church and what it stands for, where before they were ashamed of the place and many showed disgust." In fact, "the spirit of reverence has changed so much that my wife and I can't get over it." And the beautifying became contagious. In their poor community, many homes were log houses, some with dirt floors. "During the last summer" the bishop reported, "six homes were painted that have stood for years and never been painted before. Three fences were torn down (barb wire) and picket fences put in their places and painted white."[45]

As the 1930s ended, unemployment numbers were dropping. Perhaps for that reason, Church beautification releases rarely mentioned the movement's purpose to engage the unemployed. However, the March 1940 *Progress of the Church* did make note of it in an article titled "Welfare Labor in Beautification Programs," which reminded stake presidencies and bishoprics "that where able-bodied men are receiving welfare assistance and the local groups are unable to provide other work for them in exchange for the assistance rendered, that they be assigned to assist in the beautification programs in either public or private projects under the direction of the Beautification Committees of the ward or stake." A Church welfare project that spring improved the east entrance to the Manti Temple grounds. Stakes in the temple district provided work crews and trucks to haul soil. After removing steps and a retaining wall, the approach was resloped, which required one-hundred-thousand yards of soil and an enormous amount of cement and stone to be hauled one and a half miles.[46]

The Primary developed a clever springtime poem for children: "Get a rake, a garden make, and find good seeds to sow, pull a weed, plant a seed, and watch the flowers grow."[47]

During April 1940 general conference, Elder Stephen L Richards delivered a major beautification address entitled "Beautification Plan a Tribute

The Church's Beautification Movement, 1937–47

Manti Temple grounds welfare beautification project. (Deseret News, *Church section, June 15, 1940.*)

to the Pioneers," which became a Church Beautification Committee pamphlet. While nature is beautiful, he observed, "What a strange paradox it seems that civilization should be so unbeautiful." Almost all people "are sensitive to color, to form and symmetry, so that good architecture and good landscaping with trees, flowers, shrubs and lawns have a very appreciable effect, even though sometimes unconsciously, upon all persons." He also observed that "every dirty, unkept, unpainted, and shabby home; every unsightly outbuilding; every old corral and fallen fence; every scraggly dead tree; every barren and forbidding school house and church and courthouse with broken windows, curled shingles and other evidences of neglect; every littered and weedy vacant lot, street and highway is a definite liability."[48]

In May the Church committee restructured ward beautification operations and called for specific assignments for specific quorums and auxiliaries. High priests, for example, were assigned to remove fire hazards and see that chapels were painted inside and out. Relief Society sisters were to keep the building's interior clean, including floors, carpets, curtains, and the sacrament service.[49]

Beautification concerns led to a historic meeting in the Salt Lake Tabernacle on October 3, 1940. That day the First Presidency and Presiding Bishopric met with bishoprics—all of the Church's bishoprics were invited—in the largest-ever gathering of bishoprics, with 1,068 wards represented. There, the Church Beautification Committee presented illustrated talks about the upkeep, renovation, and landscaping of Church buildings.[50]

That month the committee reported that during the previous twelve months, "real progress has been made."[51] In a unique beautification project, a new stake in Riverside, California, transformed five hundred five- and ten-gallon paint cans into nicely painted trash cans for stake families.[52] A November article praised the Salt Lake City Tenth Ward, where behind their chapel ward members transformed a sunken vacant lot covered with weeds into a raised, paved recreation spot with a massive fireplace at one end for outdoor cooking and campfire suppers. "As far as possible the labor was furnished by men in the ward, many of them working under the Church Welfare Plan."⁵³

A Union Ward beautification project involved cleaning, painting, and remodeling the ward building; improving drainage, parking, and landscaping; installing a new roof; and repairing and painting interior rooms. A Wayne Stake project became a model effort that the Beautification Committee often referred to. In that stake every chapel and building became "immaculately" clean and in perfect repair, with grounds newly landscaped. A year earlier those chapels and buildings were "badly run down, clumsily patched in many places, not patched at all in others, unpainted, and generally in very bad condition." Nine tons of paint were used.⁵⁴

At the end of the year, the committee issued a warning about cleaning up fire hazards in light of the Syracuse Ward chapel in the North Davis Stake, which had recently burned to the ground. They also sent out an assurance from the state tax commission that beautification improvements would not increase property taxes, a fear many homeowners felt when considering home improvements.⁵⁵

1941: A NEW EMPHASIS ON HOME BEAUTIFICATION

With chapel upgrades going so well, the Church expanded its program to include members' homes. In March 1941, committee secretary Kirkham made a major announcement that in anticipation of the centennial, "members have been asked to beautify their homes," not only because "thousands of people are coming to our State and will visit our homes and surroundings," but also because "this beautification program is a good thing to do for our own benefit and pleasure." To help encourage home beautifying, he said, the committee had created an awards program and a one hundred-point scorecard. Each home achieving at least seventy points would receive an award from the Presiding Bishop's Office. Wards were to select awards committees from among their beautification committee members, who

A Firm Foundation

then would use the two-page scorecard (with detailed instructions for each category) and award beautification points.⁵⁶ Categories were:

- Clean-up   20 points
- Condition of Buildings   20 points
- Landscape Principles   30 points
- Care During the Season   10 points
- Condition of Lawn   10 points
- Importance of Trees   10 points

In the Church Archives are copies of a "First Year 1941 Award in the L.D.S. Church Program of Home Beautification," along with similar ones for 1942, 1943, and 1944.⁵⁷

In line with the Centennial Commission's program, Deseret Stake in Millard County set out to beautify Church properties in March and April. James Kirkham, along with the stake beautification chairman, visited all

Beautification ad, Deseret News, *March 15, 1941.*

422

the wards to help them plan. He told them that "the Church will give all the paint necessary to beautify church properties, and each ward is to put it on," inside and out.[58] However, a paint shortage developed by summer. "If there is any one thing we need in Sevier County more than another it is paint," Sevier Stake president Irvin Warnock informed the Presiding Bishopric in August 1941. His people needed paint for homes, fences, barns, outbuildings, and meetinghouses. He asked if ward and stake orders could be pooled in order to get cost reductions "either directly from the factory or thru your office."[59] What answer he received is not known.

1942–45: WORLD WAR II DISRUPTS BEAUTIFICATION

The United States formally entered World War II in December 1941. A Church editorial from 1946 said in retrospect that "at the time this country entered the war the Church had in full swing a program for improving, remodeling, repairing, beautifying and landscaping of all ward and stake property. Of necessity the wartime restrictions brought a curtailment to this program, and only needed maintenance was carried out during the past few years."[60] In March 1942, the committee admitted, "Because of war activities, conditions are changing so rapidly that it is difficult at this time to work out in detail a Beautification Program for the coming year." During 1942, the Church's beautification messages emphasized the need to keep morale up through beautiful homes, good health through cleanliness, and thorough cleanups "reaching every nook and corner" to improve the house and yard and to find salvage items to donate.[61]

Some ward beautifying continued to take place. As one example, that spring seventy-five members from two Salt Lake wards, mostly young people, spent an afternoon and evening raking debris from the grounds around their common meetinghouse and removing rocks in buckets and wheelbarrows. Older men leveled the ground and prepared it for a lawn. They could not do extensive planting of trees and shrubbery, only annual flowers.[62]

War shut down the state's Centennial Commission. It had met regularly from September 1939 to November 1940, then intermittently until June 5, 1942, when Utah's Governor Maw deactivated it for the war's duration.[63] However, the retiring commission expressed hope that the beautification part of the program could continue, carried forward by the LDS Church, the Agricultural College, and civic and women's groups.[64]

On December 7, 1942, the War Production Board in Salt Lake City wrote an urgent appeal to the Presiding Bishopric, which was soon passed along to ward bishops. The message requested "that all tin cans, fats and greases, rags, rubber, scrap iron and steel be collected for the government." Instructions called for tin cans to be taken by children to school on specific days, fats and greases to be taken to any butcher for four cents a pound, and rags, rubber, scrap iron, and steel to be sold to any junk dealer.[65]

In March 1943, the Church committee announced a clean-up and conservation program to focus on maintaining property, gardening, salvaging war materials, eliminating fire hazards, promoting tire safety (cleaning up glass fragments, nails, and debris from streets, alleys, driveways, and yards), promoting sanitation to protect health, and beautifying with materials and labor at hand.[66] A year later, in March and April 1944, the *Relief Society Magazine* published articles about home gardens and growing roses. That May, James Kirkham repeated in a *Church News* article several standard admonitions about beautifying chapels and homes and urged ward committees and bishoprics to conduct clean-up programs outside and inside meetinghouses.[67]

Late in 1944, Governor Maw reactivated the state Centennial Commission, which resumed its meetings on November 24. War continued, but with 1947 barely three years away, the Commission had planning to do. Hopes for a World's Fair–type celebration then seemed shaky.[68]

1945 AND THE WAR'S END

In March 1945, with the centennial only two years away and war still on, Governor Maw announced that war would not blot out the centennial, though it might restrict the celebration. War or not, beautification plans must be ready if manpower and materials became available. "The State must take on a holiday attire," he reminded. "There is nothing in war's demands that requires broken-down fences, filthy corrals, dilapidated outbuildings or unpainted houses," so "let Utah, then, dress up in honor of her pioneer founders."[69]

At the behest of the Church Beautification Committee, Salt Lake mayor Earl J. Glade published a beautification appeal in the May 1945 *Relief Society Magazine* titled "He's Coming Home, Let's Spruce Up!" The war in Europe had nearly ended, so he urged city and state residents to create a "brilliant homecoming" for the returning troops by dressing up parking areas, walks, and roofs; cutting down aged and decaying trees; applying fresh paint; and cleaning alleys. Businesses and industry were encouraged to dress up too, by creating new store fronts, display windows, interiors, and improved signs. "Down with shacks and dumps!" he urged; "Out with rubbish and junk." He called for improved highways, parks, and cemeteries.[70]

May 8 was V-E (Victory in Europe) Day, but Pacific warfare continued until mid-August. In August, Union Pacific Railroad general manager Randall L. Jones felt that the "most serious" cleanup problem in Utah was vacant lots, the "dumping grounds filled with rubbish and breeding grounds for mice, rats, flies, and weed."[71] That same month, referring to dilapidated "leaning-Tower-of-Pisa cow barns and sheds," Church beautification chair, Bishop Ashton, encouraged members to "fix it or burn it."[72] Owners should ask of their buildings, "Is it worth saving?" If not, they should be torn down or burned before the centennial. He penned a poem called "Fix It or Burn It" that reads in part:

> The chimney needs fixing, the roof cries for paint
> The way the porch wobbles, would make one turn faint.
> The screens all are sagging the door knobs are gone,
> The flowers are dying, and look at the lawn.
> From basement to attic, it all looks the same.
> If the thing's not worth saving, then give it the flame.

> . . . Now Utah is planning a big National Show.
> In the year forty-seven, you surely all know.
> Let's fix-up and clean-up and burn-up a bit
> And make all our homes and our premises fit.
> . . . So let's show the traveler a much better view.
> Fix it or burn it—Yes, it means you!

When the war ended, and with the centennial so near at hand, the commission reduced plans from a World's Fair with crowds of tourists, and planned instead for a celebration designed for Utahns. Both the Church committee and the Centennial Commission recommitted to beautifying Utah in time for the revised celebration.[73]

1946: THE STATE'S BEAUTIFICATION PROGRAM TAKES PRIORITY

In February 1946, the resurgent Centennial Commission established a Department on Beautification, with Donald P. Lloyd as chairman. From then until July 1947, his department directed beautification work in Utah, with the Church program following its lead.[74] Five committees composed the state committee: Clean-up, Paint-Up, Fix-Up; Publicity and Public Relations; Planning and Zoning; Landscaping; and Parks and Recreation. In February, Utah's communities were each asked to organize five such committees.[75] Mayors and town presidents responded, creating in Utah a total of 141 committees with a membership of 1,300.[76]

In March 1946, Governor Maw gave a "green light" to the centennial by making $150,000 available for the Centennial Commission until the legislature provided more. Of that total, set amounts were earmarked, with $15,000 going to beautification.[77] On April 3, 1946, by governor's proclamation, a statewide "Clean-up, Paint-Up, Fix-Up" campaign began. Designed to stimulate civic pride, beautify the state, safeguard health, and create long-term planning, it pushed communities to take action. The Church urged stake and ward authorities to cooperate in the state's activities.[78] At fifty-four local meetings held in 1946, the state "Clean-Up, Paint-Up, Fix-Up" Committee promoted spring cleanup campaigns to improve parks, clean and improve roads and sidewalks, upgrade personal property, plant trees, and eradicate weeds.[79]

A summer campaign focused on improving hotels, motels, and restaurants in cooperation with the state Department of Health. For community committee projects the state committee obtained paint from the War Assets Administration and through wholesale purchases. Autumn saw pushes for painting, cleaning ditches, planning for winter, and removing rubbish. In winter the committees concentrated on pruning and removing trees, demolishing unused sheds and outbuildings, repairing and rebuilding fences, and removing trash. The local committees directed attention to improving such municipal properties as city entrances, main streets, and public parks and grounds. The state committee arranged for landscape architects and organizations, helped by cooperating nurseries, to visit one hundred communities and give lectures, slide presentations, and demonstrations regarding shrubs, trees, planting, and pruning.[80]

On November 16, 1946, sponsored by the Utah Beautification Committee, a statewide conference took place at the Newhouse Hotel in Salt Lake City. There, two nationally recognized city planners trained and encouraged three hundred and fifty local beautification committee members (two counties were not represented). As a follow-up, regional conferences were held in seven parts of the state.[81] Beaver City's cleanup became a year-end success story. "During the fall many muddy, ungraveled streets were resurfaced with gravel hauled from the city pits two miles south of the city. Unsightly shrubs and brush were removed, new bridges and culverts installed, and larger ditches straightened and deepened." This work was done in cooperation with the centennial "beautification spirit."[82]

Nationally, Sears Roebuck and Company sponsored prizes for cleanups each year, and for Utah in 1946 the town of Hinckley won the state sweepstakes award of $200 and a trophy, one of eight regional trophies, and a county award of $100. The Hon Cropper home in Hinckley won $125 for individual home improvements.[83]

1946: THE CHURCH'S BEAUTIFICATION EFFORTS CONTINUE

War had reduced meetinghouse improvements to only essential maintenance, so when the war ended the Church announced in January 1946 a new twofold beautification program to bring stake, ward, and mission buildings up to a high standard of appearance and keep them that way. War restrictions and manpower shortages had taken their toll: "Many ward buildings need repairs, new roofs, better heating equipment, new furnishings," the announcement noted: "Floors need attention. Many buildings need to be cleaned and renovated and painted inside and out to preserve property and to improve its appearance, class rooms added and other improvements to meet recent and changing conditions. These and others will be part of program that'll be carried out." Henceforth, stake building supervisors, by then an official position, would inspect all buildings and equipment at regular intervals and report what work needed to be done. Under this program, maintenance and conservation would be continuous, with wards helping to fund the improvements.[84]

Bishops learned in February 1946 that they should give each quorum a specific building or grounds beautification assignment because so much work was needed. One ward identified twenty-seven different projects to be considered.[85] In March the Church committee promoted a "1946 push 1947" effort that focused on Church properties, while the Centennial Committee directed home beautification and public projects. Saints were to cooperate with community committees, they advised, and "help put over the 1947 celebration."[86]

For ward buildings the committee promoted a four-part attack: cleanup, repairs, painting, and beautifying. They provided to-do lists for each part. Repairs, for example, included roofs, toilets, steps, chairs, benches, pews, light fixtures, walks, fences, gates, screens, glass, plaster, locks, floors, and equipment. Because "desired material may not be available," some work might be delayed but "there need be no delay, however, on the clean up program."[87]

President McKay, chair of Utah's Centennial Commission, focused his April 1946 general conference remarks on the approaching centennial.[88] Under normal conditions, he said, the centennial exposition would invite people to behold the wonders of Utah, see the achievements of the people, and participate in various festivals and entertainments. Original plans called for a wagon train reenactment from Winter Quarters and a reenactment of the Mormon Battalion march. But the war halted planning, and when planning resumed it was too late to build roads to Utah's scenic attractions and improve parks adequately. And "due to the housing shortage, and the inability of the commission to assure comfortable accommodations for the hundreds of thousands of tourists who could be induced to visit us next year, it has been thought advisable to approach our celebration from a different angle."

Instead, the celebration would be "by and for the people of Utah, and Utahns in nearby western states." Preparations were under way, President McKay said, for the presentation of historical pageants; musical, dramatic, and educational programs; and athletic attractions. But, he reminded, "There is one important feature of the celebration which was not discontinued during the war, the duty of making the state more attractive." He urged homeowners to "all join in the campaign . . . to paint houses, fences, barns, and other buildings and to maintain a general atmosphere of tidiness and neatness about the homes, barns, and corrals." Then he proposed that Utah Saints consider a second type of beautification campaign, one to eradicate vices and bad influences.[89]

A mid-April report said that the Church Beautification Committee and the centennial "statewide clean-up organization" were in "perfect coordination" in their cleanup activities in preparation for the centennial.[90] Late in April the Presiding Bishopric explained that new government restrictions forbade new building projects and repairs on buildings "without specific

Before and after beautification, Ioka Chapel, Roosevelt Stake. (Church News, January 5, 1946.)

authorization." The maximum allowable expenditure for churches, schools, and hospitals "used exclusively for charitable purposes" was $1,000. But, "without application" and with no limit on expenditures, the Church was permitted to do "repainting, repapering, sanding floors, repairing sidewalks, fences, bridges, wells, irrigation and drainage ditches, roads and streets, and repairing of existing mechanical equipment where no change in structure is made." Likewise, "there was no government rule or regulation preventing us from cleaning up our buildings and grounds, removing all trash, weeds, ashes, etc. or cleaning inside and outside of all buildings from basement to attic."[91]

On October 7, Bishop Ashton died. Presiding Bishop Richards made Bishop Wirthlin his first counselor and Thorpe B. Isaacson his second counselor. By then Utah and the Church had but one more spring season before the centennial. "The time is short, materials are scarce, and many beautification projects will be incomplete by next summer," the Presiding Bishopric said, but they called for "beautification landscaping" wherever possible.[92]

1947: THE CENTENNIAL

The first six months of 1947 saw a flurry of final cleanup and beautification projects throughout Utah. With time running out, Utah communities received instructions in December 1946 for a statewide "face lifting" program.[93] The state's Beautification Department sent communities a manual that called for as many as twenty special committees (inspection, fire prevention, vacant lots, schools, streets and alleys, front and back yards, dilapidated buildings and signs, and so forth). Using the slogan "The Time is Now! Plan—Beautify!" the manual suggested cleanup drives of at least two weeks duration with day one assigned to a parade, day two to safety, day three to repairs, and the other days similarly assigned.[94]

Cities and counties responded. Moab, for example, cleaned up between February 23 and 28, 1947, using block captains, city trucks to haul away trash and debris, high school students who agreed to be hired to help out, and cash prizes for the best improvements.[95] Millard County conducted a two-week campaign from April 21 to May 3 with weekdays in turn devoted to safety, weed eradication, front yards, pickups, flowers and gardens, vacant lots, painting, health, businesses, and so on, culminating with a community dance and crowning of the county's centennial queen.[96] During those two weeks, ten evergreens, forty-four shrubs, and a lawn were planted at the Hinckley elementary school and high school, LDS Primary children planted shrubs around the Hinckley chapel, and the local newspaper described specific improvements made by ten homeowners in the nearby town of Sutherland.[97]

Although scaled down from the World's Fair–type commemoration that had been envisioned, grand and extended centennial celebrations filled the summer of 1947.[98] A Centennial Exposition at the state fairgrounds stayed open for four months, and more than a half million people visited.[99] The Utah Symphony Orchestra and Opera traveled the state and gave performances, and four companies of college actors presented plays statewide. The Church resurrected a pageant performed in 1930 for the Church's centennial, "Messages of the Ages," which in 1947 was performed twenty-five times in Salt Lake City.[100]

June centennial events included the Holiday on Ice; MIA drama, dance, and music festivals; a concert at Brigham Young University by the Los Angeles Philharmonic Orchestra; an NCAA track-and-field meet; a Tabernacle Choir concert with a New York Metropolitan Opera baritone as soloist; a national horse show with the Jerry Colonna Exposition; and tennis Clay Court Championships.

During July, the centennial month, Utah had Independence Day celebrations, Western Motor Boat Championships, a Wild Animal Circus, and a Tabernacle Choir concert with another Metropolitan opera star, and hosted the National Governors' Conference. From July 19 to 24, Gene Autry and his Madison Square Garden Rodeo performed in Ogden.

Four days, July 21–24, marked the climax of the centennial. On July 21 the Broadway-caliber *Promised Valley* show opened in the University of Utah stadium, with production costs of $150,000 and featuring *Oklahoma* star Alfred Drake. During seventeen performances it drew 104,000 spectators.[101] On July 22 the Sons of the Utah Pioneers car caravan reenactment of the pioneer trek arrived in Salt Lake City to great fanfare. They had left Nauvoo on July 14, their cars decorated with plywood oxen cutouts and white canvas wagon tops. On the actual centennial day, July 24, the magnificent This Is the Place Monument, sixty feet wide and eighty-four feet high, was unveiled near the mouth of Emigration Canyon, and fifty thousand people attended its three dedications. Nighttime Pioneer Day parades with sixty lighted floats took place, in addition to the release of a Utah pioneer centennial postage stamp and receptions for surviving pre-1869 pioneers. Church President George A. Smith's picture appeared on the cover of *Time* magazine. An unprecedented 183,000 July visitors to Temple Square broke all existing records.[102] In August a professional football game between the Chicago Rockets and the Brooklyn Dodgers (football team) and race-car speed-record attempts at the Bonneville Salt Flats concluded the centennial events.

END OF THE BEAUTIFICATION CAMPAIGN

With centennial events well under way, the Church Beautification Committee disbanded, ending a busy decade of work. What results had they produced? Through articles, press releases, surveys, correspondence, speeches, conferences, and personal visits, Bishop Ashton, James Kirkham, and other committee members had created workable programs. Their directives had generated stake and ward beautification committees and prodded bishops to plan, apply for Church funds, and undertake improvement projects. As a result, untold thousands of repairs, upgrades, and landscape projects improved hundreds of chapels and grounds and enhanced thousands of individual homes. Thus, the Church's program met its goal to help improve Utah's appearance for the centennial. Church efforts supplemented and sometimes prodded efforts by the Utah Centennial Commission and other organizations promoting Utah's beautification.

Through three Depression years, four war years, and three postwar years the Church expended hundreds of thousands of dollars to fund chapel and grounds improvements. Wards paid their 40 percent and then 50 percent shares of costs through the members' donated materials and money and the labor provided by thousands of children, youth, women, and men. Unknown numbers of unemployed Church members receiving Church welfare assistance worked on the ward projects. Because of the LDS beautification program, a generation of Latter-day Saints became educated about and perhaps conditioned to the importance of having well-maintained meetinghouses and homes.

Bishops' reports indicate that when buildings and grounds looked good, members enjoyed coming to church more; and where members helped to beautify chapel and grounds, reverence increased and sacrament meeting attendance rose. Lake View Ward bishop August L. Johnson, for example, said beautification produced increased sacrament meeting attendance and reverence. When members "step in the church on a nice soft carpet, instead of on old boards," he said, "they want to whisper instead of shout."[103] A Granger Ward bishop attributed "increased attendance at practically all meetings . . . almost directly to the chapel beautification program."[104] After the Church campaign started, James Kirkham noted in early 1941, "Many reports have come to us which very definitely prove that the cleanliness and beauty, the appearance of the chapel, do have an influence on Church attendance."[105]

Once the centennial ended, institutional interest in church, home, and community beautification faded and programs folded. A June 1948 Presiding Bishopric letter responding to an Idaho ward custodian seeking beautification guidelines explained that "we did have, at one time, a Beautification committee, which directed this program with regard to the homes and public places, but since the centennial we have only worked with the church property" and even for it "we have not been sending out any material for Beautification programs." The letter then acknowledged that "at the present time the Beautification Program is at a standstill."[106] Through subsequent decades, while the Church's policies for meetinghouse construction and maintenance have passed through several phases, the Church has issued an occasional beautification reminder.[107] But no major crusade has ever again materialized.

The Church's Beautification Movement, 1937–47

NOTES

1. LeGrand Richards, interviewed by William G. Hartley, March 1, 1974, typescript, 17–19, Church Oral History Program, copy in Church History Library, Salt Lake City.
2. With cleaner, more beautiful chapels and better looking homes, Church leaders probably believed that members would become more refined, more middle-class Americans, which would also improve the image of the Church for proselytizing reasons.
3. Thomas Alexander, "Sylvester Q. Cannon and the Revival of Environmental Consciousness in the Mormon Community," *Environmental History* 3, no. 4 (October 1998): 488–507.
4. The Salt Lake Women's Chamber of Commerce, headed by Cornelia S. Lund and Alice Merrill Horne, launched a vigorous campaign in 1936 to clean the city's air with the intent of having tourism replace industry and manufacturing as the city's primary economic source. Ted Moore, "Democratizing the Air: The Salt Lake Women's Chamber of Commerce and Air Pollution, 1936–1945," *Environmental History* 12, no. 1 (January 2007): 80–106.
5. "Local Organization in Each Town Will Beautify Homes," *Murray Eagle*, April 22, 1937.
6. *Addresses Delivered at a Special Meeting*, July 2, 1937, Church History Library.
7. "Centennial Program For 1947 Planned," *Moab Times Independent*, June 3, 1938.
8. Gov. Herbert B. Maw, "Are We Getting Ready for the 1947 One-Hundredth Anniversary Program?" *Relief Society Magazine*, March 1945, 136.
9. Utah Centennial Commission (1947), Agency History, Item #180, Utah State Archives, Salt Lake City.
10. Maw, "Are We Getting Ready."
11. Church Improvement and Beautification Committee, minutes, ca 1920–1949, in Presiding Bishopric Files, Church History Library. The committee is cited hereafter as CIBC.
12. Marvin O. Ashton, "A Thousand Wards Join the Church-Wide Improvement Procession," *Improvement Era*, June 1937, 348–49.

13. The Church offered a hundred-dollar cash prize to the most improved building in each stake, fifty dollars for second and twenty-five dollars for third, with special awards for seminary buildings and mission homes.
14. M. O. Ashton, "L.D.S. Church Outlines Beautification Program," *Murray Eagle*, July 8, 1937.
15. See Mary R. Jack, "Opportunities for the Child in Beautification," *Deseret News*, Church section, August 7, 1937; and Annie Wells Cannon, "A Lilac Tree for Every Church Yard," *Deseret News*, Church section, September 11, 1937.
16. CIBC, minutes, May 27, 1937.
17. CIBC, minutes, June 9, July 21, and October 11, 1937.
18. CIBC, minutes, October 4, 11, and 18, 1937.
19. Clifton Ward, Oneida Stake, Bishop's Report to the Church Improvement and Beautification Committee, June 28, 1937, in CIBC Files.
20. "Addresses Delivered at a Special Meeting," July 2, 1937, Church History Library.
21. Preston Fourth Ward, Bishop's Report to the Church Improvement and Beautification Committee, 1937, in CIBC Files.
22. Church Improvement and Beautification Committee to the First Presidency, December 16, 1937, in CIBC files.
23. *Our Churches Shall Be Beautiful* (Salt Lake City: Improvement and Beautification Committee of the Church Security Program of The Church of Jesus Christ of Latter-day Saints, 1938), 1.
24. The "blossom as the rose" phrase comes from Isaiah 35:1. The March 1938 *Relief Society Magazine* quoted Brigham Young: "Beautify your gardens, your houses, your farms; beautify the city." See also "Beautification Program Started with the Arrival of Pioneers in Utah," *Deseret News*, Church section, March 9, 1940, which carried April 14, 1861, quote by pioneer Church leader Daniel H. Wells, and James M. Kirkham's "Home and Community Beautification Was the Pride of the Pioneers," *Improvement Era*, August 1940, 450.
25. "Clean-Up! Paint-Up! Rake-Up!" *Improvement Era*, March 1938, 179.
26. Mary R. Jack, "Children's Part in Church Beautification," *Deseret News*, Church section, September 24, 1938. The August 1938 issue of *Progress of the Church*

included before and after pictures of a beautified chapel. In the September issue Idaho Primary boys with shovels were pictured in front of a church.

27. "Beautification at St. George Temple," *Deseret News*, Church section, January 14, 1939.

28. CIBC Minutes, August 18, 1939. James Mercer Kirkham (1873–1957) began full-time work for the Presiding Bishopric after filling a genealogical mission in Europe in 1937. He had been a Lehi businessman and newspaper publisher, Genealogical Society director, *Church News* assistant general manager, and mission president (1934–37). See El Moine W. Kirkham booklet *James Mercer Kirkham: Highlights of His Successful Life* (1961).

29. "Beautification Landscaping Essential," *Church News*, November 9, 1946.

30. A report about the Grandview Ward said the Church paid 50 percent of landscaping costs; see "Successful Beautification Program Follows Construction of Grandview Ward Chapel." *Deseret News*, Church section, November 25, 1939. An undated form with Presiding Bishopric 1940 materials says the Presiding Bishop's office participated in 50 percent of the cost of a renovation program and 50 percent of landscaping expenses except for soil.

31. "Welfare Project Provides Beautiful Chapel," *Progress of the Church*, January 1939.

32. "Beauty Lends Interest to Temple Block," *Deseret News*, Church section, September 23, 1939.

33. "Successful Beautification Program."

34. "Milton Ward Members United Through Successful Building and Beautification Campaign," *Deseret News*, Church section, December 9, 1939.

35. "Churches Improved During Decade through Progressive Architecture, Beautification," *Deseret News*, Church section, December 16, 1939. Members of the beautification committee then were Clyde Edmunds of the General Church Security committee; Oscar A. Kirkham, Jennie B. Knight, Relief Society; Axel A. Madsen, YMMIA; Rose Bennett, YWMIA; Mary Jack, Primary; George A. Holt, Sunday School; Irving T. Nelson, Church landscape architect; and Howard J. McKean, building committee.

36. "County Agent Column: General Clean-Up Plan," *Millard County Chronicle*, February 16, 1939.

37. "Organizations Pledge to Support Landscaping," 1940, CIBC.
38. "Editorial: Beautification," *Relief Society Magazine*, April 1940, 254–55.
39. "Salt Lakers Join JayCee Drive," *Deseret News*, April 13, 1940, 7.
40. "Beautification Committee Explains Procedure in Improvement Campaigns," *Deseret News*, Church section, January 27, 1940; James Kirkham, "Women's Part in the Church Beautification Program," *Relief Society Magazine*, March 1941, 209–10.
41. "Importance of a Fall Clean-up in Beautification Program," *Relief Society Magazine*, October 1940, 701–2.
42. "Beautification Program Activities," *Progress of the Church*, January 1940.
43. Robert C. Marchant, "Flowers in Church Beautification," *Deseret News*, Church section, January 20, 1940.
44. Walter Kerksiek, "Students Figure in Beautification Program at Altamont Seminary," *Deseret News*, Church section, February 24, 1940; see also clipping from *Week Day Religious Education*, CIBC.
45. Bishop Walter Kersiek to Irving Nelson, Presiding Bishop's Office, September 19, 1940, CIBC.
46. "Church Welfare Project Improves Manti Temple Grounds," *Deseret News*, Church section, June 29, 1940.
47. "Now Is the Time to Beautify," *Progress of the Church*, April 1940.
48. Apostle Stephen L. Richards, conference address, April 7, 1940, "The Beautification Plan: A Tribute to the Pioneers," *Deseret News*, Church section, April 27, 1940.
49. "A Division of Responsibility for Beautification Work," *Progress of the Church*, May 1940.
50. "Special Meeting for All Bishoprics October 3," *Improvement Era*, October 1940, 616, and "Righteous Living Keynote of October Conference," *Improvement Era*, November 1940, 670.
51. "Zion Must Be Beautiful," *Progress of the Church*, October 1940.
52. "Novel Beautification Aid in Riverside," *Improvement Era*, October 1940, 603.
53. "Unusual Beautification Project," *Deseret News*, Church section, November 16, 1940.

54. "Union Ward Works on Beautification," *Deseret News*, Church section, December 14, 1940; "Wayne Stake Beautification," *Deseret News*, Church section, December 21, 1940; the report of nine tons of paint is in "Commence Work on Beautification Church Edifaces," *Millard County Chronicle*, April 3, 1941.
55. "Beautification Will Not Increase Taxes," and "Could This Have Been Your Chapel?" *Progress of the Church*, November 1940.
56. James M. Kirkham, "Clean-Up Fix-Up Paint-Up and Plant for the Centennial," *Deseret News*, Church section, March 15, 1941.
57. CIBC. Further research might show if the home awards program continued after 1944.
58. "Commence Work on Beautification of Church Edifices," *Millard County Chronicle*, April 3, 1941.
59. Irvin Warnock, Sevier Stake President, to the Presiding Bishopric, August 31, 1941, CIBC.
60. "New Two-Fold Beautification Program Will Be Church-Wide," *Church News*, January 5, 1946.
61. "Beautification Program as an Aid to Morale," *Progress of the Church*, February 1942; "Clean-Up To Receive Most Stress: Beautification of Homes, Churches to Continue," *Deseret News*, Church section, March 28, 1942. In the May 1942 *Relief Society Magazine*, James Kirkham named four "Weapons Women May Use" to help secure victory for the democracies: promoting good health, growing victory gardens, cleaning homes and surroundings, and salvaging materials needed by the war effort.
62. "Clean-Up Drive Made by S. L. Ward," *Deseret News*, May 2, 1942.
63. Centennial Commission Reports, Utah State Archives.
64. Centennial Commission, minutes, June 5, 1942, in Centennial Commission (1947) Minutes, 1939–48, Utah State Archives.
65. "Bishops Should Urge Cooperation in Government Salvage Drive," *Progress of the Church*, January 1943.
66. "Clean-up and Conservation Program for 1943," *Progress of the Church*, March 1943. These instructions were repeated in "Church Clean-up Drive: Suggestions Given for Spring Campaign," *Church News*, Church section, April 3, 1943. After

August 1943, the *Progress of the Church* ceased publication, replaced by an expanded Church section of the *Deseret News* (later called *Church News*).

67. James M. Kirkham, "Church Stresses Beautifying Homes, Chapels," *Church News*, May 27, 1944.
68. Maw, "Are We Getting Ready."
69. Maw, "Are We Getting Ready."
70. Mayor Earl J. Glade, "He's Coming Home, Let's Spruce Up!" *Relief Society Magazine*, May 1945, 282–83.
71. Randall L. Jones, "The Vacant Lot—Something Must Be Done about It," *Relief Society Magazine*, August 1945, 465–67.
72. Marvin O. Ashton, "Fix It or Burn It," *Improvement Era*, August 1945, 446–47.
73. As explained in David O. McKay, "The Utah Centennial," Sunday morning session of conference, *Church News*, April 13, 1946.
74. "Beautification Urged by Leaders," *Church News*, March 9, 1949.
75. "Communities Requested to Name Committees for Beautification Program," *Murray Eagle*, February 7, 1946.
76. Final Report of the Utah Centennial Committee for Beautification, 1947, Centennial Commission (1947) Reports, Utah State Archives, 55.
77. "Centennial Gets Green Light," *Murray Eagle*, March 21, 1946.
78. "Statewide Cleanup Pushed," *Davis County Clipper*, April 12, 1946.
79. Department on Beautification Final Report, 1947, in Centennial Commission 1947 Reports, Utah State Archives, 57.
80. Department on Beautification Final Report.
81. Department on Beautification Final Report. The planners were Carl Feiss of Denver and L. Deming Tipton of San Francisco. Feiss criticized the highway from Ogden to Salt Lake City for a lack of planning that made it a "hodgepodge of signs and uncontrolled building which has wrecked the efficiency of the road and spoiled the beautiful scenery of the mountains and the valleys." See an account of the meeting in "Utahns Vow Support to Beautification," *Deseret News*, November 18, 1946.
82. "Beaver City Cleans Up For Centennial," *Murray Eagle*, December 19, 1946.

The Church's Beautification Movement, 1937–47

83. "Hinckley Wins State Awards for Clean-Up," *Millard County Chronicle*, August 28, 1947.
84. "New Two-Fold Beautification Program."
85. "On Beautifying Our Surroundings," *Church News*, February 23, 1946.
86. "Church Program for Improvement and Beautification," *Church News*, March 16, 1946.
87. "Church Program for Improvement and Beautification" and "Suggestions on Beautification Made from Presiding Bishop's Office," *Church News*, March 30, 1946.
88. McKay, "The Utah Centennial."
89. McKay, "The Utah Centennial." In line with President McKay's suggestion, Salt Lake City's police chief asked the city council to revoke the licensing of card playing tables and marble games in the city's taverns. The city had granted ninety-one licenses for card tables to fifteen establishments, earning $3,600 in fees. The police chief said revocations would help control gambling during the Centennial. The city council concurred with his request. See "Police Chief Opens Drive on Gambling, Marble Games, Card Tables to Be Cleared Out," *Deseret News*, August 8, 1946, 1.
90. "Statewide Cleanup Rushed," *Davis County Clipper*, April 12, 1946.
91. "Presiding Bishopric Endorse 'Clean-up' for Centennial," *Church News*, April 27, 1946.
92. "Beautification Landscaping Essential," *Church News*, November 9, 1946.
93. Editorial, "Will 'Dress Up' Utah," *Murray Eagle*, December 6, 1945.
94. J. B. Carlos, comp. and ed., Utah Centennial Commission Beautification Department, *Working Manual*, Utah Centennial Commission, 1946, CHL, 31–50.
95. "Centennial Clean-up Campaign For Next Week Mapped; All Citizens Urged to Join the Drive," *Moab Times Independent*, February 20, 1947.
96. "Communities Join Forces to Clean up and Beautify," *Millard County Chronicle*, April 17, 1947.
97. In 1949, the Presiding Bishopric urged ward bishops and stake building supervisors, using ward organizations, to devote a "day or two" to repair, clean, paint, and plant but not do major landscaping or painting projects; "Beautification Urged by

Leaders," *Church News*, March 9, 1949; "Planting Done at Hinckley Schools" and "Sutherland Tells of Beautification," *Millard County Chronicle*, April 24, 1947.

98. General Report 1947 Utah Centennial Commission, 1948, Utah State Archives. The summary of Centennial events given here is drawn from weekly listings of the upcoming Centennial events posted in local newspapers in June, July, and August.
99. "Exposition Attendance High," *Davis County Clipper*, September 19, 1947.
100. "Centennial Pageant Ends, Is Seen by 130,000 in 25 Nights," *Deseret News*, June 7, 1947.
101. "Promised Valley Success," *Tooele County Chronicle*, August 22, 1947.
102. "Monument Attracts Visitors," *Davis County Clipper*, August 15, 1947.
103. "Lake View Ward Writes Page of Success in History of Church Beautification Program," *Deseret News*, Church section, November 18, 1939, 5.
104. "Chapel Beautification Increases Attendance," *Deseret News*, Church section, October 21, 1939.
105. James M. Kirkham, "The Value of Appearances," *Improvement Era*, February 1941, 82, 120–21.
106. Presiding Bishopric to Ernest Blaser, Rexburg, Idaho, June 14, 1948, CIBC.
107. During the 1970s, President Spencer W. Kimball, in several major addresses, urged members to beautify church buildings, homes, and communities. See *Ensign*, May 1975, 4–5; November 1975, 4–6; May 1976, 124–25; November 1977, 4; and November 1979, 4.

Jessica Christensen and Mary Jane Woodger

19

Ardeth Greene Kapp's Influence on the Young Women Organization

T̲ʜᴇ Church of Jesus Christ of Latter-day Saints welcomes inspiration from members in leadership positions to influence the Church as a whole. Ardeth Greene Kapp epitomizes such leader-members in her ecclesiastical calling as ninth president of the Young Women organization (1984–92). Exerting her gifts and skills to direct this organization, Kapp developed major elements in the Young Women program, including the revised *Personal Progress* book and official motto, logo, and theme.[1] Her life experiences previous to this call primed her to lead the Young Women organization and make these contributions. Kapp herself expressed this idea: "I didn't recognize [how parts of my life led up to later events] until I looked back. And I thought, oh my goodness, the Lord does lead our lives."[2] Long before she revised the Young Women program, Kapp practiced foundational elements encouraged in

---

Jessica Christensen is a graduate of Brigham Young University. Mary Jane Woodger is a professor of Church history and doctrine at Brigham Young University.

the Personal Progress program, including keeping a journal, developing personal interests, and worshipping in the temple. Her early life evidences her personal tendency to innovate, respect the priesthood, lead with a plan, and sincerely connect with those she led. Furthermore, her educational pursuits enhanced her later success where she learned about the necessity of cooperation between teacher and student and the importance of being attentive to individuals. Kapp's family, specifically her parents and sisters, cultivated the traits that later defined her leadership. Though Kapp acknowledges that hers has been "just an ordinary life, anybody could relate to it, it's not [the life of] somebody that is born brilliant or born wealthy," it is apparent that her life experiences prepared her for leadership of the Young Women organization.[3]

Several notable events occurred in the Church during Kapp's service as general Young Women president. The first Young Women satellite broadcast in 1985 introduced the new Young Women values and theme. That year the new *Personal Progress* book was released with age-group mission statements, an official motto, and an official logo. The following year, the first Young Women worldwide celebration was observed.[4] Kapp's unique background and personality proved complimentary to each of these events.

Before Kapp served as general Young Women president and revised the organization, Personal Progress consisted of these areas of focus: spiritual awareness, service and compassion, homemaking arts, recreation and the world of nature, cultural arts and education, and personal and social refinement. Young women received a certificate of progress indicating their accomplishments in the program each year. They were expected to set goals, record regular church attendance, and live standards of personal worthiness.[5] When she was a ward MIA president, Kapp felt that "the individual awards seemed to be based mostly on attendance and other measurable things" and that the Mutual program focused on self-improvement rather than the gospel. Also, she noted that "activities were the things that had first priority" during her service at the ward level.[6]

Ardeth Greene Kapp's Influence on the Young Women Organization

Kapp's presidency revised the Personal Progress program in 1989. The new program consisted of age-group responsibilities called value experiences that promoted gospel standards and directed young women to use the scriptures often. The book presented an official Young Women theme outlining seven values: faith, divine nature, individual worth, knowledge, choice and accountability, good works, and integrity. Young women were to select at least two experiences for each of the seven values every year in the program. A motto, "Stand for Truth and Righteousness," and logo, featuring the silhouette of a young women's face in the flame of a torch, were also introduced. This logo was used on a medallion that young women were given upon earning the Young Womanhood Recognition award.

"Much of what [Kapp] and her presidency put in place . . . remains to guide young girls," such as the basic structure of the *Personal Progress* book, the jewelry awarded to participants who complete the program, and the theme which is still recited at local and general Young Women gatherings today in a modified version. Her focus on the temple and celebration of sisterhood both continue to be major concepts promoted in the contemporary Young Women program. But in response to revelation, leaders since Kapp have modified aspects of the program, including the theme.[7] Just as Kapp felt that "everything that had been done before was right for that time" and that she was "building on the foundation of those who had done a wonderful job before," subsequent general Young Women presidencies have revised the program.[8] For instance, the Young Women general presidency added the clause "strengthen home and family" to the theme in 2001; this decision reflected "a desire to encourage young women to use their influence for good to bless their families and prepare for their future roles."[9] Later, in November 2008, the value "virtue" was incorporated in the theme because it provided "a pattern of thought and behavior based on high moral standards."[10] Before the general Young Women presidency announced this addition, they informed Kapp, who responded to their decision with faith in them as leaders. She said, "I believe in continuing revelation."[11]

A Firm Foundation

In addition, a new *Personal Progress* book was created in 2001 under the direction of Margaret D. Nadauld, who said, "This is not a new program. It is simply a revision." A record sheet was instituted, ten-hour projects became required for each value, more value experiences were elective, the three age-group pendants were discontinued, and the Young Womanhood medallion changed from the silhouette of a young woman to the spires of a temple.[12] Recently the *Personal Progress* booklet was revised again and now invites young women to complete experiences for the new eighth value, virtue. The medallion now depicts a beehive, rose, and wreath centered with a ruby, symbolizing virtue.[13]

Kapp's influence continues with the Young Women medallion that girls receive upon completing their Young Womanhood Recognition requirements. Recently this practice affected a young Brazilian woman, Liriel Domiciano, who received national recognition at Brazil's largest televised talent competition, *Raul Gil Amateur Show*. Although she was forbidden to discuss her religion on the air, she wore her Young Women medallion to let people know she was a member of the Church. She won the competition with her partner Rinaldo Viana, and many viewers noticed her jewelry and inquired how to obtain such a necklace.[14]

Clearly young women continue to encounter and be blessed by the Personal Progress program, Young Women medallion, and Young Women theme, all of which Kapp directed her attention to as general Young Women president.

INFLUENCE OF KAPP'S CHARACTER

Examining prominent focuses of the Personal Progress program reveals Kapp's direct influence. Many of the values promoted therein clearly correspond with her upbringing.

Journal keeping and letter writing. We first note that journal keeping is a major aspect of Personal Progress and an activity which Kapp faithfully engaged in throughout her life. Having accrued forty-seven personal journals, she counsels that "everybody should keep a journal."[15] The introduction to the 1989 *Personal Progress* book instructs young women that "keeping a journal is an important part of Personal Progress."[16] Most value experiences required the young woman to "record [her] feelings in [her] journal."[17] Furthermore, several forms were provided to assist young women in recording their personal and family histories.[18]

Value experiences asked young women to pen letters. One value experience suggested they "write a letter of appreciation" and another instructed them to "participate in activities that help you keep the Sabbath day holy [such as] . . . writ[ing] letters."[19] Kapp's legacy parallels these assignments; it has been described as a "ministry by mail." She has collected boxes of letters from young women and continues to correspond with several of these women today.[20] An avid letter writer, she exchanged letters with her husband, Heber, who began their correspondence when he wrote a thank-you letter after he was a guest in the Greene home as a young missionary. Ardeth responded by "thanking Heber for the thank-you letter."[21] As general Young Women president, she infused this personal mantra of the importance of letter writing into Young Women goals.

Interest development. The Personal Progress program encourages young women to develop interests and learn about subjects they are unfamiliar with. They are urged to create unique projects or experiences, allowing them to pursue personal interests. For instance, one value experience in the 1989 edition suggested that young women "start learning about a subject you might be interested in, such as medicine, computer science, teaching, retail sales, law, child development, scientific research, secretarial work, engineering, the fine arts, or writing."[22] While earlier editions focused on developing specific domestic skills, such as homemaking, dance, music, and literature, the program under Kapp's leadership expanded to encompass any worthwhile pursuit.[23]

An inherently curious youth, Kapp tenaciously studied and pursued her talents. For instance, as a child, she practiced writing a talk like the ones Elder Richard L. Evans gave during *Music and the Spoken Word*, the weekly broadcast of the Mormon Tabernacle Choir. She later tutored herself as she and Heber built their own home. Together they "drew house plans and put them on the ceiling in the bedroom. And then [they] got pieces of wood from a church [building] that was being built and then [they] built a model home."[24] Such eagerness to learn infiltrated the revised Personal Progress program by inviting young women to likewise develop a willingness to study.

Temple emphasis. While Kapp was still very young, her parents "gave [her] an eternal perspective" and highlighted the paramount presence of temple worship in one's life. This emphasis prepared her to construct Personal Progress as an avenue toward temple worship for young women.[25] Family trips to the Cardston Alberta Temple "taught [Kapp] to view the temple as the university of the Lord." As a child she developed a serious health condition mandating immediate surgery; her mother explained that she would arrange to have Ardeth's name placed on the temple prayer roll. Although she was then unfamiliar with the temple prayer roll, Kapp recognized something in the tone of her mother's voice that assured her all would be well.[26] As an adult, Kapp continued to value the temple: "In the temple, my soul has found peace concerning questions for which my mind had no answers."[27]

The temple became the most prominent aspect of the program Kapp revised. The Young Women theme conspicuously declared a goal to prepare young women to "make and keep sacred covenants, receive the ordinances of the temple, and enjoy the blessings of exaltation." Furthermore, the design of the *Personal Progress* book identified the desired outcomes of the young women's experience; the first page featured a tissue embossed with the outline of the Salt Lake Temple.[28] More value experiences directing young women to temple preparation were integrated in the updated version of the program. In addition to inviting girls to talk to a couple recently sealed in the temple about "the blessings an eternal marriage brings" or to "learn how to submit names for temple ordinances," the program prepared girls to be worthy to enter the temple by encouraging them to dress modestly, be honest, and pay a full tithe.[29] Kapp's fervent appreciation for the temple clearly contributed to the program's emphasis on temple preparation.

Ardeth Greene Kapp's Influence on the Young Women Organization

Recent revisions continue to prepare young women for the temple. When virtue was added to the theme, Elaine S. Dalton, general Young Women president, said, "We cannot get caught up with this new value of virtue without saying the reason for the value is the temple. . . . And the temple is the reason for everything we are doing in Young Women, because it will help these young women to come unto Christ."[30] The current Young Womanhood medallion features the spires of a temple. Additionally, the updated *Personal Progress* book features the temple on the cover because "the temple is the symbol for the youth of the Church."[31]

INFLUENCE OF KAPP'S PERSONALITY

Kapp's personal convictions fully equipped her to be a spiritual and logistical administrator in the Young Women organization. Certain that the priesthood represented God's authority, Kapp faithfully supported and adhered to the Brethren throughout her leadership, as seen in several episodes from her life. A woman who had consistently constructed detailed plans and responded to problems with unique solutions, Kapp used her skills to assist the Young Women organization. Her personality proved to be immensely influential in her leadership.

Women and the priesthood. Kapp acquired an understanding of how women and priesthood holders should interact early in life. When her father was called as a bishop, "her mom helped to make it possible" by doing the "behind-the-scenes things," and Kapp realized that her mother "was always in the wings, playing a major role."[32] Kapp later asserted, "There is only one organizational channel; . . . that's the priesthood channel." She added that it is "important for us to be in line with the present prophet."[33] This attitude was exhibited when priesthood leaders turned down a proposed Churchwide satellite broadcast for young women. Rather than indulging in bitterness and regret, she reported the unexpected news to the general board at a meeting that began with the hymn "We Thank Thee, O God, for a Prophet," followed by her testimony about adhering to priesthood leadership. She is clearly sincere when she says, "I believe in who the Brethren are and I don't question the revelation they receive."[34]

Purposeful planning. Although submissive to priesthood leadership, Kapp had developed strong leadership techniques of her own. Throughout her experience as a teacher, she developed creative, successful planning methods. In her childhood, she "learned to plan with a purpose, always asking what is it that we want to have happen."[35] As an elementary school teacher, Kapp "sequenced the lesson manuals and determined the rate of progress required to reach the goals [she] had set. [She] then marked the calendar accordingly in carefully measured portions" before the school year began. In short, her "goals for the year were clearly in mind."[36]

Kapp also used her planning skills while serving as general Young Women president by instituting a strategic planning room, where "white butcher paper lined the walls [and] the presidency and board members brainstormed ideas and created blueprints."[37] Furthermore, Kapp established a tradition of using the first board meeting of every year to "review, update, and [articulate] the vision of their calling."[38] She hoped her administration would be remembered for "changing the mindset from saying 'What shall we do?' to the question 'What do we want to have happen?'" so that the focus for Young Women would shift from activities to outcomes.[39]

Creative innovations. An innovator, Kapp enjoyed calculating how to respond directly to the needs of those around her. Several experiences before her role as Young Women president primed her to identify problems and address them. Perhaps the first time Kapp exercised this skill occurred when she commandeered phone equipment her grandmother used as the town operator to reconnect Bill and Sarah, young lovers who were recently separated and publicly refused to speak to each other unless the other person spoke first. Explaining that this seemed to be an emergency, Kapp relates that she allowed Bill to believe Sarah was calling him and Sarah to believe that Bill was calling her, thus resolving the conflict between the two.[40] On another occasion when she was employed as a training instructor for new service representatives at the Mountain States Telephone Company, Kapp again designed a remedy to a threatening malady. Noticing that several colleagues were disheartened, she instigated the Sunshine Club and "cheered up the whole office by leaving notes and complimenting and building up their associates." To gain admittance to the club, associates agreed to refrain from complaining and substitute positive comments for negative ones.[41]

These episodes display Kapp's resourceful abilities and inclination to resolve problems. When she was called as general Young Women president, she noted a lack of organized attention toward young women during a "critical time" when "women and a woman's role" were not understood. She felt that during the "struggling teenage years when things sometimes seem to be in turmoil" young women need to have access to "experiences that build confidence in their individual worth." In response, she organized a program aimed at strengthening young women's spirituality. With her board, she "studied [for the new Young Women program] for about a year . . . before [they] even came forward with a plan."[42] That plan consisted of a revised program with its motto, theme, and logo.

Universality. Kapp's leadership also notably respected the diverse backgrounds of the young women of the Church. Her Canadian hometown, Glenwood, Alberta, neighbored the Blood Indian Reservation and housed immigrants, including Kapp's German schoolmates.[43] Twice her father, Kent, gave cows to Australian immigrants.[44] Many of these people came to Greene's General Store, a family-operated community convenience store, and Kapp's mother taught her "to treat them all the same."[45] Here Kapp became conscious of diversity and the need to help people in their unique circumstances. As Kapp's presidency revised Personal Progress, they asked themselves, "Is it universal?," a question that seemed to drive all their decisions as leaders of a worldwide Church.[46]

During the Young Women satellite broadcast on November 10, 1985, "seven young women, each representing a different nationality, came out in native costume and recited one of the values."[47] Moreover, her speeches addressed every young woman "in every corner of the earth, in every family, every classroom."[48] In an invitation to all of the young women of the

Church to participate in a worldwide celebration, the general Young Women's presidency specifically stated that they "hoped this experience [would] help young women of every nation feel a bond of sisterhood by participating in the same event on the same day."[49] This statement indicates Kapp's understanding that young women are united in the gospel despite their various backgrounds.

In 1990, Kapp and her administrative assistant Carolyn Rasmus traveled to Asia, where they noted that "the principles of the Young Women's program [were] universal and applicable to young women in every culture." Every group of young women Kapp visited recited the theme, and many meetinghouses hung the banner or colors of the values.[50]

Elder Vaughn J. Featherstone of the First Quorum of the Seventy accurately describes Kapp as a woman who "feels deeply for people, and it doesn't matter what race, what nationality, what color they are."[51] This empathy and openness became integral in the programs Kapp developed, which embraced all cultures. Today young women can listen to talks from the annual general meeting online in their own language; there are dozens of options.[52]

INFLUENCE OF KAPP'S FORMAL EDUCATION ON HER TEACHING

Kapp's educational pursuits prepared her to serve as general Young Women president. Having acquired a bachelor's degree in elementary education from the University of Utah in 1964, Kapp additionally earned a master's degree in curriculum development from Brigham Young University in 1971. Subsequently she worked as a schoolteacher in Bountiful, Utah, and then became a supervisor in teacher education at Brigham Young University in 1966.[53] With her background as both a student and a teacher, she adopted effective didactic techniques designed to facilitate young people's development.

Equality between leaders and youth. Kapp believed in maintaining equality, respect, and cooperation. As a teacher, she once told her students they would receive extra credit points if they corrected words she misspelled on the board.[54] She asserts that her many students "taught [her] as much as [she] endeavored to teach them."[55]

This refusal to exalt herself as a leader presented itself during her tenure in the Young Women organization. Notice how the Young Women theme uses the pronoun "we." Leaders recite this with the girls, which shows that as leaders they are also striving for righteousness and are aware of their divinity.[56] Furthermore, Kapp candidly referred to her general board as "Young Women Servants of the Lord."[57]

Youth involvement. Kapp's unique technique of preparing opportunities for youth to learn, articulate, and live gospel standards greatly shaped her leadership. When she was a teacher she took her pupils outside to experience nature firsthand.[58] She related that "sometimes sharing important things with others is like seeing those things for the first time in renewed splendor."[59]

Likewise, again consider the Young Women theme, which invites girls to verbalize truth rather than just hear it recited, and the *Personal Progress* book, which necessitates that girls incorporate gospel principles into their lives rather than just talk about doing so. Furthermore, the Young Women presidency declared that the purpose of the worldwide celebration was to "provide every Latter-day Saint young woman with the opportunity to express her feelings concerning the Church and the Young Women Values." Young Women wrote their testimonies, then attached these messages to helium-filled balloons that were released at the same time worldwide on October 11, 1986.[60] Clearly Kapp's habit of directly involving her students in the acceptance of truth appeared during her leadership as general Young Women president.

Attention to individuals. Always conscious that the circumstances of those she led were varied, Kapp respected the individuals she interacted with. Kapp acquired an understanding of the need for such individualized attention as a young child in school. When her third-grade teacher became ill, Kapp and her classmates were advanced to the next class although they did not complete the year's work; as a result she felt like she was never able to catch up and subsequently struggled in school. Later she found that overcoming this challenge allowed her to "follow her [students'] thought patterns" and be sensitive to their lack of confidence. Countless anecdotes present Kapp's gracious attention to youth she encountered, whether at a youth camp, an institute class she taught, or letters seeking help when she served as general Young Women president.[61] For instance, when she noticed a young student apathetic to math but enthusiastic about vehicles, Kapp engaged him by "talking about numbers of jeeps and how many tires were needed to supply a fleet of jeeps."[62] In the preface to her book *The Gentle Touch*, Kapp writes her belief that "if a teacher is ever to be allowed into the private, sacred realm of a child's heart, . . . where lasting changes take place and lasting imprints are made, a sensitivity to the inner spirit of each child . . . is required."[63] The revised *Personal Progress* book instructs Young Women leaders that "each young women must feel that she is able to succeed in Personal Progress. There may be times when adjustments to Personal Progress requirements may be necessary to meet the needs of individual young women."[64] Kapp's childhood struggles in school served as an asset to her teaching in the classroom and from the pulpit at general conference by yielding an understanding of reaching the one and showing consideration for individual needs and circumstances.

INFLUENCE OF KAPP'S FAMILIAL RELATIONSHIPS

Kapp's upbringing substantially contributed to her leadership. Many of her grandparents, aunts, uncles, and cousins lived nearby her childhood home. Particularly appreciative of her ancestors, Kapp once responded to her father's comment that her hands looked like Grandma Greene's by saying "I hope my spirit looks like hers also."[65] While her family history evidently contributed to her desires for righteousness, her immediate family directly shaped her leadership abilities.

Her mother. Kapp concedes that her mother Julia (June) Leavitt Greene was "not the traditional kind of mother" but was "the best kind of mom" for her. June did not have hot cookies in the oven when her children came home from school, but at Greene's General Store she often put store-bought cookies in the bags of children who could not afford them. While Ardeth does not recall her mother reading stories to her, she does remember that June initiated the first lending library in Glenwood. And although June did not close her store to attend her children's school plays, she was instrumental in convincing the school district to hire reputable teachers.[66] June's unconventional methods of mothering showed Kapp that women can be capable, adroit, and influential, using their talents, interests, and personal styles to bless their families in unique ways.

Kapp's belief that "the spiritual dimension of a woman's faith weaves itself through the tapestry of eternity from one generation to the next" is validated in her reception of her mother's legacy.[67] Kapp was never blessed with her own children and perhaps her mother's unconventional mothering illustrated that she could strengthen home and family in various avenues as well. Always an active figure in young women's lives, Kapp consciously avoided taking the place of their mothers; rather, she "helped to forge bonds between the parents and their children."[68] As a teacher, she began parent-teacher conferences "by asking each parent how [she] might be of help, since [her] role was to assist the parent in his responsibility, rather than the parent accounting to [her], the teacher."[69] Kapp contributed to her sister Sharon's family by developing a close friendship with her niece Shelly. Sharon relates that "during Shelly's teenage years . . . she would talk to Ardeth. She would tell Shelly the same things I would have, but it was more credible coming from her."[70] Kapp pursued this concept of creative motherhood through her popular booklet titled *All Kinds of Mothers*, which discusses women's responsibility to nurture others, regardless of whether or not they have children of their own.[71] Furthermore, rather than specifically preparing young women to be mothers, the revised Personal Progress value experiences and theme assist young women in developing a nurturing character and a strong testimony of the gospel. If these ambitions were realized, young women would be prepared to contribute to families and to the kingdom of God whether or not they married or bore children.

Kapp's mother, June, further contributed to the leader Kapp became by recruiting her to work at Greene's General Store, a responsibility that made her feel "needed in the family."[72] When President Harold B. Lee "emphasized that it was time for the youth to assume greater leadership roles than in the past" Kapp was prepared as general Young Women president to promote this change.[73] She enthusiastically encouraged Young Women leaders to delegate responsibility to the girls as her mother had done in the country store. Kapp personally believed in making sure members "feel like they are an intricate part of building the kingdom."[74]

Her father. From her father, Edwin Kent Greene, Kapp adopted what she affectionately called his "wonderful teaching way" of using everyday experiences to explain gospel principles.[75] She says that the most valuable lessons occurred outside of the classroom when she was with her father in the field, and that "every moment with him was a teaching moment."[76] For instance, on one occasion Kapp accompanied her father to build a fire in the store's coal stove at a time when she was feeling left out of a particular social group. He addressed her concerns by explaining he had to put wood in the stove before they felt any heat—she also must feed a friendship before she felt its warmth.[77] Another day he taught her how to jump the irrigation ditch and related it to overcoming obstacles in life; the key, he said, is to "keep your eye on the other side."[78] Kapp came to excel at identifying truth in daily circumstances for the Young Women as her father had done for her. She claims that his "reservoir of experiences seemed limitless" and related many anecdotes of how he taught her through simple, daily occurrences.[79] In the acknowledgments of *Miracles in Pinafores and Bluejeans*, Kapp addresses her father and expresses her appreciation that he "ha[d] over the years revealed beauty in common things and miracles in every day."[80]

Kapp used the same approach her father had when she became a Young Women leader. When working with young women on a major fashion show event, Kapp compared the girls to coyotes, who could overtake a rabbit by "uniting their resources and working together."[81] Her addresses as general Young Women president often related an interaction she had with a particular young woman and then explained how this interaction revealed a gospel principle. For instance, Kapp paired a didactic statement about the effect of sacrifice on a family with an anecdote about a young woman who responded to her family's poverty by working long and frequent shifts until she could afford her own college tuition and contribute to the family finances.[82] Additionally, the Young Women worldwide celebration, titled *The Rising Generation*, was scheduled to "take place at sunrise or in the early morning to symbolize the dawning of a new day for Latter-day Saint young women."[83] Kapp's appreciation of symbolism, acquired from her father, exhibits itself with this decision. When Kapp was released as general Young Women president, she thanked her father for "the part he had played from the beginning of her life in her preparation for that calling."[84]

June and Edwin's unique characteristics clearly aided in the development of their daughter's leadership. As her mother's life drew to a close, Kapp "thought about eternity and the importance of this life, and how quickly it passes."[85] Her parents' deaths, which occurred before her call as president, facilitated her concern for the young women's eternal, not just temporal, lives.[86]

Her sisters. Kapp's love, appreciation, and admiration for women seems apparent in her interactions with her own sisters. Kapp's "deep feelings" for her sisters were strong "ever since they were tiny"; she feels that they were "precious friends in the pre-existence." Kapp delighted in caring for and protecting her younger sisters, who recall that she washed their hair, got them ready for school, and let them watch her get ready for parties and dances. Even after she married, Kapp continued to fondly associate with her sisters by inviting the girls to stay at her home.[87] Just as Kapp blessed her sisters, she later blessed many other young women. Furthermore, she was accustomed to being an example and leader to girls because of her relationship with her sisters.

During her service in the Young Women organization, Kapp developed close relationships with the women she served with,[88] and the *Personal Progress* booklet begins with a reminder that young women are "part of a great and wonderful worldwide sisterhood."[89] These sentiments were evidenced as she officially represented women's issues. As a chairman of the Advisory Committee on Women's Concerns at Brigham Young University, her advocacy of education for women was reaffirmed. When US Attorney General Edwin Meese's commission on pornography held its final hearing in January 1986, Kapp delivered a powerful fifteen-minute presentation outlining the damaging effects of pornography on women.[90] In short, she believes in the power of women to lead, inspire, and stand as witnesses. In her interactions with young women, she exhibited confidence in them by assuring them that "yes, girls, you are old enough" to make a difference.[91] Formal events she coordinated, including the first Young Women satellite broadcast and the first and second Young Women worldwide celebrations (1986, 1989), yielded an opportunity for young women to be recognized and honored.[92] These events communicated the message that young women are valuable assets to the Church and worth celebrating. Modern general Young Women leaders have maintained Kapp's legacy of celebrating femininity by instituting a pink cover on the most recent *Personal Progress* book. They specifically did this to remind young women of their feminine characteristics, gifts, and roles.[93] Furthermore, a general Young Women meeting takes place every spring at the end of March to specifically address young women ages twelve to eighteen. Talks are broadcast by satellite to meetinghouses throughout the world for millions of girls.

CONCLUSION

As ninth president of the Young Women organization, Ardeth Greene Kapp used her gifts and skills to oversee the development of the 1989 *Personal Progress* book as well as the official motto, logo, and theme.[94] Her personal habits, specifically journal keeping, developing interests, and temple worship, as well as her individual character, consisting of creative and purposeful planning, respect for the priesthood, and sincere interest in individuals, defined her leadership. Kapp's formal education also prepared her by alerting her to the need for cooperation between leaders and youth and need for attentiveness to individuals. Furthermore, Kapp's family aided in the attainment of traits which contributed to her leadership techniques. In the preface

Ardeth Greene Kapp's Influence on the Young Women Organization

of *Miracles in Pinafores and Bluejeans*, Kapp affirms her conviction that her life experiences primed her to serve as general Young Women president: "I have found that seemingly unimportant events linked together at a later time with other seemingly common events become evidence of eternal principles on which faith is built."[95] Each opportunity in her life prepared her and developed talents she used as Young Women general president.

NOTES

1. Anita Thompson, *Stand as a Witness: The Biography of Ardeth Greene Kapp* (Salt Lake City: Deseret Book, 2005), 268.
2. Ardeth Greene Kapp, interviewed by Jessica Christensen, 1, December 3, 2009, Bountiful, Utah, transcript in Jessica Christensen's possession (hereafter referred to as Christensen interview).
3. Christensen interview, 1.
4. "Presidents of the Young Women Organization through the Years," *Ensign*, June 2008, 40–45.
5. *My Personal Progress* (Salt Lake City: The Church of Jesus Christ of Latter-day Saints, 1977), 10–11, 14.
6. Ardeth Greene Kapp, interviewed by Gordon Irving, 1978–79, 25, 43, typescript, James Moyle Oral History Program, Church History Library, The Church of Jesus Christ of Latter-day Saints, Salt Lake City (hereafter Irving interview).
7. Carrie A. Moore, "Ex-Young Women Leader Is a Revered Role Model," *Deseret Morning News*, March 31, 2006, A1.
8. Christensen interview, 5.
9. "Teaming Up for Youth," *Ensign*, January 2002, 7–12; "Making Progress," *New Era*, January 2002, 16.
10. Heather Whittle Wrigley, "Changing the World One Virtuous Woman at a Time," *Ensign*, January 2010, 74–75; *Young Women Personal Progress* (Salt Lake City: The Church of Jesus Christ of Latter-day Saints, 2009), 70.
11. Christensen interview, 7.
12. "Teaming Up for Youth," 7.
13. Wrigley, "Changing the World One Virtuous Woman at a Time," 74–75.

14. Jeannette N. Oakes, "A Voice for Values," *New Era*, August 2004, 12.
15. Christensen interview, 1.
16. *Personal Progress* (Salt Lake City: The Church of Jesus Christ of Latter-day Saints, 1989), 10.
17. *Personal Progress*, 19–20.
18. *Personal Progress*, 18, 30, 45.
19. *Personal Progress*, 66, 51.
20. Christensen interview, 10.
21. Thompson, *Stand as a Witness*, 189.
22. *Personal Progress*, 62, 51.
23. *My Personal Progress*, 35.
24. Christensen interview, 10.
25. Christensen interview, 10.
26. Thompson, *Stand as a Witness*, 59, 65.
27. Ardeth Greene Kapp, "Temples Like 'No Other Places in World,'" *Church News*, June 29, 1991, 10.
28. Thompson, *Stand as a Witness*, 273.
29. *Personal Progress*, 48, 59, 61.
30. Wrigley, "Changing the World One Virtuous Woman at a Time," 74–75.
31. Elaine S. Dalton, "What's New in Personal Progress?," *New Era*, January 2010, 32–35.
32. Thompson, *Stand as a Witness*, 42.
33. Christensen interview, 4.
34. Thompson, *Stand as a Witness*, 276–77.
35. Christensen interview, 9.
36. Ardeth Greene Kapp, *The Gentle Touch* (Salt Lake City: Deseret Book, 1978), 1–2.
37. Thompson, *Stand as a Witness*, 269.
38. Thompson, *Stand as a Witness*, 316.
39. Janet Peterson and LaRene Gaunt, *Keepers of the Flame* (Salt Lake City: Deseret Book, 1993), 155.
40. Ardeth Greene Kapp, *Echoes from My Prairie* (Salt Lake City: Bookcraft, 1979), 58.

41. Peterson and Gaunt, *Keepers of the Flame*, 144–45; Thompson, *Stand as a Witness*, 120.
42. Christensen interview, 6.
43. Kapp, *Echoes from My Prairie*, 18 and 22.
44. Karen Thomas Arnesen, "Ardeth Greene Kapp: A Prairie Girl, a Young Woman Still," *Ensign*, September 1985, 36.
45. Irving interview, 7.
46. Thompson, *Stand as a Witness*, 269.
47. Thompson, *Stand as a Witness*, 280.
48. Ardeth G. Kapp, "Young Women Striving Together," *Ensign*, November 1984, 96.
49. *Young Women Worldwide Celebration* (Salt Lake City: The Church of Jesus Christ of Latter-day Saints, 1985), 1.
50. "Young Women Principles Applicable in Every Culture," *Church News*, July 21, 1990, 3.
51. Thompson, *Stand as a Witness*, 296.
52. Young Women broadcasts are available at http://www.lds.org/broadcast/gywm/0,7726,2298-1-101-1641,00.html.
53. Irving interview, preface.
54. Thompson, *Stand as a Witness*, 44.
55. Kapp, *The Gentle Touch*, acknowledgments.
56. *Personal Progress*, 6.
57. Thompson, *Stand as a Witness*, 268, 295.
58. Ardeth Greene Kapp, *Miracles in Pinafores and Bluejeans* (Salt Lake City: Deseret Book, 1977), 7–9.
59. Kapp, *Echoes from My Prairie*, 50.
60. *Young Women Worldwide Celebration*, 1, 3.
61. Thompson, *Stand as a Witness*, 44, 306–8, 356–57.
62. Kapp, *Gentle Touch*, 82.
63. Kapp, *Gentle Touch*, preface.
64. *Personal Progress*, 88.
65. Thompson, *Stand as a Witness*, 236.
66. Peterson and Gaunt, *Keepers of the Flame*, 139.

67. "Examining Faith, Hope and Charity," *Church News*, April 12, 1991, 12.
68. Thompson, *Stand as a Witness*, 149.
69. Kapp, *Gentle Touch*, 13.
70. Thompson, *Stand as a Witness*, 178.
71. See Ardeth Greene Kapp, *All Kinds of Mothers* (Salt Lake City: Deseret Book, 1979).
72. Christensen interview, 3.
73. Thompson, *Stand as a Witness*, 214.
74. Christensen interview, 3.
75. Christensen interview, 3.
76. Irving interview, 5.
77. Kapp, *Miracles in Pinafores and Bluejeans*, 13.
78. Kapp, *Gentle Touch*, 100–104.
79. Kapp, *Echoes from My Prairie*, 25.
80. Kapp, *Miracles in Pinafores and Bluejeans*, acknowledgments.
81. Kapp, *Miracles in Pinafores and Bluejeans*, 23.
82. Ardeth G. Kapp, "Young Women Striving Together," *Ensign*, November 1984, 96.
83. *Young Women Worldwide Celebration*, 1.
84. Thompson, *Stand as a Witness*, 238–39.
85. Thompson, *Stand as a Witness*, 256.
86. Christensen interview, 1.
87. Thompson, *Stand as a Witness*, 228–29, 184, 19–21, 110.
88. Thompson, *Stand as a Witness*, 290–95.
89. *Personal Progress*, 4.
90. Thompson, *Stand as a Witness*, 251–52, 288–89.
91. Kapp, *Miracles in Pinafores and Bluejeans*, 3, 41–42.
92. "Presidents of the Young Women Organization through the Years," *Ensign*, June 2008, 40–45.
93. Wrigley, "Changing the World One Virtuous Woman at a Time," 74–75.
94. Thompson, *Stand as a Witness*, 268.
95. Kapp, *Miracles in Pinafores and Bluejeans*, preface.

Scott C. Esplin

20

TYING IT TO THE PRIESTHOOD: HAROLD B. LEE'S RESTRUCTURING OF THE YOUNG MEN ORGANIZATION

A MONTH after the unexpected passing of President Harold B. Lee, Elder Boyd K. Packer observed, "The work of President Harold B. Lee will have effect just as long as this Church endures; until the Lord Himself says, 'It is finished,' until His work is done. Never through all generations can it be minimized or mitigated. Never will the Church be the same, always it will run with more precision, more power."[1] Indeed, a hallmark of the Lee presidency remains the organizational changes that led some to call him the "great innovator."[2]

Though President Lee's administration was brief, one of the lasting changes effected during his tenure was the restructuring of the Young Men's Mutual Improvement Association (YMMIA). Organized nearly a hundred years earlier at the direction of President Brigham Young, the YMMIA initially operated "separate from the Priesthood,

---

Scott C. Esplin is an assistant professor of Church history and doctrine at Brigham Young University.

and yet so organized that they should be under its guidance, and tend to its strength and aid."³ Under President Lee's authorization, significant changes were made to this relationship. In 1972, President Lee directed an organizational restructuring of the Young Men organization, seeking to connect it more effectively to the priesthood. Later, at the June 1973 MIA conference, President Lee and others explained the impact of the changes. Speaking about the reorganization, Presiding Bishop Victor L. Brown noted: "Now, through inspiration from the Lord through His mouthpiece President Harold B. Lee, a most significant change has been brought about in this organization. The MIA is no longer auxiliary to the priesthood. It has now been brought directly under the umbrella of the priesthood. It is priesthood oriented and priesthood directed."⁴ The youth of the Church were more closely connected to their priesthood leaders, accomplishing the desire of President Lee, who, "from the beginning of his involvement with Church organization at the general level, . . . was anxious to tie all organizations of the Church securely to the priesthood."⁵

Looking back nearly forty years since these changes, what did President Lee see in the Young Men organization that needed restructuring? How could an organization formed under the direction of President Brigham Young find itself detached from the priesthood? Was there anything, either in its founding or in the intervening ninety-seven years, that raised Church leaders' concern regarding the organization? Finally, how, as Elder Packer taught, has the Young Men organization run with "more precision, more power" in the thirty-eight years since its restructuring?

FORERUNNERS TO A CHURCH YOUTH ORGANIZATION

The formation of the Young Men's Mutual Improvement Association began its unique relationship of being guided by the priesthood of the Church but remaining a separate entity. Histories of the movement trace the organization's beginning to a founding meeting in Salt Lake City's Thirteenth Ward on June 10, 1875. However, many leaders, including founding father Junius F. Wells, have argued that forerunners to the organization stretch as far back as Joseph Smith and Nauvoo. In the winter of 1843, some youth of the Church met at the Heber C. Kimball home "lamenting the loose style of their morals—the frivolous manner in which they spent their time—and their too frequent attendance at balls, parties, &c. &c."[6] Elder Kimball proposed that they begin meeting to address these concerns and receive instruction. Throughout January and February 1843, the group met regularly under Kimball's direction, moving meeting locations as the popularity of the organization increased, and finally gathering in the room above Joseph Smith's red brick store. In March 1843, the Prophet attended and "praised their good conduct, and taught them how to behave in all places, explained to them their duty, and advised them to organize themselves into a society for the relief of the poor."[7] Specifically, the Prophet proposed that the youth begin by collecting funds to build a home for a crippled immigrant from England, the artist Sutclife Maudsley. The youth rallied to the cause, and a society composed of single young men and women under the age of thirty, known as the Young Gentlemen's and Ladies' Relief Society of Nauvoo, was formally organized on March 21, 1843.

The benevolent society sought to transform social life in Nauvoo. The *Times and Seasons* reported, "Instead of the young people spending their evenings at parties, balls, &c., they would now leave all, and attend to their meeting. Instead of hearing about this party and that party, this dance and that dance, in different parts of the city; their name was scarcely mentioned, and the Young People's Meetings became the chief topic of conversation."[8] Short lived, it dissolved like its counterpart, the Female Relief Society of Nauvoo, with the death of the Prophet and the westward exodus of the Saints.[9] However, while editing the *History of the Church*, B. H. Roberts linked this Nauvoo organization for the youth to its Utah counterpart, noting that the minutes "more clearly describe a Mutual Improvement Association than a Relief Society; and this incident may not improperly be regarded as the first step towards that great movement in the Church which has been such a mighty aid in holding to the faith of their fathers the youth of Israel."[10]

In Utah, improvement associations and organizations also flourished before the Church's formal founding of the Young Men's Mutual Improvement Association in 1875. Early in the pioneer era, Elder Orson Pratt formed the Universal Scientific Society. Later, to promote intellectual advancement and appreciation for the arts, Elder Lorenzo Snow organized the Polysophical Society in the winter of 1852. After four years, the society was transformed by the First Presidency in 1856 into the Deseret Theological Class. An early participant, Henry W. Naisbitt, later attributed the success of the Mutual Improvement Association to these forerunning organizations: "This was the basis upon which all the Mutual Improvement Associations have been built; to it they were indebted for their ideas, which, utilizing the varied gifts and endowments found in gathering Israel, gave them a greater scope and mightier influence, providing recreation and scattering intelligence, being the nursery also for junior aspirants of both sexes, in the direction and presentation of their thoughts, as to art, literature, science, religion, politics, and amusement; refining, purifying, enlarging, under the control of the Priesthood, the mental forces and intellectual thrift of Israel in this our day and time."[11]

Naisbitt's claim that his organization acted as the genesis for the YMMIA was not alone. In 1907 the Mutual Improvement Association's official periodical, the *Improvement Era*, published a letter by Samuel L. Adams to President Joseph F. Smith acknowledging their joint involvement in an early mutual improvement society formed by President Heber C. Kimball in Salt Lake City in the fall of 1853. "President Heber C. Kimball called upon a brother by the name of George Gardner," Adams recalled. President Kimball then charged him "to hunt up all the young men in and around the Church Farm, Mill Creek and Canyon Creek, and get them together at least once a week, and get them on their feet bearing testimony to the truth of the gospel. We want these young men for the harness." Noting that he "sometimes sees matters which [he] think[s] are placed to the credit of those to whom they do not belong," Adams concluded that he believed theirs "was the first M. I. A. started in these mountains."[12]

More formal Mutual Improvement Associations abounded in the early 1870s prior to general Church organization. Reminiscing on the founding of YMMIA, Edward H. Anderson, former general secretary of the Mutual Improvement Association, recalled, "In 1873 it became the rule in some of the more thickly populated settlements of the Saints for the young people to form associations for entertainments and improvement. These were called night schools, literary societies, debating clubs, young men's clubs, or any other name that indicated the object of the gathering. Frequently they were solely for amusement, and, taking pattern after the early efforts in Salt Lake City, were formed to instruct the people by theatrical exhibitions and dramatic performances."[13] Institutes, literary associations, and instruction associations were formed in the sixth, tenth, thirteenth, sixteenth, and twentieth wards of the city, with prominent participants including the Cannons, Taylors, Lamberts, Goddards, Parks, and Morrises.[14] Eventually, Church leaders became involved in these early attempts at organization when President George Q. Cannon and Elder Franklin D. Richards created a youth association in Weber County in April 1873. All of these forerunners highlight the independence from central priesthood guidance of the original youth organizations.

FORMAL FOUNDING OF THE YOUNG MEN'S MUTUAL IMPROVEMENT ASSOCIATION

While acknowledging these forerunners, President Joseph F. Smith stressed that something different existed in the formation of the Young Men's Mutual Improvement Association. In an editorial addressing controversies surrounding the founding, President Smith noted, "From time to time we are reminded that the origin of mutual improvement work does not date from June 10, 1875, when Elder Junius F. Wells, by instruction of President Brigham Young, called a meeting in the 13th ward, Salt Lake City, and organized the first Mutual Improvement Association in the

Church. A number of people have written and protested that this, that, and the other organization was the origin, or first, from which grew the Mutual Improvement Associations." An early participant in some of these YMMIA predecessors, Smith acknowledged, "All these preliminary organizations, as we may term them, were truly forerunners, and their history is interesting as pointing the way to the present proficient Young Men's Mutual Improvement Association's." However, he also said:

> Many of these organizations in the early 70's degenerated into debating societies, in which much ill feeling was engendered, and while great good was obtained from them, they threatened to create considerable division and ill feeling. It was therefore, no doubt, evident to President Young that there existed a necessity for a general organization of the young people, for their mutual improvement, into associations that should be separate from the Priesthood, and yet so organized that they should be under its guidance, and tend to its strength and aid. Hence the call, in 1875, to organize the improvement associations.... This movement may very appropriately be called the first general movement to organize mutual improvement associations as we now have them throughout the Church.[15]

Junius F. Wells, the organization's founder, likewise emphatically defended the organization's genesis. "The inspiration of the general organization of the Young Men's Mutual Improvement Association was from God, expressed by the President of the Church of Jesus Christ of Latter-day Saints. It was not derived from any other society then in existence either in or out of the Church.... Whatever rivalry, therefore, there might be in claims for priority of organization should be relegated to these and other societies like them. Upon none [of the earlier organizations] was the general organization inaugurated by President Brigham Young in 1875 built."[16]

The founding of a formal, Church-sanctioned organization for young men is tied directly to the inspiration of President Brigham Young, a significant difference frequently stressed by those comparing it to various forerunners. Josiah Burrows wrote, "In responding to the sentiment 'The Origin, Mission, and Object of the Y. M. M. I. A,' I will state that the origin can very readily be traced to President Brigham Young, who, as the humble instrument in the hands of God, first inaugurated this work in the summer of 1875. . . . There had been, however, prior to this time mutual improvement societies, debating societies, etc. . . . But not until this time did the organization of such societies become specially ordered under the general direction of the President of the Church."[17]

On the fiftieth anniversary of the organization's founding, Junius F. Wells further testified of President Young's hand in the organization's formation: "The inspiration of the general organization of the Young Men's Mutual Improvement Association was from God, expressed by the President of the Church of Jesus Christ of Latter-day Saints." Describing his own call to be involved, Wells, then a twenty-one-year-old recently returned missionary, continued, "On Saturday morning, June sixth, 1875, President Brigham Young, upon parting with his second counselor, President Daniel H. Wells [Junius's father], sent the following message to me: 'Tell Junius that I want him to organize the young men.' . . . The spirit of the work fell upon me from the moment I was chosen to undertake it. I seemed at once to know what I should do. Nevertheless, I asked my father, and he replied, laconically: 'I think, if I were in your place I'd do it.' After conferring further with him I proceeded to arrange for a meeting to be held in the Thirteenth ward meetinghouse." Seeking further direction from President Young, Wells met with the Church President, who informed him, "We want to have our young men enrolled and organized throughout the Church, so that we shall know who and where they are, so that we can put our hands upon them at any time for any service that may be required. We want them to hold meetings where they will stand up and speak—get into the habit of speaking—and of bearing testimony. These meetings are to be for our young men, to be composed of young men for their improvement—for their mutual improvement—a society of young men for mutual improvement. There is your name: The

Young Men's Mutual Improvement Soci—Association."[18] Following his direction, Wells met with interested youth on Thursday, June 10, 1875, in the thirteenth ward meetinghouse, where the first ward Young Men organization was formed with an initial membership of eighteen. Henry A. Woolley was selected as president, with B. Morris Young and Heber J. Grant serving as counselors, and Hyrum H. Goddard as secretary.[19] Shortly thereafter, under President Young's direction, Wells, together with Elders John Henry Smith, Milton H. Hardy, and B. Morris Young, began traveling the territory forming Mutual Improvement Associations in every ward and stake. By the organization's first general conference on April 8, 1876, fifty-seven organizations had been formed with a membership of twelve hundred young men.[20] Five years later, the organization boasted a membership of more than nine thousand.[21]

PURPOSE AND PRACTICE OF THE ORIGINAL MUTUAL IMPROVEMENT ASSOCIATION

Those guiding the new organization continued to look to President Young for leadership. Early leaders reported his original instructions, including an emphasis on spiritual development: "We want you to organize yourselves into associations for mutual improvement. Let the keynote of your work be the establishment in the youth of individual testimony of the truth and magnitude of the great Latter-day work; the development of the gifts within them, that have been bestowed upon them by the laying on of hands of the servants of God; cultivating a knowledge and an application of the eternal principles of the great science of life."[22]

The development of individual testimony seems to have been the guiding factor for President Young in pushing the work of the Mutual Improvement Association forward. B. Morris Young, Brigham Young's son and an officer in the first YMMIA, recalled his father's motivation: "My father's mind was considerably exercised over the conduct of some of the young men of those days, not only his own sons, but those of his friends, for youth is the same yesterday today and forever. Father knew that youthful vigor and ambition needed guidance and direction into paths of safety and righteousness."[23] President Young's concern was rooted in the dangers he sensed facing the youth in 1875. Chief among them were threats from other religious bodies seeking to lead Latter-day Saint youth away from the faith of their fathers.

At the organization's founding meeting, Junius F. Wells elaborated on these concerns: "Do you realize that you are surrounded with enemies, the hireling priests who seek to ensnare you and lead you from the counsels of your parents whom they would destroy, if God would suffer them to do so? This is their object and mission here, to overthrow this Church and kingdom, if possible, and they expect to accomplish it by the influence they exert over the youth of our people. They are not our friends, neither are they the friends of God; their motives are false, and their doctrines are false; they seek to destroy the priesthood and lead the heirs of the priesthood down to perdition."[24] Wells later summarized other ills plaguing the youth that he hoped the organization could help combat. "We have unwittingly adopted many customs and some ideas that must be eliminated to make us the people we aim to become. Intemperance, swearing, uncouth language, and the memory-destroying habit of reading light literature are among the evils that we have to contend with, and that we hope to overcome by cultivating 'the gift that is within us,' that we may be examples of the believer in word, in conversation, in spirit, in purity, etc."[25]

Early activities of the YMMIA stressed the acquisition of truth and the development of testimony to attack these social blights. However, leaders also used social activities to attract pioneer youth. Edward H. Anderson, former general secretary of the YMMIA, recalled:

> The exercises at first were simple and in many places were of an entertaining character only. The young people had not been accustomed to study. The very circumstances and conditions surrounding them for the first quarter of a century after the arrival of the Pioneers, naturally tended to a species of wildness, so that horse-racing, trading, ranching, indifference to schools and

religious exercises were more the custom than were intellectual pursuits or devotion to the study of theology. As it is a fact that interest must first be secured and attention riveted before the mind can be impressed, it becomes necessary to have such programs in the associations as will enlist the attention and interest of the young who, though having rough exteriors, were men of integrity and virtue at heart. Music, songs, recitations, literary entertainments, intermingled with testimonies and religious references were employed, until the young became more thoroughly interested in intellectual pleasures, when it became an easy task to lead them on into heavier studies. Hence the lighter character of the programs of the earlier societies.[26]

Within a few years, however, greater emphasis was placed on the spiritual side of gospel study in the YMMIA. In 1877, the organization's central committee, headed by Junius F. Wells, Milton H. Hardy, and Rodney C. Badger, outlined how association meetings should be conducted. "The exercises should be such as will prepare the young people to promote the interests of the work of the Lord, and may be of a sufficiently diversified character to render them interesting," Wells instructed. "The greater portion of the time at meetings should be devoted to seeking to receive and impart a better and more extended acquaintance with the principles of the gospel. It should be considered the duty of all who have not yet received a testimony of the truth of the gospel, to take steps to obtain it, and generally a portion of time in the meetings should be devoted to bearing testimony to the truth of the work of God." The "handing in of written questions" for answer by other members was considered "a commendable exercise," as was the delivering of addresses, the writing of essays, and giving of readings. Debates, "being, in the opinion of this committee, contrary to the commandment to 'have no disputations among you,' are in opposition to the spirit and genius of this mission of mutual improvement" and were discouraged.[27] In 1879, Junius F. Wells wrote President John Taylor summarizing YMMIA priorities: "The object of this extensive organization is, to introduce our young men to an order of religious and intellectual exercises that will secure to them a knowledge of the truth, and put them in possession of the evidences to advocate and defend it.... While the above is the first object had in view, as secondary, and leading to its attainment, we have given our attention to improvement in other respects: In our manners, our entertainments, our social gatherings, our conversations, our readings and our writings, which brings me to the subject upon which I, at present, desire to confer with you."[28]

SEPARATE FROM BUT GUIDED BY PRIESTHOOD

The desire "to confer" with President Taylor highlights the final characteristic of the YMMIA's early founding. From the beginning, its relationship with the priesthood had been unique. President Joseph F. Smith, who was familiar with the organization from its founding, stressed that Brigham Young's desire was for "a general organization of the young people, for their mutual improvement, into associations that should be separate from the Priesthood, and yet so organized that they should be under its guidance, and tend to its strength and aid."[29] This separation from the priesthood was evident even in the founding meeting, which President Young authorized but did not attend. Highlighting the unique relationship, Junius F. Wells announced to the assembled body that he was acting "at the suggestion, and by the authority of President Brigham Young." However, bishops and other prominent men present declined Wells's invitation to join him on the stand, noting that it was not their meeting.[30] Indeed, though Church leaders at the highest levels gave official support to the early YMMIA, the organization seemed to go to great lengths to distinguish itself from the priesthood, a relationship that presented the body with challenges. Two years following the death of President Young, Junius Wells described having "many conversations with Elder Joseph F. Smith," who "became fully aware of the handicaps the organization was subjected to."

By March 1880, Wells was ready to make a change. Writing President Taylor and the rest of the Quorum of the Twelve Apostles, Wells confessed, "We feel that the interests of the organization require the sanction and direct recognition of the Presiding Authority of the Church." Specifically, he requested that a general superintendency for the YMMIA be created, headed by at least one Apostle. At the organization's fourth semiannual general conference in April 1880, Church leadership agreed, calling President Wilford Woodruff as the first general superintendent of the Young Men's Mutual Improvement Association, with Elders Joseph F. Smith and Moses Thatcher as his counselors.[31] From then on, the organization had central Church oversight. The listing of general superintendents leading up to President Harold B. Lee's restructuring reads like a who's who in Church leadership: Wilford Woodruff (1880–98), Lorenzo Snow (1898–1901), Joseph F. Smith (1901–18), Anthony W. Ivins (1918–21), George Albert Smith (1921–35), Albert E. Bowen (1935–37), George Q. Morris (1937–48), Elbert R. Curtis (1948–58), Joseph T. Bentley (1958–62), G. Carlos Smith (1962–69), and W. Jay Eldredge (1969–72).[32]

In establishing Church oversight for the Young Men's Mutual Improvement Association in 1880, the Quorum of the Twelve Apostles also took the opportunity to clarify the organization's place within the priesthood. Several of these declarations are significant because they highlight the separation between the youth priesthood quorums and the youth organization evident in the founding of the YMMIA. "This institution must not interfere with the priesthood of any of its members," the Council declared. "Each individual member must be subject to the quorum of which he may be a member, and to the regularly organized authorities of the stake with which he is associated." Placing it under stake control, the body further outlined, "Every stake organization [is] to be under the authority of the stake organization of the priesthood in that stake, and to have for its superintendent a High Priest selected by the president of the stake and his counselors, sanctioned by the high council of the stake, and voted for and sustained by the stake conference and associations of the stake." Finally, the Quorum announced, "It must be understood that this organization is not formed as a separate or distinct Church organization or body of priesthood, but for the purpose of mutual improvement of the members and all connected therewith."[33]

Tying It to the Priesthood

CONNECTING THE YOUNG MEN BACK TO PRIESTHOOD

With these guidelines in place, the YMMIA slowly transformed itself over its first hundred years of existence into the organization with which most Church members today are familiar. Between 1898 and 1900, the central committee became the general board. In 1901, the organization graded youth into two classes—junior and senior—and began the activity program of the YMMIA, adding social and cultural activities to theological studies. On May 21, 1913, it received a national charter from the Boy Scouts of America, a relationship that continues to influence both organizations heavily.

Becoming part of the Boy Scouts of America movement led to what Charles E. Mitchener Jr., former executive secretary of the YMMIA, called "the real beginning of the age-group departments in the YMMIA."[34] In 1920, three grades were formed: juniors (MIA Scouts) for ages twelve through sixteen, seniors (M Men) for ages seventeen though twenty-one, and advanced seniors (adult) for ages twenty-two and older. In 1928, the MIA Scouts were further divided, with the oldest age-group (fifteen and sixteen-year-olds) forming the Vanguard program (they adopted the Boy Scout name of Explorers in 1935). The 1930s and '40s saw additional restructurings, specifically in the age classifications for YMMIA members over twenty-five. Finally, in June 1950 the Church solidified the organization: Scouts (ages twelve and thirteen), Explorers (ages fourteen through sixteen), Junior M Men (ages seventeen and eighteen), M Men (ages nineteen though twenty-five), and Special Interest (ages twenty-six and over). During this restructuring, the YMMIA also significantly expanded its activity program, creating annual all-Church athletic contests for softball, basketball, volleyball, and, for a brief time, tennis. The YMMIA also strengthened its ties to the Young Women's Mutual Improvement Association, joining with them for the annual June Conference beginning in 1896. This traditional event highlighting the Young Men's and Young Women's Mutual Improvement Associations flourished for the next seven decades, combining instructional sessions by

Church leaders with a variety of dance, music, drama, and speech festivals to rival the all-Church athletic events.[35]

With a growing and flourishing program, the changes enacted by President Harold B. Lee to the Young Men's Mutual Improvement Association on November 9, 1972, when he restructured the program must have been shocking. In fact, the response may explain President Lee's general conference plea the following April: "Just a word now about what has been said regarding the Aaronic Priesthood MIA and the Melchizedek Priesthood MIA. . . . We are asking you to . . . not go out as a Monday morning quarterback and try to do all the second-guessing. I want to say to you that there is no topic that has received longer and more searching, prayerful discussion by the General Authorities of the Church than the matters that pertain to the young people of the Aaronic and Melchizedek Priesthood groups, and the women of similar ages. . . . Suspend judgment, then, and ponder what has been said tonight until you receive further instructions." Concluding his priesthood session address, President Lee further testified, "I bear you my solemn witness, my beloved brethren, that these things that have been spoken tonight have been spoken under the inspiration of the Lord, and we give it to you for your pondering, for your prayerful consideration, suspending judgment, and not raising your voices in criticism, but carrying on the youth organizations as they now exist until these brethren have given you the full details of just what lies ahead; then you can begin to see the merits of what it is all about."[36]

In explaining the changes, Church periodicals noted that the restructuring of the Young Men organization was done "to meet the increasing demands of a fast-growing, worldwide Church and to improve priesthood correlation."[37] To accomplish this end, in 1972 the First Presidency created two separate priesthood-oriented MIAs. The Aaronic Priesthood Mutual Improvement Association served youth ages twelve through seventeen, and the Melchizedek Priesthood Mutual Interest Association assisted young single adults ages eighteen through twenty-five as well as special interest groups of single persons twenty-six and older (generally including widowers, divorcés, and others with special situations). Describing the change at the following general conference, President Lee stressed that "these announced Aaronic Priesthood and Melchizedek Priesthood MIAs do not do away with the Young Men's and Young Women's Mutual Improvement Associations." Rather, two separate general Church bodies were created to oversee the new organizations. At the Aaronic Priesthood level, a new YMMIA presidency was created, headed by President Robert L. Backman, with LeGrand R. Curtis and Jack H. Goaslind Jr. as counselors. For the Melchizedek Priesthood MIA, Elders James E. Faust, Marion D. Hanks, and L. Tom Perry, all Assistants to the Twelve, formed the leadership committee. However, priesthood quorums took specific guidance of each group, with the Presiding Bishopric overseeing the Young Men organization and a committee of four Apostles (Elders Thomas S. Monson, Boyd K. Packer, Marvin J. Ashton, and Bruce R. McConkie) directing the Melchizedek Priesthood MIA. Of this change, President Lee concluded, "What is intended, as you see this unfold, is that the programs will go forward, but with priesthood identity the like of which they have not enjoyed before."[38]

As outlined by President Lee, tying the youth of the Church to the priesthood became the overarching theme of the change. Describing the "crazy mixed-up world" the youth face, President Lee stressed that "in these new movements with our young people, our only hope is that by intensifying the responsibility of the priesthood with the youth organizations we can strengthen their hands and reach out to these young men and women who need so much the shepherding influence of the priesthood."[39] Presiding Bishop Victor L. Brown expressed similar faith that the change would better connect the youth to priesthood: "The MIA is no longer auxiliary to the priesthood. It has now been brought directly under the umbrella of the priesthood. It is priesthood oriented and priesthood directed. . . . By clarifying and shortening the priesthood lines of responsibility on the ward and stake levels, the influence of the priesthood will be felt in the lives of young men and women. The priesthood is the power to act in the name of God. It is important that our young people understand that it is the power unto salvation for everyone, both men and women."[40]

Ultimately, the change accomplished two purposes. On the one hand, it blessed the lives of youth by bringing them in closer connection to the priesthood and priesthood leaders. Elder Perry, associate director of the newly formed Melchizedek Priesthood MIA committee, stressed that youth "have found themselves on tributaries lined with sharp rocks, rapids and swift currents that have tossed them to and fro." Comparing the priesthood to a safe harbor, Elder Perry continued, "Now a channel has been cut to bring them into the main stream of the church where the waters are deep and the ride can be smooth with many new ports of opportunity, study, activity, service and spirituality."[41] For the bishoprics, however, the change also served as a blessing, as noted by Robert L. Backman, Aaronic Priesthood MIA Young Men president. "What a marvelous opportunity this gives for the presidency of the Aaronic Priesthood to help our youth leaders learn the duties and responsibilities of their respective callings," Backman declared. "And what a blessing it will be for our youth leaders to enjoy a close relationship with the great youth leaders of the ward."[42]

The direct connections between the youth and the priesthood were further solidified less than two years later, when, at the June 1974 MIA conference, the term "MIA" was discontinued altogether, replaced by the name "Aaronic Priesthood". At the same time, Church President Spencer W. Kimball released entirely the general presidencies and boards of both the Young Men's and Young Women's MIAs, placing them instead under the direction of the Presiding Bishopric. "These changes will provide greater priesthood direction and involvement," President Kimball explained. "We have placed the responsibility directly upon the Presiding Bishopric who, by revelation, constitute the presidency of the Aaronic Priesthood." Hoping that the change would have the same effect at the ward level, President Kimball stressed, "It is the utmost importance that the bishops realize that their first and foremost responsibility is to the Aaronic Priesthood and Young Women of their wards. . . . It is our intent that no one stand between the bishopric, at either the general or ward level, and their ministry with the Aaronic Priesthood."[43]

Tying It to the Priesthood

As founders of the YMMIA had done with Brigham Young, Church leaders during the Lee and Kimball organizational changes stressed the inspiration attendant to the restructuring. Explaining the change, President Lee affirmed divine guidance in the programs of the Church.[44] President Lee, Bishop Brown, and Elder Perry all linked the change to prophecy, connecting the restructuring to President Joseph F. Smith's prediction:

> We expect to see the day, if we live long enough (and if some of us do not live long enough to see it, there are others who will), when every council of the Priesthood in the Church of Jesus Christ of Latter-day Saints will understand its duty; will assume its own responsibility, will magnify its calling, and fill its place in the Church, to the uttermost, according to the intelligence and ability possessed by it. When that day shall come, there will not be so much necessity for work that is now being done by the auxiliary organizations, because it will be done by the regular quorums of the Priesthood. The Lord designed and comprehended it from the beginning, and he has made provision in the Church whereby every need may be met and satisfied through the regular organizations of the Priesthood.[45]

Bishop Brown further noted that "now, through inspiration from the Lord through His mouthpiece President Harold B. Lee, a most significant change has been brought about."[46]

CONCLUSION

"It is change in the heart and not a change on a chart," President Kimball emphasized, "which really makes a lasting difference."[47] While the organizational changes effected in the Young Men's Mutual Improvement Association in the early 1970s may seem like semantics, the results should have eternal implications. By shortening the lines of responsibility, the restructuring brought the youth of the Church in closer contact to local priesthood leaders and, importantly, to the keys they exercise. Bishop Brown, participant witness to it all, highlighted the effect these changes would have: "This decision by the First Presidency and the Council of the Twelve will have great impact on the lives of the members of the Church in years to come. President Lee referred to it as potentially one of the most significant changes in the Church in our lifetime. Having been involved in the development of the plan, I can testify to you that it came through inspiration from the Lord."[48]

Over the course of nearly one hundred years of existence, the Young Men's Mutual Improvement Association enjoyed a unique relationship with the priesthood. Formed at the insistence of President Brigham Young, it originally enjoyed priesthood blessing and, with the formation of a general superintendency, priesthood oversight. However, without connection to the revealed priesthood quorums for deacons, teachers, and priests, the organization was separated from the priesthood at the ward and stake levels, something that appears to have worried President Harold B. Lee. Describing President Lee's concerns, Elder Boyd K. Packer noted, "He saw some drifting and felt some anxiety, and he carried that concern with him for years."[49] In the early 1970s, President Lee acted on the situation, closing the gap between the youth and the priesthood by replacing the Mutual Improvement Association with an Aaronic Priesthood model connected directly to the bishops of the Church. Near the end of his brief administration, President Lee sensed that the changes he effected were nearly complete. "Brethren, we must begin to gear down," Elder Packer reported him saying. "We must begin to reduce the pattern of changes. We must now turn from restructuring, remodeling, and overhauling, and dedicate ourselves and employ ourselves to maintenance and to operation."[50]

To allay the concerns of those impacted by President Lee's brief tenure and the extensive administrative changes it produced, Elder Packer offered an instructive parable:

> Imagine a group of people who are going on a journey through a territory that is dangerous and unplotted. They have a large bus for transportation, and they are making preparations. They find among them a master mechanic. He is appointed to get their vehicle ready, with all of us to help. He insists that it be stripped down

Tying It to the Priesthood

completely, every part taken from the other part and inspected carefully, cleaned, renewed, repaired, and some of them replaced.

Some of the gears are not efficient. They are not producing the power they should for the amount of fuel they use. And so they are replaced. This means a change in linkage, a change in the pattern of connections and delivering the power. So they go to work, with this master mechanic directing the retooling and refitting of this vehicle.

There are steep inclines that must be made and there has to be sufficient power. There will be curves and switchbacks, there will be places where control will have to be perfect, where the braking will have to be perfect.

So, painstakingly and deliberately, without undue pressure, the bus is disassembled and ultimately put together again.

Then comes the time when there has to be a shakedown, a test run, if you will. The signal comes that this master mechanic will also be appointed the driver. He will head the journey.

So the test is run. It is not a very long one, but there are some very difficult obstacles in it so that it is a full test. All of us, as we stand by, are delighted with the result. It is roadworthy. Now we know that it will make every hill and it will go over and, if necessary, through any obstacle in its way.

We see the master mechanic, pleased with his work, step down, and say that it's ready. He dusts a little dust off the radiator cap.

Then comes the signal that another will drive. And the protest comes: "Oh, but not another! We need him to drive. There's never been anyone who has seen so much and knows so much about the vehicle we are going to use. No man in all history has so completely gone through this vehicle and no one knows as much as he knows. No one is so thoroughly familiar with it."

But the command is definite. Another will drive. Some protest that the new driver isn't so much a mechanic. "What if there is trouble along the way?" And the answer comes back, "Perhaps that's all to the good that he may not be a mechanic. It may well be, for should there be a little grinding of the gears he won't be quite so inclined to strip it down, take out all the gears, and start to overhaul it again. He'll try first a little lubrication perhaps, a little grease here and there, and that will be all it needs." . . .

We must now move forward and move out. The signal comes to all of us who are on the crew. "Climb aboard. Another's been appointed to drive." We obediently and with acceptance move out into that journey.[51]

With the passing of the master organizational mechanic President Lee, the Church, and the Young Men organization he restructured moved on. However, "never will the Church be the same," Elder Packer declared regarding the changes. "Always it will run with more precision, more power."[52] Hopefully, the closer connection between the youth of the Church and their priesthood leaders will lead to the sort of experience described by YMMIA participant B. Morris Young: "My early association with the Young Men's Mutual Improvement Association made a profound impression upon my mind and left upon my character an influence for righteousness which has enriched all my life, strengthened my testimony, and aided me in developing and maintaining the principles of truth in my home and in all my public and private affairs."[53]

NOTES

1. Boyd K. Packer, *That All May Be Edified* (Salt Lake City: Bookcraft, 1982), 124.
2. Francis M. Gibbons, *Harold B. Lee: Man of Vision, Prophet of God* (Salt Lake City: Deseret Book, 1993), 478.
3. Joseph F. Smith, "Origin of Mutual Improvement," *Improvement Era*, October 1907, 985–86.
4. "Priesthood MIA Era Opens," *Church News*, June 23, 1973, 3.
5. Gibbons, *Harold B. Lee*, 478.
6. James M. Monroe, "A Short Sketch of the Rise of the Young Gentlemen and Ladies Relief Society of Nauvoo," *Times and Seasons*, April 1, 1843, 154.

7. Monroe, "Short Sketch of the Rise," 155.
8. Monroe, "Short Sketch of the Rise," 156.
9. Glen M. Leonard, *Nauvoo: A Place of Peace, A People of Promise* (Salt Lake City: Deseret Book, 2002), 226–27.
10. *History of the Church of Jesus Christ of Latter-day Saints*, ed. B. H. Roberts, 2nd ed. rev. (Salt Lake City: Deseret Book, 1957), 5:320–21, footnote.
11. Henry W. Naisbitt, "'Polysophical' and 'Mutual,'" *Improvement Era*, August 1899, 747.
12. Smith, "Origin of Mutual Improvement," 986–87.
13. Edward H. Anderson, "The Past of Mutual Improvement," *Improvement Era*, November 1897, 1.
14. Junius F. Wells, "Historic Sketch of the Y. M. M. I. A.," *Improvement Era*, June 1925, 714.
15. Smith, "Origin of Mutual Improvement," 985–86.
16. Wells, "Historic Sketch, June 1925, 713–14.
17. Josiah Burrows, "Origin and Mission of the Y. M. M. I. A.," *Contributor*, August 1890, 384.
18. Wells, "Historic Sketch," June 1925, 713–15.
19. Wells, "Historic Sketch," June 1925, 716.
20. Wells, "Historic Sketch," June 1925, 721–22.
21. "Report of the Young Men's Mutual Improvement Associations for the Year Ending March 31, 1880," *Contributor*, June 1880, 214–15.
22. Anderson, "The Past of Mutual Improvement," 2–3.
23. B. Morris Young, "Recollections," *Improvement Era*, August 1925, 955.
24. Wells, "Historic Sketch," June 1925, 717.
25. Wells, "Historic Sketch," *Improvement Era*, September 1925, 1070.
26. Edward H. Anderson, "The Past of Mutual Improvement," *Improvement Era*, December 1897, 85.
27. Wells, "Historic Sketch," June 1925, 728.
28. Wells, "Historic Sketch," September 1925, 1069.
29. Smith, "Origin of Mutual Improvement," 985–86.
30. Wells, "Historic Sketch," June 1925, 716.

31. Wells, "Historic Sketch," *Improvement Era*, 1072–74.
32. *Deseret News 1974 Church Almanac* (Salt Lake City: Deseret News, 1974), 214.
33. Junius F. Wells, "Historic Sketch," *Improvement Era*, October 1925, 1149.
34. Charles E. Mitchener Jr., "Young Men's Mutual Improvement Association," Young Men's Mutual Improvement Association History, Church History Library, Salt Lake City, 5.
35. Mitchener, "Young Men's Mutual Improvement Association," 5.
36. Harold B. Lee, "Follow the Leadership of the Church," *Ensign*, July 1973, 96–97, 99.
37. "FYI: For Your Information," *New Era*, January 1973, 46.
38. Lee, "Follow the Leadership of the Church," 96.
39. Lee, "Follow the Leadership of the Church," 99.
40. Victor L. Brown, in "Priesthood MIA Era Opens," *Church News*, June 23, 1973, 3.
41. L. Tom Perry, in "Sessions Outline Priesthood MIA," *Church News*, June 23, 1973, 5.
42. Robert L. Backman, "Youth's Opportunity to Serve," *Ensign*, July 1973, 85.
43. Spencer W. Kimball, in J. M. Heslop, "Priesthood to Direct Youth of the Church," *Church News*, June 29, 1974, 3, 14.
44. "Priesthood MIA Era Opens," *Church News*, June 23, 1973, 3.
45. Joseph F. Smith, *Gospel Doctrine*, 5th ed. (Salt Lake City: Deseret Book, 1986), 159; see also "Priesthood MIA Era Opens," 3; Victor L. Brown, "The Aaronic Priesthood MIA," *Ensign*, July 1973, 80; and "Sessions Outline Priesthood MIA," 5.
46. Brown, quoted in "Priesthood MIA Era Opens," 3.
47. Spencer W. Kimball, in Heslop, "Changes Prepare Way for Aaronic Priesthood Lead," 14.
48. Brown, "Aaronic Priesthood MIA," 80.
49. Packer, *That All May Be Edified*, 121.
50. Packer, *That All May Be Edified*, 124.
51. Packer, *That All May Be Edified*, 122–23.
52. Packer, *That All May Be Edified*, 124.
53. Young, "Recollections," 954.

John P. Livingstone

21

N. Eldon Tanner and Church Administration

I FIRST met President N. Eldon Tanner at a youth conference when he was a member of the First Presidency and I was a young teenager. He and his wife entered the dining area, and someone around us said, "That is President Tanner!" President and Sister Tanner looked very distinguished to me back then, and I took a mental snapshot of them that day. I saw him again in close quarters when, as a sixteen-year-old, I was asked to conduct a fireside in Edmonton where he spoke. Many of my nonmember friends attended that fireside, and I remember hoping he would be a good speaker and keep them interested. I needn't have worried—he gave a wonderful speech. Later, he dedicated our local chapel.

President N. Eldon Tanner brought a significant skill set to the offices of the First Presidency of The Church of Jesus Christ of Latter-day Saints when he became a counselor, first to David O. McKay and then

---

John P. Livingstone is an associate professor of Church history and doctrine at Brigham Young University.

to three subsequent Presidents. His knowledge of corporate finance, organization, and behavior resulted in tremendous changes at Church headquarters. The principles and practices he encouraged resulted in a cultural shift in the nature of Church leadership at its highest levels.

What was it that put President Tanner in a position to effect such change? What events in his life brought about the skills that were put to such good use when he was called into general Church leadership? What personality traits allowed him to be effective in bringing about such revolutionary modifications?

EARLY YEARS

President Tanner was born in Salt Lake City on May 9, 1898. (His mother went back to her parent's home for her firstborn's arrival.) He grew up in Aetna, a small farming community a few miles southeast of Cardston, Alberta, Canada. His father was Nathan W. Tanner and his mother was Sara Edna Brown (a sister to Hugh B. Brown).

As the eldest of eight children, he became a highly responsible young man, an attribute that stayed with him through his life. His reliability and dependability were due to an upbringing by hardworking farm parents who loved their children deeply and required their help with every aspect of agricultural life in southern Alberta. Eldon did well in school and decided to become a teacher. This resulted in his attending a normal school (teachers' college) in Calgary, which was 150 miles north of his home. He had taken some of his high schooling at the Church's Knight Academy in Raymond, another Latter-day Saint community about thirty miles east of Aetna, so going to Calgary was not his first time away from home. But this time, he was not able to take small jobs to maintain his room and board.

His father encouraged him to take out a loan to attend the normal school in Calgary. This may well have been a pivotal point in Eldon's interest in and facility with finances. He recorded:

After I finished my schooling in Raymond, I wanted to go to Normal School in Calgary. Father said, "Well, we need you on the farm," He said, "If you can arrange the money, we can't finance it, but if you can arrange to borrow the money, we'll sacrifice your help on the farm." So I went to the bank—I was frightened to death—I'd never talked to a banker before, and here I was talking to the manager of the Bank! I told him what I wanted and he said, "Are you Carl Tanner's boy?" I said, "No, I'm N. W. Tanner's boy." He said, "Well, when could you pay this loan back?" I said, "I'll start as soon as I start teaching school." So, he let me have the money that I needed. That was a very, very significant thing in my life. When he knew that I was N. W. Tanner's son, I made up my mind right then that I would try to live so that I would have that kind of name when my children came along.[1]

It is clear that the responsibility he felt to maintain his father's good name and to pay back the school loan began a lifetime of honesty and integrity as well as an appreciation of business ethics, which became a powerful tool in his life. This school loan was the harbinger of a life of financial responsibility and acumen that would ultimately bless millions of people in his later government, business, and Church affairs.

POLITICAL INVOLVEMENT AND SOCIAL CREDIT

When Eldon finished normal school, he began teaching in Hill Spring, where he fell in love with a pretty fellow teacher, Sara (Sally) Merrill. He continued to court Sally until they were married in 1919. After their marriage, he returned to Cardston to complete what Canadians call grade twelve. They returned to Hill Spring, where he taught school and became involved in other businesses to the point that he quit teaching for a time to concentrate on running a general store, an eighty-acre farm, a gas station, a butcher shop, and a farm machinery business. These early businesses provided lessons and experience that would come into play later in his government, business, and Church responsibilities. He sold these businesses in 1927, and he and his family moved back to Cardston, where Eldon became the principal of the high school. By this time, he and his wife had had four daughters. He also sold men's suits, insurance, and milk on the side. He was called into the bishopric of the Cardston First Ward, ultimately becoming bishop of the ward in 1933. He also successfully ran for town council.

In 1935 a significant political meeting was held in the basement of the Cardston Tabernacle that would change Tanner's life forever. Eldon was asked to chair the meeting and became acquainted with a visitor from Calgary, William Aberhart. He was an Ontario-born schoolteacher who was principal at Crescent Heights School in Calgary. He was a highly organized, commanding figure at six feet tall and about 260 pounds. Religion was the mainstay of his life, and he was a radio preacher with a two-hour program every Sunday which, at its peak in the mid- to late-1920s, was heard by about 350,000 listeners. Academic higher criticism was becoming popular in Alberta, and Aberhart, as a fundamentalist scriptorian, won a large following toward practical Christianity in his "Back to the Bible" radio program. Bible study groups popped up around Alberta based on Aberhart's efforts, creating a grassroots organization that would become politically expedient later. The economic downturn of the late 1920s and early 1930s seemed to create greater spiritual concern among citizens of the province, and the popularity of his program only strengthened. Airtime expanded to five hours each Sunday afternoon, and Aberhart and his radio program became virtually an Alberta institution.

While grading departmental examinations in Edmonton in the summer of 1932, Aberhart was introduced to a Christian-based political movement called Social Credit. A friend shared a book with him that outlined the theories of Clifford Hugh Douglas, a Scottish engineer and cost accountant who theorized that a major flaw of capitalism was that economic production could never generate enough income for the economy to buy itself back.

Douglas described Social Credit as "a policy of a philosophy," calling it "practical Christianity." Douglas believed that "there would be a chronic deficiency of purchasing power," allowing the banking system to capitalize by issuing loans and thereby controlling the economic system and credit.[2] As a solution to the Great Depression, he advocated government control of credit and prices by issuing social credit to citizens based on the actual wealth of the economy in a nation or state. This social credit would be granted to citizens via a national dividend to enable them to buy goods and services. William Aberhart began to talk about social credit on his Sunday radio show and piqued the interest of his listeners. When his Bible study groups began to study social credit, a grassroots movement emerged and formed an actual political party known simply as Social Credit. Ultimately, Aberhart proposed that Albertans be given a twenty-five-dollar-per-month dividend based on this theory. That offer remained in the minds of Albertans and later fueled the initial success of the Social Credit party in the 1935 provincial election.

This applied or practical Christianity no doubt made Social Credit attractive to William Aberhart as well as N. Eldon Tanner. The 1935 meeting in the basement of the Cardston Tabernacle placed these two school principals in touch with each other, and the principles of Social Credit interested Bishop Tanner so much that he established a study group with a few men in town, which met one night a week for several weeks.

In the early 1930s, the dividend proposal gained traction with the populace, who could see that although they were impoverished there were plenty of goods and supplies around them due to the efficiencies of the industrial age, which seemed to produce goods ad infinitum. The idea of a Christian economic system that allowed the population to benefit from the wealth of all without adopting socialism began to take off, and it seemed the new Social Credit Party was about to be elected by a landslide. Aberhart had already asked Eldon Tanner to stand as a party candidate in Cardston, and Eldon accepted.

A Firm Foundation

Sure enough, on August 23, 1935, Alberta elected the first Social Credit government in the world. William Aberhart eventually became the premier of the province (he did not actually run in the election, but the elected candidate stepped aside to allow him to take over the riding in a by-election) as well as the education minister. He asked N. Eldon Tanner to serve as speaker of the legislature, and a year later asked him to take the post of minister of lands and mines. Newspapers around the country and in Great Britain announced the birth of Social Credit as a bona fide government, and the Alberta Social Credit Party realized they must put their money where their mouth was.

Speaker Tanner quickly borrowed a robe and chair and spent late nights over the next few weeks learning parliamentary protocol. None of those elected in the first Social Credit government had even been in the legislative building, let alone served in any kind of provincial office. But they had soundly defeated the United Farmers of Alberta Party, and they sprang into activity to get ready for the upcoming legislative session. N. Eldon Tanner distinguished himself as an able speaker, taking firm control of the house and regulating all the affairs of the same. This moderating, monitoring role as speaker would become very useful in later years in both business and Church leadership.

NEW RESPONSIBILITIES

Only a year later, William Aberhardt had a disagreement with C. C. Ross, the minister of lands and mines, and asked for Ross's resignation. Both Aberhart and Ross felt that N. Eldon Tanner would be a good replacement minister. So, with only one year's experience as house speaker, Eldon was asked if he would be willing to serve as Alberta minister of lands and mines. Always self-effacing, Eldon told the premier he was happy to continue as speaker, but Aberhart insisted and the speaker became the minister.

The Alberta Department of Lands and Mines controlled fish and game interests on behalf of the government as well as forestry and public lands. When he took the reins of the ministry, Tanner once again dedicated himself to learning the various facets of his new assignment. By meeting with the former minister, civil servants working in the department, and experts in the field outside of government, Tanner was able to gather the resources necessary to run the department with efficiency and confidence. One of his former government accountants commented, "President Tanner knew every detail of his budget for Lands and Mines. He wanted to be able to defend every dollar. His budget requests never came back with any adjustments I can remember. He was a real detail man."[3]

In his new ministerial role, Tanner interacted with industry leaders, the public, and the press. On one occasion when a reporter did not keep confidence and published an upcoming action, he was called into the minister's office and told he would not be privy to any more information. This commitment to principles and integrity would be a feature of Tanner's future leadership, both in industry and in Church affairs.

Conservation and thrift was another feature of Tanner's time in the minister's office. In the early years of his service, Eldon Tanner and his department leaders formulated an ingenious leasing, drilling, and royalty plan that would prove to be remarkably effective in controlling oil and gas development in Alberta. His policies would add 2.35 billion dollars to the Alberta general revenue coffers between 1950 and 1968. Even now the policies' benefits remain evident. N. Eldon Tanner's oil policies and legislation, which resulted from much consultation with American and British oil interests, made Alberta rich and placed it in a financial position above every other province and territory in Canada, which remains the case even today.

In 1952, Tanner retired from the Alberta Social Credit government, but not before the then-current premier, Ernest C. Manning, privately offered to step down and offer Eldon the premiership. He then became the president of an oil company financed by Charles Merrill (of Merrill Lynch fame) in which his son-in-law Clifford Walker was a principal manager. Tanner had met Charles Merrill while consulting with American oil industry leaders. Tanner's position resulted in a move for his family from Edmonton, the capital city of Alberta and seat of the provincial government, to Calgary, 180 miles to the south, where he had attended normal school in earlier days. It also placed him in a location to be called as the first president of the Calgary Stake, which was formed on November 14, 1953, by Elders Harold B. Lee and Mark E. Petersen. By this time, Eldon was serving on boards for numerous companies and associations, and his leadership talents and ability were obvious to all.

Tanner worked as president of the oil company until early 1954, when it merged with another company to form Trans-Canada Pipe Lines Company Limited. Both the premier of Alberta and the Canadian minister of trade and commerce urged Tanner to accept the position of president of Trans-Canada, whose commission was to build a natural gas pipeline from Alberta to Quebec. Business associates wanted him to move to Toronto, closer to business and financial interests, but Tanner insisted on staying in Calgary, pointing to the importance of his Church calling as stake president as his reason for staying in Alberta.

Canadian nationalism at the time strongly opposed American financing or control of the pipeline project, resulting in a terrific political ruckus in the Canadian Parliament over the economics of the project. The speaker of the national parliament, René Beaudoin, had allowed a debate on the passing of pipeline financing, which the opposition hoped would delay the passing of finance legislation and block the pipeline from being constructed that year, and then reversed himself, retracting his decision and creating the major furor that ultimately facilitated the pipeline financing. The action ruined Beaudoin's career and later brought down the Liberal government and brought in a Conservative government led by John F. Diefenbaker.[4]

Tanner watched from the gallery of Canadian Parliament during the debate and became incensed at the seeming indifference of the sitting prime minister, Louis St. Laurent, and at one time left the gallery to confront him. His biographer would later report Eldon as saying, "I have never talked straighter to a man in my life."[5] Again, whenever he sensed integrity being compromised, Eldon could not be restrained from taking action, no matter who the offending party might be.

The passing of the legislation allowed Trans-Canada Pipeline to proceed with construction. By October 27, 1958, after many additional financing maneuvers, Alberta gas arrived in Toronto. While many personalities came together to bring about the project, the firm, calm, persistent leadership of N. Eldon Tanner brought it all together. The *Calgary Albertan* remembered:

> When a gas pipeline across Canada was being proposed and negotiated, the project was bogged down for a time by confusion and rivalry, and by difficult government conditions. It was agreed at the time that the one man in all Canada who could bring the various interests together and build the line conforming to government policy was Mr. Tanner. . . . The line has been built and is now in operation. It is a national institution, a major force in the economy of the country. And again, the chief architect has been Mr. Tanner. . . . We move a vote of thanks for the work he has done for Canada.[6]

The sensitive but firm hand of N. Eldon Tanner guided a difficult project to fruition in a relatively short length of time and blessed the entire country of Canada.

CHURCH SERVICE

No less impressive than his rise within the business community of Canada was N. Eldon Tanner's rise within the leadership of The Church of Jesus Christ of Latter-day Saints. With the completion of the Trans-Canada pipeline, the Tanners planned on enjoying a well-earned retirement on Calgary's west side, overlooking the foothills of the rugged Rocky Mountains. They had property, horses, and grandchildren to enjoy. But after living for only eight months in the new dream home, everything changed. While attending general conference in October 1960, the Tanners dined with Eldon's uncle Hugh B. Brown of the Quorum of the Twelve Apostles. At the end of the evening, Elder Brown said that President David O. McKay wished to see Eldon in his office at 9:00 the next morning.

Within a few minutes of his arrival at the Church Administration Building the next morning, Tanner was called by President McKay as an Assistant to the Quorum of the Twelve. This essentially meant that he would spend the rest of his life in full-time Church service. Later in the day, he would stand at the pulpit of the Tabernacle and humbly accept the call and "dedicate my life and my best to the work of the Lord."[7]

This would begin a swift rise to service in the First Presidency. Six months after his call as a General Authority, Eldon was called as president of the Western European Mission in London, where he supervised seven other mission presidents, toured their missions, and conducted Church business between them and Church headquarters. The Tanners arrived in London as a spirited building program was under way. Land had been purchased for Latter-day Saint meetinghouses, and members were excited to move away from rented halls. Elder Tanner encouraged local members to be better missionaries and to help with the construction projects. This became a good preparatory experience for the years ahead.

After serving for eighteen months in London, Elder Tanner was called in for another interview with President McKay in October 1962. On that occasion, President McKay called him to fill the vacancy in the Quorum of the Twelve Apostles created by the death of Elder George Q. Morris the previous April. He became the seventy-sixth Apostle to be ordained in this dispensation. The Tanners returned to England to prepare to turn the Western European Mission over to Elder Mark E. Petersen.

Elder Tanner was also asked to investigate the situation in Nigeria, where entire congregations of Africans had formed themselves into branches. At this time, the priesthood had not been extended to all worthy males, and Church leaders in Salt Lake City wanted an on-the-ground assessment of these branches and their earnest requests for baptism. Elder Tanner had previously met with Nigerian officials who were inquiring about Alberta's oil and gas policies. The Tanners spent two weeks in Nigeria, meeting with the leaders and members of these unofficial branches. Upon returning to Utah, Elder Tanner recommended caution in moving the work forward in black Africa. President McKay recorded, "After listening to Elder Tanner's report, I was deeply impressed that it was most fortunate that I had appointed Elder Tanner to go to Nigeria to look into the opening of the work there. I do not know of another man who could have met the conditions so favorably and intelligently as Brother Tanner did."[8]

One must wonder if this Nigerian report did not have a lasting effect on the mind and heart of President McKay, for less than a year later, with the sudden death of President McKay's counselor Henry D. Moyle, he spoke to his other counselor, Hugh B. Brown: "'I'm being urged on this side and that side to appoint this man or that man. I'm going across to the temple to find out whom the Lord wants.' When he came back, he went in to see [Hugh B. Brown] and said, 'The Lord wants N. Eldon Tanner. Can you work with him?' [Pres. Brown] said, 'Well, President McKay, you may have forgotten, but this is my nephew. I've known him all my life. He is like a son to me. Of course I can work with him.' 'Oh, he's your nephew? Well, he's the man the Lord wants.'"[9]

And so on October 3, 1963, having received a phone call from his uncle Hugh the evening before, N. Eldon Tanner met at 7:30 a.m. with President McKay, who asked if he would serve as second counselor in the First Presidency. Having served in the Quorum of the Twelve for only a year, President Tanner was now in the position of leading those who had much more general Church leadership experience than he. But time would reveal the inspiration behind his call to the leading council in the kingdom.

As a member of the First Presidency, N. Eldon Tanner was thrust into financial affairs as he served on various committees such as the Church Budget Committee, the Committee on Expenditures, and several others. His ability to ask good questions and honestly acknowledge his need to understand operations endeared him to those with whom he met. No doubt his years of experience in government and business prepared him to ask searching questions and to evaluate operations of Church departments and businesses with some insight and acumen.

Upon meeting with the Budget Committee and Financial Department leaders, President Tanner became aware that expenditures were dangerously high and that Church budgeting was in need of some realignment. The dramatic growth of the Church both in America and in Europe called for new policies and procedures. President Tanner's experience in education, business, and government had prepared him to help formulate new policies for the Church. His attention to detail, combined with a strong sense of financial accountability, allowed him to sensitively encourage change both organizationally and financially. He was unafraid to take strong action if necessary. Perhaps his strongest action early on was to declare a moratorium on brick-and-mortar construction (including delaying the construction of the Church Office Building) until the Building Committee budget could be stabilized and controlled. He also wanted to strengthen the Church's financial reserve so it could withstand the strain of surging growth and provide a safety net when necessary. He called for an evaluation of current investments and a review of current financial practices.

As he began to see improved stability, an incident occurred which was reminiscent of his confrontation with the prime minister of Canada. President McKay met with Elder Thorpe B. Isaacson, who later became a counselor in the First Presidency. Elder Isaacson was aware of Church building problems in California and came to the President of the Church with a suggestion that the current head of the Church Building Department be released and new leadership be called. Without consulting his counselors, President McKay gave authorization to Elder Isaacson to move ahead and organize a committee to review the building issues in the Church. President Tanner wished to meet with President McKay privately on the issue, but scheduling difficulties prevented this, and the issue came before a meeting of the First Presidency on January 5, 1965. President Tanner freely spoke his mind:

N. Eldon Tanner and Church Administration

> I came in here twice last year and recommended to you that we set up a committee to work with the Building Committee. Nothing was done about it. [Elder] Isaacson comes in and recommends we set up a committee and you set it up immediately and the wrong kind of a committee in my opinion. . . .
>
> I wanted to talk to you alone but it has come up this way and I want to express it here. . . . It is not the kind of committee that will do the job, it is only set up to get rid of [Wendell] Mendenhall and reorganize the Building Committee.[10]

The fact that he would address a difficult situation so directly clearly shows President Tanner's courage; he was unafraid to approach difficulties with whomever he felt needed addressing. He felt for a time that perhaps he might be released over the situation, but in spite of some hurt feelings, President McKay kept his counselor in place, knowing that there was one in his presidency who would bring issues directly to the table and not simply tell him what he wanted to hear. It may well be that this incident firmly rooted a protocol that matters coming before the First Presidency required unanimity before being acted upon. It also underscored the need for correlation among Church councils that would reduce special agreements or actions for individuals appealing directly to the President of the Church. In the end, Brother Mendenhall was still released, a new Building Committee chair was called, and Thorpe B. Isaacson later served in the First Presidency. Yet President Tanner's strong position on issues such as this illustrated the need for the President of the burgeoning Church to relinquish some personal control over Church programs and departments to his counselors, the Twelve, and the Seventy, as occurred under subsequent presidents.

It was not long before the Church budget was better balanced, spending was better controlled and monitored, and finances were subject to close cost accounting procedures. President Tanner took the scattered budgeting of the Church and brought it into correlation. His strong influence in implementing a more exacting corporate finance model to Church headquarters during his tenure cannot be overstated.

Another financial blessing for the Church, which President Tanner helped initiate working under the direction of President Harold B. Lee, was the formation of a fund-raising effort at BYU which eventually became LDS Philanthropies and the LDS Foundation. Designed to encourage donations and development funds from wealthy Church members, these foundations have raised millions of dollars for BYU and other Church entities, freeing up tithing funds to be used for direct ecclesiastical purposes. As one who accumulated wealth through his business career, President Tanner could appreciate the desire many members have to be able to share their financial blessings in building the kingdom.

President Tanner also took a personal interest in Church farms and ranches that were part of the Church's welfare efforts. His interest in cost accounting led him to examine the cost-per-animal estimates for feed and other resources. He loved to visit the Church's properties and personally examine their operations and settings. Just like back in his government days in Alberta, President Tanner would ask insightful questions of operators to learn more about their duties, planning, and ideas for improvement.

Learning and recommending as he went along, his personable and approachable style encouraged a steady flow of new ideas for improvement and thrift in Church-owned facilities. He applied his talents for garnering ideas, financial analysis, and discernment to every aspect of the Church programs for which he bore responsibility. Again, his affable style and sensitivity to the feelings of others encouraged the sharing of ideas for improvement and the application of those ideas to Church programs with timeliness and orderliness.

His delegation skills with those he worked with also followed a particular pattern. He believed in the need to not only assign individuals a responsibility but also to give them the time and space to do the job, and make sure they know how and when to report back. After meetings, President Tanner would create memos and ensure they were delivered to those who had received assignments.[11]

President Tanner was not so pragmatic that he would follow protocol just for tradition's sake. His biographer notes, "In observing transactions at Church headquarters, he sometimes asked Elder Joseph Anderson, who had been secretary to the First Presidency nearly half a century, 'Now, why do we do it this way?' Elder Anderson would reply, 'Well, we have just always done it this way.' And President Tanner would respond, 'Well, that's no reason.'"[12]

His years in education, government, and business taught President Tanner that people and their feelings were important, but that methods and systems could and should be improved when necessary. He was not afraid to say no when occasion required, but he ruled on principle, keeping in mind the feelings of those affected by his decisions.

I will not forget a situation that involved President Tanner and affected me very personally. I was serving as a counselor to a mission president who was enjoying significant success among Native Americans. The president of a university in the mission approached me and asked if Church leaders would consider providing housing in which missionary couples would serve as dorm parents for Native American students. I said I would take it up with my superiors. Church leaders deliberated over the request, but the mission president was eager to move forward.

The other counselor in the mission presidency had just sold a business for a sizable amount, and the sale was still being reviewed by business and government regulators. In a mission presidency meeting, he offered to provide funds to purchase property for the Native American student living facility. And though the Church had not approved the project, he invited me to look around for a home or facility that could house Native American students. I was able to locate what I thought was an appropriate building and met with a real estate agent and completed the purchase. A missionary couple then moved in to the home, began assembling furniture, and applied to the Church for reimbursement for the purchase.

As the application worked its way through Church offices, the mission president finished his assignment and returned home, and later the new mission president received word that the reimbursement application had been denied.

A few days later, the other counselor in the mission presidency called me, saying that he had been contacted by a national newspaper and asked about the loan he gave me to purchase the home. Because the sale of his corporation was a matter of public record, the loan for the Native American student facility looked like an insider trading violation, and he needed resolution on the matter quickly. Pressure mounted.

The real estate agent, who became my good friend through this process, was highly alarmed at the developments and asked me what I thought might happen. I said that I did not know, but I remember having a calm assurance that everything would work out just fine. He did not seem assured at all. In fact, he felt the Church had abandoned me.

When the former mission president was apprised of the situation, he made a visit to Church headquarters, where he met personally with President Tanner. In a very kind interview, President Tanner said that funds had been set aside for just such a contingency and that the Church would indeed purchase the property and then resell it as soon as possible. This, of course, was a great comfort to all involved. The real estate agent saw it as nothing less than a miracle and came away with much better feelings about the Church and its leaders, especially when he was able to resell the home for several thousand dollars more than the original purchase price. I sensed that I had literally felt the merciful hand of the Lord through President N. Eldon Tanner. Great relief was afforded through the kindness extended through this member of the First Presidency; perhaps this personal account helps highlight the height and the depth of the Church leader some called "Mr. Integrity."[13]

CONCLUSION

As the years go by and we review twentieth-century Church history with additional perspective, it seems clear that N. Eldon Tanner was especially prepared in his character and life experiences to play a very significant role in bringing The Church of Jesus Christ of Latter-day Saints into better organizational and financial practices. He established a foundation of fiscal development and responsibility that continues today. Significant Church projects may not have been possible without the influence and direction of President Tanner. Many Church departments and programs were deeply affected by his stellar service, and his memory continues to loom large over the Church even today.

NOTES

1. *An Interview with President N. Eldon Tanner*, Church History Library AV 1401 (Salt Lake City: Intellectual Reserve, Inc. 1979), DVD (2009).
2. John J. Barr, *The Dynasty: The Rise and Fall of Social Credit in Alberta* (Toronto: McClelland and Stewart, 1974), 26.
3. Telephone interview with Harold E. Bennett, January 4, 2010. Bennett was an assistant accountant in lands and mines, later registrar of lands and forests in Lethbridge, Alberta. He also served as a counselor when President Tanner was the president of the Edmonton Branch.
4. See Mark Maloney, "A Tragic Fall from Grace," *Toronto Star*, February 24, 2007; http://globalpublicaffairs.ca/article022407.html.
5. G. Homer Durham, *N. Eldon Tanner, His Life and Service* (Salt Lake City: Deseret Book, 1982), 158.
6. Durham, *N. Eldon Tanner*, 163.
7. N. Eldon Tanner, in Conference Report, October 1960, 46.
8. Gregory A. Prince and William Robert Wright, *David O. McKay and the Rise of Modern Mormonism* (Salt Lake City: University of Utah Press, 2005), 85.
9. Prince and Wright, *Rise of Modern Mormonism*, 25.
10. Prince and Wright, *Rise of Modern Mormonism*, 218–19.
11. Dee F. Andersen, interviewed by author, February 9, 2010.
12. Durham, *N. Eldon Tanner*, 257.
13. Thomas S. Monson, "How Firm a Foundation," *Ensign*, November 2006, 62, 67–68.

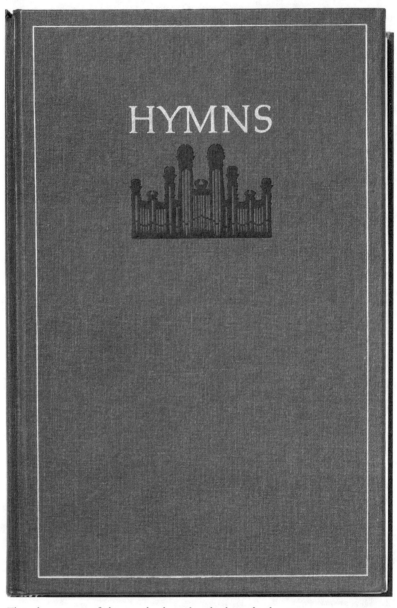

Though not part of the standard works, the hymnbook represents an important part of Latter-day Saint ideas and worship. (© 2005 Intellectual Reserve, Inc. All rights reserved.)

Michael Hicks

22

How to Make (and Unmake) a Mormon Hymnbook

The hymnbook holds an odd place among Mormon works. In some ways it resembles the standard works because it contains the authorized sacred words and music used in virtually all Church meetings throughout the world. But, unlike scripture, it can change dramatically from one generation to the next. And even the means by which it changes vary over time, from the one-person hymnbook compilers of the early Church to the bureaucratic committees of our day. The only constant is that the making of one hymnbook is the unmaking of its forerunner. Our current book, though, supplanted not only the 1950 edition but also an aborted 1970s edition, whose history reveals some chronic tensions among aesthetic, populist, and pragmatic ideals in a growing church.

Michael Hicks is a professor of music composition and theory at Brigham Young University.

A Firm Foundation

For most of the Mormon nineteenth century, ambitious individuals or ad-hoc collaborators produced hymnbooks for the general Church, its missions, and its auxiliaries. The best-known of these was the British text-only pocketbook that went through twenty-five editions from 1840 to 1912. In 1889, President Wilford Woodruff authorized a committee of well-trained British musicians to publish the *Latter-day Saints' Psalmody*, the first complete book of four-part *musical* settings for every text in the British hymnal. Other hymnbooks with printed music soon competed with the *Psalmody* for Church use—especially *Songs of Zion* (1908) and *Deseret Sunday School Songs* (1909). In 1920 the First Presidency created the General Music Committee, a group that within seven years produced a more modern and serviceable hymnbook called *Latter-day Saint Hymns* (1927). In 1948 it was replaced by *Hymns: The Church of Jesus Christ of Latter-day Saints*, and then a 1950 revision by the same name. *Hymns* was the first collection to do away with all other adult hymnbooks in the Church. For the first time in Church history, the First Presidency wrote a preface to the book as a kind of imprimatur.[1]

In October 1972, President Harold B. Lee called O. Leslie Stone as an Assistant to the Twelve Apostles and in December made him managing director of a huge new Church Music Department. This department consisted mainly of a new Church Music Committee (headed by Harold Goodman) with nine "specialized areas," including composition, headed by Merrill Bradshaw.[2] In December 1973, after the First Presidency told Elder Stone to have the Music Department "proceed in making guidelines and preparation for a new hymnal," Goodman appointed Bradshaw as the head of a new four-member hymn committee. They held their first meeting in the boardroom of the twentieth floor of the Church Office Building one week before Christmas.[3]

Bradshaw had definite ideas: he wanted the committee to review about ten thousand hymns, new and old, choose about five hundred that would appeal to an international church, and have a new book ready to issue in the fall of 1975. Committee members immediately brought up problems Bradshaw had not thought of. For example, the racks on the back of pews were sized for books of four hundred or fewer hymns. So they had to trim Bradshaw's ideal size. The timetable was also questionable, because the Church would have to coordinate with Deseret Book to make sure the stock of old hymnbooks was depleted when the new one came out. Other questions followed, including that of what to call the book. Bradshaw favored "hymnal." But should it be "hymn book"? "Hymnbook"? What about a broader title that allowed for a wider spectrum of music—"Songs for Worship"?

Bradshaw gave the committee an ambitious flowchart of how the new hymnal—or "hymnbook," as they decided to call it—would progress (see fig. 1). As they proceeded through the chart and made preliminary decisions, the committee felt momentum gathering. But eight days after the first meeting, their sponsor, President Lee, suddenly died.

Elder Stone hastily wrote to the new Church president, Spencer W. Kimball, to get the project reapproved. The rationale he offered favored genuinely new hymns, "hymns that proclaim the revealed truth in this day and time, hymns that are most meaningful to the present worldwide church. This would mean less Protestant-type hymns."[4] At the same time, the committee began to define its mission, stated succinctly by Goodman: "We will proceed from the assumption that all hymns, present and past[,] are to be deleted from the Hymn book. Only those will be put into the new Hymn book which can be justified."[5] To be justified meant to meet one or more of six criteria. Two criteria were the musical quality and the "doctrinal value and poetry" of the text. Two others were the "appropriateness" and "usefulness" of the hymn for Latter-day Saint services. A fifth criterion was a hymn's "traditional popularity with the Saints." And the sixth was "insistence of a general authority that a hymn must be included."

With those in mind, the Hymnbook Task Committee, as they now called themselves, began their zealous weeding and harvesting of hymns. The plan was fourfold:

1. Review all hymns in the current hymnbook.
2. Review all hymns from earlier Latter-day Saint hymnbooks and song collections.
3. Review hymns from as many Protestant hymnbooks as possible.
4. Use the *Ensign, Church News,* and even direct mailings to solicit new texts and tunes from Church poets and composers.[6]

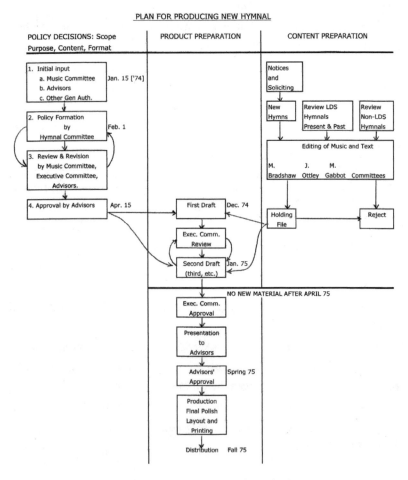

Fig. 1. Initial flowchart for planned 1975 LDS hymnbook.

As the process unfolded, the committee would decide not only which hymns to include but also whether to revise any that they chose. The most common revision, they decided, would be to lower the keys of many hymns to foster the standard practice in Protestantism: everyone sings the melody in unison rather than singing in parts.[7]

But whatever urgency the committee felt was tempered by the viscosity of working within a larger system. In April 1974, for example, the Music Department advisors (Elders Mark E. Petersen and Boyd K. Packer) finally approved the committee's fundamental document, "Specifications and Guidelines for the Preparation of a New Hymnbook," only after five drafts in as many months.[8] Still, the hymnbook committee forged ahead, meeting for three to four hours every two weeks. Each committee member had his or her assignment and, after discussing it with their subcommittees, made recommendations to the whole committee for approval. All hymn reviews were thorough and often severe. When Jerold Ottley's subcommittee looked at the first 130 songs in the 1909 *Deseret Sunday School Songs*, for example, they found only nine of them possibly worth including in the new book, and even then, all nine would need revision.[9]

The committee also had to wrestle with broader questions about content and format. Would their choices be in all international Latter-day Saint hymnbooks? They decided they should choose a core of hymns to appear in all hymnbooks and let regional committees choose the rest.[10] And what about patriotic songs like "America the Beautiful" and "Battle Hymn of the Republic"? This question was quickly answered by the First Presidency: all American patriotic songs were out.[11] The committee decided to drop the 1950 hymnbook's separation of "choral" and "congregational" hymns. Each hymn would now be headed by its actual title when that differed from its first line (e.g., "Love At Home," not "There Is Beauty All Around").[12] The new book would group hymns in sections (as the first Latter-day Saint hymnbook had done). That, in turn, would necessitate a far more elaborate set of indices and cross-references.[13]

A Firm Foundation

After a year of reviewing hymns and policies, the committee knew they would be lucky to produce even a first draft of their hymn choices by the fall of 1975—the date they had once hoped to have the book in print.[14] As personal commitments demanded more of the committee members' time, they began to meet only once a month and give each committee member more autonomy.[15] When November 1975 arrived, they had reviewed all hymns in the 1950 book twice, revoting and sometimes reversing earlier decisions.[16] An excerpt from their collation entitled "Proposed Disposition of the Materials in the Present Hymnbook" suggests the verdicts and justifications for each decision (see fig. 2).

Hymn #	Title	keep	delete	comments
241	For the Strength of	x		One of the greatest hymns of the Church; Reduce to four verses
242	Again we Meet aroun	x		Good Sacrament Hymn. Needs only four verses
243	Glorious things are		x	Not used, Music inadequate
244	Glorious things of	x*		musical setting awkward, seldom used
245	Does the Journey s		x	Music poor, text gloomy
246	God is in his holy		x	Doctrinally confusing
247	Go Ye messengers	x		Some text revisions suggested. Good missionary hymn
248	Great God attend		x	Not sung. Music beautiful, but difficult
249	Hark ten thousand		x	Not sung, music substandard for a hymnbook
250	The happy day has	x		Not widely used here, but popular overseas
251	Again our Dear Re		x	Good music, words weak and not well matched
252	Hushed was the eve	x		Samuel's call; Beautiful setting and text
253	Hark Listen to the		x	Not used, Text and Music weak
254	I'll Praise my mak		x	Music too difficult and elaborate
255	I saw a mighty ang		x	Music tricky and doesn't fit the text.
256	Give us Room that		x	Question the message of the text for our time; not used, weak text and music
257	If you could Hie to	x*		New music would certainly improve this one
258	In Rememberance of	x		Fine Sacrament Hymn
259	Jesus Lover of my		x	Bad doctrine to hide from life's ills; Lover has taken on bad connotations now.
260	Lean on my ample		x	too high and difficult for most of our congregations; not rewarding for choirs
261	I'm a pilgrim	x		difficult but rewarding
262	Let Zion in her be		x	Nice text, but not well matched with the music
263	He died the great	x		Great Sacrament hymn
264	Lo the Mighty God		x*	Very difficult to sing: high tenor, male duet in last line, awkward rhythm
265	Lord thou wilt hea		x	Text not LDS, Outdated style
266	We're not ashamed		x	not sung: Music difficult and intricate
267	Not now but in the		x	Not compatible with our theology
268	O awake my slumber		x	Not sung, music awkward, some doctrinal problems

Fig. 2. Excerpt from 1975 draft of "Proposed Disposition of the Materials in the Present Hymnbook."

The committee voted to delete over 30 percent of past congregational hymns, 67 percent of choir hymns, and 90 percent of men's and women's arrangements.[17] The hymns they cut included old Christian favorites such as "Nearer, My God, to Thee," "Come, Thou Fount of Every Blessing," "Jesus, Lover of My Soul," and "Behold, a Royal Army." They also threw out many oft-sung Latter-day Saint originals, including "Who's On the Lord's Side, Who?," "Reverently and Meekly Now," "I Saw a Mighty Angel Fly," and "Now We'll Sing with One Accord."

Their apostolic advisors asked for a list of the hymns the committee wanted to delete.[18] Bradshaw agreed to provide it but insisted that it come with detailed explanations of the committee's decisions. He also gave fourteen broad reasons for cutting hymns from the old book:

1. Their texts were "unsuitable."
2. The hymns had a "Protestant flavor" or "revivalist style."
3. They were "dated."
4. They were national anthems, state songs, etc.
5. They were too difficult or awkward to sing.
6. They were militaristic.
7. They were little used.
8. They had "excessive sentimentality."
9. They were "musically inappropriate," "incompetent," or in a "frivolous style."
10. The music or text had "uncomfortable associations" (e.g., with love songs).
11. Another setting of the same text was better (e.g., "O My Father").
12. The hymn was guilty of "preachiness" or a "moralizing flavor."
13. A better hymn with the same message was available.
14. Words and text were poorly matched.[19]

Many of these reasons seemed fair, even obvious. Others, though, must have seemed harsh and elitist, with a tone that would not sit well with some Church leaders.[20] In its report to the Twelve, the committee often used words far gentler than what it used in its internal reports, which included "gloomy," "pompous," "choppy," "racis[t]," "chauvinistic," and even "pantheistic."[21] But the committee members were still sometimes blunt in the reasons they gave to the Twelve. More than one hymn they called "musically embarrassing to the church." They deemed "Who's on the Lord's Side, Who?" to be "amateurish, jingoist [and] self congratulatory" with music that "sounds like a cheap London dance hall tune."[22] Nevertheless, since some deleted hymns might still have "historical value," the committee proposed they be published in a separate book that would "tell things about our past."[23]

With so many hymns out, the committee hoped to put as many as 175 new ones in without making the new book any longer than the old one.[24] By mid-1975 they had gathered more than three thousand potential new hymns and two thousand more new texts that could be set to music. These included Protestant favorites (especially Christmas and Thanksgiving songs); "hymns from around the world" and overtly ethnic hymns (like the Boy Scout favorite "Omaha Tribal Prayer");[25] and newly written texts and tunes, especially sacrament hymns and others that treated Latter-day Saint emphases (priesthood, prophets, fast day, tithing, genealogy, and so on). For months the committee discussed and voted on all of the hymns they had gathered. During this time, requests came from General Authorities such as Elder Thomas S. Monson, who urged them to add the hymn "How Great Thou Art."[26]

Another year passed; it was now summer of 1976 and the committee still had not completed a first draft.[27] They again revised their timetable, declaring that the book would be done by fall 1977. But for over two years unforeseen questions had kept cropping up: What would be the budget for mock-ups of the book?[28] Who was going to supervise the difficult process of translating hymn texts?[29] Could core hymns have the same numbers in all international printings?[30] What about a "simplified" hymnbook (a special edition with pared-down accompaniments)?[31] Honorariums for new hymns?[32] Thickness of the paper?[33] Who would handle the editing?[34] If they were going to lower some keys, how low and on which hymns?[35] What about other musical revisions?[36] If they were going to revise some texts, which lines would they change and how?[37] Should hymns be sung in first person singular or plural?[38] If the hymns were to be divided into topical sections, what would the topics be?[39] Should the committee field-test new hymns to see if members liked and would sing them? If so, how?[40] When a draft seemed ready to present to the Brethren, how would they do that—cassettes?[41] And how would they introduce this new hymnbook to the Church at large?[42]

But the slow pace also stemmed from knots in the administrative process. These led the committee in September 1976 to make yet another list, this one a list of six groups of questions about authority and protocol:

1. What kind of direct communication should exist between this committee and Elder Stone, managing director of the Church Music Department? Does Elder Stone understand our rationale and all of our activities?
2. On a specialized project such as the hymnbook, should the "expert," who has been selected because of his expertise with hymns and music, be allowed to sit and communicate with those higher up in the administration?
3. Exactly what authority does this committee have in relation to decisions made on the new hymnbook? What responsibility?
4. What is the role of this committee in the new hymnbook project? Will the committee be able to defend their work and rationale to those in decision-making positions?
5. What is the role of this committee in relation to Correlation and the new hymnbook? The role of the Deseret Press? The role of the Editing Section?
6. Concerning our role with Correlation, how will they react to our suggested Protestant hymns being included in the new hymnbook?[43]

Perhaps predictably, some General Authorities as well as the Correlation Committee wanted to overturn the hymnbook committee's decisions. (Elders Ezra Taft Benson and Mark E. Petersen, for example, lobbied to get patriotic songs back in.)[44] In October 1976, the committee learned that twelve hymns they had voted to delete were being put back in and three they voted to keep were being thrown out. The committee came up with three ways to respond to such overturnings: "acquiesce" (let the overturnings stand without argument), "fuss" (let the Brethren know why the committee disagreed but eventually acquiesce if compromises could be made), or "fight" ("strongly disagree with their decision, and be prepared to back up the disagreement with specific reasons and rationale"). Regarding the fifteen hymns on which they'd been overturned, the committee voted "acquiesce" on four, "fuss" on four, and "fight" on seven.[45]

As 1977 opened, the project faced a new obstacle. In February, the First Presidency divided the general Melchizedek Priesthood Executive Committee into two smaller committees, one of which, now called the Priesthood Executive Committee, was headed by Elder Gordon B. Hinckley. This committee had three subcommittees, one of which, headed by Elder Dean L. Larsen, would oversee Church publications, including music.[46] Elder Hinckley directed Elder Larsen to find out the rationale for and current status of the hymnbook project begun more than three years earlier.[47] Michael Moody, executive secretary of the Church Music Division (as it was then called) and ex-officio member of the hymnbook committee, quickly prepared a ten-point explanatory memo called "Why a New Hymnbook."[48] He and the rest of the committee also made new, detailed charts showing all the old hymns they wanted to keep, discard, or revise, and which new hymns they wanted to include.[49] On April 26, 1977, Elder Larsen told Moody that the First Presidency and Council of the Twelve seemed ready to scrap the major revision the committee had prepared and "take an entirely different direction," probably consisting of "minor modifications" to the 1950 hymnbook.[50]

The hymnbook committee stopped meeting, and the project lay fallow for another year and a half, when the Twelve suddenly reauthorized the project and called the committee back together.[51] For a few weeks they began meeting again as the "Reactivated Hymnbook Task Committee," reviewing their earlier drafts and answering a list of thirty-one questions posed to them by the Twelve.[52] For example: Number of verses for each hymn? No more than four, the committee said. Chord symbols with the hymns? No. "It encourages people to get by with less than adequate musical training in preparing themselves to serve the Kingdom musically." The color of the book? Several colors would be best, to allow wards and stakes to adapt to color schemes in their buildings. There were larger questions too, especially about what values should rule in the hymn choices the committee made. The reply was emphatic: "Every compromise with excellence will return to haunt us a thousand times."[53] Within weeks the committee submitted essentially the same plans as they had before. They received no written reply and were all released.[54]

For the next five years nothing happened with the new hymnbook. The Church's publication committee focused on new editions of Latter-day Saint scriptures: the Bible, published in 1979, and the new triple combination, published in 1982. In 1983, with the scriptures now done, the First Presidency authorized Moody to revive the hymnbook project as essentially a modest revision of the 1950 edition. Moody was not to work with any of the previous committee members, but only the current advisory committee to the Church Music Division.[55] He and they reviewed the earlier committee's work and agreed with many of their principles and decisions. Nevertheless, field-testing hymns became the dominant decider.[56] Singability and popularity trumped artistic or academic standards. Many of the hymns the earlier committee had cut now came back. The patriotic songs also returned. And the international breadth of the new hymnbook fell far short of the earlier committee's ideals.

After a comparatively swift compilation process, the hymnbook came off the presses in 1985—the sesquicentennial of the Church's first hymnbook. A period of both fanfare and adjustment began as Church members lamented the loss of a few favorites and found fresh gems among the newly added hymns. The *Ensign* heralded the book with a cover article that outlined its making, interviewed its 1980s compilers, and doted on its physical appearance.[57] Perhaps the most telling statement in the article came from the hymnbook's General Authority adviser, Elder Hugh Pinnock, who bespoke the populism of the times. The men and women that produced this book, Elder Pinnock said, had "only one disability: they knew too much about music." However, he noted, "the committee has been sensitive to select hymns of worship that people will enjoy singing."[58]

Behind the scenes, Michael Moody wrote a letter of thanks and consolation to Merrill Bradshaw. Moody said that he had never been told why the earlier version had been scrapped but that the timing of this version was right: "There were too many factors that fell into place to have it otherwise." In his reply, Bradshaw praised Moody's successful midwifing of the new hymnbook and wrote: "Knowing a little . . . of the pressures, politics, and emotions that are involved in getting such a project finished, approved, and published, I consider the final product to be little short of a miracle."[59]

"Pressures, politics, and emotions"—not sufficient for the making of a new hymnbook, to be sure, but necessary. To dismantle a greatly loved hymnbook and construct a new one in its place requires the wrenching of a whole culture of worship. And to attempt that is to confront fundamental questions of human experience: what to salvage and what to throw away. Those questions can cut especially deep where the demands of religion and the pleasures of music are concerned. The chairman of the Church Music Committee in the 1940s, explaining the choices that shaped the 1948 hymnbook, wrote that to be criticized for those choices "goes without saying." "It is a long way, I fear, from the dignity of [the great English hymns] to the triviality of some of the music we sing, . . . and it may be that our people will never, as a whole, find the same appeal in them that we musicians do." So their task in unmaking the 1927 hymnbook and making a new one was to "step forward, without being altogether too drastic." Because "we cannot make transitions to a higher plane of expression very fast in a democratic body of people."[60] But even a slow transition to a higher plane of expression is a miracle worth its share of acquiescing, fussing, and sometimes even a little fighting.

NOTES

1. A more detailed history of these various editions may be found throughout the narrative of my *Mormonism and Music: A History* (Urbana: University of Illinois Press, 1989).

2. See Specialized Areas Meeting Minutes, May 1, 1973. The specialized areas were: Text Committee, Children's Music Committee, Organ Committee, Library Committee, Choral Music Committee, Instrumental Music Committee, Composition Committee, Youth Music Committee, and Congregational Music Committee.

   The call to Bradshaw is in O. Leslie Stone to Merrill Bradshaw, January 25, 1973. These two sources and most other materials cited in this essay were given to me by Merrill Bradshaw in 1986 (and a few by Janet Bradshaw in 2009); I have placed those with many related documents in the Merrill Bradshaw Papers housed in the music area of the L. Tom Perry Special Collections, Harold B. Lee Library, Brigham Young University, Provo, Utah. All documents cited herein, except as noted, are housed in these (as yet unprocessed) Bradshaw Papers.

3. The authorization to make guidelines for the new hymnal is in Church Music Committee Minutes, December 11, 1973. All of the information in the paragraph that follows, as well as the flowchart replicated in figure 1 are from the December 18, 1973 Minutes of the Hymn Book Committee, whose name was soon changed to the Hymnbook Committee and then, for most of their existence, the Hymnbook Task Committee. Hereafter, the minutes of this committee will be cited as HTCM.

4. O. Leslie Stone to the First Presidency, January 4, 1974, Church Music Department Correspondence, Church History Library, The Church of Jesus Christ of Latter-day Saints, Salt Lake City.

5. Although the sentiment appears in the December 18, 1973, HTCM, the Goodman statement and the six criteria are from undated early holograph notes by Bradshaw. Several later lists of criteria also were drafted, with criteria varying in number and generally adding something about a hymn helping a person "feel the Spirit." The HTMC, May 15, 1974, distill the criteria for inclusion to "spirit, function, doctrine, and tradition."

6. The *Ensign* published its call for hymns in the March 1974 issue. A related flier entitled "Suggestions to Composers" appears in Church Music Department Ephemera, 1938–74, Church History Library. Bradshaw suggests letters to composers in HTCM, May 28, 1974, and calls to composers in Specialized Areas Committee Meeting Minutes, July 30, 1974. See also the undated circular letter (deadline for response is December 15, 1974) soliciting hymns for the new hymnbook:

"Although the traditional concept of a hymn imposes certain limitations, we hope that you will use your creativity in producing fresh, original hymns." Compare the letter addressed "Dear Friend" (August 1, 1945), soliciting new hymns for what became the 1948 hymnbook (both letters are in Music Department Circular Letters, Church History Library).

7. This matter was discussed from time to time. See especially the HTCM for June 4, 1974, and October 19, 1976; also the holograph. This decision ran counter to the feelings of many, of course. Elder Theodore M. Burton, for example, wrote to Elder Stone on December 13, 1973, that greater music literacy in the Church was needed and one way to get it was to place greater emphasis on singing in parts. This memo is in the Music Department Office Files, Church History Library.

8. These executive advisers to the committee approved the fourth draft, pending deletion of the committee's six-part definition of "worship" in the document. (Both the fourth and fifth drafts are in the Bradshaw Papers.) See mentions of drafts and submissions in Specialized Areas Committee Meeting Minutes, March 26, April 9 and 30, 1974.

9. The bureaucracy grows a little tangled here: the reviewing of earlier Latter-day Saint songbooks was done by the subcommittee for congregational music (chaired by Jerold Ottley), formerly one of the specialized areas of the larger Church Music Department but now under the direction of the hymnbook committee. See the Subcommittee for Congregational Music Minutes, February 21 and March 7, 1974.

10. HTCM, March 11, 1974; also, Specialized Area Committees Minutes, April 30, 1974. That core of hymns would also form the content of the simplified hymnbook.

11. HTCM, August 28, September 10, and November 12, 1974; August 21, 1976.

12. HTCM, May 15 and 28, 1974.

13. Church Music Committee Minutes, January [22?], 1974; HTCM, June 4, 1974.

14. On the pace of reviews, see especially HTCM, September 10, 1974. Blank copies of the review sheet may be found in the Bradshaw Papers. Their new completion date is discussed in HTCM, February 25, 1975.

15. HTCM, November 12, 1974.

16. HTCM, November 12, 1974.

17. These statistics come from the Hymnbook Committee, in their "Report to the Executive Committee, Church Music Department: 'Current' Hymns Recommended to Be Omitted from the New Hymnbook," undated holograph draft, whose internal and contextual evidence supports a date of about November 1975.
18. HTCM, October 26, 1975.
19. "'Current' Hymns Recommended to Be Omitted."
20. On the back of the folder containing the draft of the committee's report to the Twelve, Bradshaw made a list of President Kimball's six favorite hymns—none of which they proposed to delete.
21. These all come from "Proposed Disposition of the Materials in the Present Hymnbook."
22. From "'Current' Hymns Recommended to Be Omitted."
23. "'Current' Hymns Recommended to Be Omitted."
24. "'Current' Hymns Recommended to Be Omitted."
25. This one in particular was discussed in HTC Minutes, August 21, 1976. The "hymns from around the world" rubric for a section in the hymnbook is used in HTCM, February 25, 1975.
26. See Merrill Bradshaw, interviewed by Michael Hicks, August 11, 1986, typescript in author's possession. The committee carefully endeavored to include General Authorities' favorite hymns—see the discussion in HTCM, February 25 and October 25, 1975.
27. Project Report, Committees of the Music Department, July 1, 1976: "First draft of hymnbook is approaching completion. Initial responses from Brethren and Correlation have been received. Projected completion Fall 1977."
28. Budget issues were raised as early as February 26, 1974. See Church Music Committee Meeting Minutes for that date.
29. Translation was a recurring issue. See HTCM March 11, August 28, September 10, 1974;
30. This issue was apparently raised first by Elder A. Theodore Tuttle. See the memo to Tuttle from Michael Moody, March 8, 1974.
31. Specialized Area Committees Minutes, April 30, 1974.
32. HTCM, March 11, 1974.

33. This had come up at the first meeting, December 18, 1973, when the issue of size arose.
34. HTCM, August 21, 1976.
35. HTCM, October 19, 1976.
36. HTCM, May 15, 1974, for example, suggests (1) eliminating the rests at the end of many hymn lines, and (2) having all verses appear within the staffs, rather than some with the music and others at the page's bottom.
37. HTCM, September 10, 1974.
38. HTCM, October 19, 1976, notes that "much discussion" about this was had, then suggests these criteria: "If the congregation is singing about a general principle of the gospel, 'we' is fine—'I' for testimony-type ideas. '*I* can make the pathway bright' indicates smugness."
39. Topics (or "subject areas") are discussed in HTCM, May 28, 1974, and September 12, 1976. The criteria for sacrament hymns are discussed in HTCM, October 26, 1975.
40. HTCM, August 21 and September 12, 1976.
41. HTCM, August 21 and September 12, 1976.
42. HTCM, August 21 and September 12, 1976; see also HTCM, September 10, 1974.
43. HTCM, September 12, 1976.
44. Regarding Elder Benson's request, see HTCM, October 19, 1976. Bradshaw recalls that Elder Petersen wanted "The Star-Spangled Banner" restored to the book; Bradshaw proposed possibly printing it on the inside cover of the American edition. Bradshaw interview.
45. HTCM, October 19, 1976.
46. See "Church Policies and Announcements," *Ensign*, April 1977, 93–95.
47. This is based on a comment by Bradshaw that "when they put Elder Hinckley in charge of the Priesthood Committee the first question he asked about the Hymnbook Committee was 'Who authorized this?' So we were apparently operating with the knowledge of the President of the Church but without the knowledge of a good share of the Council of the Twelve." Bradshaw interview.

48. The pace at which these events unfolded is suggested in the dates: the Priesthood Committee reorganization (according to "Church Policies and Announcements") was announced on February 2, 1977, and "Why a New Hymnbook" is dated February 9, 1977.
49. Michael Moody to Dean L. Larsen, March 24, 1977, and the accompanying thirteen-page document, "Hymn Recommendations."
50. Michael Moody to Merrill Bradshaw, April 26, 1977.
51. Michael Moody to Merrill Bradshaw, September 18, 1978; also, Michael Moody "To Past and Present Members of the Music Committee" [e.g., the larger committee of which the Hymnbook Task Committee had been a subset], September 27, 1978.
52. Reactivated Hymnbook Task Committee Minutes, September 21, 1978. The quotations that follow in this paragraph are from "Answers to Questions about the New Hymnbook."
53. The question apparently arose partly because of one General Authority's recommendation that chord symbols accompany Primary songs in *Sing with Me*, which the Music Department's Executive Committee favored. See Michael Moody to Editors of Church Magazines and Vanja Watkins, November 30, 1974, Music Department Office Files.
54. Bradshaw interview.
55. See Michael Moody to Merrill Bradshaw, September 19, 1983.
56. See Kathleen Lubeck, "The New Hymnbook," *Ensign*, September 1985, 7–13; Michael Moody, interviewed by Michael Hicks, May 27, 1987, typescript in author's possession. For an analysis of the textual changes in this hymnbook, see Douglas Campbell, "Changes in LDS Hymns: Implications and Opportunities," *Dialogue: A Journal of Mormon Thought* 28 (Fall 1995): 65–91.
57. Lubeck, "The New Hymnbook," 7–13.
58. Lubeck, "The New Hymnbook," 11.
59. Michael Moody to Merrill Bradshaw, December 31, 1985; Merrill Bradshaw to Michael Moody, January 8, 1986.
60. Tracy Y. Cannon to G. W. Richards, October 19, 1945, in Church Music General Files, Church History Library.

Under the direction of President Spencer W. Kimball, many inspired changes were made to Church administration. (© 1976 Intellectual Reserve, Inc. All rights reserved.)

Edward L. Kimball

23

EVENTS AND CHANGES DURING THE ADMINISTRATION OF SPENCER W. KIMBALL

THE administration of Spencer W. Kimball (1973–85) proved a significant period of Church history, its highlight the 1978 revelation on priesthood. There were, however, many other developments during that time.

President Kimball's presidency began with a shock the day after Christmas in 1973. Church President Harold B. Lee felt exhausted that day, and his doctor recommended that he check into the LDS Hospital to have some tests run. The first tests showed that he was anemic and experiencing some heart distress. In the evening he sat up in bed, spoke a few words to his secretary, Arthur Haycock, and tried for a moment to get out of bed but collapsed. His heart had stopped, and, in spite of frantic efforts by the doctors to rescue him, President Lee quickly slid toward death.

Edward L. Kimball is a professor emeritus of law, Brigham Young University.

Arthur immediately called Spencer Kimball, who, as President of the Quorum of Twelve, would be the ranking Church leader if the Church President should pass away. President Kimball rushed to the hospital and, when the attending physician pronounced President Lee dead, President Kimball assumed leadership responsibility.

News of the event surprised and shocked the Church membership. In 1941, when Elder Lee became an Apostle, he was more than twenty years younger than all the men senior to him in the Quorum of Twelve. For decades it had seemed practically certain that he would one day succeed to the Church Presidency, and he did. Because of his age and apparent good health, it also seemed likely he would preside for an extended period.

That Spencer Kimball would live to succeed Harold B. Lee had always been seen as most unlikely, because Spencer was four years older and had experienced major health problems, including typhoid fever, small pox, carbuncles, transient strokes, heart valve and bypass surgery, and recurrent cancer of the throat. During all the years the two men had sat next to one another in council, it had never seemed more than a theoretical possibility that Elder Kimball would be the survivor. The event surprised him more than anyone else when it happened.

In light of his health condition and his age, people expected some sort of a caretaker presidency. Elder W. Grant Bangerter of the Seventy said, "We knew, of course, that he would manage somehow, until the next great leader arose, but it would not be easy for him. 'O Lord,' we prayed, 'please bless President Kimball. He needs all the help you can give him'" (8).[1]

Spencer had not expected the calling, but when it came he accepted it without hesitation. Years earlier, in 1951, he had said, "I am positive that the appointments of His Twelve by the Lord and the subsequent deaths control the Presidency of the Church. No man will live long enough to become President of the Church ever who is not the proper one to give it leadership. . . . No one of the Presidents had all the virtues nor all the abilities. Each in his own way and time filled a special need and made his great contributions. This I know. This I know." Although he felt himself weak and unworthy, he

Events and Changes during the Administration of Spencer W. Kimball

accepted that God had truly entrusted him to lead the Church. The calling was his, and he determined to pursue the task with all his energy, not knowing just where it would lead.

A PROPHET'S MANTLE

In April 1974, before the general conference at which he would be sustained as Church President, Spencer W. Kimball addressed the regional representatives seminar about missionary work. This was his first major address as President, and it expressed his vision of how the gospel might spread over the whole earth. Elder Bangerter described the event:

> He had not spoken very long when a new awareness seemed to fall on the congregation. We became alert to an astonishing spiritual presence. . . . It was as if, spiritually speaking, our hair began to stand on end. . . . President Kimball was opening spiritual windows and beckoning to us to come and gaze with him on the plans of eternity, . . . inviting us to view with him the destiny of the gospel and the vision of its ministry. I doubt that any person present that day will ever forget that occasion. . . . It was a message totally unlike any other in my experience.
>
> When President Kimball concluded, President Ezra Taft Benson arose and, with a voice filled with emotion echoing the feeling of all present, declared, "No greater address has been given before any seminar. . . . There is in very deed a prophet in Israel" (18–19).

MISSIONARY WORK

This prophetic address laid out the challenge of worldwide missionary work. President Kimball exhorted, "We have been proselyting now for 144 years. Are we prepared to lengthen our stride? To enlarge our vision? . . . Somehow I feel that when we have done all in our power that the Lord will find a way to open doors. This is my faith. Is anything too hard for the Lord?" (v).

He did not exclude himself from the mandate. He said, "Let *us* lengthen our stride." That became a recurrent theme during the Kimball administration.

The President taught that every healthy young man in the Church should keep his life righteous so that he could fulfill a mission. "There may be some who can't, but they *ought* to go on a mission" (115). There was no established tradition of missionary service by young men from outside the United States and Canada. In Buenos Aires he put the matter starkly: "Do you know of any reason why I should send my sons but that you shouldn't send yours? This is a great nation and great people, and it is your responsibility to teach the gospel in these nations. When you have sent all the boys from this area on missions [here], we can send all the North American missionaries to India or China, or Russia, or somewhere else" (118–19). During the Kimball administration, the number of such missionaries greatly increased. He also said, "Many young women have a desire to serve a full time mission, and they are also welcome in the Lord's service. This responsibility is not on them, as it is on the elders, but they will receive rich blessings for their unselfish service" (120).

President Kimball did not preach a new gospel of missionary work, but his administration did give that responsibility increased emphasis. In five years after he became President, the approximately seventeen thousand missionaries in the field swelled to over twenty-seven thousand. Some of the increase came from natural growth of the pool of missionary-age young men in the Church, but another part of the increase reflects the higher percentage of eligible young men who elected to accept a mission call.

In 1982, missions for men changed from twenty-four to eighteen months. I understand that the objective was to enable more young men to serve these shorter missions, particularly in countries with compulsory military service. However, after three years the practice ended. It did allow some additional young men to serve, but they were being released just when their language skills and proselyting efficiency were maturing. The Brethren quipped that they were unable to figure out how to cut off the first six months of the mission experience rather than the last six months.

Events and Changes during the Administration of Spencer W. Kimball

In 1981, the financing of missions changed. The IRS claimed that the money parents and others sent to missionaries for their support should not be considered a deductible charitable contribution to the Church but rather a nondeductible gift to the missionary. Because of the litigation, which ultimately sustained the IRS position, the Church adopted a new mechanism. Rather than sending money directly to the missionary, as had been the practice, the family or other persons providing support made contributions to the ward missionary fund, and then in turn the ward supported the missionary.

In 1974, the First Presidency called David Kennedy to serve as their special ambassador. His experience as banker, secretary of the treasury in the Nixon cabinet, and US ambassador to NATO gave him valuable international connections. For example, he was able to obtain recognition of the Church in Portugal through decree of a new military government.

AREA CONFERENCES

The administration of Spencer W. Kimball reflected his personality. He was persistent, hardworking, loving, open to change, and deeply concerned with fairness. One of the emphases of the Kimball administration was "taking the Church to the people." For several years, the Church had held annually an area general conference in some distant place, reaching people who would probably never attend a general conference and never see or hear the President of the Church in person. The fourth such conference had already been planned for Stockholm when President Kimball took office.

He believed strongly in the concept, and the next year he expanded area conferences to seven areas in South America and East Asia, which he attended personally. Even when he could not travel, the area conferences continued. Between 1975 and 1981, fifty-nine more area conferences brought members and general leaders of the Church together.

In an analogous move, President Kimball initiated a sequence of about sixty solemn assemblies between 1975 and 1978, gatherings of priesthood leaders from a designated area meeting with General Authorities for several hours of specific instruction about Church policies. During the years these were held, tens of thousands of local leaders were exposed at close range to general leaders of the Church.

BUILDING TEMPLES

In his first year as President, Spencer dedicated the Washington (DC) Temple, begun several years earlier in President McKay's time. Some large temple building continued, but the Kimball administration saw a great increase of smaller temples—another instance of taking the Church to the people. At the beginning of the twelve Kimball years there were fifteen operating temples. At the end there were thirty-six operating temples, with eleven more either under construction or announced.

The most dramatic story of temple building is that of the Freiberg temple. In 1978, Elder Henry Burkhardt met with Communist East German officials, seeking permission for six couples at a time to leave the country and be sealed in the Swiss Temple upon their solemn promise to return, but the GDR officials would allow only one individual from a couple to leave the country, not both at the same time. After petition proved futile, one of the Communist officials finally said, "Instead of going to Switzerland, why don't you just have your own temple here?" (368). Elder Thomas S. Monson reported the statement to the First Presidency, and in just a few weeks, he traveled to Germany to show local Church leaders drawings of a possible temple. Emil Fetzer, the Church architect, drew up thirteen different designs for the temple before the German state architects finally gave their approval. President Gordon B. Hinckley dedicated the temple in 1985.

The Church adopted a number of policies affecting temple attendance. Ward and stake leaders interviewing for issuance of recommends were not to set quotas for temple work to be done; it must be a matter of free will. Interviewers were told to stay with the prescribed questions and not pursue their own notions. The questions were changed to ask about proper relations with family members and about testimony (matters not addressed specifically before). And the First Presidency approved the use of two-piece temple garments. In this period the Church also created a marvelous genealogy library, perhaps the best in the world.

ORGANIZATION

Important organizational changes took place in the Kimball administration. For example, the First Council of the Seventy had repeatedly recommended to the First Presidency, without effect, that the First Quorum of the Seventy be organized. But when the recommendation was made again in 1975, President Kimball acted upon it. He organized the First Quorum of the Seventy, made up initially of the seven men in the First Council of the Seventy, the twenty-one Assistants to the Twelve, and three men newly called. Of the thirty-seven men called in the next few years, eleven were not white Americans. Men in that group spoke among them eight different mother tongues—Navajo, French, Japanese, Dutch, German, English, Spanish, and Portuguese. It appears that this reflected a deliberate choice to broaden the base of Church leadership. (255)

In 1984, on behalf of the First Presidency, President Gordon B. Hinckley announced the appointment of new members of the First Quorum of the Seventy and explained that they would serve from three to five years. These seventies did many of the tasks previously given to the Twelve. They constituted a new intermediate rank of Church leadership.

In 1978, an emeritus status was created for General Authorities who became seventy years of age or suffered ill health. However, because the Apostles stood in the line of succession to the Presidency, they were not subject to this retirement.

In 1979, the Church Patriarch received emeritus status but no one was sustained in his place, leaving the office vacant.

In 1984, the Church was divided into thirteen administrative areas supervised by Area Presidencies. Similarly the Presiding Bishopric established area or zone offices to handle the Church's temporal affairs.

A Firm Foundation

To identify locations more easily, the names of wards, stakes, missions, and temples changed form to include geographic information, such as the Provo Utah Oak Hills Ninth Ward.

MEETINGS

Meetings constitute an important aspect of Mormon worship and culture. In 1980, a three-hour block of Sunday meetings was adopted, largely to reduce the amount of travel required in areas where Church members are scattered. The area conferences that had been held all over the world and the annual general auxiliary conferences ended. Stake conferences shifted from quarterly to twice a year. General conference was reduced to two days and no longer necessarily included April 6. The installation of satellite dishes at stake centers made it possible for Church members to observe general conference in their own area. The first experimental telecast to stake centers occurred in 1975, and by the end of the Kimball administration 900 of 1,500 stakes had satellite dishes.

PUBLICITY

The Church was often in the public eye, sometimes for good, other times for ill. The Church created a Public Communications Department to deal with such matters. The Tabernacle Choir traveled overseas more than ever. *Reader's Digest* was paid to insert pamphlets concerning the Church. A disputed "Howard Hughes will" turned up in the Church Offices. Mark Hofmann followed his forgery of historical documents with murders. And murders by the Ervil LeBaron family drew attention to fundamentalist sects. Church involvement in political issues drew attention, particularly to the question of installing a long-range MX missile system in the Utah/Nevada desert (the plan was withdrawn) and the Church's opposition to ratification of the proposed Equal Rights Amendment (ratification failed). The Church agreed with the amendment's objectives while objecting to the means.

Events and Changes during the Administration of Spencer W. Kimball

WOMEN

Despite its opposition to the ERA, the Church displayed significantly increased concern for fairness to women. It convened meetings for women and girls analogous to the priesthood sessions of general conferences. General leaders of the women's organizations sat on the stand and spoke in general conference. Wards received instruction to recognize girls' achievements just as they did boys' achievements. Brigham Young University scholarships were made equally available to women. And women were invited to offer prayers in sacrament meeting.

WELFARE

The Church Welfare Program, begun in the 1930s, changed somewhat in emphasis during the Kimball administration from creating and operating stake welfare farms to individual and family preparedness. The Church disposed of many of its welfare farms and, similarly, disposed of its fifteen hospitals in three western states. The leaders realized that they could not care for even a small portion of the growing membership in a time of widespread and prolonged distress, but the Church could develop greater capacity to respond to a short-term crisis. For example, in the 1976 Teton Dam disaster, the Church called on its storehouses to feed people and recruited workers to repair the massive damage from the dam's collapse. In 1985 the drought conditions in Ethiopia brought a request from the Church that its members undertake a special fast and contribution. Six million dollars was raised for humanitarian relief in one day. This effort has continued and expanded, and the Church has now given more than a billion dollars in humanitarian aid.

DOCTRINE

During the Kimball administration, the Church published a new edition of the Bible, including a topical guide and alternate readings from the Joseph Smith Translation. The Church also issued a new edition of the other standard works. A subtitle was added to the Book of Mormon: "Another

Testament of Jesus Christ," emphasizing that the Book of Mormon is a Christian document. In the same spirit, building signs and letterheads of the Church now present "JESUS CHRIST" in larger letters than the rest.

The new edition of the Doctrine and Covenants includes three additions—a vision of Joseph Smith of his brother Alvin in the celestial kingdom (section 137), a vision of Joseph F. Smith of the redemption of the dead (section 138), and Official Declaration 2, a revelation to Spencer W. Kimball extending priesthood and temple blessings to all worthy male members of the Church.

The First Presidency said in a 1978 formal statement: "The great religious leaders of the world such as Mohammed, Confucius, and the Reformers, as well as philosophers including Socrates, Plato, and others received a portion of God's light. Moral truths were given to them by God to enlighten whole nations and to bring a higher level of understanding to individuals" (97–98).

As another doctrinal pronouncement, President Kimball stated in general conference, "We denounce that [Adam-God] theory" (95–96). He also made specific positive reference to a Mother in Heaven, reaffirming her existence (164).

REVELATION ON THE PRIESTHOOD

By my judgment, the most significant event during the Kimball administration was the revelation on priesthood, announced June 9, 1978. Like many Church members I can clearly recall the moment I first learned of it. I was in Boston visiting my son.

Over the years, my father and I had exchanged a number of letters about the priesthood restriction. Basically I was urging that we ought to be praying for change, while he was urging patience. I was talking fairness; he was talking loyalty. He said in a letter, "Perhaps what the prophet needs is not pressure, not goading, not demands. He needs in every city and place defenders—a million men and women to encourage patience, understanding and faith . . . saying, 'President, we realize we do not know all there is to be known about this problem. We have faith and confidence in you and in the Lord that if relaxation is to come, it will come when the proper time comes. We shall stand and defend as did Peter, though the whole world be against us'" (204). His position was that of a loyal follower.

When he became President in 1973, his responsibility was no longer to be loyal to and defend the President. His responsibility was to determine what the Lord wanted now. It was for him and no other person on earth to speak to this issue.

As the leader, President Kimball controlled the agenda, and in the 1970s he repeatedly directed his brethren's attention to the priesthood restriction. He made the issue a matter of extended personal prayer. He often went alone to the Salt Lake Temple. He wrestled in the night with the consequences and criticisms that would follow a decision to extend priesthood. But he gradually found all those complications and concerns dwindled in significance. He later explained, "There slowly grew a deep, abiding impression to go forward with the change" (318).

In March he reported this to his counselors but continued to pray for unity among the Church leaders. He continued to discuss the question and to pray. Then on June 1, 1978, he presented the matter to the Presidency and Twelve in the Salt Lake Temple and asked if they would pray with him for final resolution of the question. He proposed to the Lord in group prayer that the change be made, and during that prayer the men in the circle experienced confirmation, each in his own way, sharing a unique feeling of unity and of assurance that the change was to be made.

When announced to the Church, this change met with nearly universal and delighted approbation. The people were grateful for the substance of the decision, but they were also appreciative of this example of modern revelation. This crowning event, together with the other significant developments of that twelve-year period, marks the administration of Spencer W. Kimball as having signal importance in the history of the Church.

NOTE

1. This article is condensed from my book *Lengthen Your Stride: The Presidency of Spencer W. Kimball* (Salt Lake City: Deseret Book, 2005); page references are in parentheses.

Jessie L. Embry and A. LeGrand Richards

24

Global Lessons from a Local Stake

Buddy and Cindy Richards and their daughter Katie moved to southwest Provo in 1977. Two years later, Jessie Embry arrived in the area. The Franklin neighborhood, one of Provo's early pioneer settlements, included a mixture of old and new construction. The two homes owned by the Richards family and Sister Embry represented the extremes. The Richards family bought an old adobe home. Sister Embry moved into a new condo in the Richards family's backyard. A growing family and a single woman were not typical residents. Initially their neighbors were longtime residents, older couples or widows, and short-stay Brigham Young University students. Shortly after Sister Embry and the Richards family moved into the area, the Provo Utah West Stake was divided and the Provo Utah South Stake was created.

Jessie L. Embry is the associate director of the Charles Redd Center for Western Studies at Brigham Young University. A. LeGrand Richards is an associate professor of educational leadership and foundations.

Years later, in 2008, Embry, associate director at the Charles Redd Center for Western Studies at Brigham Young University, suggested to Richards, a former bishop of three wards in the Provo South Stake and then the stake president and a professor in the McKay School of Education, that she conduct "A Year in the Life of the Provo Utah South Stake" project. While the idea sounded workable at first, it became clear that Richards was in an awkward position. He knew more about the stake than he could report because of his confidential leadership position. Still, he provided important insights. Embry added her own observations and used oral histories gathered by Brigham Young University students employed by the Redd Center.[1] Even with these limitations, this study shows some of the roles that this stake provides for its wards and members in the twenty-first century and introduces some of the modern challenges of integrating diverse cultural backgrounds into the common purposes of the Church.

The Provo Utah South Stake is quite different from stakes outside the Wasatch Front, where travel takes up a great portion of the stake president's time. Richards can ride his bike around the entire circumference of the stake boundaries in just a few minutes. Despite the small geographic size, though, the Provo Utah South Stake's twelve wards are very diverse and provide unique challenges. They include two Spanish wards, the Utah Valley Deaf Ward, a Native American ward for all of Utah County, and a young single adult ward (ages 19–30) that communicates in English, ASL, and Spanish. When Richards and Embry moved to the area, the wards on the north side of the railroad tracks matched what is sometimes referred to in the Church as the "newly wed and nearly dead." South of the tracks were farms, vacant land, and trailer courts.

Over the years, the neighborhood changed. In the north, old homes were torn down and replaced with new owner-occupied dwellings.[2] While trailers remain in the south, some were replaced by townhomes, apartments, and the Provo Town Centre Mall. The major exception was the Meadow Apartments, which expanded to Pebble Creek and then with federal funds became the Boulders Apartments. In 2008 the four pioneer neighborhood wards continued to house students, older residents (although Richards and Embry have now become the older residents), and young families in new homes. Other wards split the Boulders Apartments, where 380 of its 386 units are mandated by law to be rented exclusively to low-income individuals and families (below 50 percent of the median income of the county) and most of the residents receive welfare assistance.

Embry's past research has focused on the ward, which provides a community for most members.[3] Yet the stake is a very important unit with much of its work to support wards being done in the background. As a result, most members really do not understand how a stake operates because their only contact with other wards is at conferences, large activities, or haphazard contact with other members who meet in the same buildings. Their interaction with stake leaders is limited to monthly high council speakers, annual ward conferences, youth meetings, and temple recommend interviews. They do not realize that every month the bishoprics gather as a stake for training and the elders quorum presidencies also gather for training. Monthly interviews occur between the bishops and the stake president. One of Richards's most important roles as stake president is to support the bishops, and there is about a 40 percent annual turnover in the stake membership. The turnover in stake leadership, bishoprics, elders quorums, and ward clerks means that a great deal of the stake presidency's time is spent issuing calls and reorganizing presidencies and group leadership.

Besides turnover, the stake faces other unique challenges. The highest concentration of low-income nonstudent residents in Provo City reside within its boundaries. This poses a great challenge to finding and maintaining stable leadership. It also means that the welfare demands on the bishops is constant and substantial. One ward, for example, has averaged at least one food order per day for the entire year, which makes the bishop's job almost a full-time responsibility. An additional concern is that Church welfare tries to teach self-reliance, but conditions make this almost impossible. One bishop surveyed ward members just before he was released and discovered there were "138 mentally or emotionally handicapped" members in his ward. Disabilities included schizophrenia, bipolar disorder, and multiple-personality disorder. With so many welfare cases, the potential for welfare fraud is also a constant concern, and finding a sufficient number of experienced clerks to help monitor these concerns is difficult. In 2009, the stake was assigned to sponsor the Transient Welfare Services for the Utah County area. Because of their experience with the welfare population, it makes sense that they should help develop the operating policies of this office.

Because of this concentration of welfare challenges and the lack of stable leadership, the stake was given permission in May 2006 to create its own version of Salt Lake City's Inner City Project.[4] The stake leadership requested that other stakes provide mature couples who could serve for one to two years as service missionaries. Set apart by their home ward bishops, these couples are assigned to one of the wards and the bishop can use them wherever he feels they are most needed. The bishops in the most challenged wards use the service missionaries to operate a type of welfare triage. They analyze the circumstances and fill out the needs and resources forms in preparation for meetings with the bishop. They then follow up on the bishop's request after he determines what help, if any, the Church should provide.

These service missionaries have been a huge blessing—especially in the wards south of the railroad tracks, where there are so few owner-occupied homes (other than the trailers) and stable priesthood leaders. For example, in 2009, Bishop Eric Speckhard of the Freedom Second Ward had service missionaries for both of his counselors and at least one in nearly every auxiliary presidency. The missionaries conducted home visits, taught special institute and finance classes, conducted a major canning project, and provided counseling. While the help that the missionaries provided for the stake is apparent, they also felt they benefitted. Church service missionary Jerry Bauer, who moved from California to the Grandview Neighborhood, noted that the South Stake provided more opportunities to serve than did his home ward, which included many former stake presidents, bishops, and mission presidents. He quipped that on "the hill" he had felt he was attending a Protestant church because his services were not needed.[5] The experience has been so rewarding for the missionaries that many have asked to extend their service. Elder Richard Hill was recently requested by his home ward bishop to return in 2010. Hill had served for more than four years in the Provo Utah South Stake and would have been happy to continue.

Language missionaries have also been called from other stakes to serve in the Provo Utah South Stake's Spanish units. This has had mixed reviews. Some of these missionaries have had a great experience, but others have felt underutilized. According to Richards, it has been hard for some of the bishops, especially those in the Spanish wards, to know how best to use the missionaries. In many ways the Spanish units have fewer needs than some of the Anglo wards. When Richards was called, he was told that he would preside over the highest-baptizing unit in North America—primarily because of the one Spanish ward in the stake at time.

While the language units sometimes do not know how to use the service missionaries, missionaries have learned how to help the wards. Angus Belliston, a former regional representative, and his wife, Jenny, were called to work in a Spanish ward even though they did not speak the language. They looked around at what the ward was missing and decided that they needed a Boy Scout program. The Bellistons worked very hard on instituting a program, and since then it has grown quite strong. At a special court of honor, eight Scouts—all from Spanish wards—received Eagle awards in one evening. According to Richards, this was a remarkable accomplishment by itself but especially remarkable for Spanish units that did not have a Boy Scout tradition. For the occasion, the Spanish members invited the Bellistons back and praised them for their efforts. Belliston was embarrassed because he felt the focus should be on the boys. But the ward felt that the Bellistons had gone the extra mile to make Scouting happen.

With so many wards and varieties of cultural and economic backgrounds, how does the stake meet all the needs? One of the main factors is showing love and concern. Several members of the Spanish wards especially felt that love. Manuel Jesus Castillo, a former revolutionary leader in Peru and a convert to the Church, explained, "The stake president really cares for the Hispanic people. He loves them."⁶ Brenda Beyal, a Navajo in the Franklin Second Ward and the wife of the bishop, declared: "Our stake is fantastic. President Richards is one of the most awesome stake presidents you can have. He is definitely a man of God. He's somebody who listens to the Lord. . . . We're such a unique stake because our stake president gathers everybody."⁷

One way the stake president shows this love is by including members from all the wards in stake leadership. This starts with the stake presidency. The first counselor, Kent C. Nielsen, complains that he signs with a hearing accent, but he has been involved with the Utah Valley Deaf Ward because he has children who are deaf. The second counselor, Victor A. Rodriguez, is from Guatemala. The high council and stake auxiliary leadership include members from all of the diverse cultures represented in the stake. Beyal was especially impressed. After pointing out that at one time there was only one stake leader from her ward, she continued: "Now the stake Young Men president is from our ward. . . . We have two high councilors from our ward. We have the stake Young Women camp leader director from our ward. I'm in the Young Women presidency. . . . We're in equal partnership in this stake."⁸

Another way that Richards encourages unity is by expecting the specialized units to stand on their own and provide service to their ward members and to the stake. There is a tendency for leaders to not expect as much from foreign-language units because they are unique. But Richards treats the wards as equals and expects as much from them as he does from any other ward. They are expected to accept assignments, pay their tithes and offerings, provide for the missionaries they send, and develop their own leaders.

This attitude transfers to the bishops. Randy King, a former stake clerk, explains the experience with the Native American ward. "A very unusual thing about that ward is the bishop [Anthony Beyal] actually interviews people before they can become a member of that ward. If you think about it, it's not actually racial. It's not even a special ward by Church definition. It's a regular ward. They don't have in parentheses, after the name of the ward, 'Spanish' or 'Deaf.' It is just Franklin Second Ward." In that interview, according to King, the bishop tells the Native Americans that the ward is not a place to hide. They cannot join the ward if they do not plan on attending.[9]

For Richardo Cetz, a convert from Mexico, the stake's strength is that it gives members from different cultures the opportunity to be distinct. "They have the Spanish ward and they have the hearing-impaired one. . . . I think that's a good thing to me because sometimes you just feel alienated from people trying to fit in."[10] Anglo Paul Brimhall, a lifetime member, says he enjoys "a rainbow of the Church here. We're all very colorful, and I know the Brethren are watching us with a magnifying glass to see how we do. They're praying for us. It's exciting."[11]

But as with all situations, not everyone believes the stake works all the time. Gisela Mandujano from Venezuela and her husband, Nicolas, from Mexico City are both converts to the Church. Gisela does not feel "comfortable" in the Spanish-speaking ward "because I am not Mexican. The Mexican people look at me very different. . . . They make me feel out of the group." Gisela also struggled with stake activities. She once went to a dance that "was very nice and very well organized"; however, she felt that she was not invited to share her talents. For her, the biggest barrier was language. She attends stake activities but says, "I feel weird by going to them because I don't speak English. I understand it, but I inhibit myself." Gisela's husband, Nicolas, said his sons loved attending a Boy Scout activity, "but they felt there was certain division among the American and the Hispanic kids."[12]

Other Spanish-speaking members have expressed the same concerns. Blanca Juarez pointed out that while the stake members "are very friendly towards us, there is always division among the members."[13] Juliana Cordoba, a convert from Mexico, agreed: "We just say hi to each other. . . . [The English-speaking members] don't try to make a friendship because they think that I might not understand them." But at the same time she felt that at the few stake activities that she had attended, "the sisters from the stake are very nice to us. They want to know more about us." Her husband, Alfredo, also a convert from Mexico, explains, "I have been in the United States for fifteen years; sometimes I have felt a little bit rejected by the people, even by members of the Church."[14]

Even as a member of the stake Primary presidency, Adriana Olvera, a convert from Mexico, wished for more friends. She attended an English-speaking ward for years and then transferred to a Spanish ward. She enjoyed working in the stake but she felt other members of the presidency were merely "Church-calling friends." She saw cultural differences: "[Mexicans] are more open, and we establish friendship."[15]

But should there be more interaction? Claudia Gosain from Mexico City enjoyed the stake activities and felt that the stake members "get all together and have fun." She added that she didn't have "a friend relation with all of them. We just greet [each other]." But despite that problem, she still felt it "is very nice to get together, even if you cannot talk to the people. You can feel the harmony in the stake." But it could be stronger. "I think that we as a stake should be more integrated. I think we should have an activity where we can know more about the culture of the Native Americans or the sign language ward. I think that when you know more, you love more."[16]

What activities do bring the stake members together? During the year the stake sponsored its traditional programs, including two June stake conferences, a July twenty-fourth barbeque, a Nativity performance in the Provo Tabernacle, youth programs, and a stake Relief Society dinner before the women's general conference broadcast. This study started with a stake conference in June and ended with one a year later. Neither stake conference had a General Authority visitor, so both were under the direction of the stake president. At the general meetings, members from all cultures participated. Some prayers were signed or spoken in Spanish. There were speakers from all the language groups. Just as the stake leadership represents various cultures, there is a feeling that the stake meetings should also include everyone. The presidency often asks if they are including enough representation from all the wards.

How do members feel about stake conferences? Blanca Juarez, who has attended Church since she was four in Mexico and served a mission in her home country, was impressed because she felt the topics discussed were very important.[17] Todd Roach said that stake conference was interesting because "we have a deaf interpreter signing for the deaf members. We have members who speak Spanish with earphones on listening to a translation. And occasionally we hear talks and prayers in Spanish. The prayers, of course, are not translated, so we do the best we can to appreciate the message of the Spirit. We'll have a translator, of course, for the speakers. If the deaf pray, we usually have a translator for that."[18]

Kathy Brimhall, who grew up in the area and has now moved back, enjoys all these activities. "I love stake conference. I find it entertaining because they're doing the translating with the deaf in American Sign Language. Then you've got the interpreter and the people in headphones."[19]

Stake conferences are required meetings, but the Provo South Stake has its unique traditions. For years the stake sponsored a Pioneer Day barbeque to bring members together. Alan Cherry, who has lived in the neighborhood on and off for over twenty years, was the high council member in charge. He put a lot of energy into the event because he believed it was one time that the stake could intermingle in an informal way. But he faced some problems, including the lack of a shady pavilion, although makeshift boweries provided some relief from the heat. But a bigger problem was convincing stake members who felt no connection to the pioneers to attend. For Cherry the success of 2008 was getting the Latinos involved. One way that he included Latinos was by providing both Spanish and English music.[20]

Another unique aspect of the pioneer celebration that year was the inclusion of the Native American culture. Alan Groves, a Hopi in the Franklin Second Ward, explained that a member of the bishopric, a Polynesian married to a Navajo, was very disappointed that the only member of the ward who went to the barbeque in 2007 was from the high council. He asked the ward to be more involved, but for many Native Americans, attending a party to honor the Mormons who came and took their ancestors' lands seemed a little awkward. As a youth from the Native American ward teased after being asked to participate in a handcart trek the year earlier, "And what are we supposed to do, attack the other groups?" At the same time, many wanted to support the stake that had taken them in when another stake had disbanded the ward.[21]

With encouragement from the high council and support from the stake leadership, the Native Americans played an important role at the 2008 cookout. Cherry explained: "The bishop of the Native American ward is someone I've known since he was about twelve. I know many people in the Native American ward, or Franklin Second Ward. I know that there are many warm, loving people who need to take their uniqueness and integrate into the larger group. It just is a matter of how to weave it together so that people feel comfortable and people can experience that it's an enjoyable activity. It's one that is welcomed. There's no need for us to segregate."[22]

To include the Native Americans at the 2008 celebration, stake leaders asked a group from the ward to perform in a Native American drum circle. Groves recalled that the performance was informal; there was an announcement that there would be some Native American songs that people could watch. He was impressed by how many people were interested. After performing a few songs, the leader asked if anybody wanted to participate. Since many did, the group taught some round dances and songs. The event had a great impact on Groves. He realized that the Pioneer Day celebration was less about the pioneers and more of "a chance for our ward, our stake, to get together as a whole."[23]

The Pioneer Day celebration focused especially on children. Adriana Olvera explained, "The Primary helped with the children's activities. They brought a handcart so the kids could go and pull the cart. They had pioneer games for the kids. Kids ate, played, and had fun." She added, "I don't know if the adults enjoyed it because they just ate."[24]

Isaias Rojas, a lifetime member from Mexico, could not speak for all the adults, but he felt that the barbeque strengthened the singles ward. He expected people to come and eat and leave. But when he arrived, he saw his fellow ward members serving. "That was a spiritual experience because when I saw them I just felt that I wanted to do something else, so I helped them to serve. . . . The fact that we were all serving, we made sure that everybody had eaten something, and we made sure that everybody was having a fun time. After that we ate a little bit, and after that we helped to clean."

He continued, "Why was it memorable? Because I saw the young single adults, deaf, Hispanic, Indian, American—all our members helping, all together—and that helps us to be more united as a ward in a stake activity."[25]

Another yearly stake activity is a live Nativity program. For years it was held outside the Provo Tabernacle. The audience sat on straw, and the program included a reenactment of Christ's birth, complete with animals. In 2008 the program was moved into the Tabernacle. Sharee Small, a convert from St. Louis living in the Pioneer Park Ward, enjoyed the opportunity to participate. "Last year I think was my first year doing it. . . . Hanging out like we did tonight is nice with everybody socializing." This provided an opportunity for her to meet other Latter-day Saints because she found her ward not to be very friendly.[26]

The Nativity program was special for Kathy Brimhall. She said: "I like the Nativity every Christmas. When my granddaughter got here the first time after my daughter got divorced and they were here staying for Christmas, they went to the Nativity, and she took some pieces of straw out of the bales. She brought them home and taped them in her little journal. Ever since, when she became old enough, she participates in the Nativity. So I think that the Nativity production is good and touches many hearts."[27] Stephen Howe, a young married man with children, remembered participating in the Nativity. "I think when I was in that, I played one of the prophets. I thought it was a really good activity. I enjoyed not only watching it but being involved in it."[28]

The stake also sponsors activities for priesthood and Relief Society. Rocky Steele, a young married father who was called into the bishopric as a twenty-two-year-old and has since moved, enjoyed attending the priesthood meetings. "There's just a great camaraderie in the priesthood sessions here. The reason that I mention that is because you would think that with such a transient area that might not be the case. But there are so many of the people that have gotten to know each other. There is great camaraderie, and there are always ice cream bars and Nutty Buddies they dump out on the table afterwards."[29] (Unfortunately, budget cuts have since eliminated the treats.)

Katherine Wistisen, a senior citizen living in a townhome, enjoyed the Relief Society gatherings. "When the general Relief Society meeting is held a week before general conference in the fall, the stake Relief Society has a catered meal before the meeting. There is a large group that attends the dinner and those meetings. The evening is very enjoyable. I think it's a good way to unify the women, to help them get acquainted, and to share the inspiration of the meeting."[30]

But does the event really gather people together so they can interact? When Embry attended during the year of this study, some very faithful sisters had made soups for the dinner. People stood in line and got their food and then looked for their friends. Members saved seats at tables for their friends. The Spanish-speaking and deaf sisters sat together. Embry spent most of the time observing. When she went to eat, the only space left was at a Spanish-speaking table. All she could do to communicate was to smile.

Adult activities are limited. But that is not unusual because with nearly five thousand members, it is very hard to sponsor an activity that encourages much stake interaction. The standard youth activities bring the teenagers together more often. These programs include youth conferences, girls' camp, Aaronic Priesthood encampment, and fathers and sons' activities. The big announcement in 2008 was that because there was too much snow at the campground the girls' camp was moved to the July fourth weekend. The camp was shortened because of the holiday. Interestingly, the shortened schedule allowed more young women and leaders than usual to participate. It was easier for those who work or attend summer school to participate, and some wanted to have the camp that holiday week more often.

Each year as girls' camp starts, many leaders worry about how the young women associate only with others from their own wards. Richards attended one year and especially worried that the groups would never become one. He was pleased that as the week continued, the young women broke down the barriers and worked together. Brenda Beyal remembered such a time: "[The Franklin Second Ward's] young women were playing a game. Some of the girls went down and invited the Utah Valley Deaf Ward to come, and they came and joined our ward in this game. They were laughing and just talking. Then there was another ward that came. That night there was our Franklin Second Ward, there was the Utah Valley Deaf ward, and then just a regular ward . . . with all the girls . . . laughing and having a good time. Their wards are special in their own way. We're not saying that there's not a need for a Native American ward; we're saying that we can still come together. We can still be distinct groups, but still come together as one. I think that that happens."[31] As a result, Mexican Claudia Gosain said that her daughter "is always happy to go to girls' camp."[32]

Equally important in the stake were the Aaronic Priesthood Encampment, a weeklong priesthood training session for young men, and the separate overnight fathers and sons' campout. The latter was so looked forward to that as a father of only girls, Richards used to smuggle a couple of his daughters to the campout. Now he takes grandsons. Stake member Rocky Steele enjoyed taking his son to the event because "I get to know a lot of the good brothers in the stake and take my son out. There is a great breakfast. That's a fun activity." He continued: "I like listening to Brother Alan Cherry. He's one of the high council men of the stake. I've listened to him around the campfire a couple times. He's a kind of a comedian, and so he tells some stories and jokes. Those are really good activities. I have a lot of fun at the stake fathers and sons' outings."[33]

The Aaronic Priesthood Encampment often seemed divided like the girls' camps. With a multicultural Young Men's Presidency, the leaders tried to make the encampment fun for everyone. Alan Groves said in other years the wards had done separate activities, but in 2008 he wanted everyone to be involved. The leaders planned more games so the Native Americans and Spanish-speaking members could participate. Groves recalled: "One thing we did do was have each culture come and cook dinner at night. So like one night we had a Hawaiian dinner; one night we had Indian tacos; one night the Spanish wards came up and did Carne Asada. And it was so fun for them to explain, 'This is part of our culture, and here's a way you guys can participate.' The food was really good."[34] Richards pointed out that the food arrangement also united the young women's camp, especially those from the Native American ward.

The young singles ward in the stake does not wait for stake activities to meet together. It is a ward that communicates in three languages: Spanish, English, and American Sign Language. In addition, people from all the economic and cultural backgrounds represented in the stake belong. The ward was organized at the June stake conference in 2008. Benjamin Larsen, the stake executive secretary at the time, was released and called as bishop of the new ward. Larsen served a Spanish mission and attended the Utah Valley Deaf Ward because he and his wife have a daughter who is deaf. A choir of young single adults performed at stake conference in three languages.

According to Richards, the stake presidency debated the formation of the ward. The single adults in the specialized wards, especially the Spanish and the Utah Valley Deaf wards, were very strong, but the other wards struggled with their YSA programs. Richards believed that a singles ward in the stake would be successful only if the specialty units became the core of the ward (not merely tangentially invited) and then reached out to the English-speaking young singles. A fireside was held in each of the specialty units to determine if the young people in those wards would step up to the opportunity to lead out. At first the members were a little reluctant since it was not going to be only an ASL (or Spanish or Native American) ward, but when they recognized that they were needed, they enthusiastically agreed to support the new ward.

As with other specialized wards, Richards felt the ward would only work if members were expected to provide all the Church services and recognized the vision to worship together. And many members did. Richards hopes that the single ward, with its diverse groups worshipping together, might be a model for other wards. Bryndi Cloward, who had attended the Utah Valley Deaf Ward since she could sign, was called to be the first Relief Society president of the singles ward. She had a prompting that the ward was coming and that she would have the calling. Her goal with the ward was to "bring forth what President Richards sees, but we sure pray for it and that we can accomplish the vision that the stake president had." That vision for Cloward was that we could have multicultural differences. If you think about it, there's different culture with the Spanish, there's a different culture with the Deaf, and there's a different culture with Native Americans. Everybody in between has their own culture. The biggest impression when this ward was established was that when the Savior comes, as in Third Nephi when he came to the people of Bountiful, all the people came and they were one people—one heart, one mind, combined together—and they were his people. When the Savior comes again, it's not going to be this culture and this culture and this culture. It's going to be the gospel culture. We have this little chance to have a piece of that before the Savior comes and to actually test it.[35]

Once the ward was created, the challenge was to get the single adults to attend it. Isaias Rojas from Mexico had no plans to attend the singles ward when it was announced. He liked being in a family ward, and he liked his calling. But his father encouraged him to go be with other singles. Rojas recalled: "As I started attending that ward, I realized the great blessing of being in that ward. After I transferred my records, I realized that there was something special in that ward that I needed to be part of. . . . I love the people and love the spirituality that you can feel when you are in those meetings. In sacrament meeting, Sunday School, and priesthood, you can feel the Spirit strongly."[36]

Kylee Smith, the daughter of the Franklin First Ward bishop at the time, wondered if she should go to the singles ward because she was needed to interpret for a deaf child in the family ward. But she decided to go and was impressed. "When I first went, it was a lot of fun. There were a lot of people that I'd seen but didn't really know. I'd seen them around the neighborhood or around the stores or at girls' camp. I didn't actually know they were there. There were new people too, so that was pretty cool. I just decided to check it out. The first week I went was pretty awesome. I loved from the very beginning the elders quorum and Relief Society and bishopric and all the leaders.

They wanted us to be accepted. They made sure everyone felt welcomed and everyone knew each other. It's really cool. We have a lot of fun."

Smith feared that the ward would break up into groups. "We were really worried that it was going to be cliquey, that it was going to be the deaf ward, the Navajo ward, the English ward, and the Spanish ward separately with no one really liking each other and no one really working together very well. But it was really cool. We're all friends. The deaf people are learning Spanish or Spanish people are learning sign language. The English people are learning both languages. The bishop is the perfect guy for it. He speaks the languages, and he's so wonderful. He is very inspiring. I really love that ward." Because she signs, Smith usually watches the interpreter, but she felt that everyone communicates well. She was impressed by how people jumped in to make sure that everyone understood what was being said.[37]

Embry attended the singles ward shortly after it was organized and saw some disorganization. Some of the interviewees commented about these problems when the ward first started. Sometimes interpreters were not available. Sometimes it seemed that people were caught off guard when someone spoke in Spanish.

But according to the members and the ward and other observers, those problems were overcome. Embry returned to the ward about a year later and was impressed with how organized it was. Everyone seemed to know who would sign and when they needed to use headphones. When someone spoke in Spanish, the English speakers, including the ASL interpreter, had on headsets, but the ward also provided language-specific Sunday School classes so that the ward members could communicate in their language. And there were special weekday activities so that the members could learn more than one language.

Whitney Call, a Redd Center employee, attended the ward as part of an ASL class assignment. After listening to the interviews, she knew some of the early problems in the ward. But she saw how they had been overcome. The sacrament meeting was very organized. She attended the Sunday School class for American Sign Language. The first week she was the only hearing person there, so she did not fully understand. But the next time there were several hearing people in attendance, and an interpreter translated for them. The Relief Society was also organized with headsets and a deaf interpreter. Call was impressed how the ward members, despite their language differences, interacted together.[38]

CONCLUSION

As the Church becomes more diverse, the Provo Utah South Stake gives a model of what can take place in culturally diverse units and shows some of the strengths and weaknesses of that model. Adriana Olvera looked at the stake and its wards and commented, "I don't think there's a lot of relationship with the other wards. Everybody has their own bubble, their own thing. Probably the best in that sense is the singles ward."[39] Richards's hope is that the singles ward will continue to be a model. But even if separate units continue, the Provo Utah South Stake shows ways that a stake can help bring people together. The key, according to Richards, is making sure all units have the support they need either from members or service missionaries and that the specialized units, whether they are language, age, and marital status, or geographical and economically based, are given an opportunity to stand on their own and not be treated with a "condescending benevolence." Each can be special and unique in its own ways, but "we can expect that that which unites us is greater than that which could divide us." According to Richards, when much is expected, much is delivered.

NOTES

1. Where there are no notes, the information comes from the authors' personal experiences.
2. Much of the new construction was due to the efforts of the Neighborhood Housing Service and Provo City's efforts to bring owner occupants into the pioneer neighborhoods.

3. Jessie L. Embry, *Mormon Wards as Community* (Binghamton, NY: Global Publications, Binghamton University, 2001).
4. In Salt Lake City, missionaries are called to the Inner City Project to work with Mormons and non-Mormons alike in providing basic assistance to people that live in the downtown area. For example, Embry's cousins Craig and Donna Coulson have worked with refugees to help them find housing and secure available government services. About fifteen years ago, Embry talked to Jay Haymond, who provided the same assistance. One of the reasons Richards was able to receive the assistance is that he did careful research with population results to show incomes, educational levels, crime, home values, and admission to college in the Franklin neighborhood compared to other parts of Provo.
5. Jerry and Mary Bauer oral history, interviewed by Jessie Embry, 2009, 6–7, Provo Utah South Stake Oral History Project, Charles Redd Center for Western Studies, L. Tom Perry Special Collections, Harold B. Lee Library, Brigham Young University, Provo, UT. (All of the interviews cited come from this collection or the LDS Native American Oral History Project. Interviews will be identified as Provo or LDS Native American.)
6. Manuel Jesus Castillo oral history, interviewed by Mayte Company, interview in process, 2008, Provo. (This interview was conducted in Spanish.)
7. Anthony and Brenda Beyal oral history, interviewed by Corey Smallcanyon, 2008, 7, LDS Native American.
8. Beyal interview, 25.
9. Randy King oral history, interviewed by Jessie Embry, 2009, 11, Provo.
10. Richardo Cetz oral history, interviewed by Mayte Company, 2008, 6, Provo.
11. Paul and Katherine Brimhall oral history, interviewed by Scott Marianno, 2008, 4–5, Provo.
12. Nicolas and Gisela Mandujano oral history, interviewed by Mayte Company, 2008, interview in process, Provo. (This interview was conducted in Spanish.)
13. Jairo and Blanca Juarez oral history, interviewed by Mayte Company, 2008, interview in process, Provo. (This interview was conducted in Spanish.)
14. Juliana and Alfredo Cordoba oral history, interviewed by Mayte Company, 2008, interview in process, Provo. (This interview was conducted in Spanish.)

15. Adriana Olvera oral history, interviewed by Mayte Company, 2008, 6–7, Provo.
16. Claudia Gosain oral history, interviewed by Mayte Company, 2008, interview in process, Provo. (This interview was conducted in Spanish.)
17. Jairo and Blanca Juarez interview.
18. Todd Roach oral history, interviewed by David Bolingbroke, 2008, 6, Provo.
19. Brimhall interview, 5.
20. Alan Cherry oral history, interviewed by Jessie Embry, 2009, 9–12, Provo.
21. Embry is currently researching the Franklin Second Ward and its forerunners. She presented a paper on that subject at the BYU Studies Symposium, March 12, 2010, Provo. Alan Groves oral history, interviewed by Corey Smallcanyon, 2009, 25–26, LDS Native American.
22. Cherry interview, 11.
23. Groves interview, 26.
24. Olvera interview, 9.
25. Isaias Rojas oral history, interviewed by David Bolingbroke, 2008, 6, Provo.
26. Sharee Small oral history, interviewed by Scott Marianno, 2008, 3, Provo.
27. Brimhall interview, 5–6.
28. Stephen Howe oral history, interviewed by David Bolingbroke, 2008, 13, Provo.
29. Rocky Steele oral history, interviewed by David Bolingbroke, 2008, 22, Provo.
30. Katherine Wistisen oral history, interviewed by David Bolingbroke, 2008, 9, Provo.
31. Beyal interview, 27.
32. Gosain interview.
33. Steele interview, 23.
34. Groves interview, 26.
35. Bryndi Cloward oral history, interviewed by David Bolingbroke, 2008, 9, Provo.
36. Rojas interview, 5.
37. Kylee Smith oral history, interviewed by David Bolingbroke, 2008, 6–7, Provo.
38. Whitney Call, conversation with Jessie Embry, January 2010.
39. Olvera interview, 10.

The grave of Christian Heck, former supervisor of the West German Mission (marked by arrow). He was killed by machine-gun fire from an Allied fighter plane nineteen days before the war ended. (Courtesy of Roger P. Minert.)

Roger P. Minert

25

Succession in German Mission Leadership during World War II

O̲ne of the principal tenets of the restored Church of Jesus Christ is that "a man must be called of God, by prophecy, and by the laying on of hands by those in authority, to preach the Gospel and administer in the ordinances thereof" (Articles of Faith 1:5). One application of this principle is seen in the bestowal and transfer of authority for specific callings within the Church's administrative structure. Since the early days of the Church in Kirtland, Ohio, that structure has been developed, standardized, and codified to the point that essentially no officer of the Church today is without a leader to whom he or she reports the conduct of his or her stewardship. Leaders of the Church are called with not only a specific position of service but also usually with a tenure that eventually will be terminated by release, resignation, or death. The lines of priesthood and leadership authority are now clear and almost

---

Roger P. Minert is an associate professor of Church history and doctrine at Brigham Young University.

universally observed. However, the implementation of these standards has not always been possible, as is evident from the history of the two Latter-day Saint missions in Germany during World War II. How the leaders of those missions were selected without contact with Church leaders in Salt Lake City for three and one-half years is a fascinating story.

In August 1939, with war in Europe seemingly imminent, the First Presidency issued instructions that all expatriate Latter-day Saint missionaries were to be withdrawn immediately from the East and West German Missions to Amsterdam or Copenhagen. The evacuation began on August 25, 1939, but most of those involved expected that they would return shortly, which is precisely what had happened in September and October 1938. Departing missionaries were instructed to appoint "temporary branch leaders" to serve until the missionaries could return. However, Joseph Fielding Smith, who had been traveling in Germany in his calling as an Apostle, arrived in Copenhagen on August 26. He announced in the first week of September that the missionaries would not be returning to Germany but rather to the United States. Germany had invaded Poland on September 1, and declarations of war had been issued by France, Great Britain, Poland, and Germany two days later. Back in Germany, several Church leadership positions remained unoccupied.

The two mission presidents in Germany had departed the country at the same time—M. Douglas Wood of the West German Mission from Frankfurt to Copenhagen and Thomas E. McKay of the East German Mission from Berlin to Basel, Switzerland, where he was also still serving as the president of the Swiss Mission. Each carried on correspondence with the respective mission office for some time. President McKay sent a letter dated September 8, 1939, to be read throughout the West German Mission and presumably the East German Mission as well. The conclusion of that letter reads as follows:

> All who will receive this letter, must not only take care of their own responsibilities but also of those officers, teachers and members who have been called to serve their country. We pray sincerely to

Succession in German Mission Leadership during World War II

our Heavenly Father, that He might protect and bless those that have been called to arms and that He might strengthen those who have remained at home for the additional responsibilities that rest upon your shoulders....

Thomas E. McKay, Mission President[1]

In late September, M. Douglas Wood and his family boarded a ship to return home to the United States. Joseph Fielding Smith likewise left Copenhagen for home.[2] With their departure, decisions regarding the administration of the two German missions needed to be made without delay. How, when, and by whom those decisions were made and who was asked to lead the two missions for the next six years is a complex story that reflects the talents and dedication of the men involved. The details are provided as follows for each mission.

THE EAST GERMAN MISSION LEADERSHIP IN WORLD WAR II

Before departing Berlin in August 1939, Thomas E. McKay asked Herbert Klopfer to serve as the administrator of the East German Mission. No record exists stating that Elder Klopfer was set apart by President McKay, who likely hoped to return soon. Several eyewitnesses stated in interviews conducted in 2006 that they had neither seen nor heard of any official transfer of authority. The letter of September 8 did not name a successor; thus Herbert Klopfer served more as an office manager than mission leader for the next several months.

When it became clear that President McKay would not be able to resume his work in Berlin, he clarified Elder Klopfer's title and duties in a letter written from Basel on February 13, 1940. The salient message was as follows: "All communications to the Presiding brethren and saints in the mission should go out over your name as mission supervisor."[3] (The German term was *Missionsleiter*.) He was to be paid a full-time salary, select two assistants, advise President McKay of major decisions, maintain contact with the leaders of the West German and Swiss Missions, and send a weekly letter to President McKay.

To underscore Brother Klopfer's appointment as the mission supervisor, President McKay appended a statement to be sent to the Saints in each branch of the mission "to notify them of your call, your responsibility, and your authority. They will then know that you are acting in complete coordination with the authorities here [in Basel] and that what you do and say is official."[4]

This assignment of authority over the East German Mission may have come as a surprise to the Saints in that area—the largest mission of the Church (by population) outside of the United States. Only during the Great War had the territory ever been supervised by a local priesthood leader.

The new supervisor of the East German Mission, Herbert Klopfer, was born in Werdau, Saxony, in 1911. He had served as a full-time missionary in the Austrian-German Mission and was barely twenty-eight years old when called to lead the mission. A faithful servant of the Lord, he had been a full-time employee of the Church since 1933—responsible for foreign language correspondence and translation. During his transition from part-time to full-time employment, he had moved his family from his hometown to Berlin.[5]

When Brother Klopfer received the charge to serve as mission supervisor, he was living with his wife and their two sons in an apartment adjacent to the mission office in a villa at Händelallee 6 in northwest Berlin. He chose as his counselors Richard Ranglack, a hotel employee and then president of the Berlin District; and Paul Langheinrich, a genealogist employed by the German government and a former leader in the Chemnitz District of that mission. There is no record of an official bestowal of authority upon those counselors, nor is there any surviving correspondence or autobiographical literature indicating that either of the counselors was set apart for his calling.

Beginning in August 1939, Herbert Klopfer directed mission administrative affairs from the office in Berlin with the assistance of full-time sister missionaries. Elder Ranglack and Elder Langheinrich came by in the evenings and on weekends to assist. All of those brethren and sisters were able to travel to district conferences held in cities near and far.

President Klopfer's leadership functions were hampered substantially when he was drafted into the German army in late 1940. However, he was very fortunate to be stationed in Fürstenwalde, just forty miles east of Berlin, where he served as a paymaster. From his office, he was authorized to use the telephone and the mail services to contact the mission office in Berlin as well as district and branch leaders throughout the mission. On several occasions, his counselors traveled to Fürstenwalde to report on matters requiring the supervisor's decisions and to receive instructions at his hand.

President Klopfer's wife, Erna, continued to live with their two sons in the apartment adjacent to the mission office. She also took short messages from her husband that formed the basis for detailed reports she typed and sent to Thomas E. McKay in Salt Lake City. Of course, the letters that crossed the Atlantic Ocean between Salt Lake City and Berlin were interrupted when the United States and Germany exchanged declarations of war in December 1941. There would be no communication of any kind between those offices for the next forty-two months. The leaders of the East German Mission were now on their own to keep the Church alive and functioning properly for a term they could not predict and under circumstances that would become increasingly challenging.

One significant action taken by Presidents Ranglack and Langheinrich in the absence of the mission supervisor was a visit of some ten days to the Saints in occupied Czechoslovakia. They met with members of the Church in the two branches of that country—Prag and Brünn (now Brno)—gave instruction, and ordained several men to priesthood offices. It is not clear whether the ordinations were done in response to instructions from President Klopfer or if the counselors acted on their own volition. Back in Berlin, they continued to attend district conferences in all thirteen districts and were accompanied on those occasions by several sister missionaries from the office staff.

Fig. 1. The leaders of the East German Mission at Händelallee 6 in Berlin in 1940. First row, from left: missionaries Erika Fassmann, Johanna Berger, and Ilse Reimer. Second row, from left: first counselor Richard Ranglack, supervisor Herbert Klopfer, second counselor Paul Langheinrich. (Sonntagsgruss, September 22, 1940, NR. 34 N. P.)

In February 1943, Herbert Klopfer wrote a letter to his brethren in the mission leadership that formally detailed their responsibilities in his absence. The letter was written from the mission office and began thus: "During the period of my prolonged absence and due to the hindrances caused thereby for the leadership of the mission, I would ask that my elders called to serve as mission leaders [Ranglack and Langheinrich] observe the following directives."[6] He then provided instructions in twelve specific topics, such as historical reports, communications with district and branch leaders, publications, finances, and the relationship between the two German missions. It is not impossible that Elder Klopfer had a premonition that he would soon be unable to carry out his duties as mission supervisor.

The work of the East German Mission leadership and the office staff appears from all reports to have been friendly and cooperative, but the convenience of leading the mission from Fürstenwalde ended for Herbert Klopfer when he was transferred to France in early 1943. He was no longer able to visit any Church units and no longer had access to military telephone and postal services. His counselors took over all of his functions, but their titles remained as before.

Perhaps the last time Presidents Klopfer, Ranglack, and Langheinrich were together was to observe a very sad occasion: the aftermath of the destruction of the mission office at Händelallee 6 on November 23, 1943. During the previous two nights, the neighborhood had been hit by devastating air raids by the British Royal Air Force, and all structures in the vicinity were destroyed. Fortunately, the mission staff had removed most of the important mission office property during the day on November 22, storing it in the apartment house in which the Langheinrich family lived at Rathenowerstrasse 52, about one mile to the north. The affairs of the mission were administered from that location for the next nineteen months.

In October 1944, Erna Klopfer received the letter feared by all German families—the one indicating that her husband was missing in action. His whereabouts had been unknown since July 22 and would remain so for the duration of the war.

Shortly after the arrival of the sad message that Herbert Klopfer was missing, Richard Ranglack assumed the leadership of the East German Mission, apparently in agreement with Paul Langheinrich, who became the first counselor. Again, eyewitness testimony and surviving literature support the conclusion that they were not set apart for the callings, had no authorization from Salt Lake City, and were not formally sustained in their

Fig. 2. The apartment house at Rathenowerstrasse 52 in Berlin. The mission office was established in rooms on the fourth floor in November 1943 and remained there until the summer of 1945. (Courtesy of Roger P. Minert, 2008.)

callings by the general membership of the mission. Max Jeske of Berlin was asked to serve as the second counselor.

Although President Ranglack was not officially authorized by higher officers to lead the East German Mission, it appears that the district presidents, the branch presidents, and the general membership had no objection to the new administration. Reports were continually submitted to the mission office at Rathenowerstrasse 52 by branch and district leaders and the mission leaders with their office staff continued to accept invitations to attend district conferences. The last of those wartime events took place in Dresden on May 6, 1945, while the thunder of Soviet artillery was heard all day long just east of the city.

Succession in German Mission Leadership during World War II

When the Soviet Red Army conquered Berlin on April 30, 1945, several dozen Latter-day Saint refugees were living in the apartment building at Rathenowerstrasse 52, including mission supervisor Richard Ranglack, whose apartment had been destroyed three months earlier. The Saints in that apartment house braved several harrowing experiences at the hands of the invaders, but survived the last days of the war and its aftermath in good order.

With the war over by the summer of 1945, the American occupation forces in western Berlin granted the Church the use of a fine villa in the southwest Berlin suburb of Dahlem. Several months later, Elder Ezra Taft Benson formally authorized Richard Ranglack to serve as the president of the East German Mission. The call was extended in a letter, and again there was no setting apart. President Ranglack served until 1947, when he was replaced by Walter Stover of Salt Lake City, the first American mission president in Europe after the war.

In 1948, an emaciated German POW knocked on Erna Klopfer's door in Werdau and informed her that he had been with Herbert Klopfer when the latter passed away in a squalid Russian prison camp on March 19, 1945. The veteran had promised Elder Klopfer that he would visit Erna if he survived the war. Had this promise not been fulfilled, the world would still not know the fate of the former mission supervisor.

THE WEST GERMAN MISSION LEADERSHIP IN WORLD WAR II

After West German Mission president M. Douglas Wood arrived in Copenhagen in August 1939, he immediately initiated an extensive correspondence campaign with his staff back in Frankfurt. He made assignments regarding stewardships and sent copious instructions for the conduct of mission affairs. When it was announced that President Wood could not return to Frankfurt, he designated Friedrich Ludwig Biehl of Essen to serve as the mission supervisor and instructed him to report to President McKay in Basel until further notice. Five women who were originally called as missionaries were authorized to continue to live and work in the mission home

Fig. 3. Friedrich Ludwig Biehl (1913–43) served as the supervisor of the West German Mission from September to December 1939. (Courtesy of Margaret Biehl Haurand.)

at Schaumainkai 41 on the south bank of the Main River in Frankfurt. President Wood offered each woman a monthly salary of fifty to seventy-five Reichsmark in order to give her official status as an employee and thereby prevent the government from compelling her to take other employment. Within days, each of the women responded affirmatively to her assignment.

Neither the mission supervisor nor the office staff members were set apart in a specific ceremony. Following the departure of President Wood from Copenhagen, Friedrich Biehl traveled from his home in Essen to Frankfurt each weekend (a distance of one hundred and fifty miles) to conduct mission business. Born in Essen in 1913, he was a veteran of the Swiss-German Mission, spoke excellent English, and understood thoroughly the doctrines and practices of the Church. Although only twenty-six years of

Succession in German Mission Leadership during World War II

age at the time, he possessed the qualities considered by President Wood crucial for the execution of his calling. In naming Friedrich Biehl in a letter, President Wood had requested that all of the Saints in the mission "support Brother Biehl in his work with all of your energies."[7]

The weekend travel between Essen and Frankfurt soon became inconvenient and inefficient, so Elder Biehl quit his job at a dental firm in Essen and moved into the mission office. Unfortunately, this meant that he was officially unemployed and by December, the German army called him into active military duty. His counselors, Christian Heck and Anton Huck (both older men and members of the Frankfurt Branch) carried out his duties for several months.

In February 1940, President McKay officially designated Christian Heck (born 1902) as the new supervisor of the West German Mission. Because President McKay could not travel to Germany, he made the appointment in a letter. Heck asked Anton Huck (born 1872) to serve as his counselor with no second counselor appointed at the time. In distant Russia, Friedrich Biehl was killed in an accidental fire on March 3, 1943.

The new leaders of the West German Mission were enthusiastic and dedicated men who logged thousands of miles of travel to all points of the mission. From Denmark in the north to Austria in the south, they attended branch and district meetings and assisted local leaders in their functions all over the western half of Hitler's empire. At the time of his call, Christian Heck was unemployed but soon thereafter was hired again as a traveling salesman. He constantly combined business travel with visits to local Church units. Anton Huck was a retired streetcar operator and, as such, was free to travel as often as he wished.

A curious document is found among the papers of Erwin Ruf, the president of the Stuttgart District. Entitled "Ruling" (Beschluß), the one-page statement is dated January 31, 1942, and appears to have been issued to dispel any doubt regarding Christian Heck's authority to function as the mission supervisor. The translation of the text reads as follows:

A council convened today consisting of the following brethren: Johann Thaller, president of the Munich District; Hermann Walther Pohlsander of Celle [representing the Hannover District], and Erwin Ruf, president of the Stuttgart District. The council arrived at the following decision:

We hereby recognize Elder Christian Heck of Frankfurt as the current supervisor of the West German Mission until such time as he is released from this office by Church authorities.

It has also been decided that the mission leadership be expanded to include a second counselor. Brother Johannes Thaller was nominated.

[signed] Joh. Thaller

H. W. Pohlsander

Erwin Ruf

The following brethren accept the above decision:

[signed] Anton Huck   Christian Heck

As a witness, representing the East German Mission:

[signed] Paul Langheinrich[8]

Because there is no evidence that members of the Church questioned the assignment of Elder Heck, who by then had been serving in that calling for fully two years, the document was likely produced in order to confirm the position of Elder Heck as the spokesman of the Church in the eyes of the government. The statement may also have substantiated to the government the claim made by Elder Heck that he needed to travel by rail to points all over western Germany to administer the affairs of the Church. As with the leaders of the East German Mission, there is reason to believe that no setting apart or "physical" transfer of authority took place in the cases of Elders Heck and Huck.

Despite his age, Christian Heck was drafted into the German army on May 17, 1943. While serving on the Eastern Front, he was totally isolated from the Church and thus incapable of carrying out the duties of his office. Under those circumstances, there ensued a bit of a conflict regarding

Succession in German Mission Leadership during World War II

Fig. 4. Christian Heck (1902–45, first row, left) served as the supervisor of the West German Mission from 1940 to 1943. (Courtesy of Otto Foerster.)

the leadership of the West German Mission. Thus it happened that Anton Huck convened a council of the district presidents (fourteen in number at the time) in the mission office at Schaumainkai 41. On that occasion, he proposed that Christian Heck be released as mission supervisor and that another man be chosen in his stead. Only two district presidents, Hermann Walter Pohlsander of Hanover and Otto Berndt of Hamburg, opposed the motion, insisting that Church leaders had no authority to release higher-level leaders without cause. When the motion passed with those two dissenting votes, the two men expressed their willingness to accept the decision of the majority in order to prevent a schism in the mission. Anton Huck was then selected as mission supervisor.

Several months after the war's conclusion, it was learned that Christian Heck had been wounded in combat against the Allies and had died of his wounds in a Catholic hospital in southern Germany on April 19,

1945—just three weeks before the end of the war. He lies buried in the city cemetery in Bad Imnau.

As the third wartime supervisor of the mission, Anton Huck was not set apart to this calling nor named to it in a letter. Church leaders in Salt Lake City had no knowledge of the situation in Frankfurt and no way to influence decisions made in Germany. From the statements and writings of eyewitnesses, there is no reason to believe that Anton Huck sought power but rather wished only to see the work of the mission continue. In the absence of Christian Heck, there was a great deal of work to be done among the Saints. As the war progressed, more and more members lost their homes and branches lost their meeting places. However, while a dedicated Church leader, Elder Huck was also a known member and supporter of the National Socialist (Nazi) Party, a man who did not hesitate to extol the virtues of the Third Reich. However, he apparently restricted his political comments to settings outside of Church meetings.

Elder Huck asked Johannes Thaller to serve as his first counselor while continuing as president of the Munich District. Elder Thaller had both an automobile and a small truck; as a distribution manager for two different food producers in southeast Germany, he was constantly on the road. Kurt Schneider became the second counselor in the mission leadership. As the director of the Strasbourg branch of the Rheinmetall Company, he had not only a very nice automobile but also a chauffeur to drive it. Elder Schneider retained his calling as the president of the Strasbourg District. He was a dynamic leader and frequently traveled to the homes of individual members who lived far from branch meeting places. His wife, Charlotte Bodon Schneider, recorded many of those visits in her diaries during the war years.

In the summer of 1943, Anton Huck was summoned to the Gestapo headquarters in Frankfurt and required to answer a number of questions regarding the status of the Church in Frankfurt and in Germany. This he did without further complication at a time when dealings with the dreaded secret state police were avoided wherever possible. In October, the Huck family apartment in Frankfurt was destroyed in an air raid, and Elder Huck

Succession in German Mission Leadership during World War II

Fig. 5. The West German Mission office was housed in this building at Schaumainkai 41 in Frankfurt from 1938 to 1952. The president's office window is on the ground floor on the far left. The entrance was on the west (right) side. (Courtesy of George Blake.)

moved with his family into rooms in the mission home. They were there until after the war.

The year 1944 brought ever greater challenges for mission supervisor Anton Huck. One by one, branches were losing priesthood leaders and meeting rooms. Members were scattered far from home as soldiers, evacuees, or refugees, and several branches were meeting in the homes of members. Some branches had no priesthood support and held only Sunday School meetings and prayer circles. Elder Huck was no longer able to travel as freely

Fig. 7. Christian Heck (middle of front row) represented the West German Mission at a conference of the East German Mission in Berlin in 1941. To his left is East German Mission supervisor Herbert Klopfer.

as before. By early 1945, his counselors were severely hampered in their Church work: Johannes Thaller lost his automobile and Kurt Schneider was forced to evacuate Strasbourg to an isolated town high in the Black Forest. As the war neared its conclusion, Elder Huck no longer received reports from distant district presidents, and tithing remissions essentially halted.

By the time the American army entered Frankfurt on March 26, 1945, the mission office at Schaumainkai 41 housed several refugee Latter-day Saint families in addition to the Huck family and office staff members. The building escaped the many air raids with minimal damage. Anton Huck remained the mission supervisor until June 1945. He was then relieved by Max Zimmer, a leader of the Swiss Mission who had been authorized by the leadership of the Church in Salt Lake City to go to Frankfurt as soon as

Succession in German Mission Leadership during World War II

practicable. Elder Zimmer established communications with the Saints who had lived without such connections for forty-two months.

CONCLUSION

In both missions of The Church of Jesus Christ of Latter-day Saints in war-torn Germany, worthy priesthood holders were called to replace the American expatriate mission presidents. In both missions, the first supervisor called (Herbert Klopfer for the East and Friedrich Biehl for the West) was drafted into the German army and eventually died in the service of his country. In the West German Mission, this happened a second time—to Christian Heck. In all three cases where a German member of the Church succeeded another German, it was done without any formal call from a higher authority, either in person or in writing.

In all cases, the administrative services of the mission offices were not interrupted for more than a day or two.[9] It has been reliably reported that all five mission supervisors carried out their stewardships with dedication and integrity and were instrumental in sustaining the existence of the Church in Germany for five years and nine months of war and during the initial postwar era. Perhaps Richard Ranglack spoke for the other four in suggesting the formula for success for mission leaders who did not enjoy the benefit of a formal setting apart: "When I look back on those years, I have to say that I could never have found the energy to do those things without the help of my [German] brethren."[10]

Perhaps a crucial element in the acceptance of these mission leaders by the general membership is the fact that they were well known in their respective missions. The names of supervisors and counselors alike are seen on the programs of essentially all district conferences during the war, as well as in the minutes of meetings held in even the smallest branches.[11] The typical branch in those days had about a hundred registered members and an average attendance at Sunday School of about forty people. With such small groups, everybody in attendance knew everybody else. When visitors came, they were introduced and (if qualified) were asked to speak. When mission leaders came for branch or district conferences, they usually stayed with local families, not in fine hotels.

Mission and district leaders were also involved in personal events among the general membership. Branch and personal records indicated that those leaders were often asked to officiate at baptisms and priesthood ordinations when they came to town and to give healing blessings to local members. Many eyewitnesses recalled that those leaders were asked to preside at the traditional wedding ceremonies conducted in the branch rooms.[12] With such events common throughout both German missions, it can come as no surprise that no protests against the selection of specific mission or district leaders have been found in the existing literature.[13]

It is the author's opinion that no individual selected for mission leadership in Germany during World War II was unqualified or unworthy to serve. These were the right men who were in the right place at the right time. All served with dedication and distinction and their combined efforts kept the Church alive and functioning in isolation from the rest of the Church and under the worst of circumstances.

NOTES

1. East German Mission History, Church History Library, The Church of Jesus Christ of Latter-day Saints, Salt Lake City, CHL CR 27140.
2. It may be that before he left Copenhagen, Elder Smith authorized Thomas E. McKay to function as the European Mission president. The author has not found any record of such a transaction. Perhaps Elder McKay did not receive his charge until he arrived in Salt Lake City.
3. East German Mission History, CHL CR 27140.
4. East German Mission History, CHL CR 27140.
5. With excellent skills in English (a result of nearly a decade of living and working with American missionaries), Klopfer had interpreted for visiting General Authorities of the Church such as Heber J. Grant and J. Reuben Clark Jr. (Wolfgang Herbert Klopfer, interview by Roger P. Minert, Salt Lake City, November 3, 2006.)

6. Herbert Klopfer to mission leaders [Richard Ranglack, Paul Langheinrich, Friedrich Fischer], February 20, 1943. East German Mission History, CHL CR 27140.
7. M. Douglas Wood, papers, CHL MS 10817.
8. Stuttgart District history, CHL CR 16982/11, 166.
9. This was true even when the Gestapo shut down the West German Mission offices for two days in 1943 and when the East German Mission home was destroyed on November 22–23, 1943.
10. Richard Ranglack, autobiography (unpublished), private collection.
11. A stellar example of this is the branch in Bühl in southwestern Germany. The minutes indicate that on a Monday evening, Christian Heck visited the branch along with two friends from the East German Mission: counselors Richard Ranglack and Paul Langheinrich. No branch was farther from Berlin at that time.
12. Since 1876, only weddings conducted by the local civil registrar (*Standesbeamter*) have been valid under German law. When Latter-day Saint couples married during the war (as before and since), they did so first at the city hall. The ceremony held later that day in the Church rooms (and rarely in a home) was of ceremonial importance only. With the nearest temple in Utah, temple marriages among German Latter-day Saints before the war were rare (only one is known in the East German Mission and none in the West German Mission).
13. The question raised by Elders Pohlsander and Berndt during the discussion about the release of Christian Heck in 1943 was apparently not intended to oppose the candidacy of any potential successor but to question the validity of the process.

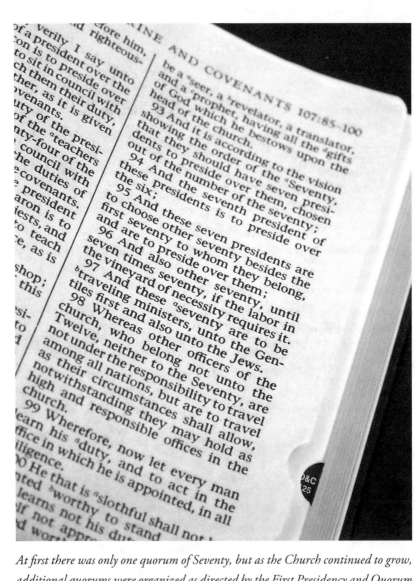

At first there was only one quorum of Seventy, but as the Church continued to grow, additional quorums were organized as directed by the First Presidency and Quorum of the Twelve.

Richard O. Cowan

26

The Seventies' Role in Worldwide Church Administration

In March 1835, when there were only a few thousand Latter-day Saints located largely in northeastern Ohio or western Missouri, the Lord revealed an administrative organization that would serve the Church well nearly two centuries later, when its members numbered in the millions and were scattered around the world. The Church was to be headed by three presiding quorums—the First Presidency, the Twelve Apostles, and the Seventy. The first of the Seventy had been called on February 28, just one month before this revelation was received,[1] were to play a key role in this administrative structure.

Like the Twelve, the Seventy were to be "especial witnesses" of Christ (D&C 107:23, 25; compare D&C 27:12). Both groups were to "build up the church, and regulate all the affairs of the same in all nations, first unto the Gentiles and secondly unto the Jews," the Twelve

---

Richard O. Cowan is a professor of Church history and doctrine at Brigham Young University.

working under the direction of the First Presidency, and the Seventy under the Twelve (D&C 107:33–34). Since both groups had almost identical assignments, the Twelve were to "call upon the Seventy . . . instead of any others" for assistance in administering the Church (D&C 107:38).

According to the 1835 revelation, the Seventy were to have an unusual organization, headed by seven presidents (see v. 93). As the demands of the work required, these seven had the authority to choose additional groups of seventy and preside over them (see v. 95). At the Kirtland Temple dedication, the presidents of the Seventy were sustained among the General Authorities as "Apostles and special witnesses to the nations, to assist the Twelve in opening the Gospel kingdom among all people."[2] Brigham Young later reaffirmed the special nature of the Seventies' office: "The Seventies are Apostles; and they stand next in authority to the Twelve."[3]

At first there was only one quorum of Seventy, but as the Church continued to grow, additional quorums were organized throughout the stakes. Eventually, these quorums numbered in the hundreds. Still, they were regarded as Churchwide quorums and were numbered accordingly; for example, the Los Angeles Stake (where I grew up) had two of these quorums—the 274th and 355th Quorums of Seventy. The seven Presidents of the original quorum presided over all these quorums and came to be known as "the First Council of the Seventy" and continued to be regarded as General Authorities.

THE FIRST COUNCIL'S ADMINISTRATIVE ROLE

As the number of stakes passed one hundred in 1928, the burden of visiting stake conferences, which were still being held quarterly at that time, overwhelmed members of the Twelve. Even though the practice of sending two visitors to each conference was phased out, the First Council of the Seventy as well as the Presiding Bishopric needed to assume a greater administrative role Churchwide.[4] Consequently, the First Council was relieved of some specific responsibilities for local seventies quorums.[5] Also, members of the First Council no longer presided personally over missions.

The Seventies' Role in Worldwide Church Administration

In contrast to the late 1920s, when three of the seven members were so engaged, a decade later all seven were available to carry out responsibilities at Church headquarters. When stake missions were organized Churchwide in March 1936, for example, this was done under the direction of the First Council of the Seventy.

In 1931, Elder B. H. Roberts had suggested that the Seventies could carry a greater portion of the administrative burden. Citing the Seventies' revealed responsibility "in building up the church and regulating all the affairs of the same in all nations" (D&C 107:34), he looked forward to the time when the Church would "get the full measure of service from the Seventy, especially from the First Council and its direct quorum," meaning the First Quorum of the Seventy which at that time existed only in theory beyond its seven presidents.[6]

During the next several years, Church leaders considered the possibility of reconstituting the First Quorum of the Seventy and designating its entire membership as General Authorities. This would have required at least thirty-six members because, according to the 1835 revelation, "a majority may form a quorum" (D&C 107:28). But as President Spencer W. Kimball later pointed out, "The scope and demands of the work at that time did not justify the reconstitution of the First Quorum of the Seventy."[7] There would need to be a different solution.

In April 1941, therefore, Church leaders made the following announcement: "The First Presidency and Twelve feel that to meet adequately their great responsibilities and to carry on efficiently this service for the Lord, they should have some help. Accordingly it has been decided to appoint Assistants to the Twelve, who shall be High Priests, who shall be set apart to act under the direction of the Twelve in the performance of such work as the First Presidency and the Twelve may place upon them."[8] The 1835 revelation had anticipated that there could be others beyond the Twelve or Seventy who "may hold as high and responsible offices in the church" (D&C 107:98). Five were initially sustained in this new calling, but their number would grow beginning in the 1950s. President Kimball later noted that they would "fill a role similar to that envisioned by the revelations for the First Quorum of the Seventy."⁹

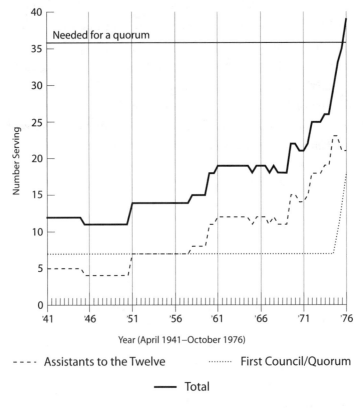

Fig. 1. Moving toward Quorum Status.

These new General Authorities and the First Council of the Seventy functioned side by side and almost interchangeably in helping to carry the administrative load. One difference was that members of the First Council were called only from among members of seventies quorums in the stakes; thus they could never have been called to serve in a bishopric or on a high council, which would require their being ordained high priests. Most of the Assistants to the Twelve, on the other hand, were seasoned Church leaders who had served as stake or mission presidents. During the 1940s and 1950s, members of the First Council of the Seventy were called at an average age of thirty-nine, while Assistants to the Twelve were an average of twenty years older.

Some suggested that members of the First Council could be ordained high priests to give them more flexibility. Others believed that this was not necessary. Elder Rulon S. Wells of the First Council, for example, insisted that the Lord had "endowed the First Quorum of Seventy with all the powers vested in the Twelve or [First] Presidency." He therefore argued that ordaining members of the First Council as high priests "would not add to their authority, nor change their status from a standpoint of Priesthood or other privileges thereunder."[10]

Nevertheless, in 1961, President David O. McKay announced: "Under the direction of the Twelve Apostles, the First Council of Seventy go to all parts of the world to set in order the affairs of the Church. That means ordaining high priests, setting apart presidents of stakes, high councilmen, setting apart president of high priests quorums, etc., and doing other things necessary for the advancement of the work. The First Presidency and Twelve recently agreed that the first Seven Presidents of Seventy under appointment by the Twelve, should have power to set in order all things pertaining to these assignments." Therefore, they were ordained to the office of high priest.[11] Even after this action was taken, members of the First Council continued to be selected only from among those serving as seventies in the stake.

When some critics pointed out that Joseph Smith had stated that it was "contrary to the order of heaven" to have high priests among the Presidents of the Seventy, Elder Harold B. Lee responded, "Had you ever thought that what might have been contrary to the order of heaven in the early 1830's might not be contrary to the order of heaven in 1960?"[12] Members of the First Council would receive new responsibilities right away.

MISSIONS, REGIONS, AND AREAS

The pattern of grouping missions for administrative purposes developed early. By the midpoint of the nineteenth century, missionary work was expanding in Europe. From the beginning, all European missions were supervised by the president of the British Mission, who typically was one of the Twelve. For example, in 1851, Elder Franklin D. Richards served as "President of the British Isles and Adjacent Countries." In 1929, a separate president was called for the British Mission; he, like presidents of neighboring missions, served under the European Mission president.

Following the disruption caused by World War II and the rapid worldwide growth of the Church during the 1950s, the concept of administrative missions returned. An Assistant to the Twelve (rather than a member of the Twelve) became president of the European Mission and established his residence at Frankfurt in 1960.[13] The following year, this mission was divided to form the West European Mission under another Assistant to the Twelve, who also moved to Europe.[14] Then, at the first worldwide mission presidents seminar in the summer of 1961, the South American Mission, the third of these administrative units, was formed, and Elder A. Theodore Tuttle of the First Council of the Seventy moved to Montevideo, Uruguay, to preside. At the same time, six other General Authorities—three members of the Twelve and three additional Assistants to the Twelve—were each assigned to supervise a particular grouping of missions. Thus there were nine administrative areas: four in the United States and Canada, and five abroad.[15]

In 1965, these mission supervisory assignments were modified to give responsibility to all twelve, rather than just three Apostles. The world was divided into twelve areas: five in the United States and Canada and seven abroad. In each area, a member of the Twelve was to be assisted by a supervisor. Nine of these supervisors were Assistants to the Twelve, while three were members of the First Council of the Seventy. All of these leaders were to reside in the Salt Lake City area, so the headquarters at Frankfurt, London, and Montevideo were closed.[16] Ten years later, as the Church continued to grow, six Assistants to the Twelve were once again assigned to live overseas in order to give more direct supervision to their respective areas.[17]

While missions were receiving this supervisory help, stakes were also given attention. In 1936, stakes had been grouped into regions to coordinate welfare projects. In 1964, the functions of these welfare regions were expanded to include other Church programs and came to be known as "Priesthood Regions."[18] Three years later, a new level of Church administration was created. The First Presidency announced "the calling of as many brethren as may be necessary, to be known as Regional Representatives of the Twelve" (later shortened to regional representatives) to provide counsel and "conduct instructional meetings in groups of stakes or regions as may be designated from time to time." Sixty-nine men, most former stake or mission presidents, received this new calling; their number would grow in coming years.[19] These brethren lived in their own homes, continued their regular employment, and served on a Church-service basis, generally in their own areas or nearby.

With the continuing growth of the Church, the General Authorities had to delegate more responsibilities to the local level. Before 1974, seventies could be ordained only by members of the First Council. In that year, stake presidents were authorized to perform this ordination following approval by the First Council. Two years later, stake presidents were permitted to ordain seventies without approval from headquarters.[20]

Writing in the *Ensign*, Dean L. Larsen, director of instructional materials for the Church who was also serving as a regional representative, noted that local leaders "come from an almost infinite variety of circumstances. Many are virtually without experience in administrative affairs" and represent "every level of education . . . , yet they are expected to learn and to administer a code of inspired principles, procedures, and policies that are determined by the General Authorities of the Church." Because it would be impossible to provide a handbook that could "make provisions for every possible contingency," the General Authorities traveled extensively to meet personally with and train local leaders. On a typical weekend in 1974, Elder Larsen noted, the Brethren traveled over 57,000 miles, visiting four continents. "Perhaps the greatest single challenge," he concluded, "is to establish and maintain a system of Church government that is universal."[21]

In 1976, the supervision of both missions and stakes worldwide was brought together into a single structure. The number of administrative areas was expanded to thirty: nineteen in the United States and Canada and eleven abroad (including the International Mission). Members of the Twelve as advisors had one to five areas. Of the thirty supervisors, nineteen were Assistants to the Twelve and eleven were Seventies.[22] However, changes were already under way that would affect the status of both the Assistants to the Twelve and members of the First Council of the Seventy.

FIRST QUORUM OF THE SEVENTY

By 1975, the combined total of Assistants to the Twelve and the First Council of the Seventy reached thirty, only six short of the minimum number to organize a quorum (see fig. 1). At the October general conference that year, President Spencer W. Kimball made this surprising announcement: "The First Quorum of the Seventy will be gradually organized, eventually with seventy members." Interestingly, this momentous development would be unfolded to the Saints step by step, allowing them time to absorb the import of what was taking place. President Kimball continued, "Three Brethren this day will be added to the First Quorum of the Seventy." He specifically pointed out that all three held the office of seventy, meaning that they had never been ordained high priests.[23] Thus these appointments followed the same pattern that had prevailed with calls to the First Council of the Seventy over the years.

However, at the next conference, April 1976, four more brethren were added to the First Quorum. Significantly, three were high priests and one was an elder, none having ever been ordained to the office of seventy. Hence, in each conference, President Kimball introduced a new precedent—first calling additional members into the First Quorum and then calling brethren who were not at the time serving as seventies. Furthermore, the First Presidency noted that members of the First Quorum of the Seventy would "hold the same authority as Assistants to the Twelve."[24]

At the October 1976 conference, the step-by-step process of organizing the First Quorum of the Seventy was completed. Four additional members were called to this quorum, bringing the total of Seventies plus the twenty-one Assistants to the Twelve to thirty-nine. President Kimball specifically noted that for the first time this exceeded the minimum number of thirty-six needed for "a quorum to do business." He announced, "Since the functions and responsibilities of the Assistants to the Twelve and the Seventy are similar, and since the accelerated, worldwide growth of the Church requires a consolidation of its administrative functions at the general level, the First Presidency and the Quorum of the Twelve . . . have felt inspired to call all of the Assistants to the Twelve into the First Quorum of the Seventy." From within the quorum, seven new presidents were chosen, five having been Assistants to the Twelve and two having served in the First Council of the Seventy. "With this move," he said, "the three governing quorums of the Church defined by the revelations—the First Presidency, the Quorum of the Twelve, and the First Quorum of the Seventy—have been set in their places as revealed by the Lord. This will make it possible to handle efficiently the present heavy workload and to prepare for the increasing expansion and acceleration of the work, anticipating the day when the Lord will return to take direct charge of His church and kingdom."[25]

At this same conference, Elder S. Dilworth Young, who had been the senior President in the First Council of the Seventy, reflected on this historic development: "It is right. It is inspired. Its time has come. It could not be stayed." He then added: "I sat in the temple Wednesday last and looked at the two presiding quorums, the First Presidency and the Twelve. I had borne in on me the great increase in the power of President Kimball, as in the third general quorum he placed some of the best-trained, most experienced, and loyal men in the Church. It thrilled me to see something come to pass for which we had so long hoped."[26]

In subsequent years, others continued to be added to the First Quorum of the Seventy. Soon the title "Presidency of the Seventy" replaced "First Council of the Seventy." In October 1978, the First Presidency announced a new status for certain members of the First Quorum. "The very rapid growth of the Church across the world, with the attendant increase in travel and responsibility, has made it necessary to consider a change in the status for some of the Brethren of the General Authorities. Some of our associates have served for many years with complete and unselfish dedication, and they deserve every honor and recognition for such devoted service." Therefore, following several years of prayerful consideration the decision was made to designate selected individuals from time to time as "emeritus members of the First Quorum of the Seventy." These brethren would not be released, but "the load of responsibility that they carry" would be reduced somewhat (for example, some became temple presidents or visitors' center directors). On this occasion, seven were given this new status.[27] In 1991, the policy was adopted of giving members emeritus status when they reached the age of seventy, although it was given earlier in a few cases, and since 2005 there have been some "year-by-year extensions as determined by the First Presidency and the Quorum of the Twelve Apostles."[28]

Traditionally, General Authorities had been called for a lifetime term of service, but in 1984 the First Presidency announced: "After much prayerful consideration, we have called six men, mature and tested through long years of service, to become members of the First Quorum of the Seventy, to serve for periods of three to five years, just as a mission president or temple president would do, and then to be released with honor and appreciation. While they so serve, they will be General Authorities with every right, power, and authority necessary to function. They will be expected to give their full time to this work while they are in office." The First Presidency believed that this practice would "provide a constant infusion of new talent and a much widened opportunity for men of ability and faith to serve in these offices."[29] Similar calls came in subsequent years (see fig. 2).

At the April 1989 conference, eight more were called on a "non-lifetime basis," bringing the total in this category to thirty-six. At the same time, four others were given a lifetime call. This brought the total number of Seventies to seventy-eight, more than can be accommodated in a single quorum; therefore, the Second Quorum of the Seventy was organized to include those serving "under a five-year call." Its members would be General

Authorities like those in the First Quorum.³⁰ "No distinction is made in the authority of members of these two quorums," the *Church News* explained.³¹

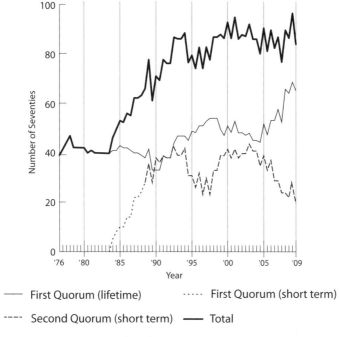

Fig. 2. *General Authority Quorums of the Seventy.*

The Presidency of the First Quorum now presided over both quorums, consistent with the instructions in the 1835 revelation (see D&C 107:95). In the future, explained Elder Earl C. Tingey, senior President of the Seventy, these presidents could be drawn from either of the General Authority quorums.³² Generally they have come from the First Quorum, but Elder Robert C. Oaks, who served as one of the seven presidents from 2004 to 2007, was a member of the Second Quorum.

With the creation of these General Authority Quorums of the Seventy in 1984 and 1989, the First Presidency decided that "the seventies quorums in the stakes of the Church are to be discontinued." Their members returned to their ward elders quorums or were ordained high priests.³³ This change eliminated any possible confusion concerning the relative authority of General Authority Seventies compared to seventies and other priesthood officers at the local level. "The office of Seventy was thus reserved for General Authorities of the Church," pointed out Elder Tingey.[34] Meanwhile, during the same year when limited-time calls were first extended, another important organizational development significantly affected the Seventies' role in worldwide Church administration.

AREA PRESIDENCIES

The pattern of having one of the Twelve serve as adviser and a member of the Seventy act as supervisor continued, although the title "supervisor" was changed to "executive administrator" in 1979 when a council was created in each area composed of the regional representatives and director of Temporal Affairs.[35] Still, there was a single Seventy responsible for each area under the supervision of a single member of the Twelve. This pattern would change, however, with a far-reaching development in 1984.

In June of that year, the First Presidency announced the formation of thirteen areas, each presided over by three members drawn from the First Quorum of the Seventy. They were to be "accountable to the First Presidency and Council of the Twelve for building up the Church and regulating its affairs in their respective areas." The structure at the area level thus became like that at other levels of Church organization—the divinely instituted pattern of a council consisting of a president with two counselors with whom he could confer. President Gordon B. Hinckley explained that "this organization lends strength to administration and brings a combined wisdom to decisions and provides flexibility in meeting challenges of growth." Presidencies of the seven areas in the United States and Canada would live near Church headquarters. Leaders of the other six areas would reside abroad, thus reducing the need for extensive travel.[36]

After the Second Quorum of the Seventy was formed, members of both quorums received assignments somewhat interchangeably. Area Presidents were most often drawn from the First Quorum, but not always. For example, for several years beginning in 1985, the entire presidency of the Pacific Area was drawn from limited-term Seventies.[37] In 1989, presidents of the Brazil and Asian Areas were drawn from the Second Quorum and had at least one counselor from the First Quorum. The following year this same arrangement was seen in the Utah South Area. Thus these unusual patterns were not limited to international areas, and the appointments underscored the fact that members of both quorums had the same authority and could be used interchangeably.

Although individual Seventies were sometimes moved to a new area after serving for only one year, they typically stayed in a given area from three to five years. Sometimes they started their service as a counselor and then became president for two or more years. Even though an individual might serve as president over one area, he could subsequently be assigned as a counselor in other areas. Sometimes Seventies were assigned to areas where they had personal experience, such as Elder John K. Carmack, who had been a stake president in Los Angeles, presiding over the North America West Area for three years beginning in 1984, and Elder F. Melvin Hammond, who had been mission president in Bolivia, being assigned to areas in South America. On the other hand, Elder Charles A. Didier, who was from Belgium, never served in the Europe West Area, nor did Elder John H. Groberg, who had been a missionary in Tonga, ever serve in the Pacific.[38]

AREA SEVENTIES

In 1995, the 284 regional representatives then serving were released and were replaced with 117 Area Authorities. Previously, regional representatives had primarily advisory "limited line authority" and were assigned to serve within specific regions consisting of only a few stakes. The new Area Authorities, on the other hand, could serve anywhere within broader geographical areas as assigned by the Area Presidency. They could create or reorganize stakes; preside at stake conferences; train stake, mission, or district presidents; and give general oversight as assigned by the Area Presidency.[39]

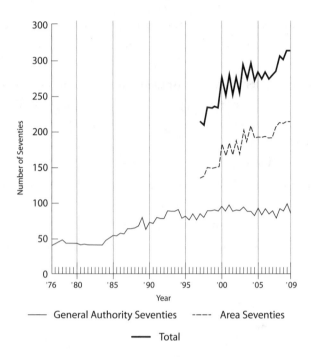

Fig. 3. General Authority and Area Seventies.

In 1997, these Area Authorities were ordained to the office of Seventy. President Hinckley explained: "They will then have a quorum relationship presided over by the Presidents of the Seventy. They will be known as Area Authority Seventies [by 2005 simplified to "Area Seventies"], to serve for a period of years in a voluntary capacity in the area in which they reside." They would serve under the direction of the Presidents of the Seventy and their respective Area Presidency.[40] Thus there were now two categories of Seventies: General Authority Seventies (in the First and Second Quorums) and Area Seventies. Nevertheless, President Boyd K. Packer has been quoted as saying, "a Seventy is a Seventy, is a Seventy."[41] The authority of these two groups was comparable. Elder L. Aldin Porter noted "that an Area Authority Seventy, within his area and by assignment of the Area Presidency or the president of the Quorum of the Twelve, can do almost anything that a General Authority Seventy can do."[42] Elder Tingey clarified that Area Authorities "receive assignments similar to those received by General Authority Seventies, with the exception that they serve in their local areas rather than worldwide."[43] Specifically, in 1997 they were authorized to preside over "member-missionary coordinating councils" which were composed of stake and mission presidents; in 2002 the jurisdiction of these councils was expanded to include all Church programs.[44]

The Area Seventies received assignments to serve in Area Presidencies. Typically Area Seventies served as second counselors in international Area Presidencies. However, the entire presidencies of the Idaho and Central America areas were composed of Area Seventies in 2001 and 2002. A significant departure from prevailing patterns took place in 2002 when two members of the Quorum of the Twelve were assigned to live abroad for two years and serve as Area Presidents. Elder Dallin H. Oaks went to the Philippines, while Elder Jeffrey R. Holland went to Chile—both areas where the Church had experienced explosive growth. Elder L. Tom Perry was similarly assigned to the Europe Central Area in 2004.

Initially there were 134 Area Seventies. The Third Quorum was composed of Area Seventies in Europe, Africa, Asia, and the Pacific; the Fourth Quorum was for those in Latin America, and the Fifth Quorum was for the United States and Canada. By 2004, the number of Area Authorities was about two hundred. In that and the following year, all three quorums were divided. The six resulting quorums covered the following areas: Third Quorum: Europe and Africa; Fourth Quorum: Mexico, Central America, and northwestern South America; Fifth Quorum: western and central United States and Canada; Sixth Quorum: southern and eastern United States and Canada; Seventh Quorum: Brazil and southern portions of South America; Eighth Quorum: Asia and the Pacific.[45]

Members of the two General Authority quorums held meetings at Church headquarters each week. Members of Area Seventy quorums met twice each year—once in Salt Lake City at the time of the April general conference, and then for the second time at a designated city within the area.

In August 2004, the stewardship of the seven Presidents of the Seventy was changed. The First Presidency relieved them of responsibility as "Executive Directors of major headquarters departments."[46] Specifically, Area Presidencies in the United States and Canada were discontinued, and those areas were to be "supervised directly by the Presidency of the Seventy under the direction of the Quorum of the Twelve."[47] The seven Presidents also assisted members of the Twelve assigned to preside over international areas by taking care of assignments, tasks, and other details.

Area Seventies increasingly are filling the role originally described for members who served for a limited time in the Second Quorum. While ranks in the First Quorum continue to grow, numbers in the Second Quorum have been dropping for several years. However, three new members were called to this quorum at the April conference in 2010 (see fig. 2).

CONCLUSION

In 1999, Elder L. Aldin Porter, the senior President of the Seventy, referred to the important 1835 revelation recorded in Doctrine and Covenants section 107: "The basics were revealed then, and continuing revelation has brought the Seventy to the present day." The Lord didn't give this revelation only for the Church in 1835; rather, "he gave it to meet the needs of the Church today and in the future. We can have 50 quorums of the Seventy, even 70 quorums of the Seventy as they are needed."[48] Thus the growth and unfolding organization of the Seventy are visible evidences of continuing revelation. As the needs of the Church change, inspired leaders will receive divine guidance in meeting them.

The Seventies' Role in Worldwide Church Administration

APPENDIX A: SEVENTIES MILESTONES

1835	Quorum of Seventies formed (February 28)
	Revelation on Church organization received: D&C 107 (March 28)
1883	Seventies quorums reorganized geographically
1931	B. H. Roberts urged that the Seventy be utilized more
1936	Stake missions organized under direction of First Council
	Regions formed to coordinate welfare projects
1941	Assistants to the Twelve called
1961	Members of First Council ordained as high priests
	Members of First Council supervised groups of missions
1967	Regional representatives of the Twelve called
1976	Both missions and stakes grouped into administrative areas
	First Quorum of the Seventy organized (October 1)
1978	Selected General Authorities receive emeritus status
1984	Seventies called to serve as General Authorities for up to five years
	Area Presidencies formed (June)
1986	Local seventies quorums discontinued
1989	Second Quorum of the Seventy formed for those with five-year calls
1991	Members of First Quorum to receive emeritus status at age of seventy
1995	Area Authorities replace regional representatives
1997	Area Authorities become Seventies, grouped into three quorums
2004	Seven Presidents preside over North America areas

APPENDIX B: AREAS OF THE CHURCH

Date Organized	Areas of the Church
July 1, 1984	Europe
	Pacific
	Asia
	Mexico and Central America
	South America North
	South America South
	North America Northeast
	North America Southeast
	North America Northwest
	Salt Lake City North (renamed Utah North)
	Salt Lake City South (renamed Utah South)
	North America Southwest
	North America West
August 15, 1987	Philippines/Micronesia
	British Isles/Africa (renamed United Kingdom/Africa) (from Europe)
	Brazil (from South America North)
	North America Central (from North America Northwest and Northeast)
November 1, 1988	Utah Central (from Utah North and South)
October 1, 1990	Mexico (Mexico and Central America divided)
	Central America (Mexico and Central America divided)
	Africa (United Kingdom/Africa divided)
	United Kingdom (UK/Africa divided)
June 1, 1991	Europe North (UK/Ireland expanded to include Scandinavia)
October 1, 1991	Asia North (from Asia)
	Europe/Mediterranean (from Europe)
August 15, 1992	Mexico North (Mexico divided)
	Mexico South (Mexico divided)
August 15, 1994	Utah Central merged into Utah North
1995	Europe East (Europe and Mediterranean realigned)
	Europe West (Europe and Mediterranean realigned)

APPENDIX B: AREAS OF THE CHURCH (CONTINUED)

Date Organized	Areas of the Church
August 15, 1996	Chile (from South America South)
August 15, 1998	Africa West (Africa divided)
	Africa Southeast (Africa divided)
August 15, 1998	Brazil North (Brazil divided)
	Brazil South (Brazil divided)
	South America West (from South America North)
	Australia/New Zealand (Pacific divided)
	Pacific Islands (Pacific divided)
	North America East (from North America Northeast and Southeast)
August 15, 2001	Europe Central (Europe North, which was discontinued)
	Idaho (from North America Northwest)
August 15, 2003	Salt Lake City (from Utah North)
August 15, 2005	Australia (New Zealand transferred to Pacific Islands)
	New Zealand/Pacific Islands (New Zealand transferred from Australia/New Zealand)
August 15, 2006	Caribbean (from North America Southeast)
August 1, 2007	Brazil (North and South recombined)
	Mexico (North and South recombined)
July 31, 2008	Middle East/Africa North
August 1, 2008	Europe (Europe West and Central recombined)
	Pacific (Australia and New Zealand/Pacific Islands recombined)
August 1, 2008	(North America East remerged)
August 1, 2009	South America Northwest (South America West and North combined)

NOTES

1. *History of the Church of Jesus Christ of Latter-day Saints*, ed. B. H. Roberts, 2nd ed. rev. (Salt Lake City: Deseret Book, 1957), 2:201.
2. *History of the Church*, 2:418.

3. Brigham Young, address, May 25, 1877, *Deseret News Weekly*, June 6, 1877, 274.
4. Stake conference appointments published in the *Church News* as early as 1942 regularly listed Presidents of the Seventy among conference visitors.
5. First Presidency to the Council of the Twelve, February 1, 1927, Church History Library, The Church of Jesus Christ of Latter-day Saints, Salt Lake City.
6. B. H. Roberts to Heber J. Grant, April 27, 1931, Church History Library, Salt Lake City.
7. Spencer W. Kimball, in Conference Report, October 1976, 10.
8. In Conference Report, April 1941, 95.
9. Kimball, in Conference Report, October 1976, 10.
10. First Council of the Seventy, minutes, March 27, 1941, 44–45, Church History Library, Salt Lake City.
11. "Status Changed for Seventy Council," *Church News*, June 17, 1961, 3.
12. Harold B. Lee, in Conference Report, September–October 1961, 81.
13. "Elder Dyer to Re-Open Europe Mission Office," *Church News*, November 28, 1959, 5.
14. "Elder Tanner to Direct W. European Mission," *Church News*, April 15, 1961, 12.
15. "New Program to Intensify Supervision of Worldwide Church Missions," *Church News*, July 1, 1961, 6.
16. "Church Enlarges World Assignments of General Authorities," *Church News*, June 19, 1965, 3–5.
17. "Six Assistants to Live Abroad," *Church News*, May 3, 1975, 3, 12; "New Mission Program," *Church News*, May 17, 1975, 3.
18. "Four-Phase Priesthood Program Set for '64," *Church News*, December 28, 1963, 6.
19. In Conference Report, October 1967, 25–26; see also 105–6.
20. Earl C. Tingey, "The Saga of Revelation: The Unfolding Role of the Seventy," *Ensign*, September 2009, 57.
21. Dean L. Larsen, "The Challenges of Administering a Worldwide Church," *Ensign*, July 1974, 20–21.
22. "Area Supervision Worldwide," *Church News*, June 26, 1976, 7, 11.
23. Kimball, in Conference Report, October 1975, 3–4.
24. N. Eldon Tanner, in Conference Report, April 1976, 29.

25. Kimball, in Conference Report, October 1976, 10.
26. S. Dilworth Young, in Conference Report, October 1976, 152.
27. Tanner, in Conference Report, October 1978, 23.
28. Tingey, "The Quorums of the Seventy," *Ensign*, August 2005, 48.
29. Conference Report, April 1984, 4.
30. Thomas S. Monson, in Conference Report, April 1989, 22.
31. Larsen, "New Quorum Is a Historic Development," *Church News*, April 15, 1989, 7.
32. Tingey, "Quorums of the Seventy," 50.
33. Conference Report, October 1986, 64.
34. Tingey, "Saga of Revelation," 58.
35. "Church Councils Now at Area, Region Level," *Church News*, April 7, 1979, 20.
36. "New Presidencies Announced for 13 Geographic Areas," *Church News*, June 24, 1984, 3.
37. Examples of Area Presidency assignments are taken from the *Church News*, which published lists of Area Presidencies in about June of each year.
38. Based on annual publications in the *Church News* of area assignments.
39. "First Presidency Names Area Authorities," *Church News*, August 5, 1995, 3.
40. Gordon B. Hinckley, in Conference Report, April 1997, 4.
41. Jay E. Jensen to author, e-mail correspondence, January 21, 2010.
42. Greg Hill, "Quorums of the Seventy Set in Place," *Church News*, May 1, 1999, 13.
43. Tingey, "Quorums of the Seventy," 49.
44. Tingey, "Saga of Revelation," 59.
45. Tingey, "Quorums of the Seventy," 49.
46. Tingey, "Saga of Revelation," 59.
47. "New Area Leadership Assignments," *Church News*, June 26, 2004, 8.
48. Hill, "Quorums of Seventy," 4; see also Tingey, "Quorums of the Seventy," 50.

The Lord has commanded missionaries, "Speak the thoughts that I shall put into your hearts, and you shall not be confounded before men; for it shall be given you in the very hour, yea, in the very moment, what ye shall say" (D&C 100:5–6).

R. Lanier Britsch

27

MISSIONS AND MISSIONARY ADMINISTRATION AND ORGANIZATION

SINCE the days of the Prophet Joseph Smith, the missionary efforts of The Church of Jesus Christ of Latter-day Saints have been guided and directly administered by the First Presidency and the Quorum of the Twelve Apostles. They make up what is called the Missionary Committee of the Church. As a group, led by the President of the Church, they give overall direction to missionary work. These fifteen men give high priority to this work. The members of the Quorum of the Twelve Apostles "are called to be the Twelve Apostles, or special witnesses of the name of Christ in all the world, . . . being sent out, holding the keys, to open the door by the proclamation of the gospel of Jesus Christ" (D&C 107:23, 35). The Twelve are assisted in their ministry by the Seventy, who "are also called to preach the gospel, and to be especial witnesses unto the Gentiles and in all the world" (D&C 107:25). As

---

R. Lanier Britsch is a professor emeritus of history, Brigham Young University.

special witnesses of the Lord Jesus Christ, they are charged with the responsibility of taking the restored gospel to every nation, kindred, tongue, and people. Every nation must receive the witness of the gospel. The Missionary Committee is very proactive. Clearly, they take missionary work very seriously, and nothing Churchwide of any significance happens without their direction and input.

The Missionary Committee carries out its work in a number of ways. They have created an action group, nicknamed "the operating piece," called the Missionary Executive Council (MEC). Until recently this council was chaired by Elder L. Tom Perry, a senior member of the Twelve. Elder Russell M. Nelson currently chairs that council. The other members are Elder Jeffrey R. Holland of the Twelve, Bishop Richard C. Edgley of the Presiding Bishopric, and Elder Richard G. Hinckley of the Seventy, who serves as executive director of the Missionary Department. This council administers missionary work for the Missionary Committee and oversees the work of the Missionary Department. This council evaluates recommendations, suggestions, and observations that may be forwarded from the Missionary Department to the Missionary Committee.

The Missionary Department works under the Missionary Executive Council. The Missionary Department does not create missionary policy, although it does forward information and recommendations to the Missionary Executive Council. The Missionary Department is a service department and functions as such. That said, it would be misleading to downplay the vital importance of this large department of the Church. The services the Missionary Department performs have a vital impact on the missionary work of the Church. In addition to general oversight and support of the current 344 missions, 15 missionary training centers (MTCs), and over 20 visitors' centers and historical sites, the Missionary Department is responsible for receiving and processing applications for all new missionaries, young and senior, male and female, proselyting and service; compilation of information regarding potential mission presidents; publication of missionary resources such as *Preach My Gospel*, the little white book titled *The*

Missions and Missionary Administration and Organization

Missionary Handbook, and the *Mission Presidents' Handbook*; compilation and evaluation of information that may lead to the creation of new missions, consolidation of existing missions, boundary changes, and changes in complements (the number of missionaries in a given mission); proselyting and media outreach; involvement in pageants; and so forth. One of the largest annual undertakings is the seminar for new mission presidents and their wives each June. A smaller seminar is held in January for new MTC presidents and visitors' center directors. It is smaller in number of participants but still a large undertaking. Each of these responsibilities deserves our attention, but let's look first at how the Missionary Department is organized.

MISSIONARY DEPARTMENT ORGANIZATION

The Missionary Department is organized with an executive director who is a Seventy. He is assisted by an indeterminate number of assistant executive directors who are General Authorities, all of whom are assigned from the First and Second Quorums of the Seventy. Currently five assistant executive directors serve. Elder Hinckley has served in the department for five years, and has been executive director for the past three years. The assistant executive directors serve from one year to several years. They are intensely busy. They each carry supervisory responsibilities in the Missionary Department. The executive director or an assistant executive director is available and on call at all times, but professional staff members in the Missionary Department who are returned mission presidents handle all but the most difficult questions that come in from the field. These brethren are called Infield Service Representatives, or IFRs.

The executive director and the assistant executive directors are supported by a compact staff of professionals. A managing director and other directors oversee the work of a number of different areas, including missionary services, proselyting, media, public programs, finances and facilities, and MTCs. A group of senior missionary couples provide much service. A retired physician oversees the medical area. He is assisted by medical missionaries—medical doctors and mental health professionals—throughout the world who provide medical and mental health counseling to the 52,500 missionaries now serving. The medical missionaries are not licensed to practice outside their home areas, but they advise mission presidents and missionaries regarding local physicians, hospitals, and procedures. They save the Church untold costs in health care every year.

THE CALL TO SERVE AS A MISSIONARY

With that introduction, we will now turn to the most important administrative responsibilities of the Missionary Department, the Missionary Executive Council, the Missionary Committee, and the First Presidency. First, the process of calling full-time missionaries: mission calls are initiated either by a bishop or branch president or by the prospective missionary himself or herself. Following successful interviews with appropriate ecclesiastical leaders and completion of medical and dental requirements, the missionary application is electronically forwarded to the Missionary Department. The Missionary Department reviews the applicant's information including a review of any medical issues (a team of volunteer doctors look at the medical information, such as allergies or required medications, and note such for evaluation). Each week a member of the Twelve reviews the information on each potential missionary and assigns him or her to a field of labor. The Missionary Department provides information on missions that need more missionaries, languages needed, restrictions on the applicant getting a visa to certain countries and any other information that will inform the Apostle(s) while making the mission assignments as part of the revelatory process.

An Apostle makes every assignment for missionaries, both single missionaries and couples. He can look at all of the information and override any piece of it. It doesn't matter; that is just informational for him. There may be a mission that is low on missionaries. He can look past that and assign that missionary to a mission that is over its complement. He has full discretion in where the assignments are made, and every assignment is made individually and by inspiration. They try to honor the financial and health constraints of couple missionaries. It takes a long time because there are hundreds a week. Assigning missionaries is rotated among the Twelve.

In April general conference of 2010, Elder Ronald A. Rasband of the Seventy spoke on missionary work. His address provided specifics regarding the process followed by members of the Twelve when they assign missionaries that are not available anywhere else. The following quotation is long, but it reveals much that is highly important regarding the assigning of missionaries to their respective fields of labor:

> With the encouragement and permission of President Henry B. Eyring, I would like to relate to you an experience, very special to me, which I had with him several years ago when he was a member of the Quorum of the Twelve. . . . Elder Eyring was assigning missionaries to their fields of labor, and as part of my training, I was invited to observe. . . .
>
> First, we knelt in prayer. I remember Elder Eyring using very sincere words, asking the Lord to bless him to know "perfectly" where the missionaries should be assigned. The word "perfectly" said much about the faith that Elder Eyring exhibited that day.
>
> As the process began, a picture of the missionary to be assigned would come up on one of the computer screens. As each picture appeared, to me it was as if the missionary were in the room with us. Elder Eyring would then greet the missionary with his kind and endearing voice: "Good morning, Elder Reier or Sister Yang. How are you today?"
>
> He told me that in his own mind he liked to think of where the missionaries would conclude their mission. This would aid him to know where they were to be assigned. Elder Eyring would then study the comments from the bishops and stake presidents, medical notes, and other issues relating to each missionary.
>
> He then referred to another screen which displayed areas and the missions across the world. Finally, as he was prompted by the Spirit, he would assign the missionary to his or her field of labor.

From others of the Twelve, I have learned that this general method is typical each week as Apostles of the Lord assign scores of missionaries to serve throughout the world. . . .

At the end of the meeting Elder Eyring bore his witness to me of the love of the Savior, which He has for each missionary assigned to go out into the world and preach the restored gospel. He said that it is by the great love of the Savior that His servants know where these wonderful young men and women, senior missionaries, and senior couple missionaries are to serve. I had a further witness that morning that every missionary called in this Church, and assigned or reassigned to a particular mission, is called by revelation from the Lord God Almighty through one of these, His servants.[1]

When the calls come back to the Missionary Department, staff members in the department prepare what is called a call packet. This call packet provides the newly called missionary with information he or she will need, including clothing requirements and travel information, to prepare for the specific mission assignment. The assignments are also immediately sent to the Travel Department, which comes under the Presiding Bishopric's Office. The Travel Department arranges transportation and visas.

THE CALLING OF MISSION PRESIDENTS

Mission presidents are called in a somewhat different manner. When General Authorities and Area Seventies visit with stake presidents at stake conferences, they suggest that the stake president might recommend two or three of the best potential mission presidents to the Missionary Department. General Authorities—the First Presidency, the Twelve, the Seventy, and Area Seventies—also see men who impress them as good candidates and bring those names back to the Missionary Department.

The Missionary Department executive directors (General Authorities) discreetly gather as much information as possible regarding each candidate's availability, health, family situation, employment and financial status, and doctrinal soundness. They look through these recommendations carefully and prayerfully. Most of this information comes from stake presidents. This process begins about eighteen months before the new mission presidents will enter the field. In 2010, the Church sent out 112 new mission presidents. More couples than needed are screened or backgrounded, as not all individual circumstances can be determined until a personal interview takes place. The six General Authorities in the Missionary Department look at the candidates together and then forward the files of the possible new mission presidents to the Missionary Executive Council, where they are carefully reviewed again. Those they choose to bring forward will be presented to the First Presidency and the Twelve. The Missionary Department's role is simply to help identify, screen, and move names forward.

Potential mission presidents are interviewed by a member of the Twelve. Although possible missionary service may be mentioned in this interview, the member of the Twelve does not extend the call to serve. Interviews with the Twelve reveal facts that could not be ascertained through the backgrounding process. Perhaps it was not known that one member of the couple or a dependent child has a serious health problem. Or the potential mission president's financial condition may have deteriorated. So for this reason, it is necessary for the Missionary Department to be prepared to provide a few more names than will be called. The process of gathering names of possible mission presidents by the Missionary Department and interviewing them by the Twelve is a very careful, time-consuming undertaking. By the time these individuals go through all the interviews and all of the screening and back to the First Presidency, they have been considered very carefully.

The call to serve as a mission president is extended only by the First Presidency, either in person or in some instances by telephone. When the call is extended, the couple normally is told whether they will serve in an English-speaking mission or in another language area. Calls are extended by the First Presidency beginning in mid-November. The actual assignment to a specific mission comes by letter from the First Presidency about the middle of February. The Missionary Department and the Twelve provide the necessary information regarding family size, which mission homes can accommodate which families, and so forth, but the First Presidency and the Twelve make all of the final decisions regarding where each couple will serve. When you realize the Presidency of the Church extends calls to over one hundred couples personally every year—they either have them in their office or talk to them over the phone—and the Twelve interview an even larger number personally, it's a daunting task. The First Presidency and the Twelve set apart mission presidents and their wives.

SEMINAR FOR NEW MISSION PRESIDENTS AND THEIR WIVES

Mission presidents are trained at the annual seminar for new mission presidents at the MTC in Provo. The Missionary Department prepares the agendas and sets everything up—housing, transportation, food, teaching schedules, arranging facilities, and so forth. Similar preparations go into the planning and implementation of the seminar for MTC presidents and visitors' center directors held in January. Elder Nelson is currently in charge. Generally, all three members of the First Presidency speak, as do several of the Twelve each year. The executive director of the Missionary Department and the five assistant executive directors teach in the classes. The seminar lasts three or four days. The classroom teachings are recorded and later sent to *all* mission presidents so they can listen to CDs and refresh their memories regarding what the Spirit conveyed and what was said. Mission presidents often understand what was meant in Provo better when they are in the thick of the work in the mission field.

One of the most important purposes of the seminar is to provide the opportunity for the new mission presidents and wives personally to be with the First Presidency and members of the Quorum of the Twelve. Mission presidents come from all over the world. Although they have spoken to the Church leaders by phone, many have never been in the same room with the President of the Church, his counselors, or the Apostles. They and their wives are able to meet these men. It is a thrill for them.

Missions and Missionary Administration and Organization

The topics covered are basic to missionary service: the purpose of missionary work, the ministry of the mission president and his wife, missionary work in the ward, working with members, teaching by the Spirit, the faith to find, media, goal setting and planning, zone conferences, strengthening missionaries, using the Book of Mormon, and so forth. New mission presidents are also informed regarding reporting lines and to whom they should turn for guidance and assistance. (Outside North America, they report to their Area Presidency. Within the United States, they report to one of the Presidency of the Seventy.) The mission presidents have the opportunity to meet with new missionaries who are going into their mission. The entire experience is formulated to give new mission presidents and their wives the administrative knowledge and tools and spiritual thrust to lead their missions successfully.

CREATION OF *PREACH MY GOSPEL*

In my interviews, I asked if there are any particular scriptures that guide and motivate their work. The answer was not surprising: "It's all of them! There are so very many that relate to missionary work. *Preach My Gospel* is filled with important scriptures."[2] With that entrée, I asked, "Let's talk about that. How did *Preach My Gospel* come into being?" The process was quite straightforward but remarkable all the same.

In 2002, President Gordon B. Hinckley met with the chairman of the Missionary Executive Council and asked him to find a way to get away from rote presentation and memorized lessons and teach with the Spirit. That was the charge given to the Missionary Executive Council by the President of the Church. They carried this charge to the executive directors and staff of the Missionary Department, who worked out the methods and content that eventually became *Preach My Gospel*. Thirteen missions around the world were involved to test the concepts—several overseas and the rest in the United States. They did so and gave their responses and evaluations back to the MEC. From time to time, the presidents of these missions met with the Missionary Executive Council, either in person or via telephone, to discuss things and this manual started to come together. It went through several drafts and did not have a title until it was finally published in English as *Preach My Gospel* in October 2004. It is a 228-page guide to missionary service. The Missionary Department immediately involved the Translation Department in preparation of language editions and by February 2005, *Preach My Gospel* was available in almost all the languages in which the Church teaches.

Preach My Gospel is a wonderful case study of how the leaders of the Church accomplish the Lord's purposes. All of the Twelve read it thoroughly and had input. The entire First Presidency of the Church read it very carefully and annotated it and made changes.

The purpose of *Preach My Gospel* is to help missionaries "speak the thoughts that I shall put into your hearts, and you shall not be confounded before men; for it shall be given you in the very hour, yea, in the very moment, what ye shall say" (D&C 100:5–6). The primary materials missionaries now receive are *Preach My Gospel* and the little white missionary handbook. (Before that, missionaries in the MTC received an array of materials adding up to over six hundred pages.) In combination with the scriptures, these foundational documents are the teaching syllabi for all missionaries. *Preach My Gospel* has clearly filled a missionary desire in many members of the Church. Over a million copies have been distributed, and the number continues to rise.

Many here today, perhaps most, will remember earlier unified teaching plans. An in-depth paper needs to be done on the development and evolution of missionary teaching materials through the years. Before World War II, missionaries did not use a uniform plan for teaching the gospel. The doctrines taught were the same everywhere, but the manner and order of presentation and emphasis varied from missionary to missionary. In the late 1940s and early 1950s, several teaching plans were developed that the missionaries memorized. Notable among these plans was the Anderson Plan developed by Richard Lloyd Anderson and Reid Bankhead. Variations of the Anderson Plan were developed all over the world. These memorized plans presented the basic Mormon doctrines clearly and efficiently. I use the word *efficiently* with caution. In Hong Kong, for example, more than sixteen lessons were developed and taught. That was before baptism. They taught new members another sixteen lessons after baptism. One advantage of the memorized plans was that when missionaries were transferred, they could simply inform their replacements which lesson any contact should receive next. These systems gave missionaries a certain sense of security, even though memorization did not always come easily to every missionary. In June 1961 (the same year that the first seminar for new mission presidents was held), the Church put forward the first unified plan for teaching the gospel. It and the second unified plan that followed in the 1970s were vetted by the Missionary Department and the Missionary Committee. These plans also required memorization and a set sequence. Refinements have been made over the years. But *Preach My Gospel* is revolutionary. The Church's missionary force worldwide is now marching together with a steady, unified beat. When the elders and sisters in the Utah Salt Lake City Mission heard that they would no longer be required to memorize teaching lessons, a cheer rang out. But their mission president said, "Just a minute. This is going to be a lot harder if you do it right." The steady beat is the unified determination to listen to and teach by the power of the Holy Spirit.

MISSION SUPPORT

Support of the missions, MTCs, and visitors' centers is an enormous responsibility and undertaking that requires a staff of missionaries and professionals to accomplish. The February 13, 2010, issue of the *LDS Church News* announced assignments for new mission presidents and also the creation of new missions. Earlier in this paper I spoke of 344 missions. That information is already out of date. Because of the creation of new missions and the consolidations of existing missions in July 2010, there are 340 missions as of this writing. For those of us who read the *Church News*, this is exciting news. But for the Missionary Department, it reflects a great amount of work. Every mission has an office and a home or apartment for the mission president's family. Cars must be procured or sold. Boundaries must be adjusted. Missionaries must be divided up, reassigned, and sent to new cities and apartments. New arrangements must be established with local priesthood leaders, and on and on. The Missionary Department is responsible for all of this. Of course, Area Presidencies, the Presidency of the Seventy, directors of Temporal Affairs, and others are much involved, but the Missionary Department is finally responsible to make sure that each mission has the right complement and the correct borders and boundaries, and that the mission president knows which stakes are assigned to his mission and so on.

MISSIONARY TRAINING CENTERS

Currently there are fifteen MTCs—one in Provo, Utah, and the remainder outside of the United States. Each MTC has a president who is called to serve for two years. MTC presidents are all returned mission presidents. They serve with local counselors. They are, of course, called and assigned by the First Presidency. The staff of each MTC varies in size. Teachers are returned missionaries who have experience teaching *Preach My Gospel*. Teachers are kept generally no longer than two years so that teaching remains fresh. Some MTCs are so small that they have, in addition to the presidency, only one staff member and a few teachers. But, in contrast, the MTC in Provo is actually over twice the size of BYU–Hawaii and has staff of considerable size and a large annual budget. It is the third largest educational institution in the Church after BYU and BYU–Idaho. MTCs in England, Brazil, and several other countries boast physical facilities and staffs of varying sizes. The four hundred dollars a month debited from the ward account for each missionary helps to offset the expenses of the MTCs as well as costs once the missionary arrives in his or her field of labor. As is true with every other part of missionary work, the curriculum at the MTCs is carefully guided and reviewed by the Missionary Department and the Missionary Committee.

Missions and Missionary Administration and Organization

VISITORS' CENTERS

The Church currently has over twenty visitors' centers and historical sites situated near temples and other places of historical importance. Visitors' centers are led by a director who serves for two years and are staffed primarily by sister missionaries and some senior couples. The Missionary Department is responsible for all aspects of construction, reconstruction, and maintenance, development of displays and literature, preparation of dialogues, and so forth. The Church History Department provides accurate historical information and archival data to enhance the interest and effectiveness of each historical site, and in some cases staffs and manages these sites.

The most visited visitors' center is Temple Square. With more than five million visitors annually, it is the most visited tourist site in the State of Utah. (By the way, Nauvoo is the second most visited Church historical site.) Because of the number of visitors and the number of missionaries required to have it function properly, Temple Square is both a visitors' center and a mission. Mission presidents hold priesthood keys to preside over their missions. Visitors' center directors do not hold keys. But in the case of Temple Square, it is presided over by a mission president who holds priesthood keys.

MEDIA AND PAGEANTS

Under the direction of the Missionary Committee of the Church, the Missionary Department has responsibility for all Church advertising efforts. These include less-direct offerings such as Homefront ads, which for many years have featured television and radio messages that promote family-related themes, and more direct, more recent media messages that invite members of other faiths to visit www.mormon.org. In recent years the Missionary Department has created and maintains this site, which presents many positive faces of Mormonism, including video testimonies, brief but powerful excerpts from talks by the Twelve and other leaders of the Church, a section on Church beliefs, and so forth. There is even a chat feature that allows participants to ask questions directly to a live missionary at the Provo MTC or at visitors' centers regarding what they are seeing on their computer screens or regarding principles of the gospel. Missionaries actually teach *Preach My Gospel* lessons over the Internet. This online missionary effort has become more and more necessary as gated communities have become the norm. How else shall we get into those homes? The Internet is one part of the answer.

The Missionary Department designs and oversees development and production of all materials used in proselyting, including developing films, pamphlets, exhibits, and other forms of media. The department has also played a major role in the production of such movies as *Legacy, The Testaments, Joseph Smith: The Prophet of the Restoration,* and other full-length films.

Pageants also come under the direction of the Missionary Department. The Hill Cumorah, Nauvoo, Manti, Castle Valley, Clarkston, Mesa, and other large pageants receive financial aid for staging, costumes, and support. The Missionary Department writes or reviews scripts, music, and other content to be sure it is appropriate. Smaller pageants receive less financial support but have the benefit of Missionary Department review and advice.

CONCLUSION

The missionary program of the Church is so large it requires a prophet's vision to grasp its magnitude. In attempting to write a suitable conclusion, I have been almost overwhelmed by the size and complexity of what is going on. It is so large yet very personal. It spans most of the nations of the earth, yet it is so personal and so individualized that the Lord's Apostles make every missionary assignment and the First Presidency calls every mission president. The work of the Missionary Department is constant in its purpose yet fluid and ever-changing in its work. In 2010, there were 340 missions. Yet the Church organized ten new missions that year. The management skills required to implement such constant changes are very demanding.

The principal message I wish to share concerns the basic organization and administration of missionary work in the Church: the First Presidency and the Quorum of the Twelve Apostles oversee all missionary efforts as the Missionary Committee of the Church. They have delegated to a select group, the Missionary Executive Council, the responsibility of moving important information back and forth between the Missionary Committee and the Missionary Department of the Church. The Missionary Executive Council also makes many decisions that do not require the consideration of the entire Missionary Committee. The Missionary Department has the responsibility to carry out the vision, plans, policies, and mandates of the Missionary Committee. The Missionary Department is a support team that services missionaries, mission presidents, the Area Presidencies, the Presidency of the Seventy, and the Missionary Committee. In sum, the system continues to accomplish remarkable work in the great effort to take the restored gospel to every nation and people.

NOTES

1. Ronald A. Rasband, "The Divine Call of a Missionary," *Ensign*, May 2010, 52–53.
2. This article about the administrative and organizational workings of the Missionary Department of the Church was written following interviews with personnel in that department. Early drafts of the manuscript were read by those individuals. For reasons of privacy, they have requested not to be identified.

MATERIALS FOR FURTHER STUDY

Allen, James B., Ronald W. Walker, and David J. Whittaker. *Studies in Mormon History, 1830–1997: An Indexed Bibliography.* Urbana and Chicago: University of Illinois Press, 2000. See particularly sections under "Missiology," 760–73, and "Missions," 773–75.

Britsch, R. Lanier. "Mormon Missions: An Introduction to the Latter-day Saints Missionary System." *Occasional Bulletin of Missionary Research* 3 (January 1979): 22–27.

———. "Missions and Missionary Work." In *Encyclopedia of Latter-day Saint History*, edited by Arnold K. Garr, Donald Q. Cannon, and Richard O. Cowan, 760–67. Salt Lake City: Deseret Book, 2000.

Cannon, Donald Q. and Richard O. Cowan. *Unto Every Nation: Gospel Light Reaches Every Land*. Salt Lake City: Deseret Book, 2003.

Cleverly, Dean B. "Missions." In *Encyclopedia of Mormonism*, edited by Daniel H. Ludlow, 2:915–20. New York: Macmillan, 1992.

Condie, Spencer J. "Missionary, Missionary Life." In *Encyclopedia of Mormonism*, 2:910–13.

Cowan, Richard O. "Missionary Training Centers." In *Encyclopedia of Mormonism*, 2:913–14.

Day, Gerald J. "Mission President." In *Encyclopedia of Mormonism*, 2:914–15.

Neilson, Reid L. *Early Mormon Missionary Activities in Japan, 1901–1924*. Salt Lake City: University of Utah Press, 2010.

———. *Global Mormonism in the 21st Century*. Provo, UT: Religious Studies Center, Brigham Young University, 2008.

Whittaker, David J. "Mormon Missiology: An Introduction and Guide to the Sources." In *The Disciple as Witness*, edited by Stephen D. Ricks and others, 435–514. Provo, UT: FARMS, 2000.

In addition to the books and articles listed above, there are numerous articles on mission history regarding various countries in the *Encyclopedia of Mormonism* and the *Encyclopedia of Latter-day Saint History*.

David J. Whittaker

28

Mormon Administrative and Organizational History: A Source Essay

One of the great strengths of The Church of Jesus Christ of Latter-day Saints is its institutional vitality. Expanding from six members in 1830 to fourteen million in 2010, its capacity to govern and manage an ever-enlarging membership with a bureaucracy flexible enough to provide for communication and growth but tight enough to ensure control and stability is an important but little-known story. The essential functions of the Church were doctrinally mandated from its earliest years, and the commands to keep records have assured that accounts of its activities have been maintained. Such historical records created the essential informational basis necessary to run the institution. These records range from membership to financial to the institutional records of the various units of the Church, from the First Presidency to branches in the mission field.

David J. Whittaker is the curator of Western and Mormon Manuscripts, L. Tom Perry Special Collections, Harold B. Lee Library, and associate professor of history at Brigham Young University.

A Firm Foundation

The study of Latter-day Saint ecclesiology has been a challenge until recently. As yet, the best studies remain in scholarly monographs, often unknown or unavailable. It is the purpose of this essay to highlight this emerging literature by complementing the essays assembled in this volume.

OUTLINE

Historical Studies
    General Histories
    1829–44
    The Succession Crisis
    1847–77
    1878–1918
    1919–2000

Contemporary Publications

Administrative Studies
    General Authorities
    Statistical and Demographic Studies
    Missiology
    Grass Roots
    Organization of the Gathering and Emigration
    Colonization and Settlement
    Meetinghouses and Temples
    The Mormon Sabbath

Specific Priesthood Offices and Quorums
    The General Pattern
    Prophet, Seer, and Revelator
    Councils and Conferences
    The First Presidency
    Scribes and Clerks
    The Presiding Patriarch
    The Quorum of the Twelve Apostles
    The First Quorum(s) of Seventy

Mormon Administrative and Organizational History: A Source Essay

    The Presiding Bishop
    Regional and Area Leaders
    Stake Presidents
    Bishops
Women and Administrative History
    The Female Relief Society
    Woman and Authority
Auxiliary Organizations
    Young Women's and Young Men's Mutual Improvement Associations
    The Primary Association
    Sunday Schools
    Church Educational System
Church Administrative Units
    Corporate Structures
    Major Departments
    Historical Department
    Family History Department/Library
The Church and Its Mission: A Theology of Church Government

HISTORICAL STUDIES

General histories. To date, this volume is the most comprehensive one-volume history of Church administration. A corrective to earlier notions that the real administrative genius of Mormonism was Brigham Young is the careful study of Joseph Smith's organizational abilities in Richard Lyman Bushman, *Joseph Smith: Rough Stone Rolling* (New York: Knopf, 2005), especially 109–26, 251–69. D. Michael Quinn has produced two volumes on the major presiding quorums: *The Mormon Hierarchy: Origins of Power* (Salt Lake City: Signature Books with Smith Research Associates, 1994) and *The Mormon Hierarchy: Extensions of Power* (Salt Lake City: Signature Books with Smith Research Associates, 1997). Quinn's studies have been influenced by Michel Foucault's work and tend to overemphasize raw administrative power (such as its use of violence and extended marriage relationships) to maintain and expand its control. His scholarship, while important, tends to move the Mormon story to peripheral areas such as criminal behavior, gender issues, and the folk beliefs of the membership. Quinn's earlier studies foreshadowing these include "Organizational Development and Social Origins of the Mormon Hierarchy, 1832–1932" (master's thesis, University of Utah, 1973); "The Mormon Hierarchy, 1832–1932: An American Elite" (PhD diss., Yale University, 1976); "From Sacred Grove to Sacral Power Structure," *Dialogue* 17 (Summer 1984): 9–34; and other articles to be noted in specific sections of this essay.

The essays of William G. Hartley gathered into *My Fellow Servants: Essays on the History of the Priesthood* (Provo, UT: BYU Studies, 2010) focus our attention on the more central areas of administrative history, as do the variety of articles on all aspects of Church administration in *Encyclopedia of Mormonism*, ed. Daniel H. Ludlow, 5 vols. (New York: Macmillan, 1992). These articles were gathered into one volume entitled *Priesthood and Church Organization: Selections from the* Encyclopedia of Mormonism (Salt Lake City: Deseret Book, 1995). A useful appendix (no. 5), "General Church Officers, A Chronology," was published in *Encyclopedia of Mormonism*, 4:1678–85. Mormon organization begins with and remains anchored to the visionary experiences and directives of Joseph Smith and his successors. The key accounts of these foundational events have been gathered into *Opening the Heavens: Accounts of Divine Manifestations, 1820–1844*, ed. John W. Welch with Erick B. Carlson (Provo, UT: BYU Press; Salt Lake City: Deseret Book, 2005). See also John A. Tvedtnes, *Organize My Kingdom: A History of the Restored Priesthood* (Bountiful, UT: Cornerstone Publishing, 2000).

Other studies which are useful for understanding the foundational structures are Neil K. Coleman, "A Study of The Church of Jesus Christ of Latter-day Saints as an Administrative System, Its Structure and Maintenance" (PhD diss., New York University, 1967); Edward Allen Warner, "Mormon Theodemocratic Elements in Early Latter-day Saint Ideology, 1827–1846" (PhD diss., University of Iowa, 1973); and Mario

DePillis, "Mormon Communitarianism, 1826–1846" (PhD diss., Yale University, 1961).

Dialogue 15 (Winter 1982) was devoted to Church administrative history. The introductory essay is called "An Introduction to Mormon Administrative History" (14–20). James B. Allen and Glen M. Leonard, *The Story of the Latter-day Saints*, 2nd ed. rev. (Salt Lake City: Deseret Book, 1992), the best one-volume history of the Church, devotes adequate space to the unfolding story of the Church administration. It also has an extensive bibliographical essay (673–762). A useful guide to the published work on Mormon ecclesiastical history can be found through various topics in James B. Allen, Ronald W. Walker, and David J. Whittaker, *Studies in Mormon History, 1830–1997: An Indexed Bibliography* (Urbana: University of Illinois Press, 2000); see the index for references to ecclesiastical topics, 617–24.

1829–44. A detailed account of the earliest years is Larry C. Porter, *A Study of the Origins of the Church of Jesus Christ of Latter-day Saints in the States of New York and Pennsylvania, 1816–1831*, Dissertations in Latter-day Saint History (Provo, UT: Joseph Fielding Smith Institute for Latter-day Saint History; BYU Studies, 2000). The development of Mormon leadership from a loose, somewhat informal grouping to a more formal hierarchy is detailed in D. Michael Quinn, "The Evolution of the Presiding Quorums of the LDS Church," *Journal of Mormon History* 1 (1974): 21–38. See also Wesley P. Lloyd, "The Rise and Development of Lay Leadership in the Latter-day Saint Movement" (PhD diss., University of Chicago, 1937); and Maurice L. Draper, *The Founding Prophet: An Administrative History of Joseph Smith* (Independence, MO: Herald House, 1991). For the extensive literature on Joseph Smith, see David J. Whittaker, "Studying Joseph Smith, Jr.: A Guide to the Sources," in *Joseph Smith Jr.: Reappraisals after Two Centuries*, ed. Reid L. Neilson and Terryl L. Givens (New York: Oxford University Press, 2008), 221–37.

The events of April 6, 1830, are detailed in Porter, "Study of the Origins of the Church," 243–53; Richard Lloyd Anderson, "Who Were the Six

Who Organized the Church on 6 April 1830?," *Ensign*, June 1930, 44–45; Anderson, "The House Where the Church Was Organized," *Improvement Era*, April 1980, 16–25. Larry C. Porter, "Was the Church Legally Incorporated at the Time It Was Organized in the State of New York?," *Ensign*, December 1978, 26–27, provides a useful overview of this topic, but for a closer look at the incorporation of the Church, see David Keith Stott, "Legal Insights into the Organization of the Church in 1830," *BYU Studies* 49, no. 2 (2010): 121–48.

A short history of the changes to the names of the Church is given by Richard Lloyd Anderson in "I Have a Question," *Ensign*, January 1979, 13– 4. Depending somewhat on Porter's pioneering study, but adding his own research and insights, is Richard L. Bushman, *Joseph Smith and the Beginnings of Mormonism* (Urbana: University of Illinois Press, 1984). An important area of divergence between Porter and Bushman is the dating of the restoration of the Melchizedek Priesthood: Porter's position of pre–April 1830 is fully presented in "Dating the Restoration of the Melchizedek Priesthood," *Ensign*, June 1979, 5–10; Bushman's review of post–April 1830 is in his books *Joseph Smith and the Beginnings of Mormonism*, 240–41, and *Joseph Smith: Rough Stone Rolling*, 118, 265–66, 588n35. See also the study by Gregory A. Prince, *Having Authority: The Origins and Development of Priesthood during the Ministry of Joseph Smith* (Independence, MO: Herald House, 1993); Orson Pratt, "Restoration of the Aaronic and Melchizedek and Priesthoods," *Millennial Star*, April 25, 1857, 258–61; John D. Giles, "Restoration of the Melchizedek Priesthood," *Improvement Era*, June 1945, 338–39, 371–74; Carter E. Grant, "Along the Susquehanna River," *Improvement Era*, May 1960, 306–9, 336–44; Robert L. Marrott, "History and Functions of the Aaronic Priesthood and the Offices of Priest, Teacher, and Deacon in the Church of Jesus Christ of Latter-day Saints, 1829–1844" (master's thesis, BYU, 1976); Richard Lloyd Anderson, "The Second Witness of Priesthood Restoration," *Improvement Era*, September 1968, 15–24; Mario S. DePillis, "The Quest for Religious Authority and the Rise of Mormonism," *Dialogue* 1 (Spring

1966): 68–88; and Mario S. DePillis, "The Social Sources of Mormonism," *Church History* 37 (March 1968): 50–78.

Developments during the Ohio period (1830–38) are detailed in Milton V. Backman Jr., *The Heavens Resound: A History of the Latter-day Saints in Ohio, 1830–1838* (Salt Lake City: Deseret Book, 1983), 237–61, 275–82; and Mark Lyman Staker, *Hearken, O Ye People: The Historical Setting of Joseph Smith's Ohio Revelations* (Salt Lake City: Greg Kofford Books, 2009). Other studies that address in various ways the early organizational history are Davis Bitton, "Kirtland as a Center of Missionary Activity, 1830–38," *BYU Studies* 11 (Summer 1971): 497–516; Donald Q. Cannon, "Licensing in the Early Church," *BYU Studies* 22, no. 1 (Winter 1982): 96–105; Gustive O. Larson, "New England in the Rise and Progress of the Church," *Improvement Era*, August 1968, 81–84; William G. Hartley, "Every Member Was a Missionary," *Ensign*, September 1978, 21–24; D. Michael Quinn, "Echoes and Foreshadowings: The Distinctiveness of the Mormon Community," *Sunstone* 3 (March–April 1978): 12–17; Davis Bitton, "The Waning of Mormon Kirtland," *BYU Studies* 12 (Summer 1972): 455–64; and Robert J. Woodford, "The Historical Development of the Doctrine and Covenants" (PhD diss., BYU, 1974). Lyndon W. Cook's *The Revelations of Joseph Smith: A Historical and Biographical Commentary of the Doctrine and Covenants* (Salt Lake City: Deseret Book, 1985) is a valuable commentary on the scriptural volume that has numerous revelations and instructions relating to organizational and administrative matters. It was the first study to take advantage of access to Woodford's dissertation on the Doctrine and Covenants.

Early economic organizations growing out of the doctrines of consecration and stewardship and showing the close connection between temporal and spiritual matters in the Church are described in Leonard J. Arrington, Dean L. May, and Feramorz Fox, *Building the City of God: Community and Cooperation among the Mormons* (Salt Lake City: Deseret Book, 1976). See also Joseph Geddes, *The United Order among the Mormons* (Salt Lake City: Deseret News, 1924); L. Dwight Israelsen, "An Economic Analysis of the United Order," *BYU Studies* 18, no. 4 (Summer 1978): 536–62; Leonard J.

Arrington, "Early Mormon Communitarianism: The Law of Consecration and Stewardship," *Western Humanities Review* 7 (Autumn 1953): 341–69; and Lyndon W. Cook, *Joseph Smith and the Law of Consecration* (Orem, UT: Grandin, 1985). Most fully, Max Parkin examines the initial developments in both organization and leadership prior to the emergence of high-level leadership quorums in "Joseph Smith and the United Firm: The Growth and Decline of the Church's Master Plan of Business and Finance, Ohio and Missouri, 1832–1834," *BYU Studies* 46, no. 3 (2007): 4–66. The later nineteenth-century developments and their interweaving into all aspects of temporal Mormonism are analyzed in Leonard J. Arrington, *Great Basin Kingdom: An Economic History of the Latter-day Saints, 1830–1900* (Cambridge: Harvard University Press, 1958).

The Kirtland Bank as a Church organizational entity is detailed in D. A. Dudley, "Bank Born of Revelation: The Kirtland Safety Society Anti-Banking Co.," *Journal of Economic History* 30 (December 1970): 848–53, and most fully in Marvin S. Hill, C. Keith Rooker, and Larry T. Wimmer, "The Kirtland Economy Revisited: A Market Critique of Sectarian Economics," *BYU Studies* 17 (Summer 1977): 391–475. A larger view of the Kirtland conflict is presented in Marvin S. Hill, "Cultural Crisis in the Mormon Kingdom: A Reconsideration of the Cases of Kirtland Dissent," *Church History* 49 (September 1980): 286–97, which sees early dissent growing out of the Zion's Camp march to Missouri in 1834.

Early Mormon city planning as evidenced in the Mormon village is detailed in Richard H. Jackson, "The Mormon Village: Genesis and Antecedents of the City of Zion Plan," *BYU Studies* 17 (Winter 1977): 223–40; Stephen L. Olsen, "The Mormon Ideology of Place: Cosmic Symbolism of the City of Zion" (PhD diss., University of Chicago, 1985); Leonard J. Arrington, "Joseph Smith, Builder of Ideal Communities," in *The Prophet Joseph: Essays on the Life and Mission of Joseph Smith*, ed. Larry C. Porter and Susan Easton Black (Salt Lake City: Deseret Book, 1988), 115–37; and C. Mark Hamilton, *Nineteenth-Century Mormon Architecture and City Planning* (New York: Oxford University Press, 1995).

Mormon Administrative and Organizational History: A Source Essay

Mormons gathered converts throughout the nineteenth century into these centers to be near their prophet and to apply the teachings of the gospel of Jesus Christ in their lives: the goal of these Mormon communities was to provide sacred space for the making of Saints. While the ward replaced the village ideal in the twentieth century, the goals have remained the same.

The organizational aspects of the move of many of the Kirtland members to Missouri in 1838 is the subject of Gordon Orville Hill, "A History of Kirtland Camp: Its Initial Purpose and Notable Accomplishments" (master's thesis, BYU, 1975).

The Church's military or quasi-militia organizational history must include Zion's Camp's march to Missouri. See Wilburn D. Talbot, "Zion's Camp" (master's thesis, BYU, 1973); Roger D. Launius, "Zion's Camp and the Redemption of Jackson County, Missouri" (master's thesis, Louisiana State University, 1978); Warren A. Jennings, "The Army of Israel Marches into Missouri," *Missouri Historical Review* 62 (January 1968): 107–35; and Peter Crawley and Richard Lloyd Anderson, "The Political and Social Realities of Zion's Camp," *BYU Studies* 14, no. 4 (Summer 1974): 406–20. Brigham Young would later say that he learned to lead modern Israel from the lessons of Zion's Camp. The so-called Danite Band in the late Missouri period is considered from an apologetic perspective in Leland H. Gentry, "The Danite Band of 1838," *BYU Studies* 14 (Summer 1974): 421–50, an abridgment of a chapter in his "A History of the Latter-day Saints in Northern Missouri from 1836 to 1839" (PhD diss., BYU, 1965); as a more sinister group in Stephen C. LeSueur, *The 1838 Mormon War in Missouri* (Columbia: University of Missouri Press, 1987); and in a larger context and a more positive sense in David J. Whittaker, "The Book of Daniel in Early Mormon Thought," in *By Study and Also by Faith: Essays in Honor of Hugh Nibley*, ed. John M. Lundquist and Stephen D. Ricks (Salt Lake City: Deseret Book; Provo, UT: FARMS, 1990), 1:155–201. The Nauvoo Legion is the subject of John Sweeney Jr., "A History of the Nauvoo Legion in Illinois" (master's thesis, BYU, 1974); most fully in Richard E. Bennett, Susan Easton Black, and Donald Q. Cannon, *The Nauvoo Legion in Illinois: A History of the Mormon Militia, 1841–1846* (Norman, OK: Arthur H. Clark, 2010). The history of the Mormon Battalion's activities in the Mexican War is Sherman L. Fleek, *History May Be Searched in Vain: A Military History of the Mormon Battalion* (Spokane, WA: Arthur H. Clark, 2006). The Utah version of the Nauvoo Legion is described in Ralph Hansen, "Administrative History of the Nauvoo Legion in Utah" (master's thesis, BYU, 1954). For later Mormon connections with the US military, see Joseph F. Boone, "The Roles of the Church in Relation to the United States Military, 1900–1975" (PhD diss., BYU, 1975).

Specific Church administrative developments during the Nauvoo period are treated in William G. Hartley, "Nauvoo Stake, Priesthood Quorums, and the Church's First Wards," *BYU Studies* 32, no. 1 (Winter/Spring 1991): 57–80; and in Glen M. Leonard, *Nauvoo: A Place of Peace, a People of Promise* (Salt Lake City: Deseret Book; Provo, UT: BYU Press, 2002). Lyndon W. Cook treats the development and administrative priesthood changes with a strong focus on the calling of the Seventy, showing their relative decline by 1844 (only one quorum) and subsequent revival (thirty-five quorums by January 1845) under Brigham Young's leadership, in *A Tentative Inquiry into the Office of Seventy, 1835–1845* (Provo, UT: Grandin Book, 2010). Mormon settlements on the western side of the Mississippi River in Iowa (the Zarahemla Stake) are discussed in Stanley B. Kimball "Nauvoo West: The Mormons of the Iowa Shore," *BYU Studies* 18, no. 2 (Winter 1978): 132–42. A study focusing on the Philadelphia area and its leader is David J. Whittaker, "East of Nauvoo: Benjamin Winchester and the Early Mormon Church," *Journal of Mormon History* 21, no. 2 (Fall 1995): 31–83.

The succession crisis. The crisis in the Church at the time of Joseph Smith's sudden death in June 1844 can be explained in large measure by the evolutionary nature of Church government prior to 1844. Joseph Smith had apparently thought of at least eight different ways or modes of succession as reflected in the changing nature of Church administration. While recent study shows that the most immediately viable leadership mode was by the Quorum of the Twelve Apostles, their position at the time was not publicly obvious to everyone. This public administrative uncertainty helps explain other leadership claims after 1844.

D. Michael Quinn surveys eight different modes of succession in "The Mormon Succession Crisis of 1844," *BYU Studies* 16, no. 2 (Winter 1976): 187–233. Essays specifically addressing the special blessing motif are D. Michael Quinn, "Joseph Smith III's 1844 Blessing and the Mormons of Utah," *John Whitmer Historical Association Journal* 1 (1981): 12–27, reprinted in *Dialogue* 15 (Summer 1982): 69–90; and Roger Launius, "Joseph Smith III and the Mormon Succession Crises, 1844–1846," *Western Illinois Regional Studies* 6 (Spring 1983): 5–22. Both essays were written with the assumption that a recently found account of the blessing was authentic, but the item turned out to be a Mark Hofmann forgery. These are included here because there were special blessings or rumors of such when Joseph Smith was alive, and these, no doubt, will be the topic of future research.

The semisecret Council of Fifty, organized by Joseph Smith in 1844 and for years thought to be the real administrative and political power behind the scenes, has been the subject of a number of studies. The first were James R. Clark, "The Kingdom of God, the Council of Fifty, and the State of Deseret," *Utah Historical Quarterly* 26 (April 1958): 131–48; and Hyrum L. Andrus, *Joseph Smith and World Government* (Salt Lake City: Deseret Book, 1958). In 1967 the most scholarly study appeared: Klaus J. Hansen, *Quest for Empire: The Political Kingdom of God and the Council of Fifty in Mormon History* (East Lansing: Michigan State University Press, 1967). All these presented a monolithic model of a religio-political machine actively seeking for world domination. But the availability of new documents has forced a major revision in the understanding of this organization, beginning with D. Michael Quinn, "The Council of Fifty and Its Members, 1844 to 1945," *BYU Studies* 20, no. 2 (Winter 1980): 163–97; and Andrew F. Ehat, "'It Seems Like Heaven Began on Earth': Joseph Smith and the Constitution of the Kingdom of God," *BYU Studies* 20 (Spring 1980): 253–79. See also Marvin S. Hill, "Quest for Refuge: An Hypothesis as to the Social Origins and Nature of the Mormon Political Kingdom," *Journal of Mormon History* 2 (1975): 3–20, and Peter Crawley, "The Constitution of the State of Deseret," *Friends of the Harold B. Lee Library Newsletter* 19 (1982), reprinted in *BYU Studies* 29, no. 4 (Fall 1989): 7–22. Current thinking suggests that this council was more symbolic than actual; perhaps a kind of contingent millennial organization in Mormon thinking given their expectations of the possible ending of the governments of the world. All of this must remain speculative until the original minute book of the Council of Fifty, owned by the Church, is made available for research.

Another group, known as the Quorum of the Anointed, was also semi-secret in Nauvoo before Joseph Smith's death. Andrew F. Ehat suggests how central the temple and its sacred ordinances were for those claiming succession in "Joseph Smith's Introduction of Temple Ordinances and the 1844 Mormon Succession Question" (master's thesis, BYU, 1982). For more information on those Joseph Smith invited into this initial select group, see Devery S. Anderson, "The Anointed Quorum in Nauvoo, 1842–45," *Journal of Mormon History* 29 (Fall 2003): 137–57; and *Joseph Smith's Quorum of the Anointed, 1842–1845: A Documentary History*, ed. Devery S. Anderson and Gary James Bergera (Salt Lake City: Signature Books, 2005).

More recent scholarship has shown that the Quorum of the Twelve Apostles were the key leaders of both the Council of Fifty and the Quorum of the Anointed. Ronald K. Esplin looks at the development of the Quorum of the Twelve Apostles in "The Emergence of Brigham Young and the Twelve to Mormon Leadership, 1830–1841" (PhD diss., BYU, 1981). Esplin brings the story past 1841 in "Joseph, Brigham and the Twelve: A Succession of Continuity," *BYU Studies* 21 (Summer 1981): 304–41; and in "'A Place Prepared': Joseph, Brigham and the Quest for Promised Refuge in the West," *Journal of Mormon History* 9 (1982): 85–111. The full story of the first apostolic missions to the British Isles and their impact on the preparation and emergence of the Quorum of the Twelve Apostles to Church leadership is presented in great detail in James B. Allen, Ronald K. Esplin, and David J. Whittaker, *Men with a Mission: The Quorum of the Twelve*

Apostles in the British Isles, 1837–1841 (Salt Lake City: Deseret Book, 1992). Other studies of apostolic-prophetic succession include Reed C. Durham Jr. and Steven H. Heath, *Succession in the Church* (Salt Lake City: Bookcraft, 1970); Steven H. Heath, "Notes on Apostolic Succession," *Dialogue* 20 (Summer 1987): 44–57; and B. H. Roberts, *Succession in the Presidency of the Church*, 2nd ed. (Salt Lake City: George Q. Cannon and Sons, 1900); Hoyt W. Brewster Jr., *Prophets, Priesthood Keys, and Succession* (Salt Lake City: Deseret Book, 1991); and Brent L. Top and Lawrence R. Flake, "'The Kingdom of God Will Roll On': Succession in the Presidency," *Ensign*, August 1996, 22–35. See also Richard Neitzel Holzapfel, "The Prophet's Final Charge to the Twelve, 1844," in *Joseph Smith, the Prophet and Seer*, ed. Richard Neitzel Holzapfel and Kent P. Jackson (Provo, UT: Religious Studies Center, BYU; Salt Lake City: Deseret Book, 2010), 495–524; and Alexander L. Baugh and Richard Neitzel Holzapfel, "'I Roll the Burthen and Responsibility of Leading This Church Off from My Shoulders on to Yours': The 1844/1845 Declaration of the Quorum of the Twelve Regarding Apostolic Succession," *BYU Studies* 49, no. 3 (2010): 4–19. For accounts of the August 1844 conference and the key role of Brigham Young, see the essay by Ronald W. Walker in this volume. See also Lynne Watkins Jorgensen, "The Mantle of the Prophet Joseph Passes to Brother Brigham: One Hundred Twenty-one Testimonies of a Collective Spiritual Witness," in *Opening the Heavens*, 373–477.

The events of Winter Quarters and the 1847 sustaining of Brigham Young as the second president of the Church are treated in Richard E. Bennett, "'I Am Going to Go It, the Lord Being My Helper': The Reestablishment of the First Presidency," in *Mormons at the Missouri: Winter Quarters, 1846–1852* (Norman: University of Oklahoma Press, 1987), 199–214; Bennett, "Winter Quarters: Church Headquarters, 1846–1848," *Ensign*, September 1997, 42–53; and William G. Hartley, "Council Bluffs/Kanesville, Iowa: A Hub for Mormon Settlements, Operations, and Emigration, 1846–1852," *John Whitmer Historical Association Journal* 26 (2006): 17–47. A useful introduction to those individuals and groups who did not follow the Church west with Brigham Young is Steven L. Shields, *Divergent Paths of the Restoration*, 3rd ed. (Bountiful, UT: Restoration, 1982); and *Scattering of the Saints: Schism within Mormonism*, ed. Newell G. Bringhurst and John C. Hamer (Independence, MO: John Whitmer Books, 2007). Most of the dissenters were unable to sustain a viable organization, and thus few of the new churches survived the death of their founders. The complex history of modern fundamentalism, dating from the era when the practice of plural marriage was abandoned by the Church, is detailed in Brian C. Hales, *Modern Polygamy and Mormon Fundamentalism: The Generations after the Manifesto* (Salt Lake City: Greg Kofford Books, 2006).

1847–77. No complete study exists that deals with Brigham Young as an administrator. The early attempt in Utah in the 1850s under Brigham Young's direction to establish the law of consecration, its general failure, and the subsequent Mormon Reformation to recommit members to their covenant obligations in 1856 are important to understanding both the deep religiosity of President Young and the zeal and rhetoric that were a part of the sermonizing of the time. These matters are discussed in Paul H. Peterson, "The Mormon Reformation" (PhD diss., BYU, 1981); Peterson, "The Mormon Reformation of 1856–57: The Rhetoric and the Reality," *Journal of Mormon History* 15 (1989): 59–87; Peterson, "Brigham Young and the Mormon Reformation," in *The Lion of the Lord, Essays on the Life and Service of Brigham Young*, ed. Susan Easton Black and Larry C. Porter (Salt Lake City: Deseret Book, 1995), 244–61. The first appearance of catechisms for teaching the children of Mormon families first appeared during this time. They were published by John Jaques, *Catechism for Children. . . .* (Liverpool: Franklin D. Richards, 1854). They were printed in large editions into the 1870s. See also Davis Bitton, "Mormon Catechisms," in *Revelation, Reason, and Faith, Essays in Honor of Truman G. Madsen*, ed. Donald W. Perry, Daniel C. Peterson, and Stephen D. Ricks (Provo, UT: FARMS, 2002), 407–32; and the essay by Ken Alford in this volume. For a useful introduction of administrative structures in England, see William G. Hartley, "LDS Pastors and Pastorates,

1852–1855," in *Mormons in Early Victorian Britain*, ed. Richard L. Jensen and Malcolm R. Thorp (Salt Lake City: University of Utah Press, 1989), 194–210.

Additional insights on Young's administrative skills are provided in Leonard J. Arrington and Ronald K. Esplin, "The Role of the Quorum of the Twelve During Brigham Young's Presidency of the Church of Jesus Christ of Latter-day Saints," *Task Papers in LDS History*, no. 31 (Salt Lake City: Historical Department of the Church of Jesus Christ of Latter-day Saints, 1979); Leonard J. Arrington, *Brigham Young: American Moses* (New York: Knopf, 1985), especially 192–209; Eugene England, *Brother Brigham* (Salt Lake City: Bookcraft, 1980), 193–230; and William G. Hartley, "Brigham Young and Priesthood Work at the General and Local Levels," in *Lion of the Lord*, 338-70. Leonard J. Arrington, *Great Basin Kingdom: An Economic History of the Latter-day Saints, 1830–1900* (Cambridge, MA: Harvard University Press, 1958), considers the many religious/economic programs of Brigham Young's administration. From personal observation, non-Mormon Elizabeth W. Kane provided important insights in 1874 into Brigham Young's leadership in her comments on his eye for detail, his personal interest in his people, and his great memory. See *Twelve Mormon Homes Visited in Succession on a Journey through Utah to Arizona*, introduction and notes by Everett L. Cooley (Salt Lake City: Tanner Trust Fund, University of Utah Library, 1974), 5, 6, 101. Brigham Young's regular trips throughout the Great Basin to visit with his people were important to his administrative successes. Greater detail is given in Leonard J. Arrington and Ronald K. Esplin, "Building a Commonwealth: The Secular Leadership of Brigham Young," *Utah Historical Quarterly* 45 (Summer 1977): 216–32; Gordon Irving, "Encouraging the Saints: Brigham Young's Annual Tours of Mormon Settlements," *Utah Historical Quarterly* 45 (Summer 1977): 233–51; and Ronald W. Walker, "Raining Pitchforks: Brigham Young as Preacher," *Sunstone* 8 (May–June 1983): 5–9. For a slightly different perspective, see also David L. Bigler, *Forgotten Kingdom: The Mormon Theocracy in the American West, 1847–1896* (Spokane, WA: Arthur H. Clark, 1998).

Brigham Young's family organization, in which many Church programs were first developed, is detailed in its earliest years in Dean C. Jessee, "Brigham Young's Family: Part I, 1824–1845," *BYU Studies* 18 (Spring 1978): 311–27; and Dean C. Jessee, "Brigham Young's Family: The Wilderness Years," *BYU Studies* 19 (Summer 1979): 474–500. See also Ronald K. Esplin, "Inside Brigham Young: Abrahamic Tests as Preparation for Leadership," *BYU Studies* 20, no. 3 (Spring 1980): 300–310; and Hugh W. Nibley, "Brigham Young as a Leader," in *Brother Brigham Challenges the Saints*, vol. 13 in *The Collected Works of Hugh Nibley*, ed. Don E. Norton and Shirley S. Ricks (Salt Lake City: Deseret Book; Provo, UT: FARMS, 1994), 449–90.

Aaronic Priesthood callings, held mostly by adult males during this period, are detailed in William G. Hartley, "Ordained and Acting Teachers in the Lesser Priesthood, 1851–1883," *BYU Studies* 16, no. 3 (Spring 1976): 375–98; Douglas Gene Pace, "The LDS Presiding Bishopric, 1851–1888: An Administrative Study" (master's thesis, BYU, 1978); Douglas Gene Pace, "Community Leadership on the Mormon Frontier: Mormon Bishops and the Political, Economic, and Social Development of Utah Before Statehood" (PhD diss., Ohio State University, 1983); and Douglas Gene Pace, "Changing Patterns of Mormon Financial Administration: Traveling Bishops, Regional Bishops and Bishop's Agents, 1857–88," *BYU Studies* 23, no. 2 (Spring 1983): 183–95. Also valuable are the essays on Bishop Edward Hunter by William Hartley and on Elijah Sheets, the longest-serving bishop in Mormon history (forty-eight years!) by Gene Pace in Donald Q. Cannon and David J. Whittaker, eds., *Supporting Saints: Life Stories of Nineteenth-Century Mormons* (Provo, UT: Religious Studies Center, BYU, 1985). Until the end of the 1850s, Mormon wards had two leaders: a bishop with Aaronic Priesthood functions and a presiding high priest with Melchizedek Priesthood functions. Having two leaders did not always work out well, and Brigham Young finally combined the two functions under one office, a pattern that has continued down to the present.

Mormon Administrative and Organizational History: A Source Essay

Tensions and challenges to Brigham Young's policies are suggested in a number of studies, including Gary James Bergera, *Conflict in the Quorum: Orson Pratt, Brigham Young, Joseph Smith* (Salt Lake City: Signature Books, 2002); Gary James Bergera, "The Orson Pratt-Brigham Young Controversies: Conflict within the Quorums, 1853 to 1868," *Dialogue* 13 (Summer 1980): 7–49; C. LeRoy Anderson, *For Christ Will Come Tomorrow: The Sage of the Morrisites* (Logan: Utah State University Press, 1981); and Ronald W. Walker, *Wayward Saints: The Godbeites and Brigham Young* (Urbana: University of Illinois Press, 1998).

The major administrative changes at the end of Brigham Young's life are treated in Gary James Bergera, "Seniority in the Twelve: The 1875 Realignment of Orson Pratt," *Journal of Mormon History* 18 (Spring 1992): 19–58; Todd Compton, "John Willard Young, Brigham Young, and the Development of Priesthood Succession in the LDS Church," *Dialogue* 35 (Winter 2002): 111–33; and William G. Hartley, "The Priesthood Reorganization of 1877: Brigham Young's Last Achievement," *BYU Studies* 20, no. 1 (Fall 1979): 3–36. See also Dale Glen Wood, "Brigham Young's Activities in St. George during the Later Years of his Life" (master's thesis, BYU, 1963). The influence of Thomas L. Kane, a non-Mormon adviser to Brigham Young, on such areas as education and finances is suggested in David J. Whittaker, "'My Dear Friend': The Friendship and Correspondence of Brigham Young and Thomas L. Kane," *BYU Studies* 48, no. 4 (2009): 193–225.

1878–1918. William G. Hartley discusses the important changes to the Seventies during John Taylor's administration in "The Seventies in the 1880s: Revelations and Reorganizing," *Dialogue* 16 (Spring 1983): 62–88. Two recent studies give good coverage to these critical years: Edward Leo Lyman, *Political Deliverance: The Mormon Quest for Utah Statehood* (Urbana: University of Illinois Press, 1986); and Thomas G. Alexander, *Mormonism in Transition: A History of the Latter-day Saints, 1890–1930* (Urbana: University of Illinois Press, 1986), both of which suggest the various ways the leadership of the Church sought accommodation with American political culture and various challenges of modernization.

Specialized studies which illuminate changes and tensions in LDS administrative history during this period include Thomas G. Alexander, "'To Maintain Harmony': Adjusting to External and Internal Stress, 1890–1930," *Dialogue* 15 (Winter 1982): 44–58; D. Michael Quinn, "LDS Church Authority and New Plural Marriages, 1890–1904," *Dialogue* 18 (Spring 1985): 9–105; Victor W. Jorgensen and B. Carmon Hardy, "The Taylor-Cowley Affair and the Watershed of Mormon History," *Utah Historical Quarterly* 48 (Winter 1980): 4–36; Kenneth Cannon III, "Beyond the Manifesto: Polygamous Cohabitation among the General Authorities after 1890," *Utah Historical Quarterly* 46 (Winter 1978): 24–36; Cannon, "After the Manifesto: Mormon Polygamy, 1890–1906," *Sunstone* 8 (January–April 1983): 27–35; James B. Allen, "'Good Guys' vs. 'Good Guys': Rudger Clawson, John Sharp, and Civil Disobedience in Nineteenth-century Utah," *Utah Historical Quarterly* 48 (Spring 1980): 148–74; and Edward Leo Lyman, "The Alienation of an Apostle from His Quorum: The Moses Thatcher Case," *Dialogue* 18 (Summer 1985): 67–91. See also B. Carmon Hardy, *Solemn Covenant: The Mormon Polygamous Passage* (Urbana: University of Illinois Press, 1992); and Kathryn M. Daynes, *More Wives than One: Transformation of the Mormon Marriage System, 1840–1910* (Urbana: University of Illinois Press, 2001).

Church financial and administrative challenges during this period are surveyed in Leonard J. Arrington, *Great Basin Kingdom*, 353–412; Leonard J. Arrington, "The Settlement of the Brigham Young Estate," *Pacific Historical Review* 21 (February 1952): 1–20; Ronald W. Walker, "Crisis in Zion: Heber J. Grant and the Panic of 1893," *Arizona and the West* 21 (Autumn 1979): 257–78; Walker, "Young Heber J. Grant and His Call to the Apostleship," *BYU Studies* 18, no. 1 (Fall 1977): 121–26; and Walker, "Grant's Watershed: Succession the Presidency, 1887–1889," *BYU Studies* 43, no. 1 (2004): 195–229.

The continuing changes to the priesthood structures (especially in the emergence of the Aaronic Priesthood as a useful avenue for the training of the young men as missionaries and for leadership responsibilities) beginning with the administration of Joseph F. Smith are detailed in David J. Whittaker, "Joseph B. Keeler, Print Culture, and the Modernization of Mormonism, 1885–1918," in *Religion and the Culture of Print in Modern America*, ed. Charles L. Cohen and Paul S. Boyer (Madison: University of Wisconsin Press, 2008), 105–27; William G. Hartley, "The Priesthood Reform Movement, 1908–1922," *BYU Studies* 13, no. 2 (Winter 1973): 137–56; Vernon L. Israelson, "Changes in the Numbers and the Priesthood Affiliation of the Men Used as Ward Teachers in the Church of Jesus Christ of Latter-day Saints, 1920 to 1935" (master's thesis, BYU, 1937); Dale C. Mouritsen, "A Symbol of New Directions: George F. Richards and the Mormon Church, 1861–1950" (PhD diss., BYU, 1982); Shirlee H. Shields, "History of the General Activities Committee of the Church of Jesus Christ of Latter-day Saints (PhD diss., BYU, 1986); Gary L. Phelps, "Home Teaching: Attempts by the Latter-day Saints to Establish an Effective Program during the Nineteenth Century" (master's thesis, BYU, 1975); and James N. Baumgarten, "The Role and Function of the Seventies in L.D.S. Church History" (master's thesis, BYU, 1960), 52–72.

1919–2000. No comprehensive study exists on the creation of the Corporation of the President in 1921 or Zion's Security Corporation in 1922, or for that matter any of the corporate structures that dominate the administrative structure of the contemporary Church. Some of the basic information is presented in Richard O. Cowan, *The Church in the Twentieth Century* (Salt Lake City: Bookcraft, 1985). This work includes information on Church education, the building programs, welfare programs, missionary work, correlation, and much information on Church statistics. Another useful volume of information is Richard O. Cowan and Wilson K. Anderson, *The Unfolding Programs and Organization of the Church of Jesus Christ of Latter-day Saints During the Twentieth Century* (Provo, UT: BYU Press, 1974).

The Church has selectively borrowed and adapted from other organizations programs that seem to offer assistance for its goals. For example, the Methodist Sunday School program was brought into the Church by British converts and remains an important program today. Another study of the impact of non-Mormon programs on the Church is found in Thomas G. Alexander, "Between Revivalism and the Social Gospel: The Social Advisory Committee, 1916–1922," *BYU Studies* 23, no. 1 (Winter 1983): 19–39. The adoption of the Boy Scout program by the Church, its largest corporate sponsor today, is another example. See, for example, Orval Leonard Nelson, "A Study of Boy Scout and Aaronic Priesthood Activity (Boys Age Twelve to Fourteen) in Selected L.D.S. Wards" (master's thesis, BYU, 1964)

Richard O. Cowan looks at important developments under Heber J. Grant in "The Priesthood Auxiliary Movement, 1928–1938," *BYU Studies* 19, no. 1 (Fall 1978): 106–20. D. Michael Quinn's biography *Elder Statesman: A Biography of J. Reuben Clark* (Salt Lake City: Signature Books, 2002) has much information on Clark's key role in the administration of the Church from the 1930s to the 1960s. The leadership of the eighth President of the Church is studied in Glen R. Stubbs, "A Biography of George Albert Smith, 1870 to 1951" (PhD diss., BYU 1974). G. Homer Durham provides two contemporary scholarly studies on Church organization: "Administrative Organization of the Mormon Church," *Political Science Quarterly* 57 (March 1942): 51–71; and "Coordination by Special Representatives of the Chief Executive," *Public Administration Review* 8 (Summer 1948): 176–80. See also F. R. Johnson, "Mormon Church as a Central Command System," *Review of Social Economy* 37 (April 1979): 79–94.

Students of the welfare program of the Church must begin with the programs of Joseph Smith. The best place to begin to study the developments from the 1930s on is with Arrington, Fox, and May, *Building the City of God*, 337–58. The Church Securities Program of 1936, which launched the modern Mormon welfare program, can be understood as more of a Utah complement to the New Deal programs of Franklin D. Roosevelt rather than as alternative to them. See also Albert L. Fisher, "Mormon Welfare Programs: Past and Present," *Social Science Journal* 15 (April 1978): 75–99; Jessie L. Embry, "Relief Society Grain Storage Program, 1876–1940" (master's thesis, BYU, 1974); David R. Hall, "Amy Brown Lyman and Social Service Work in the Relief Society" (master's thesis, BYU,

1992); Bruce D. Blumell, "Welfare Before Welfare: Twentieth Century LDS Church Charity before the Great Depression," *Journal of Mormon History* 6 (1976): 89–106; Leonard J. Arrington and Wayne K. Hinton, "Origin of the Welfare Plan of the Church of Jesus Christ of Latter-day Saints," *BYU Studies* 5, no. 2 (Winter 1964): 67–85; Maylo Rogers Wiltenberger, "Some Aspects of Welfare Activities of the Church of Jesus Christ of Latter-day Saints" (master's thesis, Tulane University, 1938); and Betty L. Barton, "Mormon Poor Relief: A Social Welfare Interlude," *BYU Studies* 18, no. 1 (Fall 1977): 77–82. The most comprehensive study is Garth Mangum and Bruce Blumell, *The Mormons' War on Poverty: A History of LDS Welfare, 1830–1990* (Salt Lake City: University of Utah Press, 1993); see also Dean L. May, "Body and Soul: The Record of Mormon Religious Philanthropy," *Church History* 57 (September 1988): 322–36. Recent activities of the Church in such areas as international relief for victims of earthquakes or floods, or in the work of the recently established Perpetual Education Fund are clearly building on earlier examples and divine directives.

An early examination of the modern temporal affairs of the Church was E. E. Erickson, "The Church and Business," in his *Psychological and Ethical Aspects of Mormon Group Life* (Chicago: University of Chicago Press, 1922), 66–72. Recent overviews are Leonard J. Arrington and Davis Bitton, "The Temporal Foundations," in *The Mormon Experience: A History of the Latter-day Saints* (New York: Knopf, 1980), 262–83; and, more critically, Robert Gottlieb and Peter Wiley, *America's Saints: The Rise of Mormon Power* (New York: Putnam's Sons, 1984), 95–128; and John Heinerman and Anson Shupe, *The Mormon Corporate Empire* (Boston: Beacon Press, 1985). See further D. Michael Quinn, "LDS Church Finances from the 1830s to the 1990s," *Sunstone* 19 (June 1996): 17–29.

More recent developments are treated in Gordon Irving, "Administration of President Joseph Fielding Smith," *Ensign*, August 1972, 40–41; James B. Allen, "Harold B. Lee: An Appreciation, Both Historical and Personal," *Dialogue* 8 (Autumn–Winter 1974): 14–17; H. Brent Goates, *Harold B. Lee: Prophet and Seer* (Salt Lake City: Bookcraft, 1985); "A Decade of

Growth [1973–1983]," *Ensign*, January 1984, 10–15; Edward L. Kimball, *Lengthen Your Stride: The Presidency of Spencer W. Kimball* (Salt Lake City: Deseret Book, 2005); and Boyd K. Packer, "President Spencer W. Kimball: No Ordinary Man," *Ensign*, March 1974, 21–31.

The Priesthood Correlation Program was announced to the Church by Harold B. Lee in 1961: "New Plan of Coordination," *Improvement Era*, January 1962, 34–37. Some of the background is described in Jerry J. Rose, "The Correlation Program of the Church of Jesus Christ of Jesus Christ of Latter-day Saints During the Twentieth Century" (master's thesis, BYU, 1973), and in the essay by Michael Goodman in this volume. A more millennial interpretation is given in Dale C. Morritsen, *A Defense and a Refuge: Priesthood Correlation and the Establishment of Zion* (Provo, UT: BYU Publications, 1972). Other studies include John P. Fugal, comp., *A Review of Priesthood Correlation* (Provo, UT: BYU Press, 1968); and Gottlieb and Wiley, *America's Saints*, 56–64, much of which appears as "The Lee Revolution and the Rise of Correlation," *Sunstone* 10, no. 1 (1984–85): 19–22. An especially valuable study is Bruce D. Blumell, "Priesthood Correlation, 1960–1974" (unpublished manuscript, copy in Church History Library). See also Carol H. Cannon, comp., "Correlation Chronology as Reflected in Minutes of Correlation Executive Committee Meetings, 1960–1971" (unpublished manuscript, copy in Church History Library). Armand L. Mauss has studied the background and consequences (some intentional, some not) of the correlation program on all levels of Church administration and membership in *The Angel and the Beehive: The Mormon Struggle with Assimilation* (Urbana: University of Illinois Press, 1994). Mauss, like O'Dea before him, seeks to understand the dynamic tension of Mormonism's struggle to maintain its unique claims and status as a "peculiar people" while at the same time seeking to be "in the world." O'Dea found the Mormon ability to avoid sectarian stagnation by keeping at least one foot in the pioneer heritage and ideals of the nineteenth century, which allowed members to combine the sacred with the secular in their daily lives; Mauss sees modern Mormonism seeking to maintain its identity by drawing closer to Protestant fundamentalism, and in effect, coming dangerously close to losing its historic identity. For Thomas O'Dea's ideas, see *The Mormons* (Chicago: University of Chicago Press, 1957); and "Sources of Strain in Mormon History Reconsidered," in *Mormonism and American Culture*, ed. Marvin S. Hill and James B. Allen (New York: Harper and Row, 1972), 147–68. The issues are too complex to discuss here, but the bibliography in Mauss's work will lead the researcher to the larger literature.

The extending of the priesthood to all worthy males (June 1978) is treated historically and sociologically in a volume of collected essays: Lester E. Bush Jr. and Armand L. Mauss, eds., *Neither White nor Black: Mormon Scholars Confront the Race Issue in a Universal Church* (Midvale, UT: Signature Books, 1984), which also has an extensive bibliography. The larger story is presented in Armand L. Mauss, *All Abraham's Children: Changing Mormon Conceptions of Race and Lineage* (Urbana: University of Illinois Press, 2003).

Reflections on the recent developments to simplify Church programs are James B. Allen, "'Course Corrections': Some Personal Reflections," *Sunstone* 14 (October 1990): 34–40, as well as the essays by J. Lynn England and Marie Cornwall in the same issue. See also John P. Livingstone, "Establishing the Church Simply," *BYU Studies* 39, no. 4 (2000): 127–63. While there are important reasons for the simplifying of Church meetings and activities to a three-hour block on Sunday, Armand Mauss has argued that the reduction in Church meetings, which in the past could require almost daily Church meetings and activities has significantly challenged and thereby weakened the Mormon historic sense of community.

CONTEMPORARY PUBLICATIONS

No historical study exists which surveys the addresses and various contemporary publications on the priesthood and Church government. A useful essay is "Mormon Imprints as Sources for Research: A History and Evaluation," in Ronald W. Walker, David J. Whittaker, and James B. Allen, *Mormon History* (Urbana: University of Illinois Press, 2001), 199–238. The earliest material can be found in the revelations and addresses of Joseph Smith. These include several key sections of the Doctrine and Covenants: 13, 20, 84, 105, 107–112, 121, 124, 127–29, 132. Several unpublished revelations of Joseph Smith are also important, including those dated March 1832 (in Newel K. Whitney Collection, L. Tom Perry Special Collections, Harold B. Lee Library, BYU), January 5, [1833] (in Church Archives), and January 12, 1838 (three on this date in "Scriptory Book of Joseph Smith," manuscript in Church History Library). Most are available in Robin Scott Jensen, Robert J. Woodford, and Steven C. Harper, eds., *Manuscript Revelation Book*, vol. 1 of the Revelations and Translations series of *The Joseph Smith Papers*, ed. Dean C. Jessee, Ronald K. Esplin, and Richard Lyman Bushman (Salt Lake City: The Church Historian's Press, 2009). The difficulty of communications in the earliest years (but which continued to be a reality through much of the nineteenth-century) is described in William G. Hartley, "Letters and Mail between Kirtland and Independence: A Mormon Postal System, 1831–1833," *Journal of Mormon History* 35 (Summer 2009): 163–89.

Joseph Smith's administrative leadership can be seen in the various minute books of early Church and quorum meetings and conferences and in his correspondence, but he also addressed a number of priesthood and administrative matters in his sermons. Many can be found in Andrew F. Ehat and Lyndon W. Cook, comps., *The Words of Joseph Smith* (Provo, UT: Religious Studies Center, BYU, 1980), under the following dates: August 8, 1839; October 5, 1840 (the only known address Joseph specifically prepared a text for); January 5, 1841; January 29, 1843; August 27, 1843; March 10, 1844; April 7, 1844; May 12, 1844; and June 16, 1844. There are also his more private addresses to the Quorum of the Twelve Apostles, many of which are contained in the journals and notebooks of Willard Richards and Wilford Woodruff, manuscripts in the Church History Library.

Some of the Prophet's addresses and editorials appeared in early Mormon publications such as *The Evening and the Morning Star*, the *Latter-day Saints' Messenger and Advocate*, the *Elders' Journal*, and the *Times and Seasons*; some were reprinted in the *Millennial Star* in England.

Several of Joseph Smith's early followers also published on these topics. One of the earliest and perhaps the most influential was Parley P. Pratt, who issued his *Voice of Warning* in New York City in 1837. Chapter 3, "The Kingdom of God," influenced a number of writers and pamphleteers in early Mormonism, including his brother Orson as well as Benjamin Winchester, a Church leader in Philadelphia, whose *A History of the Priesthood from the Beginning of the World to the Present Time* (Philadelphia: Brown, Bicking, and Guilbert, 1843) was the first book-length study of the subject. Orson Pratt's pamphlet series on *Divine Authority, or the Question, Was Joseph Smith Sent of God?* (Liverpool: R. James, 1848) and *The Kingdom of God* (Liverpool: S. W. Richards, 1848–49) were probably the main channels through which Joseph Smith's and Parley Pratt's ideas reached the majority of Latter-day Saint converts in the nineteenth century.

Brigham Young also left a mountain of documentary records which detail his administrative and organizational leadership. For his sermons, see *The Complete Discourses of Brigham Young*, ed. Richard S. Van Wagoner, 5 vols. (Salt Lake City: Smith-Pettit Foundation, 2010). Administrative record books, financial records, and extensive correspondence will provide some future historian all the material needed to tell the full story.

John Taylor, the third President of the Church, was the author of three works on this topic: *The Government of God* (Liverpool: S. W. Richards, 1852), *Items on Priesthood Presented to the Latter-day Saints* (Salt Lake City, 1881), and *Succession in the Priesthood*, a discourse of October 7, 1881 (Salt Lake City: Deseret News, 1902).

Many of these publications came as a result of a growing need within the Church for more information and internal coordination on various aspects of Church administration as it grew in size and complexity. Writers and editors of Church publications had tried at various times to address various questions relating to Church governance. While no survey of their work has been done, the following are representative of these attempts: Erastus Snow, "On Priesthood," *Gospel Reflector* (Philadelphia), April 15, 1841, 204–12; Thomas Ward, "On the Correction of Errors in Priesthood,"

Millennial Star, February 1842, 157–58; Ward, "On the False Prophets of the Last Days," *Millennial Star*, April 1842, 177–84; Orson Spencer answered various administrative questions in the mission field in *Millennial Star*, June 1, 1847, 167–71; John Taylor, "On Priesthood," *Millennial Star*, November 1, 1847, 321–26; Thomas Smith, "Questions and Answers for the Children of the LDS School," *Millennial Star*, June 15, 1848, 183–84; Orson Pratt, "Power and Eternity of the Priesthood," *The Seer*, October 1853, 145–52; and Wilford Woodruff, *The Keys of the Kingdom . . . the Prophet's Last Instructions to the Quorum of Apostles. Remarks Made at Young New Improvement Conference, Sunday, June 2[1], 1889* (Salt Lake City, 1889). More lengthy works which addressed administrative questions included John Jaques, *Catechism for Children. Exhibiting the Prominent Doctrines for the Church of Jesus Christ of Latter-day Saints* (Liverpool, 1854); Joseph Young, *History of the Organization of the Seventy* (Salt Lake City, 1878); John Jaques, *The Church of Jesus Christ of Latter-day Saints: Its Priesthood Organization, Doctrines, Ordinance, and History* (Salt Lake City, 1882); and B. H. Roberts, *Succession in the Presidency* (Salt Lake City, 1894).

A rich source of contemporary addresses of Church leaders is the *Journal of Discourses*, 26 vols. (Liverpool: R. James, 1854–1886). Most of the official statements of the Presidents of the Church to 1951, many of which deal with administrative and organizational matters, are gathered in James R. Clark, ed., *Messages of the First Presidency*, 6 vols. (Salt Lake City: Bookcraft, 1965–75). Addresses of Church leaders after about 1880 were printed as Conference Reports, at first irregularly, but generally twice a year after 1900 to the present. In more recent years, the May and November issues of the *Ensign* are devoted to the April and October conferences respectively. Reports were also published for the Area Conferences held throughout the world in the 1970s. The importance of Church conferences for administrative history cannot be overemphasized, for in these public settings new programs were announced and counsel for success in the older ones were given. Important studies include Jay R. Lowe, "A Study of the General Conferences of the Church of Jesus Christ of Latter-day Saints" (PhD diss.,

Mormon Administrative and Organizational History: A Source Essay

BYU, 1972); Kenneth W. Godfrey, "150 Years of General Conference," *Ensign*, February 1981, 66–71; and the studies of Gordon and Gary Shepherd: *A Kingdom Transformed: Themes in the Development of Mormonism* (Salt Lake City: University of Utah Press, 1984); "Mormonism in Secular Society: Changing Patterns in Official Ecclesiastical Rhetoric," *Review of Religious Research* 26 (September 1984): 28–42; and "Modes of Leader Rhetoric in the Institutional Development of Mormonism," *Sociological Analysis* 47 (Summer 1986): 125–36.

One of the key factors in the vitality of the Church is the notion of living prophets, leaders that hold the keys of authority and revelation. Catholic and Protestant views of a closed canon have given rise to suspicion of the Mormon view of living prophets and an open canon, but these beliefs are critical to understanding Mormon administrative history and much more. General conference has been one of the major channels of the institutional glue for the Mormon community, a biannual meeting of all members where counsel, direction, new programs, and spiritual food are offered to the membership. A reporter from *Harper's Weekly* caught the meaning of these conferences early when it reported that these meetings were "the post-office, newspaper, legislature, Bible, almanac, temporal, spiritual, and social director of the people" (*Harper's Weekly*, December 4, 1858, 781, in Arrington, *Great Basin Kingdom*, 31). For a historical perspective of these matters, see James B. Allen, "Line upon Line: Church History Reveals How the Lord Has Continually Added to His People's Knowledge and Understanding," *Ensign*, July 1979, 32–39. For an overview of the physical locations of Church headquarters, see Keith W. Perkins, "From New York to Utah: Seven Church Headquarters," *Ensign*, August 2001, 52–58. See also D. Michael Quinn, "LDS 'Headquarters Culture' and the Rest of Mormonism: Past and Present," *Dialogue* 34 (Fall–Winter 2001): 135–64.

Members regularly sustain their leaders by voting in Church meetings and conferences. The idea of "common consent" is not fully democratic, as members are in reality sustaining the decisions already made by their leaders. But the notion of giving approval to the decisions always implies the option to not give it. For the larger picture, see Wilson K. Anderson, "Voting within the Restored Church of Christ," in *Hearken, O Ye My People: Discourses on the Doctrine and Covenants* (Sandy, UT: Randall Book, 1984), 65–77; Martin B. Hickman, "Reciprocal Loyalty: The Administrative Imperative," in *To the Glory of God: Mormon Essays on Great Issues* (Salt Lake City: Deseret Book, 1974), 181–96; Neal A. Maxwell, *A More Excellent Way* (Salt Lake City: Deseret Book, 1968); Matthew O. Richardson, "The Law of Common Consent," in *Doctrine and Covenants, a Book of Answers: The 25th Annual Sidney B. Sperry Symposium* (Provo, UT: Religious Education, BYU, 1996), 75–83; and Hugh W. Nibley, "Criticizing the Brethren," in *Brother Brigham Challenges the Saints* (Salt Lake City: Deseret Book, 1994), 407–48. The topics of discipleship and dissent are also treated in Robert A. Rees, "'Lord, to Whom Shall We Go?' The Challenges of Discipleship and Church Membership," *Dialogue* 39 (Fall 2000): 103–14; Nathan B. Oman, "A Defense of the Authority of Church Doctrine," *Dialogue* 40 (Winter 2007): 1–28; and Matthew B. Bowman, "Toward a Theology of Dissent: An Ecclesiological Interpretation," *Dialogue* 42 (Fall 2009): 21–36. By the turn of the century, as the membership was moving out of the villages and rural settings of the nineteenth century, it was clear that a more systematic approach was needed for administrative matters in the Church. Thus the first Church handbooks began to appear at this time. The important work of Joseph B. Keeler must be seen in this light. Keeler produced four significant works at the turn of the century: *The Bishop's Court: Its History and Proceedings* (Provo, UT: Skelton, 1902); *The Lesser Priesthood and Notes on Church Government; also a Concordance of the Doctrine and Covenants, for the Use of the Church School and Priesthood Quorums* (Salt Lake City: Deseret News, 1904); *First Steps in Church Government: What Church Government Is and What It Does; A Book for Young Members of the Lesser Priesthood* (Salt Lake City: Deseret News, 1906); and *Notes on Lesser Priesthood and Church Government* (Salt Lake City: Deseret News, 1929). Several of these works went through many editions and were even adopted as manuals for the Aaronic Priesthood by the Church. Keeler's work was an important influence on the appearance and content of John A. Widtsoe, comp., *Priesthood and Church Government* (Salt Lake City: Deseret Book, 1939). Keeler's contributions are discussed in Whittaker, "Joseph B. Keeler."

Priesthood quorums of the Church at first selected their own course of study. The first seventy's quorum study guide was B. H. Roberts, *The Seventy's Course in Theology* (Salt Lake City: Deseret News, 1907). Appendix 3 in Widtsoe's *Priesthood and Church Government* (1965 printing), 370–73, gives the study courses for the Melchizedek Priesthood quorums from 1908 to 1963. Since the 1960s, the Church has issued manuals for study in the priesthood quorums. Most recently, they have focused on the teachings of the presidents of the Church.

In addition to Church Correlation–produced manuals, more recent publications on this topic include Harold Glen Clark, *Millions of Meetings* (Salt Lake City: Deseret Book, 1955); Oscar W. McConkie Jr., *The Kingdom of God* (Salt Lake City: The Presiding Bishopric, 1962); Oscar W. McConkie Jr., *God and Man* (Salt Lake City: The Presiding Bishopric, 1963); Bruce R. McConkie, *Common Consent* (Salt Lake City: The Church of Jesus Christ of Latter-day Saints, 1973); Lee A. Palmer, *Aaronic Priesthood through the Centuries* (Salt Lake City: Deseret Book, 1964); Sterling W. Sill, *Leadership*, 3 vols. (Salt Lake City: Bookcraft, 1958–1978); Harold Glen Clark, *The Art of Governing Zion* (Provo, UT: BYU, 1966); Bruce R. McConkie, *Let Every Man Learn His Duty: The Ten Commandments of Priesthood Correlation and the Home Teaching Constitution* (Salt Lake City: Deseret Book, 1976); *Priesthood* (essays by the General Authorities of the Church) (Salt Lake City: Deseret Book, 1981); Rulon G. Craven, *Called to the Work: Guidelines for Effective Leadership in the Church* (Salt Lake City: Bookcraft, 1985); and M. Russell Ballard, *Counseling with Our Councils: Learning to Minister Together in the Church and in the Family* (Salt Lake City: Deseret Book, 1997). Hugh Nibley's classic essay still serves as a useful reminder of the challenges of leading versus managing and of the key importance of the role of the Spirit in Church government: "Leaders to Managers: The Fatal Shift," *Dialogue* 16 (Winter 1983): 12–21.

Given the Latter-day Saint belief in living prophets and the regular printing of the counsel given by their leaders on organizational and administrative matters, it is not possible to provide more than a few examples here. A sampling, mostly from more recent LDS general conferences, include Bruce R. McConkie, "Only an Elder," *Ensign*, 1975, 66–69; Ezra Taft Benson, "Church Government through Councils," *Ensign*, May 1979, 86–89; Benson, "To the Home Teachers of the Church," *Ensign*, May 1987, 48–51; Gordon B. Hinckley, "The State of the Church," *Ensign*, May 1991, 51–54; Hinckley, "The Shepherds of the Flock" *Ensign*, May 1999, 51–53; Boyd K. Packer, "The Bishop and His Counselors," *Ensign*, May 1999, 57–63; Gordon B. Hinckley, "The Stake President," *Ensign*, May 2000, 49–51; Spencer W. Kimball, "President Kimball Speaks Out on Administration to the Sick," *New Era*, October 1981, 45–50; Dallin H. Oaks, "Priesthood Blessings," *Ensign*, May 1987, 36–39; Oaks, "Healing the Sick," *Ensign*, May 2010, 47–50; Oaks, "Spiritual Gifts," *Ensign*, September 1986, 68–72; Oaks, "Gospel Teaching," *Ensign*, November 1999, 78–80; Boyd K. Packer, "Reverence Invites Revelation," *Ensign*, November 1991, 21–23 ; Packer, "The Unwritten Order of Things" (devotional address, BYU, October 15, 1996); Packer, "A Defense and a Refuge," *Ensign*, November 2006, 85–88; Packer, "The Weak and the Simple of the Church," *Ensign*, November 2007, 6–9; Packer, "The Power of the Priesthood," *Ensign*, May 2010, 6–10; Russell M. Nelson, "Keys of the Priesthood," *Ensign*, November 1987, 36–39; and James E. Faust, "The Lord's Day," *Ensign*, November 1991, 33–35.

The various manuals for the priesthood quorums for the Church, especially those since the mid-1960s that have been especially written by Church writing committees, can be found in the Church History Library or the Harold B. Lee Library. Also valuable are the addresses by General Authorities at special seminars for regional representatives of the Twelve and for mission presidents, most of which are available in the Church History Library.

The early issues of the *Improvement Era* regularly published a series "Priesthood Quorum Table," which kept leaders and members informed regarding administrative matters. Finally, the in-house communication bulletins, including those issued by the Presiding Bishop's office, *Progress of the Church* (monthly, 1938–43), and *The Messenger* (monthly, 1957–64), and following the introduction of priesthood correlation in the 1960s, the *Priesthood Bulletin* (1965–74, issued six times per year) and *Bulletin* (1980–present) are important sources for more recent developments. A detailed index to the ten volumes of the *Priesthood Bulletin* prepared by Thomas G. Alexander is available in the L. Tom Perry Special Collections, Harold B. Lee Library. Also important are the various editions of the *General Handbook of Instructions* (1976–2006), and various handbooks issued in recent years for each organization and priesthood leadership unit in the Church. In November 2010, two new Church Handbooks of Instruction were issued by the Church (see *Ensign*, November 2010, 74–75). Manuals remain important guidelines for leaders throughout the Church, but they are never to take the place of the scriptures or the critical role of continuing revelation in the Church. As President Packer explains, "There is a spiritual element beyond the procedures in the handbook. . . . There are principles of the gospel underlying every phase of Church administration. These are *not* explained in the handbooks [italics in original]." See Boyd K. Packer, "Principles," *Ensign*, March 1985, 6-8.

ADMINISTRATIVE STUDIES

General Authorities. In addition to the thesis and dissertation by D. Michael Quinn cited above, see his "From Sacred Grove to Sacral Power Structure," *Dialogue* 17 (Summer 1984): 9–34, for a group portrait of the General Authorities to the 1930s. Most of the biographies of Church leaders have been "gestas," or life histories that subordinated the organizational history itself. Thus most of the biographies written of General Authorities have lacked detailed information on administrative history. The exceptions are worth noting: D. Michael Quinn, *J. Reuben Clark: The Church Years* (Provo,

UT: BYU Press, 1983); Andrew Karl Larson, *Erastus Snow: Pioneer and Missionary for the Early Mormon Church* (Salt Lake City: University of Utah Press, 1972); G. Homer Durham, *N. Eldon Tanner, His Life and Service* (Salt Lake City: Deseret Book, 1982); Arrington, *Brigham Young: American Moses*; David Dryden, "Biographical Essays on Three General Authorities of the Early Twentieth Century" and "Biographical Essays on Four General Authorities of the Early Twentieth Century," *Task Papers in LDS History*, nos. 11 and 12 (Salt Lake City: Historical Department of the Church of Jesus Christ of Latter-day Saints, 1976); and Edward Leo Lyman, *Amasa Mason Lyman, Mormon Apostle and Apostate: A Study in Dedication* (Salt Lake City: University of Utah Press, 2009). Biographical studies of more recent Church Presidents include *The Presidents of the Church: Essays on the Lives and Messages of the Prophets*, ed. Leonard J. Arrington (Salt Lake City: Deseret Book, 1986); *The Presidents of the Church: The Lives and Teachings of the Modern Prophets*, ed. Craig Manscill, Robert Freeman, and Dennis Wright (Springville, UT: Cedar Fort, 2008); Gregory A. Prince and Wm. Robert Wright, *David O. McKay and the Rise of Modern Mormonism* (Salt Lake City: University of Utah Press, 2005); Edward L. Kimball and Andrew E. Kimball, *Spencer W. Kimball: Twelfth President of the Church of Jesus Christ of Latter-day Saints* (Salt Lake City: Bookcraft, 1977); L. Brent Goates, *Harold B. Lee: Prophet & Seer* (Salt Lake City: Bookcraft, 1985); Sheri L. Dew, *Ezra Taft Benson: A Biography* (Salt Lake City: Deseret Book, 1987); Eleanor Knowles, *Howard W. Hunter* (Salt Lake City: Deseret Book, 1994); Sheri L. Dew, *Go Forward with Faith: The Biography of Gordon B. Hinckley* (Salt Lake City: Deseret Book, 1996); Heidi S. Swinton, *To the Rescue: The Biography of Thomas S. Monson* (Salt Lake City: Deseret Book, 2010). Francis M. Gibbons has written a multi-volume biographical series on the Presidents of the Church, including some of the more recent Presidents that he knew personally, and his volumes do treat administrative history. See also Joseph Anderson, *Prophets I Have Known* (Salt Lake City: Deseret Book, 1973). Both Gibbons and Anderson served as secretaries to the First Presidency.

Mormon Administrative and Organizational History: A Source Essay

There have been over seven hundred individuals called to be General Authorities of the Church. Biographical information on many of them can be found in Andrew Jenson, *LDS Biographical Encyclopedia*, 4 vols. (Salt Lake City: Andrew Jensen History, 1901–39); Orson F. Whitney, *History of Utah* (Salt Lake City: George Q. Cannon & Sons, 1904), vol. 4; Lawrence R. Flake, *Mighty Men of Zion: General Authorities of the Last Dispensation* (Salt Lake City: Karl D. Butler, 1974); Wilbur D. Talbot, *The Acts of Modern Apostles* (Salt Lake City: Randall Book, 1985); Michael K. Winder, comp., *Counselors to the Prophets* (Roy, UT: Eborn Books, 2001); and Lawrence R. Flake, *Prophets and Apostles of the Last Dispensation* (Provo, UT: Religious Studies Center, BYU, 2001). For a listing of "Biographical Register of General Church Officers" and of "General Church Officers, A Chronology," see Appendices 1 and 5 in *Encyclopedia of Mormonism*, 4:1, 631–51, 1, 678–85. See the annually issued *Deseret News Church Almanac* (Salt Lake City: Deseret News) for recent callings and releases and short biographical information. A biographical index to published biographies can lead the researcher to information on just about all the Church leaders to the 1980s: Marvin E. Wiggins, comp., *Mormons and Their Neighbors: An Index to Over 75,000 Biographical Sketches from 1820 to the Present*, 2 vols. (Provo, UT: Harold B. Lee Library, 1984). Little serious research has been done on the leadership levels below the highest presiding quorums. One useful study is Joseph Walker, "A Statistical Look at Regional Representatives," *Church News*, January 16, 1983, 8–10. Andrew Jenson, *Encyclopedic History of the Church of Jesus Christ of Latter-day Saints* (Salt Lake City: Deseret News, 1941) contains much information on Church administration and leaders to the time of its publication. Steven Sorensen has written an administrative/statistical study: "LDS Stake Presidents, 1850–1930: A Preliminary Demographic Survey" (December 1983, unpublished manuscript, copy in Church History Library). A suggestive look at the local functioning of priesthood quorums in the contemporary Church is Joseph B. Wirthlin, "The Work of Our Priesthood Quorums," *Ensign*, August 1984, 8–13; and L. Tom Perry, "What Is a Quorum?," *Ensign*, November 2004, 23–26.

Statistical and demographic studies. Basic figures on recent Church growth are part of the semiannual conference reports. Miscellaneous statistical information is also available in the *Deseret News Church Almanac.* Comparative chartings with other American religions are in Edwin S. Gaustad, *Historical Atlas of Religion in America*, 2nd ed. (New York: Harper and Row, 1976), updated with Philip L. Barlow in 2001 (Oxford University Press); and Jackson W. Carrol and others, *Religion in America, 1950 to the Present* (New York: Harper and Row, 1979). The Church has commissioned a variety of internal studies, but few have been made public. An *Atlas of Mormonism* is currently in preparation at BYU which will replace the *Historical Atlas of Mormonism*, ed. S. Kent Brown, Donald Q. Cannon, and Richard H. Jackson (New York: Simon and Schuster, 1994).

Other studies include Dean R. Louder, "A Distributional and Diffusionary Analysis of the Mormon Church, 1850–1970" (PhD diss., University of Washington, 1972); Paul Timothy Johnson, "An Analysis of the Spread of the Church of Jesus Christ of Latter-day Saints from Salt Lake City, Utilizing a Diffusion Model" (PhD diss., University of Iowa, 1966); Lowell C. Bennion, "Mormon Country a Century Ago: A Geographer's View," in Thomas G. Alexander, ed., *The Mormon People, Their Character and Traditions* (Provo, UT: BYU Press, 1980), 1–26; D. W. Meining, "The Mormon Culture Region: Strategies and Patterns in the Geography of the American West, 1847–1864," *Annals of the Association of American Geographers* 55 (June 1965): 191–220; Lowell C. Bennion, "The Geographic Dynamics of Mormondom, 1965–95," *Sunstone* 18 (December 1995): 21–32; and Ethan R. Yorgason, *Transformation of the Mormon Culture Region* (Urbana: University of Illinois Press, 2003). See also Lee L. Bean, "The Mormon Historical Demography Project," *Historical Methods* 11 (Winter 1978): 45–53; and G. Wesley Johnson and Marian Ashby Johnson, "On the Trail of the Twentieth-century Mormon Outmigration," *BYU Studies* 46, no. 1 (2007): 41–83. There are a number of essays related to the current dynamics of the Church in *Contemporary Mormonism*, ed. Marie Cornwall, Tim B. Heaton, and Lawrence A. Young (Urbana: University of Illinois

Press, 1994). See also Claudia L. Bushman, *Contemporary Mormonism: Latter-day Saints in Modern America* (Westport, CT: Praeger, 2006).

Key sources for studying these matters are in the Church History Library. A useful overview is Gladys Noyce, *Guide to Sources for Studies of Church Statistics* (Salt Lake City: Historical Department, The Church of Jesus Christ of Latter-day Saints, n.d.). A historical overview of the Church reporting forms is Dennis H. Smith, "Formal Reporting Systems of the Church of Jesus Christ of Latter-day Saints, 1830–1975" (master's thesis, BYU, 1976). See also Floyd A. Hill, "Keeping Track of the Lord's Sheep," *Ensign*, July 1990, 14–17.

Missiology. Mormon history is mission history. From the Church's earliest days, converts were commissioned to preach the gospel, and they gradually spread into the villages and hamlets of New York, Pennsylvania, Ohio, Missouri, and Upper Canada. By 1837, Mormon missionaries were moving into the larger cities and in 1837 undertook the first mission to England. The success of their missionary efforts forced leaders to address a variety of institutional and organizational matters. It was in a missionary context than many of the Church's programs were first tried. Thus organization, emigration, publication, and finances were natural outgrowths of missionary work. There are many studies devoted to Mormon missiology. The first scholarly study was S. George Ellsworth, "A History of Mormon Missions in the United States and Canada, 1830–1860" (PhD diss., University of California–Berkeley, 1951); a more recent study with much information on the makeup of the early missionary force is Rex Thomas Price Jr., "The Mormon Missionary of the Nineteenth Century" (PhD diss., University of Wisconsin–Madison, 1991). Gordon Irving, "Numerical Strength and Geographical Distribution of the LDS Missionary Force, 1830–1974," *Task Papers in LDS History*, no. 1 (Salt Lake City: Historical Department, The Church of Jesus Christ of Latter-day Saints, 1975), is a very useful compilation of missionary statistics. An extensive guide is David J. Whittaker, "Mormon Missiology: An Introduction and Guide to the Sources," in *The Disciple as Witness: Essays on Latter-day Saint History and Doctrine in Honor of Richard Lloyd Anderson*, ed. Stephen D. Ricks, Donald W. Parry, and Andrew H. Hedges (Provo, UT: FARMS, 2000), 459–538. The growing trend among scholars to use economic models to understand the growth and development of religious movements has only recently been applied to the Church. To see prophets as religious entrepreneurs and investigators as potential consumers for whom the gospel must be "packaged" to obtain their market share can be seen as offensive or at least an incomplete way of understanding the process to most Latter-day Saints. This is especially so when they believe in the key role of the Holy Spirit in the conversion experience. A useful introduction to all these matters is Larry Witham, *Marketplace of the Gods: How Economics Explains Religion* (New York: Oxford University Press, 2010).

Much of the more recent scholarship on the growth of the Church has taken a closer look at the diversity of both members and those called to lead them. In the 1970s, a time when the first large-scale surveys were beginning to be done, one study compared the beliefs and attitudes of a ward in the Oakland, California, with a ward on the Wasatch Front in Utah. Among other things, the survey found more liberal political and social attitudes (for example, on birth control, labor unions, and war) among members of the Bay Area ward than among the Utah ward. The survey also found a growing tendency of the Church to call white-collar workers rather than blue-collar laborers to leadership positions. Here, time constraints and educational backgrounds seem to have been a factor in their callings. This survey was based on a small sampling, but these matters are important for those who study Mormon organizational and administrative matters. For an overview, see the appendix "Survey Methods and Measurements" in Mauss, *The Beehive and the Angel*, 215–28. For the early studies, see Armand L. Mauss, "Moderation in All Things: Political and Social Outlooks of Modern Urban Mormons," *Dialogue* 7 (Spring 1972): 57–69; Mauss, "Saints, Cities, and Secularism: Religious Attitudes and Behavior of Modern Urban Mormons," *Dialogue* 7 (Summer 1972): 8–27; and J. Kenneth Davies, "The Accommodation of Mormonism and Political-Economic Reality," *Dialogue* 3 (Spring

1968): 42–54. See also Marie Cornwall and Perry H. Cunningham, "Surveying Latter-day Saints: A Review of Methodological Issues," *Review of Religious Research* 31 (December 1989): 162–72; and Mauss, "Flowers, Weeds, and Thistles: The State of Social Science Literature on the Mormons," in Ronald W. Walker, David J. Whittaker, and James B. Allen, eds., *Mormon History* (Urbana: University of Illinois Press, 2001), 153–97.

The growing scholarship on international Mormonism, with essays that focus on a variety of administrative topics, includes Dean L. Larsen, "The Challenges of Administrating a Worldwide Church," *Ensign*, July 1974, 18–22; Garth N. Jones, "'Acres of Diamonds': Studies of Development Administration and the Mormon Experience," in *Portraits of Human Behavior and Performance: The Human Factor in Action*, ed. Senyo B-S. K. Adjibolosoo (Lanham, NJ: University Press of America, 2001), 271–313; and *Out of Obscurity: The LDS Church in the Twentieth Century*, The 29th Annual Sidney B. Sperry Symposium (Salt Lake City: Deseret Book, 2000); and *Global Mormonism in the Twenty-first Century*, ed. Reid L. Neilson (Provo, UT: Religious Studies Center, BYU, 2008). See also Reid L. Neilson, "Authority, Organization, and Societal Context in Multinational Churches," *Administrative Science Quarterly* 38 (December 1993): 653–82; and Jessie L. Embry, *Asian American Mormons: Bridging Cultures* (Provo, UT: Charles Redd Center for Western Studies, BYU, 1999).

Communications and public relations remain important topics for administrative history. How the Church presents itself to the world, how it responds to criticism, and especially how it has used the most current forms of mass communication since its founding are important subjects of study, even though they are just beginning to go on the agendas of scholars. Several publications by Sherry Pack Baker will lead researchers to this literature: "Mormon Media History Timeline: 1827–2007," *BYU Studies* 47, no. 4 (2008): 117–23; and "Mormons and the Media, 1898–2003: A Selected, Annotated and Indexed Bibliography," *BYU Studies* 42, nos. 3 and 4 (2003): 125–89 (with Daniel Stout). Especially useful is James B. Allen, "Technology and the Church: A Steady Revolution," in *Deseret Morning News 2007*

Church Almanac (Salt Lake City: Deseret Morning News, 2006), 118–58. For the larger American context, see *Communication and Change in American Religious History*, ed. Leonard I. Sweet (Grand Rapids, MI: Eerdmans, 1993), particularly in the essay by Sweet, "Communication and Change in American Religious History: A Historiographical Probe," 1–49.

Grass roots. Following similar trends in the study of social history, Mormon scholars have been turning to new methods and sources to recover the lives and experiences of common members of the Church. Much of this has centered on the local community where Saints were gathered and shaped through much of Mormon history. Here the values of Mormonism were taught and fostered in the village of the nineteenth century and in the wards of more recent times. Mormon group solidarity and loyalty in the nineteenth century came from extended family connections, temple sealings, and a sense of being part of a covenant community. Its focus on the small community meant that there was less need for either an extensive bureaucracy or coordinated programs. This changed as membership grew and gradually came to be settled in more urban and modern locales, making the ward less autonomous and more connected to the larger centralized structure. One of the consequences of the correlation movement in the 1960s was the gradual loss of local autonomy and the standardizing of lesson materials prepared by centralized Church writing committees.

One of the main ways that members and their leaders, both local and general, have kept in touch with each other is the home teaching program. As a program for teachers (mostly adults in the nineteenth century) "watching over the Church" (D&C 20:53, 84:111), it has gone by various names: block teaching, home missionaries, ward teaching, and home teaching. Mostly informal in the earliest years, the concern of Church leaders in the 1850s to more systematically visit and teach members during the Mormon Reformation saw the program more firmly established. Concern with the laxness of members entering into the consecration program as well as a concern with some members wishing to leave the fold, pairs of priesthood holders would visit various homes to maintain contact with and to watch over those families assigned to them. These home missionaries worked to get members recommitted to their covenants and to help them reevaluate their spiritual worthiness. Using printed catechisms, these teachers would, by asking questions, encourage personal repentance and renewed dedication. Most members were rebaptized during this period as part of this effort at reformation. As a program for caring, teaching and communication, it remains a major channel for Church leaders to feel the pulse of the membership; locally, it provides the bishops with regular contact with ward members, and if done right, can lift some of the burdens of leadership and administering from the bishop's shoulders. Useful sources on this program include Gary L. Phelps, "Home Teaching: Attempts by the Latter-day Saints to Establish an Effective Program during the Nineteenth Century," (master's thesis, BYU, 1975); Rex A. Anderson, "A Documentary History of the Lord's Way of Watching over the Church by the Priesthood through the Ages" (master's thesis, BYU, 1974); Vernon L. Israelsen, "Changes in the Numbers and the Priesthood Affiliation of the Men used as Ward Teachers in the Church of Jesus Christ of Latter-day Saints, 1920 to 1935" (master's thesis, BYU, 1937). For the Mormon Reformation, see Paul H. Peterson, "The Mormon Reformation of 1856–1857: The Rhetoric and the Reality," *Journal of Mormon History* 15 (1989): 59–87. The Church has issued guide lines for home teaching throughout the twentieth century, and the importance of the program has been regularly addressed in general, stake and ward conferences. At its heart was always the strengthening of the family in matters relating to the principles of the Gospel of Jesus Christ. A sampling of the home teaching literature includes David O. McKay, *Suggestions on Ward Teaching* (Salt Lake City: Presiding Bishop's Office, General Committee on Priesthood Outlines, 1912); Bryant S. Hinckley, *Ward Teachers Handbook, 1946* (Salt Lake City: Presiding Bishop's Office, 1946); *Suggestions for Home Teachers, 1965* (Salt Lake City: Deseret News Press, 1964); *Priesthood Home Teaching Handbook of Instructions* (Salt lake City: Priesthood Home Teaching Committee, Church of Jesus Christ of Latter-day Saints, 1972); *Guidelines for Priesthood Home Teaching* (Salt Lake City: The

Church of Jesus Christ of Latter-day Saints, 1980); *The Home Teaching Visit: A Guide for Home Teachers* (Salt Lake City: Church of Jesus Christ of Latter-day Saints, 1983); Bruce R. McConkie, *Let Every Man Learn His Duty: The Ten Commandments of Priesthood Correlation and the Home Teaching Constitution* (Salt Lake City: Deseret Book, 1976); Ezra Taft Benson, "To the Home Teachers of the Church" *Ensign*, May 1987, 48-51; Thomas S. Monson, "Home Teaching—A Divine Service," *Ensign*, November 1997, 46–48; and Richard J. Marshall, *Home Teaching with Purpose and Power* (Salt Lake City: Deseret Book, 1990). A similar program, coordinated by the ward Female Relief Society, is visiting teaching, wherein women in pairs are assigned to visit their sisters in the ward each month. Monthly messages from Church leaders for both programs are contained in the *Ensign*.

Like their biblical models and their Puritan forebears, Mormons stressed the covenant in their relationships with each other and with their God. An understanding of this is central to studying Mormon history. An overview of the concept in the Church is presented in David J. Whittaker, "A Covenant People," in *The Seventh Annual Sidney B. Sperry Symposium: The Doctrine and Covenants* (Provo, UT: Religious Instruction, BYU; Salt Lake City: Church Educational System, 1979), 196–216; and in shorter form in *Ensign*, August 1980, 36–40. See also Rex Eugene Cooper, *Promises Made to the Fathers: Mormon Covenant Organization* (Salt Lake City: University of Utah Press, 1990).

The early attempts of Mormons to establish their own communities are studied in Warren A. Jennings, "Zion Is Fled: the Expulsion of the Mormons from Jackson County, Missouri" (PhD diss., University of Florida, 1962); Backman, *The Heavens Resound*, 63–81, 125–74, 262–83; David E. Miller and Della S. Miller, *Nauvoo: The City of Joseph* (Santa Barbara, CA; Salt Lake City: Peregrine Smith, 1974); Robert B. Flanders, *Nauvoo: Kingdom on the Mississippi* (Urbana: University of Illinois Press, 1965); and Glen M. Leonard, *Nauvoo: A Place of Peace, A People of Promise* (Salt Lake City: Deseret Book; Provo, UT: BYU Press, 2002).

Mormon Administrative and Organizational History: A Source Essay

The organization of gathering and emigration. The great ability of Mormon organizational skill is no better seen than in the nineteenth-century programs for bringing new converts to the Great Basin and then settling them in some 450 communities in the West. We mention only a few of the numerous studies on this topic. The key areas of Britain and Scandinavia are treated in Philip A. M. Taylor, *Expectations Westward: The Mormons and the Emigration of Their British Converts in the Nineteenth Century* (Ithaca, NY: Cornell University Press, 1966); and William Mulder, *Homeward to Zion: The Mormon Migration from Scandinavia* (Minneapolis: University of Minnesota Press, 1957). An early study of the Perpetual Emigrating Fund Company is Gustive O. Larson, *Prelude to the Kingdom: Mormon Desert Conquest, a Chapter in American Cooperative Experience* (Francestown, NH: Marshall Jones, 1947). More recent studies by Stanley B. Kimball, William G. Hartley, and Fred E. Woods can be located in *Studies in Mormon History* (2000). The story of the Mormon exodus west in 1846–47 is told well in two books by Richard E. Bennett: *Mormons at the Missouri, 1846–52: "And Should We Die . . ."* (Norman: University of Oklahoma Press, 1987); and *We'll Find the Place: The Mormon Exodus, 1846–1848* (Salt Lake City: Deseret Book, 1997). For detailed studies of the organized Mormon emigration, see Conway Sonne, *Ships, Saints and Mariners: A Maritime Encyclopedia of Mormon Migration, 1830–1890* (Salt Lake City: University of Utah Press, 1987); Sonne, *Saints on the Seas: A Maritime History of Mormon Migration, 1830–1890* (Salt Lake City: University of Utah Press, 1983). Andrew Jenson provided yearly summaries of Church emigration from 1840 to 1860 in a series of twenty-three articles published in the *Contributor*, vols. 12–14 (June 1891–September 1893). See also William G. Hartley, "LDS Emigration in 1852: The Keokuk Encampment and Outfitting Ten Wagon Trains for Utah," *Mormon Historical Studies* 4 (Fall 2003): 43–76; Hartley, "The Great Florence Fitout of 1861," *BYU Studies* 24, no. 3 (Summer 1984): 341–71; John K. Hulmston, "Transplain Migration: The Church Trains in Mormon Immigration, 1861–1868" (master's thesis, Utah State University, 1985); Don H. Smith, "Leadership, Planning and Management of the 1856

Handcart Emigration," *Annals of Iowa* 65 (Spring/Summer 2006 [published in June 2007]): 124–61; and Hartley, "Brigham Young's Overland Trails Revolution: The Creation of the 'Down-and-Back' Wagon Train System, 1860–61," *Journal of Mormon History* 28, no. 1 (2002): 1–30.

Of particular value are the recent studies that look at the function and organization of Mormon towns. A good place to begin is with Dean L. May, "The Making of Saints: The Mormon Town as a Setting for the Study of Cultural Change," *Utah Historical Quarterly* 45 (Winter 1977): 75–92, and Wayne L. Wahlquist, "A Review of Mormon Settlement Literature," *Utah Historical Quarterly* 45 (Winter 1977): 3–21. Other studies include Lowry Nelson, *The Mormon Village: A Pattern and Technique of Land Settlement* (Salt Lake City: University of Utah Press, 1952); Mark P. Leone, "The Evolution of Mormon Culture in Eastern Arizona," *Utah Historical Quarterly* 40 (Spring 1972): 122–41; Wilfrid C. Bailey, "The Social Organization of the Mormon Village" (PhD diss., University of Chicago, 1955); Dean L. May, "People on the Mormon Frontier: Kanab's Families of 1874," *Journal of Family History* 1 (December 1976): 169–79; May, "Utah Writ Small: Challenge and Change in Kane County's Past," *Utah Historical Quarterly* 53 (Spring 1985): 170–83; Cindy Rice, "Spring City: A Look at a Nineteenth Century Mormon Village," *Utah Historical Quarterly* 43 (Summer 1975): 260–77; Lester D. Campbell, "Perception and Land Use: the Case of the Mormon Culture Region" (master's thesis, BYU, 1974); Michael S. Raber, "Religious Polity and Local Production: The Origins of a Mormon Town" (PhD diss., Yale University, 1978); Charles S. Peterson, "Life in a Village Society, 1877–1920," *Utah Historical Quarterly* 49 (Winter 1981): 78–96; Peterson, "A Mormon Village: One Man's West," *Journal of Mormon History* 3 (1976): 3–12; and Larry M. Logue, *A Sermon in the Desert: Belief and Behavior in Early St. George, Utah* (Urbana: University of Illinois Press, 1988).

In the twentieth century, the form of the Mormon community shifted from the village to the ecclesiastical ward. An interesting perspective is provided in Douglas D. Alder, "The Mormon Ward: Congregation or

Community?," *Journal of Mormon History* 5 (1978): 61–78. See also James B. Allen, "The Mormon Search for Community in the Modern World," *The Restoration Movement*, 307–40; Jan Shipps, Cheryll L. May, and Dean L. May, "Sugarhouse Ward: A Latter-day Saint Congregation," in *American Congregations*, vol. 1, *Portraits of Twelve Religious Communities*, ed. James P. Wind and James W. Lewis (Chicago: University of Chicago Press: 1994), 293–348; Ron Molen, "Franchising the Faith: From Village Unity to the Global Village," *Sunstone* 10 (August 1986): 30–37; and Mario S. DePillis, "The Persistence of Mormon Community into the 1990s," *Sunstone* 15 (October 1991): 28–49.

Colonization and settlement. Until recently both Mormon and non-Mormon historians have seen Latter-day Saint western colonization as a monolithic process directed by Brigham Young from Church headquarters in Salt Lake City. According to this scenario, Young established a firm base along the Wasatch Front and gradually expanded the Mormon settlements north and south, eventually penetrating the interior valleys. As an administrator and empire builder, Young wished to further control the main points of entry into the Great Basin, so he established further colonies at Las Vegas and San Bernardino to the southwest, in Carson Valley to the west, and in southern Idaho to the north. In all, Brigham Young is said to have established or planned about 360 settlements by his death in 1877. The traditional story is told most fully in Milton R. Hunter's works, and especially in *Brigham Young the Colonizer*, 4th ed. (Salt Lake City: Peregrine Smith, 1973).

One of the first scholars to challenge the traditional view was Eugene E. Campbell, "Brigham Young's Outer Cordon—A Reappraisal," *Utah Historical Quarterly* 41 (Summer 1973): 220–53. Campbell pointed out that most of the outer settlements were not initially established under Brigham Young's direction nor as part of a concerted effort at empire building. Some were established by disaffected members acting on their own, and others were established to control threats from Indians. Richard Sherlock, "Mormon Migration and Settlement after 1875," *Journal of Mormon History* 2 (1975): 53–68, shows that later colonization was often undertaken by the initiative of various local leaders who felt the need to acquire new locations for their own rising generations.

Other studies have modified or changed traditional views such as the "trackless wilderness" as they have shown that the Mormons did not blaze any new trails in their westward immigration, nor did they find the Salt Lake Valley to be a treeless desert in 1847. See, for example, Lewis Clark Christian, "A Study of Mormon Knowledge of the Far West Prior to the Exodus (1830–February, 1846)" (master's thesis, BYU, 1972); and Richard H. Jackson, "Myth and Reality: Environmental Perception of the Mormons, 1840–1865: An Historical Geosophy" (PhD diss., Clark University, 1970).

All of this is not to discredit Brigham Young's administrative genius. As a colonizer he has no peers in American history, and a student of organizational history must not ignore this major dimension of early LDS history, for here few details were left to chance. From immigration and exploration to initial colonizing missions, Young did preside over the rapidly increasing settlement process. To say that not all colonies were under his direction is not to diminish his large accomplishments. Little wonder that almost all of his life was spent in administering the multitude of details of the Mormon settlement of the West. The variety of problems he confronted were intimately related to the evolving structure of the institution itself. Brigham Young's extensive correspondence files in the Church History Library provide the details.

John Reps, *Town Planning in Frontier America* (Princeton, NJ: Princeton University Press, 1969), is an excellent comparative study which allows the student to grasp the larger organizational picture. Studies which bring the Mormon settlement patterns into clearer focus include the essays in Richard H. Jackson, ed., *The Mormon Role in the Settlement of the West* (Provo, UT: BYU Press, 1978); Joel E. Ricks, *Forms and Methods of Early Mormon Settlement* (Logan: Utah State University Press, 1964); Wayne L. Wahlquist, "Settlement Processes in the Mormon Core Area, 1847–1890" (PhD diss., University of Nebraska, 1974); Richard H. Jackson, "Mormon Perceptions and Settlement," *Annals of the Association of American Geographers* 68

(September 1978): 317–34; Charles L. Sellers, "Early Mormon Community Planning," *Journal of the American Institute of Planners* 28 (1962): 24–30; Richard V. Francaviglia, "The Mormon Landscape: Existence, Creation and Perception of a Unique Image in the American West" (PhD diss., University of Oregon, 1970; New York: AMS Press, 1974); Francaviglia, "The City of Zion in the Mountain West," *Improvement Era*, December 1969, 10–17; Francaviglia, "Passing Mormon Village," *Landscape* 22 (Spring 1978): 40–47; and Dean L. May, "A Demographic Portrait of the Mormons, 1830–1980," in *After 150 Years: The Latter-day Saints in Sesquicentennial Perspective*, ed. Thomas G. Alexander and Jessie L. Embry (Provo, UT: Charles Redd Center for Western Studies; Midvale, UT: Signature Books, 1983), 37–69.

Steve Olsen has written on the Mormon theological sense of place in "Community Celebrations and Mormon Ideology of Place," *Sunstone* 5 (May/June 1980): 40–45; and "Zion, the Structure of a Theological Revolution," *Sunstone* 6 (November/December 1981): 21–26. See also Martha Sonntag Bradley, "Creating the Sacred Space of Zion," *Journal of Mormon History* 31 (Spring 2005): 1–30. For evidence that the Church continues its interest in Missouri as a special place, see Craig S. Campbell, *Images of the New Jerusalem: Latter Day Saint Faction Interpretations of Independence, Missouri* (Knoxville: University of Tennessee Press, 2004), especially chapters 5 and 6.

Meetinghouses and temples. The first structures built for worship were temples, and they and the sacred ordinances performed therein remain at the core of Mormon theology. The first structures for regular worship were not constructed until the Utah era. These meetinghouses varied in size and structure, being first built of wood, then brick, and then stone. The first large structures were tabernacles, temporary structures at first, then more solid buildings in Utah. The best place for a history and visual presentation of these important facilities for both worship and recreation is Richard W. Jackson, *Places of Worship: 150 Years of Latter-day Saint Architecture* (Provo, UT: Religious Studies Center, BYU, 2003). For a valuable guide to both ecclesiastical and vernacular structures of the Latter-day Saints, see Brad

Westwood, "Mormon Architectural Records," in *Mormon Americana: A Guide to Sources and Collections in the United States*, David J. Whittaker, ed. (Provo, UT: BYU Studies, 1995), 336–405. The Church expends a significant portion of its resources on ecclesiastical structures for its membership and its larger mission, including not only the construction of chapels, temples, mission homes, but also their maintenance throughout the world. The first chapels were constructed in Utah, and for over a century the major responsibility for their financing and construction lay with the members, who were expected to provide both the funding and the labor. In recent years the Church has taken over the building and maintenance of the chapels. Insights to this potential rich topic for future researchers are in David W. Cummings, *Mighty Missionary of the Pacific: The Building Program of the Church of Jesus Christ of Latter-day Saints, Its History, Scope and Significance* (Salt Lake City: Bookcraft, 1961); Edward A. Geary, "The Last Days of the Coalville Tabernacle," *Dialogue* 5 (Winter 1970): 42–50; Dennis L. Lythgoe, "Battling the Bureaucracy: Building a Mormon Chapel," *Dialogue* 15 (Winter 1982): 68–78; Brad Westwood, "Historic Tabernacles," *Ensign*, October 1997, 32–37; Ronald W. Walker, "The Salt Lake Tabernacle in the Nineteenth Century: A Glimpse of Early Mormonism," *Journal of Mormon History* 32 (Fall 2005): 198–240; Westwood, "Houses of the Lord," *Ensign*, June 1997, 9–17; and Westwood's study of Utah's first trained architect: "The Early Life and Career of Joseph Don Carlos Young (1855–1938): A Study of Utah's First Institutionally Trained Architect to 1884" (master's thesis, University of Pennsylvania, 1994).

The Mormon Sabbath. Before about 1852, Mormon Sunday meetings were less structured, and because there were no meetinghouses, meetings were usually held in the largest homes of members (much like the house churches of the New Testament). Larger meetings, where members could be instructed by their leaders, occurred in the Kirtland Temple, in barns of members, or in open areas, such as the "Grove" adjacent to the Nauvoo Temple. In 1852, Mormon meetings were standardized and were held on a community-wide basis in the tabernacle at 10 a.m. and 2 p.m. The nineteen bishops in Salt Lake City took turns administering the sacrament during the afternoon meeting. One Thursday of each month, the ward met separately for fast and testimony meeting. This was the only time the members took the sacrament as a ward. Unlike today, the sacrament was prepared and passed to the congregation while the speaker gave his remarks to those assembled. In Edward Hunter's ward, the speaker spoke while the bread was passed, and if he finished, the congregation sang a hymn while the water was being passed. After the sacrament came the closing prayer and the dismissal of the congregation. This summary is taken from Leonard J. Arrington, *From Quaker to Latter-day Saint: Bishop Edwin D. Woolley* (Salt Lake City: Deseret Book, 1976), 326–29.

To better understand the Mormon Sabbath, see Russel J. Thomsen, "History of the Sabbath in Mormonism" (master's thesis, Loma Linda University, 1968); William G. Hartley, "Mormon Sundays: A Historian Looks at How We've Observed the Sabbath Since 1830," *Ensign*, January 1978, 19–25; Hartley, "Common People: Church Activity during the Brigham Young Era," in *Nearly Everything Imaginable: The Everyday Life of Utah's Mormon Pioneers*, ed. Ronald W. Walker and Doris R. Dant (Provo, UT: BYU Press, 1999), 249–95; and Ronald W. Walker, "'Going to Meeting' in Salt Lake City's Thirteenth Ward, 1849–1881: A Microanalysis," in *New Views of Mormon History: A Collection of Essays in Honor of Leonard J. Arrington*, ed. Davis Bitton and Maureen Ursenbach Beecher (Salt Lake City: University of Utah Press, 1987), 138–61. For contemporary accounts, one in the Oakland, California, area and the other in Delaware, see Claudia L. Bushman, "The Sunset Ward," *Dialogue* 22 (Summer 1989): 119–30; Susan B. Taber, "Becoming Mormon: The Elkton Branch, 1876–81," *Dialogue* 25 (Fall 1992): 87–112; and Taber, *Mormon Lives: A Year in the Elkton Ward* (Urbana: University of Illinois Press, 1993). See also Claudia L. Bushman, *Contemporary Mormonism: Latter-day Saints in Modern America* (Westport, CT: Praeger, 2006).

SPECIFIC OFFICES AND QUORUMS

General pattern. Before April 1830, Joseph Smith, with help from Oliver Cowdery, had outlined key doctrines and Church organization in a document now known as Doctrine and Covenants section 20. They drew heavily from the Book of Mormon. Having been given the necessary priesthood authority from heavenly messengers, Joseph Smith and Oliver Cowdery officially organized the Church according to laws of the state of New York on April 6, 1830.

For the first few months, government for the infant organization was informal. Joseph Smith was recognized as the prophet and leader; Oliver Cowdery was his assistant and spokesman. The first years of Mormon history are the story of the growth from this informal government to an "oligarchy of leading elders." By 1835, the basic contours of the Church's administrative structure, the presiding quorums, were in place.

The Church began with five priesthood offices in 1830: Apostle, elder, priest, teacher, and deacon. The offices of bishop and high priest were added in 1831. But all of these early positions were local, held by lay members with no presiding authority. By 1831, Joseph Smith's ecclesiastical position had been more clearly defined, but it was not until January 1832 that he was formally sustained by a conference vote as "president of the high priesthood." Two weeks later he officially chose and ordained Jesse Gause and Sidney Rigdon as counselors. The Mormon hierarchy officially began with these March 8, 1832, calls. Early revelations and instructions from Joseph Smith established this First Presidency as the supreme authority on all matters relating to the Church.

The next major development was the organization of the Quorum of the Twelve Apostles on February 14, 1835. While men had been earlier ordained as Apostles, this act established a special unit of Church government. Although their responsibilities as a "traveling high council" were limited during the next six years to areas outside organized stakes, in time this quorum stood next to the First Presidency, and its senior member has become, upon the death of every president beginning with Joseph Smith, the new leader of the Church.

The third presiding quorum in the Mormon hierarchy, the Seventy, was organized in 1835, two weeks after the organization of the Apostles into a quorum, when Joseph Smith began ordaining men to the office of Seventy. Their task was missionary work. They were organized into quorums of seventy men, with the first quorum as the presiding quorum and its first seven members as presidents of all the seventies in the Church. From the beginning, they were to receive instructions and directions from the Quorum of the Twelve Apostles but were to "form a quorum equal in authority" to them (D&C 107:26). During the nineteenth century, most of the Church's proselyting missionaries were seventies, yet with the exception of the Patriarch, the office of the Seventy in Church history is least understood. In 1985, all local seventies quorums were discontinued, but the first and second quorums were expanded and filled with General Authorities who have been given greater responsibility in managing the affairs of the Church worldwide. This pattern has continued with eight quorums in the Church today.

The fourth presiding unit in the Church hierarchy is the Presiding Bishopric. Edward Partridge, called on February 4, 1831, was the first bishop in the Church. He was joined in 1831 by Newel K. Whitney. Only gradually did their responsibilities become known to them and to the Church. Very early they were assigned to "watch over the Church" and to take an interest in the poor, with the special assignment of administering the donations received for the needy. By 1835, Joseph Smith had revealed that the bishops should also be judges in the Church and were to be responsible to the First Presidency. They were to preside over the lesser priesthood offices of deacon, teacher, and priest, and were to be increasingly concerned with the "temporal" or economic affairs of the Church (see D&C 107:15–17, 68–76, 88; Joseph Smith later added vv. 76–93 to this section). By 1839, two more bishops were called, but each had geographical responsibility

(Missouri and Ohio) for a loose group of members. Presiding authority remained undefined.

It was during the Nauvoo period (1839–46) that, originally for voting and labor tithing purposes, wards were first organized. In time these subdivisions became useful ecclesiastical units over which a bishop took responsibility. The office of Presiding Bishop was first designated in 1840, but no Presiding Bishop *functioned* until 1847.

A useful overview of the general contours of these early developments is D. Michael Quinn, "The Evolution of the Presiding Quorums of the LDS Church," *Journal of Mormon History* 1 (1974): 21–38.

Prophet, seer, revelator. In a revelation to the Church on April 6, 1830, Joseph Smith Jr. was designated "a seer, a translator, a prophet, an apostle of Jesus Christ" (D&C 21:1). The Hebrew word for prophet is *nabi* and literally translates as "to bubble, or to boil," and seems to be related to the Akkadian *nabu* "to call, or announce." Hence the title is given to one who is called or one who announces, as in revealing the divine will. The Old Testament speaks of certain individuals who were called of God, those who spoke to and for God. In his perceptive study of the prophets of ancient Israel, Abraham Heschel spoke of the prophet as a witness, a messenger, and an assayer. His greatness "lies not only in the ideas he expressed, but also in the moments he experienced." Abraham Joshua Heschel, *The Prophets: An Introduction* (New York: Harper and Row, 1962), 1:20–22.

The Old Testament suggests a development from ecstatic seers to prophets (1 Samuel 9:9). As Joseph Smith sought to understand his gifts, he surely looked to the Bible and Book of Mormon for models of religious leadership. It should not surprise us that his own sense of calling was worked out within the context of Biblical precedents as he received additional revelation and divine tutoring on specific matters. This helps explain the heavy emphasis on the Old Testament in the earliest years of Mormonism, for it was there that the clearest prophetic models were found. Also critical was the Book of Mormon, as John Welch's essay herein clearly shows. Joseph only gradually moved the Church from a loose, rather democratic movement to a more hierarchical, pyramidal structure, the outlines of which were in place by 1835.

Thus the Hirum Page episode in September 1830 (see D&C 28) is best seen as the first serious challenge to Joseph's leadership, when a follower had his own seer stone through which he was receiving revelation. This was consistent in the early years, as everyone stood somewhat equal in these matters. But in section 28, Joseph's revelations were to be given priority over everyone else's for the Church as a whole. This was surely a necessary development, if for no other reason than to keep some order in the growing movement. But it also helped to push the early democratic elements back. Early associates of Joseph Smith came to interpret this growing authoritarianism as a serious breach of the origins of the movement. On Hirum Page, see Bruce G. Stewart, "Hiram Page: An Historical and Sociological Analysis of an Early Mormon Prototype" (master's thesis, BYU, 1987); for the attitudes of the Whitmers, see David Whitmer, *An Address to All Believers in Christ* (1888); John Whitmer, *From Historian to Dissident: The Book of John Whitmer*, ed. Bruce N. Westergren (Salt Lake City: Signature Books, 1995). For further analysis of this point see Whittaker, "The Book of Daniel in Early Mormon Thought."

From an administrative perspective, these changes not only reveal Joseph Smith's organizational genius but also surely enabled the movement to survive and grow during periods of strong criticism and forced moves throughout the nineteenth century and to adjust to the changing world of the twentieth century.

Councils and conferences. In the earliest months following the organization of the Church, Joseph Smith regularly gathered members into meetings that he identified as conferences (the term was also used for geographical divisions in the mission field). In these meetings, business was conducted, various matters were discussed and voted on, and individuals were given various Church assignments. On a smaller scale, these meetings were called councils (in the beginning, these terms were interchangeable), and a leader was appointed to preside over these meetings, as was a clerk to take minutes of the proceedings. In 1831, twelve conferences were held in about three months in addition to a general conference in November. In these meetings men were trained in administrative matters and also brought to accountability for misconduct. In these meetings, members were to seek revelation for themselves as they made decisions regarding administrative matters. As Richard Bushman suggests, it was these councils that made the Church self-governing, as Joseph Smith did not need to be present for the councils to function.

As the Church membership grew and as Joseph identified two centers of gathering, it was necessary to expand the governing capacity of these councils. The first step was to form high councils (composed of twelve high priests, with a president and two counselors) to regulate Church affairs in two locations: the Kirtland high council was organized in February 1834, and a few months later a second high council was organized in Clay County, Missouri. The Kirtland high council seems to have been intended as a council for the whole Church, and it seems that both high councils were intended to function as city councils for the two centers of Mormon gathering. These two governing bodies were to provide leadership where the Church was established, but there still remained two problems for the Church organization to address: what group should have jurisdiction in the mission field, and just what was the relationship of these high councils to Joseph Smith? Developments after 1834 addressed many of these concerns. For more information on the early councils and conferences, see Bushman, *Rough Stone Rolling*, 251–69; Bushman, "The Theology of Councils," 433–45; Kathleen Flake, "From Conferences to Councils: The Development of LDS Church Organization, 1830–1835," in *Archive of Restoration Culture: Summer Fellows' Papers, 1997–1999* (Provo, UT: Joseph Fielding Smith Institute of Latter-day Saint History, BYU, 2000), 1–8; David Holland, "Priest, Pastor, and Power: Joseph Smith and the Question of Priesthood," in *Archive of Restoration Culture*, 91–96; Jason Lindquist, "'Unlocking the Door of the Gospel': The Concept of 'Keys' in Mormonism and Early American Culture," in *Archive of Restoration Culture*, 29–42; J. Spencer Fluhman,

Mormon Administrative and Organizational History: A Source Essay

"Authority, Power, and 'Government of the Church of Christ,' 1835," in *Joseph Smith, the Prophet and Seer*, ed. Richard Neitzel Holzapfel and Kent P. Jackson (Provo, UT: Religious Studies Center, BYU, 2010), 195–231; and the essay by Joseph F. Darowski in this volume.

The First Presidency. On January 25, 1832, Joseph Smith was officially sustained by a Church conference as president of the high priesthood. On March 8, 1832, he chose Jesse Gause and Sidney Rigdon as his counselors, and with these calls the Mormon hierarchy began. Together they comprised the First Presidency. The early revelations clearly established this quorum as the top administrative unit in the Church, with final say on all matters regarding the Church (see D&C 107:8, 22, 79–80).

Early direction to the office of counselor was given in a revelation dated March 15, 1832, to Jesse Gause (see D&C 81). Frederick G. Williams replaced Gause the next year, and Gause seems to have disappeared from history. Two studies that discuss the life of the first man called as a counselor in the First Presidency are Robert J. Woodford, "Jesse Gause—Counselor to the Prophet," *BYU Studies* 15, no. 3 (Spring 1975): 362–64; D. Michael Quinn, "Jesse Gause: Joseph Smith's Little-Known Counselor," *BYU Studies* 23, no. 4 (Fall 1983): 487–93; and most completely, Erin B. Jennings, "The Consequential Counselor: Restoring the Root(s) of Jesse Gause," *Journal of Mormon History* 34 (Spring 2008): 182–227. On Williams, see Frederick G. Williams, "Frederick Granger Williams of the First Presidency of the Church," *BYU Studies* 12, no. 3 (Spring 1972): 243–61.

The first real challenge to Joseph Smith's claims to hold the keys, or directing and presiding authority, of the priesthood came shortly after the organizing of the First Presidency. In early July, 1832, with Gause absent on a mission and Joseph Smith living in Hiram, Ohio, Rigdon called a meeting in Kirtland in which he claimed that the Church no longer had the keys of the priesthood. Hyrum rode south to get Joseph, who returned to Kirtland and spent the next few weeks doing damage control. Rigdon was released from the First Presidency, and Joseph spent part of the month thinking about these matters. Joseph's first autobiographical statement was prepared during this time, and it centers on his right for claiming the keys of the priesthood: "the Keeys of the Kingdom conferred upon him" was a forceful if short summary of the visionary experiences that brought the heavenly keys to him (in it he outlines his revelatory experiences: a testimony from on high, the ministering of angels, the reception of the holy priesthood, and a confirmation and reception of the holy priesthood), and it provides the only account we have of his First Vision in his own hand. For the text of this history, see *Personal Writings of Joseph Smith*, comp. and ed. Dean C. Jessee, rev. ed. (Salt Lake City: Deseret Book; Provo, UT: BYU Press, 2002), 9–20; on Rigdon's release and reinstatement, see Joseph Smith to William W. Phelps, July 31, 1832, in *Personal Writings of Joseph Smith*, 273 ("after repenting like Peter of old, has been restored to his high standing"), and Hyrum Smith, diary, July 29, 1832, L. Tom Perry Special Collections, Harold B. Lee Library, BYU). The scribe for this early history was Frederick G. Williams, who would become Joseph Smith's counselor the next year, replacing Gause.

Few good studies have been done on the men who have served as counselors to the President of the Church. Important exceptions are Jeffrey S. O'Driscoll, *Hyrum Smith: A Life of Integrity* (Salt Lake City: Deseret Book, 2003); Andrew F. Smith, *The Saintly Scoundrel: The Life and Times of Dr. John Cook Bennett* (Urbana: University of Illinois Press, 1997); Stanley B. Kimball, *Heber C. Kimball: Mormon Patriarch and Pioneer* (Urbana: University of Illinois Press, 1981); Kimball, "Brigham and Heber," *BYU Studies* 18, no. 3 (Spring 1978): 396–409; Gene A. Sessions, *Mormon Thunder: A Documentary History of Jedediah Morgan Grant* (Urbana: University of Illinois Press, 1982); Michael K. Winder, *John R. Winder: Member of the First Presidency, Pioneer, Temple Builder, Dairyman* (Bountiful, UT: Horizon Publishers, 1999); D. Michael Quinn, *Elder Statesman: A Biography of J. Reuben Clark* (Salt Lake City: Signature Books, 2002); Eugene E. Campbell and Richard D. Poll, *Hugh B. Brown: His Life and Thought* (Salt Lake City: Bookcraft, 1975); G. Homer Durham, *N. Eldon Tanner: His Life and Service* (Salt Lake City: Deseret Book, 1982). See also N. Eldon Tanner,

Mormon Administrative and Organizational History: A Source Essay

"The Administration of the Church," *Ensign*, November 1979, 42–48; and Gordon B. Hinckley, "In . . . Counselors There Is Safety," *Ensign*, November 1990, 48–51.

The office of Assistant or Associate President in the early Church also provided extra counselors for the President. Oliver Cowdery was appointed as Assistant President on December 5, 1834. The next day Joseph Smith Sr. and Hyrum Smith were called to the same position. Of the three, only Oliver's calling was one of joint leadership with Joseph Smith with rights of succession. See Quinn, "Evolution of the Presiding Quorums," 25. Also valuable is Robert Glen Mouritsen, "The Office of Associate President of the Church of Jesus Christ of Latter-day Saints" (master's thesis, BYU, 1972).

Scribes and clerks. An important dimension in Mormon administrative history is the critical role that clerks and scribes and secretaries played in the creation and maintenance of Church records. Joseph Smith depended on personal scribes and secretaries during his presidency, as have his successors. One could almost suggest the existence of a scribal culture in Mormonism, from the important work of Oliver Cowdery in the earliest years to those who continue this nonpublic function in Mormon organizational/administrative history. Joseph Smith used such individuals as William W. Phelps to draft letters and documents for him, and the key role of Willard Richards in keeping the Prophet's Nauvoo journals and in the shaping of his history is critical for understanding the records and history of his presidency. For information on the calling/assignment, the following works are suggestive: Robin S. Jensen, "'Rely upon the Things Which Are Written': Text, Context, and the Creation of Mormon Revelatory Records" (master's thesis, University of Wisconsin–Milwaukee, 2009); Stanley R. Gunn, *Oliver Cowdery: Second Elder and Scribe* (Salt Lake City: Bookcraft, 1962); *Days Never to Be Forgotten: Oliver Cowdery*, ed. Alexander Baugh (Provo, UT: Religious Studies Center, BYU, 2009); Howard C. Searle, "Willard Richards as Historian," *BYU Studies* 31, no. 2 (Spring 1991): 41–62; Jerald F. Simon, "Thomas Bullock as an Early Mormon Historian," *BYU Studies* 30 (Winter 1990): 71–88; James B. Allen, *Trials of Discipleship: The Story of William Clayton* (Urbana: University of Illinois Press, 1987); Allen, " William Clayton and the Records of Mormon History," in *Preserving the History of the Latter-day Saints*, ed. Richard E. Turley Jr. and Steven C. Harper (Provo, UT: Religious Studies Center, BYU; Salt Lake City: Deseret Book, 2010), 83–114; Bruce A. Van Orden, "William W. Phelps's Service in Nauvoo as Joseph Smith's Political Clerk," *BYU Studies* 32, nos. 1–2 (Winter/Spring 1992): 81–94; Elizabeth Ann Anderson, "Howard and Martha Coray: Chroniclers of the Words and Life of the Prophet Joseph Smith," *Journal of Mormon History* 33 (Fall 2007): 83–113; Ronald G. Watt, *The Mormon Passage of George D. Watt: First British Convert, Scribe for Zion* (Logan: Utah State University Press, 2009); Watt, "Calligraphy in Brigham Young's Office," *Utah Historical Quarterly* 45 (Summer 1977): 265–69; Van Orden, *Prisoner for Conscience' Sake: The Life of George Reynolds* (Salt Lake City: Deseret Book, 1992); Clarence G. Jensen, "A Biographical Study of Leonard John Nuttall, Private Secretary to Presidents John Taylor and Wilford Woodruff" (master's thesis, BYU, 1962); and Jack Walsh, "D. Arthur Haycock: Aide to Four Prophets," *Ensign*, August 1984, 22–27.

The presiding patriarch. Probably the least understood office in the Church, the first patriarch was designated by Joseph Smith in December 1833 or 1834. In a blessing on his own father's head, Joseph said "he shall be called a prince over his posterity, holding the keys of the patriarchal Priesthood over the Kingdom of God on earth, even the Church of the Latter-day Saints." "Patriarchal Blessing Book," 1:9–10, manuscript, Church History Library. That same day, December 18, Joseph Smith Sr. was ordained "Patriarch and President of the High Priesthood." There is some question as to the exact date of these events, whether it was December 1833 or December 1834, the earliest mention of Joseph Smith Sr. actually giving patriarchal blessings. It is unclear just whom he was to preside over; perhaps this is why he was also called as an Assistant President. See Irene M. Bates, "Patriarchal Blessings and the Routinization of Charisma," *Dialogue* 26 (Fall 1993): 1–29.

Mormon Administrative and Organizational History: A Source Essay

The undefined nature of the presiding role of the Church Patriarch came into focus at Joseph Smith's death and during the succession crisis that followed. William Smith's claims that his position as Church Patriarch made him the new leader was denied by Brigham Young and the Quorum of the Twelve Apostles. The potential tension remained in the Church until recently, when Eldred G. Smith was made patriarch emeritus in October 1979 and no replacement was called.

The history of the office of Church Patriarch is found in the following studies: Andrew Jenson, "Presiding Patriarchs," *Historical Record* 5 (August 1886): 89; Ernest M. Skinner, "Joseph Smith, Sr., First Patriarch to the Church" (master's thesis, BYU, 1958); Pearson H. Corbett, *Hyrum Smith, Patriarch* (Salt Lake City: Deseret Book, 1963); Thomas Jay Kemp, *The Office of Patriarch to the Church, in the Church of Jesus Christ of Latter-day Saints* (Stanford, CT: Thomas J. Kemp, 1972); Irene M. Bates, "William Smith, 1811–93: Problematic Patriarch," *Dialogue* 16 (Summer 1983): 11–23; Bates, "Uncle John Smith, 1781–1854: Patriarchal Bridge," *Dialogue* 20 (Fall 1987): 79–89; E. Gary Smith, "The Patriarchal Crisis of 1845," *Dialogue*, 24–35; Paul M. Edwards, "William B. Smith: Persistent 'Pretender,'" *Dialogue* 18 (Summer 1985): 128–39; and most comprehensively, Irene M. Bates, "Transformation of Charisma in the Mormon Church: A History of the Office of Presiding Patriarch, 1833–1879" (PhD diss., UCLA, 1991); and Irene M. Bates and E. Gary Smith, *Lost Legacy: The Mormon Office of Presiding Patriarch* (Urbana: University of Illinois Press, 1996).

The office of stake patriarch has continued to function in the Church from its earliest days. Following the calling of the first Quorum of the Twelve Apostles in 1835 they were told in a revelation that "It is the duty of the Twelve in all the branches of the Church, to ordain evangelical ministers [defined by Joseph Smith as patriarchs] as they shall be designated unto them by revelation" (D&C 107:39). Their calling includes pronouncing special blessings, revealing or assigning lineages connected with the House of Israel, and giving inspired counsel to Church members. While worthy fathers are also patriarchs to their families and in that role can give blessings to their family members, stake patriarchs also serve as fathers to those who lack either a living or an active earthly father. See Boyd K. Packer, "The Stake Patriarch," *Ensign*, November 2002, 42-45.

The Quorum of the Twelve Apostles. As early as 1830 the calling of Apostle was referred to in the revelations (see D&C 18:26–39; 20:2–3). In February 1835, following the New Testament pattern, twelve men were called to constitute a quorum of Church government. At first they were not given any presiding authority over already-organized stakes, but by 1842 Joseph brought the quorum into its position of key importance next to the First Presidency. After the initial years in the Great Basin, Brigham Young geographically decentralized the Quorum of the Twelve Apostles by assigning them to preside over various areas of Mormon settlement or on various missions. It was only in the 1890s that the quorum returned to its earlier unified structure. The full story of these early years is told in Quinn, "The Evolution of the Presiding Quorums," 26–31; T. Edgar Lyon, "Nauvoo and the Council of the Twelve," in *The Restoration Movement: Essays in Mormon History*, comp. F. Mark McKiernan, Alma Blair, and Paul M. Edwards (Lawrence, KS: Coronado Press, 1973), 167–205; Ronald K. Esplin, "The Emergence of Brigham Young and the Twelve to Mormon Leadership, 1830–1841" (PhD diss., BYU, 1981); Wilbur D. Talbot, "The Duties and Responsibilities of Apostles of the Church of Jesus Christ of Latter-day Saints, 1835–1945" (PhD diss., BYU, 1977); and Talbot, *The Acts of the Apostles* (Salt Lake City: Randall Books, 1985).

A few of the individual Apostles have received scholarly treatment. Among the more important studies, beyond those already cited above, include Merlo J. Pusey, *Builders of the Kingdom: George A. Smith, John Henry Smith, George Albert Smith* (Provo, UT: BYU Press, 1981); Leonard J. Arrington, *Charles C. Rich: Mormon General and Western Frontiersman* (Provo, UT: BYU Press, 1974); Breck England, *The Life and Thought of Orson Pratt* (Salt Lake City: University of Utah Press, 1985); Parley P. Pratt, *Autobiography* (New York: Russell, 1874); David S. Hoopes and Roy Hoopes, *The Making of a Mormon Apostle: The Story of Rudger Clawson* (Lanham, MD:

Mormon Administrative and Organizational History: A Source Essay

Madison Books, 1990); Myrtle Stevens Hyde, *Orson Hyde: The Olive Branch of Israel* (Salt Lake City: Agreka Books, 2000); and Edward Leo Lyman, *Amasa Mason Lyman: Mormon Apostle and Apostate* (Salt Lake City: University of Utah Press, 2009). Lucile C. Tate authored several biographies of modern Apostles: *LeGrand Richards: Beloved Apostle* (Salt Lake City: Bookcraft, 1982); *David B. Haight: The Life Story of a Disciple* (Salt Lake City: Bookcraft, 1987); and *Boyd K. Packer: A Watchman on the Tower* (Salt Lake City: Bookcraft, 1995).

The First Quorum(s) of Seventy. Shortly after the first Quorum of Twelve Apostles was called, Joseph Smith began calling men to be Seventies. On March 28, 1835, a revelation spelled out their duties: "The Seventy are also called to preach the gospel, and to be especial witness unto the Gentiles in all the world—thus differing from other offices in the church in the duties of their calling. And they form a quorum equal in authority to that of the Twelve special witnesses or Apostles just named" (D&C 107:25–26).

From 1835, the Seventy were considered subordinate to the Quorum of the Twelve (see D&C 107:25–26). Seven men were to preside as presidents over the quorum (see D&C 107:93–96). The fascinating history of this quorum has yet to be fully told. A useful general history is James Norman Baumgarten, "The Role and Function of the Seventies in L.D.S. Church History" (master's thesis, BYU, 1960). See also Quinn, "The Evolution of the Presiding Quorums," 31–32; Lyndon W. Cook, *A Tentative Inquiry into the Office of the Seventy, 1835–1845* (Provo, UT: Grandin Book, 2010); Joseph Young, *History of the Organization of the Seventies* (Salt Lake City: Deseret News, 1878); Hartley, "The Seventies in the 1880s," *Dialogue* 16 (Spring 1983): 62–88; S. Dilworth Young, "The Seventies: A Historical Perspective," *Ensign*, July 1976, 14–21; Bruce Van Orden, "Preparing for a Worldwide Ministry," *Ensign*, October 1999, 33–39; L. Aldin Porter, "A History of the Latter-day Seventy," *Ensign*, August 2000, 14–20; Earl C. Tingey, "The Saga of Revelation: The Unfolding Role of the Seventy," *Ensign*, September 2009, 54–60; and Richard O. Cowan, "Administrating the International Church," in *Unto Every Nation: Gospel Light Reaches*

Every Land, ed. Donald Q. Cannon and Richard O. Cowan (Salt Lake City: Deseret Book, 2003), 482–501. A valuable chronological compilation of documents on the history of the Seventies to 1970 is John L. Lund, "An Extensive Annotated Bibliography of Literature Relative to the Office and Calling of the Seventy" (unpublished manuscript), L. Tom Perry Special Collections. Recent developments, including the expansion of the First Quorum and the organization of the Second and others that followed, can be traced in *Church News*, especially November 8, 1975; October 9, 1976; and October 16, 1975, and in subsequent general conference reports. Also Spencer W. Kimball, "The Reconstitution of the First Quorum of the Seventy," *Ensign*, November 1976; "Organizational Principles Pertaining to the First Quorum of the Seventy," manuscript in Church History Library, dated December 7, 1978.

The best-known members of the Seventy are the subjects of Truman G. Madsen, *Defender of the Faith: The B. H. Roberts Story* (Salt Lake City: Bookcraft, 1980); and J. Claude Richards, *J. Golden Kimball* (Salt Lake City: Bookcraft, 1966).

The Presiding Bishop. There was no functioning Presiding Bishop while Joseph Smith was alive. While Edward Partridge was appointed bishop on February 4, 1831, and Newel K. Whitney was called in December 1831, neither man was given authority over the other. Rather, they had regional responsibilities, one in Ohio, the other in Missouri. Only gradually did their duties become defined: they were to answer to the First Presidency; they were to preside over the lesser offices of deacon, teacher, and priest; and they were to concern themselves exclusively with the temporal affairs of the Church.

The first man to be designated as Presiding Bishop of the Church was Vinson Knight. This was in 1841, but his name was never presented to the Church for a vote, and it is clear he never functioned in this capacity before his death in July 1842. While there was some seniority ranking among the other bishops during the Nauvoo period, Newel K. Whitney was sustained as the first functioning Presiding Bishop in April 1847. He was succeeded by Edward Hunter in April 1851.

The complex details of these early events are told in Quinn, "The Evolution of the Presiding Quorums," 32–38. See also Quinn, "Was Edward Partridge the First Presiding Bishop?," *Ensign*, December 1972, 32; Donald Gene Pace, "The LDS Presiding Bishopric, 1851–1888: An Administrative Study" (master's thesis, BYU, 1978); Larry N. Poulsen, "The Life and Contributions of Newel Kimball Whitney" (master's thesis, BYU, 1966); D. Brent Collette, "In Search of Zion: A Description of Early Mormon Millennial Utopianism as Revealed through the Life of Edward Partridge" (master's thesis, BYU, 1977); William G. Hartley, "Edward Hunter: Pioneer Presiding Bishop," in *Supporting Saints: Life Stories of Nineteenth-Century Mormons*, ed. Donald Q. Cannon and David J. Whittaker (Provo, UT: Religious Studies Center, BYU, 1985), 275–304; William E. Hunter, *Edward Hunter, Faithful Servant* (Salt Lake City: Publishers Press for the Hunter Family, 1970); D. Gene Pace, "Changing Patterns of Mormon Financial Administration: Traveling Bishops, Regional Bishops and Bishops Agents, 1851–1888," *BYU Studies* 23, no. 2 (Spring 1983): 183–92; Janet Burton Seegmiller, *"Be Kind to the Poor": The Life of Robert Taylor Burton* (Salt Lake City: Robert Taylor Burton Family Organization, 1988); and Michael E. Christensen, "The Making of a Leader: A Biography of Charles W. Nibley to 1890" (PhD diss., University of Utah, 1978). A useful biographical compilation is Michael R. Winder, *Presiding Bishops* (Salt Lake City: Eborn Books, 2003). Two unpublished manuscripts in the Church History Library are also useful: Elden J. Watson, "Early Development of the Presiding Bishopric"; and Ronald G. Watt, "The Presiding Bishopric to 1888."

Regional and area leaders. Reflective of the growth of the Church in the twentieth century was the creating of large geographical units to help facilitate the administration of the Church worldwide. Supervised and staffed by members of the Seventies quorums and responsible to the Quorum of the Twelve Apostles, these regional leaders have proved essential for the governing of an ever-enlarging Church.

An earlier attempt to provide General Authority leadership came in 1941, when Assistants to the Quorum of the Twelve Apostles were first called. Some thirty-eight men served in these callings before it was merged with the expansion of the Seventies quorums in 1976. A number of those who served as Assistants to the Twelve were later called into the Quorum of the Twelve. See John A. Widtsoe, "Assistants to the Twelve," *Improvement Era*, May 1941, 288; and Spencer W. Kimball, "The Reconstitution of the First Quorum of the Seventy," *Ensign*, November 1976, 9.

The best overview of the current developments is Kahlile B. Mehr, "Area Supervision: Administration of the Worldwide Church, 1860–2000," *Journal of Mormon History* 27 (Spring 2001): 192–214. The shifting boundaries and those who are called to lead these areas can be followed in the *Deseret News Church Almanac* and in the *Ensign*. There is also much useful information in Francis M. Gibbons, *The Expanding Church: Three Decades of Remarkable Growth among the Latter-day Saints, 1970–1999* (Bountiful, UT: Horizon Publishers, 1999).

The history of the calling of mission president has received little attention in Mormon scholarship. There is much indirect information in the many histories of Mormon missions, easily located in Whittaker, "Mormon Missiology." Very useful profiles of those who served missions, a number of whom later became mission presidents themselves, is William E. Hughes, "A Profile of the Missionaries of the Church of Jesus Christ of Latter-day Saints, 1849–1900" (master's thesis, BYU, 1986); and Rex Thomas Price Jr., "The Mormon Missionary of the Nineteenth Century" (PhD diss., University of Wisconsin–Madison, 1991). For more specific studies of the leadership, see George D. Pace, "The Effectiveness of Mission Presidents of the Church of Jesus Christ of Latter-day Saints Measured by Six Selected Criteria" (DRE dissertation, BYU, 1976), part of which was published in *Review of Religious Research* 19 (December 1978): 209–19. For several perspectives on what can go wrong, see D. Michael Quinn, "I-Thou vs. I-It Conversions: The Mormon 'Baseball Baptism' Era," *Sunstone* 16 (December 1993): 30–44; Richard Mavin, "The Woodbury Years: An Insider's Look as

Mormon Administrative and Organizational History: A Source Essay

Baseball Baptisms in Britain," *Sunstone* 19 (March 1996): 56–60; Kahlile Mehr, "The Trial of the French Mission," *Dialogue* 21 (Fall 1988): 27–45. Fortunately, these have been the exception in Mormon mission history. A useful introduction to Mormon missiology is R. Lanier Britsch, "Mormon Missions: An Introduction to the Latter-day Saints Missionary System," *Occasional Bulletin of Missionary Research* 3 (January 1979): 22–27, and Britsch's essay in this volume.

Stake presidents. The organization of stakes, with a president and two counselors and a high council of twelve members, dates from 1834. The first wards were created in 1839, through the gradual movement to their modern function took a little time. Both organizations were fluid geographically, and while these governing units began to coalesce during the Nauvoo period, it was not until the Saints settled in the Salt Lake Valley that they came to function like today. But there were still changes and modifications. For example, the Salt Lake Stake functioned as the center stake, with a higher status than other stakes, until 1876, when Brigham Young announced that all stakes were to be considered on equal footing. The rich history of stakes, still not fully told, can be seen in two essays by William G. Hartley: "Organization of Wards and Stakes: A Historical Approach," in *Religious Educators Symposium on LDS Church History* (Salt Lake City: Church Educational System, 1977), 53–55; and "Nauvoo Stake, Priesthood Quorums, and the Church's First Wards," *BYU Studies* 32, nos. 1–2 (1992): 57–80. Donald Q. Cannon studies the powerful nineteenth-century president of the Salt Lake Stake in "Angus M. Cannon: Pioneer, President, Patriarch," in *Supporting Saints*, 369–401.

Bishops. The most important grassroots leader in the Church is the bishop. In the modern Church his responsibilities center in five areas, (1) acting as the presiding high priest or father of the ward; (2) acting as head of the Aaronic Priesthood in his ward, (3) caring for the needy as he administers the welfare program on the local level, (4) overseeing ward finances, and (5) acting as a common judge in Israel. These are summarized in the March 22, 1974, oral history interview of J. Thomas Fyans, in the James Moyle

Oral History Program, Church History Library. These five areas were made the core of the Bishop's Self-Help Training Course in the Church (ca. 1980).

Written revelations of the Church specified that the bishop was divinely authorized to administer the temporal and financial resources of the Church, in addition to certain other duties. The precise jurisdiction of the office of bishop was not specified, and the Presidents of the Church often distinguished various types of bishops. The student should be aware of the following titles used in Church history: (1) *ward bishop*—a lay leader whose jurisdiction was limited to a local ecclesiastical unit called a ward. This type of bishop has been recognized in Latter-day Saint terminology and practice from 1839 to the present; (2) *regional presiding bishop*—a leader who served as bishop over a region, generally a county or a stake. The regional presiding bishop was responsible for the regional storehouse, in which the voluntary donations of Church members were received and disbursed. This designation was used from the early 1850s to 1877; (3) *bishop's agent*—an agent of the Presiding Bishop who was directly responsible to the Presiding Bishop for the condition of the resources and records in the stake to which the agent was assigned. The title and function date back to 1831, when one of the general bishops had an agent as authorized in a written revelation, but the number of such officers was largest after 1851. An organized system of bishop's agents was used extensively in Utah during the period 1877–1888; (4) *Presiding Bishop*—a bishop who was responsible for the administration of temporal affairs of the entire Church and who presided under the First Presidency over the entire Church. He and his two counselors comprised the Presiding Bishopric. As stated earlier, there was no *functioning* Presiding Bishop while Joseph Smith was alive. Newel K. Whitney was sustained as the first functioning Presiding Bishop in April 1847. He was succeeded by Edward Hunter in April 1851; (5) *Assistant Presiding Bishop*—bishop who served as an assistant to the Presiding Bishop of the Church. When sustained by the vote of the general membership of the Church, these assistants were also General Authorities. This title was first designated in 1851, lasted from one to two years, and became firmly established in 1856 as permanent counselors to the Presiding Bishopric; (6)

traveling bishop—a bishop whose jurisdiction was not limited to a ward or stake. The traveling bishop was to be as "a father to the people" and to supervise temporal matters in the settlements he visited. This position was authorized in a written revelation of 1830, and men periodically served in this role for the next several decades; (7) *traveling agent for the General Tithing Office*—a traveling auditor who gave instruction on bookkeeping to the ward bishops, compiled financial summaries, and helped with the supervision of temporal affairs in the areas he visited. Traveling agents for the General Tithing Office were used from 1860 to 1876. This summary of bishops' roles is taken from D. Gene Pace, "Changing Patterns of Mormon Financial Administration: Traveling Bishops, Regional Bishops, and Bishop's Agents, 1851–1888," *BYU Studies* 23, no. 2 (Spring 1983): 183–95.

The historical roles of bishops can be seen in the following studies: Dale F. Beecher, "The Office of a Bishop: An Example of Organizational Development in the Church," *Task Papers in LDS History*, no. 21 (Salt Lake City: Historical Department, The Church of Jesus Christ of Latter-day Saints, 1978); Beecher, "The Office of Bishop," *Dialogue* 15 (Winter 1982): 103–15; D. Gene Pace, "Community Leadership on the Mormon Frontier: Mormon Bishops and the Political, Economic and Social Development of Utah before Statehood" (PhD diss., Ohio State University, 1983); Steven J. Sorenson, "Civil and Criminal Jurisdiction of LDS Bishops and High Council Courts, 1847–1852," *Task Papers in LDS History*, no. 17 (Salt Lake City: Historical Department, The Church of Jesus Christ of Latter-day Saints, 1977); Jerry C. Higginson, "Abraham Alonzo Kimball: A Nineteenth Century Mormon Bishop" (master's thesis, BYU, 1963); Blaine M. Yorgason, "The Impact of Polygamy upon the Life of James Yorgason: A Nineteenth-century Mormon Bishop" (master's thesis, BYU, 1980); D. Gene Pace, "Elijah F. Sheets: The Half-century Bishop," in Cannon and Whittaker, *Supporting Saints*, 255–73; Leonard J. Arrington, *From Quaker to Latter-day Saint: Bishop Edwin D. Woolley* (Salt Lake City: Deseret Book, 1976); Alan P. Johnson, *Aaron Johnson, Faithful Steward: A Documentary History* (Salt Lake City: Publishers Press, 1991); William G. Hartley, *My Best for the Kingdom: The History and Autobiography of John Lowe Butler, a Mormon Frontiersman* (Salt Lake City: Aspen Books, 1993); William G. Hartley and Lorna Call Alder, *Anson Bowen Call: Bishop of Colonia Dublan* (Provo, UT: Lorna Call Alder, 2007); William G. Hartley, "The Miller, the Bishop, and the 'Move South,'" *BYU Studies* 20, no. 1 (Fall 1979): 99–105; William G. Hartley, "Ward Bishops and the Localizing of LDS Tithing, 1847–1856," in *New Views of Mormon History* 96–114; Dean L. May, "Brigham Young and the Bishops: The United Order in the City," in *New Views of Mormon History*, 115–37; P. T. Reilly, "Kanab United Order: The President's Nephew and the Bishop," *Utah Historical Quarterly* 42 (Spring 1974): 144–64; and Leonard J. Arrington and Richard Jensen, "Lorenzo Hill Hatch: Pioneer Bishop of Franklin," *Idaho Yesterdays* 17 (Summer 1973): 2–8. William G. Hartley's forthcoming biography of Albert King Thurber focuses on his service as a bishop in Spanish Fork for fourteen years and then as a stake president in Richfield from 1875 to 1888.

Four of the seven interviews of William Woolf taken in 1973–74 by William G. Hartley for the oral history program of the Church Historical Department detail Woolf's experiences as the bishop of the Manhattan Ward in New York in the 1940s. They are frank and contain good insights into the role of a more contemporary urban bishop. Valuable insights are in Pilar Rich (pseud.), *The Saints of Snowville: Story of a Mormon Bishop* (New York: Exposition Press, 1970). The rural ward discussed here was in Star Valley, Wyoming. A guide to nineteenth-century bishops is Ronald G. Watt and Rachel Whitmore, comps., "LDS Bishop's Directory, 1848–1890" (unpublished manuscript, Church History Library, 1979). A contemporary look at the history of one ward in Delaware for one year is Susan Buhler Taber, *Mormon Lives: A Year in the Elkton Ward* (Urbana: University of Illinois Press, 1993). See also Jessie L. Embry, *Mormons Wards as Community* (Binghamton, NY: Global Publications, Binghamton University, 2001). Lorin K. Hanson and Lila J. Bringhurst's history of the Fremont, California, stakes provides an overview of the growth of one area outside the Wasatch Front to branches and districts and then to stakes and wards: *Let This Be Zion:*

Mormon Administrative and Organizational History: A Source Essay

Mormon Pioneers and Modern Saints in Southern Alameda California: From a Colony of Refugees in Gold Rush California to "Stakes of Zion" in a World-wide Church (Newark, CA: Fremont California and Fremont California South Stakes of the Church of Jesus Christ of Latter-day Saints, 1996).

The key role of the bishop as a common judge in counseling members, hearing confessions of members, and assisting members of his congregation with the repentance process is discussed in great detail in Lester E. Bush Jr., "Excommunication and Church Courts: A Note from the General Handbook of Instruction," *Dialogue* 14 (Summer 1981): 74–98; Edward L. Kimball, "Confession in LDS Doctrine and Practice," *BYU Studies* 36, no. 2 (1996–97): 7–73; and Kimball, "The History of LDS Temple Admission Standards," *Journal of Mormon History* 24 (Spring 1998): 135–79. See also R. Collin Mangrum, "Furthering the Cause of Zion: An Overview of the Mormon Ecclesiastical Court System in Early Utah," *Journal of Mormon History* 10 (1983): 79–90. While ward bishops have counseled their ward members since the earliest days of the Church, due to its private and generally confidential nature, very little study has been done on this aspect of their job. Recent studies, of uneven quality, include Peter Wendel Johnson, "Counseling Attitudes of Bishops and Seminary Instructors of the Church of Jesus Christ of Latter-day Saints," (EdD diss., Boston University, 1973); Franklin Kelso Meadows, "A Study of the Status, as Counselors, of One Hundred Bishops in the Church of Jesus Christ of Latter-day Saints" (master's thesis, BYU, 1958); Philip Dayton Thorpe, "The Brigham Young University Ward Bishops and Professional Counselors as Helping Persons" (PhD diss., BYU, 1967); and Jerry Allen Wilson, "A Fault Free Approach to Analysis of Counselor Training for Bishops in the Church of Jesus Christ of Latter-day Saints" (EdD diss., BYU, 1976). The Church has commissioned a variety of studies on wards and on bishops, but almost none of them have been made public. The growing interests and concerns of professional counselors, many of whom are used by bishops in referral situations, can be seen in the publications and meetings of the Association of Mormon Counselors and Psychotherapists (AMCAP). See also Scott Ashby Speakman, "A

History of the Youth Guidance Program of the Church of Jesus Christ of Latter-day Saints" (master's thesis, University of Utah, 1968); Harold C. Brown, "New Developments in L.D.S. Social Services," *AMCAP* 7 (January 1982): 11–13, 31, 32. See also Eric Gottrid Swedin, *Healing Souls: Psychotherapy in the Latter-day Saint Community* (Urbana: University of Illinois Press, 2003).

WOMEN AND ADMINISTRATIVE HISTORY

From Mormon institutional beginnings, women have been encouraged to participate in Church government. They were to vote in conferences on matters of policy and doctrine, and Mormon scripture never suggested that revelation or inspiration was a function of one's gender. From the earliest days, women have played a major role in virtually all aspects of Latter-day Saint history, but their lives and contributions have only begun to catch the attention of scholars. This judgment is true whether the topic is a single biography, women organized, or in the more sociological areas of the role and function of sisterhood in the Mormon experience.

A good place to begin is with Carol Cornwall Madsen and David J. Whittaker, "History's Sequel: A Source Essay on Women in Mormon History," *Journal of Mormon History* 6 (1979): 123–45. An updated listing of studies since 1977 has been compiled by Patricia Lyn Scott and Maureen Ursenbach Beecher, "Mormon Women: A Bibliography in Process, 1977–1985," *Journal of Mormon History* 12 (1985): 113–27. See also Karen Purser Frazier, compiler, *Bibliography of Social, Scientific, Historical, and Popular Writings about Mormon Women* (Provo, UT: Women's Research Institute, BYU, 1990). These bibliographies contain material on the administrative and organizational dimensions of women's activities. A useful overview of women in Church history is Leonard J. Arrington and Davis Bitton, *The Mormon Experience: A History of the Latter-day Saints* (New York: Knopf, 1979), 220–40. Valuable essays are gathered in Maureen Ursenbach Beecher and Lavina Fielding Anderson, eds., *Sisters in Spirit: Mormon Women in Historical and Cultural Perspective* (Urbana: University of Illinois Press,

1987); *Mormon Sister, Women in Early Utah*, Claudia L. Bushman, ed. (Logan, UT: Utah State University Press, 1997); and Vicky Burgess-Olson, ed., *Sister Saints* (Provo, UT: BYU Press, 1978). See also Jill Mulvay Derr and C. Brooklyn Derr, "Outside the Mormon Hierarchy: Alternative Aspects of Institutional Power," *Dialogue* 15 (Winter 1982): 21–43;

The Female Relief Society. The most important women's organization has been the Relief Society. *History of the Relief Society, 1842–1966* (Salt Lake City, 1966) was published by the General Board of the Relief Society, but it covers only the essential programs and highlights in the development of this organization. Insights into its origin are in Maureen Ursenbach Beecher and James L. Kimball Jr., "The First Relief Society: A Diversity of Women," *Ensign*, March 1979, 25–29; and Jill Mulvay Derr and Carol Cornwall Madsen, "Preserving the Record and Memory of the Female Relief Society of Nauvoo, 1842–92," *Journal of Mormon History* 35 (Summer 2009): 88–117. The life of the first president is treated in Linda King Newell and Valeen Tippetts Avery, *Mormon Enigma: Emma Hale Smith* (Garden City, NY: Doubleday, 1984). Emma's use of the Relief Society to condemn plural marriage led Brigham Young to suspend its operations after Joseph Smith's death. Its history to 1868 when it was again organized more fully by Brigham Young is considered in Richard L. Jensen, "Forgotten Relief Societies, 1844–67," *Dialogue* 16 (Spring 1983): 105–25. Biographical information on the presidents is in Janet Peterson and LaRene Gaunt, *Elect Ladies* (Salt Lake City: Deseret Book, 1990); and Janet Peterson, *Faith, Hope and Charity: Inspiration from the Lives of General Relief Society Presidents* (American Fork, UT: Covenant Communications, 2008). Economic responsibilities after 1868 are studied in Leonard J. Arrington, *Great Basin Kingdom* (Cambridge, MA: Harvard University Press, 1958), 251–54; and Jessie L. Embry, "Grain Storage: The Balance of Power between Priesthood Authority and Relief Society Autonomy," *Dialogue* 15 (Winter 1982): 59–67.

Other studies which reveal the richness of the organizational experiences of the Relief Society are Maureen Ursenbach Beecher, "The Leading Sisters': A Female Hierarchy in Nineteenth Century Mormon Society,"

Journal of Mormon History 9 (1982): 26–39; Beecher, "Women at Winter Quarters," *Sunstone* 8 (July–August 1983): 11–19; Jill Mulvay Derr and Susan Staker Oman, "The Nauvoo Generation: Our First Five Relief Society Presidents," *Ensign*, December 1977, 36–43; Derr, "These Three Women: They Presided over Relief Society in the Twentieth Century," *Ensign*, February 1978, 66–70; Maureen Ursenbach Beecher, "Priestess among the Patriarchs: Eliza R. Snow and the Mormon Female Relief Society, 1842–1887," in *Religion and Society in the American West: Historical Essays*, ed. Carl Guarneri and David Alvarez (Lanhan, MD: University Press of America, 1987), 153–70; Carol Cornwall Madsen, "A Mormon Woman in Victorian America [Emmeline B. Wells]" (PhD diss., University of Utah, 1985); Dixie Shaw Huefner, "Survey of Women General Board Members," *Dialogue* 6 (Summer 1971): 60–70; Carol Lois Clark, "The Effect of Secular Education upon Relief Society Curriculum, 1914–1940" (PhD diss., University of Utah, 1979); Lorretta L. Huefner, "The Decade Was Different: Relief Society's Social Services Department, 1919–1929," *Dialogue* 15 (Autumn 1982): 64–73; Jill Mulvay Derr, "Changing Relief Society Charity to Make Way for Welfare, 1930–1944," in *New Views of Mormon History*, 242–72; David R. Hall, "From Home Service to Social Service: Amy Brown Lyman and the Development of Social Work in the LDS Church," *Mormon Historical Studies* 9 (Fall 2008): 67–88; Hall, "A Crossroads for Mormon Women: Amy Brown Lyman, J. Reuben Clark, and the Decline of Organized Women's Activism in the Relief Society," *Journal of Mormon History* 36 (Spring 2010): 205–49; Tina Hatch, "'Changing Times Bring Changing Conditions': Relief Society, 1910 to the Present," *Dialogue* 37 (Fall 2004): 65–98; Jean Anne Waterstradt, "Relief Society's Golden Years: The Magazine," *Dialogue* 37 (Fall 2004): 99–107; and Barbara B. Smith, "The Relief Society Role in Priesthood Councils," *Ensign*, November 1979, 83–85. For its more complete history, see Jill Mulvay Derr, Janath R. Cannon, and Maureen Ursenbach Beecher, *Women of Covenant: The Story of Relief Society* (Salt Lake City: Deseret Book, 1992).

Mormon Administrative and Organizational History: A Source Essay

Women and authority. To date, the administrative priesthood is held only by males, but there have been interesting aberrations in Mormon history. See Linda King Newell, "A Gift Given, A Gift Taken: Washing, Anointing, and Blessing the Sick among Mormon Women," *Sunstone* 6 (September–October 1980): 16–24; Newell and Valeen Tippetts Avery, "Sweet Counsel and Seas of Tribulation: The Religious Life of Women in Kirtland," *BYU Studies* 20, no. 2 (Winter 1980): 151–62; Maureen Ursenbach Beecher, "A Decade of Mormon Women in the 1870s," *New Era*, April 1978, 34–39; Gail Farr Casterline, "'In the Toils' or 'Onward for Zion': Images of the Mormon Woman, 1852–1890" (master's thesis, Utah State University, 1974); Dixie Shaw Huefner, "Church and Politics and the IWY Conference," *Dialogue* 11 (Spring 1978): 58–75; Linda Sillitoe, "Women Scorned: Inside Utah's IWY Conference," *Utah Holiday*, August 1977, 26ff; and Robert Gottlieb and Peter Wiley, *America's Saints*, 187–213. An important essay on a relevant topic is Linda Wilcox, "The Mormon Concept of a Mother in Heaven," *Sunstone* 5 (September–October 1980): 9–15. See also Maxine Hanks, ed., *Women and Authority: Re-emerging Mormon Feminism* (Salt Lake City: Signature Books, 1992). For a study of a divorced, single, professional Latter-day Saint woman who was able to work within the Church and was able to influence some temple clothing designs and missionary approaches, see the biography of a world-famous swimsuit designer, Carole Reid Burr and Roger K. Petersen, *Rose Marie Reid: An Extraordinary Life Story* (American Fork, UT: Covenant Communications, 1995). The history of Mormon women missionaries and Church policy is surveyed in Calvin S. Kunz, "A History of Female Missionary Activity in the Church of Jesus Christ of Latter-day Saints 1830-1898," (master's thesis: BYU, 1976); Rebecca L. Johns, "A Study of Coded Messages in the Personal Narratives of Female Mormon Missionaries" (PhD diss., University of Utah, 2001); Jessie L. Embry, "LDS Sister Missionaries [1930–70]: An Oral History Response," in *Journal of Mormon History* 23 (Spring, 1997), 100–139; and Tania Rands Lyon and Mary Ann Shumway McFarland, "'Not Invited, But

Welcome': The History and Impact of Church Policy on Sister Missionaries," *Dialogue* 36 (Fall 2003): 71–101.

In recent years, scholars have been looking more closely at the historical and scriptural record on women and priesthood ordination. These include Anthony A. Hutchinson, "Women and Ordination: Introduction to the Biblical Context," *Dialogue* 14 (Winter 1981): 58–74; Nadine Hanson, "Women and the Priesthood," *Dialogue* 14 (Winter 1981): 48–57; Melodie Moench Charles, "Scriptural Precedents for Priesthood," *Dialogue* 18 (Fall 1985): 15–20; Linda King Newell, "The Historical Relationship of Mormon Women and Priesthood," *Dialogue* 18 (Fall 1985): 21–32; Meg Wheatley-Pesci, "An Expanded Definition of Priesthood: Some Present and Future Consequences," *Dialogue*, 33–42; and Shane B. Inglesby, "Priesthood Prescription for Women: The Role of Women as Prescribed in Aaronic Quorum Lesson Manuals," *Sunstone* 10 (March 1985): 28–33. Also valuable are Jill Mulvay Derr and C. Brooklyn Derr, "Outside the Mormon Hierarchy: Alternative Aspects of Institutional Power," *Dialogue* 15 (Winter 1982): 21–43; and Ian G. Barber, "The Ecclesiastical Position of Women in Two Mormon Trajectories," *Journal of Mormon History* 14 (1988): 63–79.

AUXILIARY ORGANIZATIONS

Young Women's and Young Men's Mutual Improvement Associations. The Young Women's organization began in November 1869 as the Cooperative Retrenchment Association, when Brigham Young organized his own daughters into the group. Initially concerned with matters of dress and deportment, it was supervised by Eliza R. Snow. By 1870, each ward in Salt Lake City had a women's organization, and in 1871 it was renamed the Young Ladies' Retrenchment Association. In 1875, a similar organization for the young men was organized. A useful summary is Elaine Anderson Cannon, "Young Women," in the *Encyclopedia of Mormonism*, 4:1616–19. Susa Young Gates wrote the first history of the YWMIA: *History of the Young Ladies' Mutual Improvement Association, November 1869 to June 1910* (Salt Lake City: Deseret News, 1911). In 1955, Marba C. Josephson brought the history up to date in her *History of the Y. W.*

Mormon Administrative and Organizational History: A Source Essay

M. I. A. In 1969, the General Board of the YWMIA published a chronological pictorial collage entitled *A Century of Sisterhood*. A useful study which treats both the men's and women's MIAs is Scott Kenney, "The Mutual Improvement Association: A Preliminary History, 1900–1950," *Task Papers in LDS History*, no. 6 (Salt Lake City: Historical Department, The Church of Jesus Christ of Latter-day Saints, 1976). For information of the young men's organization, organized under the direction of the Priesthood, see Leon M. Strong, "A History of the Young Men's Mutual Improvement Association, 1875–1938" (master's thesis, BYU, 1939); John Kent Williams, "A History of the Young Men's Mutual Improvement Association 1939 to 1974" (master's thesis, BYU, 1976); and Elbert R. Curtis, "The Young Men's Mutual Improvement Association," *Improvement Era*, November 1956, 802ff. See also Asael T. Hansen, "The Role of the Auxiliary Organizations in the Mormon System of Social Control" (PhD diss., University of Wisconsin, 1930). See further, Richard Ian Kimball, *Sports in Zion: Mormon Recreation, 1890–1940* (Urbana: University of Illinois Press, 2003).

Primary Association. Under the direction of President John Taylor, the Primary Association began in 1878, and by the 1880s this organization for young children was functioning in most Mormon wards. Until recently, the only history of the Primary was the personal history of the founder, Aurelia Spencer Rogers, *Life Sketches of Orson Spencer and Others, and History of Primary Work* (Salt Lake City: George Q. Cannon and Sons, 1898). While this work is valuable, the serious student will want to read Carol Cornwall Madsen and Susan Staker Oman, *Sisters and Little Saints: One Hundred Years of Primary* (Salt Lake City: Deseret Book, 1979), and Janet Peterson, *Children's Friends: Primary Presidents and Their Lives of Service* (Salt Lake City: Deseret Book, 1996). See also Jill Mulvay Derr, "Sisters and Little Saints: One Hundred Years of Mormon Primaries," *Task Papers in LDS History*, no. 20 (Salt Lake City: Historical Department, The Church of Jesus Christ of Latter-day Saints, 1978); Susan Staker Oman, "Nurturing LDS Primaries: Louie Felt and May Anderson, 1880–1940," *Utah Historical Quarterly* 49 (Summer 1981): 262–75; Susan Oman and Carol Cornwall Madsen, "One Hundred

Years of Primary," *Ensign*, April 1978, 32–43; and Conrad Afton Harward, "A History of the Growth and Development of the Primary Association of the LDS Church from 1878 to 1928" (master's thesis, BYU, 1976). The official magazine of the Primary Association was published as the *Children's Friend* from 1902–1970 and as the *Friend* from 1971 onward.

Sunday Schools. There is no adequate one-volume history of the Church's Sunday School programs. Borrowed from British-Canadian examples in the 1830s and first established in the Salt Lake Valley in 1849, the Sunday Schools were formally centralized in 1867 when Brigham Young established the "Parent Sunday School Union Society." Thereafter the organization was modified and its name was changed to the Deseret Sunday School Union. In 1971 its name was changed to its current form, the Sunday School of The Church of Jesus Christ of Latter-day Saints. The Sunday Schools have remained important channels for weekly socialization and gospel instruction for all ages in the Church beyond Primary. Two publications have served as official organs of the organization: the *Juvenile Instructor* (1866–1930) and the *Instructor* (1931–70). For many years the lessons and guidelines for the classrooms and organizations were printed in these magazines. Since 1944 separate manuals have been issued for the various classes.

The American context is explored in Anne M. Boylan, *Sunday School: The Formation of an American Institution, 1790–1880* (New Haven: Yale University Press, 1988). An early history was published by George Reynolds and Levi W. Richards, "Historical Review of the Deseret Sunday School Union," *Juvenile Instructor*, October–November 1884, three-part series. In 1900 the first book-length history was published: *Jubilee History of Latter-day Saint Sunday Schools, 1849–1899* (Salt Lake City: Deseret Sunday School Union). Other, shorter studies are A. Hamer Reiser, "Latter-day Saint Sunday Schools," *Improvement Era*, April 1935, 241, 262–63; "Sunday School Centennial Edition, 1849–1949," *Instructor* 84 (December 1949); and J. N. Washburn, "'Ye Have Need That One Teach You': A History of the Sunday Schools of the Church of Jesus Christ of Latter-day Saints," *Instructor*, January–November 1949.

Mormon Administrative and Organizational History: A Source Essay

Church Educational System. From its earliset years, Church leaders have fostered education among its members. Schools were established in Kirtland and Nauvoo, which were followed by others in the Great Basin. Academies or high schools were organized in the 1880s and some became colleges or universities later. Religious education remains a paramount concern as reflected in the existence of seminaries for high-school-age youth and institutes for college-age today. The student of Mormon educational programs should begin with the sources surveyed in David J. Whittaker, "Bibliography: History [of the] Educational System of the LDS Church," *Mormon History Association Newsletter*, no. 68 (April 1988): 2–5. Basic works include Orlen Curtis Peterson, "A History of the Schools and Educational Programs of the Church of Jesus Christ of Latter-day Saints in Ohio and Missouri, 1831–1839" (master's thesis, BYU, 1972); Paul Thomas Smith, "A Historical Study of the Nauvoo, Illinois, Public School System" (master's thesis, BYU, 1969); John Danel Monnett, "The Mormon Church and Its Private School System in Utah: The Emergence of the Academies, 1880–1892" (PhD diss., University of Utah, 1984); Milton Lynn Bennion, "The Origin, Growth, and Extension of the Educational Program of the Mormon Church in Utah" (PhD diss., University of California–Berkeley, 1935); Leonard J. Arrington, "The Founding of the LDS Institutes of Religion," *Dialogue* 2 (Summer 1967): 137–47; William E. Berrett, *A Miracle in Weekday Religious Education: A History of the Church Educational System* (Salt Lake City: printed by the author, 1988); Frank M. Bradshaw, "The Administrative Organization of the Latter-day Saints' Institutes of Religion" (PhD diss., University of Southern California, 1966); Gary James Bergera and Ronald Priddis, *Brigham Young University, A House of Faith* (Salt Lake City: Signature Books, 1985); John L. Fowles, "A Study Concerning the Mission of the Weekday Religious Educational Programs of The Church of Jesus Christ of Latter-day Saints from 1890–1990: A Response to Secular Education" (PhD diss., University of Missouri–Columbia, 1990); and Thomas W. Simpson, "Mormons Study 'Abroad': Latter-day Saints in American Higher Education, 1870–1940" (PhD diss., University of Virginia, 2004).

A Firm Foundation

CHURCH ADMINISTRATIVE UNITS

Introduction. As the Church increased in size and complexity, various administrative units were either created or given additional responsibilities. At the beginning of the twentieth century, as American society was modernizing and bureaucratizing, the Church moved in the same direction by creating specialized departments to handle various chores of the kingdom. Today many of the day-to-day functions of the Church are carried out by these departments. Hence no student of administrative history can ignore these bureaucracies that seek to implement the directives from Church leaders.

Corporate structure. Today the corporate structure of the Church is controlled by the Corporation of the President, which was created in 1921. Under this lead corporation are three major corporations: (1) the *Cooperative Security Program*, which runs the vast welfare program of the Church, including Deseret Industries, Deseret Mines and Elevators, Deseret Transportation, and about 650 separate corporate welfare related corporations; (2) *Deseret Trust*, which administers all the nontaxable ecclesiastical Church properties, including chapels, temples, mission homes, and other nontaxable properties; and (3) *Deseret Management Corporation*, which is responsible for a variety of income-producing properties. The three major subsidiaries of Deseret Management Corporation are (1) *Zion's Securities Corporation* created in 1922, which was responsible for such entities as ZCMI, Beneficial Development Company, Utah Home and Fire, U & I Sugar, Utah Hotel Corporation, Beneficial Life, and other properties and securities; (2) *Bonneville International*, the major communications arm of the Church, which includes BEI Productions, Bonneville Productions, twenty-eight affiliate radio and TV stations and two shortwave stations; and (3) *Deseret News*, which includes Deseret Press, Deseret Book Company, and Deseret Enterprises LTD. A diagram of this corporate structure at the time of the Church's sesquicentennial is in *Dialogue* 15 (Winter 1982): 16. Deseret Trust and Deseret Management Corp. were mistakenly reversed on the printed chart. Very little scholarly attention has been devoted to these corporate structures, which have continued to grow and change, including the 2009 formation of two new operating divisions of Deseret Management Corporation: KSL Broadcasting (split off from Bonneville International and focusing only on KSL-TV and KSL News Radio), and Deseret Digital Media (which will manage the websites and business operations of Deseret News, Deseret Book, and new KSL Broadcasting subsidiaries). Thus Deseret Management has begun to function as an active operating company rather than as a holding company, as it had in the past. See *Deseret News*, September 10, 2009, for the announcement. With the creation of these new divisions, Deseret Management Corporation now comprises nine for-profit divisions: Bonneville International, Deseret Book, Deseret Digital Media, Deseret News, KSL Broadcasting, Beneficial Financial Group, Temple Square Hospitality, Hawaii Reserves Inc., and Zion's Securities. A useful overview in 1979 is in Arrington and Bitton, "The Temporal Foundation" in *The Mormon Experience*, 262–83. The key role of N. Eldon Tanner in Mormon administrative and financial history is suggested in G. Homer Durham, *N. Eldon Tanner, His Life and Service* (Salt Lake City: Deseret Book, 1982).

The Church has not released financial figures for public consumption since 1952. The veil over the financial dealings has led to all kinds of misunderstanding, particularly among the critics of the Church. Studies that attempt to penetrate this veil include Bill Beechan and David Briscoe, "Mormon Money and How It's Made," *Utah Holiday*, March 22, 1976, 4–11; "Change Comes to Zion's Empire," *Business Week*, November 23, 1957, 103–16; Jeffrey Kaye, "An Invisible Empire: Mormon Money in California," *New West*, May 8, 1978, 36–41; Gottlieb and Wiley, *America's Saints*, 95–128; "Leaders of Mormonism Double as Overseers of a Financial Empire," *Wall Street Journal*, November 9; 1983, H. Henderson, "Managing the Mormon Millions," *Executive*, November 1976, 32–35; Randall Hatch, "The Mormon Church: Managing the Lord's Work" *MBA*, June 1977, 33–37; Fred Esplin, "The Saints Go Marching On: Learning to Live with Success," *Utah Holiday* 10 (June 1981): 33–48; John Heinerman and Anson Shupe, *The Mormon Corporate Empire* (Boston: Beacon Press, 1985); "Mormons Inc.: Finances and Faith," a four-part series, *Denver Post*, June

30–July 3, 1991; "Mormons Inc.: The Secret of America's Most Prosperous Religion," *Time Magazine*, July 28, 1997; and D. Michael Quinn, "LDS Church Finances from the 1830s to the 1990s," *Sunstone* 19 (June 1996): 17–29.

A full study of the financial affairs of the Church must begin with Joseph Smith, the first trustee-in-trust. There are insights on Joseph Smith's financial affairs and philosophy in Lyndon W. Cook, *Joseph Smith and the Law of Consecration* (Provo, UT: Grandin Book, 1985); Max Parkin, "Joseph Smith and the United Firm,"; Dallin H. Oaks and Joseph T. Bentley, "Joseph Smith and Legal Process: In the Wake of the Steamboat Nauvoo," *BYU Studies* 19, no. 2 (Winter 1979): 167–99; and Edwin B. Firmage and R. Collin Mangrum, *Zion in the Courts: A Legal History of the Church of Jesus Christ of Latter-day Saints, 1830–1900* (Urbana: University of Illinois Press, 1988). Brigham Young's financial activities are treated in David James Croft, "The Private Business Activities of Brigham Young, 1847–1887," *Journal of the West* 16 (October 1977): 36–51; Arrington, *Great Basin Kingdom*; Arrington, "Mormondom's Financial Records," *This People*, Summer 1991, 46–47; Arrington, "Mormon Finance and the Utah War," *Utah Historical Quarterly* 20 (July 1952): 219–37; Arrington and Ralph W. Hanson, "Mormon Economic Organization: A Sheaf of Illustrative Documents," *Utah Historical Quarterly* 28 (January 1960): 41–55; Arrington, "The Settlement of the Brigham Young Estate 1877–1879," *Pacific Historical Review* 21 (February 1952): 1–20; Dwight L. Israelsen, "Economic Stabilization Through Tithing Prices: Utah 1855–1900," *Encyclia* 54, no. 1 (1977): 75–88. With the stability of Mormon settlement in the Great Basin, more formal administrative structures were established. Because economic prosperity was vital, the organizational devices for managing economic programs were often incorporated into the ecclesiastical structure. In "The Six Pillars of Utah's Pioneer Economy," *Encyclia* 54, no. 1 (1977): 9–24, Arrington identified six organizational devices: the office of trustee-in-trust; the department of public works; the tithing office (later the Presiding Bishop's Office); the Perpetual Emigration Fund; the Relief Society; and the office of Brigham Young, who, as both President of the Church and as a private entrepreneur, sought to apply correct spiritual principles to all areas of life. Each of these institutions needs further study.

The economic wealth of the Church has always depended heavily on the tithes and offerings of individual members. In the nineteenth century tithing came in three forms: cash, commodity, and labor. Since cash was hard to come by, commodities and personal labor (ideally every tenth day individuals or wards donated their labor for a Church-assigned project) were the most common forms of capital. Thus the tithing house was *the* main economic institution. Its early functions are the subject of Arrington, "The Mormon Tithing House: A Frontier Business Institution," *Business History Review* 28 (March 1954): 24–58. As Arrington shows, the functioning of tithing houses delayed the development of commercial banking in Utah. See further, William G. Hartley, "Ward Bishops and the Localizing of LDS Tithing," in *New Views of Mormon History*, 96–114; L. Dwight Israelsen, "Economic Depression, Tithe paying and the Mormon Debt Problem of the 1890s," *Encyclia* 70 (1993): 115–22; E. Jay Bell, "The Window of Heaven Revisited: The 1899 Tithing Reformations," *Journal of Mormon History* 20 (Spring 1994): 45–83; and O. Kendall White Jr., "The Institutionalization of Mormon Tithing: Tithing Settlement, Worthiness Interviews, and Temple Recommends," *Virginia Social Science Journal* 31 (Winter 1996): 38–52.

The Cooperative and United Order movements under Brigham Young are studied in Arrington, *Great Basin Kingdom*, 293–349; and more fully in Arrington, Fox, and May, *Building the City of God*. The movement to a centralized economic board under John Taylor, Zion's Central Board of Trade, is detailed in Leonard J. Arrington, "Zion's Board of Trade: A Third United Order," *Western Humanities Review* 5 (Winter 1950–51): 1–20; and *Building the City of God*, 311–35.

Corporate responses to the economic challenges of the twentieth Century are the subjects of a variety of studies: Albert L. Fisher, "Mormon Welfare Programs: Past and Present," *Social Science Journal* 15 (April 1978): 75–99; Jessie L. Embry, "Relief Society Grain Storage Program, 1876–1940" (master's thesis, BYU, 1974); Bruce D. Blumell, "Welfare before Welfare: Twentieth-Century LDS Church Charity before the Great Depression," *Journal of Mormon History* 6 (1979): 89–106; Betty L. Barton, "Mormon Poor Relief: A Social Welfare Interlude," *BYU Studies* 18, no. 1 (Fall 1977): 66–88; Wayne K. Hinton, "Some Historical Perspective on Mormon Responses to the Great Depression," *Journal of the West* 24 (October 1985): 19–26; Leonard J. Arrington and Wayne K. Hinton, "Origin of the Welfare Plan of the Church of Jesus Christ of Latter-day Saints," *BYU Studies* 5, no. 2 (Winter 1964): 67–85; Paul C. Child, "Physical Beginnings of the Church Welfare Program," *BYU Studies* 14, no. 3 (Spring 1974): 383–85; Vearl Gordon McBride, "The Welfare Program of the Church of Jesus Christ of Latter-day Saints" (master's thesis, Arizona State University, 1970); M. Randall Rathjen, "Evolution and Development of the Mormon Welfare Farms" (PhD diss., Michigan State University, 1969); Dan Larue Free, "The Sources, Organization and Operation of the Mormon Welfare Program in Utah and Colorado, 1936–1959" (master's thesis, Denver University, 1961); Garth L. Mangum and Bruce D. Blumell, *The Mormons' War on Poverty: A History of LDS Welfare, 1830–1990* (Salt Lake City: University of Utah Press, 1993); William G. Hartley, "Saints and the San Francisco Earthquake," *BYU Studies* 23, no. 4 (Fall 1983): 430–59; Bruce D. Blumell, "The Latter-day Saint Response to the Teton, Idaho, Flood, 1976," *Task Papers in LDS History*, no. 16 (Salt Lake City: Historical Department, The Church of Jesus Christ of Latter-day Saints, 1976); Blumell, "The LDS Response to the Teton Dam Disaster in Idaho," *Sunstone* 5 (March–April 1980): 35–42; and Janet Thomas and others, eds., *That Day in June: Reflections on the Teton Dam Disaster* (Rexburg, ID: Ricks College Press, 1977).

From 1982 to 1984, the whole system of welfare farms was reevaluated by Church leaders and in November 1984 it was announced that about 70 percent of these farms were to be sold or leased to avoid competition with private farmers. The shift of the Church membership to the south of the United States border in recent years has also witnessed changes in the administration of welfare programs. See Bradley Walker, "Spreading Zion Southward: Improving Efficiency and Equity in the Allocation of Church Welfare Resources,"

Dialogue 35 (Winter 2002): 91–109; Walker, "Spreading Zion Southward, Part II: Sharing Our Loaves and Fishes," *Dialogue* 36 (Spring 2003): 33–47; and Walker, "First, Mothers and Children: A Postscript to 'Moving Zion Southward, Parts I and II,'" *Dialogue* 36 (Fall 2003): 217–23.

Major Departments. Today, the administrative structure of the Church is directed by Church leaders through a number of professionally staffed departments. These departments include Audiovisual, Church Auditing, Church Educational System (includes BYU, BYU–Idaho, BYU–Hawaii, and LDS Business College, in addition to the extensive Seminaries and Institutes of Religion programs), Church Security, City Creek Reserve Inc., Correlation, Curriculum, Temporal Affairs, Family and Church History Department (including the Church Museum), Finance and Records, Human Resources, Information and Communication Systems, Investment Properties, Investment Securities, LDS Family Services, LDS Philanthropies, Materials Management, Missionary, Perpetual Education Fund, Physical Facilities, Priesthood (which oversees military relations, Music and Cultural Arts, Primary, Relief Society, Sunday School, Young Men, and Young Women), Public Affairs, Tabernacle Choir, Temple Department, Translation, and Welfare Services. In addition, there is an office of General Counsel. This organizational reality reflects the size and breadth of the Church, but it also suggests that the initial organization under Joseph Smith was flexible enough to permit growth and adjustment to new challenges. It all remains under the leadership of the First Presidency and Quorum of the Twelve Apostles, just as it did under Joseph Smith by 1844.

Here we can only look at two departments; we focus on them because of their critical role in record keeping.

Historical Department. On the day the Church was organized, Joseph Smith revealed to his followers a commandment that a record should be kept of the movement (D&C 21:1). While personal records have been maintained, large quantities of institutional records have been kept on just about every aspect of the Church. Most of these records are now housed in the Church History Library in Salt Lake City.

Various individuals have received assignments to be the Church historian and recorder since Joseph Smith's day. The Office of Church Historian has been given the major responsibility of record keeping, the writing of histories, and the care and preservation of these records. The existence of a large quantity of records today testifies to their dedication and hard work.

No one study covers the entire history of this department. An overview of its activities in the nineteenth century is in Charles D. Adams and Gustive O. Larson, "A Study of the LDS Church Historians Office, 1830–1900," *Utah Historical Quarterly* 40 (Fall 1972): 370–89. A list of Church historians and general Church recorders was compiled by Leonard J. Arrington in *Dialogue* 3 (Summer 1968): 66. An overview, with detailed bibliography, of the history of Mormon historical writing which considers both institutional and private Mormon histories and historians within the larger context of American historical work is found in Leonard J. Arrington and Davis Bitton, *The Mormons and Their Historians* (Salt Lake City: University of Utah Press, 1988); and Ronald W. Walker, David J. Whittaker, and James B. Allen, *Mormon History* (Urbana: University of Illinois Press, 2002).

The more recent years are surveyed in Peggy Fletcher, "Church Historian: Evolution of a Calling," *Sunstone* 10, no. 4 (April 1985): 46–48; Leonard J. Arrington, "Joseph Fielding Smith: Faithful Historian," *Dialogue* 7 (Spring 1972): 21–24; Arrington, "Historian as Entrepreneur: A Personal Essay," *BYU Studies* 17 (Winter 1977): 193–209; "History Is Then and Now: A Conversation with Leonard J. Arrington, Church Historian," *Ensign*, July 1975, 8–13; Davis Bitton, "Ten Years in Camelot: A Personal Memoir," *Dialogue* 16 (Fall 1983): 933; and T. Edgar Lyon, "Church Historians I Have Known," *Dialogue* 11 (Winter 1978): 14–22. See also Leonard J. Arrington, *Adventures of a Church Historian* (Urbana: University of Illinois Press, 1998); and Marlin K. Jensen, "Church History: Past, Present and Future," *Journal of Mormon History* 34 (Spring 2008): 20–42.

As assistant Church historian, Andrew Jenson was responsible for a variety of projects that are important for students of administrative history.

Mormon Administrative and Organizational History: A Source Essay

During his tenure in the Historical Department (1893–1941), he traveled extensively and compiled histories of wards, stakes, missions, and organizations of the Church, many of which remain unpublished. A useful study of Jenson's work is Keith W. Perkins, "A Study of the Contributions of Andrew Jenson to the Writing and Preservation of LDS Church History" (master's thesis, BYU, 1971). More broadly, see Richard E. Turley, "Assistant Church Historians and the Publication of Church History," in *Preserving the History of Latter-day Saints* (Provo, UT: Religious Studies Center, BYU; Salt Lake City: Deseret Book, 2010), 19–47.

Family History Department/Library. Also of great value is the Family History Library of the Church, both because of its central role in gathering genealogical information in the Mormon practice of vicarious work for the dead and because of the great amount of Church energy and money that have been invested in its growth and operation. It has become the largest genealogical library in the world. The best overviews currently available are Merrill S. Lofthouse, "A History of the Genealogical Society of the Church of Jesus Christ of Latter-day Saints" (master's thesis, BYU, 1971); Elizabeth L. Nicholls, "The Genealogical Society of the Church of Jesus Christ of Latter-day Saints," *Genealogical Journal*, 1972, 108–12; William R. Bruce, "The Utah Genealogical Society" (master's thesis, University of Chicago, 1956); and James B. Allen, Jessie L. Embry, and Kalile Mehr, *Hearts Turned to the Fathers: A History of the Genealogical Society of The Church of Jesus Christ of Latter-day Saints* (Provo, UT: BYU Press, 1994). Information on its various activities, including its worldwide micro-filming activities are Archibald F. Bennett, "The Record Copying Program of the Utah Genealogical Society," *The American Archivist* 16 (July 1953): 227–32; JoAnn Jolley, "The World Conference on Records: Writing the History of the Heart," *Ensign*, February 1980, 72–75; and Kahlile B. Mehr, "Preserving the Source, Early Microfilming Efforts of the Genealogical Society of Utah" (master's thesis, BYU, 1985). Also valuable is the oral history of James M. Black, a Church microfilmer from 1938 to 1972, manuscript in Church History Library.

A Firm Foundation

THE CHURCH AND ITS MISSION: A THEOLOGY OF CHURCH GOVERNMENT

Central to its divine mission are three goals that have been enunciated in recent years: to preach the gospel, to perfect the Saints, and to redeem the dead. See Spencer W. Kimball, "A Report of My Stewardship," *Ensign*, May 1981, 5. A fourth goal, always implied but more recently stated, is to care for the poor. Everything else the Church as an organization does is subsumed by and subordinated to these four central areas. All were preached during Joseph Smith's presidency, and while the programs used to achieve them have been changed and modified in the years since, they remain the core vocation and errand of its leaders and members. These goals, founded on the rock of revelation and restored priesthood authority, remain the firm foundation of the Church. As President Gordon B. Hinckley noted in 2005: "The remarkable organization of the Church was framed by him as he was directed by revelation, and no modification or adaption of that organization is ever considered without searching the revelations set forth by the Prophet" (*Ensign*, December 2005, 2).

From its earliest years, Joseph Smith's approach to Church government was to combine divine direction with a deep love for the membership. "I teach them correct principles and they govern themselves," Joseph Smith is reported to have taught, according to John Taylor ("The Organization of the Church," *Millennial Star*, November 15, 1851, 339). He further said, "Sectarian priests cry out concerning me, and ask, 'Why is it that babbler gains so many followers, and retains them?' I answer, it is because I possess the principle of love" (Discourse, July 9, 1843, in Joseph Smith diary, kept by Willard Richards, Church History Library). He also said, "A man of God should be endowed with wisdom, knowledge, and understanding, in order to teach and lead the people of God" (June 11, 1843, in Wilford Woodruff, journal, Church History Library). Faithful Latter-day Saints strongly believe that their leaders are the men of God Joseph spoke of.

At the heart of all these concerns about organization was Joseph Smith's teaching that it was the purpose of the priesthood "to direct man to godliness"

Mormon Administrative and Organizational History: A Source Essay

(Joseph Smith discourse, May 12, 1844, report of Thomas Bullock, cited in *The Words of Joseph Smith*, 366), to have the divine authority to administer the saving ordinances and correct teachings for mankind to be exalted. An early revelation (June 1830) informed Joseph Smith that it was God's purpose "to bring to pass the immortality and eternal life of man." (Moses 1:39)

Wilson K. Anderson, who taught a course on priesthood and Church government at BYU for years, suggested that the priesthood could be studied under five definitions: (1) priesthood is *authority*, the exclusive right, recognized and commissioned by God, to act in his name; (2) priesthood is *an organization*, a brotherhood, a government, organized by quorums and conducted by councils; (3) priesthood is the *divine channel of communication*; (4) priesthood is *a divine physical and spiritual power* delegated to intelligences; and (5) priesthood is the *foundation of the rights, powers, and privileges of the family*, both in time and in the eternities. Each of these aspects could be the subject of a book, as each lay at the heart of Mormon administrative history. With Brigham Young, we could say:

> There is no other people on this earth under such deep obligation to their Creator, as are the Latter-day Saints. The Gospel has brought to us the holy Priesthood, which is again restored to the children of men. The keys of the Priesthood are here; we have them in our possession; we can unlock, and we can shut up. We can obtain salvation, and we can administer it. We have the power within our own hands, and this has been my deepest mortification, one that I have frequently spoke of, to think that a people, having in their possession all the principles, keys and powers of eternal life, should neglect so great salvation. We have these blessings, they are with us. (in *Journal of Discourses*, 4:299, discourse of March 29, 1857)

NOTE

I would like to thank Arnold K. Garr, William G. Hartley, and James B. Allen for their reviews of an earlier draft of this essay.

Index

Italicized page numbers refer to images.

Aaronic Priesthood: in Book of Mormon, 37–38; restoration of, 60, 68, 118; keys to, 71–77; during progressive period, 303–4; under Brigham Young, 626; historical studies on, 628–29

Aaronic Priesthood Encampment, 545

Aaronic Priesthood Mutual Improvement Association, 476–77

Aberhart, William, 488–90

accountability, age of, 40

Acre, Nelson, 47

Adams, George J., 163

Adams, Samuel L., 466–67

administrative history: general histories, 613–20; succession crisis and, 620–24; of Brigham Young, 624–27; 1878–1918 period, 627–29; 1919–2000 period, 629–33; contemporary publications on, 633–41; administrative studies, 641–58; of priesthood offices and quorums, 658–78; women and, 678–82; of auxiliary organizations, 682–86; of Church administrative units, 686–94

Alexander, Thomas G., 251

Allen, James B., 342

Amalgamated Correlation–Social Advisory Committee, 326–29

Amherst conference, 105, 127–28, 130

Anderson, Edward H., 307, 467, 471–72

Anderson, Joseph, 499

Anderson, Richard Lloyd, 604

Anderson, Wilson K., 695

Anderson Plan, 604–5

Angell, Truman O., 144

Apostasy, 62–64, 78n9, 79n15

Apostle(s): Joseph Smith and Oliver Cowdery ordained as, 62, 116; priesthood keys and, 71–77;

Index

Three Witnesses as, 120–21; in early Church, 135nn21–22; missionary work and, 595–96, 598–600; mission presidents and, 601–2; as title, 61, 135n21. *See also* Quorum of the Twelve Apostles; Quorums of the Seventies

Aquinas, Thomas, 224

architects, for meetinghouses, 311

Area Authorities, 585–88

area conferences, 525–26

area leaders, 671–73

Area Presidencies, 584–85

areas, 577–80, 590–91

Area Seventies, 585–88

Arrington, Leonard J., 342

Articles and Covenants: basic unit program and, 93–94; Church organization and administration in, 89–93; conferences and councils in, 100; in early Church, 85–89; writing and revelation of, 84–85; "Articles of the Church of Christ," 17–24, 51nn3–4

Ashton, Marvin J., 477

Ashton, Marvin O., 405, *406*, 407–9, 411–12, 425–26, 431

Assistant President, 111, 132, 176, 665, 666

Assistant Presiding Bishop, 674

Assistants to the Twelve, 575–77, 578, 581, 672

Associate President, 665

auditing committee, 297

auxiliary organizations, 300, 309, 322, 479, 682–86. *See also* correlation; specific organizations

babies: blessing, 41, 92; health work for, 364, 366–69; Utah infant mortality rates, 374n27

backbiting, 91–92

Backman, Gus P., 405

Backman, Robert L., 477, 478

Badger, Rodney C., 472

Ballantyne, Richard, 322

Ballard, Melvin, 405

Ballard, M. Russell, 355

Bangerter, W. Grant, 522, 523

Bankhead, Reid, 604

baptism: of Joseph Smith and Oliver Cowdery, 60, 68–69; ordinance of, 38–40; qualifications and authority for, 37–38, 90

basic unit program, 93–94

Bauer, Jerry, 536

Beaudoin, René, 492

beautification movement: Church Improvement and Beautification Committee and, 407, 410–12; continuation of, 428–31; effects of, 415–21; end of, 433–34; home beautification and, 421–23; launch and promotion of, 407–10;

non-LDS organizations and, 414–15; pioneer centennial and, 405–7; under Presiding Bishopric, 412–13; as priority, 426–28; in Utah, 404–5; welfare program and, 405; World War II and, 423–26
Beehive program, 281
Belliston, Angus, 537
Belliston, Jenny, 537
Bennett, Richard E., 202
Bennett, Rose W., 407
Bennion, Adam S., 334, 383, 384, 387, 399n16
Benson, Ezra T., 116, 182–83
Benson, Ezra Taft, 350–51, 511, 523
Bentley, Joseph T., 474
Berger, Johanna, 558
Berndt, Otto, 565
Beyal, Anthony, 538–39
Beyal, Brenda, 538, 544–45
Bible Questions and Answers for Children (Snow), 232–34, *234*, 262–63
Biehl, Friedrich Ludwig, 561, *562*, 562–63, 569
bishop of the Church. *See* Presiding Bishop
bishops, 11–12, 104, 105, 673–78
bishop's agent, 674
Blakesley, James, 182
Blanchard, James, 46–47
blessing(s): of babies, 41, 92; patriarchal, 41
Blood, Henry H., 405
Bolt, Robert, 59
bonds, 296
Bonneville International Corporation, 347, 352, 686
Book of Commandments, 85, 102
Book of Mormon: administrative principles in, 15–17, 33–49; in "Articles of the Church of Christ," 17–24; in Doctrine and Covenants, 24–25; *Questions and Answers on the Book of Mormon* (Cannon), 234–36; use of, in early Church, 25–33, 53n34
Bowen, Albert, 405, 474
Boynton, John, 28
Boy Scouts of America, 475, 537, 630
Bradshaw, Merrill, 504–5, 509, 514
branches, 93–94
Branch Guidebook, 93
Brigham Young University, 346, 388–89, 498
Brimhall, Kathy, 541, 543
Brimhall, Paul, 539
British Mission, 213–14, 215n2, 578
British Saints. *See* emigration
broadcast media. *See* electronic media
Brown, Hugh B., 493–94, 495
Brown, Sara Edna, 486
Brown, Victor L., 287, 464, 477, 479–80
Budge, William, 211, 214
Building Committee, 496–97

Bulletin, 641
bureaucratic government, 2–6
Burkhardt, Henry, 526
Burrows, Josiah, 469
Burton, Robert T., 298
Burton, William, 186
Bushman, Richard L., 44, 56n64, 662
BYU Television, 346, 347, 352, 358n29, 358n42

Cahoon, Reynolds, 41
Calkin, Asa, 213
Call, Whitney, 548–49
callings: authority for, 553–54; in early Church, 36; sustaining, 8–9, 92, 122, 637–38; transformation after, 12; volunteerism and, 43–44
Cameron, Averil, 340
Campbell, Alexander, 165
Cannon, Abraham H., 234–36
Cannon, Elaine Anderson, 288–89
Cannon, George Q.: emigration and, 210, 219n35; on Holy Ghost and priesthood ordinations, 69; improvement associations and, 467; as president of British Mission, 214
Cannon, Lucy Grant, 283–84
Cannon, Sylvester Q., 308, 405
Cannon, Tracy Y., 514
Carmack, John K., 585
Carrington, Albert, 211, 214
Carter, Simeon, 87

Castillo, Manuel Jesus, 537–38
Castle Garden Immigration Depot, 207
Catechism for Children, Exhibiting the Prominent Doctrines of the Church of Jesus Christ of Latter-day Saints (Jaques), 229–31, *230*
"Catechism of New England, The," 224
catechism(s): Christian tradition of, 224–25; decline of LDS, 240; historical studies on, 624; influence of, 237–40; LDS, publications, 229–31; LDS tradition of, 225–28; in modern Church, 240–41; Primary Association and, 262–63; proliferation of, 231–37; reformation and, 228–29
centennial, of Church, 405–7, 411, 429, 431–33, 441n89
Centennial Commission, 414–15, 424, 426
Cetz, Richardo, 539
charisma, 2–7, 12, 13n5
Cherry, Alan, 541, 542, 545
children: Ardeth G. Kapp and, 453–54; as congregation members, 43; health work for, 364, 366–69. *See also* Primary Association
Children's Primary Hymn Book, 261–62
Children's Primary Tune Book, 262
cholera, 139, 205, 207

Index

Christensen, D. H., 392
Church Building Committee, 496–97
Church courts, 306. *See also* disciplinary procedures
Church Educational System: Commissioners of Church Schools and, 399n16; establishment of institute program, 384–86; historical studies on, 685; preservation of Church schools, 386–91; seminary program, 381–83, 391–95
Church Handbook of Instructions, 34–35, 42, 46, 48, 50
Church handbooks, 638–41. *See also Church Handbook of Instructions*
Church Historian, 692–93
Church Improvement and Beautification Committee, 407, 410–12
church meetings, 42–43, 89, 304–5, 528, 633
Church membership, 40, 92, 298–99
Church Music Committee, 504–12
Church Music Department, 504
Church of Christ: administrative principles for, 33–49; Articles and Covenants in, 85–89; Book of Mormon use in, 25–33; conferences and councils in, 100–104; names, leaders, and congregations of, 35–37; priesthood offices in, 658; studies on organization of, 615–16
Church of Jesus Christ of Latter-day Saints: administrative units of, 686–94; authority in, 7–9; debts of, 295–97; disciplinary procedures in, 46–47, 92–93; expansion of, 313; form of government in, 1–2, 12; growth of, 286, 345, 347, 353, 354, 644–45; mission of, 694–95. *See also* administrative history; names of, 616; organization of, 3–6; practices and policies for, 48–49; prerequisites for joining, 38–39; property of, 308–12
Church Radio, Publicity and Mission Literature Committee, 343
Church Security Plan, 404, 405, 630
Church Welfare Plan, 370, 405, 421, 529
city planning, 618
Clark, J. Reuben Jr., 330–32, 333
Clawson, Rudger, 297, 308
Clayton, William, 167, 175, 180, 183
clerks, 665–66
Cloward, Bryndi, 546–47
colonization, 653–55. *See also* emigration
Committee of Correlation and Coordination, 330–31
Committee on Publications, 333
common consent, 8–9, 43, 92, 101, 107, 122, 637–38

communication media. *See* electronic media

community, 648–50

conferences and councils: defined, 99–100; in early Church, 100–104; high priesthood and, 104–6; historical studies on, 661–63; organization of, 106–7; publications on, 636–37; organization of first High Council, 108–11; questions and answers on, 92; confirmation, 91, 119, 134n13

congregations, according to Book of Mormon, 36–37, 42–43

Conrad, Clara, 267

consecration, 42, 617–18, 624

Constitution of the United States, 84

Cooperative Security Program, 686

Cordoba, Alfredo, 539

Cordoba, Juliana, 539

Corporation of the President, 310, 313, 629, 686

correlation: Amalgamated Correlation–Social Advisory Committee and, 326–29; Committee of Correlation and Coordination and, 330–31; Committee on Publications and, 333; Correlation Committee and, 325–26; curriculum and, 322–23; establishment of, 285–86; General Priesthood Committee on Outlines and, 323–25; Harold B. Lee committee and, 334–35; historical studies on, 632–33; impetus for, 321–22; as inspired development, 320–21; Social Advisory Committee and, 326; Sunday School cooperative and, 329–30; Union Board of the Auxiliaries and, 331–32

Correlation Committee, 325–26

Corrill, John, 124, 125

Cotton, John, 224

Council of Fifty, 147, 176–77, 178, 180, 621–22

Cowdery, Oliver: as Apostle, 71–77, 116, 117; Articles and Covenants and, 84–85; "Articles of the Church of Christ" and, 18–22; as Assistant President, 132, 665; authority of, 124–25; authorized as elder, 35; Book of Mormon and, 49; on catechisms, 227; in conferences and councils, 101, 102, 103; organization of Church and, 16, 23, 658; Orson Pratt's correspondence with, 63–64; as presiding council member, 106; on priesthood and missionary work, 65; priesthood ordination of, 60, 61–62, 118–19; on priesthood restoration, 66–68; receives baptism and Holy Ghost, 68–69; revelation

and, 120, 134n18; as scribe, 665; as second elder, 120, 121
Crosby, Caroline, 144
Cullertson, Robert, 87–88
Curtis, Elbert R., 474
Curtis, LeGrand R., 477

Dalton, Elaine S., 291, 449
Danite Band, 619
deacons, 302–3
deaf ward, 544–45, 546–47
debt, 295–97
democracy, 7–11
demographic studies, 644–45
Department on Beautification, 426
Deseret Digital Media, 687
Deseret Gymnasium, 310–11
Deseret Management Corporation, 686, 687
Deseret Theological Class, 466
Deseret Trust, 686
Dew, Sheri L., 350
Didier, Charles A., 585
Diefenbaker, John F., 492
disciplinary procedures, 46–47, 92–93
dispersion, 313
diversity, 451–52, 533–49, 646
Doctrine and Covenants, 24–25
Domiciano, Liriel, 446
Douglas, Clifford Hugh, 488–89
Driggs, Howard R., 326
Dwyke, Sister, 257

early Church. *See* Church of Christ
East German Mission, 555–61, 569–70
Edgley, Richard C., 596
Edmunds-Tucker Act (1887), 295
education: of Ardeth G. Kapp, 452–54; in Church, 47–48; Relief Society and, 361–71. *See also* Church Educational System
Eldredge, Horace S., 214
Eldridge, Jay G., 386, 474
election, 122
electronic media: David O. McKay and, 345–47; Ezra Taft Benson and, 350–51; future of Church and, 354–56; George Albert Smith and, 345; Gordon B. Hinckley and, 351–53; Harold B. Lee and, 348; Heber J. Grant and, 342–45; Howard W. Hunter and, 351; Joseph Fielding Smith and, 348; missionary work and, 607–8; religion and, 340–42; Spencer W. Kimball and, 348–50
Elliott, Bradford, 140
Embry, Jessie, 533–35, 544, 548
emigration: cost and needs of, 204–6; Erastus Snow and, 206–7; James H. Hart and, 211–13; John Taylor and, 208–10; organization and administration of, 199–204; port changes in, 207–8; studies on,

651–55; William C. Staines and, 210–11
endowment, 142–43, 153–54, 180
equality, 452–53
Equal Rights Amendment, 528–29
Esplin, Ronald K., 176
European Mission, 577–78
Evans, Richard L., 447
Evening and Morning Star, 86, 87–88
Everett, Addison, 70–71
excommunication, 46–47, 92–93
Eyring, Henry B., 599–600

faith, 226
Family Guidebook, 93–94
Family History Department/Library, 693–94
Fassmann, Erika, *558*
Faust, James E., 477
Fayette conference, 100–101
Featherstone, Vaughn J., 452
Federal Maternity and Infancy Act (1921), 365–69, 370
Felt, Joseph, 266
Felt, Louie B., 245–46, 254, 264–69
Felt, Nathaniel H., 206, 210
Female Relief Society, 176, 465, 679–80
Fetzer, Emil, 526
Fielding, Joseph, 213
financial affairs, of Church, 295–97, 687–91

Finke, Roger, 340
First Council of the Seventy, 300–302, 527, 574–80
First Presidency: bishop of the Church and, 123–25; establishment of, 130–31, 321; historical studies on, 663–65; Joseph Smith and, 119–22, 125–30; mission presidents and, 601; precursors to, 118–19; Seventies administrative changes and, 301–2; succession and, 76–77, 166, 306–8
First Quorum(s) of the Seventy: area presidencies and, 584–85; beginnings of, 140–43; historical studies on, 669–70; organization of, 98, 527, 580–84
"Fix It or Burn It" (Ashton), 425–26
Follett, King, 144
Fordham, George, 140
foreign-language wards, 537–41, 544–45
For the Strength of Youth, 241, 285, 288, 290
Fox, Ruth May, 268, 282–83
Franklin Second Ward, 538–39, 541–42, 544–45
Freeze, Lillie Tuckett, 265, 267
Freeze, Mary Ann, 266, 267
Freiberg Temple, 526
Frontier Guardian, 204
Funk, Ruth Hardy, 284, 287–88

Index

Gabbott, Mabel Jones, 240–41
Gardner, George, 466
Gates, Susa Young, 268, 280, 292, 362
gathering: cost and needs of, 204–6; Erastus Snow and, 206–7; historical studies on, 619, 651–55; James H. Hart and, 211–13; John Taylor and, 208–10; organization and administration of, 199–204; port changes in, 207–8; William C. Staines and, 210–11
Gause, Jesse, 105, 128–29, 130, 658, 663
Gee, Elias, 260
genealogy, 693
General Authorities: authority of, 7; dispersion of Saints and, 313; emeritus status for, 527; living allowance for, 312, 330; responsibilities of, 579; Seventies as, 574–76, 582–84; studies on, 641–43
General Conference, 102, 346, 636–37
General Handbook of Instruction, 641
General Music Committee, 504
General Priesthood Committee on Outlines, 323–25
George III, 11
Gibbons, Francis M., 346
Gibson, William, 203
Gilbert, Algernon Sidney, 106
girls' camp, 545
Glade, Earl J., 425

Goaslind, Jack H. Jr., 477
Goddard, Hyrum H., 470
godly power, 9–10
Goodman, Harold, 504, 505
Gosain, Claudia, 540, 545
government(s): according to Book of Mormon, 35–37; charismatic, 2–3; form of, in Church, 1–2, 12; Joseph Smith and, 3–6; purpose and authority of, 227
Grant, Brigham F., 307
Grant, Heber J.: administrative changes under, 309; blesses Ruth May Fox, 282; catechisms and, 238–39; Church education and, 378, 388, 392; Church finances and, 296, 297; correlation and, 327–28, 330–31; electronic media and, 342–45, 353, 357n19; meetinghouses and, 311–12; succession and, 306–8; YMMIA and, 470
Grant, Jedediah M., 163, 164
grass roots, 648–50
Greene, Edwin Kent, 456–57
Greene, Julia (June) Leavitt, 454–56, 457
Greenwood, Joshua, 392
Groberg, John H., 585
Groves, Alan, 541, 542, 545

Hafen, Bruce C., 319
Hales, Janette Callister, 289–90

Hammond, F. Melvin, 585
handbooks, 638–41. See also *Church Handbook of Instructions*
Hanks, Marion D., 477
Harding, Warren G., 343
Hardy, Milton H., 470, 472
Harris, Franklin S., 388–89
Harris, Martin, 120
Hart, Edward L., 212
Hart, James H., 211–13
Hatch, Nathan, 341
Haun's Mill Massacre, 146
Haycock, Arthur, 521–22
healing the sick, 41
health work, Relief Society and, 361–71
Heck, Christian, *552*, 563–66, *565*, *568*, 569
Hedlock, Reuben, 213
Herrick, Lester J., 214
Heschel, Abraham, 660
"He Sent His Son," 240–41
Hess, John W., 247, 248, 249
High Council of the Church of Christ, 98, 106, 108–11
high councils, 662
high priesthood, 104–11, 124, 126–30, 577
Hill, Richard, 537
Hinckley, Gordon B.: on Area Authorities, 586; on Church presidencies, 584; electronic media and, 343, 346, 347, 348, 351–53; First Quorum of the Seventy and, 527; Freiberg Temple and, 526; hymnbook and, 512, 518n47; Joseph F. Merrill and, 397; on LDS youth, 291; *Preach My Gospel* and, 603; on organization of Church, 694
Hinckley, Richard G., 596, 597
Historical Department, 692–93
historical studies: on 1878–1918 period, 627–29; on 1919–2000 period, 629–33; administrative studies, 641–58; on auxiliary organizations, 682–86; on Brigham Young, 624–27; on Church administrative units, 686–94; general histories, 613–20; on priesthood offices and quorums, 658–78; on succession crisis, 620–24; on women and Church, 678–82
Hofmann, Mark, 528, 621
holiness, walking in, 88
Holland, Jeffrey R., 587, 596
Hollingsworth, C. R., 387
Holt, George A., 407
Holy Ghost, 38, 40, 68–69, 91
home economics, 363
Homefront series, 248
homes, beautification of, 421–23
home teaching program, 648–50
Horn, Mary I., 265
Howe, Stephen, 543

Index

Huck, Anton, 563, 565, 566–68
Hughes, Howard, 528
Hunter, Edward, 147, 158nn29–30, 626, 671, 674
Hunter, Howard W., 351
Huntsman, Jesse, 140
Hurlbut, Philastus, 106
Hutchings, Elias, 140
Hyde, Annie Laura, 380
Hyde, Jeannette Acord, 362, 369
Hyde, Orson: on Apostasy, 62, 63; baptism and, 29; *Frontier Guardian* and, 204; mission of, 78n9; as president of British Mission, 213; on priesthood restoration, 65; revelation for, 102–3
hymnbook, 261–62, *502*, 503–14
Hymnbook Task Committee, 505–12
Hymns and Songs: Selected from Various Authors for the Primary Associations of Children of Zion, 261–62
Hymns: The Church of Jesus Christ of Latter-day Saints, 504

Improvement Era, 287, 302, 330, 641
Innis, Harold, 341
innovation, 339, 450–51
institute, establishment of, 384–86
Instructor, 684
interests, developing, 447–48
Internet, 352, 354, 355–56, 608
Isaacson, Thorpe B., 431, 496–97

Israel, gathering. *See* gathering
Ivins, Anthony W., 308, 309, 327–28, 474

Jack, Mary R., 407, 412
Jacobsen, Florence Smith, 286–87
James, 60–62
Jaques, John, 229–31
Jenson, Andrew, 693
Jeske, Max, 560
Johnson, August L., 434
Johnson, Benjamin, 144–45, 183
Johnson, James H., 212
Johnson, Noah, 140
John the Baptist, 60–61
John the Beloved, 60–62
Jones, Nathaniel V., 214
Jones, Randall L., 425
Josephson, Marba C., 278
journal keeping, 26–29, 446–47
Juarez, Blanca, 539, 540
Juvenile Instructor, 236, 684

Kane, Thomas L., 627
Kapp, Ardeth Greene: administration of, 289; correlation and, 285–86; on Young Women organization, 287
Kapp, Heber, 447
Kaw Township conference, 127
Kays-Burden, Angela, 291
Keeler, Joseph B., 638–39

Index

Kennedy, David, 525
Kent, Nancy, 170
Kerksiek, Walter, 416–18
keys: First Presidency and, 131, 663–64; Oliver Cowdery and, 121; restoration of, 71–77, 118–19, 134n12; succession crisis and, 172–73
Kimball, Heber C.: Aurelia Spencer Rogers and, 246; on authority of Joseph Smith, 73; on Brigham Young as prophet, 6; called to First Presidency, 117; on ease of Joseph Smith, 177; emigration and, 215n2; on First Presidency, 117; mission of, 164; on ordination of Apostles, 120; as president of British Mission, 213; on priesthood restoration, 135n20; on Seventies, 149; succession crisis and, 168, 183; YMMIA and, 465, 466–67; Young Women program and, 278
Kimball, J. Golden, 300–301
Kimball, J. LeRoy, 155
Kimball, Spencer W., *520*; area conferences and, 525–26; assumes Church presidency, 521–23; beautification and, 442n107; church meeting changes under, 528; Church Welfare Program and, 529; doctrine under, 529–30; electronic media and, 340, 348–50, 353;

hymnbook and, 505, 517n20; missionary work and, 523–25; organizational changes under, 527–28; on priesthood and correlation, 285; publicity and, 528; Quorums of the Seventy and, 321, 575–76, 581; revelation on priesthood and, 530–31; temple building and, 526–27; YMMIA and, 288–89, 478, 479
King, Randy, 538–39
King, William H., 370
Kirkham, James M., *406*, 412, 421–23, 424, 434, 437n28
Kirtland Camp, 146
Kirtland high council, 662
Kirtland Safety Society Anti-Banking Company, 144, 145–46, 618
Kirtland Temple, 98, 142–43
Klopfer, Erna, 557, 559, 561
Klopfer, Herbert, 555–59, *558*, *568*, 569
Knight, Jennie B., 407
Knight, Vinson, 670
KSL Broadcasting, 342–43, 345, 352, 687

Langheinrich, Paul, 556–60, *558*, 564
Larsen, Benjamin, 546
Larsen, Dean L., 512, 579
Larsen, J. H., 409–10
last charge, 172–73, 174
Latter-day Saints' Psalmody, 504

Latter-day Saints' Sunday School Treatise, The, 236–37
Law, William, 178
LDS College, 390
LDS Foundation, 498
LDS Philanthropies, 498
leadership: according to Book of Mormon, 35–37; charismatic, 2–3; form of, in Church, 1–2, 12; Joseph Smith and, 3–6
LeBaron, Ervil, 528
Lectures on Faith, 226–27
Lee, Ann, 180
Lee, Harold B., *318*; Church Music Department and, 504; on Church organization, xi–xii; correlation and, 285, 320, 322–23, 333, 334–35; death of, 521–22; electronic media and, 348; First Council of the Seventy and, 577; influence of, 463–64; N. Eldon Tanner and, 492, 498; YMMIA and, 476–77, 479, 480; on youth and leadership, 456
Lee, John D., 147–49, 152, 153, 154
letter writing, 446–47
Livingstone, John P., 93
Lloyd, Donald P., 426
lottery ticket, 205
Lund, Anthon H., 214, 217n17, 297, 306, 307–8
Lyman, Amasa, 153, 167, 185, 214

Lyman, Amy Brown, 362, 364–65, 369
Lyman, Francis M., 236, 297, 303
Lyman, Platt D., 214
Lyman, Richard R., 309, 380–81

Mabey, Charles R., 406
Madison, James, 10
Madsen, Arch, 347
Madsen, Axel A., 407
Mandujano, Gisela, 539
Mandujano, Nicolas, 539
Man for All Seasons, A (Bolt), 59, 78
Manning, Ernest C., 491
Manti Temple, 418, *419*
Marchant, Robert C., 416
Markham, Stephen, 182
Marks, William, 164, 166, 167, 175–76, 178–79, 183
Marsh, Thomas B., 88–89
Martin Handcart Company, 204, 218n18
Mather, Cotton, 224
Maudsley, Sutclife, 465
Mauss, Armand L., 632–33
Maw, Herbert B., 424, 426
Maxwell, Neal A., 320
McConkie, Bruce R., 477
McCracken, Chancellor, 239
McCune, George W., 313
McKay, David O., *318*; beautification movement and, 405, 429; Church

708

education and, 378, 388, 390, 399n16; correlation and, 285, 320, 324, 325, 326, 330–31; electronic media and, 340, 345–47, 353; First Council of the Seventy and, 577; missionary work and, 286; N. Eldon Tanner and, 494, 495, 496–97; succession and, 306; Sunday School and, 309

McKay, Thomas E., 554–56, 557, 561–62, 563

McKean, Howard J., 407, 408

McLellin, William, 26–29, 60–61, 63, 65, 79n9

McLuhan, Marshall, 341

McMurrin, Joseph W., 301

media. *See* electronic media

Meese, Edwin, 458

meetinghouses, 310, 311–12, 496–97, 655–56. *See also* beautification movement

Melchizedek Priesthood: Apostasy and, 62–64; in Book of Mormon, 38, 56n64; during progressive period, 303–4; keys to, 71–77; restoration of, 59–62, 68–71, 77–78, 80n33, 118–19, 616–17

Melchizedek Priesthood Mutual Interest Association, 476–77

membership, 40, 92, 298–99

Mendenhall, Wendell, 497

Merrill, Charles, 491

Merrill, Joseph F., *376*; educational background of, 379–81; establishment of first seminary and, 381–83; as Commissioner of Church Schools, 383–84; establishment of institute program and, 384–86; preservation of Church schools and, 386–91; defends seminary program, 391–95; called as Apostle, 396–97

Merrill, Marriner W., 379

Merrill, Sara (Sally), 487

Messenger, The, 641

MIA (Mutual Improvement Associations), 466–67. *See also* Young Men's Mutual Improvement Association (YMMIA); Young Women program

military organization, 619–20. *See also* Zion's Camp

Millennial Star, 199–201, 216nn7–8, 229

Miller, George, 184–85

Miller, Orrin P., 298

Milton Ward, 413

missiology, 645–48

missionaries. *See* missionary work

Missionary Committee, 596, 609

Missionary Department: advertising efforts under, 607–8; mission calls and, 598–600; mission presidents and, 600–603; mission support

and, 605–6; organization of, 597–98; *Preach My Gospel* and, 603–5; visitors' centers and, 607; Missionary Executive Council, 596, 601, 603–4, 609
missionary training centers, 606
missionary work: Apostasy and, 78n9; Apostles and, 595–96; in Book of Mormon, 45–46; of Brigham Young, 169–72; calls to, 598–600; in early Church, 659; media and pageants and, 607–8; mission presidents and, 600–603; mission support and, 605–6; missionary training centers and, 606; of N. Eldon Tanner, 494; *Preach My Gospel* and, 603–5; restoration of priesthood and, 64–66; service missions, 536–37; Seventies and, 141–42, 147, 150, 153, 577–80; Spencer W. Kimball and, 523–25; studies on, 645–48; visitors' centers and, 607
mission presidents, 600–603, 672–73
Missouri conference, 127, 130
Mitchener, Charles E. Jr., 475
Moffat, David, 229
Molen, Jane E. Hyde, 257–58
monarchy, 2–3
Monroe, James M., 153
Monson, Thomas S., 292, 477, 510, 526
Moody, Michael, 512, 513, 514

Moore, Beatrice Young, 259–60
More, Thomas, 59, 78
Moreland Ward, 413
Morley, Isaac, 124
Mormon, 208–9, 219n35
Mormon Battalion, 620
Mormon migration. *See* gathering
Mormon village, 618
Morris, Colin, 340–41
Morris, George Q., 331, 474, 494
mothers, 454–56
Moyle, Henry D., 495
MTCs, 606
music books, 261–62, 503–14

Nadauld, Margaret Dyreng, 290, 446
Naisbitt, Henry W., 466
National Council on Social Work (1917), 364
Native American students, 499–500
Native American ward, 538–39, 541–42, 544–45
Nativity program, 543
Nauvoo Legion, 620
Nauvoo Neighbor, 152, 153, 154
Nauvoo Temple, 154
Nelson, Irving T., 407
Nelson, Russell M., 596, 602
New Era, 287
New York, 207–8
Nibley, Charles W., 298, 299, 308, 309
Nielsen, Kent C., 538

Nielson, Joseph, 311
Nigeria, 494–95

Oaks, Dallin H., 587
Oaks, Robert C., 583
O'Dea, Thomas, 632–33
Ohio period, 617
Olvera, Adriana, 540, 542, 549
Ong, Walter, 341
Orange conference, 102, 127
ordinances, 38–41
Orton, Roger, 142–43
Ottley, Jerold, 507
Our Churches Shall Be Beautiful, 410–11
Overman, Lee S., 224
oxen, 169

Packer, Boyd K.: on handbooks, 641; on Harold B. Lee, 463; hymnbook and, 507; on seminary and institute programs, 377; on Seventies, 586; on today's challenges, 291; YMMIA and, 477, 480–82
Page, Hiram, 4, 5, 61, 101, 121, 661
Page, John E., 164
pageants, 608
Painesville Telegraph, 25, 86
Parker, L. K., 155
Parkin, Bonnie D., 290
Partridge, Edward, 98, 106, 123–25, 130, 659, 670

patriarchal blessings, 41
patriarchs, 666–68
Patten, David W., 29
Peirce, Eli, 239–40
Penrose, Charles W., 306, 307, 327–28
Perpetual Emigrating Fund, 204
Perry, L. Tom, 477, 478, 479, 587, 596
Personal Progress, 443–49, 453, 454, 458
Peter, 60–62
Petersen, Mark E., 492, 494, 507, 511
Peterson, Paul, 229
Peterson, Ziba, 61
Phelps, William W.: on Apostasy, 63, 79n15; in conferences and councils, 110; difficulties with Joseph Smith, 98; mission of, 79n9; as president of high priesthood, 111; as presiding council member, 106; as scribe, 665; succession crisis and, 185; "Voice from the Prophet, A: Come to Me," 151
Pilgrims, 224
Pinnock, Hugh, 513–14
pioneer centennial, 405–7, 411, 429, 431–33, 441n89
Pioneer Day cookout, 541–43
Pittsburgh, Pennsylvania, 163
Pohlsander, Hermann Walter, 564, 565
Polysophical Society, 466
Porter, Larry C., 69
Porter, N. Aldin, 586, 588

711

Index

Postman, Neil, 341–42
power: in Church and democracy, 7–10; godly, 9–11; moral terms of, 11–12
Pratt, Addison, 153
Pratt, Orson: as Apostle, 135n22; on apostleship, 74; on Apostasy, 63–64; catechism and, 229; First Presidency and, 116; George A. Smith's correspondence with, 66–67; improvement associations and, 466; mission of, 164, 172; as president of British Mission, 213; on priesthood restoration, 65; *Seer, The,* and, 219n35; succession crisis and, 168
Pratt, Parley P.: on Apostasy, 64; as Apostle, 135n22; emigration and, 198, 215n2; *Millennial Star* and, 199; mission of, 79n9, 164–65; preaches from Book of Mormon, 30; as president of British Mission, 213; on priesthood keys, 73; on priesthood restoration, 65; reports to Joseph Smith, 110; succession crisis and, 167, 185; William E. McLellin and, 27–28
Pratt, William D., 140
preacher's license, 174–75
Preach My Gospel, 603–5
presidential campaign, 163, 170–71
president of the high priesthood, 104–5, 107, 126–30

Presiding Bishop, 123–25, 660, 670–71, 674
Presiding Bishopric, 298, 412–13, 659–60
presiding patriarch, 666–68
Preston, William B., 298
priestcrafts, 44
priesthood: ordinations to, 37–38, 56n64, 91, 92; restoration of, 64–69, 77–78, 80n33, 118–19, 616–17; Articles and Covenants and, 88; high priesthood, 104–6; revelation on, 125–26, 530–31, 633; controversy over, authority, 145–46; during progressive period, 299–300; new priesthood movement, 303–5; development of offices, 321; Ardeth G. Kapp and, 449–50; YMMIA and, 473–79; authority, 553–54; contemporary publications on, 633–40; studies on, offices and quorums, 658–78; women and, 681–82; mission of Church and, 695–96. *See also* Aaronic Priesthood; correlation; Melchizedek Priesthood
Priesthood Bulletin, 641
Priesthood Executive Committee, 512
priesthood keys: First Presidency and, 131, 663–64; Oliver Cowdery and, 121; restoration of, 71–77, 118–19,

Index

134n12; succession crisis and, 172–73
Priesthood Regions, 578–79
Primary Association: establishment of, 246–54; expansion of, 254–64; greater organization of, 264–67; historical studies on, 683–84; materials for, 259–61; music books for, 261–62
Primary Conference of Cache Stake, 257–59
Primary Speaker Book No. 1, 264
Primary Speaker Book No. 2, 264
Prince, Gregory A., 345–46, 347
progressive period (1898–1930), 295–314
Progress of the Church, 641
property: of Church, 308–12; ward and stake, 299
prophecy, gift of, 4–6, 101, 119–22
prophets, 637, 660–61
Public Communications Department, 528
public health, 361–71
public relations, 345, 607–8, 647–48
Pulsipher, John, 146
Puritans, 224
Pyper, George, 309

Quarter, William, 155
Questions and Answers on the Book of Mormon (Cannon), 234–36
Questions and Answers on the Life and Mission of the Prophet Joseph Smith, 234
Quinn, D. Michael, 60–61, 178
Quorum of the Anointed, 177, 622
Quorum of the Twelve Apostles: Assistants to, 575–77, 578, 581, 672; development of, 321; in early Church, 135n21; emigration and, 198–99; historical studies on, 668–69; mission calls and, 598–600; mission presidents and, 601–2; N. Eldon Tanner called to, 494; organization of, 658–59; restoration of office, 5–6, 74, 98; succession and, 184, 185–87, 306–8, 622–23; YMMIA and, 474
quorums, during progressive period, 299–300
Quorums of the Seventies: beginnings of, 140–43; development of, 321, 659; discontinuation of, 583–84; during progressive period, 300–302, 303; expansion of, 143–54; milestones for, 589; scriptural references to, 156n3. *See also* First Quorum(s) of the Seventy; Second Quorum of the Seventy

radio broadcasting, 342–43
Ranglack, Richard, 556–60, *558*, 561, 569

Index

Rasband, Ronald A., 599
Rasmus, Carolyn, 452
Rathenowerstrasse 52 building, 559–61, *560*
Reactivated Hymnbook Task Committee, 512–13
Reading Committee, 333
Reagan, Ronald, 349
recitations, for Primary children, 264
recommends (records), 298–99
record keeping: Articles and Covenants and, 88–89; blessings of, 611; Church membership and, 40, 92; commandment on, x–xi, 48; Historical Department and, 692; membership records and, 298–99; William McLellin and, 26–29
Red Cross, 364
Reeder, Bertha Stone, 284–85
reformation catechism, 228–29
regional leaders, 671–73
regional presiding bishop, 674
Regional Representatives, 578–79
regions, 577–80
Reimer, Ilse, *558*
Relief Society, 255, 271n34, 300, 361–71. *See also* Female Relief Society
Relief Society Magazine, 362, 363
Repsher, D. M., 152
revelation: continuing, 637; errors in, 103; joint, 134n18; Oliver Cowdery and, 120, 121; in organization of Church, x; in Church callings, 5; on priesthood, 125–26, 530–31, 633
Rich, Charles C., 166, 167, 214
Richards, Buddy, 533–35, 537, 538, 544–46, 549
Richards, Cindy, 533
Richards, Franklin D.: blesses William C. Staines, 211; called to auditing committee, 297; emigration and, 207, 208, 221n48; improvement associations and, 467; as president of British Mission, 213, 214, 578; Primary Association and, 253
Richards, George F., 308
Richards, Katie, 533
Richards, LeGrand, 403, 411–12
Richards, Samuel W., 67–68, 202, 203, 213
Richards, Stephen L, 309, 325–27, 334, 418–20, 431
Richards, Willard: called to First Presidency, 117; correspondence with Brigham Young, 171; Quorum of the Anointed and, 177; as scribe, 665; succession crisis and, 164–65, 167, 174–75
Ricks College, 389–90
Rider, Alonzo, 46–47
Rigdon, Sidney, 98; conferences and councils and, 102, 103; as counselor to Joseph Smith, 105,

128–31, 658, 663; revelation and, 122, 126; succession crisis and, 162–69, 179–82, 183, 185–86
righteous living, 41–42
Roach, Todd, 540–41
Roberts, B. H.: catechisms and, 231; First Council of the Seventy and, 301; on priesthood restoration, 69; on Seventies, 575; on succession crisis, 185; on "Supplication to the Throne of Grace, A," 151; YMMIA and, 309, 465
Robinson, Ebenezer, 163
Robinson, Theodore, 307
Rodriguez, Victor A., 538
Rogers, Aurelia Spencer, 245–54, 264–69, 270n14
Rojas, Isaias, 542–43, 547
Romney, Antone K., 331
Romney, George, 183
Romney, Marion G., 333
Roosevelt, Franklin D., 344
Ross, C. C., 490
Ruf, Erwin, 563, 564

Sabbath, 656–57
sacrament, 23–24, 40–41, 89–90, 657
Salt Lake County Beautification Committee, 414
satellite technology, 346, 349–50
Schaumainkai 41 building, *567*, 568
Schneider, Charlotte Bodon, 566

Schneider, Kurt, 566, 568
Scofield, Brother, 212
scouting, 475, 537, 630
Scovil, Lucius, 205
scribes and clerks, 665–66
scriptures, 529–30
Second Quorum of the Seventy, 143–44, 582–85
seer, 119–22, 660–61
seminary, 381–83, 391–95
service missionaries, 536–37
Sessions, J. Wyley, 384–86
Seventies. *See* First Council of the Seventy; First Quorum(s) of the Seventy; Quorums of the Seventies; Second Quorum of the Seventy
Seventies Hall, 147–49, 151–54, 155
Sexual Revolution, 286
Sheppard-Towner Act (1921), 365–69, 370
Short Biblical Catechism, A, 225
singles ward, 546–49
Sjodahl, Janne M., 231
Small, Sharee, 543
Smith, Barbara B., 288
Smith, Bathsheba, 255
Smith, Craig S., 198–99
Smith, David A., 298, 405, 407
Smith, Eldred G., 667
Smith, Emma, 175–76, 178, 179, 183
Smith, G. Carlos, 474

Index

Smith, George A., 66–67, 164, 167, 225–26, 230, 239

Smith, George Albert, 334, 345, 433, 474

Smith, Hyrum: Articles and Covenants and, 89; as Assistant President, 665; authority of, 176; Book of Mormon and, 27, 30; death of, 162, 163, 171–72; as president of high priesthood, 132; Seventies Hall and, 147–48

Smith, Hyrum G., 306

Smith, Hyrum M., 231

Smith, Jezehi B., 140

Smith, John, 29

Smith, John Henry, 214, 297, 470

Smith, Joseph: as Apostle, 71–77; Articles and Covenants and, 84–85; authority of, 124–25; blesses Reynolds baby, 41; on Book of Mormon, 50; on church meetings, 43; Church government and, 694–95; conferences and councils and, 98, 101–4, 107–9, 661–62; contemporary publications on, 634–35; death of, 162, 163, 171–72; emigration and, 202; estate of, 175–76; on excommunication of Joseph Wood, 47; financial affairs and, 688; as first elder, 119–22; First Presidency and, 116, 117–18, 125–30, 663–64; gives last charge, 172–73; makes use of Book of Mormon, 30–33; new doctrine and organizations under, 176–78; organization of Church and, x, 3–6, 12, 16, 658–59; on power, 9–10; as president of high priesthood, 105; as presidential candidate, 163, 170–71; on priesthood, 694–695; priesthood restoration and, 60–61, 64–68, 77–78, 80n33, 118–19, 616–17; as prophet, seer, and revelator, 660–61; *Questions and Answers on the Life and Mission of the Prophet Joseph Smith*, 234; receives baptism and Holy Ghost, 68–69; on responsibility of children, 254; on Seventy, 140–41; on Sidney Rigdon, 163; success of Church and, xiii; as charismatic leader, 3, 7, 12n3; succession crisis and, 620–21; YMMIA and, 465; on Zion's Camp, 143–44

Smith, Joseph F.: catechisms and, 224; Church property and, 309, 310; correlation and, 323–24, 325; correspondence with Addison Everett, 70; death of, 306–7; as president of British Mission, 214; on priesthood and auxiliaries, 479; YMMIA and, 467–68, 473, 474

Smith, Joseph Fielding, *238*; on catechisms, 237–38; as Church

716

Index

historian, 309; Committee on Publications and, 333; electronic media and, 348; German Missions and, 554, 555; succession and, 306
Smith, Joseph III, 182
Smith, Joseph Sr., 29, 41, 665, 666
Smith, Kylee, 547–48
Smith, Lucy Mack, 60, 176
Smith, Samuel, 62, 79n9, 175, 176, 178
Smith, Sylvester, 62–63, 79n9, 142, 157n11, 158n23
Smith, Thomas, 229
Smith, William, 164, 171, 176, 667
Smith-Lever Act (1914), 363
Smoot, Margaret T., 257
Smoot, Reed, 224, 239, 308
Snow, Eliza R., *233*; catechisms and, 231–34; expansion of Primary and, 254–66; on importance of Primary, 253; Primary beginnings and, 247–48; Relief Society and, 271n34; Young Women program and, 279
Snow, Erastus, 144, 171, 206–7, 211, 217n17, 219n35
Snow, Lorenzo, 295, 296–97, 300, 466, 474
Social Advisory Committee, 326
Social Credit, 488–90
social work, 361–71
Solomon, Alfred, 214
Spanish wards, 537–40

"Special Conference," 103
Speckhard, Eric, 536
Spencer, Orson, 213
Staines, William C., 210–11
stake patriarch, 667–68
stake presidents, 673
stake property, 299
Stapley, Delbert L., 334
Stark, Rodney, 340–41
statistical and demographic studies, 644–45
Steele, Rocky, 543, 545
Stegner, Wallace, 284
Stephens, Daniel, 140
stewardship, 617–18
St. Laurent, Louis, 492
St. Louis, Missouri, 205–7
St. Louis Luminary, 206–7, 208
Stone, Barton W., 165
Stone, O. Leslie, 504, 505, 511
Stout, Hosea, 147
Stover, Walter, 561
succession crisis (1844): Brigham Young and, 169–74; decision in, 174–88; historical studies on, 620–24; Sidney Rigdon and, 162–69;
Sunday School, 327–30, 629–30, 684–85
Sunshine Club, 451
"Supplication to the Throne of Grace, A," 151
Sweet, Leonard I., 340

Tabernacle Choir, 343, 344, 349, 350, 528
talents, developing, 447–48
Talmage, James E., 240, 312, 327
Tanner, Nathan W., 486
Tanner, N. Eldon: as Alberta minister of lands and mines, 490–91; childhood of, 486–87; Church service of, 493–500; on correlation, 321; as oil company president, 491–92; political involvement of, 487–90; as president of Trans-Canada, 492–93
Tanner, Sara Edna Brown, 486
Tanner, Sara (Sally) Merrill, 487
Tanner, Susan Winder, 290
Taylor, Elmina Shepard, 280–81
Taylor, George, 210
Taylor, John: on catechisms, 225; correspondence with Junius F. Wells, 472–73; emigration and, 208–10, 211, 219n35, 220n43, 221n48; historical studies on, 627; as martyrdom witness, 164; on organization of Church, x; Seventies and, 151–52; Primary Association and, 248, 253–54, 266, 322, 683; succession crisis and, 167; Young Women program and, 279–80
Teasdale, George, 214
technological advancements, 339, 450–51. *See also* electronic media

Temple Square, 607
temples, 44–45, 448–49, 526–27, 607, 655–56
Thaller, Johannes, 564, 566, 568
Thatcher, Moses, 474
Third Quorum of the Seventy, 144–45, 157n19
Three Witnesses, 120–21
Times and Seasons, 152
Tingey, Earl C., 583, 584, 586–87
Tingey, Martha Horne, 281–82
tithes and offerings, 42, 295–98, 675, 689
tongues, gift of, 257–58
Trans-Canada Pipe Lines Company Limited, 492–93
transfiguration, of Brigham Young, 186–88
traveling agent for the General Tithing Office, 675
traveling bishop, 675
trustee-in-trust, 175–76, 178, 183
Tune Book for the Primary Associations of the Children of Zion, 262
Tuttle, A. Theodore, 578
Twelve Apostles. *See* Quorum of the Twelve Apostles

Union Board of the Auxiliaries, 331–32
Universal Scientific Society, 466

Index

Utah centennial, 405–7, 411, 429, 431–33, 441n89
Utah Centennial Commission, 405–7
Utah Landscape Improvement Committee, 414
Utah Loan and Trust Company, 296
Utah Stake Primary Association Conference, 256–57
Utah Valley Deaf Ward, 544–47

Van Der Donckt, Rev. C., 231
Van Wagoner, Richard S., 186, 187
Viana, Rinaldo, 446
visiting teaching program, 650
visitors' centers, 607
Voice, Sister, 174
"Voice from the Prophet, A: Come to Me," 151
volunteerism, 43–44

Walker, Clifford, 491
walking in holiness, 88
Ward, Thomas, 213
ward bishop, 674, 677
ward buildings, 310, 311–12, 496–97, 655–56
ward property, 299
Warnock, Irvin, 423
Weeks, William, 147
Welch, John W., 660
Welch, Robert, 231–32

welfare: beautification movement and, 405, 418; in Book of Mormon, 42; historical studies on, 630–31, 686, 690–91; N. Eldon Tanner and, 498; Provo Utah South Stake and, 535–37; regions and, 578–79; Relief Society and, 361–71; Spencer W. Kimball and, 529. *See also* Church Welfare Plan
Welling, Milton, 392–93
Wells, Daniel H., 214, 469
Wells, Emmeline B., 247, 255, 261, 266, 362, 363
Wells, John, 405
Wells, Junius F., 465, 468–74
Wells, Rulon S., 214, 301, 577
West German Mission, 561–70
"What Was Witnessed in the Heavens?," 240
White, Louisa, 265
Whitmer, David, 23, 60, 61, 110, 111, 120
Whitmer, John, 61, 106, 110, 111, 119
Whitney, Helen Mar, 181
Whitney, Newel K., 167, 178, 659, 670–71, 674
Whitney, Orson F., 238–39
Widtsoe, John A.: called as Apostle, 308; as Commissioner of Church Schools, 399n16; correlation and, 333; education of, 398n4; General

Index

Authority living allowance and, 312, 330; Relief Society and, 363
Wight, Lyman, 110, 124, 164, 168–69, 171
Wilcox, Maria Wealthy, 183
Williams, Clarissa Smith, 362, 365, 369
Williams, Frederick G., 106, 110, 117, 130–31, 663, 664
Williamson, Isaac L., 391–92, 393–94, 395, 400n36
Willie Handcart Company, 204, 218n18
Wilson, Guy C., 383
Winter, Arthur, 310
Wirthlin, Joseph B., 412, 431
Wistisen, Katherine, 544
Woman's Exponent, 251–52
women: and administrative history, 678–82; Ardeth G. Kapp and, 457–58; in Church, 529
Wood, Joseph, 47
Wood, M. Douglas, 554, 555, 561
Woodenden, Sarah, 212
Woodruff, Wilford: blesses William C. Staines, 211; Book of Mormon and, 29, 30; on Brigham Young and succession, 188; business investments under, 296; on catechisms, 225; on emigration, 198; on First Presidency succession, 306–7; grieves martyrdom, 174; hymnbook and, 504; mission of, 164; as president of British Mission, 213; on priesthood restoration, 80n33; as Seventy, 144; succession crisis and, 168, 179–80, 182, 187; YMMIA and, 474
Woolley, Henry A., 470
World's Fairs, 406–7
World War II, 423–26. *See also* German Missions
worship services, 42–43, 89, 304–5, 528, 633
Wright, William Robert, 345–46, 347

Yates, Thomas, 382
Year of the Child Campaign (1918), 364
YMMIA (Young Men's Mutual Improvement Association). *See* Young Men's Mutual Improvement Association (YMMIA)
Young, B. Morris, 470–71, 482
Young, Brigham: on apostleship and priesthood keys, 75, 77; Book of Mormon and, 29; on catechisms, 229; colonization and, 653–54; contemporary publications on, 635; death of, 248; emigration and, 202, 203, 207, 217n17, 221n48; financial affairs and, 688; First Presidency and, 115–17, 132, 133n5; on Joseph Smith as

720

Apostle, 76; mission of, 79n9, 164; on organization of Church, x; leadership of, 2–3, 5–6; as president of British Mission, 213; on priesthood, 695; on priesthood keys, 73–74; on Quorum of the Anointed, 177; on Seventies, 150, 574; Seventies Hall and, 147, 148–49, 151; stakes and, 673; succession crisis and, 168–74, 180–86, 623–24; Sunday School and, 684; on technological advances, 339; transfiguration of, 186–88; Twelve Apostles and, 668; Willie and Martin handcart companies and, 218n18; YMMIA and, 322, 468–71, 473, 480; Young Women program and, 279; on Zion's Camp, 619

Young, Brigham Jr., 214, 297

Young, John, 170

Young, Joseph: First Presidency and, 115, 116; as president of Seventies, 139–40, 146–47, 149–50; property sold to, 158n30; Seventies Hall and, 152

Young, Joseph W., 203

Young, Luna, 170

Young, Mary Ann, 170

Young, S. Dilworth, 581

Young, Vilate, 170

Young, Willard, 311

Young, Zina D. H., 253, 255, 256, 265–67

Young Gentlemen and Ladies' Relief Society of Nauvoo, 278–79, 465–66

Young Ladies' Department of the Cooperative Retrenchment Association, 279

Young Men's Mutual Improvement Association (YMMIA): beginnings of, 464–67; formal founding of, 467–70; historical studies on, 682–83; priesthood and, 473–79; purpose and practice of, 470–73

Young Womanhood Recognition, 288

Young Women program: beginnings of, 278–80; girls' camp, 545; historical studies on, 682–83. *See also* Kapp, Ardeth Greene; maturation of, 285–91; pattern for, 280–85; YMMIA and, 475–76

YWMIA (Young Women's Mutual Improvement Association). *See* Young Women program

Zimmer, Max, 568–69

Zion's Camp, 140, 143–44, 156n6, 619

Zion Securities Corporation, 309–10, 629, 686